MODERN TYRANTS

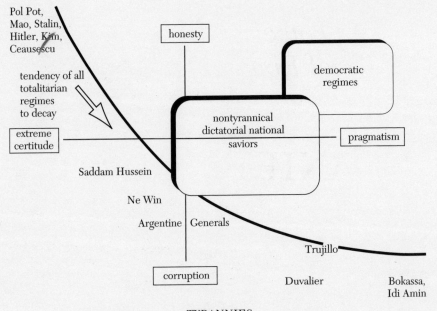

Pol Pot,
Mao, Stalin,
Hitler, Kim,
Ceausescu

tendency of all
totalitarian
regimes
to decay

honesty

democratic
regimes

nontyrannical
dictatorial national
saviors

extreme
certitude

pragmatism

Saddam Hussein

Ne Win

Argentine | Generals

Trujillo

corruption

Duvalier

Bokassa,
Idi Amin

TYRANNIES
[to the left and below the thick curved line]

MODERN TYRANTS

The Power and Prevalence of Evil in Our Age

DANIEL CHIROT

THE FREE PRESS
A Division of Macmillan, Inc.
NEW YORK

Maxwell Macmillan Canada
TORONTO

Maxwell Macmillan International
NEW YORK   OXFORD   SINGAPORE   SYDNEY

The Free Press
A Division of Macmillan, Inc.
866 Third Avenue, New York, N.Y. 10022

Maxwell Macmillan Canada, Inc.
1200 Eglinton Avenue East
Suite 200
Don Mills, Ontario M3C 3N1

Macmillan, Inc. is part of the Maxwell Communication Group of Companies.

Printed in the United States of America

printing number

1 2 3 4 5 6 7 8 9 10

Library of Congress Cataloging-in-Publication Data

Chirot, Daniel.
   Modern tyrants: the power and prevalence of evil in our age/
   Daniel Chirot.
      p. cm.
   ISBN 0-02-905477-X
   1. Dictators—History—20th century. 2. Despotism—History—20th
   century. I. Title
   JC495.C47 1994
   321.9—dc20   93–14621
                                                        CIP

Grateful acknowledgment is made for allowing permission to reprint excerpts from the following previously published works:

Samir al-Khalil, *Republic of Fear: The Politics of Modern Iraq*. Copyright ©1989, The Regents of the University of California.

Katherine Verdery, *National Ideology under Socialism: Identity and Cultural Politics in Ceausescu's Romania*. Copyright ©1991, The Regents of the University of California.

Lowell Dittmer, *China's Continuous Revolution: The Postliberation Epoch, 1949–1981*. Copyright ©1987, The Regents of the University of California.

J. P. Stern, *Hitler: The Führer and the People*. London: Peters, Fraser & Dunlop.

Robert Tucker, *Stalin as Revolutionary*. New York: W. W. Norton & Company, 1974.

Adolph Hitler, *Mein Kampf*, translated by Ralph Manheim. Copyright ©1943, renewed 1971 by Houghton Mifflin Company. Reprinted by permission of Houghton Mifflin Company, New York. All rights reserved.

Arkady Vaksberg, *Stalin's Prosecutor*. Copyright ©1990 by Arkady Vaksberg, translation copyright ©1990 by Jan Butler. Used with permission of Grove/Atlantic Monthly Press, New York.

William Carr, *Hitler: A Study in Personality and Politics*. London: Edward Arnold, 1978. By permission of Hodder & Stoughton on behalf of Edward Arnold.

Nunca Mas: The Report of the Argentinian National Commission on the Disappeared. Translation copyright ©1986 by Writers and Scholars International Ltd. Reprinted by permission of Farrar, Straus & Giroux, Inc., New York.

Paul R. Mendes-Flohr and Jehuda Reinharz (editors), *The Jew in the Modern World: A Documentary History*. New York: Oxford University Press, 1980.

TO HIRSCH AND JACOB CAHN

whose questions of long ago I have tried to answer

CONTENTS

vii

PREFACE

When I was young I would often hear older relatives and their friends discuss World War II and Nazism. Some were convinced that it was only the Germans who were capable of such things, and that now, it would never be allowed to happen again. Others were not so sure. Anti-Semitism, war, and oppression, after all, were far older than Hitler. Those who had lived in Russia through the Revolutions of 1917 would also discuss Bolshevism. Was Stalinism a uniquely Russian deformation of noble Socialist idealism? Or was there something in Marxism as a whole that created tyranny? It was only when I was in college that I realized that most of those who had lived through the momentous revolutions and political nightmares of the twentieth century did not have good explanations for what had occurred. Perhaps having been in the middle of it precluded any kind of balanced judgement.

My grandfather and his brother, to whom I have dedicated this book, spent many hours in their old age reading about their past, and discussing it with anyone curious enough to ask. They were quite learned men, but ultimately, they did not understand how such things could happen. Raised to believe in the power of rationality, educated to accept that the principles of the European Enlightenment were the most noble in history, they could not believe that human beings exposed to these ideals would renounce them and commit such atrocities.

I do not think that many of us understand the answers to these questions today. We know more than we used to about how such things happened, and how common they have been in the twentieth century, but not why. We know that the torture and the killings did not stop everywhere in the world in 1945, when World War II ended, or in

1953, when Stalin died, or in 1976 when Mao died, or in 1989 when Eastern Europe ceased to be communist. They continue even today, and in many parts of the world there are leaders, or potential leaders, ready to commit new holocausts, to open new concentration camps, and to launch new wars in the name of historical, sacred justice and truth, or for the sake of imagined utopias.

The long historical essay I have written tries to answer the questions raised by the existence and persistence of the phenomenon of tyranny. By comparing many examples, I think it is possible to gain insights that no single case, no matter how thoroughly researched, no matter how profoundly experienced, can ever answer.

I did not pick my cases arbitrarily. Hitler, Stalin, and Mao had to be included because they were tyrants who defined much of our century. Then, I wanted a selection of cases from various parts of the world. There have been far too many cases to do justice to more than a few, but those I chose were meant to illustrate particular aspects of modern tyranny.

In Southeast Asia the Khmer Rouge were an obvious choice because they were so heinous. Originally I intended to make General Suharto of Indonesia another case because I have studied his country, travelled in it quite a bit, and because it is one of the most populous in the world. But I decided that Suharto was far from being unambiguously evil; he may have saved his country from something worse than what has happened under his rule. I picked Burma as a substitute because it makes the consequences of well-meaning but misguided ideologies so clear. Burma is also an example of the problems multi-ethnic states have when they try to create united nations. Far from being exotic, in some respects it is all too typical of much of the world.

I included Nicolae Ceausescu because of all the regimes over-thrown in Eastern Europe in 1989, his was the clearest example of per-sonal tyranny. But also, I once wrote a book on the social history of Romania. I know its language, and even before he was overthrown, I knew many of the details of Ceausescu's misrule, and how most of my friends there suffered. The similarity between Ceausescu and Kim Il Sung is too obvious to miss if one knows even a little bit about North Korea. Adding material about North Korea actually clarifies some aspects of Ceausescu's rule, and about the general connection between nationalism, corporatism, communism, and tyranny.

Saddam Hussein was slated to appear in this study even before the

Iraqi invasion of Kuwait and the subsequent Gulf War. Of the many Middle Eastern dictators who have thrived in recent decades, his is one of the most clearly tyrannical regimes. But many aspects of his rule make it similar to other nationalist and militant governments in this part of the world. And Iraq's attempt, so far largely unsuccessful, to forge a common sense of nationality among its diverse peoples further reinforces the important lesson that this often insuperable problem is at the heart of many modern tyrannies.

My reason for examining Argentina was that this was a country that should never have fallen into such a condition. Favored by geography, economically well developed in the early twentieth century, isolated from the great wars and tragedies of Eurasia, it should have remained a haven of peace, prosperity, and democracy. But it did not, and more than any other case, it shows the power of misguided economic and political theories to foster the conditions that lead to brutal tyranny.

The mess in Haiti is so great that there is little need to justify its inclusion. But even in the case of the Duvalier family, whose rule seemed so purely corrupt and selfish, the original ideological impetus behind Papa Doc's rise to power serves to emphasize the role of ideology in most twentieth-century examples of tyranny. And Haiti is an almost perfect example of a country whose heavy historical burdens make happy political outcomes most unlikely. I added the Dominican Republic because, as Haiti's neighbor, there are obvious comparisons to be made, and because Rafael Trujillo in some ways typifies a large number of Latin American dictators—military men who came from obscure circumstances to bully and rob their people even as they tried to bring about order in semi-anarchic, fractured societies.

I picked Idi Amin because he was so notorious. Studying him makes it clear that no matter how arbitrary and irrational his personal rule may have seemed, it had deeper causes and was connected to a whole history, not just to a few passing coincidences or to his personality. To emphasize this, and to reinforce the connection between the colonial era and the many disasters that have occurred in Africa since then, I picked a second African case from the former French Empire. I worked in French-speaking Africa in the 1960s and learned a lot about how the French still operated there. I heard some unsavory details about how local corruption and French interference interacted in the Republic of Niger from its then President, Hamani Diori. But Diori, who was overthrown and died in exile, was himself a gentle man who was far from being a tyrant. So I decided that I could best apply what I had learned to the study of Emperor Bokassa.

Obviously, my selection does not resemble what social scientists might call "random sampling." But I do not believe that this is necessary, or even useful in picking whole societies to study. There are not thousands of cases from which to pick, and they are not all of equal importance. There have been, for example, over a dozen Latin American military dictatorships in recent times that might qualify as tyrannies, but only one Hitler. Hitler may not be as "representative" of the type "tyrant" as these more common Latin Americans, but to leave him out of a study such as mine would be foolish, and devoting too many pages to the Somozas and Trujillos of our century would add little insight into the nature of tyranny.

My method is simple. I have tried to give brief social and political histories of the places I have studied in order to explain how they became tyrannies. Then, I have discussed the effects of the tyrannies they suffered, adding some observations about the personalities of the tyrants themselves. No expert historian on any of these cases is going to find any new facts in what I say. Around most of them there exist well-worn academic arguments about the causes and consequences of what happened. Using what I have learned from reading about my examples, I have picked what I think are the most correct arguments for each of the cases, and adopted them for my own use. Thus, I hope that even a specialist on, say, Hitler, or on modern Burma, is going to find something new in what I say about those cases because my comparisons should illuminate previous academic arguments and strengthen the ones I think are correct. I am quite confident that few readers, specialists or not, are going to be very knowledgeable about more than a few of these tyrannies before they read my book.

From these studies I have drawn some general conclusions which suggest what I believe to be the main causes of modern tyranny. As I explain at the very end of the book, I do not think that tyranny is a phenomenon exclusively of the past. Our next century may be as filled with it as the twentieth. But by knowing its causes somewhat better, I think it is possible to see it coming, in ways that my grandfather's generation did not.

ACKNOWLEDGMENTS

I would like to thank three institutions for financing and encouraging my work.

The John Simon Guggenheim Memorial Foundation gave me a grant in 1991–1992 during which I wrote the first two-thirds of my book.

The Rockefeller Foundation allowed me to live in their study center overlooking Lake Como in February and March of 1992 while writing two chapters.

The Institut für die Wissenschaften vom Menschen in Vienna supported me during the fall of 1992. There I finished my first draft. My colleagues in Vienna, particularly those from Germany, helped me appreciate the fact that national cultural traits, no matter how deeply rooted in history, are not carried by genes, and can be changed by determined effort.

A number of colleagues and friends helped me. None is responsible for my errors, but some of them are definitely responsible for my better ideas.

Peter Dougherty, my first editor at The Free Press, was an immeasurable morale booster. His successor, Bruce Nichols, worked very hard to make me revise and shorten my manuscript. I owe him a lot.

Ken Jowitt and Liah Greenfeld generously shared ideas with me and commented on the manuscript. Jacek Kochanowicz, Charles Ragin, Willfried Spohn, Claudia Minoliti, Robert Hefner, and Jung-en Woo read parts of the manuscript and made many useful suggestions. My old friend Martin Seligman gave me the benefit of some of his vast store of knowledge about human psychology. Charles Keyes helped me find my way around the Southeast Asian material, Elizabeth Perry told me where to begin with China, and Hillel Kieval gave me advice about the debates on the Nazi policies toward the Jews. Kathie and Resat Kasaba suggested books I should read to be more balanced. Günter Frankenberg, Lisa Conradi, and Lonnie Johnson helped me in Vienna. Tony Judt, Jason Parker, and John Reed wrote nice letters on my behalf. Sylvana Foa, who has seen the gruesome effects of modern tyranny at close hand much more often than I have, helped me far more than she realizes with shared ideas. Cynthia Chirot was my most careful reader and practical advisor. Finally, as on other occasions, I thank Lee Bullock for making my work possible at all.

Chapter 1

On Modern Tyranny

For many decades professional analysts of political power stopped using the term "tyrant." It is an old-fashioned word, and reminds us of Plato, or Machiavelli. The emphasis on political and economic modernization in the twentieth century produced so many ideological excuses for the abuse of power by governments that most of us forgot that tyranny, rather than diminishing, was actually as common as ever, and far more abusive than in the past.

But with the collapse of European communism from 1989 to 1991, the term "tyrant" began to come back into use. It turned out that when Romanians marched through the streets of Bucharest in December of 1989, they held aloft signs proclaiming "Down with the tyrant!" They were referring to their leader, Nicolae Ceausescu, who would soon be shot with his wife. We were reminded that tyranny was not an archaic concept after all.

Nonetheless, in 1989 we hoped that the word tyranny might have reappeared, only to die once and for all. Democracy had been proved better than totalitarianism, and except for the occasional little, local despot, no one was going to return to such nightmares.

By 1993, to be sure, such naïve sentiments, so widely expressed

1

from 1989 to 1992, have already been exposed as nonsense. Brutal civil wars rage in large parts of the former communist world, and more are in store. In many places, rather than democracy we are seeing various kinds of dictatorship and political abuse that look suspiciously old-fashioned.

I believe that it is even worse than that. Along with traditional abuses of power, which today we characterize as corruption and ordinary evil, the twentieth century has been rich in ideological tyranny motivated by utopian dreams and a false sense of scientific certitude. The conditions that created these tyrannies have not passed, even if the collapse of Marxism has left the world without one of its major twentieth-century utopianisms. There will be others in the twenty-first century. It is not possible to predict the specific ideological content of future tyrannies, but by showing how these have developed in the past century, I can explain why the conditions that led to them have not vanished.

My study of tyranny will try to identify the major types of modern tyranny together with their common causes, and therefore, to conclude with a set of propositions that might allow us to spot emerging new tyrannies in the future. In order to do this, it will be necessary to examine a wide array of twentieth-century tyrants. Some were very modern and could not have existed before the twentieth century. Others seem like recent versions of very old models. Yet all have been products of our century, while exhibiting traces of an ancient evil.

THE ORIGINS OF TYRANNY

Tyranny is the abuse of power. There have always been individuals who abuse their greater strength or cleverness to inflict pain and humiliation on others, and to exploit those around them for personal gain. Even when there were no policemen or soldiers to enforce anyone's will, nor states to tax and wage war, there were surely bullies who abused their strength, jealous rages that ended in violence, and small-scale wars between the small bands of wanderers competing for resources. Those with greater strength could and often did brutalize, humiliate, rob, and kill those who were weaker.

But the scale of cruelty and the types of distress that the powerful have inflicted on others have increased as societies have become more complex. The key step toward the creation of political tyranny, the sys-

tematic abuse of power by those in positions of authority, was the creation of the state. With armed soldiers at their command, and a growing body of administrators, those in charge of states could exploit their
subjects much more thoroughly. They could tax more, demand greater
servility, and, if they so wished, were able to inflict greater cruelty.

The invention of permanent settlements, and especially of agriculture, allowed humanity to multiply quickly in a few favored areas and
put greater pressure on resources. Intensified competition increased
conflict. Simultaneously, improvements in productive technologies
necessary to grow enough food for the more densely populated regions
also made available more resources that could be hoarded by the
strong—land, houses, domesticated animals, women. There is little
question that the transition from gathering and hunting societies to
early agriculture created increasing inequalities of wealth and the subordination of the many by the strong few, and that this was accompanied by a great increase in the incidence of war.[1]

In response to greater crowding and increasing war between territo-
rially based groups, professional political and military leaders developed. To settle disputes within groups, professional adjudicators and
coordinators appeared. Those who could claim special charismatic
powers as healers, as interpreters of the supernatural, or as strong warriors within societies assumed leadership, and because of the growing
need for such individuals, they were able to consolidate their authority.
They eventually began to bequeath their expertise and accumulated
riches to their offspring. Once these elite kin groups gained the ability
to store the payments they received for their services, and to employ
professional soldiers to enforce their will and collect their tribute, they
became the rulers of states. This took a long time. The first states
began about 5,500 to 5,000 years ago in the river valleys of Mesopotamia, at least three thousand years after the appearance of agriculture and rudimentary towns. Plow agriculture developed at about the
same time as states in Mesopotamia, also to better use limited
resources. This allowed greater population concentrations, and consequently, grander states.[2]

The rulers of the early states sought to legitimize their control and
use of vast resources seized from their subjects by awing them and
claiming divinity. Fantastic displays of power became common within a
few centuries after the invention of states. Giant funerary monuments
such as pyramids, and human sacrifices on a large scale became part of

the ceremonial life of the early states from Egypt to China, and in the somewhat later, but similar civilizations that developed in the New World.[3] It is pretty clear that the standards of nutrition and well being for the majority of the populations in these states fell, partly because of the overcrowding, but also because those in command expropriated so much of production.[4] More was taken from the peasants, and in return they received the dubious advantage of having glorious, cruel, divine monarchs and officials to rule them. Large-scale slavery spread, as did the semi-slavery that many peasants were forced into. Whatever the utility of state structures in the beginning, they soon became what Michael Mann has called "gigantic protection rackets." Even though states could rise and then collapse as people took power back into their own hands and "regressed" toward egalitarianism, in the long run the institution of the state spread and took over the entire world.[5] Societies organized as states could mobilize great fighting power. They were also immensely attractive to outsiders dazzled by the splendid luster of the life enjoyed by the few at the top of the civilized heap. The existence of the state became, and has remained, an invitation to those who would abuse its powers. That has not changed in more than five thousand years.

There remained, however, in all civilizations, myths about earlier times when there were no states, no taxes, no rulers, no wars, and no cruelty or abuse of power. And the question of why the powerful so often hurt the weak became one of those eternal human problems, almost as important as the question of why we become ill and die. Perhaps, as the writer Eli Sagan claims, the human need for structure and authority in a kind of super-family, the state, overwhelmed the desire for freedom.[6] Whether it was this "need," or simply the fact that those with power are tempted to abuse it, and to legitimize their excesses by displays of awesome cruelty, the fact is that the imposition of suffering became the accepted way of exercising political power. Once this was considered normal, the exceptional nature of state power could be legitimized and rationalized so that it ceased to be viewed as exceptional, and only the unusual, egregious abuse of hierarchy continued to be interpreted as something abnormal. The humiliation and deprivation imposed on most humans in the great civilizations came to be seen as entirely normal.

As we begin a study of modern tyranny, it is well to remember this. Our democratic standards that began to be applied only in the nineteenth and twentieth centuries have begun to push back the limits of what we consider "abuse." But if what may have been normal from the invention of the state until very recently may no longer be acceptable, for most of recorded history the tyrannical abuse of power has been only too common. And even in the twentieth century, Sagan's phrase about the cruelty of the state is worth remembering. "The normal state can commit acts that only a psychotic family would allow itself."[7]

Looking at statements made about statecraft and the nature of politics across a very wide range of agrarian states around the world shows how despotic, how abusive, and how contemptuous of ordinary human lives the elites in these states actually were, and how unashamed they were of this. The state came to be viewed as the private domain of the ruler, and the people as mere tools of his power, hardly superior to domestic animals. Peter the Great of Russia, who lived from 1672 to 1725, humiliated and terrorized his nobles, maintained Russia's peasants in the strictest bondage, and murdered his son in a drunken rage, justified his life in this way:

> The Russian nation is to be maintained in a permanent state of war in order to keep soldiers battle-tested and fit; respites serve only to improve the state's finances, rebuild the army, and pick a suitable moment for attack. Thus peace is to serve war, and war peace, all in the interest of enlarging the size and prosperity of Russia.[8]

Two thousand years earlier, in the fourth century B.C., the Lord of Shang, an influential advisor to the rulers of the Qin state that was to unite China into its first great empire in the following century, had written:

> [T]he means whereby a country is made prosperous are agriculture and war. . . . The way to organize a country well is . . . to have no license of speech. This being so the people will be simple and have concentration. . . . The way to administer a country well is for the law of the officials to be clear; therefore one does not rely on intelligent and thoughtful men. The ruler makes the people single-minded and therefore they will not scheme for selfish profit. Then the strength of the country will be consolidated.[9]

Whether legitimate or not in the eyes of their people, rulers in agrarian civilizations were, for the most part, a rapacious and bloodthirsty lot who caused immense suffering. Even if some were kinder than others, and others too weak to inflict much damage, the very essence of politics in these states was, by our contemporary democratic standards, tyrannical.

Nevertheless, we cannot simply say that all state power tends toward tyranny. The first extensive, analytic treatises we have about government are a little over two thousand years old and they try to deal with the problem of the abuse of power by delineating the proper limits of power. The Greeks, who asked far more penetrating questions about their environment than any other ancient people, made the exploration of the causes of tyranny a central issue in their philosophical investigations. Plato, Xenophon, and Aristotle sought to define and explain tyranny, and to prescribe ways of avoiding it. The Chinese and Indian texts roughly contemporary with the writings of the classical Greeks were quite different in that they accepted the notion that royal absolutism was the only workable form of government. But even they tried to distinguish between good and bad rulers, between the necessary violence and cruelty that had to be imposed to maintain such rule and needless exploitation and cruelty.

The exploration of ways to limit tyranny continued to preoccupy political philosophers, and with the Renaissance and Enlightenment in Europe it became a major theme of philosophical discourse. In the eighteenth century, French and English political theorists speculated, as had the Greeks, that tyranny might be avoided altogether by creating more balanced state structures, ones in which the people at large, or at least their representatives, would be able to curb the power of the state. To accomplish this end was the stated purpose of the American and French Revolutions in the late eighteenth century.[10]

In the nineteenth century the Industrial Revolution created a few economies where it began to seem that the harsh competition for resources that had characterized agrarian societies might be ended by great abundance. Then, some theorists speculated, the dreams of the Enlightenment philosophers might actually become workable because the very need for a coordinating and war-making state would vanish. Standards of political morality had risen; populations participated more widely in politics; and the abuses of the past were understood to be "barbarian." This was a misunderstanding, of course, because the tyrannies of the past were "civilized" compared to the earlier, more egalitarian primitive societies without states. Still, some nineteenth-century thinkers believed such abuses to be unworthy of truly developed modern civilizations. Herbert Spencer, the founder of Anglo-American sociology, believed that industrial societies no longer needed wars to prosper, but on the contrary, thrived on peace and trade:

> With the absence of need for that corporate action by which the efforts of the whole society may be utilized for war, there goes the absence of need for a despotic controlling agency. Not only is such an agency unnecessary, but it cannot exist. For since, as we see, it is an essential requirement of the industrial type, that the individuality of each man shall have the fullest play compatible with the like play of other men's individualities, despotic control, showing itself as it must by otherwise restricting men's individualities, is necessarily excluded. Indeed, by his mere presence an autocratic ruler is an aggressor on citizens.[11]

Unfortunately that optimism about how much more "civilized" modern societies are than ancient or feudal ones has been exposed as hopelessly naïve in the twentieth century. On the contrary, this sad century has seen the greatest and bloodiest wars ever fought, and we only narrowly averted a final cataclysm that might have destroyed humanity forever. But more horrifying than the immense slaughter in warfare has been the even greater death toll caused by internal repressions. The level of human suffering imposed by despotic political power has been so high, so devastating in many societies, that it makes the classical discussions of tyranny by Greek or Roman authors, or later, by Machiavelli, and even more recent work by Enlightenment philosophers such as Rousseau, seem quaintly archaic and almost as naïve as Spencer.

In World War I, some 10 to 15 million people were killed, most of them soldiers, and most of the rest civilians who died of the hunger and disease brought on by war. But at least 800,000 Armenians were deliberately murdered by the Turks.[12] In World War II, a very conservative estimate of deaths would include at least 30 million in Europe and about the same number in Asia. Of these, at least half were civilians killed as part of extermination campaigns, deliberately induced famines, and the incidental destruction of economies by the war. Between five and six million of those killed for nonmilitary reasons were Jews. Perhaps up to 18 million Chinese civilians died, and 11 million in the Soviet Union (of which close to one million were Jews).[13]

The deaths caused by the Stalinist purges and persecutions in the Soviet Union in the 1930s and 1940s, not counting war-related deaths, have been estimated at between 15 and 25 million, and recent revelations in the Soviet Union indicate that the high estimate is closer to the truth.[14] Somewhere between 20 and 40 million Chinese died of famine in China during Mao's Great Leap Forward because of misguided, stubbornly imposed rural socialist policies.[15] Over one million Cambodians, at least one eighth of the entire population, were killed during the rule of Pol Pot's Khmer Rouge in the late 1970s.[16] Up to three million Bengalis, most of them civilians, may have died during the repression by the Pakistani army in the period leading up to Bangladesh's independence.[17] Several million died in Ethiopia and Eritrea in the civil wars and related famines caused by the harsh and unsuccessful attempts to build a Soviet type of socialist, united society in that country from 1975 to 1991.[18] At least a half million, perhaps one million Indonesians were killed in 1965 and 1966 as part of the purge of leftist elements. This does not count the many deaths imposed on East Timor by the Indonesian army's policy of forced starvation and deliberate persecution after that little country was invaded by the Indonesians in 1975.[19]

Yet, this is only part of the story. Massive suffering imposed on people by political power has at one time or another in our century included most of the world. When Mao Zedong died in 1976, Chinese sources estimate that 20 percent of the population of China, some 200 million souls, were suffering from chronic malnutrition for no good reason other than the failures of socialist agriculture and the chaos of the Cultural Revolution.[20] Political repression in Nazi-controlled territories throughout Europe subjected several hundred million people to terror and deprivation for six years. Political terror and murder in Central and South America have killed and tortured at least hundreds of thousands, and probably well over a million individuals, and subjected many times that number to incessant fear and misery. Repressions have jailed millions and confiscated the properties of millions more in Eastern Europe, North Korea, Vietnam, and Cuba, but also in Spain during and after the terrible Civil War of 1936–1939, in Burma since 1962, in Iran, in Syria, in Iraq, in Libya, and in many parts of Africa. Ethnic and religious wars and repressions in Uganda since 1969 have killed over a half a million, in Lebanon since 1956 a few hundred thousand, in the Sudan during the 1960s to 1990s over one million, in Rwanda and Burundi in the 1970s another few hundred thousand, and between Pakistan and India in 1947–1948 over a million.[21] Over a million were killed in the Mexican Civil War that began in 1911, and went on into the 1920s. In Afghanistan, since the late 1970s three to five million, a third of the population, have been killed, wounded, or driven into refugee camps. Many millions died or were ruined in China and Russia during their gigantic internal wars which accompanied the seizure of power by the communists. Well over a million died in the civil war that raged in Vietnam at the same time that the French, and later the Americans, were involved in combatting the communists. And even as I am writing these words, there are terrible stories of castration of prisoners, in which guards force some of the prisoners to bite off the testicles of others, public rapes, and mass murder in Bosnia, mostly committed by Serbs. Many more hundreds of thousands will die before the end of the century in the numerous wars unleashed by the collapse of communism in the former Soviet empire and in Eastern Europe.[22]

This is only a very partial, very conservative list. There have been well over 100 million deaths caused by war and political repression in the twentieth century, and over half of them have not been caused by direct military action but by the persecution and abuse of civilian populations. There have been several billions subjected to frightful regimes.

Enumerations such as these are numbing, and eventually lose all meaning. But it is essential that we study and try to understand them. If anything ties most of them together, it is the fact that political despotism, the exercise of power by small ruling elites, initiated the actions that led to these terrible outcomes. In some cases, it was error, the mistaken policies of rulers that produced such horrors. But more often than not, killing and suffering on a gigantic scale was started on purpose, to carry out specific political goals. Even when it became obvious that the amounts of suffering imposed were immense, policies were continued because leaders preferred to make their people suffer rather than to change their own goals and hence admit their own errors.

As a matter of definition I have decided to call such leaders, those responsible for the political nightmares of our century whose orders have resulted in such suffering, tyrants. The word "tyrant" is laden with a weighty and controversial history, and a good exploration of the many meanings and interpretations of "tyranny" would fill a considerable volume. This is not what I propose to do. Rather, I want to understand the causes and consequences of the political behavior that has made the twentieth century so contemptuous of human life and freedom.

CLASSICAL TYRANTS

It should be clear that the horrors inflicted on humanity by tyranny in the twentieth century are not absolutely unprecedented. Killing, torture, enslavement, the use of terror to keep dissenters in line, artificially induced famine—all of these have occurred before, sometimes on a large scale. Giovanni de Piano Carpini, an Italian Franciscan monk who travelled to the Mongol court of Karakorum in the thirteenth century, described how the Mongols treated cities they had besieged and captured.

> All those they capture in battle are killed or enslaved. They select those who are to be killed with battle axes, and their captains distribute them among the prisoners who are to be enslaved. These slaves then have to kill about ten prisoners each, more or less, according to the officers' decision.[23]

On the other hand, most Mongols took a rather practical view of killing. David Morgan, the author of a recent book about them, has emphasized this by writing:

> But normally Chingiz Khan had neither the time nor the inclination for such expedients as cementing people alive into towers, which Tamerlane is said to have enjoyed. Chingiz's principle seems to have been much the same as President Truman's over Hiroshima and Nagasaki. The apparent rationale was that if the population of one city was subjected to a frightful massacre, the next city would be more likely to surrender. . . . thus avoiding unnecessary Mongol casualties.[24]

The Romans, who were the greatest power in the Mediterranean world from about 200 B.C. to about A.D. 400, were known for their fierce brutality. But they also tended to be practical. They destroyed Carthage out of fear that a dangerous rival might revive. But once that was done, there was no attempt to destroy the Carthaginian people as a whole. Their language continued to be spoken in North Africa until after the end of the Roman Empire. Similarly, when the Jews revolted in the late first century and again in the early second, they were brutally repressed. Tacitus estimates that 600,000 were killed, probably an exaggeration, but indicative of the vast numbers involved. But once they had been scattered and rendered powerless, there was no further attempt to exterminate, or even to convert the Jews into Latin-speaking Romans.

So it was in all of the agrarian empires. Submission of subject peoples was the object; if they paid their taxes, humbled themselves, and did not interfere with affairs of state, they could remain relatively safe. This could entail immense suffering, and the very form of government in these states would be considered unbearable tyranny by people living in modern democracies. But it was normal, and there may have been no other way to rule or maintain state structures when resources were so limited.

Cases of exceptional cruelty were common enough. Often, they were deliberately aimed at potential rivals of rulers. Many of the princes who have remained in our historical memory as monsters did so because they viciously persecuted elite nobles, and even members of their own families in order to conquer and maintain themselves in power.

Recent scholarship about Caligula, the notorious Roman Emperor who ruled in the middle of the first century and whose name has become almost synonymous with irrational tyranny, shows that he was neither mad nor destructive on a large scale. He was selfish, sometimes cruel, and, as Anthony Barrett has put it, "so obsessed with a sense of his own importance as to be practically devoid of any sense of moral responsibility." He was hated and feared by that portion of the senatorial nobility engaged in a desperate effort to bring back the old republican form of government by overthrowing the empire. Some of his enemies were viciously persecuted, but there is no evidence that he harmed large numbers of people. The malicious gossip of Suetonius (the source for Robert Graves's brilliant but misleading novels about the first Roman imperial dynasty, the Julio-Claudians) notwithstanding, there is little evidence that Caligula was clinically mad.[25]

There are two important lessons for us in the story of Caligula. One is that malicious persecution of fairly small numbers of potential rivals and insubordinate elites, as opposed to the routine oppression of slaves and peasants, which was considered a normal part of social life, can easily mislead us into thinking that the tyrants of the past committed crimes as great as those of the twentieth century. Secondly, it is clear that tyrannical personalities, self-absorbed, suspicious to the point of paranoia, and vindictive, were not necessarily unsuited to rule. On the contrary, that type of personality may have been well adapted to the competition for power in agrarian states, and may, indeed, be well suited in general to compete for power. It would be the greatest error to confound this kind of personality with madness, even though, when it results in cruel tyranny, it comforts us to think that the perpetrator is crazy. In a very few cases, this may have been true, but on the whole, the truly insane are unable to keep themselves in power long enough to do much harm.

Eli Sagan, in describing the nineteenth-century kingdom of Buganda (from which the name of the modern country of Uganda was derived), where the *Kabaka*, or King, frequently displayed extreme cruelty, makes the point that "License is implicit in omnipotence. The two great licenses are the sexual and aggressive, and early kings were expected to exercise both."[26] But that did not mean that those who exercised such license were in any sense psychotic, only that they had the power to do what they wanted, and it was accepted as long as their behavior did not endanger the state. On the other hand, kings, and not just early ones, were always threatened by rivals, and extreme cruelty could sometimes be perfectly functional in order to keep potential opponents in check.

This point could be made by looking at the story of another famous historical tyrant, Sultan Muhammad bin Tughluq of Delhi who ruled in the fourteenth century, probably after having his father murdered. The noted Arab traveller Ibn Batuta, who served him, wrote that he was exceptionally generous and that he cared about the fate of his people. But Ibn Batuta also describes how Sultan Muhammad tortured his enemies, sometimes killing hundreds at a time. He was called a tyrant by his foes, and blamed for a particularly heinous act which Ibn Batuta describes as follows:

> [H]e forced the inhabitants of Delhi into exile [because they wrote him anonymous letters] containing abuses and scandals. . . . So he resolved to lay Delhi to waste. . . . Then he ordered the inhabitants to leave Delhi and move to Daulatabad. . . . [A] blind man [who had not left was ordered] to be dragged from Delhi to Daulatabad—a distance of forty days' journey. He was torn to pieces on the way, and only a leg of his reached Daulatabad.[27]

Later Sultan Muhammad brought the province of Sind under control, reputedly by having his enemies flayed to death.[28]

But later historians have found that these stories were greatly exaggerated. Sultan Muhammad's venom was directed primarily against what he considered rebellious elites trying to resist his centralizing autocracy. He was certainly a tyrant by the standards of his day, and of ours, but it is because the literary sources of his epoch considered only the interests of the elites that he was depicted as a monster.[29]

Whether in Europe, India, China, the Near East, or Africa, many of the ruling figures who have been called tyrants were centralizers of their states who fought their aristocracies and cultural elites in order to strengthen royal power. Some famous European examples were Louis XI of France in the fifteenth century and his contemporary, the unsuccessful but historically famous prince of the little principality of Wallachia in southern Romania who is remembered by the Romanians as Vlad the Impaler and by the rest of the world as Dracula. Impaling enemies by having a metal tipped stake driven up the anus, through the body, and out near the shoulders so that the victim continued to live for hours, to be put up, much as the Romans had put up their crucified victims, seems to have been a form of execution occasionally used by the Turks in the Balkans during this time, and Vlad was not that original. But when West Europeans, who were not familiar with this particular form of torture, heard of it, they were suitably horrified and spread stories about the monster "Dracula." In the sixteenth century, the Russian Tsar Ivan IV (the "Terrible") loved to have stories about the famous Dracula told to him. He was himself a successful centralizer of his state who brought his nobles under control by slaughtering many of them and intimidating the others.[30]

In more recent times, these three—Louis XI, Vlad, and Ivan IV—have been lionized by nationalist French, Romanian, and Russian historians as great and far-sighted patriots. But this is as anachronistic a view as trying to interpret them as medieval Stalins or Hitlers. Despots and tyrants they were, but they were motivated by personal and dynastic ambitions in a time when politics were conducted cruelly and the wishes of the common people were not taken into account. Their wars caused much death and destruction, but in this they were not so different from other princes. There is little or no evidence that they tried to change the fundamental social order in which they lived.

Even without resorting to extreme examples, it can be shown that pre-modern politics could result in awful human catastrophes. Up to one-third of the population of Central Germany died as a result of the

Thirty Years' War from 1618 to 1648. For all of the theological and great power politics involved, it is clear that a major motivation for this war was the search by high-ranking nobles throughout Europe for states to rule in order to support themselves, and of ruthless imperial state builders such as Gustavus Adolfus of Sweden and Richelieu of France who were trying to acquire new revenue-producing lands to finance their ambitions.[31] From our point of view, these glorious episodes of warfare and conquest were examples of tyranny in that they imposed human suffering on a large scale in order to satisfy the ambitions of small, selfish elites. Within their own world, however, these leaders were pragmatic, and their suspicion of others and great cruelty were quite rational.

Tyrannies of the past can be explained in three ways. One, that Spencer and other naïve nineteenth-century European optimists understood well, was the simple fact that there really was no other known way of maintaining elites than by plundering and abusing the majority of their people. Economies could only grow slowly, and sometimes not at all. Elites in the settled and nomadic states that lived from the labor of peasant majorities were essentially parasites, as William H. McNeill has pointed out.[32] If they misjudged the extent to which they could drain their human resources, they pushed their masses below subsistence. If the elites overpopulated themselves, they tended to do the same thing, much as general overpopulation results in overuse of the environment. The only defense of the population was to rebel, though this was generally futile, and only produced more suffering.[33]

In order to maintain order, such elites had to be truly awesome and frightening. This, no doubt, partly explains the wanton brutality in agrarian states, particularly early ones that were still insecure. If they failed to frighten, elites invited predation from other potential elites, and rebellion from the peasants. But modern industrial economies do not need to do this. If properly managed they can grow quickly and satisfy elites as well as increasing the well-being of large proportions of the entire population. Thus, when modern states behave as did the Mongols, or the desperate princelings of Europe in the seventeenth century, or the *Kabakas* of Buganda, they have less of an excuse. Spencer was right, we do have a right to expect better political behavior than did our ancestors.

A second category of political abuse in the pre-modern world was the inevitable result of the extreme concentration of power into a few hands, and the transmission of power by heredity. Insanity, sadism, and incompetence were bound to crop up, and unelected, powerful rulers were then likely to cause suffering simply because there was no way to remove them without bloodshed. There is no inherent way of preventing this, even in modern societies, except by limiting the power of those in charge of the state, and by subjecting power holders to frequent review by the general population through elections. Sadistic and incompetent rulers may still exist, but in a democratic political system that hedges power with many restrictions, they are likely to do less harm, and to be more easily removed than in nondemocratic states. Whereas in the past it was almost universally accepted that only tiny elites should participate in governing the state, today it is generally admitted, even in some of the most despotic systems devised, that the "people" or the "masses" should have a say in governance. Therefore, the kind of abuse that used to be common and could simply be ascribed to bad luck, to the presence of a "bad king," needs to be explained in the modern era when most rulers claim to have been selected and kept in power by popular acclaim.

Finally, there was corruption. When greed or excessive ambition led the powerful to take much more than what was considered reasonable in their societies, they were abusing their power. Aristotle wrote, "As of oligarchy, so of tyranny, the end is wealth. Both distrust the people and so deprive them of their arms. Both agree, too, in injuring the people and driving them out of the city."[34] To be sure, the line between "normal" exploitation of the populace and "excessive" greed was not always clear. In democratic societies the notion of corruption is more sharply delineated than in monarchies where the prince's and the state's purses were indistinguishable. Therefore, much of what used to be considered acceptable behavior by rulers would now be considered corrupt. Nevertheless, even in the past corruption by the powerful was recognized as one of the types of tyranny.

Given that democracy has been more widely praised than practiced in the twentieth century, it may well be that one of the reasons for the widespread presence of tyranny is simply that our ethical standards are higher, but that politics in many, perhaps most countries continue to be run as in the past. And there is no question that some of the egregious tyrants of our times have really been nothing more than classically corrupt, sadistic, or incompetent "bad kings."

Of the Dominican Republic's Rafael Trujillo, or of Uganda's Idi

Amin, it can truly be said that they were examples of "Aristotelian tyranny"—the purpose of which was to accumulate wealth for a few corrupt individuals. As we will see later, Idi Amin and Trujillo were also sadistic torturers. Other twentieth-century tyrants, such as Duvalier of Haiti, or Ne Win of Burma, began with every intention of being "good kings," but through incompetence and corruption degenerated into "bad" ones who did immense amounts of harm to their societies. Despite their ideological pretensions to being modern revolutionaries, these four, in fact, came to resemble classical tyrants.

Because the old-fashioned tyranny of incompetence, corruption, and wanton brutality still exists on a large scale, it is necessary to explore it in order to understand the twentieth century. Also, newer kinds of tyranny, to which most of this study will be devoted, have a tendency to degenerate into incompetence and corruption, and to begin to resemble classical tyranny. There is a continuum between the new and the old, and it is hard to identify the originality of some modern tyrannies without adequate contrast. Yet, the similarities between the important ideological tyrannies of the twentieth century and their older, more classical relatives should not obscure the fact that our century has seen the large-scale development of a kind of tyranny that was rare in the past, if it existed at all.

MODERN IDEOLOGICAL TYRANNY, NATIONALISM, AND SCIENCE

Hitler and Stalin, the two greatest murderers in history, were not in it "for the money," and they most certainly were not just old-fashioned monarchs who happened to survive into the twentieth century because their societies were backward. They were neither Aristotelian tyrants nor anachronisms. Nor were Mao, Kim Il Sung of North Korea, or the Khmer Rouge, and it is unlikely that Augusto Pinochet, who killed and tortured on a far lesser scale, but still committed many atrocities, can be explained in terms of corruption. Trujillo may have been a gangster who seized a country and exploited it, as was Idi Amin of Uganda, but Hitler, Stalin, Mao, and the other ideological tyrants of our century were revolutionary idealists who wanted something much more.

Revolutionary idealism that turns into tyranny is not an entirely new phenomenon. What is required for this is an absolute sense of moral superiority based on an ideology, or a religion that claims to explain everything perfectly. This sense of certitude can justify the worst horrors in the name of sanctity, purity, and the general improvement of life for the multitudes. Before Hitler and Stalin, there were Torquemada,[35] the Dominicans who inspired the Albigensian Crusade, and the Church leaders who preached the massacres and expulsion of the Jews. Religions that came out of the Near East—Christianity and Islam, and perhaps Zoroastrianism and Judaism before them—have been particularly prone to such absolutist interpretations of the world. Monotheism seems to be congenial to the exercise of ideological tyranny, which might be labelled more correctly as the tyranny of certitude.[36]

But even so, the Spanish Inquisition probably killed no more than 30,000 people over a century and a half.[37] The various Christian Crusades, the first of which also began in Europe with the mass murder of Jews, were initially characterized by great ideological fervor, and then gradually turned into the normal kinds of plundering expeditions by rapacious nobles that can be explained without the ideological certitude that may have started them.[38] No ideological tyranny in the past was ever as absolute and devastating as twentieth-century Nazism and communism. There is little question that in the twentieth century the tyranny of certitude became much more widespread than at any time in the past.

If the old-fashioned type of tyranny that still exists in the twentieth century would have been recognized easily by Plato or Aristotle, the newer kind, the tyranny of certitude and revolutionary idealism, would have been unfamiliar to them. Whereas the tyranny of corruption and incompetence needs little new theory to explain it beyond that offered by political philosophers over the past two and a half thousand years, ideological tyranny, its growth, and its destructive potential have only been understood and studied since the French Revolution, and its practitioners only exposed their enormously destructive potential in the twentieth century.

There are two elements of modern ideological tyranny that explain why it has produced such mayhem. These are fundamental aspects of modern thought and life, and are unlikely to disappear quickly. One is nationalism, the other the way in which modern science has been applied to social and political programs. Both have to be understood by seeing how intellectuals, that is those with higher education of one sort or another who read and think about alternative social and political models, interpret the modern world. Ideological tyranny, or the tyranny of certitude, in fact, relies first of all on intellectuals, and might just as easily be called the tyranny of thought.

Most of those who have analyzed nationalism, easily the most important ideologically binding force in the modern world, generally have neglected the degree to which so much of it is based on a combination of resentment and insecurity. The first strong nationalisms—in England in the sixteenth and seventeenth centuries, and in the United States and France in the eighteenth—were not like this. These were nations that saw themselves from the start as advanced, powerful entities, feelings that were confirmed by their economic strengths, security from foreign invasion, and significant international successes. But the nations that followed England, France, and the United States developed their sense of nationhood as economically and politically backward places, always trying to catch up to and avoid being dominated by the more advanced nations.

Nationalism replaced older ways people used to identify themselves, by family or clan, by village or town, and by religion. Nationalism is at once more sweeping, encompassing the great majority of people in large territories, and more exclusive as the ultimate source of defense people have against the vagaries of social, economic, and political misfortune. Modern nations base their enormous claims to their citizens' loyalties on the fact that they are the ultimate protectors of cultural integrity, economic well-being, and freedom from political humiliation by outside forces. In societies that are self-confident, nationalism is only occasionally jingoistic and aggressive. In those that come into being as nations sensing that they are backward and threatened, nationalism is fundamentally envious and angry. To create strong feelings of cultural identity with, dependence on, and loyalty to a political entity born of resentment and fear, and to teach, at the same time, that "our" nation should be recognized as being inherently superior to others, is to create the essential political and ideological contradiction that has plagued the modern world.[39]

Germany, starting in the early nineteenth century, developed a particularly resentful, self-pitying form of nationalism. First the French, and later the English, were seen as unfairly dominating Europe. At the same time, the Germans felt themselves to be, at least while German nationalism was developing, economically backward, but also more deserving and superior to the more advanced French and English. Fritz Stern's account of how some key German intellectuals nursed this sense of grievance and a powerful but insecure belief in their own superiority goes a long way toward explaining what propelled Germany toward Nazism.[40]

But as Liah Greenfeld explains, Germany was not the only "resentful" nation. Russia was similar. As higher education was developed in the eighteenth and nineteenth centuries to train a service aristocracy capable of running this vast empire, the elite were taught that theirs was an inherently superior nation, purer and less affected by the ills of modernism, but also a backward one permanently endangered by a hostile, outside world, particularly the more advanced Western powers in Europe. The sense of angry insecurity toward the West and romantic idealization about their own communal, Russian Orthodox, rural tradition that infected Russian intellectuals made them reject crass modern Western capitalism as a solution to their backwardness. By the late nineteenth century, though the Russian intelligentsia was divided between so-called Westernizers and Slavophiles, in fact, both groups shared a deep contempt for the political and economic systems that prevailed in the more advanced countries.[41]

In one way or another, almost all the new nationalisms that were formed subsequently resembled the German and Russian patterns. The Hungarians and Poles led the way in Eastern Europe, to be followed by Romanians, Serbs, Bulgarians, and others. Everywhere there was a similar pattern. Nationalistic intellectuals "discovered" that theirs was an ancient people, once possessors of proud empires in the forefront of civilization, and then treated unfairly by fate, and sacrificed or exploited by the selfish, undeserving Western nations (the French, the English, and eventually, too, the Germans). Born of envy and frustration about being small, backward, and weak, these nationalist historian-intellectuals created persuasive fantasies that were taught in their countries' growing school systems.

Then the same sentiment developed as the basis for anti-Western, anti-colonial resentment and national unity in the non-European world. The sense of persecution and resentment may have had more objective justification among many colonial peoples than among the Germans and Russians, but in any case, it was the powerful myth of past national grandeur (even if, in the past, there were no "nations," but only loosely integrated imperial structures) and latter-day persecution that shaped the intellectuals who spread nationalism throughout Asia, Africa, and Latin America.[42]

This was not sufficient to produce fully developed ideological tyranny, but it was an important aspect of political development in much of the world. Leaders who could appeal to that kind of nationalist sentiment, and promise to carry out its goals of catching up and gaining revenge, as well as recapturing past grandeur, could count on intellectual support, and it was intellectuals who occupied the leading ideological and technical positions almost everywhere. The more the world has modernized, the more important education has become and the more schools there have been to be staffed by nationalist intellectuals training whole new generations of converts.

Nationalist ideologies built on resentment are conducive to tyranny for two reasons. One is that the anger of the resentful and vengeful tends easily toward violence. The other is that if the external world (imperialism, the world communist conspiracy, international Jewry, high finance, American multinationals, or whatever) is viewed as dangerously threatening, this is a good argument for demanding internal unanimity and conformity. The consequent suppression of dissent is favorable to the abuse of power.

Along with nationalism, the other major element in the development of modern ideological tyranny has been the success of modern science in convincing intellectuals that final answers can be found. It was the adaptation of misunderstood Darwinian evolutionary theory and the emerging genetic sciences in the late nineteenth and early twentieth centuries that created an intellectual climate in Europe conducive to the growth of virulent racism. This was not the only cause of the rise of Nazism, of course, but the general acceptance of theories about the importance of race, of remaining strong in the competition for survival, and of maintaining genetic purity in order to maintain national vigor, when combined with resentful nationalism, produced the base without which vengeful hatred and extreme racial exclusivity could not have gained a significant number of followers.

Marxism has been another great "science" that has lent itself to tyranny. It was ideally suited to backward countries wishing to catch up to and surpass a West that was assumed to be persecuting them. It blamed the injustices so evident in industrializing societies on capitalism itself, and presented the leading capitalist nations as fundamentally rotten and evil. Once Lenin had adapted Marxist science to Russia, the model could be presented as a way of leaping over capitalist nations.

For nationalists from backward countries all over the world, Marxism-Leninism promised the benefits of economic development without the defects of capitalism; it also promised the ultimate revenge, that the great colonial powers would be destroyed by the progressive forces that would bypass and isolate them.

Had the Russian intelligentsia not been so deeply nationalistic and anti-Western, so eager to catch up but also so contemptuous of the moral failings of bourgeois capitalism, it is unlikely that either Lenin, or later Stalin would have been able to impose themselves. But Marxism's appeal was greater than this because it could also present itself as the epitome of modern, advanced scientific thought even as it was anti-capitalist, and hostile to the existing powers in the West.

The essential element in the development of these tyrannical ideologies is the contradictory feelings of admiration and hatred of European modernity. The Nazis could present themselves as technological and scientific virtuosi unleashing vast modern armies on the world. Yet, at the same time, Wagnerian nostalgia for a fantasized past and contempt of bourgeois democracy appealed to all those alienated by the vagaries of modern market forces and the seeming collapse of traditional communal solidarities. Communism, which may seem to be so different, is pretty much the same in this respect. In its most extreme form, such as Pol Pot's Khmer Rouge, communism abandoned modernity entirely in favor of a return to communal, rural solidarity. But the promotion of communalism over individualism, of status assigned by virtue rather than through market-induced class differences, and the rejection of soft, "degenerate" bourgeois consumerism has been central to communism in Europe, too, as it was to fascism in the 1920s and 1930s.

To hatred and jealousy directed against the advanced, that is bourgeois, democratic, and capitalist nations of the West, has been added the sense of scientific certitude that, paradoxically, is a critical element of Western thought. Without such certitude, it would have been impossible for Stalin or Hitler, Mao or Pol Pot, Ceausescu or Kim Il Sung to carry on with such determination, such willingness to impose mass suffering against all the evidence of the harm their policies were producing.

It is easy to understand why such a sense of certitude is conducive to tyranny. Those who are sure that theirs is the only truth, and a scientific truth at that, can justify tyranny more easily than those who are unsure of their beliefs. The appeal to "science" can transform the utili-

tarian calculus used to legitimate imposed suffering. After all, if, ultimately, the "race" or the "people" will benefit, and this is a scientific
certainty, it matters little what the immediate costs may be.

Science since the eighteenth-century Enlightenment has convinced
a large number of intellectuals that it is possible to formulate perfect
social and economic models, and that society can be "engineered."
Karl Popper's demonstration that it is impossible to predict "scientifically" what the future will be, is accurate. But this has not prevented
most intellectuals from believing the contrary because modern science
and technology are so evidently powerful, and increasingly able to
change the world. It is true, as Popper has shown, that the transposi-
tion of science to theories justifying massive social engineering leads to
tyranny. Yet, the error of unreasonable faith in the power of certain
social theories, chiefly Marxism, has proved to be extremely persuasive
throughout almost all of the twentieth century.[43]

The combination of resentment, nationalist xenophobia, and "scientific" intellectual intolerance and certitude makes a potent brew
responsible for the proliferation of ideological tyrannies in the twentieth century. Nor is the latter part of our century better in this respect
than the first half.

There are still those who cling to the belief that the age of modern
ideological tyranny has drawn to a close.[44] We are said to be more skeptical about science, and social engineering. Nationalism is said to be
giving way to the recognition that free trade and supra-national institutions such as the European Community are better for us than the narrow competition between nations that dominated most of the
nineteenth and twentieth centuries. I agree that in the societies that
are the democratic heirs of the Enlightenment in Western Europe and
North America this is so, at least for now.

But the many tragedies that have occurred in the former communist
states since 1989 suggest that nationalism may have increased its
power to produce tyranny. And I doubt that the fascination with science and the belief in social engineering are as dead as optimists might
think. So much of the success of the most advanced societies in the
world is so obviously based on the wonders of technology and science
that it is difficult to believe that intellectuals will abandon the idea that
the same methods can be applied to social reform as well. It is not as if
the problems of poverty and inequality, or of frustrated rage and
resentment, have been put aside once and for all. There continue to be

winners and losers, and new ideologies that claim to be able to tap sup-posedly scientific certitudes will surely arise.

In the past two decades we have witnessed the large-scale revival of religious ideologies of certitude. Bolstered by the examples of both communism and fascism, taking advantage of extreme nationalism, and using the modern technological methods of coercion developed in our century, the Iranians have developed a tyranny of certitude that calls itself traditional but is actually entirely new. The sense that Islam can adopt what is useful in Western science and technology without giving up its religious certitude may be the prelude to a similar phenomenon throughout much of the world.

Understanding what happened in the past will not help us predict the tragedies of the next century; but it may prepare us better than simply pretending, as did so many late nineteenth-century optimists, that we have evolved too far to repeat the nightmares of the past.

Chapter 2

Moderation Abandoned

Adolf Hitler and Joseph Stalin were the two most influential politicians of the twentieth century. Only Mao Zedong rivalled them in importance. They rank with the greatest conquerors in history who revolutionized politics in their age. Yet, like Alexander of Macedonia, whose empire fractured immediately after his death, Shi Huangdi, who created the first unified Chinese Empire but whose dynasty collapsed soon after him, Charlemagne, whose empire was divided and reduced to impotence two generations after he had ruled most of Europe, or Napoleon, who ended his life as a prisoner on a lonely island, Hitler and Stalin were also colossal failures. The new types of societies they tried to create did not survive long.

Hitler's tyranny only lasted a dozen years. His dramatic fall, combined with the much later collapse of the Soviet Empire, seventy-four years after its creation and thirty-eight after Stalin's death, gave optimists around the world a false sense that tyranny so colossal could not possibly arise again. I obviously disagree, and I devote the first part of this book to studying Hitler and Stalin, not merely as appalling examples of tyranny, but as models for a century that produced many others like them.

Hitler and Stalin killed on a titanic, unprecedented scale. Alan Bullock's recent book, *Hitler and Stalin: Parallel Lives*, estimates that between them they were responsible for 40 to 50 million deaths between 1930 and 1950, and that over half of these were not due to military battles. They were both worshipped, as were Mao and Lenin, in ways that no mortal had been since the great religious prophets of the past, Jesus Christ, Buddha, and Mohammed. Yet they are reviled and hated as no successful religious leader could be.

Like many of the greatest leaders of the past, especially Napoleon, they came from marginal border lands that were not fully part of the countries they came to rule. In a real sense they were foreigners in the states they seized. Furthermore, like Napoleon, they were born in circumstances that made it almost inconceivable that they would attain such power.

Compared to the two other great leaders in World War II, Franklin Roosevelt and Winston Churchill, both of whom were born as members of their countries' most elite class, Hitler and Stalin were totally self-made men. It is one of the great ironies of Hitler's and Stalin's careers that these two greatest enemies of democracy could only have reached such heights in a revolutionary democratic age that devalued the role of traditional elites, while their great democratic contemporaries, Roosevelt and Churchill, were hereditary aristocrats.

Because of their astonishing accomplishments, their almost magical, unbelievable rise to total power, and the destruction and misery they caused, it is easy to think that they were unique, terrible miracles. This is even truer of Hitler, who created his party by himself, almost from nothing, than of Stalin, who was preceded in power by another political genius, Lenin. But like all great leaders, including the greatest charismatic religious prophets of the past, Hitler and Stalin operated in societies that were ready and willing to grant them such powers. Like religious prophets, they did not create their ideologies alone, but were a part of the major intellectual and political currents of their time. This is not to deny their exceptional abilities, but only to emphasize that neither Stalin nor Hitler was as original in his thinking as in his ability to create novel forms of administration and political rule.

To explain them requires a knowledge of European, German, and Russian history before them, of the circumstances that created such violent revolutionary conditions in the early twentieth century, and of the nature of their rule. If it requires no fantastic leap of the imagination to understand why Winston Churchill believed in democracy and was able to mobilize England behind him, the originality and scope of Hitler's and Stalin's tyrannies make it much harder to understand them. Yet, we must try, because their tyrannies resulted from the conflicting and contradictory forces of the modern era that combined in the 1930s to reshape our world permanently. The main forces at work were nationalism, a belief that modern science could be used to engineer a perfect social world, and hatred of the social and economic transformations wrought by capitalist industrialization since the start of the nineteenth century.

Explanation is made at once easier and much harder by the enormous amount of popular and scholarly literature about these characters. It is hardly possible to say anything original about Hitler and Stalin, and even impossible to read all the works about them. Yet, amid all this material, it is necessary to choose an interpretation that makes sense. There is no escaping the fact that these two men were the original architects of modern tyranny whose astonishing careers inspired all tyrants who were their contemporaries as well as those who came after them.

CRITICISMS OF CAPITALISM AND OF LIBERAL DEMOCRACY

What the late nineteenth-century optimists like Herbert Spencer missed was that, even as they were writing, deep currents of dissatisfaction against capitalism, liberalism, and democracy were gaining ground. They would eventually overwhelm and almost extinguish the forces of the European Enlightenment.

It is not difficult to see why the growth of capitalism would have been unpopular at many levels of society. For the old landed aristocracies, whose positions had been under assault since the French Revolution of 1789, first of all in France, but eventually everywhere in Europe, the predominance of money over inherited status associated with landed titles threatened their very existence. An appeal by the Prussian People's Association to the legislature in the 1860s, pleading for the continued legal control of interest rates, summarizes the essence of the conservative position which was anti-democratic, anti-capitalist, and which increasingly tended to blame these modern misfortunes on some alien and mysterious presence in the midst of their pure and supposedly previously well-behaved and passive people.

In the name of the Christian foundation of the state, in the name of the
morals of the concept of justice of our people, in the interest of landed
property, which nourishes and maintains the state, and finally, in the
interest of all who still have not and do not want to fall under the sway
of the speculating moneyed economy, the undersigned hope and ask
that it may please the honorable house to protect our fatherland by its
vote against this new pernicious gift of "progress"! . . . Should Christian
law hand over Christian inhabitants of the land to speculating Jewry?[1]

Subjecting landed property to market forces meant that self-preservation of the old elites would depend on their economic skills, not on
their blood or sacred right to ancient titles. If rich industrialists and
bankers could buy political power and land, and afford to imitate the
style of life of the high nobility, then the old nobilities would have
nothing left but their fading prestige. This is why, in so many countries
of Europe, the sons of the nobility preferred the army to other professions. There, old feudal virtues, honor, military skills, and loyalty to ideals higher than crass materialism were still worth something; and
through military careers, it was possible to maintain political influence as
well. To be sure, some members of old aristocratic families became modern entrepreneurs, and others married new wealth. But in so doing they
transferred their disgust of mere money grubbing to those who had done
so well in the market that they could now afford to deny their origins.

The high bourgeoisie that increasingly dominated economic life in
nineteenth-century Europe (and in North America) actually wished to
gain the prestige formerly held by aristocrats. It developed a whole set
of institutions to mark its newly gained social eminence. These
attempted to recreate aspects of aristocratic behavior through an
emphasis on honor, the development of martial values in athletic com-
petitions, and exclusive patterns of marriage and socializing. These values were taught in expensive schools and perpetuated in social clubs
where only the rich or well born were supposed to mingle. Thus, it was
in the nineteenth century that many of the supposedly "traditional"
habits of the aristocracy came to be widely practiced by the new rich
as well as by the aristocrats with whom they mixed. Sporting contests
between universities in the Anglo-American world and duelling in
German universities were among the most characteristics practices
developed for such purposes. But more than this, a whole style of education that emphasized history and letters for the upper classes, that

instilled patriotic mythology and taught that it was the responsibility of the well born to maintain national honor, and that prepared the high bourgeoisie for a quasi-aristocratic role also systematically devalued the ethical basis of modern capitalism on which these institutions were really built. It was particularly in the last quarter of the nineteenth century that this happened, at the very time when the political and economic successes of the bourgeoisie in the most advanced Western European countries were creating this felt need to separate the most successful capitalists from their mercantile and decidedly unaristocratic origins.[2]

For much of the ordinary middle class, but particularly for small owners of shops and small manufacturing enterprises, the economic fluctuations of the nineteenth century were alarming and difficult to understand. Even the most advanced economic thinkers of the early nineteenth century, David Ricardo and Karl Marx, had believed that a product's value was based on how much labor, and what resources went into its production. Yet, as we now know, there is no such thing as absolute value. Any good is worth exactly what the market will pay for it, so that a valuable item one day may lose much of its worth if too many appear on the market, or replacement products appear the next day.[3] For those who have labored to produce, and who work as hard no matter what price the market assigns to their labor, this is a fact that is almost impossible to accept.

There were severe economic dislocations in the industrial world from the 1820s to the 1840s, as the leading edge of technology shifted from textile production to railroad and iron. This led to serious unemployment in the old textile centers, a drop in profits, and great political upheavals throughout much of Europe.[4] As severe, or perhaps more so, were the economic dislocations that accompanied the next great industrial shift.

The 1870s and 1880s were again a time of difficult adjustment as new high-technology industries, steel, organic chemistry, and electrical machinery, replaced railroads and iron as the key products, and as Germany and the United States replaced Great Britain as the world's most advanced economic centers. From 1873 to 1896 there was a drop in wholesale prices of 43 percent in France, 40 percent in Germany, and 42 percent in Great Britain.[5] Though this did not result in any lasting economic harm, and was, in fact, the result of rapid advances in productivity, it was perceived at that time to be catastrophic because it put downward pressure on profits and wages. So, throughout Europe, there was a sense that during much of this period, or at least well into the 1880s, the industrial world was going through a terminal crisis that might bring it down.[6] This perceived crisis was particularly threatening to the lower middle classes who feared being pushed, as Karl Marx had predicted, into the ranks of the poor working class, bereft of property or dignity.

Similarly, agricultural prices also increasingly fluctuated according the seeming whim of distant, misunderstood forces. In the last part of the nineteenth century, North American, Argentine, and Australian grain production became so efficient, and sea transport so cheap, that grain prices were forced down all over the world. It was hard to understand why a given amount of wheat could be sold at profit one year, but not the next. This had always been true to a certain extent, but the improvements in transportation as steam ships became the main carriers of bulk goods, and as rail networks saturated Western Europe, made it much more so in the last quarter of the century. From 1867 to 1894 the price of wheat fell by almost two-thirds.[7]

For the masses of industrial workers, particularly the unskilled new arrivals from the countryside, life in nineteenth-century cities was unpleasant and dangerous. If they had been poor in the countryside (and that, after all, is why millions of peasants left the land to seek work in the industrial cities, or, for the more adventurous, in the faraway Americas), at least life had been somewhat more comprehensible, based as it was on ancient yearly cycles and the vagaries of the weather. It is not easy to explain why there were sudden shifts in business cycles that rapidly created unemployment, or, just as capriciously, produced prosperity. If the weather that affects farming is no easier to explain, it is at least God's work, not that of the human manipulators who seemed to be behind wild swings in the stock market, or in employment, or in the very value of all products. The workers and the middle classes may have had different political allegiances, but they suffered similarly at the hands of incomprehensible economic forces. And if, in the long run, the very large majority of people were becoming more prosperous, short-run fluctuations could wreak havoc on millions of individual lives.

Added to this was the tempo of modern urban life. It seemed to many observers that rapid change, mass migration to cities, and the impersonality of the cities were producing social disorder and restlessness.

Thus, for the advanced European societies, among most social classes, from the rich to the poor, the late nineteenth century was utterly
paradoxical. There was immense progress; standards of health rose and
death rates declined; productivity increased spectacularly and a host of
new products came onto the market to make life easier; schooling
increased rapidly.[8] Yet there was a sense that something was not right,
that modern industrial society was somehow unnatural, and that drastic solutions were necessary in order to remedy its problems.

There were two broad ways of protesting against capitalism, from
the right and from the left. The right rejected capitalism as alienating
and unnatural because it destroyed traditional communal bonds and
values, because it made money dominant over honor and morality, and
because it corrupted society. The right also rejected the liberal political
changes that had injected democracy into the advanced world. Democracy denied the values of established, traditional hierarchy and subjected politics to sudden, irrational bouts of mass hysteria. Edmund
Burke's horror of the French Revolution in 1790 expressed this
loathing of democracy which remained essential for the critics of the
right. Burke wrote:

> Nobility is a graceful ornament to the civil order. . . . He feels no
> ennobling principle in his own heart who wishes to level all the artificial
> institutions which have been adopted for giving a body to opinion, and
> permanence to fugitive esteem. It is a sour, malignant, envious disposi-
> tion, without taste for the reality or for any image or representation of
> virtue, that sees with joy the unmerited fall of what had long flourished
> in splendor or in honor. I do not like to see anything destroyed, any void
> produced in society, any ruin on the face of the land.[9]

The left, on the other hand, believed that capitalism merely bred a
new form of inequality and that it was exploitative. It disliked parliamentary democracy because it did not go far enough and remained the
political tool of a hypocritical bourgeoisie intent on denying power to
the growing working class and to the poor. Rather than wanting to
recreate the old order of hereditary noble power and monarchy, the
left proposed to push modern rationality further, to democratize far
more, and to use modern science and technology to solve the problems
of industrial capitalism, particularly the swings of boom and depression, unemployment and social displacement, and inequality. Yet, however divergent the political aims of the leftist and rightist critique of

modern capitalism and democracy may have been, there was substantial agreement about the connection between capitalism, industrialization, and alienation. Karl Marx wrote in 1844:

> The worker becomes poorer the more wealth he produces, the more his production increases in power and extent. The worker becomes an ever cheaper commodity the more commodities he produces. The *devaluation* of the human world grows in direct proportion to the *increase in value* of the world of things. Labour not only produces commodities; it also produces itself and the worker as a *commodity.* . . . This fact simply means that the object that labour produces . . . stands opposed to it as *something alien*, as a *power independent* of the producer. . . . [T]he worker loses his reality to the point of dying of starvation. (Emphasis in original)[10]

Alienation, lack of roots, inauthenticity—these were some of the key words used to express the pervasive sense among intellectuals that modern industrial society was unnatural and inhuman, and that it was necessary to find something better. In the 1890s, Emile Durkheim, the French sociologist and moderate socialist, virtually created the field of modern empirical sociology on the basis of this sense that capitalist industrial society lacked unifying institutions and established rules. His chief studies, *The Division of Labor in Society* and *Suicide*, were meant to show that it was necessary to recreate what older societies had had, stabilizing and integrating corporate bodies.

On the right the sense of alienation and uprootedness made intellectuals favor greater attachment to traditional communal bonds and unity with the original, unsullied "folk" of their native lands. Increasing nationalism and the celebration of primitive virtues supposedly rooted in the true "people" suggested solutions to the problems of modernity that were quite different from the ideals of Marxist socialism, but were based on a similar, mystical faith that it should be possible to return to a more natural type of social organization.

In Germany, this blend of opposition to modern society, attachment to nationalism, and search for roots in a hereditary community led to what came to be called *Völkisch* ideology. The historian George Mosse has anglicized this word to "Volkish" because it cannot be translated. It suggests nationalism, racial consciousness, right-wing hostility to big capitalists and foreigners, and a kind of populism that also rejected the aristocrats' disdain for the masses. It is a central concept that can be applied to a strain of ideology that became very widespread, not just in Germany, but throughout Europe, and in the twentieth century throughout most of the world.

> The term "rooted" was constantly invoked by Volkish thinkers—and with good reason. Such rootedness conveyed the sense of man's correspondence with the landscape through his soul and thus with the Volk, which embodied the life spirit of the cosmos. . . . Moreover, rural rootedness served as a contrast to urban dislocation, or what was termed "uprootedness." It also furnished a convenient criterion for excluding foreigners from the Volk. . . . Volkish thinkers tended to contrast the idyllic medieval Volk with the actual modern present.[11]

Many of the greatest critics of modern Western life throughout Europe accepted this ideology, both on the left and the right, though of course, the idealized "folk" varied according to the nationality of the thinker. For Feodor Dostoevsky Western capitalism had to be kept out of Russia because it would "upset the old order and give rise to divisive class conflict." Russian intellectuals, he felt, should remain rooted in the people and avoid Western liberalism which could only lead to alienation.[12]

In France, where the whole modern notion of a "left"—in favor of the French Revolution, greater equality and democracy, and the anticlerical acceptance of Enlightenment *reason* as the main guide for human action rather than received Catholic faith—and a "right"—opposition to the Revolution, approval of hereditary nobility and monarchy, and acceptance of the primacy of religious faith as a moral guide to action—was born, there was also an evolution in the same direction. In the late eighteenth and early nineteenth centuries the ideologues of the right, most prominently Joseph de Maistre and Louis Bonald, were ultra-royalists and Catholics. But this was not sufficient to attract the growing middle classes, or even vaguely appeal to the masses in the nineteenth century. Gradually, there emerged a more nationalistic form of the right that finally hit a proper populist tone when it combined nationalism with hostility to big capitalists and to foreign manipulators who were polluting and destroying the common Frenchman. What provided a bond between the old clerical, monarchist right and large numbers of followers in the middle and even working classes was the identification of Jews as the real culprits. Religious anti-Semitism in Europe was very old, but only in the nineteenth century were Jews tied to the evils of modernity and capitalism.[13]

Edouard Drumont's *Jewish France*, published in 1886, was the first best-selling book to associate Jews with the ills of capitalism in this way. It went through over one hundred editions and may have been the most widely read book of its time in France. Its basic thesis was this:

> The Jews possess half of the capital in the world. Now the wealth of France. . . . is possibly worth one hundred and fifty billion francs, of which the Jews possess at least eighty billion. . . . [The expropriation of Jewish wealth] would allow the workers to test their social doctrines in optimal conditions in that there would be no violent revolution, and no unemployment would be created. . . . In effect, no one could seriously deny that Jewish wealth has . . . special character. It is essentially parasitical and usurious. . . . It is the result of speculation and fraud. It is not created by labor, but extracted with marvelous cleverness from the pocket of real workers by financial institutions, which have enriched their founders by ruining their stockholders. . . . [F]ive hundred determined men in the suburbs of Paris and a regiment surrounding the Jewish banks would suffice to carry out the most fruitful revolution of modern times. . . . [P]eople would embrace in the streets.[14]

But even with respect to the "Jewish Question," which increased steadily in importance as the criticism of capitalism intensified, it should not be thought that the right and the left were all that different from each other, at least at first. Pierre-Joseph Proudhon, an early nineteenth-century French socialist, identified Jews with all that was evil about money and greed. And the greatest of all socialist theoreticians, Karl Marx, wrote in 1843:

> The god of the Jews has been secularized and become the god of the world. Exchange is the true god of the Jew. The view of nature which has grown up under the regime of private property and of money is an actual contempt for and practical degradation of nature. . . . What is present in an abstract form in the Jewish religion—contempt for theory, for art, for history, for man as an end in himself—is the *actual* and *conscious* standpoint, the virtue, of the man of money. The *chimerical* nationality of the Jew is the nationality of the merchant, of the man of money in general.[15]

The point is not to suggest that there was no difference between left and right, or that the doctrines worked out in the nineteenth century provided immutable guidelines to twentieth-century political action, because neither statement could be supported by historical evidence. Rather, it is important to understand that by the early twentieth century there was a set of well worked-out critiques of capitalism and liberal democracy, despite the material and political successes that these had experienced. Whether on the left or right, the intellectuals who formulated these positions shared a hostility to capitalism that expressed itself in a wish for a better integrated, more harmonious, purer life. Critics of capitalism thought they could identify forces to blame for the sad collapse of morality and stability. Jews, capitalists, foreigners, secret manipulators, Freemasons, socialists (from the right's point of view), or other sinister actors could be identified and fought. These intellectual constructions provided the programs for political movements and were of real political consequence.

The identification of "the Jew" with all the ills of modern liberal capitalism is a testimony to the power of symbolism in the ideological transformation that was occurring in the late nineteenth century. Though Jews were disproportionately successful in commerce and finance, and by the end of the century in some intellectual and cultural fields in the big cities of Europe, they were a very small portion of the population in Western Europe. In 1900 just under 1 percent of the total population in Germany and Great Britain was Jewish, and only about one half of 1 percent in France. Only in the western parts of the Russian Empire and in Austria-Hungary were Jews as much as 5 to 10 percent of the population. It was the success of a relatively small number of Jews who embraced Enlightenment values and assimilated into the economic and cultural elites of their countries that most frightened and angered those who were turning against liberalism and the Enlightenment. That Jews, foreigners with no homeland of their own, totally unrooted in the folk cultures that were supposed to form the heart of national communities, could assimilate the new values well enough to succeed was proof that these values were wrong. If a few Jews could do it, there were many other Jews in Central and Eastern Europe who were not yet emancipated from their traditional religious and isolated ways, and if they adapted as easily, then there would be millions of these dangerous agents of modernity, money, and liberalism flooding the cities of Europe. That was the perceived danger, and raw numbers were far less important than the image of agents of the new type of society worming their way into the healthy nation to destroy it.[16]

Yet, important as the growing criticism of capitalism from the left and the right may have been, at no time in the late nineteenth century did the forces of the radical left or right come close to obtaining power through reasonably free and democratic elections, wherever these were held. The middle classes, after all, had too much to lose from drastic alteration of a system that was benefitting them, and the working classes, who turned increasingly to socialism, began to gain the benefits that they were demanding without revolution. This is why the intellectual leaders of the radically anti-capitalist movements of the right and the left excoriated the timidity and narrow self-interest of the masses that were supposed to follow them, and why they came to understand that "bourgeois democracy" was incapable of bringing about their goals.

Vladimir Ilyich Lenin in 1902, writing the program of action for his party, fifteen years before it was to take power, spent a good part of his tract *What Is to Be Done?* savagely attacking what he called "economism," that is, the tendency of workers' associations to concentrate more on improving wages and working conditions than on preparing revolution. Georges Sorel, the French anarcho-syndicalist who considered himself a man of the left, but who came to be much admired by fascists as a prophet of violent anti-bourgeois revolution, wrote in 1906:

> When working-class circles are *reasonable*, as the professional sociologists wish them to be [he is attacking Durkheim, whom he had mentioned by name a few pages earlier], when conflicts are confined to disputes about material interests, there is no more opportunity for heroism than when agricultural syndicates discuss the subject of the price of guano with manure merchants. It has never been thought that discussions about prices could possibly exercise any ethical influence on men.[17]

One of the most serious accusations made against liberal democracy by many intellectuals was that it was humdrum, practical, and boring, lacking the heroic virtues of both feudal aristocracy and of revolutionary socialism. Indeed, it fit the mentality of the little merchant, who sought the better deal, the incremental, calculated improvement of profit, and who avoided the grand gesture, the bold risk, or the noble disdain for mere material benefits.

If, for ordinary people, the growing, if uneven prosperity of capitalism, and the tendency of parliamentary liberalism to compromise its way toward accommodation and slow progress, were satisfactory, for growing numbers of intellectuals with larger ideas and programs, they were anathema. That, no doubt, was why in the late nineteenth century democratic, practical England, and distant America, even more capitalist and democratic, were the objects of such contempt by so many European intellectuals. As that great hater of everything liberal, Friedrich Nietzsche, put it in *Beyond Good and Evil*, the English were "profoundly mediocre," their great liberal philosophers, Hume and Locke, were capable only of "mechanical stultification of the world," and their scientists capable of little more than "narrowness, aridity, and industrious carefulness." In the *Genealogy of Morals*, Nietzsche called on Germany to unite with autocratic Russia to become masters of the world, to give up "the English principle of the people's right of representation," and above all, he added, "No American future!"[18]

The growing intellectual discontent with liberalism and capitalism might not have led to such upheavals had it not been for two other crucial changes in Europe's, and later the world's, ideological configuration. One was the rapid spread of nationalism in the nineteenth century, and the second was the demonstrated success of modern science and the popularization of the idea that its methods could be applied to social, economic, and political questions and problems. It is to these two changes that we now have to turn.

NATIONALISMS: GERMAN, RUSSIAN, AND OTHER VARIETIES

Nationality is a very powerful identity. There are other, often overlapping ways for people to identify themselves—sex, age, religion, clan, language, residence, class, profession, and more. But in the modern world, for most, though not all people, one's nationality is the most basic political and cultural identity.

Nationalism is a relatively new concept. All contemporary "nations" are derived from entities that previously possessed quite different identities.[19] In the past there were tribes based on extended kinship and small city-states capable of generating loyalty and a sense of common identity among their members. But there were no large political and territorial units able to do this except among their small ruling elites. The most successful "world religions"—Buddhism, Islam, Christianity, and Hinduism—provided strong cultural identities for their followers, but they broke up into competing political units. The nation was supposed to replace, or absorb older religious identities, and to become more exclusive, more territorial, and more solidly united. The nation was also supposed to consist of all of the people, masses as well as elites.

Nationalism generates conflict. It claims territory, proclaims sovereignty, and expects full support from its people, but it is bound to run into sharply competing claims over cultural and territorial boundaries. It produces clashes over personal loyalties, and creates rivalry with other political structures. Furthermore, nationalism's demands threaten those who are defined as "aliens," or who, because of previously established interests, do not wish to be incorporated.

England and France

Modern nationalism began in England. It then spread to France, partly, though not entirely because of conscious imitation, and to the United States, an offshoot of England. In Russia and Germany, the spread of nationalism was more a matter of deliberate reproduction of established nationalism, particularly France's. Subsequently, just as the international political success of England and France made the model so appealing, so did the extraordinary dominance of the world by Europeans in the nineteenth century spread the notion of nationalism. It is still spreading, and it remains the most powerful political organizing principle in the world. But from the very start, there were different kinds of nationalism, depending on the circumstances in which they developed.

In the late fifteenth and early sixteenth century England's political elite had to find a new way to legitimize itself. There was a new dynasty, the Tudors, an almost entirely new ruling class replacing the old aristocracy decimated by the Wars of the Roses, and a new religion, Protestantism. But there were also a well-established Parliament dating back several centuries, a strong urban, mercantile class, a high level of local self-rule, and with the spread of Protestantism, a relatively high degree of literacy. Therefore English nationalism developed along what was, for its time, democratic lines, at least for the landowning and mercantile urban elites. This was to prove especially useful in the nineteenth century when English political institutions proved to be highly adaptable to the growth of the middle class, which was rather easily incorporated into the political process.[20]

English nationalism further developed in the seventeenth century in tandem with a growing faith in scientific rationality. Protestantism, especially Puritanism, promoted the idea that finding order in the natural world proved the existence of God, and that the individual was responsible for proving his own faith to himself. But there was also the coincidence that this was the period of growing scientific research. The English seaborne empire encouraged a practical interest in science, and the Puritan Protestant tradition fostered it. Seventeenth-century English scientific advances were interpreted by the elite intellectual culture as a proud part of England's unique virtue.[21]

So at the elite if not yet at the mass level, English nationalism was built on a participatory notion of parliamentarism, on a belief in law, and on a respect for rationalizing religion and science. Together all these added up to a confidence that decisions arrived at by individual reason were good for the national community. As these notions spread they came to characterize broad segments of the population. This may be contrasted, at the opposite end of Europe, to the nationalism that eventually developed in Russia, where the autocrat, and later the community as a whole (which again means an autocrat who embodies communal needs) were totally superior to individual rationality and opinions. It may also be contrasted to German nationalism, which developed with a strong streak of anti-individualistic mysticism, and in the nineteenth century came to feel contempt for its great rivals in European affairs, England and France.

French nationalism was developed in the eighteenth century by an aristocracy that sought to find a role for itself. It had been politically defeated by the monarchy during the reigns of Louis XIII and XIV in the seventeenth century, and was forced to give up its political power to the absolutist, anti-parliamentarian monarchy. The aristocracy tried to adapt by claiming to be the natural defender of a political entity even greater than the king, that is, the "nation." French political philosophers of the Enlightenment, inspired by the English example, further elaborated on the idea of a nation independent of the King. But their vision was more parliamentary than aristocratic and warlike, creating two contradictory strands of nationalist sentiment in France.[22]

The French Revolution combined these two strands of nationalism; to the aristocratic idea of patriotic and warlike nationalism it added the notion of democratic mass participation in politics. It brought down the monarchy, but it kept and further rationalized the centralized bureaucratic apparatus it inherited from the royal absolutist state. In the hands of Napoleon, this combination of mass nationalism and political centralization was used to try to conquer Europe.

In a sense, French politics for the 150 years after Napoleon continued to be a battle between the restrained, liberal parliamentary vision of nationalism promoted by the some of the eighteenth-century philosophers—Montesquieu, Diderot, and Voltaire—and the grandiose, aggressive, absolutist vision of the nation taken over from the aristocracy and monarchy.

Napoleon's military success, however ephemeral, spread the ideal of nationalism further and much faster than the example of England could have done alone. It was because France was nationalistic that it could mobilize such energies and threaten all of Europe. So, instead of the cautious, limited, parliamentary form of nationalism embodied by England, it was the most aggressive aspect of French nationalism that was most admired. This combined the vainglory of Louis XIV with a Rousseauian cult of the collective will acting in unison, a worship of liberating science and education, and at the same time, mass military mobilization. It was a dangerous brew.

Germany

In the eighteenth century Germany was split into so many political units that there was barely any semblance of unity, and its kings, princes, nobles, and other rulers were hardly nationalistic at all, but rather, defenders of their own local power. The early carriers of German nationalism were, instead, intellectuals. This class became significant in the eighteenth century, when the Enlightenment combined with an older Protestant tradition to produce a large demand for highly educated teachers, preachers, and other professionals. Those trained for such positions by the universities, which themselves became sources of regional pride, became a distinct class, the *Bildungsbürger*, the educated or "cultured" bourgeois.

The *Bildungsbürger* in northern, non-Catholic Germany carried a contradictory cultural tradition. On the one hand, there was the Pietistic background from which most of its members came. Unlike its Protestant cousin, English Puritanism, German Pietism had become the religion of static, economically unsuccessful strata. Particularly because of the disasters of the Thirty Years' War from 1618 to 1648, and the ensuing depression in northern and central Germany, Pietism had turned much more to mysticism and fatalism than English Puritanism, which was a religion of the economically upwardly mobile. Resignation to one's fate and mysticism bred an emotionalism and distrust of theological rationalization which was inconsistent with the rationalizing aspects of Protestantism, and particularly Puritanism.

The German eighteenth-century Enlightenment therefore had elements absent in France or England. The educated *Bildungsbürger* combined it with their Pietistic upbringing to produce an original and powerful movement, German Romanticism. The result fit well with this class's yearning for high status based on its education and understanding of modern science, and with its gloom caused by its inferiority to and dependence on the political and social elites in Germany. Dark, brooding mysticism and pessimism combined with an exaltation about the possibilities offered by modern science and art to produce a strong sense of resentful inferiority. The situation was worsened in the late eighteenth century by the overproduction of intellectuals and the consequent decline of opportunities. As the spirit and language of German Romanticism were pan-German, not merely limited to the smaller political institutions, and its carriers were intellectuals who could travel throughout the land to universities and other posts, it had the potential to become the base of German nationalism.[23]

This latent potential was activated by the French Revolutionary invasion of Germany. At first, most of the German Romantic intellectuals admired the French, and saw the Revolution as their salvation. But of course, the French were nationalists, and their policies did not produce the opportunities and rewards, much less the recognition, so ardently wished for. In bitter frustration, German intellectuals turned very quickly to German nationalism. Johann Fichte's was perhaps the prototypical case of a rapid conversion from admiration of the French Revolution to intense German nationalism. After Prussia's defeat in 1806, he became the great philosopher of German nationalism, which could now become a tool of the Prussian state as it tried to rebuild itself to ward off the French menace.

German nationalism, then, combined the frustrations of the class of intellectuals who had developed its grandiose, romantic dreams about Germany's special role, and the politically practical ambitions of revived Prussian militarism. It directed its anger against the forces arrayed against Germany—the French Enlightenment, liberalism, and eventually, successful English capitalism. Therefore, even as it was itself a product of the Enlightenment, German nationalism rejected it. It also sought, from the start, to find the agent, the causes of the decay of pure German virtue that had led Germany to fall so low. This quickly became the Jews. Legally emancipated by the French armies that occupied most of Germany under Napoleon, these formerly despised but tolerated "foreigners" came to embody the insidious liberal forces said to be subverting German purity and strength from the inside. In large measure this was because many Jews now adapted so well to the new circumstances of greater liberty and growing economic opportunities.

Indeed, as early as 1793, while he was still a supporter of the French Revolution, Fichte wrote, "A powerful, hostilely disposed nation is infiltrating almost every country in Europe. This nation is in a perpetual war with all these countries, severely afflicting their citizenry. I am referring to the Jewish Nation [das Judentum]."[24]

German nationalism always remained partly wed to the Enlightenment, to scientific progress and education, and to high artistic achievement. In the nineteenth century, even before German unification, the German states were much more conscientious promoters of university research and higher education than other parts of Europe. This was a great source of pride, and it is one of the main explanations for Germany's astonishing economic success in the latter part of that century.[25]

On the other hand, the dark, xenophobic, mystical, romantic strain that lay at the heart of German nationalism also remained, and grew. As the nineteenth-century aristocracy, primarily in Prussia, but then throughout united Germany after 1871 redefined its mission in military-nationalist terms, and as the growing bourgeoisie was educated according to the ideals of the early German nationalist intellectuals, the original contradiction between Enlightenment and anti-Enlightenment became a part of the German character. Despite the growing strength of the German capitalist economy, this combination of its intellectual roots and the addition of the Prussian military tradition to

German nationalism insured that it would remain as deeply suspicious of capitalism as it was of liberal democracy.[26] This was the cultural legacy that lay at the base of the development of Volkish ideology.

That Germany was then united through a series of successful, aggressive wars managed by a highly militarized Prussian state, and that it emerged in the twentieth century as the leading European industrial power, even as it maintained its original sense of resentful frustration against the French and English, had much to do with the willingness, even eagerness, of Germany to go to war in 1914. That is not the entire story, of course, but it is an important part.

Germany's unexpected loss of the Great War in 1918 reinforced all that was most dangerous about its nationalism. Nazism was neither inevitable nor accepted by all Germans, but it is not difficult to see that its spiritual antecedents were well rooted in German culture.[27] German nationalism was, in a real sense, born aggressive and angry in the early nineteenth century. After 1918 it became angrier still. And yet, even with this reinforced Volkish ideology, the sense that there was somehow a "scientific" solution to all of Germany's problems persisted. The kind of "science" this produced was something few could have expected in the nineteenth century.

Russia

From its earliest days Russia was economically backward compared to Western or Central Europe. Its population density was low, its agricultural technology was centuries behind the West's, and its best agricultural lands were only very gradually freed from nomadic rule, because they were on the edge of, and inside the steppe zone that was so ideally suited to the horse empires of Mongol and Turkic peoples. Russia's geography made its communications primitive, even by medieval European standards. The density of urban settlement was far less than what it was in Western and Central Europe.[28]

Since at least the twelfth or thirteenth century, there has been a kind of technological, economic, and philosophical "slope" running from a Northwestern European heartland to its peripheries, mostly to the south and east. Whether it is a matter of the introduction of the three-field system and the mouldboard plow, of independent towns and advanced artisanal skills, or of innovative religious and scientific thought, the part of Europe including northern Italy, running through the Alps to southern and western Germany, including Burgundy and northern France, going to the Netherlands, and touching southeastern England and southern Scandinavia has long been more advanced than the rest of Europe.[29] Russia was often near the bottom end of that slope, along with parts of the Balkans and Iberia.

Sixteenth-century Muscovy became a strong state based on autocratic, centralized, military rule under the Tsars (the Russian version of Caesar) Ivan III, Vasilii III, and Ivan IV, the "Terrible" or "Awesome." Such autocracy was possible because the Russian nobility was a service nobility without sufficient claim to land and local power to stand up to the power of the Tsars, or, if left unprotected by the state, to resist foreigners on the one hand or peasant revolt and flight on the other. During the Time of Troubles in the early seventeenth century, provoked by the devastation of Ivan IV's ferocious and deadly internal war against his own nobility and his long series of costly, foreign wars, the Russian state virtually collapsed, and it was almost seized by Poland-Lithuania. This was also a time of immense rebellion, migration, and flight. But the Poles were expelled, and the nobility, unable to protect its interests in any other way, recreated an autocratic monarchy under the Romanovs.

This can be contrasted to the opposite experience of the Polish high nobility. Its interests were not seriously threatened by outside forces until much later, and it resisted the creation of an autocratic, militarized, that is, absolutist state. Only in the eighteenth century did it become obvious that the absolutist monarchies of Austria, Prussia, and Russia were terribly dangerous. By then, it was too late to build a strong Polish state.[30]

In Russia, to assure a steady supply of noble warriors who would be maintained by the peasants, and to satisfy their own need for very scarce labor, the Tsars increased the obligations on the peasantry, and by the mid-seventeenth century, they had completed the long process of turning what had once been relatively free peasants into serfs. (In Poland, local lords did the same thing, but without a strong state, and this further strengthened them against their monarchy.)

This centralization and reduction of both nobles and peasants to the subjugated status of servants of the Tsars was to have grave consequences for Russia. It merged with an older, Byzantine Orthodox tradition of Church servility to the Emperor and produced what was in a way Europe's strongest, most absolutist state based on one of its most backward and weakest economic bases. It was also from Byzantium, the Eastern Roman Empire, that the Russians had gotten the idea that after the fall of that Empire to the Muslim Ottoman Turks in 1453 they, the Russians, were to become the new Rome, the home of true Christianity. Thus their Kings were entitled to call themselves "Caesars."[31]

Into this setting there came Peter the Great who reigned from 1689 to 1725. He decided to force Russia to Westernize so that it could catch up to the advanced Europeans. Using the levers available to the Tsar, the servility of his subjects, and the enormous potential resources of Russia, he redefined and reshaped Russia into a modern state, and its service nobility into the heart of the new nation. He also created industries to build his army and navy. The transition took several generations, but by obliging his nobles to dress and act as Westerners, to educate themselves, and to serve in military and civil institutions based on a Western model, he changed their perception of themselves. They were separated from their tradition, from whatever local roots they still had, and turned into the new nation that Peter and his successors wanted to rule.

His work was finished by Catherine the Great from 1762 to 1796. Catherine, like Peter, was enamored of Western, in her case mostly French, ideas. Under her, the nobility completed the transition it had begun under Peter. Fundamentally, it had no role to play other than as servants of the state. The nobility had been constantly humiliated under Peter, shorn of its peculiarly Russian old habits, and obliged to behave in strange foreign ways. Under Catherine, even though it was treated better, and some of its obligations were lifted, it continued to be thoroughly dominated by an autocrat who was actually a German (she had married into the Russian royal family) and a promoter of new ideas. But Catherine, like Peter, was also a very successful player in international affairs and took over most of the vast territory of Poland-Lithuania (the other parts went to Prussia and Austria) and portions of Ottoman borderlands along the Black Sea, including the Crimea. It is not surprising, therefore, that the Russian nobility, which was now nothing but a highly militarized bureaucratic elite, came to see itself in the image of its Tsars, as a nationalist elite dedicated to the military success of the Russian Empire. The Western, particularly French, philosophical ideals inculcated in the last third of the eighteenth century were themselves highly nationalistic, and it was not a long step to adapt them to Russian needs.[32]

There were two problems with Russian nationalism. One was that it identified the whole of the Russian people as part of the nation, as French and English nationalism did. But the vast bulk of the Russians were illiterate, poor serfs. If it took a leap of the imagination for French intellectuals to think that they somehow represented their whole nation, in the case of the Russians the gap was that much greater, especially because there were far fewer bourgeois or even independent, prosperous peasants between the elite and the serfs. And if had taken a good three or four generations to Westernize and educate the nobility, it was going to take a lot longer to do this with the common people.

The other, related problem was that for anyone who looked closely, Russia remained terribly backward in almost every respect when compared with the West. Not only were its masses illiterate, but its technology was never quite up to the highest Western standards. Nor were the governing institutions of Russia Western, no matter how much European styles of dress were imitated, because the Tsars remained such absolute rulers. Neither the nobility nor the towns had any political power or liberties at all. Thus the Enlightenment ideas from France absorbed by the aristocracy and court were stripped of much of their content. The idea of progress and of the nation made sense to the Russians, but not the idea that the power of the state ought to be limited. In fact, the state seemed to be the only potent institution able to forward the cause of the nation.

Since Russian nobles had been trained to be patriotic and love the idea of the Russian nation, they had to glorify and be proud of what must have seemed to be an inferior product. This resulted in a bizarre combination of pride in the uniquely Russian traits of the population—mysticism, communalism and anti-individualism, Orthodoxy, servility, and ignorance—and resentment of the individualistic, educated, more prosperous, and politically freer West. Since the Russian intelligentsia which began to emerge in the late eighteenth century was the product of the education devised for the noble servants of the Tsars, it developed with the same contradictory sense of nationalism—proud but deeply ashamed, wanting to emulate the West but also aggressively contemptuous of it, eager to impress other Europeans but very resentful of them as well.[33]

By the time of the Decembrist uprising of 1825, in which a pathetically small and unprepared group of young nobles tried to seize power in order to reform the Russian autocracy, the pattern of nationalism was set. Russia's great rulers, Peter, Catherine II, and the recently deceased Alexander I, who had ruled from 1801 to 1825, had been astonishingly successful in international affairs. Each had defeated the great European powers that had challenged them—Sweden, Prussia, and finally Napoleonic France. They had pushed the Ottoman Empire back into the Balkans, opened the Black Sea to Russia, eliminated the border nomads once and for all, and made Russia a great power, the only power England identified as a potential threat to its global hegemony after 1815. They had also made serfdom ever more onerous, crushed peasant protest, and humiliated the most enlightened members of the aristocracy who had reformist ideals. They had created a modern military juggernaut on a backward mass of virtual slaves and staffed it with a proud, patriotic, deeply shamed and insecure noble elite.

If this sounds like a description of the Communist Party bureaucracy built by Stalin, that is not entirely a coincidence. In effect, he reproduced the same pattern. There are many who believe that the pattern will reassert itself in a nationalist, post-communist Russia in the twenty-first century.

It is no wonder, then, that the intelligentsia, that is, the class that grew rapidly in the nineteenth century because of the state's constant need for more educated and technically competent officials, should be full of the contradictions that characterized Russian nationalism from the start. And to add to the combination of nationalistic pride and shame, of the wish to emulate the West even as it was resented, there was also an increasing sense of guilt about the fact that Russian power was built on so much suffering. With the guilt, and the grandiose nationalistic ambition to make Russia great and modern, there was also a chronic sense of frustration about Russia's problems. This made many believe in the need for drastic revolutionary change.

The murder in 1881 of Alexander II, the Tsar who had liberated the serfs twenty years earlier, by impatient radicals, was only the most extreme case of what turned into an unending, shadowy war of plots, murders, and multiple betrayals between the revolutionary part of the intelligentsia and an autocracy that reacted by continuing to consider all opposition as unpatriotic treachery.

The Russian intelligentsia, which became the carrier of those revolutionary ideas that eventually overthrew the Romanov Tsars, represented what seemed to be a wide array of opinions. There were the

"Slavophiles" who emphasized the purity and virtue of the Russian peasant commune and of Orthodoxy. The "Westernizers" wanted to continue the work of Peter the Great and further modernize Russia. There were anarchists, populists, nihilists, and eventually, Marxists of various types. The extraordinary cultural vigor of this class, which was reflected by its amazing productivity in literature, music, painting, and science in the latter part of the nineteenth century and in the early twentieth, was paralleled by its range of great political and social thinkers. Perhaps the difficulties of reconciling the various aspects of Russian nationalism contributed to this explosive productivity of what was, after all, a very small intellectual elite. In 1860 there were no more than 20,000 in the intelligentsia, out of a population of some 60 million.[34]

But in all this there was agreement about certain key points. One was that Russia had to be drastically reformed, and the "people" had to be integrated into the Russian nation. Second, there was a widespread feeling that the capitalist bourgeois West was corrupt, tired, and that Russia was destined to surpass the rest of Europe because it was somehow younger. Whether on the right or the left, among "Slavophiles" or "Westernizers," the intelligentsia shared a distaste for capitalism, and a belief that Russia's anti-individualism was a benefit. Dostoevsky, the greatest of the "Slavophile" literary figures, wrote his *Notes from Underground* to expose the shallowness and futility of following Western rationalism, and to debunk the very popular novel *What Is to Be Done?* by Nikolai Chernyshevsky, a "Westernizer" who was to greatly influence the leftist intelligentsia, and especially Lenin.[35] But Chernyshevsky also disliked Western individualism and the idea of an economic system based on private property and the market rather than on communalism.

Alexander Herzen, the intellectual grandfather of the later nineteenth-century Russian radical revolutionary intelligentsia (Chernyshevsky, in the next generation, was their "father"), was convinced that Western Europe was hopelessly decayed because of its materialism, and that "youthful" Russia could show the way to a better world.[36] Adam Ulam summarized Herzen's thought, which remained at the heart of the revolutionary intelligentsia's worldview, in these words:

> And so backward Russia could still one day show the world the way to a
> higher and freer civilization than the one created in the West. The peas-

ant, the representative Russian man, was fortunately free of the materialistic craving of the French or English bourgeois or, for that matter, worker. The idea of private property, in the corrupt Western sense, was alien to the peasant; he was in fact an instinctive socialist.[37]

There were never many moderate liberals among the Russian intelligentsia, and Ivan Turgenev remained a lonely exception.[38] Mired in conflicting emotions of love and disgust for their own society, the intelligentsia accepted a highly romanticized vision of their nation that made it seem as if it corresponded to their imagined models.

Unfortunately, romantic nationalism that so idealized the community while despising liberal moderation, skepticism, and individualism disregarded the costs of making the "nation" great. Cultivation of glory and patriotism combined with a disregard for the practical interests of the population were mixed with a messianic sense of Russia's unique greatness and a deep resentment against the rest of Europe. Such a Russia, sufficiently advanced in science and technology to maintain a powerful modern army, and possessing enormous human and physical resources, was bound to be dangerous. When it won wars, this confirmed its sense of mission and superiority. When it lost, as in the Crimean and Russo-Japanese Wars, or World War I, this provoked revolutionary reforms and deep soul searching. Nor was this pattern changed by communism. The success of the 1941–1945 "Great Patriotic War" consolidated Stalinism and created a sense of enthusiasm that allowed a fundamentally unworkable system to go on for another 45 years as one of the world's two great superpowers. The failure in Afghanistan in the 1980s, which was quite minor in military and strategic terms, began the rapid unravelling of the communist state.

Russia's nationalism, then, while modelled on France's and England's, was quite different. Twentieth-century history was shaped by the fact that this romantic, aggressive, contradictory, resentful big power nationalism happened to be located right next to another—in some ways equally paranoid and contradictory—nationalism, Germany's.

It is not true that all nationalism leads to tyranny. But if based on jealous and vengeful resentment, on memories of past wrongs, real or imagined, on a conviction that somehow "the nation" is capable of being superior but is frustrated and blocked from being so because of powerful alien forces, the probability that tyranny will ensue is high.

This is particularly the case when the discrepancy between the imagined glory of the nation contrasts sharply with the squalid reality of poverty and backwardness. If, furthermore, nationalistic elites absorb the Western idea of nationalism while discarding the Enlightenment concept of the rights of the individual against the community, tyranny is more likely. And if "democracy" is taken to mean mass support for decisions taken by an elite on behalf of the "nation," instead of a means by which individuals can defend themselves against the power of government, then the prospects of avoiding tyranny dim further. That is what happened in Germany and Russia, has happened elsewhere, and will continue to happen in many countries.

TWO SOCIAL SCIENCES: BIOLOGICAL AND ECONOMIC HISTORICISM

The eighteenth-century European Enlightenment was an age of science. Political philosophers were inspired by advances in the natural sciences, and Newton, or rather an idealized Newton, became the hero of thinkers throughout Europe. Empiricism, skepticism about received truth, intellectual modesty in the face of the vast complexities of existence, but faith that progress could be made in understanding how the natural and human universes worked, were the main qualities preached by the Enlightenment.[39] But if the eighteenth century witnessed the birth of scientific popularization, it was only in the second half of the nineteenth that the spread of education and the growth of the middle class created a more substantial market for this kind of writing, and that the idea of science as a guide to political and personal action spread beyond narrow elites.[40]

Yet, as natural science's accomplishments grew ever more impressive, and its links with the immense technological revolution sweeping Europe more obvious, the original skeptical modesty and open empiricism were lost, especially in its popularized versions. As science progressed, and became more specialized, it became ever more difficult for the nonspecialist to keep up with what was really going on. The illusion was created that the amazing success of science and technology prefigured equally decisive advances in the study of society, and therefore, in the solution of human problems. This led many intellectuals into desperate attempts to discover moral and philosophical certainty. These were meant to replace the old faiths in religion, and to be consistent with the new age of science.

In the late eighteenth and early nineteenth centuries, a series of great builders of theoretical social systems tried to imitate Newton. Eventually, these efforts led to Auguste Comte and Karl Marx, both of whom believed that they had unlocked the secret laws of history and could thereby predict the future. Both were enamored of natural science and were convinced that this is what they were practicing. Both created elaborate, complex models that reduced individual human action to insignificance because history was determined by larger, impersonal forces that could, at best, be perceived only by the very most enlightened of scientists (for example, Comte and Marx). Both also conceived of history as something that moved from lower to higher stages, and that would culminate in a perfectly engineered, scientifically determined future utopia.[41]

It was not new to believe that all of past history had a purpose, that it was preparing mankind for a greater future, and that the force propelling history could ultimately explain all that was going on. Christianity offers precisely such a teleology, as do some other religions, particularly those that emerged from the ancient Near East.[42] A growing number of intellectuals, disenchanted by the conservatism of the main Christian churches almost everywhere, and religion's inability to grapple with the implications of rapid technological and scientific change, turned, therefore, to teleological social sciences.

The substitution of teleological science for teleological religion, however, removes one of the restraints imposed on the religious. If scientific understanding reveals the motive force of history and its inevitable direction, as Isaiah Berlin has written, then:

> The growth of knowledge brings with it relief from moral burdens, for if powers beyond and above us are at work, it is wild presumption to claim responsibility for their activity or blame ourselves for failing in it. Original sin is thus transferred to an impersonal plane, and acts hitherto regarded as wicked or unjustifiable are seen in a a more "objective" fashion—in a larger context—as part of the process of history which, being responsible for providing us with our scale of values, must not therefore itself be judged in terms of it; and viewed in this new light they turn out no longer wicked but right and good because necessitated by the whole.[43]

The mid-nineteenth century saw sensational advances in biology. Unlike physics or chemistry, this work seemed more directly relevant to the human experience, and was eagerly seized upon at the very time when popular science was becoming an accepted part of general, not merely elite culture.

In 1859 Charles Darwin published *The Origin of Species by Means of Natural Selection or the Preservation of Favored Races in the Struggle for Life*. The book was a sensation even though it said almost nothing about human society, politics, or history. Within a short time, Darwin had become the best-known scientist in Europe, and his theories started to be applied to human affairs. His work was translated into German in 1860, with the term "struggle for life" emerging as *"Kampf ums Dasein,"* which suggests much more of a direct combat for existence than Darwin's subtler meaning.[44]

In the early 1860s Louis Pasteur developed bacteriology and the modern theory of disease based on micro-organisms. Though Pasteur's theories did not lend themselves to grand social theorizing, as did Darwin's, the notion of hidden infectious agents sneaking about to destroy us caught the popular imagination. He became, after Darwin, the second most famous European scientist.[45]

A few years before these scientific advances became so famous, Joseph Arthur de Gobineau had published his *Essay on the Inequality of Human Races* (1853–1855). Gobineau was a social theorist, not a natural scientist, but his idea that blond northern Europeans were a superior race, and that there was a hierarchy of racial worthiness, seemed to acquire scientific validity because of the spread of Darwinism.

After the introduction of the new biological theories, it became possible for one of the leading German Volkish ideologues, Paul de Lagarde, to write that Jews were bacilli who had to be exterminated to save the Germans.[46] If this is very far from what Pasteur meant to imply with his work on disease, the notion that invisible "germs" were inserting themselves into the "pure" races, spreading disease and pollution, would have been impossible without popularizations of his discoveries.

There have been so many misuses of Darwin that it seems unfair to pin his name to much that claimed to be inspired by *The Origin*. Yet, there is little doubt that, whatever his intentions, his work was a major impetus to what should be called "biological historicism." "Historicism" is the notion that history is governed by laws that can be known and interpreted in such a way as to yield accurate predictions about future change.[47] "Biological historicism," then, sees biological laws as the main causes of social historical change.

Biological historicism was only one of several historicist teleologies elaborated in the mid-nineteenth century. But along with "economic historicism," best presented by Karl Marx, and now simply called Marxism, it was the most important. Biological historicism and Marxism were by no means mutually exclusive; they reinforced each other, and became an important part of the ideological baggage of political intellectuals in the late nineteenth century and early twentieth. Since Nazism was ultimately based on the former, and Communism, of course, on the latter, it is worth outlining the theories of each, though this is not easy for biological historicism because it never acquired as great and unifying a theoretician as Karl Marx.

The Struggle of Races Against Infection and for Living Space

At first neo-Darwinism was favored by the left and by middle-of-the-road liberals. Marx was very appreciative of Darwin, and his colleague Friedrich Engels could think of no higher praise in his eulogy at Marx's funeral in 1883 than to say, "Just as Darwin discovered the law of evolution in organic nature, so Marx discovered the law of evolution in human history."[48] Spencer, who used Darwinian notions to explain why liberal capitalism was a superior social system, and believed that it would lead to a peaceful world without war, became the founder of "social Darwinism."

In no country did popularized Darwinism take hold as firmly as in Germany, where its chief spokesman was the widely read Ernst Haeckel. Haeckel was much admired by the German Social Democrats, particularly by Karl Kautsky, the party's leading theoretician in the early twentieth century.[49] One of Haeckel's disciples, who turned Darwinism into a kind of worship of nature and sexuality, became Germany's best-selling nonfiction author, with over one and a half million of his books sold by 1914.[50] But as Alfred Kelly has pointed out, the many attempts to link these authors directly to Volkish ideology, and thus to Nazism, is based on a misunderstanding. Almost anything can be made out of popularized Darwinism. Biological historicism provided a legitimating, scientific explanation for a variety of ideologies.

An important concept was added to popularized versions of Darwinian theory at around the turn of the century with the acceptance of heredity as the principal determinant of human characteristics. This led to the eugenics movement. All the undesirable social traits, it seemed, might be cured by appropriate sterilization of those who had such vices as "imbecility," "poverty," and "immorality." Gobineau's old racist theories, the Darwinian concept of "struggle for life," and fear of insidious infection of the healthy European racial stock by the "inferior" or "degenerate" races were then combined. Inhumane proposals for "cleansing" society were put forward. Their nastiness was excused by the "scientific" principles that supposedly justified them.[51] This was not just in Germany, but throughout Europe, and in the United States as well, where it led to renewed calls to control immigration of "undesirable races" and to forced sterilizations of "undesirables." But it was in Germany that this new version of Darwinism established itself most strongly.[52]

The prevalence of biological historicism in European thought contributed to making the late nineteenth century an age of intense nationalism and imperialism. In response to the perceived economic crises of the 1870s and 1880s, European powers had conquered most of the vast parts of Africa and Asia that had previously remained free of European domination. That this was an inappropriate and unprofitable response to the new age of steel, chemistry, and electrical machinery hardly mattered; European leaders believed that colonies were important for economic survival. Pushed on by growing nationalism, and the continued domination of the military by aristocrats imbued with feudal notions of honor and glory, the advanced countries of the world pressed on with their colonizing projects, and increased the tensions between them as their ambitions clashed.

After all, those who failed to expand would be proved inferior, and would be overcome by their competitors. From 1875 to 1913 expenditures for arms tripled in Germany and the United Kingdom, and doubled in France, as a near hysteria seized the European powers in their fear of being left out of the race.[53] In 1879, a German imperialist had written:

Every virile people has established colonial power. . . . All real nations in the fullness of their strength have desired to set their mark upon barbarian lands and those who fail to participate in this great rivalry will play a pitiable role in time to come. The colonizing impulse has become a vital question for every great nation.[54]

The popularized science of the late nineteenth and early twentieth centuries did not invent imperialism or racism; but it did give them the sense of infallibility and assurance that came with the cachet of "science." For intellectuals as well as for the less educated Europeans, the overwhelming technological superiority of the "white races" over the rest of the world seemed to be explained by a kind of simplified Darwinism. Reality and theory appeared to match, and the implications for the future were clear. Racial superiority had to be maintained, or else the nation faced ruin.

That this was particularly true in Germany was due in part to the greater role played in German politics by the army, the powerful Volkish strain in German nationalism, and the receptivity to anti-Semitism and the disdain for the Catholic Slavs along the eastern borders of the German Empire. It was also helped, no doubt, by the very qualities in German life that had made Germany so prosperous and economically progressive—a high level of education and literacy, and respect and support for advanced scientific research in universities. Fortified by generally accepted scientific principles about the struggle for survival between higher and lower races, frightened by the rapidity of social change and blaming much of it on the infection of foreign elements, Germany, and much of the rest of Europe, were prepared to accept this violent and combative version of Darwinism as the truth.

Economic Historicism

Karl Marx became the nineteenth century's most influential social analyst because he managed to present economic historicism in so powerful a way that he persuaded generations of his followers that he had discovered a true social science. At the same time, the basic elements of the theory could be simplified and grasped by millions who were unable to follow his complicated arguments and Germanic philosophizing.

The essence of Marxist theory, taken from Georg Hegel (Fichte's successor in Berlin), is that there are stages of human history, with each one containing within it the forces that will make it obsolete and lead to a higher, synthetic stage that keeps the advances of the old stage while incorporating the progress of the new one. This, stripped of its subtleties, is the dialectic process of history. The main forces, according to Marx and to his friend and collaborator Friedrich Engels, were economic. Each economic stage was characterized by a mode of production, a particular technology and a ruling class that exploited the labor of the masses. But each stage produced new classes that could grow and undermine the old system until it was fatally weakened. The rising class would revolt against the old system, and create the new one. Thus, there had been an ancient, "communal" stage without private property, states, or classes. With a rising surplus of production it had become possible for a ruling class to enslave the others, and produce the "ancient" or "slave" mode of production, which reached its height in Greece and Rome. This, in turn, was undermined by the barbarian, German invasions of Rome, which had produced a new synthesis, feudalism. In feudalism, which was the first stage to count in Marx's analysis (though not for Engels, who was more interested in anthropology and ancient history), a rural nobility controlled the land and exploited peasant serfs. But within feudalism there grew cities dominated by bourgeois merchants who increasingly resisted the domination of feudal lords and the restrictions on trade and movement imposed by feudal law. The bourgeoisie eventually revolted, and created capitalism.

In his study of *Capital*, Marx laboriously explained that capitalist profits are based on the extraction of surplus value from workers. Investments in machinery may produce short-term profits, but in the longer run, competitors learn to copy the same advanced technology, so that none have any advantage. In order to meet competition and maintain profits, capitalists are obliged to reduce the wages of labor to a bare minimum. Only the most efficient and ruthless producers survive, and they concentrate ever more economic power in their hands as small firms fail and are replaced by a small number of giant businesses. Capitalism's harsh need to maintain profits leads, therefore, to the creation of ever larger numbers of propertyless, impoverished workers, or proletariat. Peasants, artisans, small owners of businesses are all swept into this giant infernal machine until society consists only of a few very rich capitalists and a giant mass of struggling, poor industrial workers. But these workers, unlike the feudal peasants or slaves in past systems, are concentrated into cities, literate, and able to organize. Eventually, they unite, overthrow the system, and bring about socialism. Socialism, or ownership of the means of production by the masses producing for their own sake, not for blind profits, does away with the cruel vagaries of the market, it ends wild cycles of overproduction and depression, and it allows the rational utilization of modern technology.

Capitalism alienates people. It strips workers of pride in their work, because they become mere cogs in a vast, impersonal machine. It is more efficient than feudalism, but it also breaks the old patrimonial, communal ties that once bound lords and serfs. Socialism will recreate communal bonds, end alienation, and thus, aside from being even more efficient than capitalism, it will be much more humane.

Later, Rosa Luxemburg, trying to explain why capitalism still survived into the twentieth century, noted in 1913 that it was the imperialism of the late nineteenth century that had saved it. Capitalists, she said, had discovered how to prolong their system by exploiting new sources of surplus labor and easy markets in the colonies. Thus, they had postponed the death of capitalism by being able to buy off workers in their own countries with the cruel exploitation of the non-European world; but this, too, had to end. Capitalist powers controlled by their big financiers and capitalists were thrown into ever more desperate competition for colonies in order to keep their economies afloat.[55] As the world was filled up by colonies, this would lead to great wars between the capitalists, and eventually, to the collapse heralded by Marx. In his 1916 pamphlet, *Imperialism, the Highest Stage of Capitalism*, this is how Lenin explained the First World War.[56]

The Marxist view of the world is extremely persuasive. It explains the dynamic of history and makes predictions that, throughout much of the twentieth century, and certainly in its first half, seemed to be correct. There were wild business cycles. There was concentration of ownership into giant firms. There was frenetic imperialism, culminating in two terrible world wars. But workers were organizing, socialist parties were growing, and the fantastic advances in technology made it seem that, surely, there must be a more rational, benign way of organizing the world. First, of course, there had to be revolution. And because humans are dominated by their material interests, the bourgeoisie, or what was left of it, could be expected to fight ferociously to maintain itself in power.

Marxist prophecy strongly resembles Christian teleology. There was once a perfect state of being, when there was no property, no class war, and no alienation. This was a kind of Eden. Then, there was the sin of the private appropriation of the means of production by an elite, and mankind was thrown into slavery. After a long struggle, the forces of righteousness began to organize themselves. They found a prophet, Karl Marx, who showed them the way to promised redemption that would recapture Eden. But first, as in Christianity, there had to be a final struggle, a terrible war to the finish between the forces of good and evil. The forces of good, however, would win an inevitable victory, and the good would be saved, to live in perfect bliss. The coincidence between Marxism and Christian prophecy, and, it turned out, with the prophetic hopes of many other religions, made it appealing to masses of its followers who had been raised religiously but who were looking for a more modern, more scientific, solution to their problems. It also freed those who suffered, or who wished to abolish suffering, from the bonds imposed by official Christian churches that everywhere seemed so tied to the conservative establishment. It was not just because Marxism did not believe in the Christian, or any other metaphysical God, that Marxists in power were to turn so viciously against religion, but also because they recognized that religion was their main ideological competitor among the poor.

Marx and his followers in the nineteenth and early twentieth centuries, found Darwinism perfectly congenial. But instead of races fighting for survival, as in the interpretation of the biological historicists at the turn of the century, classes were the main actors. History, said Marx, was the story of class conflict. And the dominant classes would stop at nothing to save themselves. Thus, many, if not all Marxists came to feel that almost anything was justified to overthrow capitalism, and that mere reformism only delayed the inevitable, and therefore prolonged unnecessary human suffering.

Organized labor movements and socialist parties won significant victories in Western Europe in the 1890s and early 1900s. In several countries, though not in Germany, they were either brought into government or at last turned into partial allies of moderate liberal forces. This was most evident in France where some socialist leaders became ministers. In Great Britain, workers won important concessions and reforms.[57] But even in Germany, where the Social Democratic Party was frozen out of power, it was able to gain one-third of the vote in the parliamentary election of 1912, and to organize some four and a half million workers in its trade unions.[58]

This progress made socialists more moderate in practice, but not in theory. On the contrary, except to some extent in England, socialism became more Marxist. Revolutionary Marxist ideology was accepted as the official theoretical position of all the major continental European socialist parties.[59] The tension between moderate action and revolutionary rhetoric was particularly evident in Germany, where the leading socialist ideologue, Karl Kautsky, maintained a firmly orthodox Marxist line.[60] This made it possible for a Marxist as intransigent as Lenin, who was operating in the very different environment of Russia, where workers were both much poorer and more repressed than in Western Europe, to admire the German Social Democrats for their ideological purity.

Marxism was not merely successful in the most highly industrialized countries, but in less advanced countries as well. The theory combined what seemed to be best about the West, scientific certitude and precision, with a condemnation of the West's imperialism. It promised greater equality and fairness, and it condemned the evils of a system driven by market forces instead of by nobler human instincts. Yet, unlike more traditional rejections of capitalism that relied on old religious concepts and on sheer resistance to modernization, Marxism seemed entirely modern and progressive. It could therefore be used to attack the West, to reject established local elites, and to condemn old superstitions at the same time that it promoted the best of what the West had to offer.

This combination was particularly attractive to the "Westernizing" Russian revolutionary intelligentsia. It appealed at once to their desire to catch up and surpass the West, to their disgust for the inequities and bondage of the Tsarist autocracy, to their contempt for crass Western materialism, and to their admiration for modern science. Tibor Szamuely, one of the finest analysts of Russian intellectual history, has written:

> For the nineteenth-century European rationalist science was king—for the Russian intelligentsia it was also God. They were, of course, atheists almost by definition: religion represented the most malevolent of superstitions, to be combated with the same intense ferocity and dogmatism that the Church itself had displayed in its suppression of heresy. But pure intellectual rationalism was foreign to the Russian nature: it gave no moral satisfaction, it inhibited fervour and excluded faith. There was a strong mystical streak that required an object of veneration, even if the

object was nothing more than the mental process of reasoning itself. Science became the secular religion of the Russian intelligentsia. Its philosophical expression was a rather primitive materialism [that] opened up limitless vistas of a brave new scientific world, whose guiding principles of absolute justice would be based on immutable laws of nature. Messianism and scientism blended into a potent brew . . . further fortified by the addition of social-Darwinism and the positivism of Comte and Spencer.[61]

This was true even before the introduction of Marxism, and it was the expression of such sentiments that made Chernyshevky's *What Is to Be Done?* so popular.

Marxism became widely influential among the Russian intelligentsia in the 1880s and 1890s. It was not merely the merits of the doctrine, as such, nor the way it fit so many of the radical intelligentsia's needs that made Marxism so strong, but also the failure of previous, less theoretically sound forms of political action. There had been an attempt to "go to the people," to send out young idealists to the countryside to stir up revolution. This had ended in tragicomic failure. There had been violent plots and murders that were supposed to provoke revolution by themselves. Indeed, Tsar Alexander II was murdered by a bomb in 1881. But he was succeeded by the far more reactionary Alexander III, and the hoped-for revolution did not come.[62] In 1887 there was a botched, amateurish plot to assassinate Alexander III. One of its leaders was a young student, Alexander Ulyanov, who was hanged. As a result, his little brother, Vladimir, later named Lenin, became a dedicated revolutionary or so he himself claimed.[63] But even by 1887, it was increasingly clear that violence alone was quite insufficient, and that Marxist theory was a sounder base from which to begin to organize a revolution.

So, by the start of the early twentieth century, there were two powerful "sciences," one based on the notion that races competed ferociously for life, and the other on the notion that classes were engaged in an apocalyptic struggle. These ideas had spread far beyond the small circle of Western European intellectuals who had originated them. The prevalence of biological thinking contributed to an atmosphere that saw war as healthy and imperialism as natural. Marxism's revolutionary eschatology gave hope to its followers, and frightened its enemies, who saw socialism's potential for destroying their world. Both of these ideologies contributed strongly to increasing the widespread intellectual disdain for capitalism, liberalism, and democracy, which were viewed as increasingly obsolete and unable to cope with the modern world.

In general, the stronger the ideologies of inevitable conflict between communities—be they races, nations, economic classes, or religions—the more likely it is that tyranny will ensue. The very notion of preordained conflict to the death between groups makes such conflict far more likely, and persuades intellectuals and political activists to accept and promote the most ruthless means of control to insure the necessary unity in the face of danger. Those who follow them are pulled along by the fears such apocalyptic ideologies inevitably generate.

Yet, for all this, before 1914 it hardly seemed as if a racial or class Armageddon would really take place. If there had been no great war in 1914, both biological and economic historicism might have aged more gracefully. In Germany, the violently anti-Semitic right seemed to have passed its peak by the 1910s.[64] In Western Europe socialism was becoming more moderate, and more widely accepted. None of the previous international crises had led to a great war between the major powers. The Russian Marxists were divided and even Lenin believed in 1912 that the chances for revolution in his lifetime were small. In 1913 he said, "A war between Austria and Russia would be a very useful thing for the revolution, but it is not likely that Franz Joseph [Emperor of Austria-Hungary] and Nikolasha [Nicholas, Tsar of Russia] will give us that pleasure."[65]

But the idea that either class or biological war could happen, or might even be fated because of the impersonal forces of "history," was firmly implanted. It was part of the prevailing intellectual atmosphere. All that was needed to confirm what had so far been only intellectual speculations was a major disruption in the established world order. This Franz Joseph, "Nikolasha," and many other statesmen, generals, and other leaders gave to Europe over the summer of 1914.

THE CAUSES AND IMMEDIATE CONSEQUENCES OF THE FIRST WORLD WAR

Without World War I neither Hitler nor Stalin would have had any chance of achieving power.

Adolf Hitler, whose personal life was aimless and apolitical before the war, became an exceptionally courageous and decorated soldier whose bitterness at Germany's loss galvanized him into action.[66]

Though his political opinions had been formed over many years, beginning with his conversion to anti-Semitic, pan-German nationalism in the Vienna of his youth, his opportunity to enter politics came later. After moving to Munich, in 1913, he joined the German army at the start of the war in 1914. In 1919 the military unit to which he still belonged in Munich sent him to report on the political potential of a tiny political movement, which he joined, and turned into the National Socialist German Workers' Party.[67] In the disillusioned, paranoid atmosphere of post-war Germany, hundreds of groups like the fledgling Nazi Party (short for *Nationalsozialistische Deutsche Arbeiterpartei*, or NSDAP) thrived. It was Hitler's brilliantly charismatic speeches as well as extraordinary ability to win over supporters from other right-wing, extreme nationalist groups that raised the Nazis above the others, at first in Munich, then throughout Germany. Even then, Hitler did not achieve power until January 1933, after the Great Depression of 1929 had further disorganized and frightened Germany.

Stalin also would have remained obscure without the war, though by 1914 he was already an experienced and prominent Bolshevik revolutionary. Lenin's Bolsheviks, however, would have been unlikely candidates for power in a nonrevolutionary situation. But in 1917, as a result of three years of devastating war, Russia was in ferment, with a disintegrating army, a disgraced government and political elite, and a war-weary population ready to accept a new order. The revolution of March 1917 did not, at first, bring Lenin to power. The weak, insecure government that ruled after the overthrow of the Tsar remained in the war, and continued to lose. In November, Lenin's Party seized power in a second revolution.[68] (The old Russian calendar was slightly different so that usually these revolutions are called the February and October revolutions.) Lenin died in 1924, and Stalin, by then one of his top lieutenants, maneuvered himself into absolute power over the next four years.[69]

That leaves the question: Why did this terrible war begin?

The Marxist explanation of World War I was that advanced capitalist economies were becoming the domain of monopolistic firms increasingly unable to extract sufficient profit from their workers. So, the main capitalist powers had spent the previous fifty or so years expanding their colonial empires in order to find new peoples, resources, and markets to exploit. Now, by 1914, they were running out of areas to seize and exploit because the world had been filled up, and almost all of it lay within the colonial empire or sphere of influence of one of the industrialized powers. Driven to desperation in order to assure their profits, the large capitalist enterprises pushed their countries into war.[70]

A somewhat more simplistic version of this argument, but one that had great popular appeal after that war, was that arms merchants had caused the war to increase their profits. But there is no evidence that Krupp or Vickers, the two biggest armaments firms in Germany and England, really determined policy, or that they were in much danger of failing before 1914.

Though appealing because it seems to account for the frenetic imperialism of the late nineteenth century, and the catastrophic war that ensued between the European powers in 1914, the Marxist, or more simply, the economic explanation of the war has almost no empirical basis. Rather than being a period of increasing economic crisis, the years before World War I were ones of tremendous technological progress and economic growth throughout the industrialized world. Steel production, at that time the best single indicator of economic strength, increased sixteen-fold in Russia from 1880 to 1913, six-fold in the United Kingdom, twelve-fold in France, twenty-six-fold in Germany, and twenty-one-fold in Austria. These were the five biggest steel producers in Europe in 1913. In terms of general industrial progress, growth during that period in Russia was 455 percent, in the United Kingdom (which had started well ahead of the others) it was 99 percent, in France 102 percent, in Germany 285 percent, and in Austria 250 percent. The United States had an even more impressive record of industrial growth during this period.[71] No amount of hedging and explaining can demonstrate that there was any obvious economic crisis brewing among Europe's five major powers at this time, and especially not in Germany and Austria, which were the two powers that ultimately made the decision to go to war.

But there is little question, as Eric Hobsbawm has maintained, that there was a general *perception* that colonies, and perhaps permanent expansion, were necessary for economic well-being.[72] Not only Marxists, but more conservative elites believed the same thing. Elites believed in one or another of the versions of historical "science" that made conflict seem inevitable.

Joseph Schumpeter explained modern imperialism in advanced industrialized countries as an anachronism.[73] Military officers, and most of the kings and princes who were so influential in 1914, were the products of feudal agrarian traditions. The education of the rich along such lines perpetuated and furthered the attitudes that went with these traditions. But in agrarian societies, when economic growth was so slow and erratic as to be imperceptible, and elites had to control an adequate number of peasants in order to maintain their standards of living, making war on neighboring domains could make perfect sense. In an age of rapid economic growth promoted by technological progress, the rationale for such wars was far less clear. But even if the obsessively aristocratic and anti-bourgeois sentiments prevalent among European elites at this time were anachronistic, they were strong among the influential decisions makers in Europe who perceived the world in terms of honor, feudal combat, and maintaining their positions through warfare. Even worse, because so many of the leading intellectuals believed in the inevitability of conflict between nations, a large portion of those who should have been able to see through the nonsense of the feudal pretensions of their aristocrats were themselves in favor of war.

In no case was the anachronism of feudal honor more evident than in Austria-Hungary. After the heir to their throne, Franz Ferdinand, was assassinated by a young Serb while on an official visit to Sarajevo, the Austro-Hungarians presented a harsh ultimatum to Serbia for compensation and guarantees, which the Serbs accepted. But the Austro-Hungarians wanted war. Their elderly Emperor, who had been occupying his position since 1848, and who still viewed his domain as a personal family enterprise supported by the empire's only unifying force, the army, believed that war would cut through all the ethnic and nationalistic passions tearing his domains apart. War would end the seemingly endless, tedious, and threatening squabbles between Austria-Hungary's German, Italian, Romanian, Hungarian, South Slav, Czech, Ukrainian, and other subjects.[74]

As Austria-Hungary was not strong enough to face Serbia's ally, Russia, alone, Germany had to go along. Here, the explanation becomes more complex, because Germany, quite unlike Austria-Hungary, was a unified state supported by intense German nationalism. It was in no danger of disintegration. The overwhelming majority of its population was German, and Germany was clearly moving into the forefront of Europe as its most dynamic, most rapidly growing economy, with a population second only to Russia's. Some German historians have since claimed that the German government thought it only a matter of time until Russia surpassed them in absolute strength, and that defeating Russia before it was too late was its most important goal.[75] That some of Germany's leaders may have felt this way is undoubtedly correct. But the feeling was nonsense. Germany was much stronger in every respect, and far more unified than the Russian Empire which was itself a multi-ethnic, divided state. Only an ideological atmosphere which saw conflict between nations as an inevitable, biological imperative could support such a sentiment.

Germany was ruled by an Emperor, Kaiser Wilhelm II, who had behind him an army suffused with concepts of feudal glory. Germany had been preparing for war for so long that this time it gave its approval. The key was not any perception of economic, or even of immediate political problems, but a vague, long-term fear of Russia and a sense of grievance against France and England. England, which had dominated the early part of the Industrial Revolution, from the 1780s until the 1870s, had lost its edge after this. It was slower than Germany (or the United States) in developing new chemical and electrical industries, and though still immensely rich and the pre-eminent naval power in the world, it had fallen behind Germany in the leading-edge technologies of its day. Germany was larger and more dynamic, so the Germans felt it unfair that the British, and to a lesser extent, the French, had bigger overseas empires.[76] The German upper classes, including many intellectuals, so despised bourgeois capitalist democracies that they were convinced that England and France were obsolete, decaying, old powers, ready to be pushed out of the way by a more deserving, more martial Germany. In other words, the very nature of German nationalism, its resentment against the older dominant powers, a contempt for the weaker Slavs to the East, and a sense that Germany deserved to be the only great European power, all contributed to making the Germans sanction Austro-Hungarian aggression.

There was more, of course. Much of late nineteenth-century imperialism in Europe can be explained in terms of the increasingly popular Darwinian view of social life. If all was struggle, and the world was being organized into competing nations, then it stood to reason that, as in the evolutionary jungle, only the strongest would survive. That such a modern, "scientific" view corresponded so well to the archaic sense of feudal honor which was more prevalent than Darwinism among military elites is ironic. It explains why such a large portion of the educated middle classes, and even working classes, especially in Germany (where, it will be recalled, such biological explanations of social life were extremely popular), went along with their leaders and loyally went to war to save "their" version of civilization against all others. World War I, then, was caused less by direct economic competition than by nationalist perceptions that saw conflict as an almost inevitable outcome of competition. It ought to be noted that in the end, when a very small number of leaders were making the rapid, fateful decisions that led to war, the German Kaiser was fatalistic about what even he realized to be a terribly risky undertaking. War was inevitable sooner or later, so it might as well come sooner when Germany was ready.[77]

Russia, the last great European power ruled by an absolutist Emperor, Nicholas II, was politically archaic, and not as economically advanced as the other great powers. But its nationalism, at least among the bureaucratic and small educated elite, was, as we have already seen, just as resentful and active as in Germany. Furthermore, this fit very well with Tsar Nicholas's sense of personal honor, and his government's worry about the rising push for democratic reforms. So Russia honored its commitment to Serbia, and went to war. The French, fearful of Germany, and influenced by decades of nationalist propaganda since it had suffered defeat in the Franco-Prussian War of 1870–1871, mobilized to help its ally Russia. The British were forced in to help France and stop Germany from its threatened conquest of Europe.

The fact that well before the war a system of interlocking alliances, pitting France, the United Kingdom, and Russia against Germany, Austria-Hungary, and Italy (which abandoned its alliance when the war started, and eventually joined the other side), has been used to explain the inevitable march to war. In this respect, it is unfair to place blame exclusively on Austria-Hungary or Germany. In general, the widespread admiration of aristocratic-feudal tradition and the sense that national competition was akin to the supposedly vicious struggle for survival that took place in the jungle were pan-European, and perhaps even global phenomena. Japan and the United States were as much a part of the armaments race and the scramble for colonies as the European powers of this time. And it is true, as George Kennan has asserted, that the growing insecurity of the British and French, as they watched Germany's economic power growing, pushed them into an alliance with Russia that could only increase Germany's sense of being surrounded by enemies who would have to be dealt with one way or the other.[78]

The cause of World War I, in conclusion, was a mistaken worldview that combined nationalism with a widespread sense that national survival depended on struggling against other nations. In this respect, sentimental aristocratic values, popular nationalism, Marxism, and pseudo-Darwinist interpretations of nature all agreed. Even Austria-Hungary's pathetic attempts to expand its own colonial empire as best it could in the Balkans was part of a much larger world trend, and is what led young Serb extremists to plot the famous murder in Sarajevo.

A list of the colonies seized by the British, French, Germans, Russians, Italians, Spaniards, Dutch, Belgians, Japanese, and by the United States between 1860 and 1913 includes over sixty territories. More than three-quarters of these were annexed between 1878, the year Austria took control of Bosnia-Herzegovina, of which Sarajevo is the capital, and 1908, when Austria formally annexed that province. The British and French got the lion's share of the overseas European empires, not the Austro-Hungarians, who only got this one particularly troublesome Balkan province, or the Germans, who entered the race for colonies later than the other two big Western European powers.[79] Though the economic benefits of all these conquests were negligible, there was, as Rosa Luxemburg and Lenin argued, and as the biological historicists claimed, a real sense that the competition for empire was becoming ever fiercer, and the losers would face eventual conquest by the winners.

Beyond the competition for empire, there were also the attacks on modern bourgeois capitalism from both the left and right. To its critics modern society was poorly integrated and should try to recapture the sense of wholeness and community that had existed in the past. As the literature of that time testifies, there were many who saw glorious, natural, patriotic war as something that could do precisely that—recreate community, spontaneity, and a long-lost purity that had been sullied by crass materialism and social modernization. Herbert Asquith, son of the British Prime Minister at the start of the war, wrote:

Here lies a clerk who half his life had spent
Toiling at ledgers in a city grey,
Thinking that so his days would drift away

With no lance broken in life's tournament.
Yet ever 'twixt the books and his bright eyes
The gleaming eagles of the legions came,
And horsemen, charging under phantom skies,
Went thundering past beneath the oriflamme.
And now those waiting dreams are satisfied;
From twilight to the halls of dawn he went;
His lance is broken; but he lies content
With that high hour, in which he lived and died.[80]

The reality was not anything like that. The results were horrifying. Military tacticians were not prepared for the consequences of all the technological advances that had been made since the last round of major European wars in the mid-nineteenth century. They did not realize that railroads, heavy artillery, and machine guns gave the defense an overwhelming advantage that could only be broken once tanks and air power had been perfected, as they were in the next world war. Once attackers broke through an enemy's lines, they had to advance on foot, or with horses, while in Western Europe, namely France or Germany, the rear lines could be reinforced by rail, and large numbers of men moved around quite quickly to shore up defensive lines. That, combined with the massive destructive powers of new weapons, condemned millions of men to senseless deaths as they charged, and counter-charged across the bloody, muddy fields of northern France and Belgium. When the Americans finally joined the French and British in 1917, and poured their huge resources into the effort against the Germans in 1918, the war ended because of Germany's exhaustion. But so many had died, and for such meager results on both sides, that the war enormously reinforced the sense of despair and cynicism about modern capitalism and democracy that had existed before.

Rough figures (and that is all that is possible) show that about 1,800,000 Germans, over 1,700,000 from the Russian Empire, 1,400,000 Frenchmen, 1,300,000 Austro-Hungarians, 950,000 from the British Empire, 670,000 Italians, 335,000 Romanians, over 325,000 Turks, 45,000 Serbs, and 90,000 Bulgarians died in the fighting. The Americans had 116,000 killed. This is a total of 8,700,000, but it does not take into account civilian deaths, the certain undercount of military deaths, particularly in Russia and Turkey, and the vast number of injured who survived. Nor does it indicate the proportionate effect on one sector of the population, young men. Some 18 percent of Frenchmen of military age, 13 percent of all German young men, 12 percent of the Austro-Hungarians, and about 10 percent of the young men in several other participating countries died. The Americans were an exception. Only about one-half of 1 percent of the men of military age in the United States were killed.[81] By the end the poetry was different. Siegfried Sassoon, in one of his most quoted poems, wrote:

You smug-faced crowds with kindling eye
Who cheer when soldier lads march by,
Sneak home and pray you'll never know
The hell where youth and laughter go.[82]

As a result of the war, the Austro-Hungarian Empire disintegrated into several new countries. Romania's size doubled, including pieces of Russia and previously Hungarian Transylvania. A new South Slav state, Yugoslavia, was formed uniting Serbia and parts of the previous Austro-Hungarian domain. Czechoslovakia, and the small, now separated countries of Austria and Hungary were carved out of the Empire. A new Polish state was formed from parts of the Austro-Hungarian, German, and Russian Empires. Three new Baltic states and Finland left the Russian Empire and became independent. Less important border adjustments were made elsewhere, and the Ottoman Empire also disintegrated. Russia was taken over by Lenin's communists, while Germany became a republic and lost its overseas colonies. Onerous reparation payments were imposed on Germany.[83]

Many of the participant countries were angered by the outcome. The Germans, who had believed themselves to be on the verge of victory until the summer of 1918, just before their unexpected collapse, thought they had been betrayed by a domestic enemy—communists, Jews, or other sinister forces. Russia, which had been on the victors' side, lost much of its European territory. Hungary, the equal of Austria in the old Austro-Hungarian Empire, lost over half its territory. Austria, previously the center of a great power, was shorn of this distinction, but now that it had become almost entirely German, was prohibited from joining Germany. Italy, which had entered the war late on the side of the winners, expected to be more abundantly rewarded, and to gain much of the Adriatic Coast of what became Yugoslavia. Bulgaria, a German ally, lost territory. Even France, a major winner, was frustrated by its inability to turn its sacrifice into immediate prosperity and security.[84]

It is an unfortunate aspect of nationalist passions that territorial exchanges that please one side are invariably viewed as historical injustices by the other. Further, many of the new or enlarged countries of Eastern and Central Europe contained large linguistic and religious minorities which were not pleased to find themselves in these new, highly nationalistic entities.

It was in these difficult circumstances, and after much destruction, that the Bolsheviks tried to begin carrying out their plans for change in Russia, and that, in Germany, Hitler began his rise to power.

Among all the other tragedies inflicted by World War I, the harsh conditions imposed on Germany, and more indirectly on Russia, by the victors, and the seeming increase in international tension after the unsatisfactory peace, seemed to confirm the views of those who interpreted social life as unending conflict, either on racial and biological grounds, or as a result of class warfare. If aristocratic pretensions, and the prestige of the old nobilities, kings, and emperors in Europe were seriously damaged by the war, the newer pseudo-scientific explanations of why wars exist and must be fought were confirmed. Nations, classes, and races did, indeed, seem to be locked in life-threatening combat. Europe and the world learned this lesson, and acted accordingly.

Chapter 3

In the Beginning Was the Word

Neither Joseph Stalin, born in 1879, nor Adolf Hitler, born in 1889, had early lives that gave clues about their futures. Born in obscure circumstances, they would have remained unknown if they had not come to embody revolutionary theories that saw human history and social life as the product of violent conflicts between races and classes. Once in power, they condemned millions of humans who were in the wrong category—the wrong race, the wrong class, or the wrong place—to death.

Hitler was exceptionally narcissistic. He had the capacity to see himself as a vessel for all the social and political forces at work in his world, and thus, believe that he was at its center. Ernst Nolte, a postwar German historian of fascism, has written that, "The dominant trait in Hitler's personality was infantilism." Yet Nolte added that "there are thousands of monomaniacal and infantile types in every large community, but they seldom play a role."[1]

Hitler's obsessive sense that he embodied all the aspirations of the Germans allowed him to concentrate on presenting himself as the savior he believed himself to be. But this trait was shared by Stalin who came to identify himself with socialism's future. This kind of "infantil-

71

ism" is useful for those who want to become great leaders. The competition for power is rarely won by those who are considerate of their enemies, who lack self-confidence, or who think they do not have something important to contribute to the problems of the group they want to rule. And when kindly, insecure, or purely opportunistic politicians with no particular agenda except to enjoy power happen to take control, they rarely, if ever, make memorable or successful leaders. This is particularly the case in turbulent situations in which routine administrative skills are inadequate. And for those of very lowly origins to reach the summit of power, they must, after all, possess exceptionally strong personalities, that is, forceful self-confidence in their own importance and programs. It is easy, after the fact, to call Hitler and Stalin obsessed egocentrics. At the height of their powers, to their millions of admirers, their absolute dedication to their causes was a source of wonder and admiration.

Hitler had a frustrating youth that embittered him, especially when his dreams of becoming an artist or architect came to naught.[2] Stalin grew up in great poverty, and his strong personality made him a rebel in the disciplined atmosphere of the religious seminary to which he was sent for his education.[3] But these kinds of youthful frustrations and anger are the stuff of most human lives, and cannot explain the political power these men came to wield.

Hitler and Stalin in the early years of their rule were not the isolated, semi-senile, half-crazed tyrants they became in their last years. Though both were angry and driven individuals for most, perhaps all of their lives, this gave them much of their energy, without which they would have accomplished little; and it did not preclude their being flexible compromisers when this was necessary, at least until their final years. In short, despite their character, they could seem entirely reasonable.

It was partly in their ability to convince others that they were trustworthy and could solve difficult problems that these men were political geniuses. Adam Ulam has written about Stalin that "this apparently choleric and obsessed man was at the same time perceptive and eminently practical." And "[he] was a man of uncommonly good sense and unusually vile as well as brooding temper."[4] Joachim Fest has written about Hitler that he possessed exceptional "tactical ability . . . artistry in handling people . . . hypnotic talent."[5] Saying this, however, merely emphasizes the obvious. Of course they had these abilities, otherwise no one would have heard of them. The angry and obsessed individuals who abound in every society but who lack unusual good sense or the ability to handle people may create personal tragedies around themselves, but they do not turn the world upside down.

On the other hand, skillfully handled anger and resentment, when attuned to broader, popular social theories that view the world in terms of permanent conflict, will strike other believers as neither irrational nor harmful, but as basically correct. Hitler's rage, whatever its psychological origin, fit the mood of many Germans very well. Not only was resentment an important element in German nationalism, but it was vastly augmented by the tragedy of World War I. Stalin's conviction that the whole world was an arena for class conflict, and that his Party's brand of socialism was bound to arouse the dangerous opposition of every other class and country, was shared by his fellow Bolsheviks, and eventually came to be seen as a sad fact of life by many Soviets as well. There was much to be angry about in Russia before the Revolution, and in Germany right after World War I. And later, as Hitler and Stalin became more successful, they created ever more enemies, and more alarm. Both men found ways to channel their anger, ambition, and idealism into political movements without which they would have remained insignificant. Hitler and Stalin were able to turn their own personal rages into terrible tyrannies because they had so many followers who agreed with them, not just because they were obsessed monomaniacs.

In other words, as far as these two tyrants are concerned, looking for psychological pathologies in their character does not add much to our understanding of how they achieved power, though it can be useful in understanding how they later abused it so terribly. It is especially important to point out that Hitler's rise to power belies his supposed irrationality because, as William Carr has written, he is largely remembered as "a ranting mob orator, a demoniacal figure carried away by the elemental power of his own oratory and utterly incapable of controlling his own emotions." But the film extracts we are used to seeing, small bits taken from the climactic end of his speeches, deceive us, and:

> one is left to infer either that Germans are peculiarly vulnerable to hysterical oratory, or else that Hitler was an unsophisticated rabble-rouser. . . . Almost exactly the reverse is the truth. Sophistication in the use of the techniques of public speaking and care in the preparation of

speeches were the hallmarks of his oratory. . . . He did not rant and rave all the time—a physical impossibility for a man who spoke normally two hours and more—but addressed his audiences in quiet tones at first, even hesitantly, developing his chosen theme with occasional shafts of humour and invariably with lucidity and skill.[6]

Hitler did not try to convince his opponents that he was right, but to address those who were inclined to agree with his facts and reasoning in order to confirm and strengthen their beliefs. "Hitler's aim in the early years," writes Carr, "was quite simply to arouse and mobilize the emotions of his audience." The meetings at which he spoke in his early political life transformed the Nazi Party into a powerful force because of his ability to do this, and in that sense, they were like religious revivalist gatherings. "For Hitler politics, like Wagnerian opera, was essentially a systematization of illusions to capture the total allegiance of the audience."[7]

THE YOUNG HITLER

The relationship between Hitler and the mother he evidently adored but found weak, and the father who occasionally beat him, makes for fascinating reading, but tells us little. He had an unexceptional childhood in a family that was, for its time, normally hypocritical, quite respectable on the outside but riven by tensions and some brutality within itself. As an adult he had a magnetic personality, but little time for anything other than his work, so it is not surprising that the women who fell in love with him also felt ignored and lonely. The generally perceptive analysis of him done in secret for the American government during World War II by the psychiatrist Walter C. Langer (he correctly predicted that Hitler would commit suicide rather than trying to survive his defeat) concluded from the available material that he was masochistic and had a deep desire to have women urinate and defecate on him, though there is nothing but the most circumstantial evidence to suggest that this was the case. Langer used this conclusion to explain Hitler's known obsessions with pollution and disease, which he expressed in *Mein Kampf* (My Struggle) with reference to the dangers of syphilis, and particularly, in discussing the pollution of the Aryan race by inferior races, particularly Jews, who were portrayed by Hitler as the epitome of filth.[8]

Following Langer, other psychoanalytic explanations have sought to explain Hitler in similar ways. Erik Erickson, and more recently Robert Waite, adopted a similar perspective.[9] In the late twentieth century a Freudian analysis that concentrates on anal fixations and unresolved mother-love seems less compelling that it did at mid-century. But even if correct, as it may well be, it explains relatively little. The image of Jews as diseased polluters was a common one among anti-Semites at the turn of the century, while fathers who occasionally beat their sons, drank too much, and acted overbearingly toward their wives were hardly unusual. Sentimentality and considerable hypocrisy about idealized mothers and womanhood were a staple of late nineteenth- and early twentieth-century European and North American culture. And since the sexual perversions of one generation may become the liberation movement of another, it is misleading to emphasize veiled allusions to what might have been anxieties and tastes that were only slightly beyond the normal range for that period.

Whatever Hitler's sexual proclivities may have been, as far as anyone can tell, and as Langer and others have admitted, sex was a minor part of his life. Hitler, unlike some of his highly placed followers, never seems to have shown much interest in exploiting his power for sexual ends. But then, Stalin was the same. For both men, as for Lenin, politics and power were vastly more interesting than sex. Hitler's recorded dinner conversations and accounts by his closest collaborators, such as Albert Speer, indicate that he liked the company of old friends and of pretty women, but that he most enjoyed talking about history, politics, and his own career.[10] What struck observers was his absolute faith in biological historicism and the inevitability of racial war, his hatred of Jews, and his determination to assure the dominant place of Aryans in the world once and for all. It is only if we believe that these theories are themselves psychopathic that we can justify explaining Hitler and Nazism as strange psychological anomalies. As these ideas were widely shared by millions of Europeans at the time, particularly, but not only, in Germany, it is unconvincing to suggest that abnormal psychology can help us understand why anyone should believe in them. It is an endearing, but analytically wrong aspect of liberalism to think that if an ideological position can be shown to be based on dubious scientific principles, then it must be irrational. If that were so, not only Nazi racial theories, but also Marxism, and most other strong faiths would have to be described as irrational.

If Hitler's early psycho-sexual development cannot tell us much about his later success and policies, the political and moral climate in Vienna to which Hitler moved in 1907, when he was 18, can tell us more. It is in the late teens and early twenties that one's political ideology is usually formed, largely on the basis of the world one observes at that time.[11]

The political atmosphere in Vienna—liberal, bourgeois, and expansively optimistic in the 1860s and 1870s—had become anti-liberal and pessimistic by the end of the nineteenth century and the early twentieth.[12] German nationalism, epitomized by the popular Mayor of that city, Karl Lueger, and earlier by Georg von Schönerer's pan-Germanism, had set itself against the Austro-Hungarian Empire's efforts to accommodate to the multi-ethnic and multi-cultural nature of the lands it ruled. This was part of the general trend against tolerance and loss of confidence in the ability of economic and political liberalism to solve Europe's problems. Such sentiments were particularly acute in Austria-Hungary because of the stalemated competition between the various ethnic groups for political advantage, and because the political elite's need to accept any support it could get had made it exceptionally willing to accept Jews as near equals, going so far as to make some of them nobles, and allowing them to become military officers in greater numbers, by far, than in other European armies of that time.[13] Furthermore, the official tolerance toward Jews in Vienna allowed educated, emancipated Jews to move into important cultural positions in the world of music, theater, literature, art, medicine, the sciences, education, and journalism. It was even easier if Jews converted to Catholicism, as many culturally prominent ones did. A large minority, and in some fields even a majority of the leading cultural and scientific positions in Vienna came to be occupied by Jews or converted Jews.[14]

The young Hitler, who wanted to be an artist, was denied admission to the Vienna Academy of Fine Arts. Frustrated by his inability to break into the artistic intelligentsia, and observing the prominence of Jews in high cultural positions, he became an admirer of Schönerer and Lueger, and received his political education reading nationalist, pan-German, anti-Semitic literature.[15]

But it was after emigrating to Munich in 1913, serving in the German army with great courage, and being seriously gassed near the end of the war, that Hitler's frustrations with Germany's bleak prospects took their final shape. It seemed to him, as it did to many other Germans, that the outcome of the war was unbelievable. How could the strongest, best army in the world, after it had crushed Russia in 1917, and launched a successful new offensive in France in the spring of 1918, be reduced to impotence in a few short months?

Erich Ludendorff, the de facto military ruler of Germany in 1918, realized in September of that year that Germany could not go on, now that the Americans were pouring in men and supplies. The last offensive had failed, and though Germany could certainly resist longer, the odds had changed, and ultimate defeat was inevitable. Hardly anyone else in Germany understood this, so when he told Germany's leading political leaders on September 29 that an armistice had to be sought at any cost, he shocked them. Whether or not Germany could have received better terms if Ludendorff had not lost his nerve must remain an unanswered question, but there is little doubt that the possibility of a final victory had evaporated. The German army, exhausted by four years of war and the cost of its last great offensive, could no longer hope to prevail. Given the surprise of Germany's elite in the face of this news, it is not at all astonishing that ordinary Germans, including Hitler, could hardly believe what happened.[16]

The terms imposed on Germany were harsh, though from the French viewpoint, because they had suffered such enormous casualties, not entirely unreasonable. Germany lost territory, mainly to France and to the newly established Poland; it had to establish a republic, disband most of its army, and promise to pay steep reparations. It lost all of its overseas colonies. Given this, and the mood of disgust and disbelief, Field Marshal Paul von Hindenburg, who had been Ludendorff's (largely ceremonial) superior, was able to claim in public testimony a year later, in November of 1919, that Germany had been "stabbed in the back," that is, betrayed by internal forces that had stolen Germany's victory. He was believed, because this seemed to make more sense than the unanticipated reality of what had actually happened.[17] Most people in countries that have experienced a catastrophe prefer to believe that some sinister plot, rather than the dreary reality of their leaders' mistakes, is responsible for their misfortunes.

Having lost credibility, the German political establishment ceded power to the socialists, who had been seen as the party of peace, and then immediately blamed them for having lost the war.[18]

In fact, the dominant moderate Social Democrats allied themselves to the remnants of the army, reimposed order, and brutally eliminated the centers of radical left-wing revolt, thus preventing a repetition of what had happened a year earlier in Russia where the communists had seized power. Then, with the help of the army, they brought right-wing extremist violence under control. But this did not satisfy the German establishment, and particularly not army officers, most of whom were now threatened with unemployment after years of fighting bravely. The new constitution that was established in July of 1919 in Weimar, and which created the republic that was to last only fourteen years, thus came into being tarnished by defeat and disgrace, and, in the eyes of the nationalists, by treason.[19]

Now, German Volkish ideology—anti-liberal, anti-democratic, anti-capitalist, and anti-Semitic—asserted itself. Rather than blaming their catastrophe on military failure, the nationalists were convinced that it was only because they had been betrayed by evil foreign forces, chiefly socialists and Jews who had been undermining Germany for a long time, that they were faced with ruin. It is quite possible that if the German army had had a long string of failures, and only gradually disintegrated, as did the Russian army during the war, the extreme nationalists and the military officers would have been discredited. Instead, they could present themselves as wronged martyrs whose success had been unfairly stolen from them.

It was in this atmosphere, with many rightist, nationalist, Volkish groups operating in Germany, that Hitler began his rise to power.

THE RISE OF THE NAZIS

Revolutionary groups never appear out of nowhere to seize power alone. When such events happen, it always turns out that there are many such groups competing for attention in a general situation of chaos and ideological confusion. They thrive on general social and political ferment. Christianity triumphed in Rome in such a troubled environment; Islam came to the fore in Arabia after a long period of intense and increasing religious competition between Jews, Christians, Zoroastrians, and more traditional Arab religious beliefs. The Bolsheviks in Russia were only one of a growing number of revolutionary groups when they took power. Similarly, the Nazis were only the most successful of what were at first hundreds of such groups in Germany.

In popular belief, Nazism is sometimes thought to have emerged "out of the gutter." More scholarly accounts emphasize the "petty

bourgeois" nature of its followers, and claim that Nazism was a movement of the frustrated, endangered, lower middle class. Joachim Fest,
the major post–World War II German biographer of Hitler, has written
about the brown-shirt SA troops led by Ernst Röhm who, after Hitler's
rise to power "[gave] vent to all the sadistic ingenuity of inhibited petty
bourgeois feelings" that they had presumably kept under some control
before 1933.[20]

Marxists, on the other hand, say that the real onus for Nazism rests
on the large corporations that supported the Nazis in order to destroy
democracy and socialism, and thus, insure their own positions. The
lower middle class, by these accounts, was a tool of the economic
elites.[21]

But neither explanation is satisfactory. Nazism eventually came to
appeal to a very broad range of Germans, not just to one or two classes.
It was neither predominantly lower middle-class, nor was it a plot by
big business. Henry A. Turner's carefully documented research demol-
ishes the idea that Hitler came to power as the result of support from
large business interests.[22] Rather, as the Nazis became the main Volkish
party, a wide spectrum of German opinion swung to the belief that
they were the only political group able to save Germany from ruin. Big
business, the aristocracy, the army, the lower middle classes, farmers,
and even significant portions of the working class eventually voted for
the Nazis.

Young men from a variety of classes, at first mostly disillusioned,
recently demobilized soldiers like Hitler himself, or Ernst Röhm and
Hermann Göring (both of whom, as officers, had distinguished war
careers marked by heroism and decorations) were at the heart of the
early Nazi movement. A few years later a new generation of youths
seeking solutions to Germany's many problems—the Baldur von
Schirachs, Reinhard Heydrichs, Heinrich Himmlers, and Albert
Speers—became the activists of the movement. These were not monsters from the "gutter," or even primarily frustrated petty bourgeois,
but, at first, idealists who had grown up in an intellectual environment
that rejected stale bourgeois habits and ideology and who sought
something better. The catastrophe of the First World War, and then the
disorders and limited opportunities for escape in the 1920s confirmed
their belief that the old system was *too* bourgeois, that capitalism and
parliamentary niceties led to failure, not success.[23]

It is the young who make revolutions, even if they are inspired by their elders' ideas. No revolutionary movement can succeed if it fails to mobilize the discontent of the young who alone have the energy, strength, and spare time to provide the movement with its troops. The Nazis were not a children's crusade, but their appeal to young adults stood out in marked contrast to the more established German parties of the 1920s.

Peter Merkl's tabulations of the class origins of Nazi Party members in 1933, based on party archives, show that though workers and farmers were under-represented, they were still in the party in large numbers, and that in general, the party represented a fair cross section of society in terms of occupation.[24] Workers and artisans, who were some 46 percent of the general working population, provided 32 percent of the Nazi Party's members. White-collar employees, who were 12 percent of the working population, made up 21 percent of the party members. Also over-represented were those in the liberal professions and students—10 percent of the population but 20 percent of the party; and civil servants, which included teachers, who were 5 percent of the population but 13 percent of the party. Farmers, with 21 percent of the population, were the most under-represented group, as they made up only 11 percent of the party.

On the other hand, the Nazis differed markedly from the general population, and from the other parties, in terms of age representation. Merkl presents the age distribution of the Social Democratic Party to contrast it with the Nazis, and considers the socialists to have had a typical age distribution for the German political parties of that time.[25] Among those 18 years or older, 31 percent of the whole population were between the ages of 18 and 30 in 1933. Whereas only 18 percent of the Social Democratic Party's membership were in that age group, 43 percent of the Nazi Party were that young. At the other end, 47 percent of the adult population were over 40 years old, but of the Social Democrats, 55 percent were over 40, while in the Nazi Party only 30 percent were that old.

That the Nazis captured the enthusiasm of youth, then, was more important than any specific class basis for the movement. But how did they accomplish this? After all, other radical movements of the right and left were trying to capture the same clientele.

In the years from 1919 to 1923, Hitler's political activities were almost entirely confined to Munich and Bavaria. Through his oratorical talents, he attracted growing numbers of followers, and became one of the major Volkish leaders.

This was a time when all the moorings of normal social life in Germany seemed to have become detached. There were attempted coups by various paramilitary groups and political assassinations. There was economic disruption, and the serious threat that Germany might be dismembered. Refugees were arriving from the eastern territories that had been German or had had large, privileged German minorities, but were now in the hands of newly independent states.[26]

Hitler's speeches and proposed program for action were consistent. It was the fault of the Jews, the Marxists, and the French. The great German people were being ruined by their enemies, and it was necessary to mobilize for combat to rid the nation of these forces.

There was nothing unusual in the substance of the Nazi program. The most influential political writer in Germany in the early 1920s was Oswald Spengler whose biting contempt for liberal democracy ascribed Germany's miseries to softness and lack of will. Even more than in his two volumes on *The Decline of the West*, this view was expressed in his widely read *Preussentum und Sozialismus* (Prussianism and Socialism) in which he called for a return to military discipline and centralization, a "Prussian socialism" that would reject both liberalism and Marxist materialism. This was a revolt against the Enlightenment, not simply a political program for the solution of temporary problems.[27]

Hitler's own single-minded belief that at the bottom of it all was racial war, fought by Jews covertly for centuries and now coming to a climax, enabled him to cut through the contradictory philosophical issues raised by Germans who opposed the Enlightenment while simultaneously defending German civilization as the epitome of high European culture standing against the encroaching barbarism of Bolshevism. Race rather than class or ideology was the master concept that explained everything. The association of Bolshevism with the Jews justified the German race's push eastward to secure its necessary *Lebensraum* (living space). Given the extraordinary complexity of what was happening in Germany and Europe, this ability to simplify and find a common thread running through everything gave Hitler an ideological consistency and force which were at the heart of his personal charisma. Those open to his ideas, but uncertain and confused by the march of events, would hear him and feel a sudden flash of insight that reordered their world.[28]

In early 1920, the Nazi newspaper in Munich, the *Völkischer Beobachter* (Volkish Observer) began to print the German translation of *The Protocols of the Elders of Zion*. This was a work probably written in Paris in the late nineteenth century by the Russian secret police, and disseminated in Russia and elsewhere by the Russian government in the first decade of the century. Now, in 1920,it suddenly struck a chord among Europeans disgusted by the fruits of modernity. Even the London *Times* described it as genuine, though it would retract this claim in 1921. It first appeared in the United States in 1920, too, in carmaker Henry Ford's *Dearborn Independent*.[29]

The work was supposed to be an account of the Jewish program to take over the world. It purported to show that since the French Revolution Jews had been using the slogans of the Enlightenment and the Revolution to destroy traditional privileges and communal solidarities. This was going to leave Europe unprotected from the power of money which the Jews controlled. Jews would set nations against each other in destructive wars, subvert public opinion through their control of the press, seduce non-Jewish intellectuals by propagating complicated scientific theories that would blind them to the empirical truth of what was going on, and they would promote class warfare by keeping workers poor in order to hasten the internal disintegration of every nation.[30]

Hitler, however, went further than *The Protocols* which were hostile not only to Jews but to Darwin and Nietzsche as well. Hitler put his theory of a Jewish conspiracy on what was meant to be a more modern, scientific and biological basis. Much of this, at least as it was expressed in his autobiographical political statement written in 1924, *Mein Kampf*, was taken from *Foundations of the Twentieth Century* by Houston Stewart Chamberlain. Chamberlain, an Englishman who emigrated to Germany and married Richard Wagner's daughter, combined elements of Gobineau's racial theory with pan-German nationalism and anti-Semitism. His work was excerpted for Hitler to read by Alfred Rosenberg, a Russian-speaking, German émigré from Estonia, who also wrote the commentary for the German publication of *The Protocols* in the *Völkischer Beobachter* and was one of Hitler's early ideological companions.[31]

In *Mein Kampf* Hitler distilled the content of his speeches and thoughts of the past five years. He wrote:

The Jew has always been a people with definite racial characteristics and never a religion; only in order to get ahead he early sought for a means which could distract unpleasant attention from his person . . . . Indeed, the Talmud is not a book to prepare a man for the hereafter, but only for a practical and profitable life in this world. . . . The Jewish religious doctrine consists primarily in prescriptions for keeping the blood of Jewry pure.[32]

Hitler was obsessed with the notion that Jews were seeking to destroy the German race by any means, including seduction of "pure" Aryan girls. He wrote:

With Satanic joy in his face, the black-haired Jewish youth lurks in wait for the unsuspecting girl whom he defiles with his blood, thus stealing her from her people. With every means he tries to destroy the racial foundations of the people he has set out to subjugate. . . . It was and it is Jews who bring the Negroes in the Rhineland, always with the same secret thought and clear aim of ruining the hated white race by the necessarily resulting bastardization, throwing it down from its cultural and political height, and himself rising to be its master. . . . And in politics he begins to replace the idea of democracy by the dictatorship of the proletariat. In the organized mass of Marxism he has found the weapon which lets him dispense with democracy and in its stead allows him to subjugate and govern the peoples with a dictatorial and brutal fist. . . . In economics he undermines the state. . . . In the political field he refuses the state the means for its self-preservation, destroys the foundations of all national self-maintenance and defense, destroys faith in the leadership, scoffs at its history and past, and drags everything that is truly great into the gutter. . . . Culturally he contaminates art, literature, the theater. . . . Religion is ridiculed. . . . The most frightful example of this kind is offered by Russia, where he killed or starved about thirty million people with positively fanatical savagery, in part amid inhuman tortures, in order to give a gang of Jewish journalists and stock exchange bandits domination over a great people.[33]

There was a suspicion that Hitler was partly Jewish himself. His paternal grandmother may have worked as a servant in a Jewish household. At that time, she conceived an illegitimate child, Hitler's father. The man who later married her and gave Hitler's father his family name of Hitler was not the real father. Therefore, it is possible that she was impregnated by someone from a Jewish family. There is no way of knowing. To further complicate matters, Hitler's mother was also a Hitler, through her mother who was the niece of his legal (but not real) paternal grandfather.[34] Whatever the truth, Adolf Hitler was terrified by the possibility that he might be part Jewish. His fear of "blood poisoning," and of the "Satanic . . . black-haired" Jew lurking in the darkness to seduce and violate the fair Aryan maiden was very real for him, and not a mere rhetorical trick. After annexing Austria in 1938 Hitler ordered that the village where his paternal grandmother was buried be turned into an artillery range and obliterated.[35]

However, there was much more than hatred of the Jews in Hitler's doctrine. There was also a foreign policy based on the notion of a racial struggle for survival. He wrote:

> The foreign policy of the folkish state must safeguard the existence on this planet of the race embodied in the state, by creating a healthy, viable natural relation between the nation's population and growth on the one hand and the quantity and quality of its soil on the other. . . . Only an adequately large space on this earth assures a nation of freedom of existence.[36]

Much of *Mein Kampf* was prophetic, because in power Hitler continued to be guided by the same principles. He believed that the Jews had subverted England and America, and turned them away from their Aryan heritage by weakening them through racial bastardization and political democracy run for the benefit of Jewish money. In Japan, however, Hitler believed that the Jews had met their match because, unlike in European societies, they could not blend in and weaken national will. This was why the Jews in England and America were pushing so strongly against Japan, he believed.[37] In fact, those who have claimed, like A. J. P. Taylor, that World War II resulted from a series of accidents and blunders made by the French and English, rather from Hitler's fundamental worldview, have the heavy burden of Hitler's own writings against them.[38] By the mid-1920s he had unfolded, and publicly revealed the policy of racial war, expansion to the East, and alliance with Japan and Italy that he was to follow to the end.

Much of Hitler's appeal to broad portions of the German population and to idealistic youth was based on the fact that he did not accept the old privileges of the rich and aristocratic. On the contrary, for him, the whole German race, if it maintained its purity, was worthy, peasant and worker as much as bourgeois or aristocrat. Equality of opportunity alone could guarantee that the strongest elements would come to the fore, and this, too, was part of his racial theory of the survival of the fittest, and of building a stronger race.[39]

Hitler also discussed why it was best to have a single leader, the virtues of physical fitness, and his program for the militarization of Germany: "The German army does not exist to be a school for the preservation of tribal peculiarities, but should rather be a school for the mutual understanding of all Germans."[40] And in his discussion of his brown-shirted *Sturmabteilung* (Storm Troops), or SA, who acted as his guards, as fighters to control the streets, and as a kind of vanguard of the Nazis, he wrote:

> What we needed and still need were and are not a hundred or two hundred reckless conspirators, but a hundred thousand and a second hundred thousand fighters for our philosophy of life. We should not work in secret conventicles, but in mighty mass demonstrations. . . . We must teach the Marxists that the future master of the streets is National Socialism, just as it will some day be the master of the state.[41]

Of course, these writings are not the highly systematized work of a great philosopher, or of a practiced journalist or academic. They are the work, as his translator Ralph Mannheim wrote, of a "self-educated modern South German."[42] Nor are they exact predictions, because Hitler was a practical politician who learned how to adapt to circumstances. But it does our understanding of twentieth-century history little good to claim that this was just hot air and venom, or that its history and science were mediocre and often wrong. Hitler was an intellectual who lived by his words and thoughts. His education, however informal, captured the elements of Volkish nationalism, of popularized biological determinism, and the striving for equal opportunity of most Germans in a society that had, before the war, maintained rigid class lines.

Many of the same claims of banality and opportunism have been made about Stalin, too, and they are just as wrong in both cases. This is how political and social theory works—it remains academic unless it can be transformed into a plan for action. Neither Hitler nor Stalin created the ideological systems they imposed on their societies. They read these ideas, discussed them, and made them work. In the beginning, with Hitler, as with Stalin, there was the word, the idea. And it was on the word that they built.

The Crisis of 1923

Nineteen twenty-three was a bad year for Germany. France invaded the Rhineland to try to force reparations payments from the Germans, and it also tried to foster a separatist movement that would have severed this rich industrial region from the rest of the country. The German government printed money to pay its bills and set off an inflation that totally destroyed, in just a few months, the value of the currency. Bond holders and those who had relied on their savings were ruined.[43]

Germany's experience with inflation was unprecedented. The wholesale price index, a good measure of the true underlying value of money, went up 293 percent (almost four times) from 1914 to 1919. This was not entirely out of line with what happened in other war economies in Europe because of massive deficit spending. But from 1919 to 1922, wholesale prices went up over 82 times. And from 1922 to 1923 wholesale prices went up 486 million times! Money had lost all value.[44]

It is difficult to exaggerate the sense of confusion and bitterness this engendered among wide segments of the population, particularly those who had always saved, who had trusted government bonds, who had always done their duty, and who now had all their work and dignity taken from them.[45]

The anger among the middle classes, the very portion of the population that might have been won over to Weimar's democracy in better circumstances, had lasting effects. This was such a betrayal of everything they had believed in about stability and righteousness that they never got over the shock. The emotional divorce between the Weimar present, that was somehow not considered a legitimate part of German history, and wide segments of the public played a decisive part in bringing the Nazis to power. But it would take another economic crisis to make it happen.

To take advantage of the crisis of 1923 the communists, with Moscow's backing, attempted to seize power in October, hoping that the combination of nationalist fervor against the French and economic hardship would reproduce the conditions that had led to success in

Russia. A series of strikes were launched in Thuringia and Saxony, while in Hamburg communists seized police stations. But the army, joined by the Social Democrats, and the unwillingness of the mass of the working class to join in a coup, re-established order in a few days.[46] The far right then decided that this was the moment to take power.

Hitler felt he had to act in order to maintain credibility, and to forestall other rightist groups. He believed that the Nazis would be supported by the local police and the Bavarian authorities. These were, in fact, sympathetic to the Volkish cause, and Hitler had General Ludendorff by his side in order to sway the army and to help extend his power beyond Munich after the seizure of that city. But the attempted revolution of November 8 failed when the Bavarian authorities refused to give in to Hitler. As Hitler, Ludendorff, and other Nazis leaders were leading a march, Bavarian state police fired on them. Hitler was marching arm-in-arm with a comrade who was killed, and who, in falling, dislocated Hitler's arm. The Nazis scattered and fled, and the next day Hitler was arrested. But the Bavarian authorities remained sympathetic to the Volkish far right, and allowed Hitler's trial to be turned into a propaganda show that gave Hitler the opportunity to disseminate his views more widely. He did this brilliantly in speeches to the court, and the reports of the trial made him much better known as a leading Volkish ideologue in the rest of Germany. He was sentenced to a year in prison in very gentle circumstances, and it was there that he wrote most of *Mein Kampf* in 1924. When he left prison, he began to rebuild the party, and, sobered by his failure of 1923, to lay a sounder political base throughout the country.[47]

But by the end of 1924, the situation had changed. The economic situation had improved, the French had withdrawn from Germany, a new currency had been established and stabilized, and the high tide of extremist Volkish sentiment seemed to have passed.

The Nazi Party shrank, though in northern Germany, under Gregor Strasser's leadership, it made progress. Strasser, who was to become Hitler's main rival in the party, was more socialist than the now cautious Hitler.[48] Hitler, who had led a bohemian, disorganized life before 1924, now purchased a house in the Alps south of Munich, put the finishing touches on *Mein Kampf* (which was published in 1925), sat back to wait, and slowly rebuilt his party, winning the allegiance of key leaders in the movement. Perhaps his seeming moderation was caused, as Fest suggests, by his falling in love with his young niece, Geli. Or it may have been the wisdom of experience, a realization that as long as the army and the established authorities were against him, no matter how sympathetic they might have been to right-wing causes, street demonstrations could never succeed in taking power.[49]

It was, in fact, during this period that his political genius was most evident, because, unlike the 1919 to 1923 period, he seemed to have a much less promising situation to work with. He outmaneuvered Gregor Strasser in 1926, conciliated the northern, more radical wing of the party, and won over Joseph Goebbels, until then one of Strasser's leading supporters in the party. Goebbels, a highly educated intellectual, became Hitler's master propagandist, and in 1926, took control of the Berlin wing of the party, reorganizing it and making it a success in what had been a largely socialist city.[50]

Hitler's moderation on the issue of socialism and the need to reassure the middle and upper classes that he did not mean to confiscate property was considered "petty bourgeois" by Nazi radicals, for example, by Goebbels himself before he was won over to Hitler's side. Alan Bullock wrote that it was part of Hitler's "cynical" attitude toward all political programs.[51] Yet, it was so consistent with Hitler's view that race was the primary historical force, not class, that there is no need to suspect cynicism. The decision to avoid alienating Germans for the sake of social policy was not only politically astute, it fit perfectly well with the ideological position expressed in *Mein Kampf*.

The Army, the Great Depression, and the Seizure of Power

No amount of tactical shrewdness or oratorical skill could have brought Hitler to power if it had not been for two problems. The first was the failure of the Weimar Republic to bring the German army under its full control, and the second was the outbreak of the Great Depression of the 1930s.

The German army was shaped by the traditions of the Prussian army. From the early eighteenth century, and especially under Frederick the Great, this army became the backbone of the Hohenzollern dynasty. It was led by nobles, whose primary duty as a class came to be to provide officers for it; and it was the loyalty of Prussia's aristocrats and the strength of its army that turned what had been a modest northern state, Brandenburg, into Prussia, a great European power. Even after the army let in commoners and became the armed force of a modern, industrializing state in the nineteenth century, it maintained its old codes of honor and sense of identity as the dynasty's army. As late as 1861, 65 percent of the officers, and 86 percent of all generals and colonels in the Prussian army were nobles. Furthermore, this army was enormously successful. Despite its reverses in the early part of the Napoleonic wars, it survived, and rebuilt itself to play a decisive role in destroying Napoleon. During the revolutionary period of 1848–1849 it stood by the King and defeated the liberals. It then fought three quick, victorious wars against Denmark, Habsburg Austria, and France from 1864 to 1871. These successes united Germany and made the King of Prussia the Emperor of the Second Reich. This took place under Bismarck's political leadership. He allied the nobility with the rising industrialist class in Germany, but he and his Emperor, Wilhelm I, were primarily beholden to, and grateful to their army for what it had done. Bismarck made sure that the army was independent of any parliamentary control or serious oversight.[52]

It may be true, as Barrington Moore has suggested, that it was one of the peculiarities of German history, at least when compared to French and English history, that the hereditary landed aristocracy, especially the Prussian Junkers, retained a disproportionate share of political influence into the late nineteenth century, even after Germany had become a major industrial power, and that this fatally weakened the liberal, middle-class political parties. But it was through the army that this influence was manifested, and even as the army became less noble in the early twentieth century, it maintained the same ethos of duty to the dynasty, staunch political and social conservatism, and admiration of aristocratic honor and landed property as the main sources of status and prestige. The fact that it was the Prussian army and King that had unified Germany gave them a degree of nationalist legitimacy that allowed this ethos to assume far greater importance in Germany than in the other European states that had not been united by their noble armies.[53] The Austro-Hungarian Empire was also dependent on its army, but this was a force, like the Empire itself, that was multi-ethnic and could claim no nationalist legitimacy at all.[54] Only Russia, the other great militarized absolutist eighteenth-century state to survive with its political system still largely intact into the twentieth century, was similar. Neither England nor France was like Germany or

Russia, because in the former there had never been a militarized absolutist state, and in the latter, the Bourbon effort, and later Napoleon's,
to construct one, failed.

Writing after World War II, the great German historian Friedrich
Meinecke would explain that, by becoming the main tool in constructing the new German Empire, the army became throughout Germany
what it had previously been in Prussia, the ideal social model: "Thus
militarism penetrated civilian life. Thus there developed a conventional Prussianism (*Borussismus*), naïve self-admiration in Prussian character, and together with it a serious narrowing of intellectual and political
outlook. Everything was dissolved into rigid conventionalism."[55]

The army did not accept the result of World War I. Forced to reduce
its numbers drastically, the supposedly new army, the Reichswehr, was
actually dominated by old-style officers. It supported the republic
against its enemies on condition that civilians not interfere with the
slow reconstruction and retraining of a new army. This was not because
of any love for the republic, but simply because if the republic had
been overthrown, there would have been a French invasion that Germany was too weak to resist. After 1925, when von Hindenburg was
elected President of Germany, the Reichswehr's sacrosanct, untouch-
able status was further strengthened.[56]

To be sure, the army was not the only German institution that did
not accept Weimar. The prevailing attitude in the universities, among
both students and professors, was anti-democratic throughout the
Weimar period. This can only be understood in terms of the intellectual trends described earlier, and was common throughout Europe. It
was all part of the revolt against stale "bourgeois" culture, against the
boredom and banal lack of heroism of liberalism, against the defeats
and frustrations of the 1920s, and in favor of community, roots, and the
nation. This was by no means limited to failed intellectuals or to those
of limited talent, but characterized the highest reaches of the professo-
rate. J. P. Stern has written, "Men like Martin Heidegger, Gottfried
Benn, and Joseph Nadler . . . all direct their aggression towards a
revival of those 'authentic' values which the modern cosmopolitan
world is destroying." They, and many others, exalted the "organic community" (*Volksgemeinschaft*). The great philosopher Karl Jaspers wrote
in 1931 that modern man was alienated by Marxism, psychoanalysis,
atheism, bureaucracy, and homosexuality, and that democracy could
only bring mob rule, egalitarianism, and hatred of excellence.[57] By 1931

the Nazis were receiving about twice as high a percentage of electoral support from universities as they were getting from the country at large, that is, a clear majority of the intellectuals.[58]

Much of the German civil service shared this same contempt for Weimar democracy, but this was particularly serious among the judges. The German judiciary remained monarchist and anti-democratic in the 1920s; the majority of its members were allied with the *Deutschnationale Volkspartei* (German National People's Party), an extreme right-wing party. Ingo Müller's recent study of the Nazi judiciary notes that "they [judges during Weimar] were quite willing to accept the version of the end of the First World War favored in conservative circles, in which an army unbeaten on the field was defeated solely by sabotage on the home front. . . . They devoted themselves to eliminating the 'enemy within.'"[59] Their bias was demonstrated repeatedly. Left-wing violence was severely sanctioned; right-wing violence, murders, and coup attempts, including Hitler's in 1923, were only lightly punished, if at all.

In the late 1920s, prosperity seemed to ease the crisis of Weimar, but this was temporary. The Great Depression set off by the collapse of prices on the New York Stock Exchange in the fall of 1929 precipitated a crisis from which Weimar could not recover. This hardly means that the Depression prevented the triumph of liberal moderation. Without it, the German army probably would have taken power on its own, as it was on the way to doing, and then carried out a war to regain Germany's dominant place in Europe. Certainly, despite the temporary accommodation going on at diplomatic levels in European affairs in the late 1920s, neither Weimar's institutions nor liberalism as a whole was on the ascendant in Germany. In other words, almost any crisis would have finished the republic.

The Great Depression was the result of a great liquidity crisis aggravated by restrictive monetary policies and increased tariffs among the leading industrialized countries. German recovery in the late 1920s had been dependent on foreign, chiefly American capital, and a market for its manufactured exports. When both of these failed, so did the German economy.[60] Unemployment rose from under 5 percent of the registered work force in 1929 to 30 percent in 1932.[61] This was not out of line with what was going elsewhere in the industrialized world, including the United States, but coming on top of the political legacy of the entire post-war period, from the "betrayal" of 1918, to the inflation of 1923, and now the Great Depression, it led to a severe break-down in the Germans' confidence in their social and political order. This is shown by the rapid rise in Nazi votes, and particularly in an analysis of what groups voted for Hitler's party, for other rightist parties, for the left, or for the rapidly shrinking middle.

In 1928 the Nazis received 2.6 percent of the vote in the parliamentary (Reichstag) elections. In May 1924 they had received 6.5 percent. In September of 1930, after the start of the Depression, they received 18.3 percent. In the July 1932 election, their vote rose to 37.3 percent, making them by far the largest single party. Even though their total fell back to 33.1 percent in the November 1932 election, they received more than half again as much as the second largest party, the Social Democrats.[62]

Richard Hamilton's analysis of German voting patterns during this period puts to rest many of the widely accepted claims made about the Nazis' rise to power. These exist largely because of the preconceptions of German Marxist intellectuals who gave us the official Marxist version of Nazism, that it was an alliance of big business and the alienated lower bourgeoisie. Hatred of the high bourgeoisie, contempt for the "petty" bourgeoisie, fear of the "lumpen proletariat" (that is, what Marxists consider the unemployed social scum—quite unlike the true proletariat, the industrial working class), and the conviction that somehow anything that does not move societies toward progressive socialism must be seen as a kind of irrational resistance to the proper march of history all contributed to this false image.[63]

What really happened is that vast portions of German society gradually had their worldview, the entire moral basis of their social existence, undermined and then shattered. The main swing in voting occurred among northern German Protestant voters, particularly in rural areas (even though Hitler was a southern, urban Catholic). Only two groups of voters held out against the Nazis. One was the Catholic Center Party which retained its strength, especially in rural Catholic areas. The other was the socialist left (Social Democratic and Communist), whose base lay among the industrial, urban, working class. Neither Catholicism's moral grounding nor socialism's were badly shaken by the collapse of what both had viewed as an essentially hostile, Prussian Protestant culture. In the case of the Catholics, this attitude had existed since Bismarck's Kulturkampf, or cultural war against them, and in the case of the socialists, it was caused by Imperial Germany's permanent refusal to accept them as legitimate, despite their rising electoral and organizational strength.[64]

The Catholic Center Party's vote in Reichstag elections from May 1924 to July 1932 fell from 13.4 percent to 12.5 percent, a rather insignificant fall given the fact that one of their leaders, Brüning, had been in power in 1930–1931, and had utterly failed to stem the economic decline through a series of conservative fiscal measures. The Social Democratic vote over this period rose from 20.5 percent in May 1924, to 29.8 percent in May, 1928, and then fell back to 21.6 percent in July 1932, and 20.4 percent in November 1932. The Communist vote was 12.6 percent in May 1924, 10.6 percent in May 1928, and 14.3 percent in July 1932. It hit a high of 16.9 percent in the November 1932 election. Combining Social Democratic and Communist votes shows that the socialist left's vote remained quite steady throughout the period from 1924 to 1932. It totalled 33.1 percent in May 1924, 40.4 percent in May 1928, 35.9 percent in July 1932, and 37.3 percent in November 1932. If, toward the end, the Social Democrats began to lose ground, the Communists gained strength, though certainly not at a spectacular rate.[65]

Those who lost ground were the non-Catholic, moderately conservative center parties. They had 14.9 percent of the vote in May 1924, reached a high of 16.4 percent in December 1924, then fell to 13.6 percent in 1928, 8.3 percent in 1930, and 2.2 percent in July 1932.

The far right was at first led by *Deutschnationale Volkspartei*. It combined anti-Semitic, nationalistic, Volkish elements with aristocratic, agrarian Prussian interests. In May and December of 1924, it was the second largest party after the Social Democrats, with 19.5 percent and 20.5 percent of the vote. In 1928, at the height of Weimar's success, it had fallen to 14.2 percent of the vote. But then, the rise of the Nazis, and its obviously elite character prevented it from reaping the benefits of the swing to the right. In 1930 it received 7 percent of the vote, and in July 1932, only 5.9 percent. Perhaps because some on the right began to be frightened by the Nazis, in the second election of 1932 it gained much of what the Nazis lost, and went back up to 8.3 percent of the vote. In 1933, however, it became an ally of the Nazis, so that their combined strength still stood at 41.4 percent, whereas in the first election of 1932 it had been 43.2 percent.

The other parties that declined during the early 1930s were the regional parties, which were mostly conservative and agrarian. Their voters moved to the Nazis.

Aside from the rural Protestants, who moved from moderately conservative or regional parties to the Nazis, another significant shift occurred among what Hamilton calls "Tory" or conservative workers. Though the majority of the working class remained socialist, those who were not voted for centrist parties in the 1920s and then moved to the Nazis. This was most evident in Berlin, where the greatest losses for middle-class parties actually took place in working-class residential districts. But this was a widespread phenomenon in other cities, too, though less so in Catholic ones.[66]

Hamilton found that the more prestigious and expensive urban residential districts were, the higher the proportion of votes obtained by the Nazis. The Nazi vote was not, therefore, "petty bourgeois," but widespread throughout the entire range of classes in Germany. It was highest among the well-to-do, and among rural Protestants, but it also captured a large proportion of those working-class voters who previously had not been committed to the socialists.[67]

The Nazi leadership was disproportionately from the upper reaches of society. In the early 1930s something on the order of 40 percent of the Nazi Gauleiters (regional leaders) were from the officially defined elite and upper-middle classes, a category that included only 2.8 percent of the German population. About 50 percent were from the "lower middle class," a group that encompassed about 43 percent of the population. In other words, the vast bulk of the middle classes was very slightly overrepresented, the lower (chiefly working) class (54.6 percent of the population) was seriously underrepresented, and the upper middle and upper classes were vastly overrepresented in the Nazi leadership.[68] The upper-middle classes and elite were more sympathetic to the Nazis than other classes. Leaving aside the Protestant rural support that swung to the Nazis in the 1930s, the lower one went on the social scale, the lower the support for the Nazis. It was not the petty bourgeoisie or the lumpen proletariat that were the electoral base of the Nazi's electoral party, but *all of the bourgeoisie*. And though the Nazis never obtained majority support from workers, they did gain the support of a large minority of them, as well the votes of non-Catholic peasants and farmers.

All the analysis of Weimar politics indicates that throughout the 1920s the middle-of-the-road parties, including the Catholic Center Party, tended to become more and more rightist in their policies. This accelerated with the coming of the Depression. It was not the Nazis who created this rightward drift, but they were its ultimate beneficiaries.

Imperial Germany, as Meinecke and many others have pointed out, including even those sympathetic to the socialists such as Guenther Roth,[69] was a society of order and discipline. This corresponds to what has come to be seen as the German national character. There is no need to exaggerate this tendency to point out that all societies are held together by a certain conception of order which includes economic predictability and validation of the society's moral concepts. If hard work, proper adherence to social conventions, and predictability were the hallmarks of a successful Germany before World War I, and after World War II, this does not in any way explain Germany's proclivity for Nazism. On the other hand, a seeming collapse of the moral order because of economic unpredictability, the absence of reward for hard work and conventional adherence to social norms, and a seemingly unjustified international persecution of Germany did lead to a search for new solutions. This is what the Nazis offered.

Both through their firm anti-socialism, which promised to guarantee private property, and their radically anti-establishment style, which promised new solutions to the evident collapse of the old order, they won over those whose world was disintegrating. They offered, in short, a new faith for the delegitimized Weimar way of life, a return to Imperial grandeur, but with a greater element of social mobility and opportunity. That the Nazi worldview was nationalistic, Volkish, and anti-Semitic gave them their most enthusiastic, committed supporters, especially among young elite intellectuals in the universities and among aspiring young professionals. But, as Hamilton points out, very few of the solid middle-class types who voted for the Nazis had any idea of what Hitler's rule would bring.[70] The same is almost certainly true among those Protestant rural voters who just wanted to regain their self-respect as good Germans and a measure of economic stability.

The "mass society" theory of Nazism, blaming its appeal on the alienation or loneliness of modern life and the marginalization of many individuals, misses the point. Thus Hannah Arendt, many of whose original insights into the nature of totalitarianism remain valid, errs in using such theories to explain the rise of the Nazis, and in claiming that totalitarianism succeeded because old class solidarities had broken down, leaving individuals alone to face modern life. What had broken down was not the old class structure, at least no more than in any other modern society, including the United States and Great Britain at that time, but a whole social model of what constituted proper social and economic behavior. Given this, people turned to a movement that promised to return Germany, as Thomas Mann had put it, to a "coherent, disciplined, historical past."[71]

That this particular "past" had been conceived as a set of Volkish ideas, and animated by a widely accepted theory about the primacy of race in human affairs, had to do with the specific trajectory of European, and particularly German intellectual history, as Arendt herself made quite clear in the first two parts of her study. The Nazis became the only anchor in a moral storm for those who had accepted the Prussian-dominated culture of order that had prevailed in Imperial Germany. They offered a new way of life that appealed to angry young people; but they also promised a return to historical certitudes in which Germany would be great, in which hard work would be rewarded, and in which everyone would be prosperous. Thus, even though energetic young elites were in the forefront of party activity, older, more sedate voters could go along, too. If one leaves aside the two socialist parties (Social Democratic and Communist) and the Catholic Center Party, all three of whom retained their own viable moral, intellectual, and theoretical explanations of how the world worked and what their role in Germany might be, the Nazis had the vast majority of the vote by 1932. In July of 1932, the Nazis received 72.2 percent of the remaining (nonleftist, non-Catholic) vote, and 65.2 percent in the following November election.

In the end, a small clique around the almost senile President von Hindenburg, led by Hindenburg's son and by Franz von Papen, who represented the Volkish non-Nazis in the German National People's Party, suggested that Hitler be made Chancellor, or Prime Minister, in order to tame his growing electoral popularity. They believed they could control him. Why they thought that the superbly organized, highly popular Nazi Party, animated by a strong ideology and a forceful leader, might be manipulated by a select group of rich but not very popular men with hardly any organization behind them must remain a mystery. The fact is that they preferred Hitler to what they perceived as the growing left-wing danger represented by the continuing strength of the socialists and the growing power of the communists.

And the vast majority of Germans, including the Catholic Center Party, agreed with that view. Better to have the right in power than the left.

Hitler became Chancellor in January 1933. Over the next year and a half, he transformed German politics and established himself as sole dictator.

Hitler's rise to power suggests that nationalist ideologies that stress resentment and social theories that view the world in terms of inevitable conflict between races or classes created a high potential for tyranny, but did not make it inevitable. Economic and political chaos were necessary to bring these ideologies to their ultimate fruition. Particularly when disorder leaves a whole population at a loss of how to react because the old rules of behavior seem to have become useless, the likelihood increases that a tyrant will emerge as a self-proclaimed savior.

Whether this conclusion applies as well to the rise of Stalin is the subject to which we now turn our attention.

THE YOUNG STALIN

Stalin's rise to power was fundamentally different from Hitler's because he did not create the organization he came to dominate, nor did he lead it when it seized power. Rather he could count on a very well-worked-out, coherent, powerful ideology. In some respects, Stalin was like Heinrich Himmler, the loyal follower and masterful bureaucrat who might have succeeded Hitler if Hitler had died in, say, 1941. Stalin was a good bureaucrat who built up institutions loyal to him and placed his allies in key positions, but at first he avoided the limelight. Stalin's success, therefore, came as a surprise to Lenin's closest and oldest companions, as Himmler's did to Hitler's old friends. But this does not mean that Stalin was in any sense an opportunist who did not believe in Marxism-Leninism, and it certainly does not suggest that his was a mediocre mind. Both of these accusations were levelled against him by those who lost the struggle for power, chiefly Trotsky. He was not as great a writer, as charismatic a speaker, or as flamboyant a personality as Lenin or many other top Bolsheviks. Though he was only nine years younger than Lenin, and older than some of his prominent revolutionary rivals, he was, institutionally, part of the second generation of leaders, working within an established, if fragile tradition, rather than starting from the beginning.

Any revolutionary faith that means to survive and thrive must establish its own institutions. It must, as Max Weber pointed out in his analysis of politics and religion, become routinized, ordinary. The original, almost magical charismatic flame cannot be sustained beyond the death of the leader unless institutions are built to sustain daily existence. Hitler never really had to do this because he remained the leader until Germany was conquered in 1945 and the movement collapsed. Also, the Nazis simply took over most of the institutional structure of the German state without destroying it. Thus, even though the Nazis later began to build an entirely new institutional structure, they never faced the structural exigencies and succession crisis that marked the early years of Bolshevism.

In the case of the Bolsheviks, the state they took over, Imperial Russia, was in collapse. Its institutions were in chaos. The discredited old bureaucratic and military elite, quite unlike the German elite which was largely favorable to the Nazis, was hostile to communism. But among the radical intelligentsia as well as among urban workers, and at first among peasants, there was clearly much sympathy for Lenin and his party. There existed a strong ideology to bind the communists together, namely the Marxist theory of the inevitability of class conflict and the ultimate triumph of socialism, and there existed a strong and dangerous form of nationalism to rally many noncommunists to any government that could claim to speak for the nation. But there were no institutions, no known way of operating a socialist political and economic system. It was Stalin's accomplishment to create just such a system. This feat was as impressive as what Lenin or Hitler accomplished. The potential for tyranny in a situation such as Russia's in the late 1910s was very high, just as it is high in the early 1990s in Russia for many of the same reasons—chaos, a discredited old system not yet replaced by a new one, rampant ideologies of nationalist resentment, and a growing sense that bitter conflict is inevitable. But it was Stalin who converted that potential into reality.

In some respects, Stalin's early life bore some uncanny resemblance to Hitler's. Stalin's father also drank and beat his mother. But Stalin's father was a poor peasant turned cobbler rather than, like Hitler's father, an established middle-class official. Like Hitler, though, he was the first (and in his case the only one) of his mother's children to survive into adulthood. Hitler's mother, too, had lost her earlier children. Both men, therefore, became the principal source of emotional attachment for their mothers, and according to Robert Tucker, this gave Stalin (and by analogy may have given Hitler) a level of self-assurance that was crucial in his later life. Tucker quotes Sigmund Freud who wrote that "a man who has been the indisputable favorite of his mother keeps for life the feeling of a conqueror, that confidence of success that often induces real success."[72] Both men also seemed to have developed a hatred for their abusive fathers, and an early resistance to authority that was the basis of their later revolutionary resentment against the established political order in which they grew up.

The Georgian Iosif Djugashvili (this was his original name, before he took on a number of revolutionary pseudonyms, of which Stalin, "Man of Steel," was the one that finally stuck) was placed by his mother in a religious preparatory school where he was an outstanding, lively student. His loutish father tried to take him out, because he did not want an educated son, but his mother put him back in after one of their many violent fights. He graduated from this to an Orthodox Seminary where he read forbidden books, from Victor Hugo to Marxist works. Many of his fellow students were like him, and the atmosphere was conducive to the formation of revolutionaries because it brought together highly literate, bright young men in a repressive, conservative, intellectually irrelevant institution. Stalin, supposedly, ceased to believe in God at thirteen after reading about Darwin's theories.[73]

The young Djugashvili also read romantic nationalist Georgian literature, and was particularly taken by a novel called *The Patricide*, by Alexander Kazbegi. It features a hero, Koba, who is a fearless sort of Robin Hood character fighting against Russian invaders and treacherous Georgians. Ultimately, he inflicts revenge on those who try to betray the noble Georgian cause. Koba, a plain mountaineer, was the enemy of the pro-Russian aristocracy. That Stalin identified with this brave, straight-shooting, exemplary hero who could bring rough justice with his pistol is evident, because "Koba" was Stalin's favorite underground name as a young communist, and the name by which his Party friends always called him.[74]

Georgia in the late nineteenth and early twentieth centuries was the most socialist and revolutionary province in the Russian Empire. Partly this was because it had an unusually large, and therefore poor aristocracy, whose educated sons turned, as did much of the young Russian intelligentsia, to Marxism. Also, the repressed nationalist sentiment of the Georgians was consistent with revolutionary sentiments. Finally, mountain peasants and shepherds, who live in physically more remote areas, tend to remain more independent and recalcitrant to authority than other peasants. Teodor Shanin has written that it was in Guria, a part of Georgia, that there flourished the first of the twentieth-century's Marxist peasant radical revolutionary "republics" from 1903 to 1906. Later on there were similar radical rural movements in China, India, Cambodia, and, most recently, in Peru.[75] When Georgia's experience was repeated on a much larger scale in 1905–1906, with spontaneous peasant uprisings in many parts of Russia, Marxist theoreticians who had expected peasants to remain passive were astonished.

Georgian revolutionaries during this time fell almost entirely under the sway of Mensheviks, who, in the subsequent years, moved apart from Lenin's Bolshevik wing of the Russian Social Democratic Party. But Stalin chose to stay with the minority of Georgian Marxists who remained Lenin's Bolshevik allies.

Mensheviks and Bolsheviks

The Menshevik-Bolshevik split, which began in 1903, but continued to develop and only really crystallized in the aftermath of the 1906 repressions, during a period when Mensheviks and Bolsheviks were formally allied (1906–1912), needs to be explained, if only briefly, because it was decisive in Stalin's rise to power that he chose to remain a Bolshevik. Perhaps he chose the Bolsheviks because his rancorous personality made it difficult for him to get along with his fellow Marxists in Georgia. Tucker suggests that Stalin found in Lenin a Russian father figure and model to emulate because Lenin's writing in *What Is to Be Done?*—his key 1902 text on how to organize a revolution—was so combative, uncompromising, and elitist, and this fit Stalin's own image of himself.[76]

At the 1903 Second Congress of the Russian Social Democratic Worker's Party, which met in Belgium, Lenin demanded a more centralized party, and his chief rival, Martov, a somewhat less centralized structure. Martov was more "inclined to take over and use existing legal institutions."[77] The Jewish socialists, who had their own wing of the party, the Bund, had walked out just before this dispute because they felt they were not being granted enough autonomy, and so Lenin's side won an accidental, thin majority of 24 to 20 among the remaining delegates. On this basis Lenin and his followers forever after called themselves the "Majority" (Bolsheviks) and their opponents the "Minority" (or Mensheviks), even though those who had walked out would have agreed with the Mensheviks and would have given Martov a majority. As the split grew more severe, the Mensheviks, who were certainly in the majority in the 1906–1912 period, accepted this nomenclature.

The Mensheviks were more heavily non-Russian than the Bolsheviks. Martov himself was Jewish, and the Mensheviks were stronger in the non-Russian periphery of the empire—in the Baltics, Poland, the Caucasus, and among Jewish revolutionaries.[78] The Bolsheviks had a large number of non-Russians, too, but Lenin was Russian, and the Bolshevik obsession with centralization meant favoring the Russian center. To begin with, the ideological differences between the two were not great, but they grew during the very repressive period from 1906 to 1912. The Mensheviks concluded that Russia was not ripe for revolution, and it was better to educate the workers and build a stronger base, following the model of the German Social Democrats. Lenin, analyzing the failures of 1905–1906 differently, concluded that the potential for revolution remained high, and that by allying his movement with the peasants and eschewing the increasingly reformist path of the Western European socialists, quicker gains could be achieved.[79]

Leonard Schapiro has summarized the differences between Bolsheviks and Mensheviks this way:

> [T]he Bolshevik temperament was closer to the traditional Russian conspiratorial revolutionary movement; while the Mensheviks looked more to the model of Western Europe, with its free institutions and its developed labour movement. . . . [T]hey still, unconsciously perhaps, embraced the doctrine of social democracy because they saw it as a powerful westernising force for backward Russia. Lenin and the Bolsheviks, closer perhaps to some traditional Russian roots, were more intent on capturing autocratic power and using it for the ends in which they believed.[80]

The Mensheviks were too Westernized. They did not realize that Lenin was not a compromiser, that he had to have complete control, and that whatever tactical peace he might make with them, in the end, he had to destroy them. They were "the first of many socialist victims of the illusion which dies hard among socialists: that a genuine cooperation is possible with communists on any terms other than complete surrender."[81]

During the period from 1912 to 1914, there was a resurgence of strike activity and worker militancy in Russia. By the time World War I had begun, Lenin's "Majority" had become exactly that among the urban workers in Russia, particularly in its big cities—St. Petersburg and Moscow. This was primarily because the workers wanted action, and the Bolshevik's militancy fit the desperate mood of the severely repressed unions.[82] By 1917, with the situation even worse for the workers, the urban proletariat backed Lenin at the moment of crisis.

The Mensheviks were a much looser party than the Bolsheviks, and therefore more willing to give autonomy to non-Russian branches, and this, probably, is what led the Georgian section of the Russian Social Democrats to side with them, even though, temperamentally, their radicalism might have made them stay with the Bolsheviks. But Stalin's loyalty and continuing admiration for Lenin, expressed in letters and articles, brought him to Lenin's attention. By then, not only had Stalin become a permanent revolutionary (he never had any other occupation), but he had already been arrested, and sent to his first Siberian exile.

The Tsarist political police were unbelievably lax by later twentieth-century standards. They allowed political exiles in remote parts of Russia to live on their own, to write abroad, to read, to study, and often, to escape. Stalin, experienced with this routine because of his many arrests, exiles, and escapes in 1902–1904, 1908, 1910–1911, 1912, and 1913–1917, would not make the same mistake when he was in power.[83]

While in exile in 1904 Stalin first corresponded with Lenin, who took notice of his pamphlet defending *What Is to Be Done?* against the Georgian Mensheviks. They first met in 1905. Stalin then helped organize some violent bank robberies in Georgia that brought considerable amounts of cash to the Bolsheviks. In 1907, probably because his role in the bank holdups made his stay in Tiflis dangerous, but also because he was not getting along with the largely Menshevik Social Democrats, Stalin moved to the industrial oil town of Baku in what is now Azerbaijan, Georgia's eastern neighbor. It was then, along with Georgia and parts of Armenia, part of the larger province of Transcaucasia.[84]

In 1912, at the Bolshevik Sixth Party Conference in Prague (then in Austria, where the authorities tolerated socialists), Lenin had Stalin appointed to the Central Committee of the Party, along with another loyal Leninist from Georgia, Ordzhonikidze, one of Stalin's closest friends. The Central Committee at that time consisted of only nine full and five associate members. There was one other Caucasian full member, Spendarian, an Armenian. The Caucasus was so important because of its revolutionary tradition, its peasant activism, and the fact that, as the center of the oil industry, it had a relatively militant working class.[85]

The Issue of Nationalism and Stalin's Solution

Part of Stalin's loyalty to Lenin and the Bolsheviks was his conversion from Georgian nationalism to identification with Russia. Though he always spoke Russian with a noticeable Georgian accent, he was not only fluent, but also learned to do all his writing in Russian. The accusation that he never learned Russian properly, made by many, including Roy Medvedev, is false, based partly on the wish to vilify him, and on the disdain of Russian urban intellectuals for those who lack the proper speaking style of those raised from within the intelligentsia.[86]

Stalin's admiration for Lenin's writing contributed to his conversion to Russianism, as did his genuine belief in Marxism and its rejection of nationalism in favor of class solidarity. Furthermore, he realized that by being a Russian he could aspire to something much more than by being a Georgian. In 1907 Stalin wrote an article pointing out with approval that the Bolsheviks had more worker adherents in big industry than the Mensheviks, and that the Bolsheviks also had a majority of real Russians, while the majority of Mensheviks were Jews, with Georgians second, and Russians only third.[87]

This is another striking similarity between the young Hitler and Stalin. Both felt that they were failures in their native, peripheral lands, and chose to identify with a larger nationality. Both despised much about their native countries. Hitler loathed the Habsburgs because most of Austria was too stuffy and provincial, and in Vienna there was too much toleration of Jews, Slavs, and other non-Germans. Stalin developed similar feelings toward most Georgian socialists because they were "soft" Mensheviks, not true proletarians, and also too narrowly nationalistic and provincial.

Marxists have always had trouble understanding nationalism which strikes them as a kind of disturbingly irrational "false consciousness." Nevertheless, the importance of such sentiments had to be recognized, and a solution found in order to foster genuine "class consciousness"

across ethnic lines. Lenin, like Marx and Engels, had a patronizing
attitude toward nationalism that was itself unconsciously nationalist in
that it recognized big and established nations such as France, Germany, and Russia as legitimate. But smaller nationalities struggling to
establish political independence he considered silly, to be used but not
respected as genuine. In the multi-ethnic Russian Empire, local
nationalists, particularly the Poles, who represented an old, established
tradition, had to be recognized. But the confusing jumble of small peoples in the Caucasus seemed to add needless tension to what was supposed to remain a class-based revolutionary party. In 1912 Stalin, who
was much better versed in such issues than Lenin, was commissioned
by Lenin to write a theoretical essay laying out the Bolshevik position
on nationalities and nationalism. The long article that Stalin produced
in 1913, while in Vienna with Lenin and other Bolsheviks, became the
major statement on the issue by communists. As late as the 1980s it
was being cited by Western Marxists as the key explanatory text and
guide to understanding how to reconcile nationalism and Marxism.[88]

The solution to local nationalism, said Stalin, was to allow regional
autonomy and the right of any minority to use its own language and
have its own schools. But the Social Democratic Party should remain
unified, and its task was to educate the proletariat to abandon such
anachronistic sentiments. Stalin particularly emphasized the absurdity
of giving every small group its own nation by pointing to the Caucasus.
There, he claimed, "backward" peoples should be brought up to a
higher cultural level by being associated with more advanced peoples.[89] Stalin wrote:

> The national question in the Caucasus can be solved only *by draw-*
> *ing the belated nations and nationalities into the common stream of*
> *higher culture* [emphasis in original]. It is the only progressive solu-
> tion. . . . Regional autonomy . . . would impel them forward and facilitate
> access to the benefits of higher culture. Cultural-national autonomy,
> however, acts in a diametrically opposite direction, because it shuts up
> the nations within their old shells, binds them to the lower stages of cul-
> tural development and prevents them from rising to the higher stages of
> culture.[90]

Later, when Stalin was in power, he would emphasize what had
been implicit all along, that Russian culture and language was the
appropriate vehicle for bringing up the lesser nationalities in the Sovi-

et Union, much as he had himself been made into a great man by his assimilation of Russian culture. His ideas laid the basis for the maintenance of the Tsarist Empire under socialist guise in the form of the Union of Soviet Socialist Republics, each with its own language and ostensibly autonomous structures, but all under the central control of the Communist Party of the Soviet Union. This system, institutionalized in 1924, would last until 1991.

Stalin's essay was much appreciated by Lenin. Anti-Stalinist Marxists, starting with Trotsky, would claim later that it was really Lenin's inspiration and Bukharin's research into the Austrian Marxist writings on nationalism that had produced the work.[91] But while there is little question that Stalin was helped in reading the Austrian Marxist literature on nationalism by the more cosmopolitan Bolshevik émigrés who knew German (he did not), the sentiments expressed in his pamphlet were genuinely his. Lenin certainly learned something from Stalin about nationalism in the Caucasus, and thus, by extension, in other remote parts of the Russian Empire.

Stalin was arrested again and exiled to Siberia in 1913. He fished, brooded, and lived with a local woman with whom he had a son who survived but remained entirely obscure. Stalin had earlier been married to a Georgian wife who had evidently worshipped him, and also bore him a son who survived, Yakov. When she had died in 1909, he is reported to have said, "this creature softened my heart of stone. She died and with her died my last warm feeling toward people." Yakov was later captured by the Germans during World War II, and Stalin would refuse a German offer to have him exchanged for a high-ranking German prisoner. Yakov was to die in a German prison, either shot by the Germans or as a suicide.[92]

In 1917, after almost three years of terrible war and suffering, Tsarism collapsed as soldiers refused to fire on crowds rioting for bread and peace in St. Petersburg (named Petrograd during the war to make it sound more Russian and less German). Stalin made his way back to the capital and, as a senior Bolshevik from the Central Committee, immediately assumed an important position.

THE RUSSIAN REVOLUTION

There was much reason to feel outrage with Tsarist Russia in the second decade of the twentieth century. It would be possible to recite the long list of historical injustices perpetrated on the people of the Russian Empire through centuries of serfdom, frequent war, and brutal police repression. The poverty of the peasantry, and of much of the working class in the cities, was a further cause for discontent. These sorts of conditions had produced a long tradition of peasant uprisings in Russia, and in the nineteenth century, as we saw in the previous chapter, a revolutionary intelligentsia disgusted by what it saw.[93] The rapid industrialization after about 1890, and Russia's evolution toward a more modern, market-based economy, away from the subsistence and forced tribute system of the past, contributed to a heightened awareness of society's inequities, particularly in the cities where workers, most of whom were migrant peasants with family ties to the villages, could see the vast gulf between the majority and the few who were well off. Writing about Russia at the start of the twentieth century, Teodor Shanin recently put it this way:

> Clearly, in Russia's villages and towns not only land, wages and abject poverty were at issue but also the societal division, fundamental and sharp, into the plebeian "us" and the variety of "them": the state and the nobility, the manor house and the "clean quarters" of the city, the uniforms, the fur coats, the gold-rimmed spectacles, or even the elegantly-rolling phrases.[94]

In European Russia just before World War I, a quarter of registered newborns died before the age of 1. This was hardly better than it had been in the late 1860s, when Russia began to keep such statistics, whereas in most of Europe, this period saw a dramatic decline in infant mortality. More prosperous European countries at that time had rates of infant mortality that were half or less of Russia's.[95] Cold numbers cannot convey the sense of misery that produces such statistics, particularly as it becomes known that it is possible to do better. The reality was almost certainly much worse than the official statistics.

But it was not simply poverty that was at issue. There was also a sense of profound alienation at almost every level of society because no one except a tiny court clique seemed to have the power to do much about Russia's problems. The Tsarist autocracy was itself an obtuse, cruel, corrupt, and overgrown, if inefficient, tyranny.

Hans Rogger has summarized Russia's government in the late nineteenth and earlier twentieth centuries by saying that it had no goal other than survival, no sense of how to treat its many national and religious minorities, no firm ideology except to repress change, and that it "behaved often in the fashion of a military occupation solely concerned with the maintenance of tranquility and order."[96]

In 1904, a dispute with Japan over control of Manchuria and Korea led to a catastrophic war, which began by a Japanese surprise attack, without a declaration of war, on the Russian far eastern naval base of Port Arthur. By 1905 Russia was being defeated. The appalling corruption and inefficiency of the Russian military was shown by the way its vaunted fleet was totally destroyed by the Japanese after sailing halfway around the world into combat. But even before the end of the war, mounting suffering, economic disruption, and the government's ineptitude had led to protest by workers and by the educated intelligentsia in both cities and the countryside. On January 9, 1905, a peaceful march by workers on the Tsar's palace in St. Petersburg ended with government troops firing on the crowd. This episode, "Bloody Sunday," provoked protests elsewhere in Russia, and soon, a workers' and peasants' revolution.[97]

At first, Nicholas II's government granted concessions, but then, it gradually and violently suppressed the insurrection and went back on its promises. It took until late 1906 or, in some cases, early 1907 to bring the countryside under control.

What had the peasants wanted then? Egalitarian division of land, the end to trading in land, elected local officials, and the end of oppression by state officials, squires, and villagers who tried to make money by destroying the egalitarian peasant communes that then prevailed.[98] That many of these wishes, particularly the desire for reinforcement of the Russian rural commune, with its absence of private, marketable land, and periodic redivision of land to prevent the emergence of rich peasants, were unrealistic and self-defeating, is hardly relevant. Peasant leaders who expressed such sentiments were arrested, beaten, and humiliated, and peasants came to feel that there was no recourse with the government. Furthermore, the belated and incomplete reforms carried out subsequently by Stolypin tried to go in the exact opposite direction, to privatize land and create a more market-based economy.[99]

But peasants never like economic modernization that breaks up their communities and eventually forces so many of them off the land. The process of alienation and protest is a common one throughout modern history all over the world.[100] In Russia, it was worse because the attempt to modernize society from above was so inefficient and failed to keep the support of any significant group.

Peter Stolypin, who was made prime minister after the 1905 Revolution, saw that it was necessary to build a rural middle class to support the monarchy, and to win the confidence of the rising class of capitalists. But he was repeatedly thwarted by the Tsar who had appointed him. Ultimately, he lost power, and was murdered by the Tsarist political police, the Okhrana, in 1911.[101]

Urban workers, who had also revolted in 1905, were equally repressed, and their organizations subjected to continual harassment, with their leaders arrested and dispersed. Strikes were met with brutality. Growing worker militancy culminated in a massacre of strikers in the Lena goldfields in 1912. There was no possibility of a reasoned dialogue or of compromise.[102]

The political treatment of the urban middle class was hardly better. They had been promised and had received a parliament, a Duma, by the Tsar, but it was also humiliated, dismissed, and when called again, manipulated by changes in the electoral law to squeeze out liberal representation. Thus, a class that would have backed the system against revolution, and was, in fact, dependent on the central government to maintain its status and wealth, was also alienated. This is why so many of the young from this and other elite groups were part of the revolutionary intelligentsia whose outstanding characteristic, along with its nationalism, was its moralism. Truth and justice for Russia were its central program, and, as Shanin has put it, "[M]any of the Russian nobles, bureaucrats and merchants shared much of its intellectual baggage."[103]

In the end, not even the nobility, the most reactionary and monarchist part of Russian society, was satisfied. As the Tsarist government turned completely against any form of parliament, even if dominated by the tiny landed elite, "power moved increasingly into the hands of a narrow circle of courtiers, the tsar's wife and kinsmen, Rasputin [a fake monk whose hypnotic powers seemed to control the bleeding of the hemophiliac crown prince, but whose whoring and corruption were legendary], and the *Camarilla* [palace clique]."[104] Tsar Nicholas II himself was partly responsible for this because of his fear of any form of liberalism. No matter how sentimentalized he has been in some biographies, no matter how much he loved his wife and family, his stubborn fear of reform, his narrow prejudices, and his sheer stupidity played a role, too.

Frightened by the events of 1905, Tsar Nicholas II increasingly placed his hopes on what he thought was his people's love for him. He sought confirmation of this in populist, right-wing groups that tried to enlist peasant as well as urban support in favor of autocracy and a return to a simpler, purer, pre-industrial Russia. Jews were identified as the carriers of evil Western ways, of financial corruption, and of the destructive effects of modernization. Though these rightist groups gained only limited popular support in Russia, they pushed the Tsar, who claimed that "inner voices" told him it was necessary to maintain legal discrimination against Jews, further into anti-Semitism.[105] The groups also strengthened his belief that the masses supported him rather than what he identified as foreign, Westernized, Jewish socialists. Such a right-wing populism might have had more success, and might have formed the base for a genuinely popular revolutionary fascist movement if it had not been so closely associated with the hated government.[106]

Leon Trotsky was not exaggerating when he wrote, "Nicholas recoiled in hostility before everything gifted and significant. He felt at ease only among completely mediocre and brainless people, saintly fakirs, holy men, to whom he did not have to look up."[107]

When world war came in 1914, millions of Russian soldiers died (by the end well over 1.7 million had been killed) and were captured in defeat after defeat because they were led by incompetents, because the system for provisioning troops had been corrupted by favoritism and theft, and because, facing Germany they were confronted by the most technologically advanced and efficient military force in the world.[108] By 1917, half of the stock of cattle, half the horses, and one-third of the pigs in Russia were gone, a good reflection on the state of agriculture and food production.[109] That the Tsarist regime survived until 1917 shows the extent to which the inertia of habit, and the absence of any reasonable alternative in a divided, alienated society can preserve a government that is no more than a walking corpse.

In March 1917, a bread riot by women in St. Petersburg turned into a general protest, as guards refused to fire on the crowds. The Duma and the army generals decided that the Tsar had to abdicate. But there were no other members of the royal family willing or able to take power. The monarchy just ended.[110]

After the fall of the Tsar in March 1917, a Provisional Government dominated by liberals and moderate socialists took power, and tried to continue the war. Not only did this fail to pacify the population, but moderation hardly stood much of a chance to begin with. There was such distrust and hatred between workers and factory owners, between landowners and peasants, and between soldiers and their officers, that even under the best of circumstances it would have been hard to reestablish order. The economy continued to collapse during 1917, and there were massive waves of strikes as well as rural expropriations in the countryside.[111]

But there were deeper causes of unrest as well. During the autocracy, various competing interest groups had never learned to talk to each other and work out compromises because everything had to go through the Tsar and his bureaucracy. There was no independent civil society, as in Western Europe, no free trade unions, no free churches, no working parties unhindered by police spies and repression. Instead, there were secretive groups of plotters, and an intelligentsia passionately committed to justice but with no experience of how to govern. The masses of workers, peasants, and soldiers were clearly discontented and revolutionary, but they had had insufficient political experience to judge between the various groups of intellectual leaders who were trying to speak for them; they listened to those who made the best promises. Indeed, their lack of experience made them respect the intelligentsia more than they should have.[112]

The Mensheviks and the other socialists who played a leading role in the Provisional Government, but not the Bolsheviks, who remained in opposition, expected the angry workers in the cities to behave like patient liberals, to debate, and compromise, and wait for Russian society to make progress. Thus, the most radical elements, the St. Petersburg and Moscow workers, the soldiers and sailors, who were organized into Soviets, or democratic, popular councils, rejected the Provisional Government.[113]

It was Lenin's intelligence, or perhaps his total devotion to his cause, that made him see the opportunity. In November of 1917, the Bolsheviks, helped by workers and sailors, seized power in St. Petersburg, and then Moscow. Again, there was relatively little fighting. Stalin, who had been assimilated into the leadership of the Party on his return from Siberia after the March Revolution, became one of the leaders of the new regime.

STALIN TAKES POWER

Though on the Central Committee of the Bolshevik Party, and an editor of *Pravda*, the Party newspaper, Stalin was not as prominent in the
Revolution as Trotsky, Zinoviev, or Kamenev. Yet, he was one of seven
elected to the "Bureau for the Political Guidance of the Insurrection"
at the Central Committee meeting of early October 1917, just before
the Bolshevik seizure of power. This was the body that became the
Politburo. He was a supporter of Lenin in what was actually a rather
divided Party elite. (Along with the three members named above, Stalin, and Lenin, the remaining two were Sokolnikov and Bubnov.) When
Stalin differed with Lenin, it was on the side of caution. He was neither flamboyant, like Trotsky, nor publicly opposed to Lenin, as
Kamenev and Zinoviev were, briefly, just before the November Revolution. He was an experienced revolutionary, a hard worker, and unlike
Trotsky, Zinoviev, Kamenev, and Sokolnikov, he was not a Jew. Bubnov,
the only real Russian in this group except Lenin, was an extreme left-
wing communist hothead who would later oppose Lenin's drive for
peace with the Germans at any cost, who had no theoretical strength,
and who would resign his posts in 1918, rejoin in 1919, be expelled,
and then drift in and out of high positions until he was arrested in 1937
and died in a Stalinist prison camp, probably in 1940.[114]

Zinoviev was considered by most who knew him to be vain, and
though a good orator, he acquired the reputation of being a shifty cow-
ard. Kamenev, Lenin's closest assistant in the years just before the Revolution, linked himself so closely with Zinoviev, who seems to have
been his inferior in most respects, that they came to be seen as one.[115]
But Zinoviev believed he could succeed Lenin, and he and Kamenev
allied themselves with Stalin after Lenin was incapacitated by strokes
in 1922 and 1923, and remained united against Trotsky after Lenin's
death in 1924. Both wound up being shot on Stalin's orders in 1936
after sham trials.

Trotsky lived until he was assassinated on Stalin's orders in 1940,
and Sokolnikov was arrested and died in a prison camp in 1939. Thus,
of the original men on the "Bureau" meant to guide the Revolution, by
1940 all had been killed by Stalin, except Lenin.

Lenin insisted on signing a humiliating peace with the Germans,
who occupied vast parts of the Russian Empire. But after being defeated in November of 1918 by the allies, the Germans pulled out. Peace

gained Lenin popularity among his core working-class supporters, but the Bolsheviks would not have been able to keep power in free elections, so they imposed a dictatorship. There then followed a long, bloody civil war as various anti-communist factions, some of them supported by armed outside intervention from France, England, the United States, and Japan, tried to overthrow the Bolsheviks. What saved communism was the immense hatred accumulated against the old regime on the part of urban workers and peasants. Even those who did not love communism feared the return of the old regime more, and as long as there was this threat, they joined the communists and fought with them. Also, there was the nationalism of the intelligentsia, which made most of them, even those who were not Bolsheviks, offer their talents to Lenin.

But the communists did not just rely on goodwill. They formed a tough political police force, the Cheka (later call the GPU, the OGPU, the NKVD, and finally the KGB) led by the Polish communist Felix Dzerzhinsky. Staffed by the toughest, most loyal Bolsheviks, the Cheka waged a ruthless war against its enemies: it shot over 8,000 political enemies without trials and arrested over 80,000 in 1918 and the first half of 1919 alone. Their enemies, the "Whites," were as brutal.[116]

Trotsky organized the Red Army, and using patriotic Tsarist officers as specialists, assembled a vast force. To feed the besieged and loyal cities, the communists militarized the economy and instituted forced food deliveries from the countryside. Had the old regime had any shred of legitimacy with the rural population, if its return had not been so feared, there is little question that the brutality of this period, called "war communism," would have destroyed the communists. How many died during the Civil War, which lasted from 1918 until 1921, or in the famines and the epidemics that followed, is not known, but it was certainly in the several millions. Trotsky, in the 1920s, would write that the communist victory was due to the peasants' preference for the lesser of two evils, not out of any love of communism.[117]

The world was astonished that this small band of inexperienced leaders won their desperate war. In large part it was because the White Army units acted as a conquering army against workers and peasants, and provoked rebellion behind their lines. The hatred left from years of repression, and particularly from the brutality of the repression in 1905–1907, played a key role, too, as did the lack of understanding on the part of the Whites about what the source of grievance might have been.[118]

The communists were also able to count on a hard core of fanatic defenders, often from those who had been persecuted by the Tsarist state because of their religion, ethnicity, or class. Sailors and metal workers in St. Petersburg, Latvian riflemen defending Lenin in 1918, and Poles, Jews, and Latvians in the Cheka were the shock troops of the Revolution.[119]

Stalin, like other top leaders, was dispatched to various fronts during this period, but did not distinguish himself either as a military strategist or as a particularly cooperative team player. But his continuing loyalty, and his very failure to sparkle made him many friends among the Bolsheviks who were becoming resentful of Trotsky. Stalin carefully built himself a group of loyal subordinates who would remain close to him later on. On the other hand, Trotsky was too busy for petty politics. "His disregard for the susceptibilities of some of his colleagues, when the interests of efficiency demanded it, were to make him enemies who were not disposed to forget or forgive. Stalin's first [open] conflict with Trotsky took place during the civil war."[120]

After the Civil War, and a war with Poland, Trotsky, who was viewed as the second man in the government after Lenin, wanted to continue war communism. Military discipline and ruthless central control of the means of production were to continue until Russia was back on its feet, and they would hasten the construction of socialism. But Russia would have cracked, and in fact, there was a serious revolt of the sailors at the main naval base near St. Petersburg, Kronstadt, near the end of the winter of 1921. It was crushed by the Cheka and the Red Army, thus ending any pretense of democracy and toleration of opposition.[121] But even before the end of this episode, rising discontent in the countryside had persuaded Lenin to go easy and end war communism. It was replaced by the New Economic Policy, or NEP, which permitted private production and trade to return.

In 1922, Lenin had Stalin appointed Secretary of the Communist Party, a post he considered to be suitable for a loyal bureaucratic technician. This put Stalin in charge of a vast patronage machine in which he could begin to place his own followers in key positions. Zinoviev, who already saw himself as Lenin's successor, but who was afraid of Trotsky, pressed Lenin to make this appointment because he did not consider Stalin dangerous.[122]

In 1921 the communists had reconquered an independent Georgia led by local Mensheviks, and in 1922, Stalin and Ordzhonikidze harshly suppressed all nationalist dissent within the Georgian Party. This struck Lenin as too reminiscent of traditional Russian Imperial rule, and his criticism of Stalin on this issue finally awakened him to what kind of person he had placed so high. At the very end of 1922, writing about the events in Georgia, Lenin said, "I think that here a fatal role was played by Stalin's hastiness and love of issuing orders, and also by his malice. . . . In general, malice usually plays the very worst role in politics."[123] But it was too late. Lenin had already had a stroke by then, and throughout the next year, he would have more, and become incapacitated before dying in January of 1924. He spent his last active months in early 1923 trying to have Stalin removed, but he was increasingly isolated and ill, and he failed. There is little doubt that if Lenin had remained healthy another six months or a year, Stalin's career would have been sidetracked, and he would never have reached supreme power.[124]

Since then there has been a debate about the degree to which it was Lenin, not just Stalin, who was responsible for the gruesome events that were to follow. There is no way of resolving this argument.[125] Lenin was a ruthlessly dictatorial leader. He had crushed whatever hope for democracy had existed in Russia. He had willingly established the Cheka, political prison camps, and a militarized form of communism to hold on to power at any cost. He, no one else, had furthered Stalin's career. In 1918, during a particularly difficult period, Stalin had been in charge of food supplies in southern Russia. Based in Tsaritsyn (later renamed Stalingrad, and now called Volgograd), he had been utterly ruthless in having anyone suspected of laxity shot without trial. Lenin had instructed him to be "merciless" against other socialists who did not accept Bolshevik rule, and Stalin had answered, "Be assured that our hand will not tremble."[126] Did Lenin have a change of heart about the need for ruthless means to save his vision of Marxist socialism? That is unlikely. But would he have wished on Russia the tragedy that was going to overwhelm it five years after his death? Certainly not, but probably Stalin himself had no idea of what would happen, either. That is the nature of ruthless ideologies that take hold in chaotic, revolutionary times—they have unanticipated, baleful consequences. There is no certainty that either Lenin or Trotsky would have taken a long-run direction different from Stalin's, and coming against some of the obstacles that faced communism, they would not have hesitated to spill blood, either. They might have killed less. Or, in extreme circumstances, the most brutal of the Bolsheviks might have seized power anyway.

Lenin's last attempts to demote Stalin were well known by the other top Bolsheviks, but still, they did not stop Stalin. Obsessed by their too careful reading of books about the French Revolution, which made them fear a new Napoleon Bonaparte, many of them identified Trotsky, the founder of the Red Army, as such a character, and by far the greater danger.[127] Stalin's conflict with Trotsky was well known, too, and he was seen as a useful counterweight precisely because he was thought to be less capable. So Stalin kept his position, and continued to build his organization, with the approval of Zinoviev and Kamenev and their supporters in the Party.[128] When the latter two woke up to the danger facing them, they tried to recruit Trotsky into an alliance against Stalin in 1925, but he refused until 1926. By then it was too late.

Stalin attacked this faction as the "leftist opposition," because they tried to discredit Stalin by claiming that he was not a rigorous enough socialist. They were demanding overly ambitious programs, the end of the New Economic Policy, renewed militancy, and therefore, Stalin claimed, a new period of disorder and suffering. Stalin was backed by Nicolae Bukharin, by then the foremost economic thinker among the top Bolsheviks, and a strong proponent of a gradualist, market-oriented mixed economy to prepare a much later drive toward full socialism.[129]

But it was not just because of maneuvering at the top that Stalin won. Robert Tucker offers this sociological explanation:

> Lenin . . . provided the Bolsheviks with charismatic—that is messianic—leadership at various key points in party history, 1917 in particular. Paradoxically, however, a leader of a messianic tendency was not what the movement required as a *successor* to Lenin. . . . Having achieved power . . . the dominant mood was one of cautious optimism about the domestic prospect, combined with fear of any international complications which might endanger the Soviet regime or interrupt internal development. This was a situation that greatly favored Stalin's victory and Trotsky's defeat in the leadership contest. For Stalin, by virtue of both his seemingly plain and earthy personality and his sanguine platform of socialist construction in one country, offered the Bolsheviks non-charismatic leadership.[130]

It was Bukharin who had formulated the notion that socialism could prosper in one country, Russia, and did not require a worldwide socialist revolution, but Stalin adopted it. To rank-and-file members of the Communist Party, Trotsky's dangerous concern with foreign revolutions, and his association with a more radical, more militarized form of socialism, appeared threatening, especially when, after the 1923 defeat of the communist uprising in Germany, it had become obvious that there would be no other socialist revolutions in Europe anytime soon.[131]

Stalin's success resulted from yet another important social phenomenon. The Communist Party had had about 24,000 members in early 1917. It had about a half a million by the time of Lenin's death, and a million in 1925. The old Bolsheviks, many of whom had died by then, were a small minority, and most of the new members were not as sophisticated in revolutionary discourse as the old group, which had been dominated by members of the intelligentsia. Stalin addressed himself directly to these new members in his writings, particularly in his *Foundations of Leninism*, which offered a somewhat simplified version of Leninism in 1923. He did the same in his speeches and debates before the Central Committee, which, by the mid-1920s, had many such "new" members.[132]

Then, too, Stalin was not a Jew. The old Bolsheviks had been largely free of anti-Semitism, but most new members were more conventional, and like most Russians, at least somewhat anti-Semitic. Trotsky, Zinoviev, and Kamenev, of course, were Jews. In any case, the old socialist intelligentsia was cosmopolitan, and seemed to many Russians to be overly Westernized. Even among much of the intelligentsia itself, this was a cause of guilt, and contradicted the Slavophile sentiment of Russian purity and superiority. Stalin, though not a Russian, was certainly a proponent of Russian nationalism, as Lenin had noted in his dying days. Most of all, Stalin, even though he appeared to the rank and file to be a good Marxist and a faithful interpreter of Leninism, was anything but a Westernized cosmopolitan. Stalin's victory, then, was partly the victory of old Russia over the West.[133]

From 1925 to 1927, Stalin was the leader of the communists, but Bukharin seemed to be his virtual equal. The problem, never quite accepted by those who have admired the intelligent, humane, brilliant, moderate Bukharin was that if his policies had prevailed, the Communist Party would have become an oligarchy with political power but no real function. The New Economic Policy was finally producing independent, land-owning peasants, as Stolypin had wanted two decades earlier. Many knowledgeable observers were fooled into thinking that all the Bolsheviks were going to accomplish was to bring capitalism to the countryside![134] And in the cities, a new merchant class was growing. To push for rapid industrialization, workers had to be fed, but if investment was to be high, it would be difficult to pay the peasant with consumer goods. To let the whole process develop slowly, moved by market forces and private entrepreneurs, meant abandoning socialism, or at least, postponing it for a long time, and accepting a long period of economic backwardness and weakness for Russia. In essence, Stalin in 1928 had to face the same dilemma that troubled communism in the 1980s: if the economy is to be run by the market, what is the Party other than one more oligarchy holding onto its privileges for no particularly good reason? Stalin would solve that problem by pushing forward with socialism, by adopting the program of his old enemies of the "left," and he would save communism in the only possible way. Hardly anyone could have anticipated the price that would be paid.

In the struggle for supremacy Stalin had solid control of the Party machinery, so that Bukharin, whose faction was labelled as the "right opposition," never really had much chance in a straight contest. But also, Stalin continued to have the support of the less educated, new members of the Party, men whose careers were now bound to the continuity and success of socialism. They did not want to become superfluous. Stalin was adopting what had been Trotsky's old program, but seven years later, after the Party machinery had been consolidated and the political situation stabilized. Stalin's ideological position was not particularly original, but his sense of timing, and his awareness of what the bulk of the Party wanted, was far better than that of his leading opponents. In other words, he turned out to be the better politician.

Trotsky, and a good many of the most intelligent, committed communist thinkers never understood that their idealism led naturally to Stalin. In 1937, writing a long and bitter attack against Stalinism, Trotsky could only claim that Stalin had betrayed the Revolution, first by supporting NEP, and then crushing it. In a section of his book called "Bonapartism as a Regime of Crisis," he wrote:

> The state support of the kulaks [prosperous peasants] (1923–28) contained a mortal danger for the socialist future. But then, with the help of the petty bourgeoisie the bureaucracy succeeded in binding the prole-

tarian vanguard hand and foot, and suppressing the Bolshevik Opposition. This "mistake" from the point of view of socialism was a pure gain
from the point of view of the bureaucracy.[135]

But if independent peasants and a growing market economy were a
"mortal danger" for socialism, why was it wrong to eliminate them?
And who else could do this if not a large Party machine? And could the
workers be allowed to protest their poor living conditions if there were
food shortages and suffering? Trotsky, after all, had sanctioned the
attack against the sailors at Kronstadt to save Bolshevism. For all his
brilliance, Trotsky fell back on irrelevant historical analogies, calling
Stalinism "petty bourgeois" and "Bonapartist," both well-worn Marxist
epithets for anything they disliked but could not define within the
framework of the Marxist model.

Stalinism might have been anticipated as a logical outcome of the
Revolution, and was, by thinkers less devoted to Leninism than Trotsky and other Bolsheviks. Maxim Gorky, who would later be seduced
by Stalin's flattery, and return to Russia to be his literary booster, wrote
in 1917 that Bolshevism would lead to one-man dictatorship. Yevgeny
Zamiatin predicted that Bolshevism would eliminate free thought, and
in 1924, he wrote a prophetic novel, *We*, predicting the nightmarish
conditions that would exist when the state controlled everything.[136]

Crudely, but consistently, Stalin would do exactly what Leninism
had promised—create a socialist powerhouse in backward Russia, and
make it serve as a model for future socialist revolutions everywhere in
the world. In a review of Isaac Deutscher's critical, Trotskyite book
about Stalin, E. H. Carr wrote:

> The most baffling feature of Stalin's career is that he carried out a revo-
> lution which was no less far-reaching than the revolution of 1917, and
> was in many senses its logical and necessary completion. . . . Yet it is
> clear that Stalin had to contend with far more apathy and disillusion-
> ment in the masses, far more opposition and intrigue in the party *élite*,
> than Lenin had ever known, and was driven to apply correspondingly
> harsher and more ruthless measures of discipline.[137]

It is not necessary to be a sophisticated apologist for Stalinism, as Carr
was, to recognize the truth of what he said, and the cold-blooded
implication: to carry out a worthy dream that is historically progressive, it may be necessary to sacrifice millions of lives.

The lessons of Hitlerism and Stalinism are similar. Ideologies and the long intellectual preparation that may lead to tyranny do not, of themselves, cause revolutions to occur. But once economic, political, and moral breakdowns occur, as they did in Germany in the 1920s and early 1930s, or in Russia during World War I, movements based on strong and coherent ideological worldviews have the opportunity to seize power. If these are based on the idea that conflict within and between societies is inevitable, and necessary in order to bring about desired utopias, the worst sorts of ideological excesses become likely.

We will see in the next chapter what some of these excesses were during Hitler's and Stalin's reigns, and in the following chapters of the book, how other ideological tyrannies in the twentieth century resembled them.

Chapter 4

Death, Lies, and Decay

S talin and Hitler were the century's worst tyrants. They caused millions to die, often after sadistic mistreatment. Many who survived were left damaged for life. They devastated whole nations, caused murderous famines, enslaved hundreds of millions, all the while feeling satisfaction about what they were doing. Once they reached their full power, there were virtually no checks on their actions, no one who could stand up to them and moderate their policies. Neither ever expressed any remorse, and both pursued their dreams of creating new types of societies ruled by their brutal notions of scientific certitude until the very end.

Hitler's last pronouncement, just before his suicide on April 30, 1945, to avoid being captured by the Soviet army closing in on his bunker in Berlin, repeated his main ideological line. He wrote in his testament:

Above all I call upon the leaders of the nation and all followers to observe the racial laws scrupulously and to implacably oppose the universal poisoner of all races, international Jewry. . . . The efforts and sacrifices of the German people in this war have been so great that I cannot believe that they have been in vain. The aim must still be to win territory in the East for the German people.[1]

Stalin's end was not as dramatic. He died in his country house outside Moscow of a stroke at 73. In his last published work, in the fall of 1952, *Economic Problems of Socialism in the USSR*, he hinted at a renewed assault on the peasantry, eliminating what little private property they had left. It is known that he died just as another massive purge was getting under way, this one centered on Jews. They were being called "rootless cosmopolitans" and "Zionist agents of American imperialism." Some Jewish doctors were accused of trying to assassinate the top leadership of the Party, and a number were arrested just before Stalin died.[2]

That Stalin also showed hatred of Jews, even though his dislike was not based on racial or biological theories, is further evidence of the extent to which Jews were identified throughout Europe as the carriers of liberal ideals, of democracy, and of economic progress. Whether identified as "Bolsheviks" or "imperialists," they were the target of all those who hated the liberating consequences of the Enlightenment.

Already in the late 1940s, Stalin had begun reducing the influence of his top lieutenants. Molotov, his highest aide, and perhaps his closest and most loyal surviving high Party friend from 1917, the long-time prime minister and foreign minister, had been unable to save his Jewish wife from being arrested. Voznesensky, his top economic aide, had been shot. All of the old crowd, including the secret police chief Beria, and Voroshilov, Stalin's friend from the Civil War days at Tsaritsyn, and many others—all were threatened.[3] Had Stalin lived past March 1953, the generation of leaders who had come to the fore in the 1930s might have shared the fate of older Bolsheviks purged in the 1930s whom they had replaced, and the Jews would have followed the kulaks, Ukrainians, Crimean Tatars, and dozens of other categories of "enemies of socialism" into the hell of concentration camps, internal exile, and death. There is no indication that Stalin was either repentant for his sins, or contemplating anything but renewed intensification of terror when he died. By then he may have been partly senile, but this did not make him gentler.[4] He was certainly afraid of his entourage, perhaps because he remembered how he had marginalized a sick Lenin in 1923, and he feared that his associates would do the same to him.[5]

Hitler and Stalin have been the subject of enormous professional historical and popular interest. As might be expected, there are also fierce arguments about what it is they did, why, and what the ultimate effects may have been. The main arguments revolve around the question: To what extent were Hitler and Stalin responsible for what went on? They were, after all, surrounded by vast, impersonal bureaucracies. Did they really know the extent of the crimes that were being carried out in their name? A less naïve question is: To what extent were the extreme measures taken by the Nazis and the communists necessary in order to make their systems survive, and thus, to what degree were they essential defensive measures forced on them by the outside world rather than inherently part of the systems they conceived? Or, for those who fully accept Stalin's and Hitler's responsibility, but who still want to salvage something from their ideologies, the question becomes: Was it perhaps just an unfortunate accident that these ideological movements were taken over by such vicious leaders? In the hands of different leaders, could the movements have been more benign? Few are prepared to say this about Hitler because he was so central to the very existence of the Nazis, but many defenders of communism have claimed that it was just bad luck that Stalin came to power.

Defenders of communism, for example E. H. Carr, long justified Stalinism, though not its excesses, as if these could be separated, by saying that this was the only way to save the noble ideal of socialism in a hostile world.

In a book published in 1942, Beatrice Webb, a well-known, elderly British socialist writer who had visited the Soviet Union in the 1930s, wrote:

> Stalin is not a dictator. . . . [H]e is the duly elected representative of one of the Moscow constituencies to the Supreme Soviet of the USSR. . . . [T]he Communist Party . . . is not an oligarchy; it is democratic in its internal structure. . . . Nor has Stalin ever claimed the position of a dictator or fuehrer. Far otherwise; he has persistently asserted in his writings and speeches that as a member of the Presidium of the Supreme Soviet of the USSR he is merely a colleague of thirty other members. . . . He has, in fact, frequently pointed out that he does no more than carry out the decisions of the Central Committee of the Com-

munist Party. . . . [T]ested by the Constitution of the Soviet Union as revised and enacted in 1936, the USSR is the most inclusive and equalized democracy in the world.[6]

She goes on to explain that the USSR is far more democratic than the United States, even though only one party is allowed, because this party represents the true interests of the people, unlike in what she dismisses (by putting it in quotation marks) as "Western Civilization." The purges, she says, were a justified reaction to the Trotsky conspiracy and German subversion of high army circles.[7] But it was not just eccentric English socialists who wrote this kind of nonsense. In a book published in 1946 and introduced by the former American ambassador to the Soviet Union, Joseph E. Davies, the writer and journalist Jerome Davis wrote this about the collectivization campaign in the late 1920s and early 1930s:

> A kind of civil war broke out between kulaks [rich peasants] and the collectives. . . . The kulaks burned collective farm buildings and slaughtered livestock. In some places overzealous communists used coercive measures and turned entire villages against collectivization. . . . The property of kulaks was confiscated, they were exiled to Siberia and the North, to work camps. It was a harsh policy and many died as a result. By 1930 the collective farm movement had triumphed. . . . In March 1930 he [Stalin] published a famous letter, "Dizziness From Success," calling for a halt to coercive measures and roundly scoring excesses.[8]

Davis concluded that since then collectivized agriculture had worked well and contributed to the success of the Soviet Union.

Ambassador Davies himself also wrote a book, *Mission to Moscow*, that praised Stalin, and, among other things, accepted the official Soviet view about the purge trials of the late 1930s, that they were justified by the evidence presented, and that the old Bolsheviks, military men, and others sentenced to prison and death had indeed been traitors.

But Robert Conquest, whose work on Stalinism has now been confirmed by revelations coming from the archives of the defunct Soviet Union, found that the crisis of collectivization was not all settled in 1930. In 1932–33 close to a quarter of the Ukrainian population on the best lands of the Soviet Union was starving to death. This was deliberate policy, carried out by the Party and the police, because forced grain delivery targets were set so high that it was impossible for the peasants to keep enough to feed themselves. In all, in the 1930s at least 14.5 million peasants died of famine, of brutal conditions in work camps to which they were deported, and of outright murder.[9] This is what "dekulakization" really meant.

Lenin believed that a class of rich peasants, called kulaks, existed, that it represented a rural bourgeois element that would be hostile to socialism, and that, therefore, at some time, it would have to be dealt with. But Teodor Shanin has shown that there never was a distinct class of kulaks. Within peasant families some prospered, but wealth tended to rotate rather than accumulate, so that the "kulak" was as likely to be a poor peasant's relative as not, and the accident of a few bad harvests, or the birth of too many children, could quickly bring down a "rich" peasant, while a formerly poor family might prosper. The egalitarian traditions of the village community also tended to work against the establishment of fixed class lines.[10] By trying to set class against class, where these did not really exist, dekulakization introduced a general war of all against all, setting family members and neighbors against each other so that Party agents from the cities could destroy the fabric of village society. Soviet agriculture never recovered, and remained the most problematic sector of the Soviet economy for the rest of the life of the USSR. A theoretical error made by Lenin in analyzing rural class structure, adapted by Stalin to his brutal notions of class warfare, doomed millions to terrible deaths.

As for the purges of "Trotskyites" and other supposed traitors, by the end of 1938 some 12 million individuals had been arrested, about one million had been executed, and two million had already died in prison camps. Most of the rest of those arrested died in the ensuing years because of the abominable conditions in these camps. On average, about 10 percent of the population in the camps died each year, though in some particularly bad camps, that rate was as high as 30 percent per year.[11]

In the late 1940s there were many more arrests and deportations to the camps, and this included most of the returned Soviet prisoners of war who had survived the German camps. Stalin labelled them traitors. Some, no doubt, had been, but millions were just ordinary prisoners of war or people who had been seized by the Germans to work as slaves. Of about five and a half million Soviets returned from German prisoner-of-war and forced labor camps, 20 percent were executed or sentenced to twenty-five years in the Stalinist camps, where most of them died.

Up to 20 percent received shorter sentences of five to ten years in the camps, and another 25 percent were sent to parts of the USSR as work conscripts under harsh conditions. Many of these died as well. That added at least another two million deaths to the total.[12]

Conquest estimates that at least 20 million died under Stalin from the purges and from collectivization, and probably up to 30 million.[13] This seemingly fantastic estimate of 30 million was confirmed by the analysis of previously concealed census figures carried out by Anton Antonov-Ovseyenko, himself the son of a former prominent Bolshevik killed by Stalin.[14] Roy Medvedev, perhaps the most thorough Russian researcher on Stalinism, estimated the total number at closer to 40 million in an article in *Argumenty i fakty* in early 1989.[15] It is safe to say that an estimate of some 20 million killed by Stalin is the lowest credible estimate, and 40 million the highest.

Vasily Grossman, the Soviet writer, wrote the following account of what he saw in Kiev, Ukraine, in the spring of 1933. Starving peasants were trying to flee to the city to find food, but the authorities wanted to keep them out. It was forbidden to help, though some townspeople tried anyway.

> In the morning hours horses pulled flattop carts through the city, and the corpses of those who had died in the night were collected. I saw one such flattop cart with children lying on it. They were just as I have described them, thin, elongated faces, like those of dead birds, with sharp beaks. These tiny birds had flown into Kiev and what good had it done them? Some of them were still muttering, and their heads still turning. I asked the driver about them, and he just waved his hands and said, "By the time they get where they are being taken they will be silent too."[16]

In retrospect the German threat would serve as an excuse for the killings; but they began well before Hitler seized power. The famine and the persecutions of peasants were deliberate—to provide food for industrializing without having to pay the peasants, to destroy the peasant class because it was considered hostile to socialism, and also to extirpate Ukrainian nationalism in what was the richest agricultural part of the USSR.

Yet, Stalin's tyranny found defenders abroad among those who were ideologically inclined to believe in the Marxist laws of history, or who simply assumed that modern history was going to be a fight to the death between fascism and communism, so it was best to have communism triumph, no matter what the cost. Those who believed in the immutable laws of racial and national conflict to the death, and who felt that in such circumstances almost anything that avoided "Bolshevism" was defensible, found similar ways of excusing Hitlerism.

Defenders of Nazism have ranged from outright racists who claim that the mass murder of Jews never took place, or was justified by racial war, to more sophisticated recent apologists who believe that they were really carried out in reaction to the communist menace. Ernst Nolte, a major German historian of European fascism, wrote in 1986:

> Did the National Socialists carry out, did Hitler perhaps carry out an "Asiatic" deed only because they regarded themselves and their kind as the potential or real victims of an "Asiatic" deed? Wasn't the "Gulag Archipelago" [the Stalinist concentration camps] more original than Auschwitz? Wasn't class murder on the part of the Bolsheviks logically and actually prior to racial murder on the part of the Nazis?[17]

Charles Maier has used a very conservative estimate of 7 to 8 million people killed in camps or by special execution squads under the Nazis.[18] This excludes deaths from military actions, which were also in the many millions. But it gives an idea of the magnitude of what happened, and shows that Stalin and Hitler, taking into account the considerably longer time Stalin had in power, were in the same league as mass murderers. The vast majority of those murdered by Hitler died during his last five years in power, whereas Stalin killed on a massive scale throughout the 1930s, and again in the late 1940s and early 1950s, over a period three times as long.

Though it would be pointless to repeat many of the well-documented accounts of what the Nazis did, one selection gives the flavor of what happened. This one is from a report of a German engineer present at the killing of about five thousand Jews by the SS and their allied Ukrainian militia in the region in Dubno in October of 1942:

> People lay so closely pressed together that only their heads could be seen. Blood was running from almost all their heads across their shoulders. Many of those who had been shot were still moving. Some raised their arms and turned their heads to show that they were still alive. I looked round for the marksman. It was an SS-man sitting on the edge of

the short side of the pit, his legs hanging down into it; on his knees lay a submachine gun, and he was smoking a cigarette. The people, entirely naked, walked down some steps which had been dug into the clay wall of the pit, and then slid across the heads of those who lay there until they reached the place which the SS-man had pointed out to them. They lay down in front of the dead and wounded, some were stroking those still alive and talking to them quietly. Then I heard a series of shots. I looked into the pit and saw bodies moving convulsively or heads which were lying quite still on the bodies in front. Blood poured down the napes of their necks.[19]

Of the five million or so Jews killed by the Nazis, about one-quarter were killed in this way. Most of the rest died in the camps, gassed, hung, beaten, shot, starved, frozen, victims of gruesome medical experiments, or just overworked to death. It is not possible to see pictures of films of the camps during their operation or just after their liberation, for example *Night and Fog* produced by Alain Renais, without being shocked.

Were the Jews being killed really a threat to the mighty German army in 1941 and 1942? Were the millions of helpless victims who died in the Stalinist terror really traitors plotting against socialism? To those of us who do not accept either class or racial war as inevitable or as the mainsprings of history, it is clear that the answer is unambiguously negative. But that is why it is impossible to explain what happened without reference to the guiding ideological principles behind Hitlerism and Stalinism, because in neither case would objective measures of self-interest on the part of the leaders lead to such outcomes if there had been no theory of history behind their governments. Perhaps even more important is that there would not have been so many willing to carry out these orders if there had not been considerable agreement, at least among elites, that the scientific principles that lay behind these ideologies were valid.

There is little question that Hitler and his chief executioners did feel that they were in a racial war to the death, and that a racially pure Germany and Europe was a most desirable goal. As for Stalin, he and his closest followers believed that they were in a class war to the death, and that a classless, socialist society was both achievable and desirable.

However disturbing it may be for us to accept, and whatever his motives may be, Nolte's apology has some truth to it from the perspective of the Nazis themselves. It only seems fantastic to those who cannot bring themselves to believe that Hitler and his entourage took their ideology seriously. For the Nazis, prior events in Russia, about which they were informed, were interpreted as the opening round of a racial, not a class war. If they did not kill first, they would be killed.

Similarly, though Stalin's defenders in the West may have lied deliberately, or been silly dupes, as Beatrice Webb, Ambassador Davies, and many leftist intellectuals outside the USSR certainly were, the fact is that a committed but bitterly anti-Stalinist Marxist like Leon Trotsky agreed that the kulaks were indeed a "mortal danger" to socialism.[20] Furthermore, the USSR was encircled by capitalist powers, and they were not friendly. And after all, if Stalin was a fount of Marxist theoretical wisdom, as he and his followers claimed, was it not so that any opposition, even by some who might have called themselves Marxist, must be counter-revolutionary? Lenin had been very hostile to "kulaks," he had believed in class warfare, and he had urged merciless repression against traitors to the cause, even if they called themselves "socialists."

Both Hitler and Stalin thought of themselves as embodiments of historical truth and inevitability. Their loyal followers also came to view them as miraculous, perfect representations of "racial" and "class" forces. This magical, irrational aspect of modern ideological tyranny, so carefully fostered by Hitler and Stalin themselves, became as much a source of their power as the historical "sciences" that created Nazism and communism in the first place. It was the mixture of revolutionary charisma and scientific certitude that gave such strength to the ideologically committed, and legitimized almost any level of horror.

DID HITLER WANT A BIG WAR? DID HE MEAN TO COMMIT GENOCIDE?

Once in power, Hitler was faced by a number of important constraints. Germany was still a military weakling compared to France and England. It had a faltering economy. Military officers, the business elite, the aristocracy, and the clique around von Hindenburg had to be managed carefully, even though they were sympathetic to Volkish nationalism, because they might object to drastic, revolutionary changes that could threaten them. They could call upon the army to help them, and they did not view the Nazis as undisputed leaders of Germany. On the other side, among the Nazis, the SA under Ernst Röhm, and the Strasser wing of the party did want drastic revolutionary measures implemented right away. This frightened the conservatives, and offended their sense of propriety. If the SA went too far, that would threaten the army, which Röhm wanted to absorb into his own units. And extremism pushed too far risked provoking foreign intervention. Furthermore, Hitler himself considered his long-range goals to be the expansion of Germany and the elimination of inferior races, chiefly Jews. Social revolution that would pit class against class was not on his agenda, particularly if it threatened German unity and strength.[21]

In all the arguments about why Hitler did not begin exterminating Jews immediately, why World War II started when it did, over six years after Hitler took power, not earlier or later, and what its aims were, it is easy to forget that ideologically committed as he may have been Hitler was also an excellent practical politician who knew when to move his agenda forward, and when to be cautious. He understood, as some of his followers did not, that the majority of Germans may have been anti-Semitic, but they did not envision an outright extermination of the entire Jewish population. The majority was nationalistic and wanted to right the perceived wrongs of the Versailles Treaty, but they did not want to repeat the dreadful experience of World War I. It required time to bring Germany under full control and to rearm it.

A. J. P. Taylor claimed in *The Origins of the Second World War* that it was really the English and French who pushed Hitler into war by giving in to him at critical moments, and then unexpectedly reversing themselves when he thought he could safely take one more prize. By Taylor's account, Hitler was a mere opportunist who had no set plan to go to war. After starting an armaments program that violated treaty obligations, after remilitarizing the Rhineland in 1936, annexing Austria in early 1938, being ceded Czechoslovakia in late 1938, and taking Memel in 1939, surely, Hitler thought, he would be allowed to seize most of Poland, too.

But there is a better explanation. Hitler was not prepared to compromise in the long run. He took his ideas too seriously for that. As a practical politician, however, he knew that premature action, like the attempted coup of 1923 that had almost cost him his career, had to be avoided. So he went step by step, consolidating his rule by eliminating and marginalizing opposition to him within Germany, and pushing against the French and British to see exactly how far they would go.

Had they threatened war in 1938 instead of giving in at Munich, he might have stepped back. He did just that, in fact, before the Munich Conference, when his first moves against Czechoslovakia had provoked a strong response from the French, British, and Czechs. A group of conservative army officers who, by then, had decided that Hitler was too dangerous, expected the French and English to remain firm and Hitler to be humiliated or defeated quickly in a war. In the ensuing debacle, they would topple him with a military coup.[22] More or less the same cast of military men did try to overthrow Hitler again in July of 1944, after it had become obvious that World War II was lost.

To recognize this, and that Hitler could have been stopped earlier, with much less bloodshed if war had begun in 1938, or better yet, in 1936, is not the same as to claim that he was a mere cynical politician drifting from one lucky gamble to another. His writings, his speeches, and the militarization of society which was part of the very structure of the Nazi Party suggested that he considered war necessary. As it was, the German rearmament program was scheduled to be completed in 1944, so that even though the war came prematurely, there would have been no way of avoiding it in any case.[23] It was the tragedy of the French and British that they did not understand Hitler's ideology or take it seriously.[24] If they had, they would have started the war earlier, on better terms for themselves.

It is true that Hitler did not expect the kind of war that actually occurred. He took his racial theories so seriously that he was puzzled by the British resolve to fight him to the bitter end. He thought that as fellow Aryans, they should be more understanding, and would be if their government could be freed of Jewish influence.[25] Had the French and English agreed to let Hitler have his way in the east, as some French and particularly English conservatives wanted, there would have been the kind of war Hitler planned for.[26] But when he signed a nonaggression pact with the Soviets in August 1939 in order to have a free hand in Poland, Hitler made a mockery of the policy of those English conservatives who wanted to use Germany as a defense against communism. They now had no choice.[27]

Hitler's aim was to take Poland quickly and then convince the English to abandon their commitments without serious fighting.[28] Stalin, on the other hand, signed the treaty of cooperation with Hitler in order to better prepare the Soviet Union. He greatly feared that a war with Germany would bring a repeat of the debacles of World War I and a new revolution, this time against him. He hoped, too, that Germany might fight a long, inconclusive war against England and France, as it had from 1914 to 1918. So the two tyrants agreed to divide Eastern Europe between them.[29] By 1940, however, Hitler was already making plans to betray his agreement with Stalin and launch a great invasion of the USSR to conquer the *Lebensraum* he felt the Germans needed.[30]

It is impossible, therefore, to come to any conclusion other than to blame Hitler for the start of the war, no matter how many mistakes all the other parties made.[31] If the start of World War I was much less clearly the fault of any single power, because much of Europe's general intellectual drift for several decades before that war had pointed toward conflict, and the various imperial claims of the major European states had created an explosively dangerous situation, this was no longer true in the 1930s. Neither the French nor the English wanted war, and they did everything to avoid it. Stalin felt the same way. Furthermore, even though the Nazis' political victory in 1933 made Volkish ideology ascendant in Germany, and the combination of militarism, desire for revenge, and racial arrogance were a recipe for aggressive war, Hitler and his party were well ahead of their public opinion in being war-like. When it all started, unlike the elation that met the opening of World War I, the German people were depressed.[32] The Nazi propaganda machine had worked hard to heighten the desire for war, but the obsession with racial purity, with cleansing the world of the diseased, dangerous, degenerate races, and the wish to enslave other non-Aryans were not yet fully shared by many Germans. Even many Volkish Germans were far from understanding the implications of Hitler's ideology.

But if the debates about who started World War II are no longer controversial, the controversy about the killing of the Jews has become more heated with the passage of time, and in some ways it reproduces the contentious issues raised by A. J. P. Taylor. Was the slaughter of the Jews something that was inherent in Nazism from the start, or perhaps in German history, or was it more a matter of chance, and perhaps even just an unfortunate aspect of a more important anti-communist drive?

Part of the debate has taken place in Germany, where it is called the *Historikerstreit*, or historians' conflict.[33] Conservative German historians like Nolte have claimed that, after all, Nazism was no worse than a number of other murderous movements around the world, and that when faced by the extreme danger of communism, which killed more people than Nazism, its reactions can be understood and, if not excused, at least put into a context that makes them seem less monstrous. Against them have been arrayed liberal Germans, led by the philosopher-sociologist Jurgen Habermas, who say that unless Germans recognize their unique guilt, modern Germany can never be a fully moral, democratic nation.

In part the essential argument of my book sides with the conservatives who claim that Nazism was not unique, especially if we accept the notion that belief in class war to the death is quite similar to that of race war to the death.

In another way, however, this conservative argument that seeks partial exoneration for Germany under the Nazis avoids the essence of the question because it tries to explain the Nazi crimes as a reaction to external events. Much of the killing that occurred, and in fact World War II itself were deliberate, precisely because of the ideological commitment to conflict, and were not a response to any realistic threat. If external contingencies, World War I and the Great Depression, can explain how Nazis came to power, it is hard to see any provocation from the outside at all in 1939, much less a real Jewish threat, except in the imaginations of the Nazi ideologues, and particularly Hitler's. Jews were less than 1 percent of the German population in 1933, and no more than one-quarter of 1 percent by 1939. Yet, Hitler's personal rage, which he had been nurturing since his youthful days in Vienna, and which had become focussed against Jews as the main "traitors" in 1919, would not have been quenched by anything other than massive violence. Nor could his dreams of "living space" in the east, and his personal fear that Aryan Germany would be overwhelmed, as he thought the Habsburgs had been, by inferior races unless it colonized Russia, ever be resolved peacefully.

The strongest, yet ultimately unsuccessful attempt to claim that the Nazi war against the Jews was somehow contingent on events rather than premeditatedly genocidal in its intent has been made recently by Arno Mayer.[34] His argument is not a conservative defense of the Germans, but one which views communism as a long-suffering, unfairly persecuted movement. Killing the Jews, according to Mayer, was an expression of frustration against the communists that Hitler initiated when he realized that he could not defeat the Soviets. Yet, by blaming the Nazi crimes on their excessive anti-communism, and only secondarily on their anti-Semitism, Mayer actually winds up agreeing with much of the conservative argument in the *Historikerstreit*. In this interpretation World War II was, first of all, part of a long attempt by Western Europe to rid itself of Soviet power. In Mayer's view, Nazi anti-Semitism was merely a well-organized version of classical prejudice against Jews. They would have been deported to Siberia, or elsewhere in Russia, if the war against the Soviets had been won, because eliminating them was of secondary concern to Hitler.

Mayer's argument has been shown to be wrong in numerous reviews, most notably by István Deák and Christopher Browning.[35] Yet, it musters enough facts in its favor so that in examining it, we can understand what really motivated Hitler.

Before 1941 there were vague German plans for sending all the Jews to Madagascar, or to set up Jewish reservations in Poland. But the unrealistic plan to ship the Jews to Madagascar was supposed to be headed by a man who actually headed the "Euthanasia Program" within Germany.[36] The nature of that program tells us what the Nazis really had in mind. Killings of non-Jews designated as feeble-minded or biologically unfit had already begun in Germany in 1939, and that was when the first experiments with killing in gas chambers disguised as showers had occurred. Something on the order of 70,000 to 80,000 Germans were killed as part of this general program.[37]

The Germans invaded the Soviet Union on June 22, 1941. Far from starting to exterminate Jews only when they realized that they were not going to win, the Germans began the mass killings in July, whereas they only began to experience reverses with the onset of winter. The summer of 1942 was again a period of advance for the Germans, and it was not until the battle of Stalingrad in the next winter of 1942–1943 that Hitler saw that he might lose the war. So the essence of Mayer's argument has to be wrong. But if so, why did the exterminations really get under way only in 1941, and why was there talk in Nazi circles of other "solutions" until then?

We know that Hitler admired Stalin personally, and felt it regrettable that, as he thought, Stalin was dominated by Jewish Bolsheviks.[38] In March 1941, gathering together his generals to discuss the impending invasion of the Soviet Union, he told them that the communist intelligentsia would have to be "liquidated" in "the most brutal fashion."[39] So in that respect, Mayer is right to point out that the "Jewish Question" was closely tied in Hitler's mind with the problem of how to deal with communism and how to conquer Russia. As soon as the German armies sliced into Soviet territory after the June invasion mass killings of Jews, as well as of communist functionaries, began. Within weeks the exterminations were well under way.[40]

Mayer has the argument backward. What bothered Hitler most about communism was not that it was in some sense "socialist," but that it was supposedly "Jewish," and as such, it represented everything the Nazis loathed. "[W]e will never be able to come to terms with Jewish Bolshevism without signing our own death warrant," said Hitler to a friend in the early 1930s.[41] And it was not when he began to fear that he might lose to Stalin that Hitler began disposing of the Jews, but precisely at the moment when he thought he was triumphant, and no longer needed to hide his ultimate intent. This we can see by going back to Hitler's Jewish policies during the 1930s.

The killing of German Jews did not begin in 1933, when Hitler seized power, though there were anti-Semitic laws passed almost immediately. Nor were German Jews herded into concentration camps for many years; and for a time, Hitler seemed to put the Jewish issue aside, at least until 1938. Then there were killings and mass jailings on the occasion of *Kristallnacht* (so called because so many storefront windows of Jewish shops were broken), a night of terror initiated by the SS. But still, only a few hundred were killed, and most German Jews who wanted to emigrate then were allowed to. Even after the war began in 1939, and Poland, with its three million Jews was conquered, a policy of mass murder was not instituted. Jews were ruthlessly herded into ghettos, they were publicly humiliated and their goods were confiscated, some were sent to camps where they were mistreated and many died, but deaths were relatively few, especially compared to what would come later, starting in mid-1941.

Why did Hitler wait so long? Because he really believed in a world Jewish conspiracy, and particularly, that Jewish financiers were very powerful in France, England, and the United States.[42] He did not wish to bring war on Germany before it was ready. So, even in 1938, he wanted to appear reasonable enough to make concessions. And after the war began in 1939, he needed to keep Stalin as a friendly neutral while he handled the French and British and prepared for the invasion of the USSR. If Jews were powerful in Western Europe and the United States, Hitler believed, they were even more dominant in the Soviet Union, as Bolshevism, in his opinion, was primarily a Jewish plot.

Given that war with the Soviets was inevitable when he was ready, but not before, systematic exterminations would have to wait until that part of the war had begun. In effect, the invasion of the Soviet Union opened the campaign to eliminate Jews.[43]

It was in the summer of 1941, after coming back from Hitler's headquarters in East Prussia where Hitler had gone to oversee the launching of the attack against Russia, that Heinrich Himmler, head of the SS, of the political police, and of the existing network of concentration camps, told the commander of Auschwitz that Hitler had ordered the start of the "Final Solution" (*Endlösung*) to the Jewish Question. The SS would be called upon to carry this out, and the facilities in the east were not adequate, so Auschwitz would have to be readied for the task.[44]

The wholesale murder began in the eastern territories being overrun by the German army. Special SS detachments, *Einsatzgruppen* (literally, operation or special action groups), were dispatched on extermination campaigns. This is when the mass killings began in the newly occupied Russian, Ukrainian, Belorussian, and Baltic lands.[45] The stories of bodies heaped on top of each other in trenches, stripped naked, some of them still living but left to smother to death, were hardly believed when they first reached the outside world in 1942. "In the territory wrested from Russia in 1941," writes Lucy Dawidowicz, terror became systematic and massive." And:

> Within days of the German invasion, thousands upon thousands of Jews in Vilna, Kovno, Riga, Bialystok, Minsk, and hundreds of other towns, disappeared in raids carried out by Lithuanians, White Russians, and Ukrainians under German orders. It was said that Jews were taken away to work. By mid-July a survivor here or there staggered back, physically maimed, psychically scarred, to report the mass execution of Jews. In Bialystok some 7,000 Jews were killed by the *Einsatzgruppen* in July; in Kovno, some 6,000 to 7,000; in Vilna, 20,000 or more, nearly half the city's Jewish population—were swallowed up in the death pits at Ponary. . . . The reports were hard to believe; once believed they were still harder to assimilate.[46]

But this was just the beginning. Soon, because shooting was going too slowly, the Germans began using special buses in which the motor's carbon monoxide was fed back into the passenger area. By the end of the summer of 1941, some 300,000 had been killed in these ways, but still, it was too slow.[47]

As the *Einsatzgruppen* were doing their job in the east, it became evident that there was a lot of work to be done in Central and newly occupied Western Europe (taken mostly in May and June of 1940, as a result of a stunningly successful invasion of the Low Countries and France). So, the process was carefully and methodically organized. It was neither a panicked reaction to defeats in the east, which began later on, nor, as some Germans would have it, in reaction to Bolshevik atrocities. There were plenty of these, to be sure, but they had never affected Germany, only the Soviets themselves.

Once Hitler invaded the Soviet Union, this greatest of dangers, Jewish Bolshevism, was about to be brought under control. It is more likely that it was Hitler's overconfidence that precipitated the start of this genocidal campaign, not a looming perception of defeat, which only came 18 months after the invasion, at Stalingrad. By the summer of 1941, there was no one left to fool or stall. Hitler controlled most of Europe, and his armies were slicing deep into Russia.

In January 1939, Hitler had warned Jews that they would be destroyed if there was a new war. The previous November, in preparation for *Kristallnacht*, Himmler had told his SS:

> We must be clear that in the next ten years, we face unprecedented conflicts of a critical nature. It is not only the battle of the nations . . . [but that against] Jewry, freemasonry, Marxism and churches of the world. These forces—of which I assume the Jews to be the driving spirit, the origin of all the negatives—are clear that if Germany and Italy are not eradicated, *they* will be eradicated. . . . We will drive them out more and more with unexampled ruthlessness.[48]

At that time, in late 1938 and early 1939, there was not yet a definitive plan on how to carry out the coming slaughter. In any case, by September 1939, there were no more than 200,000 Jews left in Germany and 60,000 in Austria, so the issue was not pressing.[49] It was only with the conquest of Poland that significant numbers of them fell under German control.

But as Michael Burleigh and Wolfgang Wippermann's study on the systematic enactment of racial and biological laws in Nazi Germany shows, the psychological preparation for these horrors was under way long before they took place. Not only did the entire Nazi worldview point in that direction, but it was part of a larger plan in which the feeble-minded, those with hereditary diseases, Sinti and Roma (more commonly called Gypsies, a term they do not like), and homosexuals were to be wiped out. Thousands of these people were killed as a result of Nazi policies. Furthermore, there were plans to sterilize large categories of other people, including any who were part black, so that these "mongrelized" individuals would no longer be able to pollute the Aryan race.[50]

Up to 250,000 Sinti and Roma were murdered along with Jews during the war. Somewhere between 10,000 and 15,000 homosexuals were sent to the concentration camps. If the Germans had won the war, there were plans for an extension of this purification project that would have engulfed many more. The Jews were, of course, the most persecuted because they were considered by far the most dangerous and hated, but it is certain that killing them was part of a larger scheme to create a racially pure, perfectly "healthy" ideal world.[51]

Yet, for all this, there were obviously contradictions in the policies carried out by the Nazis. For one thing, some leading Nazis, most notably Göring, did not take Hitler's racial theories all that seriously, and they were more concerned with the rational exploitation of labor for war production than with any racial program. They resisted the projects to destroy Jews whom they preferred to simply enslave and put to work. With respect to this issue, as with many others, Hitler tended to let his subordinates fight it out among themselves rather than insisting on complete centralization. Therefore, it was only gradually that Himmler and the SS took control of Jewish policy, and that Göring's more pragmatic policies were shunted aside.[52]

In order to straighten out conflicting claims over the disposal of the "Jewish Question" a meeting was suggested by Göring himself on July 31, 1941, though it was delayed for logistical reasons until January of 1942. It was chaired by Reinhard Heydrich, Himmler's chief assistant, and the SS's organizer of concentration camps. This meeting did not mark the decision to engage in the "Final Solution." That had been done before, and mass gassing of Jews had begun in the fall of 1941.[53] But it did mark the victory of Himmler's SS over competing institutions and policies with respect to this issue, and the extension of the "Final Solution" to occupied Western Europe. That meant, in other words, that now the work of the *Einsatzgruppen* would be supplemented and vastly enlarged by the concentration camps.[54]

Heydrich himself was one of the few top Nazi leaders who outward-ly conformed to the image of the Aryan "blond beast." He was tall, handsome, blond, young, and strikingly heartless. The historian Joachim Fest and, evidently, the top Nazi leadership, both Hitler and Himmler, believed that Heydrich was one-quarter Jewish. Fest's evi-dence is convincing. Not only were there rumors about Heydrich's ancestry, but his personal file kept by Martin Bormann, Hitler's secre-tary, was left blank where it should have listed information about his maternal grandmother. Heydrich was taunted about being Jewish as a schoolboy, and as he grew to be a fervent Volkish nationalist, he greatly resented this. Heydrich, like his immediate boss, Himmler, came from a successful upper-middle-class family. His father was a well-known musician, singer, and composer, and he was himself a good violinist who loved to play chamber music, especially Haydn and Mozart.[55]

There have been some popular interpretations of the Nazis claiming that they were misfits who came "out of the gutter." No doubt, there were some, but this is certainly not true of those who organized the killings. Heydrich was from a prominent, highly cultured family. Himmler's father was a respected *Gymnasium* professor, and later head of a *Gymnasium*, or elite secondary school, an honored position in Germany.[56]

At the January meeting, named after the Berlin suburb where it took place, the Wannsee Conference, the SS were told by Heydrich that Hermann Göring, Hitler's official second-in-command, had ordered the preparation for the "Final Solution of the European Jewish ques-tion." Heydrich envisioned the deportation of some 11 million Jews, carefully enumerated by country, from throughout Europe into camps. The minutes of the conference specify:

> With adequate management the Final Solution is expected to result in Jews being put to appropriate work in the East. In large groups of work-ers, the sexes separated, able-bodied Jews should be made to build roads in these areas, which would doubtless lead to the natural diminu-tion of numbers at a considerable rate.[57]

This was ostensibly a compromise to please those, like Göring, who wanted to exploit the Jews' labor, but the phrase about "natural diminution of numbers" was more to the point.

Even at this late date, the discussion avoided giving the horrible details of what was in store for these deportees, though the mass

killings had already begun six months earlier. But there was no doubt
in the minds of the participants about the ultimate goal. Adolf Eichmann, who acted as secretary at the meeting, later testified at his trial
in Israel that what actually happened was that the various high civil
servants delegated to attend put forward proposals for what their min-
istries should do with respect to the "Final Solution." Future actions, it
was decided, would be coordinated by Heydrich and the SS. Heydrich
was delighted by the results. Eichmann himself, it seems, was not personally disgusted by Jews. He had a Jewish mistress in Vienna at the
very time that he was organizing the rounding up of the Viennese Jewish community. He would later claim that he had doubts about the
bloody solutions previously proposed for resolving the Jewish Question, but at Wannsee he saw that the "most prominent people had spoken," so the issue was settled once and for all.[58]

Why were the discussions not more explicit, even though everyone
understood what was being decided? This is not because there was
anything spontaneous and unplanned about the murder of millions that
was to occur, but because even the SS understood fully that what they
were doing was awful, and ought not be publicized for fear of destroying German morale. But then, Stalin also wanted the extent of his
crimes kept secret from his people, even though they were on such a
scale that everyone had some idea of what was happening.

In October of 1943 Himmler would make a speech to SS leaders in
which he would say:

> I shall speak to you here with all frankness of a very serious subject. We
> shall now discuss it absolutely openly among ourselves, nevertheless we
> shall never speak of it in public. I mean the evacuation of the Jews, the
> extermination of the Jewish people. It is one of those things which it is
> easy to say. "The Jewish people is to be exterminated," says every party
> member. "That's clear, it's part of our programme, elimination of the
> Jews, extermination, right, we'll do it." And then they all come along,
> the eighty million good Germans, and each one has his decent Jew. Of
> course the others are swine, but this one is a first-class Jew. Of all those
> who talk like this, not one has watched, not one has stood up to it. Most
> of you know what it means to see a hundred corpses lying together, five
> hundred, or a thousand. To have gone through this and yet—apart from
> a few exceptions, examples of human weakness—to have remained

decent, this has made us hard. This is a glorious page in our history that has never been written and never shall be written.[59]

Though the extermination campaign involved enormous logistical problems, and significant resources had to be devoted for rounding up, transporting, and killing Jews, the machinery was enlarged and perfected to do the job. Not only special SS detachments but also older German soldiers from the reserves were thrown into the effort. To help with many of the most unpleasant tasks, Ukrainians, Lithuanians, Belorussians, and Latvians were recruited from prisoner-of-war camps after being "screened on the basis of their anti-Communist—and hence almost invariably anti-Semitic—sentiments." These *Hilfswillige* (auxiliary volunteers, called "Hiwis" by the Germans), however, had German officers to train and lead them.[60]

Terrible atrocities were committed at every stage of the procedure. Extreme sadism and brutality were the rule, not the exception. Christopher Browning's study of the men in a reserve police battalion who played a major role in rounding up and hunting down Jews in Poland shows that many of those who carried out these orders were, as he put it, "ordinary men," from every walk of life. Many were at first sickened by the brains that splattered them when they shot Jews at close range, by the mindless brutality of the Hiwis (auxiliaries) who assisted them as they drank themselves into a stupor while executing Jews, and by the cruel scenes as families were driven into packed cattle cars for the trips to the death camps. But most of them got quite used to what they were doing, and those few who could not stand it were rotated to less demanding jobs.[61]

In the camps themselves, many inmates were gassed immediately, while others were put to work and starved or beaten to death. There were gruesome, useless medical experiments conducted by SS doctors. Lucy Dawidowicz's description corresponds to thousands of testimonials, and these are now so well known that it is unnecessary to repeat them. Elie Wiesel's memoirs of his stay in the camps, first published in 1958, give us a particularly powerful image of what it was like. The short stories of Ida Fink, who lived through all this, tell us how the Polish Jews felt as this was being done to them.[62]

Three million Polish Jews (according to the pre-war Polish boundaries), 700,000 from the Soviet Union, 270,000 Romanian Jews,

260,000 from Czechoslovakia, over 180,000 Hungarian Jews, 130,000 from Lithuania, over 170,000 from Germany and Austria, 200,000 from the occupied Western European countries, including 75,000 from France, and over 120,000 from the Balkans (not counting Romania) were killed. The total was somewhat over 5.1 million, of whom about 3 million died in the camps. About 1.3 million of the rest were killed by the *Einsatzgruppen* or related groups such as the reserve police battalion studied by Browning. The remainder, about 800,000, died of starvation or disease in the ghettos set up by the Germans.[63]

An estimate of the total number who died in the camps is 5.4 million. This would mean that up to 2,400,000 non-Jews, mostly Gypsies and Slavs, died there, too. The entire Slavic east was slated for slavery. Even those populations from whom the Germans were willing to take soldiers and concentration camp guards and "Hiwis," such as Ukrainians, were not spared. Three million Soviet prisoners of war were killed, starved, or frozen to death in their own camps where the Germans neglected them. The Germans treated Western European and American prisoners much better.[64]

In Poland, occupied for five years, such a policy was carried out with devastating thoroughness. Leading intellectuals, political figures, and churchmen were sought out and killed. Higher schools were abolished. Opportunities for Poles were reduced to a bare minimum. And if Christian Poles did not suffer on the whole as much as Jewish ones, it was bad enough to push the population into one of the most determined underground wars the Germans had to face anywhere. The Poles had no choice between enslavement and slow starvation on one hand, and revolt on the other.[65]

Even in Western Europe, which received lighter treatment, the German occupation was a time of forced labor conscription, hunger, and terror for those who did not cooperate fully. Of course, in countries whose people were not deemed racially inferior, or not too much, like France, a great many locals collaborated with the Germans, and did quite well during the war.[66] In countries openly allied to the Germans, life during the war could be quite bearable, too. What a Nazi Europe would have been, however, is clear. All Jews, Gypsies, homosexuals, and other "inferior," "mongrel," or "diseased" people would have been dead. Most Slavs would have been enslaved and consigned to slow death through abuse and starvation. Other non-Germans would have been heavily taxed and their economies put at the disposal of Germany's. German colonists would have spread out to the east, and would have taken over elite positions everywhere in Europe. This is, in fact, the system that existed from 1940 to 1944 over most of the continent.

The killing of the Jews was not just planned; it was the cornerstone of Hitler's entire policy. Hitler began his political career with an idea, and he carried it out. This is the essence of the "tyranny of certitude." The Nazi version combined, as did Marxism, an absolute faith in itself, utter ruthlessness, and a conviction that it was all justified by modern science. On February 22, 1942, at dinner with Himmler, Hitler said:

> The discovery of the Jewish virus is one of the greatest revolutions that have taken place in the world. The battle in which we are engaged to-day is of the same sort as the battle waged during the last century by Pasteur and Koch. How many diseases have their origin in the Jewish virus![67]

Stalin's tyranny was similarly rooted in a conviction that the scientific validity of his ideology justified his ruthless policies.

DID STALIN HAVE TO MURDER MILLIONS OF CLASS ENEMIES?

The murder of millions of people in the Soviet Union under Stalinism is more difficult to explain than the killings by the Nazis. Hitler's entire political career was based on his blaming the Jews for Germany's and the world's ills. His speeches and writings were suffused with violent threats. Most of his close associates expressed similar sentiments, and he made sure that it was a true believer in racially based theories of history, Himmler, who was put in charge of the exterminations, not a faceless and possibly indifferent bureaucrat or opportunist. But there is much less in the body of Marxist-Leninist-Stalinist writing that prefigures the massacres that occurred.

It is possible, by stretching definitions and trying to empathize with the thinking of the communist, to see how rich peasants could be defined as dangerous class enemies, and as such, in a world where class warfare was all-important, a legitimate target for persecution. But by Marxist criteria, elite classes, not the run-of-the-mill poor, should have been persecuted. Of the millions of peasants who died, not many could have been considered elites. Even more astonishing is that after 1933, the killings continued and spread. In the 1935 to 1938 purges

millions more died, mostly from the cities, and including the majority
of the older members of the Bolshevik Party itself. Then, tens of thousands of army officers were killed. After World War II, millions more
were arrested and died. In all, something on the order of a million
Party members may have been arrested, and the majority were shot or
died because of brutal treatment. And millions more who were of no
conceivable importance, but who were working class, or other categories of nonthreatening individuals, and their families, were arrested,
brutalized, exiled, and murdered.

Hitler did not do anything remotely like this. The killings of former
Nazi Party comrades during the purges in 1934 did not exceed, at
most, a couple of hundred, and the violence had a political logic to it
which is easily understood. They directly or indirectly threatened
Hitler's hold on power. Subsequently, if one was not a Jew, a Gypsy, a
communist, a Slav, a homosexual, or one of the other categories considered racially unfit, that is to say, if one was part of the overwhelming
majority of Germans, there was little danger of direct, life threatening
persecution under Hitler. That is not to say that Hitler was any less
guilty of mass murder, but that in terms of his own ideology, and that of
the Nazis, what he did made obvious sense.

In 1935, Stalin began a campaign of killing his loyal supporters and
huge numbers of his own people who had nothing at all to do with politics, who had never been singled out by communist theoreticians as
dangerous, and he continued even though he was securely ensconced
in a position of absolute power. No attempt to explain this has been
entirely successful, and no matter how many documents are uncovered
from that period, there will be always be questions about why it happened.

We now know that what first occurred under Stalin later happened
elsewhere, in Cambodia under the Khmer Rouge, and to some extent
during Mao's Cultural Revolution in China. So even if Stalin's personal
role remains a vital part of the explanation, and even if one supposes
that in the hands of a different Leninist, a Trotsky, say, or a Kirov, there
would have been fewer deaths, there still would have been millions.
Collectivization, the militarization of society, and suspicions about
internal and external threats would have occurred in any case.

Also, once a tyrant is in power, whatever his original motivation, the
tendency toward increasing isolation from reality, growing impatience
and frustration at the reverses he inevitably suffers, and mounting

intolerance of criticism, tend to make him suspicious of all those around him. We see this in the career of every tyrant, and in fact, of every individual who is in power for too long.

In Plato's *The Republic* Plato has Socrates and Adeimantus discussing tyranny:

> SOCRATES: Has he [the tyrant] not also another object, which is that they [the citizens] may be impoverished by payment of taxes, and thus compelled to devote themselves to their daily wants and therefore less likely to conspire against him?
>
> ADEIMANTUS: Clearly.
>
> S: And if any of them are suspected by him of having notions of freedom, and of resistance to his authority, he will have a good pretext for destroying them by placing them at the mercy of the enemy; and for all these reasons the tyrant must be always getting up a war.
>
> A: He must.
>
> S: Now he begins to grow unpopular.
>
> A: A necessary result.
>
> S: Then some of those who joined in setting him up, and who are in power, speak their minds to him and to one another, and the more courageous of them cast in his teeth what is being done.
>
> A: Yes, that may be expected.
>
> S: And the tyrant, if he means to rule, must get rid of them; he cannot stop while he has a friend or an enemy who is good for anything.
>
> A: He cannot . . .
>
> S: What a blessed alternative, I said:—to be compelled to dwell only with the many bad, and to be by them hated, or not to live at all!
>
> A: Yes, that is the alternative.
>
> S: And the more detestable his actions are to the citizens the more satellites and the devotion in them will he require?
>
> A: Certainly.[68]

We cannot forget that however modern the ideologies of a Hitler or Stalin, much about their behavior was the inevitable result of giving an individual too much power. On the other hand, a Stalin placed in the role of Greek tyrant or Roman emperor might have murdered his former friends and close associates, but he would not have felt compelled to annihilate millions of people along with them, and there would have been no intellectuals eager to justify his murderous rages on the grounds of historical and scientific necessity.

We can trace the road Stalin and the Bolsheviks took toward mass murder and explain how the combination of ideology, immediate contingency, Stalin's personality, and the general psychology of tyranny that applied even in the ancient, classical cases all combined to produce such an outcome.

By 1928 Stalin and the Bolshevik Party were in secure control of the USSR. Then, Stalin decided to collectivize the countryside. The decision was to prove catastrophic for Soviet agriculture, but in the context of Marxist-Leninist ideology, it was neither irrational nor should it have been unexpected. Peasants were not liked by the Party; they were viewed as "petty bourgeois." Not only Stalin, but Trotsky, Kamenev, Zinoviev, and Preobrazhensky, the leading Bolshevik economist after Bukharin, all favored forced industrialization and strict control of the peasantry in order to extract a surplus for investment.[69]

The daring step of plunging into socialist industrialization and abandoning the relatively free markets of the NEP period promised to bring the Party back to its days of revolutionary fervor, and particularly appealed to the young members who had missed the earlier period of glory, as well as to those who were already in leadership positions and for whom the period of war communism had been the headiest days of their lives. Their nationalism also would have led them to accept the notion that the USSR needed to be strengthened against its potential enemies. Furthermore, the violence that began almost from the first, when it turned out that the peasants were not willingly going to give up their produce for nothing, reinforced the fortress mentality of the Party, "us against them," the class of the future against the old, resistant bourgeoisie. Bukharin urged gentler treatment of the peasants to avoid what he called "military-feudal exploitation." But the Party leadership as a whole could not accept accommodation with a class enemy or reliance on market forces to solve their problems.[70]

In a discussion at a Central Committee plenum in 1929, Stalin told the following story:

> At a recent village assembly in Kazakhstan, after an agitator had tried for
> two hours to persuade the local holders of grain stocks to turn them over

[writes Tucker, summarizing], a kulak stepped forward with a pipe in his mouth and said: "Dance a little jig for us, young fellow, and I'll give you two poods [measures of grain]." At this point in Stalin's speech, a voice from the plenum audience exclaimed "The son-of-a-bitch!" and Stalin went on: "Try and persuade people like that. Yes, comrades, a class is a class. There's no getting away from it."[71]

But as the campaign of suffering developed many Party functionaries were traumatized by what was going on, even though they had originally approved. Many adapted by accepting the need for terror.[72]

Surely they had expected a better outcome, and probably so had Stalin. For him, and for the Party, there was no return. Robert Tucker has argued that Stalin had not only admired Lenin, but also come to resent his revolutionary greatness and to wish to imitate and perhaps surpass it. He also had begun to identify himself with Tsar Peter the Great, who had carried out an industrialization campaign to build Russia into a great, modern, military power in the early eighteenth century. The decision to force industrialization and to squeeze a surplus out of the peasantry through collectivization, while destroying a dangerous class enemy, was Stalin's way of matching the deeds of his heroes, those who had replaced the less sophisticated, early "Koba" as subjects to emulate. Collectivization was a return, also, to the glorious, dangerous days of militarized war communism, but now, with him in charge. To admit defeat and retreat in any meaningful way would be a personal admission of failure, and endanger his hold on power.[73]

It was war, and as in any war, the leader that begins it must show results to justify the frightful carnage and cost of war, or be discredited. To be sure, there is another alternative. If the results are not satisfactory, it is possible, for a time, to lie about them, or to blame subordinates, as Stalin did in his "Dizziness From Success" article in early 1930. But beyond a certain limit, when lying becomes insufficient, the unsuccessful leader must use much greater repression in order to stay in power after failure.

Stalin had begun to prepare for some sort of purge, accompanied by show trials, with the accused being beaten and tortured into making fabricated confessions, as early as 1928, though there is no way of knowing how far such trials would have gone if collectivization had worked smoothly. That was the year when foreign and Soviet specialists were supposedly found to have been plotting systematic sabotage.

In this so-called Shakhty case, the procedure for later trials had been worked out, with Andrei Vyshinski as the presiding judge. (Vyshinski, a former Menshevik lawyer totally subservient to Stalin because of his own politically suspect past, would later be the chief prosecutor in the much larger trials of the 1930s.) The purpose of this trial had been to disgrace the technical specialists Bukharin wanted to protect and use, just as earlier, Trotsky had wanted to protect and use former Tsarist officers to build up the Red Army, against Stalin's wishes. There were more trials in 1930.[74] But again, there is no indication that at that time Stalin expected the massive purges of later years.

Whatever Stalin's plan was for the future beyond forcing collectivization, industrialization, and rendering his political rivals totally helpless, it is suggestive that in 1932 there was another awful crisis in his personal life. He had remarried in 1919. His wife, Nadezhda Alliluyeva, was the daughter of an old Bolshevik friend of Stalin's, and was only in her late teens. By all accounts, she was devoted, beautiful, and an idealistic, intelligent Bolshevik herself. During the 1920s Stalin seems to have led a reasonably normal, even happy life that may have relaxed him somewhat. He had two more children. His daughter Svetlana later published her memoirs, and they make her home life when she was a little girl seem pleasant. Despite the likely exaggerations of what were, after all, the memories of a pampered little girl surrounded by attention, there are other accounts that confirm her descriptions.[75] But by the early 1930s Nadezhda seems to have been deeply disturbed by what was happening around her, and by the brutalization caused by collectivization. In November of 1932 she committed suicide, and though there were rumors that Stalin killed her, his grief was obvious. His daughter, and his own subsequent behavior suggest he never got over this episode, and that he blamed some of the people in his close circle of friends, particularly Molotov's wife Polina, Nadezhda's dear friend. Perhaps this is why Polina Molotova was later arrested.[76]

Stalin's rage against perceived enemies, his suspicious nature, his growing sense of being a world historical figure—all of these existed before. Now, in his anger and personal isolation, they increased. Those who did not totally agree with him became enemies; those old friends who would not flatter him became suspect; class warfare and personal anguish, old desires for revenge and new problems raised by the failure of collectivization, combined to create the Stalin of the 1930s.[77]

But Stalin's slow, patient, methodical style did not abandon him. He pressed on with his policies, but did not turn on the Party itself until the end of 1934, when Sergei Kirov, the popular Party boss in Leningrad, was murdered in December.

There may always remain doubts about who had Sergei Kirov killed. But it is at least very likely that Stalin ordered it, and that whatever Kirov's own intentions may have been, he was a serious potential threat to Stalin. He was a Russian, a popular and effective Bolshevik leader, and by 1932, and especially 1933, there was some sentiment in the Party that Stalin might have gone too far. Even those who felt that he had held the Party and the Soviet Union together during the very difficult days of 1929–1933 had begun to think that in the future it would be appropriate to follow a more gradual, less traumatizing policy. Kirov would have emerged as a natural new leader, and Stalin could have been turned into a partially retired elder statesman after 1934.[78] In late 1933 and early 1934, furthermore, Stalin suffered from what was probably angina pectoris, or heart problems that included pain and difficult breathing. The Politburo considered naming Kirov as the successor in case Stalin's illness got worse.[79]

In the early 1960s, after a catastrophic policy failure that also produced millions of peasant deaths from starvation, loyal Chinese communist leaders would try to move Mao Zedong into benign semi-retirement in order to pursue a more rational-technical policy. In retaliation, an aging Mao, who wanted to maintain personal control, set off the Cultural Revolution and a whole series of party purges which claimed many lives. Something like this happened with Stalin.

Stalin probably organized a plot to murder Kirov, and then blamed opposition forces within the Party to begin a purge. Even without direct documentary proof that Stalin ordered the murder, the way in which every potential direct witness was soon killed or died of a suspicious accident, as well as the immediate reaction of Stalin to the news of the murder and the launch of mass arrests, as if the event had been anticipated, suggest that Conquest's analysis about the Kirov case is correct.[80]

All those who had been critical of Stalin, or who might have formed a nucleus around which to express and organize opposition, were purged. Trials began almost immediately after Kirov's murder, and large-scale shootings in 1935. By 1936, much of the old leadership was gone, replaced by younger, more loyal Stalinists without the stature to threaten his rule. Of the old leadership, only those most subservient to

Stalin remained in positions of authority, though gradually, even close friends who dared speak their mind, like Ordzhonikidze (who is presumed to have shot himself before being arrested), were being arrested and tried.[81]

What was required to remain on his good side can be guessed by a letter Vyshinski wrote to Stalin to thank him for the promotion to chief procurator of the Soviet Union in 1935:

> Dear Iosif Vissarionovich,
>
> Embarking upon my new appointment . . . I feel an insuperable desire to express to you my most profound gratitude, touching me to the very depths of my soul, to the Party, to the Government and to yourself, our leader and beloved teacher, for the trust you have bestowed upon me.
>
> For fifteen years I have served our Communist Party and the cause of the working class, which has been working miracles under your great leadership.
>
> Sparing neither my strength nor my life, I am ready to serve the great cause of Lenin-Stalin to the end of my days.
>
> Please accept, deeply respected teacher and beloved leader, dear Iosif Vissarionovich, once again this expression of my sincere gratitude.
>
> A. Vyshinski[82]

If this is what it took to gain his trust, Stalin must have been already well on his way toward thinking that he was super-human. To trust that kind of obvious flattery from an opportunist rather than the decades of loyal, but more straightforward friendship, such as that shown by Ordzhonikidze, or other old Georgian comrades who were executed in the purges, is a sign of extraordinary suspicion and a certain lack of judgement. Or perhaps those of us who have not had this kind of power are not competent to evaluate what is required to hold onto it. After all, the cynical Vyshinski, who continued in positions of very high power for the rest of Stalin's life, had not been an old political ally. His obvious boot-licking meant that he was all the more likely to do exactly what he was told. Perhaps instead of being deluded, Stalin understood exactly what he was doing. Subsequently, he would appoint Lavrenti Beria, a Georgian with a suspicious political past who had proved himself a vicious police enforcer, and who had written an extravagantly praiseworthy, false account of Stalin's early Caucasian revolutionary career, as head of the political police and the concentration camps. Ultimately, as minister of the interior, Beria would command vast police and military power as well as the slave labor camps. Yet Beria was also, by all accounts, personally corrupt, and an opportunist as well as a lecher and sadistic torturer.[83]

In his deeply suspicious frame of mind, his anger, and his sense that everything was based on conflict to the death, Stalin confounded old grudges against Party comrades who had contradicted him, or had made him seem dull because he was less cosmopolitan and brilliant, or had simply failed to flatter him, with class enemies, sabotage, and resistance to the march of history. With the purges, he got even, arresting even those who had entirely lost power, subjecting many of the most famous old Bolsheviks to spectacular, well-publicized show trials, and then having them executed. Often their entire families went with them.

But the very public nature of the show trials of leading old Bolsheviks shows that they were not simply intended to humiliate his opponents, but to show the world, and even more the Soviet people, that there were traitors, and that vigilance as well as continued efforts in the class war were essential. Similarly, Mao during the Cultural Revolution would turn his personal grudges into major public spectacles because, above all, like Stalin, he was not simply vindictive, but an ideologue intent on using his personal power to create the kind of utopian world he envisioned. On the whole it seems to have worked, as many in the Party, and among sympathetic foreign observers, believed the allegations made in these trials, just as later, sympathetic intellectuals throughout the world would believe Mao's charges against his previous close associates.

Going through the transcripts of the trials, for example, of Bukharin and those tried with him in March of 1938, it is evident that much attention was paid to making them seem like real judicial inquiries.[84] The Party, the people, and foreign Marxists needed to have their faith in the theory confirmed, and mere power politics would not have been adequate grounds for purging so many former Bolsheviks. Part of Stalin's political genius was that he remembered that one aspect of his role was to be what Adam Ulam has called "a great educator." Thus, at the very moment when Stalin most needed the support of the Party officials, he found a way to reinforce their belief in the correctness of the official ideology.[85]

But it was not just a few hundred, or a few thousand potential opposition leaders who were purged. The purges spread to include minor officials, and millions of others. Why? Surely, the extremely suspicious nature of just one man, Stalin, cannot explain this, even if it is perfectly obvious that he initiated the process and knew what was happening.

In part, he was consciously imitating Ivan the Terrible, who had destroyed large parts of his nobility and set up his own personal political police force, the Oprichnina, to terrorize his enemies, real and imagined.[86] *Time* magazine, in a well-informed, but undocumented story on January 1, 1940, in which he was declared "Man of the Year" for 1939, has Stalin supposedly saying, "Ivan the Terrible was right. You cannot rule Russia without a secret police."[87] But in part, also, his subordinates understood that to prove their loyalty, they had to engage in their share of killing, and this spread downward through the bureaucracy so that every little local Stalin had to secure himself by conducting little local purges.

Once the most minor official, or a mere worker, clerk, or peasant had been denounced as a Trotskyite, or a Japanese spy, even if he had never quite understood who Trotsky was, or ever seen a foreigner in his town or village, this guilty individual could not just be returned home, for fear that an official who did not continue the charade might himself be condemned by a rival, jealous subordinate, or frightened superior. There must have been many who protested, but not enough to stop it, so that those who showed insufficient enthusiasm were packed off to camps and prisons. Denunciation and fear spread, to the point that local initiatives could often sweep victims up without having any direct orders from the top. And in this climate of growing fear and paranoia, officials from the center would visit outlying parts of the Union and order purges, not only to show the boss, Stalin, that they were loyal, but to secure themselves against potential rivals.

But why, in such circumstances, did local officials not realize that to protect themselves they should oppose the center? There was such talk, to be sure, but as the purges proceeded, those local officials who had failed to take the initiative and start to purge their own districts risked falling when the central authorities examined their actions.[88]

Stalin had some believing communists, such as Molotov, Kaganovich, and younger men like Mikoyan, Khrushchev, and many others to back him and carry out his orders. But even they had to be totally submissive, because there were always corrupt weaklings like Yezhov, Beria, and Vyshinski to execute any possible order. In fact, throughout the hierarchy, from top to bottom, this pattern of revolting subservience, cruelty, corruption, and fear was replicated. And even those who believed in communism, and who were slavishly loyal, had to be broken and intimidated by having relatives arrested or killed, by being forced to sign compromising documents, and by having to write servile praises of their boss that could only demean any intelligent person. No doubt, also, Stalin enjoyed such spectacles which fed his exceptionally malicious sense of humor.[89]

Milovan Djilas tells the story of how he was sitting near Kalinin, by then a decrepit old man, but still formally President of the Soviet Union, at a dinner in Stalin's presence. Kalinin asked Tito, Djilas's boss and then head of communist Yugoslavia, for a cigarette. "Don't take any —those are capitalist cigarettes," said Stalin. Kalinin immediately dropped the cigarette from his trembling fingers, and Stalin laughed. "[H]is physiognomy," writes Djilas, "took on the expression of a satyr. A bit later none other than Stalin raised a toast in honor of 'our President,' Kalinin."[90]

Only Stalin could enjoy such jokes, because so often, they were not just for fun. Mikoyan's brother was jailed; Kaganovich's brother was to be arrested but shot himself first; Poskrebyshev, his longtime, totally devoted personal secretary, saw his wife arrested by Beria, and after three years in prison she was shot. When Poskrebyshev asked Stalin for her release, Stalin told him it was out of his hands.[91]

Stalin, unlike Hitler (who knew what was going on in his camps but who paid no attention to the details, and left that to Himmler, Heydrich, and other loyal subordinates), took personal care of a lot of the details of the purges. Many of the executions, jailings, and deportations to camps were conducted in an ostensibly legal way, with signed orders, and Stalin often reviewed death sentences and approved them. Some were reviewed and approved by other top leaders, including the only Bolshevik senior who survived in a high position, Kalinin, who is said to have cried when signing many of the orders, but who signed anyway.[92]

In 1938 it was the army's turn. By then it was the only organization that might have stood against Stalin. As it was preparing for the growing menace of Germany, Stalin struck it, and this again needs to be explained. There was a provocation by German intelligence that fed false information to the Russians, using the Czech government, about a subversive military plot. But this was clearly fabricated, and may, in fact, have originated as a Soviet plot to create false information about leading generals. In any case, there is no evidence that there ever was a real plot, and Stalin certainly knew this.[93] The reason he decided to purge the military is that he was aware of the growing danger of war, and feared that the Soviet army would be mauled by the Germans, repeating the pattern of World War I. Then, angry soldiers and officers would threaten his hold on power. So he began to move simultaneously in two directions, to purge the army and render it incapable of opposing him in any way, and also to pacify Hitler in order to postpone or avoid war. It was, in a sense, a repetition of the Party purges. It was necessary to destroy potential opposition that might have risen against failure. Those who had the potential strength to resist Stalin, then, became traitors even before they had thought of treachery themselves. For a man as suspicious as Stalin, in an atmosphere of general fear and terror, it was not difficult to jump from suspicion to the perception of a real threat.[94]

In 1938, three of the five marshalls, including the top one, Tukhachevsky, were executed, as well as 15 of 16 army commanders, 60 of 67 corps commanders, and 136 of 199 divisional commanders. In all, about 40,000 officers below that were killed, too, and many of their families.[95]

There is little question that by 1938, Stalin's fear of being overthrown must have been magnified many times over, for indeed, he had created legions of enemies. Thus, the tendency to persecute whole families may have seemed justified. Furthermore, the millions deported to labor camps provided what then seemed to be a useful source of investment, particularly for building roads and dams, and mining and lumbering in very difficult parts of the Soviet Union. Hannah Arendt was only partly right, but nevertheless had an important insight when she wrote that the Soviet secret police came to rely on forced labor to finance itself, and that this was comparable to the spoils extracted by the Nazi SS from confiscations of Jewish and other "enemy" property. In fact, that is one of the mechanisms by which any abuse of power by any bureaucratized police force begins to feed on itself, no matter what the original ideology behind the creation of that force.[96] Secret police forces allowed to steal and blackmail will always fall prey to this kind of corruption. That was one reason why, even after Stalin's death and Beria's execution by his colleagues, the system of political prisons and slave labor camps was only very slowly dismantled in the USSR. That any serious economic analysis would have shown that the forced labor camps were inefficient was almost beside the point.[97]

The stories that subsequently came out of the prisons and camps show how much sadism and wanton cruelty there was on the part of the police interrogators, and within the camps, by the guards. As in Nazi Germany, the trips to the camps were themselves nightmares of overcrowding, famine, and thirst, with many perishing on the way. Nevertheless, these were not death camps as were the German ones, because there was no plan to systematically exterminate all the prisoners. Those who were not shot in prison, who survived the trips to the camps, who were not sent to the harshest camps where 30 percent died each year, and who were physically tough had some chance of surviving, as Solzhenitsyn's short novel *One Day in the Life of Ivan Denisovich* shows.[98] Still, Conquest estimates that over 10, perhaps more than 20 million died in these camps.[99]

Later, the same methods of torture and brutality were to be used in the East European countries conquered by the Red Army at the end of World War II.[100]

Roy Medvedev tells the following two stories from the Soviet experience:

> Stanislav Kosior's . . . captors, unable to break him with torture, brought his sixteen-year old daughter into the room where the investigation was taking place and raped her before her father's eyes. Afterward Kosior signed the entire "confession," and his daughter, having been released from prison, committed suicide by throwing herself under a train.

And:

> When sadistic investigators in Butyrskaya prison did not obtain the testimony they needed from one Communist, they tortured him in front of his wife and then tortured her in front of him. A. V. Snegov tells about torture chambers of the Leningrad NKVD where prisoners would be put on a concrete floor and covered by a box with nails driven in. . . . One NKVD colonel, on getting a prisoner for interrogation, would urinate in a glass and force the prisoner to drink the urine. . . . Soso Buachidze, commander of a Georgian division and son of a hero of the revolution [would not confess, so] his stomach was ripped open, and he was thrown, dying, into a cell.[101]

There were thousands of such stories.

Many of those involved in the torturing personally enjoyed it and behaved sadistically. Others simply carried out what they considered to be their duty, and believed that they were protecting socialism, as they were told. Yet others were too frightened to protest, and so followed orders. Many hardly thought about what they were doing.

Studies of those who tortured and killed Jews in Nazi Germany show the same pattern. On the whole they did not much like Jews, and they believed they were carrying out their duty, whether they enjoyed it, as some did, or just did what they were told. Though there is a vast literature that tries to understand how humans could do this to each other, there is no indication whatsoever that it is difficult to find plenty of jailers and killers around. Their motivations vary greatly, but killing and torturing are neither unusual human activities nor are they particularly unique to Stalinist Russia or Nazi Germany.[102] What stands out in the history of Hitlerism and Stalinism, as in some other cases of modern ideological tyranny, is that such behavior was organized, sanctioned, and furthered by deliberate policy on behalf of a specific ideological goal. Only when it is a matter of policy can so many be killed in this way.

This brings us back to the question: Did Stalin have to do so much harm? Obviously not, but in view of his ideology, his personality, and his increasing need to cover up failures with more purges, and to meet threats from inside or outside with more terror, all the killing and suffering took on a momentum of its own. After 1938, everyone around him was too terrified and too broken to try to stop him. With the coming of World War II, the Party and his country felt that he was really needed, once again, to save the situation, as he had during the catastrophe of collectivization. The USSR did win, so that in the end he could justify his behavior to himself, and his supporters, both within and outside the Soviet Union. By then, terror had become his way of ruling, so that even after his great victories of 1945, he continued. He no longer had any other model before him, so he just kept on going. What had begun as a function of the Marxist-Leninist worldview, that history was shaped by class struggle to the death, had become the way of life of Stalin's regime.

In the early 1980s, Jakub Berman, an old Party member, who was one of the top leaders of communist Poland from World War II until 1956, and who knew Stalin, Molotov, and much of the top Soviet leadership, was interviewed and asked to answer questions about his past.

Berman was a Polish Jew; many in his family were killed by the Nazis. His belief in communism remained sincere to the end, and in his interview he insisted that what he had done in Poland was for the best. Teresa Torańska, who was interviewing him, asked:

> And what did you feel in 1937 and 1938, when thousands of communists were being murdered in the USSR?

Berman answered:

> I assumed that the terror of the Great Purge was a side effect of the search for a solution to the Soviet Union's extremely difficult international situation, and possibly as a result of Stalin's own internal struggles and contradictions; they in turn may well have been connected with his extreme suspiciousness, which had become pathological. I didn't try to justify what was happening; rather I accepted that it was a tragic web of circumstances which drew an enormous number of victims into it. Naturally, I tried desperately to cling to the thought that you can't make omelettes without breaking eggs— a superficial little saying, actually, but at that time, in 1938, it was current among us, and I imagine that there were some who found consolation in it in the situation that had arisen.[103]

If Berman, a learned historian who was a highly intelligent, dedicated activist could explain these terrible events to himself like this, in perfectly good faith, is it any wonder that ordinary policemen, guards, and soldiers went along, too? If, at the top, there were enough men and women who believed in the underlying, "scientific" theory of history that was causing these crimes to occur, that was enough to continue on the same path. For Stalin and for Hitler, once they had fully consolidated their power, no level of criminality would have made most of those closest to them revolt.

SOCIAL REVOLUTION, CULTURAL TOTALITARIANISM, AND THE CULT OF THE LEADER

The suffering they imposed is sufficient to make us accept the idea that Hitler and Stalin were tyrants. But an important part of their agendas was not just to destroy but to change their societies by building new institutions.

Ralf Dahrendorf has argued that Germany was not a fully modern society in 1933 because there were so many restraints on social and physical mobility, because traditional local elites still held considerable political and social power, and because the surviving institutions of Imperial Germany—such as the army, the courts, the churches, and the universities—reserved considerable privileges and powers for themselves. Hitler and the Nazis sought to remove possible barriers to their rule, and to mobilize the energies of the nation for their own ends. In order to do this, they had to abolish all these old privileges, centralizing and modernizing Germany's institutions. This was done under the principle of "coordination" (*Gleichschaltung*).[104]

"Coordinating" society, however, was no simple matter of slight reform. The Nazis seriously undermined capitalism by creating giant state-owned enterprises that increasingly took over vital parts of the economy, and made the surviving large private concerns their servants. Hermann Göring was put in charge of a "Four-year plan" modelled after the Stalinist system of creating five-year plans to promote heavy industry required by the military. A huge state firm, the Reichswerke-Hermann Göring, was created. To produce automobiles for the masses, Volkswagen, or "people's car," was set up as a state enterprise, and it produced a great little model that went on to fabulous international success after the war, and was still being produced in essentially the same form by Volkswagen of Mexico and Brazil in the 1990s. In the important chemical industry, I. G. Farben, which became notorious for its use of concentration camp slave labor, survived as an ostensibly private firm, but in fact it was so closely entwined with the government, and so dependent on high Nazis for patronage, that it became a virtual state firm, too. Huge state orders for armaments, public investment, and a giant road-building program increased public investment from 1933 to 1938 from 6.8 percent to 25.6 percent of national income. After World War II, such projects were widely imitated elsewhere in Europe. By 1938 Germany had the highest proportion of public spending relative to national product of any industrialized country except the Soviet Union. Furthermore, as labor unions were broken, the work force became subject to direct state control more rigorous than anywhere else except in the USSR.[105]

Though not as massive as the transfer of power to centralized state institutions in the Soviet Union, Nazi Germany was very much on the same path toward a state-controlled economy. Similar, also, was the attempt to weaken the family. The Hitler Youth movement was like the

Komsomol (Communist Youth) in trying to produce loyal, militarized young people ready to do their duty for the Party and leader, and to subordinate loyalty felt by young people to any institution other than the Party and state.[106] The social transformations carried out by Nazis and communists gave a sense of the enormous power and success of their leaders and aimed at the total control of society. Thus the term "totalitarian," originally invented by Mussolini, fit Hitler's Germany as it did Stalin's Soviet Union.

There was also the homogenization of culture. There were so many similarities between Nazi and Soviet communist cultures—the taste for grandiose architectural monuments, dislike of abstract art and modern music, love of huge sports spectacles, the cult of a highly artificial "folk" culture, and underneath it all, the continual fostering of deliberate lies and deceptions about the reality of life—that we are justified in supposing that there is a common totalitarian style and culture that overcomes many local, historical, and even ideological differences. Both Hitler and Stalin considered themselves cultural experts. Hitler was particularly concerned with architecture and the plastic arts, and had pronounced musical tastes.[107] Art, according to Hitler, was supposed to reflect "eternal" beauty and not follow passing fashion. It was to be "German," "healthy," and untainted by "Jewish intimidation."[108] "Modern" art, as Hitler understood it, was bad because it was negative, ugly, and cosmopolitan. What he liked was quite similar to what would later be called "socialist realism," and was similar to what Stalin, and later Mao Zedong and Kim Il Sung also liked.

Stalin was far more brutal in his treatment of artists and interfered with every aspect of the arts—with film, literature, music, and the drama—so that after the late 1930s it was impossible to get any artistic work produced that did not meet with his personal approval or that of his immediate appointees. He also had a large portion of the productive cultural elite, much of which had been enthusiastically communist in the 1920s, physically liquidated.[109]

It is a fact that the same attributes turned out to exist in other twentieth-century ideological tyrannies, and there is little difference between the deliberate, mendacious cult of Hitler, Kim Il Sung, Ceausescu, Saddam Hussein, or of Stalin.[110] In all these cases, by placing the leader at the center of cultural life his image is projected more forcefully, and this enhances the aura of worship created around him. That much of the art this produces is simplistic and crude does not detract from its popular appeal. Sophisticates may laugh at "socialist" or "fascist" realism, but this does not mean it lacked appeal.

To be sure, as critics of the concept of totalitarianism have pointed out, not even Stalin, much less Hitler, ever assumed total control over their societies. Nor could they hope to. They were able to mobilize their populations and economies into making gigantic efforts, at very great costs, but they could not will everything, and no individual with as much power as either of them had could keep up with all the details. Nevertheless, they tried, and by using brutal means, they certainly affected every major institution in their societies, ruined millions of lives, and altered the history of the twentieth century. Other modern industrial societies have been able to mobilize millions into their armies, to bring about gigantic economic transformations, and to alter the way in which all of us live. But without the omnipresent tentacles of totalitarianism, it is unlikely that either Russia or Germany would have been able to do so much damage, ultimately to themselves, with so little visible protest.

As the population at large was not expected to understand the finer points of the intellectual discourse which lay behind Nazi racial and communist class theories, except in the most simplified forms, and in order to strengthen their own personal positions, both Stalin and Hitler encouraged fawning worship of their own persons. They probably both came to believe all the flattery, which, in a sense, they deserved. After all, they had done all this, and destroyed their enemies, against overwhelming odds. In his anthropological study of early states, Eli Sagan claimed that one reason people accepted great cruelty on the part of their kings was that it reassured them that they had an omnipotent father watching over them. The death of the king brought disorder and tragedy, so that almost anything was better than regicide.[111] Studying popular reaction to Stalin and Hitler, and to the fantastic cults of their personality, gives some credence to this belief. As they ruled in times of enormous crisis, and in fact greatly increased the level of tension by their own actions, their people did, to a certain extent, come to think of them as playing a vital role. They were terrible, but life without them might be even more terrible.

Roy Medvedev cites the writer Aleksandr Zinoviev's book, *The Flight of Our Youth*, on this. Zinoviev writes that to claim Stalinism was just based on force and deception is wrong because "at [the] bottom it was the voluntary creation of the many-millioned masses who could be

organized into a single stream only by means of force and deception."
Though on the face of it, this seems exaggerated, Zinoviev is perhaps
thinking of his own mother. In his earlier book, *The Radiant Future*, he
described how she kept a picture of Stalin in her illegal Bible![112] Perhaps the masses did not wish Stalinism on themselves, but once they
had him, they did accept, to some extent, the image he tried to give of
himself as their great and protective father, an image which in many
cases approached religious veneration.[113]

If anything, the worship of Hitler was more intense and more genuine. Most Germans, even those who were not Nazis, were grateful to
him early in his rule for bringing back what they considered normali-
ty—order and strength.[114] But then it went much further. "What they
felt for him," writes the historian Eberhard Jäckel, "especially during
the war years, was an almost childlike devotion to a beloved father, a
devotion that could easily dissolve into compassion." Jäckel adds that
the prevailing opinion after 1945 denied that this was so, but nevertheless, even in the dark days of 1944, when it became clear that the war
was being lost, German opinion was, on the whole, outraged that some
army officers tried to kill Hitler. The popular reaction was, "The
Führer is really spared nothing."[115] After the unsuccessful attempt on
his life, he got on the radio to tell Germany what had happened, and
he totally regained control over his people and army.[116]

As with Stalin, of course people were not told the whole truth. There
was endless propaganda, and the cult of the leader was deliberately fostered from the start. On the other hand, there was much less terror than
in the USSR under Stalin. This has posed a problem for historians who
cannot believe that such an evil man was loved. But he was.

Is Eli Sagan's insight about cruel father-kings correct? Not only in
early states or in modern tyrannies, but everywhere, people want to
believe, to hope, that their leaders are good. In democracies as well as
in totalitarian tyrannies public opinion rallies to the leader in a time of
crisis, and it is easy to arouse sympathy for leaders when they are
struck by tragedy, especially if they seem to have accomplished great
things. Americans cried when Franklin Roosevelt died; they cried
when Jack Kennedy was shot. Lenin understood perfectly well that
even a failed and unpopular Tsar might arouse sympathy, so he ordered
him and his entire family secretly shot to prevent his resurrection as a
symbol.

Hitler and Stalin accomplished so much, they steered their societies through such troubled times, they brought such glory, and all the time, at least in public, they remained above the petty squalor of daily life so well that many did think of them as saintly fathers. The circumstances of Hitler's death did not lend themselves to public demonstrations of grief because Germany had just been conquered by enemy armies. Stalin's death, on the other hand, did produce real grief.

When Stalin died many wept, even in the concentration camps! Millions of people crowded into central Moscow to pay their last respects and grieve, and hundreds, perhaps thousands of Soviet citizens were crushed to death in the frenzy that ensued.[117] Stalin's death left his people and true believers throughout the world without a father to lead them through the troubled future.

THE DECAY OF TOTALITARIANISM AND THE PROLIFERATION OF MAFIAS

But this picture of totalitarian social and cultural revolution, buttressed by extravagant, cult-like praise of the supreme, omniscient, omnipresent leader, correct as it may be in accounting for the transforming effects of such regimes, conceals a darker side that springs from the very nature of all tyranny, and was exacerbated by the thoroughness of the Nazi and Soviet communist versions. They were not, of course, the perfectly efficient totalitarian machines they were trying to be. The reliance on the leader, instead, could paralyze efficiency because subordinates did not dare to initiate too much on their own, or to criticize. Information flows from the bottom to the top, vital for adjustment of policy, were impeded. And at lower levels, every little leader imitated the same style, thus spreading the corrupting and inefficient aspects of tyranny at the top.

Aside from the cautious bureaucratism and paralysis, this also created a massive potential for corruption, because there was no public scrutiny at any level of management or leadership. Control commissions from the center could intervene, but since they were themselves more interested in political obedience than in efficiency, and since each leader and administrator in the chain of command was trying to build up a personal clique of followers who could be counted on for support, totalitarian regimes actually soon turned into vast patronage pyramids. Add to this the fact that the Party, whether Nazi or Communist, could not be effectively questioned, and that complaints were likely to bring swift retribution. This made it inevitable that Mafia-like societies ever more dependent on vast protection rackets, systematic lies, and intimidation were created. As Detlev Peukert has put it for Nazi Germany, "In place of the promised 'just' national community and a government of 'order,' it provided an economy of privilege, boss rule and chaotically conflicting spheres of jurisdiction."[118] We know that this is exactly what Stalinism degenerated into as well, especially after his death and the end of the terror.[119] But even under Stalin, corruption was rampant, and sinister. Alexandr Solzhenitsyn has described in excruciatingly painful detail the way in which officers in labor camps picked out their slave concubines from among arriving prisoners, how they could be bribed, and how the guards stole, and sanctioned a system of theft and brutalization among the prisoners, too.[120] Many more stories like this are told by Gustaw Herling-Grudzinski in *The World Apart*.[121]

It was not just in the Gulag that these things happened. Stalin sanctioned a growing difference in the standard of living between the *nomenklatura*, those officially approved by the Communist Party for high managerial and political positions, and the rest of the population. This included special stores, schools, hospitals, rest homes, and so on. But all of this was hidden from the population because it was not "socialist." Yet, the deception and corruption involved permeated the elite from top to bottom.[122] After Stalin, when the system had time to mature, and the ruling class became more secure, it became so totally corrupt that by the end it was little more than a group of organized racketeers who lied, stole, and plundered their society into ruin.[123]

In Nazi Germany, deep corruption spread even more quickly than in the Soviet Union because there was not as much of a pretense of egalitarianism. Also, it was part of Hitler's style of rule from the beginning to allow his subordinates to do what they wished as long as they did not threaten him and remained obedient to his policies. There was never any serious threat of rectification by purges, as under Stalin, so in Nazi Germany there were no effective limits on corruption at all. Only a few minor functionaries were occasionally disciplined, and then not usually very severely. Hermann Göring was the worst thief among the Nazis, accumulating a vast treasure of artworks, palaces, and jewelry, but many of the others were greedy takers of state funds and of bribes, and this extended from top to bottom.[124]

Hitler and Stalin were personally not corrupt in a financial sense.

They lived well, but so do all heads of state. However, the further down the ladder of bosses one went, the more time passed, and the more practical and less ideological the personal motivation of the individuals in positions of authority, the more corruption became pervasive. Tyranny at the top made this inevitable.

But if neither Hitler nor Stalin was financially corrupt, the adulation and lying that went on around them so corrupted their judgement that they lost the ability to govern effectively. By the end, everyone was too afraid to speak the truth. The ruling bureaucracies were too protective of their privileges and ill-gotten gains to risk endangering themselves, and there was a paralysis at the top that turned the tiny groups of confidants around these two leaders into little madhouses of fear and deception, as each maneuvered against the others, promoted his pyramid of clients and clients' clients to support his position, spread rumors, and concentrated on trying to remain alive and close to the leader.

The tendency of those in positions of authority to appoint yes-men is widespread, and is one of the most common causes of failure of leadership in all social systems. But turning the one in power into a god whom everyone fears, and who can justify his actions by claiming, and eventually believing himself to represent the force of fated history, magnifies the problem. Albert Speer, who went from being Hitler's private architect to the very powerful position of minister of armaments, and who, in the end, was almost the only capable technician close to his boss, wrote in his memoirs: "Since he [Hitler] regularly responded to opposition by choosing someone more amenable, over the years he assembled around himself a group of associates who more and more surrendered to his arguments and translated them into action more and more unscrupulously."[125]

Perhaps as early as 1943, after the loss of the decisive battle of Stalingrad in Russia, but certainly after the attempt on his life in July of 1944, Hitler lost touch with reality, and it became almost impossible to discuss policy with him in a way that took into account the catastrophic war losses. Yet, there was such paralysis around the leader that no one dared do anything to contradict him, and even Speer remained loyal until almost the very end.[126]

For Stalin, similar stories have been told by Nikita Khrushchev, one of his top aides who became his successor, and who hated him, and more recently by Stalin's biographers. As early as 1962, however, the

Yugoslav communist leader Milovan Djilas, who met several times with Stalin, wrote that by 1948, at least, the same process was well under way. Stalin could sometimes still be shrewd, but at other times, he could make absurd errors of fact, which would be allowed to pass, because no one could contradict him.[127]

Both Hitler and Stalin were so much in charge that they could not be displaced, even as their judgement weakened, and as the flatterers around them gained the upper hand and they began to lose touch with reality. They were gods, and gods do not age. In the end, as Hugh Trevor-Roper has described in *The Last Days of Hitler*, his bunker had become a bin of lunatics. As for Stalin, Roy Medvedev has written:

> In the last years of his life Stalin was often ill and took very little part in the affairs of state. He occupied his time with various amusements. He liked to cut out colored pictures and photos in magazines, make montages of them, and paste them up on the walls of his bedroom and office. Guests were often invited to play chess with Stalin, but warned never to win.[128]

Yet, the arrests went on, and more purges were being planned. His murderous rage was never quenched.

When Hitler finally killed himself to avoid capture by the Soviet army, his life's work had collapsed, and his death left nothing but ruin behind. Germany recovered from his rule, as did the rest of Europe, but it took over a decade.

Stalin was much more successful; he left behind a gigantic structure. The Soviet Union was industrialized and, in some ways, a quarter of a century after the beginning of collectivization, it had become a modern society. But the model society Stalin had created was an imitation of late nineteenth- and early twentieth-century advanced industrial nations: giant steel mills and electric generating plants, a massive armaments industry, heavily polluting chemical industries, and an agriculture dependent on massive industrial inputs, but incapable of feeding the country. Soviet industry was labor- and capital-intensive, but inefficiently wasteful and outdated even as it was under construction. Stalin left a society where the truth could not be spoken for fear that the whole structure would collapse if it were known, a people shamed by the humiliation of terror and having to respect the local little tyrants who ran the Party, and a whole country so thoroughly afraid of itself and the outside world that it had to keep itself shut up within its borders, and on a constant state of military alert in order to survive. It would take more than thirty years before the mounting crisis from this legacy forced the Party to reform itself, and to face the moral and physical rot left by Stalin's legacy. Then, when the lid was raised on the infestation underlying the Soviet state, Stalin's instincts were proved to have been absolutely right. Without terror and purges to rejuvenate its cadres, Soviet communism had become little more than one vast set of Mafia families, each controlling some part of the empire, cheating and lying as the economy eroded. Without continual lies about how things were going, the fragile legitimacy of Leninism-Stalinism collapsed as ordinary people discovered that all the suffering had been for nothing, that it had all been a monstrous hoax.[129]

No doubt Stalin would have laughed to see Gorbachev trying to pursue Bukharin's strategy, a kinder, moral, market-oriented socialism—a contradiction in terms—and utterly failing. In effect, we can suspect, though never prove, that Stalinism probably saved Leninism and made it work as well as possible. Bukharin in 1928 would have accomplished what Gorbachev did sixty years later, and just as unwittingly—the dissolution of the Bolshevik Revolution.

Chapter 5

A Typological Map of Tyranny

Hitler and Stalin were radical innovators because they created societies in which the abuse of power was taken to such extremes, because the number of people killed or whose lives were irreparably damaged was so high, and because their tyrannies were meant to impose their utopian, supposedly scientific visions of the world on the populations they controlled. Later in the century there were other rulers who matched their extremism and frightening ideological sense of certitude. Mao Zedong and his Chinese Communist Party were responsible for tens of millions of deaths and the persecution of tens of millions more in the name of their own form of Marxism. Pol Pot and his Cambodian communists, the Khmer Rouge, ruled a much smaller society, but they probably caused an even larger proportion of their people to die than Stalin did of his. Kim Il Sung of North Korea, who is thought to have killed on a considerably lesser scale, has nevertheless created an even more regimented and totalitarian society than Stalin did.

But not all twentieth-century tyrants have been as ideologically driven as these extreme cases. Some, of course, have been merely corrupt, old-fashioned tyrants who would have been entirely comprehen-

167

sible to ancient political philosophers like Aristotle. In the last parts of this book I shall discuss some interesting cases of classical corruption and evil, such as Idi Amin of Uganda.

There have also been many intermediate cases in which ideology and corruption, the new tyranny of certitude and the old one of greed, have been thoroughly mixed together. In some of these cases rulers have come to power with genuine ideological goals, with thoughtful and idealistic plans, but they have slipped into corruption and incompetence on such a scale that they did their people great damage. Ne Win of Burma is an example of this. In his case, however, even though there came to be much corruption, it was primarily his regime's incompetence, not its inherent dishonesty, that led to Burma's tragedy. But an important part of that incompetence was the refusal to see that the original ideology of the regime was fatally flawed. Ne Win's inflexibility contributed as much to his failures as either the increasing corruption over which he ruled or any of his other personal failings.

Even though today Nicolae Ceausescu of Romania is considered to have been a corrupt tyrant, and indeed there was considerable corruption under his rule, he was actually much more of an ideological tyrant. The devastating effects of his rule on Romania were much more the result of his utopian and nationalist vision than of any petty personal corruption he exhibited. Similarly, even though Saddam Hussein of Iraq came to rule over an increasingly corrupt and notoriously nepotistic regime, the impetus and binding glue of his rule has always been extreme nationalism and the vision of a greater Arab nation that has beguiled Arab intellectuals for most of the latter half of the twentieth century.

The extreme and violent nationalism of the Argentine generals who ruled in the late 1970s and early 1980s degenerated so quickly into corruption and incompetence that it is difficult to remember that in this case, too, a modern ideology similar to fascism, including strong overtones of racist anti-Semitism, played an important role in creating and sustaining the regime.

Thus the line between the tyranny of corruption and the tyranny of ideological certitude is not always obvious. Even in Nazi Germany and Stalin's Soviet Union, as we have seen, corruption was rampant, and tended to get worse with time. At almost the other extreme of tyranny, the regime of the notorious "Papa Doc" Duvalier of Haiti may seem to us to have been entirely corrupt, but it actually began with an ideological vision of sorts, even though this was quickly corrupted so that none of it was left by the end.

Another difficult but important distinction exists between some rather brutal dictators who have nevertheless proved flexible and capable enough to stop far short of doing great damage to their societies, and others who left behind tragic legacies with few redeeming features. Some dictators may actually be considered to have been national saviors who have left positive legacies. All modern dictators, and in fact most rulers have made such claims, but in some cases there are reasons for accepting them, while in others there are not. Because of this, any evaluation of tyranny must be partly subjective. Why should I include the Argentine generals and General Ne Win as tyrants, but not General Francisco Franco of Spain, or Atatürk of Turkey? Both of the latter were brutal with their enemies, and Franco in particular can be blamed for hundreds of thousands of deaths during the Spanish Civil War of 1936-1939 and in its aftermath. Yet both Franco and Atatürk also left behind them societies that were better for the majority of their people than what they found when they began their rule. Atatürk may be considered an unambiguously genuine national savior who controlled his impulses toward arbitrary brutality and dictatorial behavior enough to leave a nation in much better condition than when he began his rule.

The fickleness of history is shown by the career of Benito Mussolini. Had he died in 1935, before the Italian invasion of Ethiopia, and well before the disaster of World War II into which he pushed Italy, he might well be remembered as an effective and great leader who brought social order and stability to Italy, and who took giant steps to modernize its economy. But Mussolini lived too long, and his impulse toward violent glory-seeking ruined his country. He is remembered by Italians as a nasty and incompetent tyrant, and had I had enough room, I would have included him in this study.

It is easy to label certain regimes, such as Hitler's, or Idi Amin's as tyrannies. It is more difficult to draw a precise line between relatively more benign and successful dictatorships on one side and tyrannies on the other whose behavior has been bad, but not as unequivocally evil as Hitler's. In any case that line would be drawn differently by various observers. But it is important to see that some such line must exist. At one extreme there is a Lee Kuan Yew of Singapore, an authoritarian, bullying ruler who has often expressed his lack of faith in democracy, but who has, nevertheless, allowed free elections, persecuted only a very few of his political opponents, and guided his little country to unimaginable prosperity. At the other, there is a Ne Win of Burma, who almost certainly meant to do better, but who ruled over an increasingly brutal regime, who bears considerable responsibility for the economic ruin of his country, and whose behavior with time came to be increasingly out of touch and unresponsive to the needs of his country. Somewhere in between these two, the line between tyranny and benevolent authoritarianism exists.

Though I intend to argue that all benevolent dictatorships risk becoming tyrannies, and that with time this has happened with many cases we know about, the fact that some rulers have managed to stop short of tyranny needs to be remembered. Various kinds of ideologies, of social and political situations, and of political personalities are more or less likely to become tyrannical, and knowing which are or are not contributes greatly to our understanding of the nature of tyranny. Comparing only extremes makes these distinctions seem too easily drawn, and therefore weakens the analysis of tyranny. More confusing examples need to be studied as well.

In order to make the distinctions between various types of tyranny clearer, and also to explain the organization of the remainder of this book, I have drawn a schematic map. It is oriented around two axes, each of which defines a particular type of tyranny.

On one axis, the limits are extreme ideological certitude at one end, and extreme pragmatism at the other. The more pragmatic, the more willing to listen to contending arguments, and the more open to compromise a ruler is, the less tyrannical. This is, after all, the essence of how democracy really works—a wide variety of positions and arguments must be listened to and taken into account when wielding power. Tolerance and pragmatism are closely related to each other, as are the ability of a political system to tolerate different interests and points of view and the sustenance of formal democracy.

There have been tyrants, such as Rafael Trujillo of the Dominican Republic, who were actually quite flexible about their ideologies, as long as they retained complete power. But their greed, and the brutality they used to exploit the countries they ruled, nevertheless made them tyrants. In fact, even though we often think of democracies as corrupt, they can never become as corrupt as regimes such as Trujillo's or that of Duvalier in Haiti because they are too open for inspection.

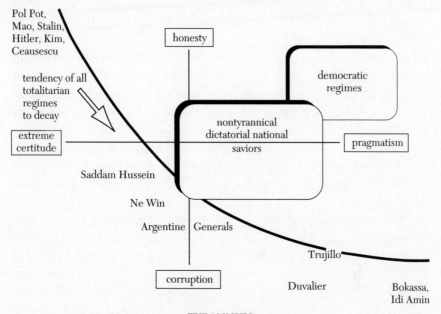

TYRANNIES

[to the left and below the thick curved line]

When brutality, torture, and terror are used to allow the ruler to stay in power in order to further his corrupt ends, tyranny exists. This is the second axis which defines tyranny, with corruption at one end and honesty at the other.

Because democracies, for all their imperfections, impose a certain ideological pragmatism and compromise, and because they are open, they cannot become tyrannies unless the rules of democracy are overthrown, that is, unless open discourse, free voting, and the ability of the population to inspect the workings of government are abolished.

More problematic are those very imperfect democratic political systems, or even outright dictatorships, which nevertheless maintain sufficient standards of honesty, and enough pragmatic flexibility to fall outside the range of tyranny. This is especially true if they contribute significantly to the general well-being of the societies they rule. These types of regimes, which I have labelled those of "national saviors," are located in the middle of the schematic map I am proposing. In some ways they resemble the degenerate ideological tyrannies that have slipped toward corruption and some flexibility. But they are just somewhat less corrupt, or less ideologically rigid, and therefore fall on the other side of the line which separates tyrannies from other dictatorships.

It is easy to identify and label the tyrannies of extreme certitude and extreme corruption, though being at either end of one of these axes rules out being at the tyrannical end of the other. That is to say that Hitler's and Stalin's regimes became less utopian, less ideological as they became more corrupt. Degenerate Stalinism under the rule of Leonid Brezhnev became very corrupt indeed, and in that sense was far along the path toward the middle of the typological map of tyrannies. It is almost certainly impossible to maintain highly ideological, utopian tyrannies for much longer than one, or at most two generations.

At the other extreme, no one would take seriously the notion that regimes such as those of Rafael Trujillo or Emperor Bokassa could ever be taken seriously as ideological regimes, so they are as easy to label as Hitler's and Stalin's.

The remaining chapters will explain the causes and working of twentieth-century tyranny in much the same way, but with somewhat less detail than the chapters about Hitler and Stalin. I shall follow the typological map I have laid out, going from the most ideological to the most clearly corrupt tyrants I have placed on this map. As I do this, I shall try to clarify the many questions that such a map inevitably raises, as well to move toward a set of propositions which will allow us to understand the main causes of tyranny in the twentieth century. In my concluding chapter I shall assemble these propositions in a series of formal statements. These should help predict the likely future of tyranny in the next century.

Aside from this, I shall remain as close as I can to my typology, even to the point of discussing in the same chapters what may at first sight seem to be tyrants far removed from each other, such as Romania's Ceausescu and North Korea's Kim Il Sung, or Saddam Hussein and the Argentine generals. I believe that the ways in which they exercised their rule, and the ways they used and misused their ideologies—in the first instance of national communism, and in the second of militant, militarized nationalism—justify these pairings.

Throughout the remainder of the book I intend to continue to use a method of analysis similar to that used in the chapters on Hitler and Stalin. It is necessary to know something about the history of these countries in order to know why tyrants were able to take power. It is also vital in the case of ideologically motivated tyrants to know something about the content of their ideologies. Finally, even though these studies are obviously not primarily about the individual psychologies of the tyrants I am examining, some biographical details, and some discussion of the psychology of power and what it does to individuals is a necessary part of any study of tyranny. The psychology of the individual in power matters, even if it is not the only determining factor in deciding how a tyrant will rule. As I have with Hitler and Stalin, so shall I try, where appropriate, to include some information about the personalities who have ruled over the evil regimes I am analyzing.

Chapter 6

Imagined Egalitarian Hells

Maoism and the Khmer Rouge

When news of China's Cultural Revolution began to spread to the West in the late 1960s, leftist intellectuals happily embraced and glorified it. The Soviet experiment had been tarnished by the gradual revelations of Stalin's viciousness, then by the crushing of the liberation movement in Hungary in 1956, and even more by the brutal suppression of attempted reforms in Czechoslovakia in 1968. There was growing evidence that the whole system was becoming bogged down in corrupt bureaucratic sloth. Jean-Paul Sartre, the eminent Parisian philosopher and guru of student radicals in the late 1960s, believed that now, at last, real communism was going to come, a utopia without bureaucrats or alienation, filled with spontaneous solidarity and joyous work on behalf of mankind.[1] On university campuses throughout the world Mao buttons sprouted, and serious young idealists diligently studied the thoughts of Chairman Mao.[2]

Chinese foreign policy was reoriented in favor of indigenous extremist revolutionaries throughout the Third World, in Latin America, Africa, and Asia. The rift between the Soviets and the Chinese, already serious since the late 1950s, now became a quasi-religious conflict between two competing dogmas, each of which claimed to be the

175

true heir of Marxist revolution, and each of which asserted that the other side had become dangerously heretical.[3]

The change in China's foreign policy was particularly notable in countries near China. It produced an open split between China and the Vietnamese communists, who now had to rely increasingly on the Soviets for help in their war against the Americans. The Khmer Rouge (Cambodian communists), who were beholden to the much more powerful Vietnamese for support, had been chafing under the guidance of their Vietnamese allies who wanted to stay on good terms with the noncommunist government of Cambodia led by Prince Sihanouk.[4]

But as the Chinese and Soviets turned against each other with increasing bitterness, so their Southeast Asian allies—the Khmer Rouge and Vietnamese communists—allowed their enmity to surface, with the Chinese encouraging the Khmer Rouge. As long as the Americans were there to be fought, this hostility between ostensible allies in Southeast Asia was kept under control. Later, in the mid-1970s, the Khmer Rouge's wish to emulate and surpass even China in ideological purity, and the hatred felt toward the Vietnamese would have dire consequences.[5]

Chinese and Cambodian communism had dissimilar origins, and the differences between the two countries are enormous. Cambodia, with eight million inhabitants in the 1960s, had fewer people than the city of Shanghai, while China contained close to one-fifth of all of the human race. Cambodia in the first half of the twentieth century was a quiet, obscure, and economically very backward little French colony; China was not only the scene of immense revolutionary movements and wrenching civil wars, but also a major participant in World War II. Their ancient histories were different, their forms of Buddhism were not the same, and Cambodia was never influenced by Chinese Confucianism, unlike Vietnam.

But in both countries a blend of extreme utopianism and nationalism resulted in massive catastrophe. In proportionate terms, the million and a half or so people who were murdered, starved, and beaten to death under Khmer Rouge rule from 1975 to 1978—close to 20 percent of Cambodia's entire population—were the victims of one of the most murderous episodes of political tyranny in the twentieth century. By comparison, the Cultural Revolution was responsible for a relatively smaller number of deaths, perhaps as few as a million, and certainly not more than a few million. But the earlier, and closely connected

Great Leap Forward in China from 1958 to 1960 probably caused a minimum of 20 million, and perhaps as many as 40 million Chinese to die of starvation, from 2 to 4 percent of the population.

The ideologies that led to such tragedies provide further proof that the propositions suggested so far to account for modern tyranny are not only valid but are as applicable in the late twentieth century as earlier. They combined large doses of resentment against real or imagined enemies, internal class enemies, and, in the case of Cambodia, racial ones as well. They stressed strong communal over individual values, they were born of chaotic and desperate circumstances, they were intensely nationalistic and paranoid about foreign intervention, and they were formulated by elites who somehow believed that by emphasizing "pure" domestic as opposed to "corrupt" foreign values they could work miracles.

FROM REVOLUTION TO CULTURAL REVOLUTION IN CHINA

China's path to communism was even more complicated and lengthy than Russia's. Founded in 1921, and a significant political force by the mid-1920s, the Chinese Communist Party (CCP) was a partner of the main Chinese nationalist party, the Kuomintang (KMT), until 1927, when the KMT turned on the communists and almost exterminated them. From 1927 until 1949 the CCP fought a civil war against its Chinese enemies, but also a war against the Japanese in the 1930s and 1940s, during which it was nominally but not really an ally of the KMT. After 1945, in the culmination of the long civil war, the CCP mounted a large conventional war against the KMT which brought it final victory. It took twenty-eight years of almost continual struggle, extreme hardship and sacrifice, and millions of casualties for the communists to win. They came to power, then, with much experience governing some of China's provinces, with an admirably dedicated, disciplined, and huge army, and with a long history of internal party political struggles and developed mechanisms for resolving them. By 1949, the top Party leadership was fully unified behind Mao Zedong, determined to modernize China and make it catch up to the advanced societies of the world, and confident of its abilities. The Communist Party and the Red Army were further tested by the Korean War that China fought against the United States from 1950 to 1953. Forcing the mighty Americans into a stalemate was further evidence of their success.

For ten years after coming to power, the CCP avoided major internal disputes, at least among the top echelons of the Party. Even after a serious conflict between top leaders, and a purge in 1959—a result of the catastrophe brought about by the Great Leap Forward—the leaders who lost power were not treated brutally. It was not until the Cultural Revolution that began in 1966 that Party purges became deadly for the top participants.

But then, despite all the deaths that had resulted from collectivization in Stalin's Soviet Union, it was not until the Kirov murder there in 1934, seventeen years after the Bolshevik Revolution, that Stalin had begun openly to jail and execute the top veterans of the Party he did not trust. Mao began his purge seventeen years after the triumph of his revolution, too, and for some of the same reasons. The Soviet and Chinese parties had just experienced major human disasters because of the failed rural policies of the top leadership, and, in both cases, there was some sentiment that the senior leaders responsible for these mistakes, Stalin and Mao, ought to be gracefully retired to an honorific but relatively powerless post.

But the Cultural Revolution of the late 1960s and the great Stalinist purges of the late 1930s had very different consequences, and they were carried out in quite opposite ways. Stalin's purges were secretive and closed off what little political access the population and ordinary Communist Party members might have had to the top. The Cultural Revolution, on the other hand, was out in the open, it mobilized millions of Chinese, primarily youth, and it brought virtual anarchy to this vast country. This is what appealed to Western leftists, especially young ones: the fact that the "masses" and youth were genuinely involved.

What few outsiders realized, however, was that the suffering, personal humiliations, beatings, and deaths brought about by the Cultural Revolution set back China's development efforts by at least a decade. Between the misguided policies of the Great Leap Forward and the anarchy of the Cultural Revolution, the real standard of living of most Chinese was lower in 1976 than it had been in 1956. In the Soviet Union, the purges also unsettled the society and caused massive suffering, but an iron discipline was imposed on the population, and this allowed Stalin to construct an industrial and social system that would last a half century. In China's case, the Cultural Revolution made that impossible, and within a few years after Mao's death in 1976 his version of communism had been demolished as land was turned back to private peasant hands and, in the 1980s, the economy was largely taken out of centralized state control.[6]

The origins of the CCP in China's traumatic confrontation with modern Europe and Japan, its combination of traditional Chinese culture with new Western scientism, and Mao's personal ideas all played a role in propelling China in a different direction from the Soviet Union.

The Fall of Imperial China, the Failure of Youthful Idealism, and the Rise of the Communists

The decline of China in the nineteenth century might have simply become one more of the many dynastic cycles that had governed the rhythm of Chinese history for at least two thousand years. The dynasty in power, the Qing, were Sinicized Manchurians who, like the Mongols in the thirteenth and fourteenth centuries, conquered China and ruled it using traditional Chinese bureaucratic techniques and Chinese Confucian intellectuals. But like the dynasties the preceded them, the Qing were unable to control the pace of social and demographic change. In peaceful times, the population tended to grow faster than agricultural production because technological progress was slow. The resulting discontent and poverty in the countryside made it harder to collect taxes, and this tended to weaken the central government. With time, the upper classes also grew in number, and competition for office became fiercer, producing divisions within the elite and growing corruption as shrinking revenues had to be divided among more claimants. Shortage of funds made it harder to maintain the massive irrigation works on which northern China depended for survival, magnifying the disruptive effects of droughts and floods. That made peasant misery all the more common, further reduced tax collection, and produced banditism and rebellion as desperate peasants sought to alleviate their situation.[7]

All agrarian civilizations have been subjected to such tribulations, and to more or less predictable cycles of rise and decay. After a bad period, population would decline from war, famine, and disease, and a new dynasty would bring back peace and prosperity.[8] In China the educated elites, whose respect for Chinese Confucian tradition and quasi-sacred texts always provided the basis for reunification of the country after episodes of civil wars and catastrophe, interpreted dynastic cycles as the granting and withdrawal of the "mandate of heaven" to ruling dynasties. New dynasties had the moral legitimacy needed to rule. They were fresh and honest, vigorous and virtuous, and they cared for the people. Later, as the cycle would be repeated, dynasties were thought to have become morally corrupt, to have lost their legitimacy, and so to be bringing renewed chaos to the land.[9]

By the early 1800s the Qing had been in power for over a century and a half and there were signs that the cycle of decay was under way once more. But this time, there was a new element—the intrusion of the West. From 1839 to 1842 a war was waged by Great Britain to keep the Chinese market open to the very profitable opium trade from British India. The Chinese wanted to stop the spread of the debilitating addiction encouraged by the trade, and the British did not want to lose the revenues from their main export to China. The ease with which a small number of well-armed European troops disposed of larger Chinese armies was a shock, and revealed the weakness of the government.[10]

A vast rebellion took shape in the south, led by a Confucian intellectual who had failed his exams and was thus denied access to office. Hong Xiuquan combined a traditional Chinese belief in China's cultural superiority with a recognition of Europe's temporary advantage. This was, he claimed, because the true Christian religion was actually Chinese, but had been lost. Now he, as the new son of God, the younger brother of Christ, would bring it back to its rightful home, and reclaim Chinese supremacy. He announced:

> Father [God] had ordained the heavenly Kingdom to be in China; since China was originally the home of the Heavenly Kingdom. Before Father descended to the earth, China belonged to Father, and yet the barbarian devils [the Manchus] stole into Father's Heavenly Kingdom. This is the reason Father decreed that I should come to destroy them.[11]

From 1850 to 1864, his rebellion, called Taiping (Great Peace), ruled a large part of southern China, and came close to toppling the Manchus. It is significant, and perhaps not accidental, that the Taiping advocated a communal society in which private property and the traditional family would disappear, and in which a kind of egalitarianism was supposed to prevail, at least among the common people. Maoism, especially during the Great Leap Forward, proposed to revolutionize society in the same way, as did the Khmer Rouge in Cambodia. And as in the two later cases, the Taiping regime tended to bring to the fore homicidal leaders whose feuding factions engaged in repeated purges that degenerated into massacres of thousands of Taiping followers.[12]

Simultaneously there was another great peasant movement, the Nien Rebellion, that controlled a part of the north Chinese plain from 1851 to 1863. This movement was less ideological that the Taiping, and more a matter of sheer desperation as peasants sought to survive in a region subject to terrible natural disasters worsened by the decline of central power. For a while, however, the Nien also threatened to end the rule of Qing.[13]

The Manchus recovered, for a time, but there were other humiliating wars with Europeans and then with the Japanese, and a growing number of concessions forced on China. It lost control of its most important coastal cities and of its foreign trade. Had World War I not intervened, China would have been divided between the various European powers and Japan.[14]

In 1911 the Manchus were overthrown, but the growth of local power in the decades that preceded this event made unity impossible. A variety of local warlords, and a weak central republican government competed for power. It would not be until a strong Nationalist Party (the KMT) was built by the followers of Sun Yat-sen along Leninist, centralized lines in the 1920s, and taken over by Sun's successor, General Chiang Kai-shek, that a reasonably strong, but still insecure central government emerged.[15]

But it is not directly in the details of Chinese politics in the 1910s and 1920s that the origins of later ideological movements are to be found. Rather, it was the reaction of successive generations of young Chinese intellectuals to these events, and to the persisting humiliation of China by foreign power that shaped the evolving debates about how to modernize and save China.

It was only in the late nineteenth century that a significant number of Chinese began to study the West, and not until China was humbled by Japan in war in 1895 that they began to wield some influence. But few reforms were actually carried out because the Imperial court and the overwhelming majority of the old intelligentsia trained in the Confucian classics had too much to lose by admitting the superiority of Western rather than traditional learning. Nevertheless, in 1898 a new type of university was created in Beijing modelled on Western institutions of higher learning. Some Westerners were brought in to teach there, and positions were opened for Chinese scholars versed in European and Japanese learning.[16]

The most influential of the early reforming intellectuals was Kang Yuwei (1858–1927). Kang and his fellow reformer, Liang Qichao, were, along with the then revolutionary leader Sun Yat-sen, Mao Zedong's political heroes when he was in his late teens and becoming interested in politics.[17] Kang proposed to put Chinese learning on a rational, scientific basis. But, like many other Chinese intellectuals, he believed that in order to reform China a fundamental change in human behavior was necessary. The old autocracy was based on a patriarchal family structure that would have to be dissolved; it was also based on the selfish exploitation of property rights by the rich and powerful, and these would have to be eliminated. He advocated a kind of utopian communal society, without property or conventional family ties, in which people's lives would be coordinated by military work brigades. Then, perfect "democratic" harmony would reign, and conflict would end.[18]

It is not that there is a direct line from the speculations of Kang, or of any other of the many Chinese intellectuals of this period, to later events in China. Nor was there any unanimity about how to proceed. But something which emerges from the study of Chinese intellectual reformers of this period is that for them Western rationality and science were presumed to lead to some absolute truths that would replace older Confucian truth. Somehow, there had to be a scientific answer to China's problems. Democracy, which was assumed to be superior to traditional autocratic government because the great Western powers were democratic, was interpreted as the achievement of greater harmony and unity through mass participation and coordination. That firm coordination and harmony might imply something less than genuine democracy was not widely recognized by these intellectuals, who, in that respect, were much like the old-fashioned Confucian intellectuals they were fighting. But after all, in Europe at that time, there existed substantial anti-liberal currents too, and it was natural that the Chinese who were studying the West should be impressed by those seemingly "scientific" and rational Westerners whose conception of society was closer to that of traditional Chinese thought than to the disorganized pluralism implied by liberal thought.

On May 4, 1919, about three thousand students, led by a contingent from Beijing University, and later joined by workers, demonstrated in Beijing against the treaty arrangements being made in Paris to hand over Germany's chief base in China, Qingdao (still the place where China's best beer is made) to the Japanese. This marked the emergence of a new generation of young intellectual reformers, sickened by the failures of the past, but filled with optimism and determined to modernize China.[19] Exactly seventy years later, when I was teaching at National Taiwan University in Taipei, my students still spoke in awe of this magical moment that had, in their view, marked the real beginning of modern China. It was, they felt, symbolically appropriate that at the same time on the mainland, in May of 1989, Beijing students were occupying Tiananmen Square in favor of democracy.

That such a small event in 1919 had major repercussions testifies to the role of reformist intellectuals, because at the time, the political consequences of the demonstration were small. But the students were determined to keep their movement going by writing and teaching their views. At the heart of their beliefs was a rejection of old ways of thinking, and, unlike the generation that preceded them, some of these students openly admired the liberal tradition of the European Enlightenment. Common sense, toleration of differences, and an experimental approach to science characterized their thinking. They were less inclined to believe in absolute solutions than their predecessors or successors, and they rejected dogmatism. At the same time, in their writing they continued to reject the constraints of the patriarchal Confucian family and to promote the rights of women, something they felt was a key to reforming China.[20] This was, in fact, the golden period of Chinese liberalism, and if adequate reform and unity had been achieved, China might have evolved in a much more democratic way.

But the intellectual energies of this enlightened generation did not give them political power, or solve China's problems. They contributed, however, to a sense that reform was inevitable in the future, and that national unity through modern patriotism was possible. In the face of continuing warlord power and foreign control in the coastal cities, this was an important beacon of hope for other young students and potential reformers.

What could unite all Chinese was the dislike of foreign intervention. In May of 1925, there was a student and worker demonstration in Shanghai to protest the killing of a Chinese worker in a Japanese-owned factory. British colonial troops fired on the demonstrators, killing twelve. On May 4, 1919, no one had been killed in Beijing. Now the students were shocked to find out that their high status as intellectuals no longer protected them. In March of 1926, in another student-led demonstration against foreign imperialist demands in Beijing, the troops of the local Chinese warlord opened fire, and forty-seven demonstrators, mostly students, were killed. The generation of May Fourth, 1919, was slowly awakened to the fact that idealism and rationality were not sufficient to save China.[21]

The culmination of this brutal suppression was that of the communists by the KMT in 1927, that began with the massacres of union leaders in Shanghai in April. The hunt for radicals then continued, and was pursued for another decade, forcing reformist intellectuals to withdraw from politics, to join with the now increasingly conservative and anti-reform KMT, or to turn from liberalism to communism, as did Lu Xun, considered China's greatest writer of the twentieth century.[22] It was the failure of peaceful liberal idealism that opened the way for the eventual success of more radical intellectuals who were neither liberal nor democratic. The generation of student reformers who came to the fore in 1919 proved to be a brief interlude between two generations of reformist intellectuals who believed in much more centralized and autocratic policies to solve China's problems.

The Chinese Communist Party was formed in 1921 by young activists, most of whom had been inspired by or had participated in the May Fourth, 1919 Movement. Like their later enemy, the KMT, they received help from the Bolshevik Communist International which sent them advisors. The founding members had belonged to loose associations of radical student youths in various cities of China as well as abroad, chiefly in Paris and Tokyo. There was no sharp division between them and other May Fourth students, except that those who were among the first communists tended to be more inspired by anarchism than by either liberal or Marxist ideas.[23]

Mao Zedong, who was born in 1893, arrived in Beijing in 1918 as a radical nationalist interested in Western ideas, but with no clear ideology other than a conviction that China had to be modernized and had to rid itself of imperialist domination. He was able to obtain a position as an assistant librarian at Beijing University where he was influenced by the head librarian, Li Dazhao, who would become one of the intellectual leaders of the May Fourth Movement. Li was not a liberal, but "a nationalist who saw in the Leninist theory of imperialism a justification for his chauvinistic views."[24]

Among the early communists from Beijing, Li Dazhao's nationalism was more important than his Marxism, and though at first there seemed to be no essential difference between his followers and the more liberal May Fourth intellectuals, their approaches to China's problems were fundamentally divergent.[25] As Frederick Wakeman wrote, "It was perhaps because Mao [Zedong] began with indignation and only later acquired a revolutionary ideology that he viewed Marxism primarily as an instrumentality rather than as a revelation.[26]

The story of how Mao and rural supporters of the CCP survived the attacks on them of the late 1920s and early 1930s, how they escaped elimination at the hands of Chiang Kai-shek's army in 1934 by marching in a great arc through western China from the south to a remote part of the north, and how after this "Long March" they established themselves in Yanan, is long and complicated. The majority of those who set out on the Long March died or were killed along the way. It is an astounding tale of sacrifice, suffering, heroism, and determination.[27]

It was during the Long March that Mao established his domination over the Party because of the repeated failures of the Soviet-trained leaders who insisted on seizing the cities in order to duplicate the Bolshevik experience. Pro-Soviet leaders remained a threat to Mao's dominance until 1935 in Yanan, when he finally overcame them. Mao remained convinced until the end of his life that these experiences demonstrated the need to engage in ceaseless struggle against both internal as well as external enemies in order to survive, that losers were killed, as his first wife was by the KMT, and that the Moscow-oriented wing of the CCP would have killed him too if he had not defeated it.[28]

Yet, Mao and the communists were far from secure, and it was only the invasion of China by Japan in 1937 that saved them from slow strangulation by Chiang's armies. Until the Japanese came into northern China, the communist policy of trying to win over the peasants by giving them land was only partially successful.

As in other cases of modern tyranny, it was not just a set of cultural and ideological histories that can explain what ultimately happened, but the combination of these histories with the contingencies of actual events, and most particularly, war. Neither Hitler nor Stalin would have come to power without the chaos and tragedy left by World War I. Nor could Mao and his communists have won their revolution had it not been for the Japanese who began the Pacific part of World War II with their aggression against China.

The Japanese were never able to establish full control over the parts of China they tried to annex, but they did succeed in pushing out the KMT government, which was not ideologically or organizationally equipped to survive as a guerrilla organization in the face of superior Japanese strength. Peasants turned to the communists not only, or perhaps even chiefly, on nationalist grounds, but as the only available source of support against Japanese demands and brutalities, and in order to control the rampant banditism that spread with the withdrawal of KMT control.[29] This was the key to Mao's eventual success.

But even after the collapse of the Japanese in the Pacific War, and their surrender after the Americans dropped two atomic bombs on Japan, the Chinese communists did not have an easy time. Stalin evidently did not welcome Mao's success because his own agents in the CCP had lost power, and he was suspicious of possible competitors. In the 1930s he had massacred thousands of Chinese, many of them communists, who had fled to the USSR as refugees. After 1945 Stalin backed the KMT in international forums. Stalin never accepted Mao as an equal, and he remained suspicious of the CCP until the end of his life.[30]

Nevertheless, the communists had a better, more motivated army than the KMT because they had successfully organized the peasants in northern China during the anti-Japanese war. They had greater legitimacy as defenders of Chinese nationalism among intellectuals and the urban middle class, and they did not squander their resources in corruption as did the KMT. By 1949, they had conquered southern China in a conventional invasion.[31]

From Success to The Great Leap Forward

The peasant base of Chinese communism has often been cited to explain the differences between Maoism and Stalinism.[32] It is true that the communist success was based on their ability to mobilize peasants in northern China, but neither the social origins of the leadership nor the policies of the Party during most of Mao's rule reflected this.

The CCP's leadership, like that of other nationalist, modernizing movements in the twentieth century, was heavily dominated by intellectuals who entered the movement when they were young. They could come from a variety of classes, but, on average, simply because those who came from more prosperous families were more likely to have the time to study and engage in politics, they did not have either

poor peasant or worker origins, though of course there were excep-
tions. Mao came from a well-off peasant family, Deng Xiaoping's family
were landlords, and Zhou Enlai's were from the old Confucian elite. In
all, the Party's leadership came predominantly from either the old
bureaucratic elite, from the rich rural classes, or from merchant families. In fact, the social composition of the leading cadres of the CCP
was remarkably similar to that of its enemy, the KMT.[33] It was the ideology of the Party elite that played a much more important role than its
class interests.

What the peasants wanted was to get land and to secure their property rights. Destroying the landlords, eliminating debt and exploitation, and bettering the quality of rural life were genuine goals of the
Party, and these were popular measures. At first land was distributed to
poor peasants, and rural life returned to normalcy in the early 1950s.
Production increased, and later the Chinese would view this period as
a kind of golden early age of communism. But eventually Maoism
turned in a quite different direction which was anything but popular
with the peasants.

It was not as if the early stages of the land reform were peaceful. Far
from it! The Party deliberately exacerbated class warfare in the villages
in order to mobilize poor and middle peasant support. Public behead-
ings and beating landlords to death was common, and because the
dividing line between rich peasant and landlord was vague, this
involved millions of deaths. Zhou Enlai later estimated that 830,000
were killed between 1949 and 1956. Mao, who ordered leniency
toward rich peasants because their skills were needed, estimated a
much larger number of deaths during this period, from two to three
million.[34]

The increase in agricultural production that resulted from the successes of the early 1950s made life more comfortable, but it was insufficient to propel China toward rapid industrialization, and that was
Mao's goal, to be as successful as Stalin's Soviet Union in transforming
a backward nation into a military-industrial powerhouse. In 1955, Mao
decreed collectivization, even though many, perhaps most in the leadership thought it better to proceed slowly. We now know that if,
instead, the peasants had been given facilities for modernizing agriculture on their own they would have been more successful. That is exactly what was done in the late 1970s, after Mao's death, under the
leadership of Deng Xiaoping. But this was not considered by Mao,

who continued to insist that the best approach to economic problems was to mobilize the masses the way he had during the revolutionary wars. Furthermore, government investment, far from being directed to the countryside, continued to be channelled largely into industry, following the Soviet model, while in the countryside the peasants were supposed to overcome their problems by collective enthusiasm and huge increases in labor inputs without accompanying investments in modern technology. Mao decided that since in the past the solution to low productivity had been to direct efforts toward water conservancy through intensive labor, this could work again, and this is what he decreed.[35]

Mao was not just a revolutionary communist, but one who believed in the power of human will over nature, of enthusiasm over technology, and of revolution over peaceful and piecemeal solutions to major problems. The Soviet communists also believed in revolutionary campaigns and mass labor efforts, but Stalin was more willing to admit the limits of voluntarism and turn instead to differential wage scales, renunciations of egalitarianism, and emphasis on technology to overcome economic problems.[36] Yet, Mao's policies in the early days of his rule, at least until about 1956, were reasonably flexible and accommodating to the material needs of his people. As long as he remained optimistic about the possibility of very rapid economic growth, he appeared less dogmatic and certainly less cruel than Stalin.[37]

In 1938 Mao said, "The theories of Marx, Engels, Lenin, and Stalin can be applied to the whole universe. Their theories are not to be looked upon as dogma but as a guide to action." Yet, he added, "The history of our great people over several millennia exhibits national peculiarities and many precious qualities . . . and we must constitute ourselves the heirs of all that is precious in this past."[38] For Mao the key to progress was the destruction of what most reformist Chinese intellectuals identified as the major cause of China's backwardness— the patriarchal, selfish, land-obsessed Chinese peasant family. In 1943 he said, "For thousands of years a system of individual production has prevailed among the peasant masses under which a family or a household forms a productive unit. This scattered, individual form of production was the economic foundation of feudal rule and has plunged the peasants into perpetual poverty. The only way to change this state of affairs is gradual collectivization." But by the mid-1950s, gradualism was out. Mao had become impatient and was calling on mass action and a faster transformation.[39]

Secure in power, he began to return to the impatient ideology of his youth, when he had written, in 1919, "The greatest force is that of the union of the popular masses. . . . The time has come! The great tide of the world is rolling ever more impetuously! . . . He who conforms to it shall survive, he who resists it will perish."[40] Thus, by combining Marxism-Leninism with voluntarism and a faith in the innate capacity of the Chinese people to revolutionize their society in order to overcome their past, Mao believed it possible to make China a great success that would revolutionize the entire world. As early as 1936 he told Edgar Snow that "the Chinese Revolution is a key factor in the world situation, and its victory is heartily anticipated by the people of every country, especially the toiling masses of the colonial countries."[41] This would become a major part of his thinking in the late 1950s and 1960s, when he felt that by accelerating revolutionary change China would undermine the entire world capitalist order more thoroughly than could the Soviets.

It is important that we be clear about why Maoism eventually caused so much damage. There is nothing in the Maoist texts that suggests he was eager to kill people, except insofar as this was necessary to win and maintain power, and to force necessary change. The greater good of China was always his goal. The problem, as in the case of the Soviet communists, was that the blueprint for a perfect society was fatally flawed. Collectivistic enthusiasm, which may be tremendously effective in mobilizing vast armies to fight a war of liberation against a hated enemy, is of limited use in making economic progress. Economic activity does not consist of a short burst of heroic activity, but of patient and long-term work. Furthermore, not even small modern economies can be effectively planned from the top because they require too much specialized knowledge that no small group of leaders can master. Then there is the fact that individuals and families need to have some sense of being able to build a secure future for themselves, and therefore to be guaranteed the fruits of their efforts, in order to keep on working efficiently. As China lurched from one desperate campaign to another in order to find the magic formula that would modernize it quickly, the work of the recent past was undone and those who had thought that they were insuring greater security for themselves and their families would find that the rules had changed. That kind of insecurity is hardly propitious for economic growth.

Some of the other members of the leadership, notably Liu Shaoqi, who was the second most powerful man in the leadership during most of the 1950s and into the early 1960s, felt that the successful war the CCP had fought for so many years was the really decisive part of saving China. The rest was supposed to be easier, and therefore, to be subject to rational calculations and planning. There was no disagreement about the ultimate goals, but Liu's approach denied the need for continuing revolutionary turmoil, especially within the Party which he thought should now concentrate on managing the economy. Mao, on the other hand, never abandoned his belief that continuing struggle, even within the Party, was the only way to mobilize the gigantic mass energies necessary to overcome the technological limitations of the Chinese economy.[42] Mao's belief in voluntarism, collectivism, and egalitarianism made him a disaster as China's guide toward modernization, so much so that after his death, unlike the Soviets after Stalin's, the CCP virtually abandoned its faith in socialism and egalitarianism.

But for all his belief in voluntarism, Mao did not renounce his faith in the scientific validity of Marxist categories of class. Struggle was good, but it should be class struggle as this was the mainspring of history. Thus, along with promoting repeated premature and catastrophic experiments in socialism and mass mobilization, he also oversaw, with the full approval of the other Marxist leaders of the CCP, the division of Chinese society into carefully defined class categories that were supposed to predict individual behavior and become the basis of action. Those labelled as bad class elements, old members of the elite, landlords, bourgeois, former KMT officials and soldiers, and rich peasants, were permanently stigmatized and excluded from advancing in society. Not only this, but their offspring were labelled as bad elements, so that vast portions of the population were permanently relegated to inferior positions, thus stripping Chinese society of many of its most talented individuals, and creating a situation of submerged, deep resentment among the disenfranchised. The population was divided into more than sixty class designations.

> This classification, based on a combination of "class status" (based on occupation during the three years prior to 1949) and "family background" (based on the class status of one's parents and grandparents),

was usually entered into each person's confidential personnel file and kept in the local unit office. As the assumptions underlying this classification became problematic upon "basic completion" of socialization of the means of production at the end of 1956, the files began to take on a life of their own.[43]

As the work unit was the all-important social unit in China, with power to decide virtually all aspects of an individual's life, and because these "files" could not be altered, this way of dividing the Chinese population into favored and disfavored classes created the basis for endless frustrations and conflict.[44]

Every communist society has done this to some extent, though in Europe, even in the Soviet Union, it became possible to overcome a bad class background after the first one or two decades of the revolution. But as Mao combined this belief in the importance of classes with the repeated need to mobilize the population, whenever his plans went awry and he needed a new struggle he would encourage various parts of the society to war with each other. This meant that the hereditary class labels assigned to individuals and their families would continue to haunt successive generations each time new scapegoats and objects of "struggle" were needed. The effects of this at every level of society became most obvious during the Cultural Revolution.

The Great Leap Forward

In 1957, partly to renew revolutionary fervor, but also in response to the troubling events in communist Europe where the Hungarian uprising and the Polish strikes had demonstrated the potential weakness of communism, Mao gave a speech in which he said:

> The policy of letting a hundred flowers bloom and a hundred schools contend is designed to promote the flourishing of the arts and the progress of science. . . . Questions of right and wrong in the arts and sciences should be settled through free discussion. . . . Marxism has developed through struggle. . . . [R]emnants of the overthrown landlord and comprador class still exist, the bourgeoisie still exists, and the petty bourgeoisie has only just begun to remould itself. The class struggle is not yet finished. Marxists are still a minority of the entire population as well as of the intellectuals. Marxism therefore must still develop

through struggle. . . . That which is correct always develops in the course of struggling against that which is wrong. . . . This is the law of the development of Marxism. Ideological struggle is not like other forms of struggle. Crude, coercive methods should not be used in this struggle, only methods of painstaking reasoning.[45]

This was Mao in his most appealing guise. The initiative for this apparent relaxation came from Zhou Enlai, always presented as Mao's most reasonable and open-minded top aide, but Mao adapted Zhou's ideas to his own purpose.[46] The trouble, of course, was that whatever it was that Zhou intended, probably only a relative relaxation of ideological fervor in order to make technically able intellectuals more productive, Mao never meant to be a liberal. He was confident that in the struggle of ideas the "truth," that is, his version of Marxism, would triumph.

There were forces in the CCP who were skeptical about allowing such freedom, but Mao pushed ahead, and a "hundred flowers" did bloom as intellectuals were encouraged to voice their complaints. The torrent of criticism about the harshness and inefficiency of Party rule, about the desires for greater freedom, and about the need for reform astonished and frightened the Party, including Mao, and he soon reversed himself, launching an "Anti-Rightist" movement to "root out all the 'weeds' that had 'bloomed.'" That is, those who had complained were to be singled out and punished.[47]

The consequences for many individual intellectuals, especially those who had naïvely gone along and criticized Party bosses, were shocking. Liang Heng, in the revealing book he wrote in 1983 with his American wife, Judith Shapiro, remembers how Mao's careless temporary enthusiasm for free expression destroyed his family when he was a little boy.

In early 1957 the "Hundred Flowers Movement" had been launched. Mother . . . really loved the Party and didn't have any criticisms to make. . . . Still, her leaders said that everyone should participate. . . . So, regarding it her duty to come up with something, she finally thought of three points she could make. . . . But then, with utterly confusing rapidity, the "Hundred Flowers Movement" changed into the "Anti-Rightist Movement." . . . Anyway, every unit was given a quota of Rightists [to be purged], and Mother's name was among those. . . . Perhaps her section head was angry at her; perhaps her unit was having trouble filling its quota. . . . But there was no court of appeal. Mother was sent away . . . for labor reform.[48]

This eventually led to divorce as Liang Heng's father desperately tried to save the family from the consequences of having a "bad element" among their close relations. But nothing worked, and they were all ruined, with the children being separated from their parents and virtually abandoned.

The Anti-Rightist movement caused a half million people to be "repressed."[49]

In late 1957 and early 1958 a campaign was launched to rid China of the "four pests": rats, sparrows, flies, and mosquitoes. Millions of people were mobilized to chase these grain-eating and disease-spreading pests. Claims which later turned out to be vastly exaggerated were made about the improvement of health as a result of this campaign. At the time, foreigners in China came back with amusing stories of thousands of people chasing flies and sparrows out of devotion to Mao, but the seeming success of this campaign fed the delusions of the Party.[50]

In early 1958 the campaign to mobilize the masses more effectively gathered steam. Targets for economic growth were raised to almost unbelievable heights. As Liu Shaoqi put it, "It should be realised that machines are made and operated by men, and materials are produced only through the efforts of men. It is man that counts; the subjective initiative of the masses is a mighty driving force."[51]

This was standard Marxist fare, as was the obsession to overcome the normal limitations of time by accelerating everything. Stalin had done the same thing, up to a point.[52] But the CCP went much further. Steel production in China in 1957 was 5.35 million tons. In early 1958 the new target of 6.2 million tons was set. In May it was increased to 8 million tons for 1958. In August Mao decided to raise the 1958 target to 10.7 million tons, and by September he was claiming that China would produce between 11 and 12 million tons in 1958, 30 million in 1959, and between 80 and 120 million tons in 1962. By the mid-seventies, he predicted, China would be producing 700 million tons of steel, or more than all other economies in the world combined! In the late 1950s and early 1960s the United States was producing about 100 million tons of steel a year.[53] How was this to be achieved? By throwing the peasants into steel production in their villages. And what resources, what labor would be used for this? Only what was locally available. By such means, developments that had taken centuries in the West, and decades in the Soviet Union, would be accomplished in a few years.

Such a great leap required fantastic agricultural progress, of course, in order to free the peasants' time so that they could become industrial workers. This was no problem because Mao believed that the liberating effects of socialism, new types of miracle rice, water conservancy, and close planting were going to increase yields so quickly that there would soon be overproduction of grain in an economy that had barely managed to feed itself for the centuries. In August, 1958, he said in a speech:

> Yesterday, I could not go to sleep. I have something to tell you all. In the past, who ever dreamed that a *mu* [one-sixth of an acre] of farmland could produce ten thousand catties of grain? [five metric tons, that is 30 tons per acre or 75 tons per hectare!] I never dreamed it. . . . If the situation is allowed to continue, I am afraid our 1.5 billion *mu* of farmland will be too much. Planting one-third of them is enough; another one-third may be turned to grassland; and let the remaining one-third lie fallow. The whole country will thus become a garden.[54]

Indeed, greatly increased yields were possible with new strains of rice, though hardly on such a scale. But added water, fertilizer, and labor were needed.[55] Without new and improved seeds there is no miracle rice. Without extra fertilizer, close planting exhausts the soil faster than traditional methods. Without either more time or machinery, the extra labor required to make improved agriculture work was not available. Mao, however, thought it unnecessary to provide the required investments because enthusiasm would overcome any difficulties.[56]

This was not all. Mao's secretary, Chen Boda, came up with the idea of consolidating village collectives into communes where people would live in dormitories and eat in communal kitchens. This would heighten socialist consciousness, and further regiment and energize the rural masses. This was an old Chinese idea already present during the time of the Taiping, and admired by Mao's intellectual idol Kang Yuwei at the turn of the century. Heavily mythologized Marxists texts about the heroic Paris Commune of 1871 provided the name for this new policy, and the People's Commune movement was approved by Mao in mid-1958. This was not only a way of advancing socialism, but it provided an argument in China's increasingly serious ideological dispute with the Soviet Union by showing that China had leapt ahead of the Soviets in creating full socialism. It also further disrupted village life.[57]

In the communes, huge increases in grain production were planned; and a miraculously accelerated industrialization program was set in motion.

Kang Sheng, Mao's secret police chief, wrote at that time:

Communism is Paradise;
The people's communes are the bridge [to it].[58]

Kang Sheng, who would play an active role in the Cultural Revolution, also happened to have been an old friend, perhaps former lover of Jiang Qing, Mao's wife, and had introduced the Jiang to Mao in the late 1930s. Later Kang Sheng and other police officials would become the main providers of sexual partners for Mao who, according to Harrison Salisbury, "about this time [the early 1960s] . . . by some accounts, began to indulge in sexual water sports, filling his heated indoor swimming pool with bevies of unclad young women." Earlier, Kang Sheng had helped Mao gather together China's best collection of classical pornography.[59] For some, it was a sort of paradise indeed, but not for the hundreds of millions of peasants who now faced the consequences of the Great Leap.

In villages throughout the land peasants were encouraged to bring their iron cooking and farming implements to be melted down to make steel; trees were cut down to be turned into charcoal for smelting; and some 90 million peasants abandoned farming for this new work. Liang Heng remarks that in some areas deforestation was so great that wood remained unavailable a decade later. The steel was of poor quality and could not be used for industrial purposes; the resources used to make it were wasted; but the target of 10.7 tons was achieved. "But in the fields," writes Roderick MacFarquhar, the foremost academic expert on this period, "bumper harvests of grain, cotton and other crops awaited collection. A massive tragedy was in the making."[60]

By 1959 those in the Party who were paying attention to what was going on in villages knew that a famine had begun. But as the frightened rural authorities falsely reported the increased yields expected from all this progress, the amount of grain demanded from the peasants actually increased.[61] Grain rations for peasants in some regions fell to 125 grams a day per person, starvation rations. Some Party officials later estimated that over 40 million died. The economist Nicholas Lardy, citing official Chinese sources, estimates that between 16 and 28 million died. But the effect was concentrated in certain regions, the most overcrowded provinces traditionally subjected to famine in times of crisis, Sichuan, Gansu, Henan, Anhui, and Shandong. In Anhui Province only 40 of 200 families survived in the average village. One-eighth of the people in Gansu Province died. The toll was higher in these regions than in the terrible famines of the early 1930s.[62]

In Chen village in the relatively less affected south, in the words of a villager, "People were so hungry they had difficulty sleeping. . . . Some people became ill, and some of the elderly died. Our village became quiet, as if the people were dead." Knowing that what they would grow in the next year would be confiscated, the peasants in Chen village did not plant for the new year and let their fields go wild.[63]

Dismissing those who worried about technical details as petty and bourgeois, the higher Party cadres came to believe their false statistics and to be impressed with their ability to mobilize hundreds of millions of peasants. As news of hardship spread, Mao and other top officials thought that the deficits were caused by the peasants hiding their surplus grain.[64]

Nevertheless, in 1959 Mao had to admit that his dreams were proving to be unrealistic. Only 8 million of the 10.7 million tons of steel produced in 1958 were any good, and future projections, while remaining fantastically unrealistic, were scaled back. With his usual folksy wisdom he said, "One does not know the difficulties of a thing without experiencing it." The commune system was quietly abandoned, and Mao urged the Party to be easier on the peasants who, he now felt, would take many years to become fully socialist. The Great Leap was not abandoned, but it was toned down.[65]

Ever since he had observed the confusing struggle for power in the Soviet Union after Stalin's death, Mao had been concerned with his own succession. Now, in 1959, Liu Shaoqi, his puritanical, workaholic number two was promoted to the position of head of state, and Mao began to reduce his own activities. But it has never been entirely clear to what extent this was a genuinely voluntary semi-retirement. In any case, in the summer of 1959 the top leaders of the Party held a dramatic conference at Lushan in which the minister of defense, Marshal Peng Dehuai, denounced Mao for his tragic mistakes during the Great

Leap, and openly accused him of having committed "leftist" mistakes because of "petty-bourgeois fanaticism." To combine the epithet of excessive leftism, which Lenin had long ago labelled as infantile, with that of "petty-bourgeois," the ultimate Marxist insult, must have been "infuriating to the originator of the Thought of Mao Zedong, whose greatest intellectual accomplishment was the 'sinification' of Marxism." Mao defended himself by launching a blistering counterattack which resulted in the purge of Peng Dehuai, and reviving Great Leap policies to vindicate himself. But Mao's reputation with his peers, as well as the Party's popularity with the population at large, were seriously damaged.[66]

Nineteen-sixty was a year of drought in the north and devastating typhoons along the coast that brought floods, insect pests, and plant diseases. These natural disasters compounded the effects of the Great Leap, and began to be reminiscent of the kind of multiple catastrophes that signalled a ruling dynasty's loss of the "mandate of heaven." Thus it was a seriously chastened Party elite that finally abandoned the Great Leap in 1960.[67]

Whatever Mao had meant by handing over greater formal power to Liu, after 1960 that became the reality, and with Liu as head of state, Deng Xiaoping as head of the Party, and Zhou Enlai as Prime Minister, Mao was eased into a kind of honored retirement. But Mao deeply resented this, and became unwilling to accept criticism. Deng Xiaoping, who would emerge as the leader of China after Mao's death, and who would dramatically open China to capitalism and the world economy in the late 1970s and 1980s, while remaining a believer in Marxist-Leninist analysis, put it this way: "He [Mao] really behaved in an unhealthy, feudal way."[68]

In his growing isolation and bitterness over his two great failures in the 1950s, the "Hundred Flowers" campaign and the "Great Leap," Mao began what, in retrospect, appears to have been a well-planned campaign to regain pre-eminence and get even with those of his comrades who had sidelined him. His tools for this were the loyalty of the new minister of defense, Marshal Lin Biao, Mao's wife Jiang Qing, who had not, until then, played a major role, his secret police chief Kang Sheng, and of course, his greatest asset, his ideological prestige with the masses of Chinese who did not know about the inner workings of the Party.[69]

The Great Proletarian Cultural Revolution

The Cultural Revolution began in 1966 and lasted, depending on one's definition, either until 1968, when the bulk of the violence and disorder ended, or 1971, when Lin Biao tried to overthrow Mao, failed, fled, and died in a plane crash on his way to the Soviet Union, or to 1976, when Mao finally died. All accounts of it, whether from a personal point of view or through detailed historical analysis, confirm that it was a massively disruptive period in Chinese life. If the loss of life was probably considerably less than in the Great Leap because bizarre and destructive economic policies were not imposed on the peasants, and there was no big famine, nevertheless, many were killed, often after being tortured, and millions were beaten, imprisoned, humiliated, forced to migrate, or otherwise harmed. About one-tenth of China's population, some 100 million, suffered. At least one million died, though some estimates of deaths go as high as 20 million.[70] The fact is that these events produced a massive sense of guilt and self-questioning that allowed Mao's successors to reverse practically all of his cherished socialist, egalitarian, and mass mobilization ideals and strategies.

Was all of this set in motion by one personally corrupted old man's vengeful, idiosyncratic ideological fantasies? There is no doubt that Mao's decisions were at the heart of the Cultural Revolution, though of course alone he could not have done all this if the society established by the communists in the preceding seventeen years had not been so inherently contradictory and conflictual. The combination of Mao's intent to shake up the system that had relegated him to secondary and symbolic importance and the existing strains in the society after so many years of induced conflict, centrally ordered struggle, and economic hardship combined to produced a national cataclysm.

After 1959 Mao's public image changed. He was increasingly deified, even as his reputation among the higher cadres sank. Lin Biao used his position as head of the army to further this image, and Mao clearly concurred. The Party seems to have gone along in order to use Mao as a charismatic, unifying symbol at a time of doubt caused by the failures of the late 1950s.[71] Obviously the rest of the leadership did not realize what was happening, or what the consequences would be. Had they studied the stories of other aging despots who were able to use their carefully nurtured charisma to settle old scores and indulge in personal fantasies, instead of believing in the scientific certitude of their own Marxism, they might have been more careful about controlling Mao.

To be sure, what happened in 1966 was hardly the beginning of
tyranny in communist China. All of the episodes of violence and turmoil
after 1949, whether the murder of millions of class enemies, the persecution of "rightists" after the "Hundred Flowers," or the deaths during
the Great Leap, conform to what we already know about what causes
modern tyranny. Communism came to power with the specific intent of
avenging old grievances, of basing the new China on a theory of society
that emphasized the centrality of inevitable conflict between classes,
and after a long period of economic and political chaos in which the
CCP in general, and Mao in particular, were viewed as national saviors.
These conditions set the stage for the rise to power of a utopian group
of ideologues sure that they had the right answer to all of China's problems, and anyone who stood in their way was in their view not only
unpatriotic, but doomed by the inevitable march of history.

Now Mao added an original element rarely if ever consciously put
in motion by a despotic ruler: he set about weakening and even
destroying much of the apparatus of administrative control built up by
the Party. This he did partly because he genuinely believed that struggle would unleash creative energies, and partly because he was a
utopian egalitarian who disliked the privileges the bureaucracy had
given itself, though evidently he never declined a diet of fine foods for
himself, or the swimming pools in all his residences, or his beautiful
young swimming companions. But also, he unleashed an attack on the
bureaucratic administrative machinery of the Party and state to get
even with his enemies who controlled it.

The result was that his own position was enhanced, and even as he
aged and began to edge toward senility, he became an omnipotent god
whose word could not be questioned. This gave an opportunity to
those below him, particularly his angry, jealous, and vengeful wife, to
exploit his name and power to exercise their vindictive, or, in some
cases, corrupt power. As the whole exercise of power was personalized
far beyond what it had been in the 1950s, and Mao became incapable
of accepting criticism of any sort, he turned on the intellectuals as a
class that might question his omniscience. Though he was an intellectual himself, and he had the backing of a substantial group of radical
young intellectuals, particularly from Shanghai, no group suffered
more during the Cultural Revolution. All higher learning, all educa-

tional attainment, all high culture were systematically devalued, and intellectuals were hounded to death, exiled to menial jobs, tortured for their past accomplishments, and dismissed as irrelevant for the construction of China's future. Mao had boasted in 1957 that the CCP had already killed 400,000 intellectuals. That was only a start.[72]

Since all of this brought more disorder and economic failure, Mao finally had to resort to military dictatorship, and he brought in Lin Biao's army to restore order. That led to the final frustration of the early 1970s, because military rule proved inadequate to foster economic growth. In the last years of his rule Mao sank into near incoherence while China was paralyzed by contradictory policies and an emerging power struggle between those who wanted to return to a semblance of well-administered order and those who sought to cling to "The Chairman's" revolutionary image in order to keep themselves in power after his demise.

It all began quietly enough in 1965 with Mao's attack against Beijing's vice-mayor, Wu Han, who had written an earlier article criticizing a Ming Emperor who had dismissed an honest official for criticizing corruption. This gradually turned into an attack against Peng Zhen, the mayor of Beijing. The political scientist Hong Yung Lee does not believe that there was a meticulous plan to begin with, but that Mao was probing for ideological weaknesses within the Party elite he opposed, and as the situation developed in early 1966, he was pushed into seizing this opportunity by Lin Biao who had been using the army to stir ideological disputes.[73]

There was also Jiang Qing, Mao's wife. In her early adult years, like Evita Perón (who will discussed in a later chapter) she had been a beautiful but minor actress. Ambitious, self-serving, and able to use sex to her advantage, she had fled to the communist region along with other young idealistic intellectuals in the late 1930s, and gotten herself into Mao's bed. When they were married (she was his third wife) the Party had insisted that she should be relegated to political insignificance. There she had remained throughout the 1940s and 1950s, as Mao lost interest in her. But now, in the early 1960s, losing power, and already ill from Parkinson's disease, he turned to her as a helpmate in his political struggle. Allied with Lin Biao and his wife, who shared Jiang Qing's hatred of Liu Shaoqi's more accomplished and politically powerful wife, Jiang helped plan the increasingly theatrical displays that were designed to enhance Mao's god-like image. She also actively cemented and co-ordinated political plots between Mao, Lin Biao, and the secret police chief Kang Sheng, her probable former lover. She found young supporters to help her, and for a few years, with Mao's help, she was able to direct policy. Much of her power was used to get revenge against old Party leaders who had crossed her, to eradicate all memory of her less than politically or morally pure past, and to foster groups of Red Guards who could be counted on to destroy the old administrative machinery. Her struggle, unlike Mao's, seems to have been based on almost pure resentment and lust for the trappings of power rather than on any considered ideology; but as Mao weakened physically, she became the critically important transmitter of his thoughts.[74]

On May 16, 1966, Mao established the "Central Cultural Revolution Small Group" to oversee propaganda and fight against "moderate" Party forces that wanted to stop the effects of the Wu Han and Peng Zhen affair from spreading. Jiang Qing and Mao's "personal secretary and alter ego for nearly thirty years, the man who personified Mao's most evil impulses," Chen Boda, the same man who had come up with the idea of the communes at the time of the Great Leap, were put in charge.[75] This organization, a kind of "kitchen cabinet" to Mao, had begun as an informal group of advisors, but now took on official functions. The Party itself, however, still remained under the control of Liu Shaoqi and Deng Xiaoping, so that the radical Maoists had to use their control over propaganda to launch their attack against it.[76]

On May 25, 1966, a lecturer in philosophy at Beijing University put up a "big-character poster" (a political commentary put up on a public wall in large characters) denouncing the university authorities for suppressing the spontaneous student movement that was emerging in support of the newly labelled Cultural Revolution. The university authorities tried to suppress this manifestation of protest, but on June 1 Mao ordered Kang Sheng to broadcast the content of the poster over Beijing Radio. This encouraged students who were opposed to the authorities to organize and demonstrate, sometimes violently, and the movement spread to other universities, colleges, and secondary schools. The authorities in the Party tried to resist and labelled the young protesters "monsters and freaks."[77] In Shanghai, China's biggest city, the mayor publicly called on "Party members, Youth League members, the masses of peasants and workers, and revolutionary cadres and intellectuals to carry the Great Proletarian Cultural Revolution through to the end."[78]

Within schools, and spreading into various cities, there were growing numbers of violent clashes between supporters of the Cultural Revolution and those backing the regular Party order. Big-character posters appeared denouncing various past abuses of power and urging more participants to join "Red Guard" groups. These were groups of protesting youths inspired by ideological fervor, by youthful exuberance, by the growing perception that such activity might lead to politically favored careers, and increasingly by the wish to get even for the hardships and humiliations in their lives. On August 8, 1966, Mao's Central Committee prohibited the public security apparatus—the police and army—from suppressing new political groups. This was the key step, because it meant that not only those from previously favored social categories, but anyone, even youths from the "seven black categories" (landlords, rich peasants, counterrevolutionaries, bad elements, rightists, bourgeois, and reactionary intellectuals) could organize and perhaps get back into political favor, or at least, take out their frustrations against the established "good elements" and cadres who had been persecuting them for so long.[79]

After this, all hell broke loose. Did Mao intend this? As usual, his pronouncements were somewhat ambiguous. Clearly, the fact that all Red Guard factions claimed to be the purest of Maoists, and that the growing disorder played into his hands against his Party enemies pleased him. But at the same time, it had always been part of his philosophy to believe in the abstract goodness of struggle. After almost two decades in which individuals were systematically persecuted, denied promotions, humiliated, and often tortured and killed because they or their families were from "black categories," he could blandly declare that "some of the students did not have terribly good family backgrounds, but were our own family backgrounds all that good?"[80] He was telling the truth, of course, and for those who had suffered from the "blood pedigree theory" of class, there was new hope. On the other hand, for the previously favored families of good workers and cadres, this was extremely dangerous, because they were now subjected to attacks by the previously disfavored. An old truth was replaced by a new one. Before, it had been:

If the father's a hero, the son's a good chap;
If the father's a reactionary, the son's a bad egg.[81]

The most loyal of the "good elements" were the cadres who were in charge of China. But now, their favored position was threatened, because, as Mao had put it in 1965 while preparing the coming changes, "The bureaucratic class is a class sharply opposed to the working class and the poor and the lower-middle peasants. These people have become or are in the process of becoming bourgeois elements sucking the blood of the workers."[82] Again, as we have known all along from studying communist societies since Milovan Djilas's pathbreaking study of the communist "New Class," there was a lot of truth to this.

Yet, to overthrow the cadres meant destroying the expertise built up over almost two decades. It meant throwing central planning away. Thus, Liu Shaoqi had tried even in the late 1950s to put forward the idea that the class struggle had been won, and in the future it would suffice to pick successors from the proper class elements. But Mao would have none of it because to accept Liu's interpretation meant that the days of revolutionary turmoil were over, and the hope of establishing full equality were ended. As the Cultural Revolution developed in 1966, students from "bad" backgrounds seized on certain parts of the Maoist texts that emphasized that class status was more a matter of how one was behaving in the present rather than one's family roots, whereas those from "good" backgrounds stressed the importance of the "good chap vs. bad egg" dichotomy based on family origin.[83]

Lynn T. White III's analysis of the Cultural Revolution in Shanghai shows that this soon became the critical fault line between relatively conservative (status quo) Red Guards and radical Red Guard groups. The latter were largely made up of youths from "bad" elements. The former were youths from proper worker or cadre backgrounds fighting to maintain their futures and those of their families from the vicious and vengeful attacks of the ultra-Maoist radicals. As long as Mao, Jiang Qing, and Lin Biao backed the ultra-leftists, they encouraged a civil war with enormous implications because its outcome could determine social stratification for the next generation. Hong Yung Lee's older study agrees, and Liang Heng's personal account of how he and his friends from "bad" backgrounds eagerly joined the radical Red Guards to salvage their futures and prove that they, not the privileged "good" elements, were the best Maoists confirms the general accuracy of this interpretation.

Heng, who was only 12 at the time, writes:

> I thought this was a great idea [to launch a local Cultural Revolution with his friends]. We would be following Chairman Mao just like the grown-ups, and Father would be proud of me. I suppose too I resented the teachers who had controlled me and criticized me for so long, and I looked forward to a little revenge.[84]

But setting loose such youths, encouraging them to go an their own little "Long Marches," to struggle and expose counterrevolutionaries among older intellectuals and cadres, was to ask for trouble. In fact the Cultural Revolution not only sparked violence, sometimes on a large scale, between opposing Red Guard bands, but also between Red Guards and workers trying to defend their factories.[85]

As disorder spread and growing numbers of teachers, managers, and even important cadres were singled out for humiliation and punishment, as millions of youths were set free from schools to join Red Guard movements, the country was paralyzed by anarchy. Youths whose lives had been hemmed in by poverty and harsh discipline imposed by their elders jumped on trains to wander around and spread revolution. In some places they were met with violence from frightened local workers and cadres, in others they were allowed to scrounge for food and lodging.[86]

Now with the bureaucracy in disgrace and central authority crumbling, Mao could take his personal revenge. In January 1967, he held a last interview with Liu Shaoqi, once his most devoted follower. He told Liu to study and read Hegel and Diderot! Then Liu and his wife, Wang Guangmei, were arrested. They were tortured, and in August 1967, Liu's children were made to watch their father and mother tortured and savagely beaten in front of thousands of screaming Red Guards. Liu's medicine for diabetes was taken away from him. His teeth were knocked out. In September Jiang Qing publicly called for Liu's death, but specified that he should die slowly "by a thousand cuts, by ten thousand cuts." Then Zhou Enlai, who was spared this fate because he had befriended Jiang Qing in the 1950s, when Mao was ignoring her, managed to get Liu some medical help. But he barely remained alive, and in November 1969, he died lying naked on the cement floor of a provincial prison to which he had been removed. His family were not told. Zhou persuaded Mao to save the life of his wife, Wang Guangmei, even though Jiang Qing and Lin Biao wanted her dead, too. But Wang Guangmei's mother was tortured to death to try to force a confession out of her about her daughter's supposed "espionage" activities. Liu's eldest son was beaten to death, and his family told he had committed suicide. Liu's second son was kept in a dark cell for eleven years. He was released in 1978 and died three months later of the tuberculosis he had contracted in prison. Wang Guangmei herself was only released in 1979, three years after Mao's death.[87]

There were thousands of other cases like this among top Chinese communists and leading intellectuals.[88] Deng Xiaoping was exiled to a village. His life was spared because Mao wanted him saved, but Deng's eldest son, Deng Pufang, a student of physics at Beijing University, was savagely tortured by student Red Guards and thrown out a window. He survived, but has been crippled ever since.[89]

Throughout the society similar episodes occurred. Liang Heng tells how Red Guards burst into his house and began to swear at his father.

> —"Shit. You've always been a liar!" Two Red Guards took him by each arm and grabbed his head, pushing it down so he was forced to kneel on the floor. They shook him by the hair so his glasses fell off, and when he groped for them, they kicked his hands away.
>
> "Liar!"
>
> —The others were already starting to go through our things. . . . Then one of them cried out.
>
> —"Quite a fox, isn't he? We said he was a liar." The Red Guard had two Western ties and a Western-style jacket. "What's the meaning of this?"
>
> —"Ties," my father mumbled.
>
> —They kicked him. "Ties! Do you think we're children? Everyone knows these are ties. Capitalist ties. Or hadn't you heard?"
>
> —Father was pointing excitedly. "They were ordered through the newspaper. For some jobs. It wasn't my idea. For receptions and—" The spring slammed down on his hand and he cringed in pain.[90]

In early 1993 evidence even surfaced of hundreds of episodes of cannibalism in Quangxi Province. One school principal was eaten by students after being murdered. The students wanted to prove how "red" they were. This may have been the most extensive case of documented cannibalism in the world in the twentieth century in which acute hunger was not a motive. Only after Mao's death were some of the perpetrators of this horror expelled from the Party.[91]

The idealism of millions of youths was used by those maneuvering for power at the top. They were encouraged to behave in shameful ways, and those among them who were violent, or vicious, were tolerated.

Then, in 1968, with Mao and his associates firmly in power, they decided to stop the whole thing because it was making China ungovernable. Between 60 and 80 percent of the cadres had been purged. Mao turned to Lin Biao's army which now imposed order, disbanded the Red Guards, and sent millions of politically active youths off to the countryside to "rusticate." This had been done before to get rid of what were thought to be excessive numbers of urban youths, but now it occurred on a much larger scale than ever before. In effect, a whole generation of students was sent off to remote villages and denied education. Military order was imposed throughout the country. This displeased Mao, it alienated Zhou Enlai who preferred to return to a more conventional form of centralized planning and control, and it also alienated the radicals around Jiang Qing who lost influence. Against these forces, Lin Biao was outnumbered, and he plotted to take power. He failed, fled, and died in an airplane crash in Mongolia.[92]

However, this did not end the nightmare. Throughout the land people tried to adapt to the rapidly changing political struggles in Beijing. First one group then another would rise to the top, only to be disgraced as campaigns against their line of action were launched. It was no longer clear who could be trusted, who were the good or bad elements, nor even what was appropriate behavior.

In Chen village the peasants tried to pick on former "bad elements," as they hoped this would save them from further troubles. But they were forced to go on. The village had had some youths from the city sent there before the Cultural Revolution, but these had gone off to join the Red Guards. Now some were sent back and became targets of persecution. Old village leaders were picked on and blamed for past or imagined political shortcomings. Finally, the villagers started to persecute those who were just unpopular, particularly a few quarrelsome old women who could be connected through family ties to bad elements.

One such woman, who was merely a helpless old shrew, was subjected to such abuse and public humiliation that she went mad and died a few weeks later of shock.[93]

The ensuing years, until Mao's death, did not see a return to stability as various forces contended for power. Jiang Qing and those around her, chiefly Kang Sheng and Chen Boda, tried to keep up the hysteria of the Cultural Revolution, while Zhou Enlai tried to bring back administrative order. Mao himself sank into semi-senility, like Stalin and Hitler in their last days. Mao had long been a virtual drug addict. Even in the 1930s he suffered from terrible constipation, for which he took medicine, and insomnia, which turned him into a sleeping pill addict. This was common among the top leaders of the CCP, partly because they had to adapt to Mao's habits and stay up all night. (Strangely, both Stalin and Hitler followed the same sleeping habits.) In fact, that had been part of the beginning of the torture of many of Mao's closest aides who were purged during the Cultural Revolution: they had been deprived of their sleeping pills. This had driven Liu Shaoqi and Peng Dehuai almost insane. Lin Biao was a morphine addict. Harrison Salisbury, who interviewed many of the top survivors from the elite, even speculates that some of the more grotesque aspects of the Cultural Revolution were the result of drug-induced delusions and paranoia.[94] But in the 1970s, Mao's condition further deteriorated.

To receive guests or appear in public, Mao had to be propped up and dressed. That was enough to impress Richard Nixon (who also befriended Ceausescu, two men who, he felt, knew how to use power). Commands continued to be issued in his name, and purges continued in fits and starts. Deng Xiaoping was brought back to power, then had to flee and go into virtual hiding to avoid retribution from Jiang Qing who wanted him out of the way. Finally Mao died, and Jiang Qing and her closest associates were arrested, tried, and sentenced to prison.[95]

In a way, the Cultural Revolution saved China. The shock and humiliation of what happened were so widely felt and open to public scrutiny that the Communist Party and its leadership were forced to admit that there was little left to be saved of Maoism. This is why Deng Xiaoping was able to change China so quickly after 1978. Presumably, if Liu Shaoqi had remained in power through the 1960s and 1970s, a more thoroughly socialist, more tightly centralized, planned economy would have survived. In the long run that might have been even worse for China than the Cultural Revolution.

Nevertheless, Mao and the system the CCP set up produced some very large tragedies which ruined the lives of hundreds of millions of people. This ultimately happened because of the ideological vision which pushed them into making terrible economic blunders. It happened because they believed that classes had to be antagonistic to each other, and that class struggle was the law of history. It happened because too much power fell into the hands of a tiny elite, and because one of them, Mao, was deified. Once this kind of system and ideology was in power, the normal play of human passions, jealousies, idealisms, and imperfections made some sort of tragedy inevitable.

Mao, like Hitler, Stalin, and other ideological despots, was disappointed when he saw that his grand ideas were not working out as he thought they should. Briefly sidelined, he took his personal and ideological revenge by making things even worse. It was left to the much more pragmatic and less ideological Deng Xiaoping to try to fix things, though it remains to be seen whether or not Mao's legacy will ever be fully exorcised.

In 1963 Mao expressed the fear that if continuing class struggle were not pursued, the Chinese Communist Party might allow capitalist restoration to take place and turn itself into a fascist organization.[96] If by this he meant what Marxists usually (even if wrongly) mean by fascism, the dictatorship of the high bourgeoisie that monopolizes wealth and privilege and suppresses discontent by any means necessary, he was not so wrong. To be sure, the Chinese Communist Party of the late 1980s and early 1990s was not the tool of a classical high bourgeoisie, but it was a substantial, corrupt elite that parasitically fed on the economy without any longer having much of a useful function, and it was determined to hold on to power at any cost, as the events of June 1989 at Tiananmen Square demonstrated. Mao was not motivated purely by his hatreds and vengefulness, though these clearly played a role. He was a far-sighted and genuine socialist idealist. He knew how difficult it would be to carry out his dream. Unfortunately, he thought he could do it, and he tried. In so doing, he not only tyrannized a billion people, but he brought them closer to the outcome he most feared. Whatever happens to China in the future, it is most unlikely that socialist idealism will ever be rekindled, even if the Party retains its privileges and power.

DELUSIONS OF UTOPIAN GRANDEUR IN
DEMOCRATIC KAMPUCHEA

The excesses of the communist government in power in Cambodia from 1975 to 1978 have become a symbol of the nightmarish excesses of late twentieth-century totalitarianism. The rule of the "Khmer Rouge" (that is, the Red or Communist Cambodians, so labelled by Prince Sihanouk when he was ruler of the country) was terrible. Ben Kiernan, a foremost expert on modern Khmer history, estimates that about one and a half million Cambodians died as a result of outright killing, starvation, and disease caused by their policies.[97] David Chandler, another specialist in this field, estimates that "in less than four years, more than one million Cambodians, or one in seven, probably died from malnutrition, overwork, and mis-diagnosed or mistreated illness. At least 100,000, and probably more, were executed for crimes against the state. Tens of thousands perished in the conflict with Vietnam, almost certainly started by the Red Khmer."[98] Michael Vickery, who among the knowledgeable historians of this subject comes closest to being an apologist of what he admits was hardly a defensible regime, considers such estimates propagandistic and somewhat unconvincingly lowers the number to 400,000.[99] Even this would mean that in a little over three years the Khmer Rouge were responsible for a slaughter in their country proportionately on the same order as was Stalin's during the collectivization drive in the early 1930s, and greater than the deaths during the Chinese Great Leap Forward. The reality is such that it is safe to call this tragedy an unprecedented case of what Jean Lacouture has called "autogenocide."[100]

Accurate enumeration of the number of dead in such tragedies is impossible. We have seen that estimates about the number killed directly or indirectly by Stalin's collectivization and purges vary considerably, as do those about the number who died in China because of Maoist policies. A more precise count is only possible in the case of Hitler, largely because practically all of the relevant records have been made available and because the Germans were far better record keepers than any other modern mass murderers. Even there, however, substantial questions remain about the number of deaths, especially with respect to communities without good records, for example the Roma. Cambodia was a largely agrarian society with poor census materials to begin with. Then it was subjected to a brutal and disruptive war before the Khmer Rouge took power. After the Khmer Rouge were over-thrown by a Vietnamese invasion in 1979, more than a decade of con-tinued fighting ensued, partly against the Vietnamese, but also a civil war. Even after a peace agreement was signed between the various Cambodian factions in 1991, fighting continued. Under such condi-tions, no accurate count of the dead can ever be made. But whether 10 or 20 percent of the population died as a result of the Khmer Rouge regime, there is no question that this was an atrocious period.

To make things worse, in the five years before 1975, when the Khmer Rouge took power, some half million Cambodians were killed by a war that was thrust on Cambodia by the United States of America as a by-product of its failed Vietnam policy. During that war over a mil-lion Cambodians were made refugees.[101]

What happened in Cambodia was as bad as anything that has hap-pened in the twentieth century. It was the product of very angry, frus-trated nationalism, some of it based on real grievances developed during Cambodia's colonial history, and then greatly exacerbated by the effects of the American war. The top ranks of the Khmer Rouge elite, however, shared a utopian vision of society that, once it was applied, turned Cambodia into a complete hell, far worse than any-thing that had happened before. This vision was based on a fabricated, idealized sense of Khmer history, a utopian, egalitarian ideology similar to, but even more extreme than Maoism, and a Maoist organizational structure well suited to fighting a long guerrilla war against better armed urban enemies.

The American bombing that began in 1969, and the invasion of Cambodia that followed in 1970, were supposed to eliminate Viet-namese communist base camps on the Cambodian-South Vietnamese border, and to break communist lines of communication from North Vietnam to the South that went through Laos and Cambodia. Instead, it pushed the Vietnamese communists more deeply into Cambodia, and the bombing followed them. There ensued a five-year war that gave the Khmer Rouge their chance by making them the only possible protectors of rural Cambodians, much as the Japanese invasion of northern China gave the Chinese communists their opportunity to take power. It was not the Americans who created the Khmer Rouge or gave them their ideology, any more than the Japanese created the Chi-nese Communists, but the American government and its South Viet-namese ally from 1970 to 1975 humiliated and ruined Cambodia and created a noncommunist government so corrupt and inefficient that its fall to the Khmer Rouge was made almost inevitable once the Americans decided the game was not worth the cost. Whatever the rationale of the American intervention in Vietnam, Richard Nixon's and Henry Kissinger's Cambodian policies had no serious prospect of yielding positive results, and in retrospect, were caused less by any serious strategic goals than by the American government's desire to save face by persuading the North Vietnamese that the Americans could be irrationally destructive unless given favorable terms for leaving Vietnam. Their policies did make life more difficult for the North Vietnamese, who had to lengthen their lines of communication by going more deeply into Cambodia, but they did not decisively damage the communist effort. They did, however, destroy whatever chance Cambodia had of escaping destruction.[102]

While this is not an appropriate work in which to discuss American policy in Indochina, there is little question that in areas where they are protected from public scrutiny democratic governments can behave tyrannically and inflict enormous, cruel damage for unworthy reasons. This was certainly the case with respect to France's colonial policy in Equatorial Africa, as we will see in a later chapter. The French government in the early part of the twentieth century worked to keep that policy hidden from its public opinion at home. Similarly, the American government tried hard to keep its people from knowing what was going on in Cambodia in the early 1970s, for many of the same reasons. The effects of American policy were cruel and contradicted democratic values, so that public knowledge could only result in a reversal of that policy. This certainly confirms the notion that the only defense against tyranny is not to count on honest rulers, but to have an open, well-informed democracy. And if democratic states are to behave properly, eschewing tyrannical behavior abroad as well as at home, the same openness is necessary in foreign as in domestic affairs.

Yet, if the results of American policy may have been that the Khmer Rouge came to power, this does not answer the question of why these particular communists had an ideology that made everything so much worse than under many other communist regimes around the world. After all, the United States did much the same to Laos as to Cambodia, and also to Vietnam, though on a larger scale. These policies did not, however, bring to power communist regimes as vicious as the Khmer Rouge. The Laotian communists were dominated by the Vietnamese, and the Vietnamese communists themselves, for all their cruelties and misguided policies, never came close to committing autogenocide. For one thing, the Vietnamese were much more self-confident, and less afraid than the Cambodians that their entire nation might be swept away. Then, by comparison, they were much more politically experienced, far less utopian, and more pragmatic. Perhaps, also, it helped the Vietnamese communists that in the Sino-Soviet dispute of the 1960s and 1970s they relied increasingly on Soviet support to help balance the power of China, and Mao's fantastic experiments during the Great Leap Forward and the Cultural Revolution had little appeal to them. Soviet communism during this period, of course, was far from being the utopian, crusading movement it had once been. Cambodia's communists, on the other hand, were more isolated than Vietnam's, they were desperately afraid that they might be taken over by the Vietnamese, they overcompensated for their insecurity by adopting extraordinarily grandiose dreams, and, insofar as they had any working model, it was Maoist China at its worst during the Cultural Revolution.[103]

Colonialism and the Origin of the Myth of Angkor

When the French made Cambodia a protectorate in 1863, as part of the project that would make all of Indochina (Vietnam, Laos, and Cambodia) part of France's Empire, it was on the verge of disappearing as a distinct political entity. Without French intervention, it would have become a part of the newly expansionist, vigorously modernizing Thai kingdom to its west. The Khmer kings were already vassals of the Thais. In the east, the Vietnamese were moving westward after having earlier conquered the Muslim Cham-speaking people in what is now southern Vietnam, and they ruled over substantial areas inhabited by Khmer speakers. At one time Khmer civilization had dominated not only Cambodia and parts of southern Vietnam, but much of modern Thailand. The Mon people, linguistically and religiously similar to the Khmer, had ruled southern Burma and also parts of Thailand. Both Thai and Burmese invaders from the north had taken much of their statecraft, Buddhism, and high civilization from the Khmer and Mon. The Vietnamese, on the other hand, were primarily influenced by Confucian Chinese civilization rather than by India which was the source of much Khmer-Mon religion and political theory.[104]

Nevertheless, French rule was not welcomed. There was no sense of nationalism, and for most of the people, whether they were ruled by this or that kingdom made little difference as long as they were not taxed more. The French, however, did impose new taxes and rules. As for the elite, particularly the provincial officials, they wanted to preserve their privileges and slaves, something the French threatened by introducing private property, centralizing taxation, and outlawing slavery.[105] The colonial period was marked by a series of uprisings and, in the 1920s and 1930s, by the spread of a Vietnamese syncretic religious movement, the Cao Dai, that was viewed as dangerously chiliastic by the French. The slumps in agricultural prices in the 1930s led to further unrest, but the level of both urbanization and education was so low that Cambodia did not, at that time, develop a major communist movement, unlike neighboring Vietnam.[106]

A movement to renovate Buddhism and make it more relevant to the modern world was, however, repressed by the French. The French also relegated the traditional Khmer Buddhist intellectuals and high court culture to irrelevancy, and they were slow to develop a modern school system or a substantial new intellectual elite. Compared to the rest of Southeast Asia, with the exception of Laos, Cambodia remained the least developed, least educated country.[107]

This meant that the more developed nationalism in neighboring countries played an important role in fostering modern Khmer nationalism. The first important independence party, the Khmer Issarak, was founded in Thailand, and Khmer Krom (that is, those from Cochinchina, the southern third of Vietnam) played a major role in developing both a nationalist doctrine and in founding, with Vietnamese help, the Cambodian communist movement. The Cochinchinese had much greater access to French higher education, and as inhabitants of a French colony, rather than of the Cambodian protectorate still bound by a traditional monarchical system, they had more rights.[108]

Tardy as it was, it was inevitable that some sort of Cambodian nationalism would emerge from colonial rule. A few intellectuals were educated, and a nationalist newspaper began publication in 1936. Contact with the powerful West, the imposition of a centralized administration, and the opening of schools to train "natives" produced this result everywhere, though, compared to other Southeast Asian colonies, Cambodia was about a generation behind.[109]

The French contributed something else: the myth of Angkor and of past Khmer greatness based on a communal, highly regimented social system able to bring in three rice crops a year because it could mobilize such concentrated labor power to irrigate and work its fields. This was actually another version of the European myth about the fabled "Asiatic" type of civilization. One of its manifestations was Karl Marx's hypothesis about the existence of an "Asiatic mode of production," a theoretical construction that was popular among Marxist historians and intellectuals in the 1950s and 1960s, especially in France, where it led to an explosion of frequently doubtful scholarship which identified this "mode of production" as having existed throughout much of the world, from the Inca Empire to Madagascar, and naturally in Indochina as well.[110] A particularly influential version of this theory, according to Ben Kiernan, was propounded by Bernard-Philippe Groslier in the 1950s, though in the 1970s he would admit that he had been wrong and that there was no evidence that the ancient irrigation canals found in central Cambodia had ever been used for more intensive rice cultivation than that practiced in modern times.[111]

It is quite true that there are magnificent temples in central Cambodia, and the complex at Angkor Wat, built in stages from the seventh to the twelfth centuries, is spectacular. When the French found it in the nineteenth century, abandoned to the tropical jungle, with its wealth of sculptures inspired by Hindu influences, they fell in love with the romantic dreams the place inspired. This fascination with ancient Khmer religion, art, and statecraft remained an inspiration for several generations of French archaeologists, historians, colonial administrators, and esthetes, the most famous of whom was André Malraux who wrote a novel about his experiences there, *La Voie Royale*. As it happened, Malraux was equally intrigued by China, and he wrote a highly romanticized novel about revolutionaries fighting against the Kuomintang in China in 1927, *La Condition Humaine*.

The reality of modern Khmer life was quite different. The mass of people in the heart of the country were poor peasants surviving at a low economic level, and around the edges of Cambodia the peasants were even more backward and hostile to the small urban elite that consisted of the royal palace and its officials, the colonial rulers, and the largely Chinese merchant class that migrated into the colony to take advantage of new opportunities, much as the Chinese had migrated into other Southeast Asian societies.[112] But for the urban intellectuals trained after World War II in France or in French schools in Cambodia's capital, Phnom Penh, the drab and backward reality of their Cambodia was much less exciting than the visions of past greatness which so appealed to the French themselves.

The theory about past greatness suggested to some intellectuals that it was possible to overcome the obvious backwardness and relative insignificance of their nation in contemporary times. It was not only Saloth Sar (who later called himself Pol Pot and would become the leader of the Khmer Rouge) who was seized by this image of the past; so were noncommunist nationalists like Lon Nol, who became the head of the anti-communist regime that was in power until 1975. The symbol of Angkor Wat has been on all Cambodian flags since independence from France.[113] The myth of the past also strengthened resentment and fear among Cambodian intellectuals. If they had been great in the past, and now were not, this meant that the trend was toward extinction, as had been the case with the neighboring Cham-speaking people, whose once great empire had vanished. The fact that in the past conquest by a new empire did not imply "racial extinction," or even forced conversion to a different culture—the Chams, for example, continued to thrive without their own empire into the twentieth century—was lost on these intellectuals. As we have seen in the chapter explaining the rise of fascism and communism in Europe in the late nineteenth and early twentieth centuries, modern nationalism in its European form had reached the conclusion by the late nineteenth century that life among nations was a matter of struggling for supremacy and either conquering or being destroyed. Khmer intellectuals imbued with French ideas believed the same thing, and consequently they identified the Vietnamese, past conquerors of the Chams, and now the most numerous and most important people in French Indochina, as their hereditary racial enemy.[114]

In 1977 when the communists, led by Pol Pot, were in power, they would declare that "The Chams are hopeless. They abandoned their country to others. they just shouldered their fishing nets and walked off, letting the Vietnamese take over their whole country."[115] That contempt and the belief that the Chams were racially untrustworthy was one of the justifications for the subsequent wholesale slaughter of the Cham minority in Cambodia by the Khmer Rouge, and for the attempt to scatter and forcefully assimilate the remainder in 1977 and 1978.[116]

But if the perception that Cambodia was threatened with racial extinction was not limited to the intellectuals who became the leaders

of the Khmer Rouge, the communists added another element to this
mythology, namely the Marxist notion that within Cambodia itself
there also had to be a class war for survival as desperate as the struggle
against foreign, that is, chiefly Vietnamese conquest. Thus, they
believed that to succeed they had to recreate Angkor's greatness, fight
off the Vietnamese, and wage class warfare, all at the same time.

Independence and Neutrality: The Sihanouk Years

Though there was considerable unrest in Cambodia after World War
II, and a lingering anti-colonial uprising, it was the better organized
and highly mobilized Vietnamese Communist Party that defeated the
French army and precipitated the rush to establish independent states
in the rest of French Indochina in 1954. The French used the seemingly docile Cambodian royal court, whose young King was Norodom
Sihanouk, to lead the new Cambodian state. Sihanouk proved to be
much better than the French had expected. He was an excellent, if
autocratic politician who made himself genuinely popular. He greatly
expanded the educational system. But Sihanouk was also intolerant of
criticism and he tightly controlled his intellectuals. Furthermore, the
Cambodian education system did not train its students for technical or
commercial work, and urban commerce remained largely Chinese, as
in most of the rest of Southeast Asia. The poorly trained, semi-educated
graduates coming out of the new Cambodian education system had
trouble finding work.

Sihanouk's foreign policy was based on befriending China and
appearing to be a supporter of "Third World" progressivism. This legitimized the spread of Maoist ideology among the young intellectuals.
Sihanouk was a kind of Khmer Tsar, like Peter or Catherine the Great.
At least this is what he wanted to be, an enlightened, modernizing
despot. He promoted nationalism, trained a newly educated, but frustrated intelligentsia, and encouraged this new elite to adopt a foreign
ideology that made the contradiction between a backward domestic
reality and that ideology's goals all the more glaring.

There were several different strands of nationalism that developed
in these circumstances. One was conservative and culturally anti-modern
and anti-western. Another was a growing communist movement that
was ostensibly, but not really, the exact opposite.[117]

It was Sihanouk's genius that he seemed, for a time, to embody these conflicting currents. Other Southeast Asians in the newly independent states after World War II tried to play similar roles, but ultimately, all failed, as did Sihanouk. Sukarno of Indonesia was at once a nationalist modernizer, a leftist, at ease with "Third World" forces and the Chinese communists, but also a traditional Hindu-Javanese leader. U Nu of Burma was a socialist, also a leading "Third World" figure, but still very much of a Buddhist whose political roots were in the revolutionary religious movement that had organized against the British in the pre-war period. U Nu, Sukarno, and Sihanouk were all overthrown, in 1962, 1965, and 1970, respectively, by military men who were less Westernized and educated than their more sophisticated predecessors. Generals Ne Win in Burma, Suharto in Indonesia, and Lon Nol in Cambodia were all deeply superstitious, traditionally authoritarian figures who rose to power as military power brokers. All three also represented a particular strain of nationalism. The most successful of them, Suharto, managed to eliminate the major competing, leftist strand of nationalism by annihilating the large Indonesian Communist Party. Lon Nol tried to do the same in Cambodia, but failed catastrophically.[118]

Much of the analysis of "Third World" nationalism has failed to recognize the depth of conservative and anti-modern (as opposed to simply "anti-imperialist") feeling that has been at its heart. Leaders like Sukarno or Sihanouk, seemingly so at ease with European ways and with the language, if not the substance of the Enlightenment, reinforced this mistaken perception. The association of nationalism with "progressive" socialism and communism during and after World War II, for example in China, Yugoslavia, Vietnam, and Cuba, seemed to confirm the error. Yet, in many cases, communism captured a significant portion of that extremely anti-Western, reactive, and bitterly resentful nationalism which was an important part of the anti-Western reaction. Where it succeeded in doing this, communism reinforced its nationalistic credentials, without which it could not effectively take power and rule. This was certainly so in the cases we have already examined in this book—Russia and China—as well as in North Korea and Romania, which will be discussed in the next chapter. It was to prove true in Cambodia as well.

Many of the Khmer Rouge elite received some higher education in France in the late 1940s and early 1950s, after attending an elite secondary school in Phnom Penh. Most of the important Khmer Rouge leaders—Saloth Sar (Pol Pot), Hu Nim, Ieng Sary (Pol Pot's brother-in-law), Khieu Samphan, and Hou Yuon—followed this trajectory. There were some Khmer Rouge leaders with little formal education, of course, such as Heng Samrin (who was installed as Cambodia's head by the Vietnamese after their war against the Khmer Rouge in the late 1970s), and the notoriously bloody Ta Mok, a peasant rebel who eventually became Pol Pot's military leader. But the intellectuals predominated. In their Marxist discussion circle in France, their ideology was more anti-royalist and nationalist than communist and internationalist. In particular, from the start in the early 1950s, these French-trained Khmer, unlike older Cambodian communists who were influenced by the Vietnamese, looked back at the idealized Khmer Empire as a model.[119]

Later, in official documents explaining Cambodian history, the Khmer Rouge would stress the wonder of Angkor, which was seen as a unique wonder of the world, built without outside influences. This made the Khmer Rouge believe that they could work miracles by returning their population to its pristine rural condition, and breaking all contacts with the outside world. To make this ideal more Marxist, the wonders of Angkor were ascribed to the "people," not to their exploitative masters. Thus, to return to an even more perfect version of the past, the Cambodian peasants would have to rid themselves of their class exploiters, who were also identified as being in league with foreign, that is, primarily Vietnamese interests.[120]

Even after the fact, after the enormous number of deaths, Pol Pot would claim that only Vietnamese and those having "Khmer bodies with Vietnamese minds" had been killed. Khieu Samphan, the formal head of state during the Khmer Rouge regime, would write later that 3,000 had been killed because of the regime's "mistakes," 30,000 had been killed by "Vietnamese agents," 11,000 had been killed because they were "Vietnamese agents," and about 1.5 million had died because of "Vietnamese aggression."[121] In 1977, when in power, Pol Pot said, "Long ago, there was Angkor. Angkor was built in the era of slavery. Slaves like us built Angkor under the exploitation of the exploiting classes, so that these royal people could be happy. If our people can make Angkor, they can make anything."[122]

Pol Pot would claim that he had been a peasant and a plantation worker. Actually, he was born in 1928 in a landowner's family. In the 1920s, one of his cousins became an important royal mistress. Later, one of Pol Pot's sisters took on the same role, and a brother became a clerk in the royal palace. Because of these important connections Pol Pot was sent to the Royal Palace at the age of six to live with his influential relatives, and he grew up as an educated, French-speaking member of the small elite. All the reports about him in his youth suggest that he was a happy, even-tempered child. There are no reported traumatic rebellions against paternal authority as in the case of Stalin, Hitler, or Mao; there was no poverty and humiliation in his early youth as with Saddam Hussein; there was no revolutionary tradition in his family or even any unusually youthful political commitment to revolutionary change, as in the case of Romania's Nicolae Ceausescu. Whatever the deep psychological origins of his later ruthlessness, there was no early sign of it. He became interested in politics in secondary school in Phnom Penh, but his ideology only took shape during his stay in France as a student from 1949 to 1953. When he won a scholarship to go to France in 1949, he was one of only about a hundred Cambodian youths to have won such an honor since 1946.[123]

Aside from joining a Marxist-nationalist discussion group in Paris, Pol Pot's other formative experience seems to have been a trip he took to Yugoslavia in 1950. This was unusual because orthodox communists at that time were anti-Titoist, and to visit Tito's country at a time when Stalin was still waging verbal war against it would not have been approved by the French Communist Party. In 1950, Yugoslavia was not the reformist communist state it would later become, but a hard line police state intent on proving that it could be more communist than the Soviet Union.[124] The mass mobilization of people, the frenetic construction projects, the unity of the masses fighting for what they perceived to be national survival against dangerous outside powers, and perhaps Tito's image as "the wild man of communism" of his time impressed Pol Pot.[125]

Pol Pot's intellectual development was quite similar to that of others in his group, though some went much further with their studies and obtained degrees. Khieu Samphan finished a doctoral dissertation in 1959 in which he tried to show that Cambodia's economic development was "dependent" and therefore unsound. The merchants and elites in the cities were parasitical, and foreign aid, particularly from America, further distorted the economy and caused agriculture to stagnate. The dissertation was not particularly radical; rather, it was vintage "Dependency Theory" of the type we will see as dominant in the thinking of intellectuals in such disparate places as Korea, Romania, and Argentina in the twentieth century. The essence of the theory, that capitalist development through foreign aid and investment is inherently bad, is not necessarily leftist or rightist. It can be both. The key is that while it has been used by Marxists, it is primarily a nationalist doctrine that Khieu Samphan used to call for greater closure of his country from Western influences, and for purification of the corrupt and parasitical urban elements.[126]

After Pol Pot's return in 1953 he joined the communist underground, which was dominated at that time by the Vietnamese. In the early 1960s he and his French-educated intellectual friends moved into leadership positions, though the history of their trajectory is not well known. Certainly, as the elite of their generation, it is not difficult to imagine why they appeared to their Vietnamese allies and advisors as natural leaders. It may be that Pol Pot's pleasant personality made him a natural consensus builder and leader. David Chandler speculates that it was precisely because he seemed more pliable and reasonable than the other, more abrasive and ultra-nationalist young Khmer Rouge leaders, that the Vietnamese communists and older Khmer communists found him easier to work with.[127] Subsequently, the Khmer Rouge would publish a *Black Book* in 1978 with a long list of anti-Vietnamese grievances and a reconstructed history of Cambodian communism. In it, the bossiness and arrogance of the Vietnamese communists are repeatedly emphasized. Whether the incidents in the *Black Book* are true or not (and much of its history is demonstrably false), the resentment of the Khmer Rouge leadership is clear.

In 1965 and early 1966 Pol Pot visited China as the Cultural Revolution, with its emphasis on perpetual class conflict, was just getting under way, and by all accounts, he was suitably impressed by the purity of China's utopian revolutionary enthusiasm. But it would not be until after 1967 that the Khmer Rouge would be able to gain a measure of independent strength, and not really until the 1970s that they began to break away from their Vietnamese communist "big brothers."[128]

The Fall of Sihanouk, the Intensification of the War,
and the Victory of the Khmer Rouge

By 1967 Sihanouk's position was fraying. In China the Cultural Revolution was under way, and pressure from the Red Guards resulted in support for revolutionary forces throughout South and Southeast Asia, even against noncommunist regimes that had been friendly with China, such as Cambodia's and Burma's. The Vietnam War was threatening Cambodia's delicate balancing game between the contending forces in Indochina. Discontent among urban intellectuals, students, and the small but growing urban middle class over Sihanouk's autocracy was becoming a problem. Inspired by the Cultural Revolution, secondary-school students, most of whom were urban ethnic Chinese, launched protest movements. The Cambodian communists now launched an open revolt, probably primarily in reaction to the fact that Sihanouk was trying to crack down on the opposition to restore his authority. But the Khmer Rouge had too little rural support to go far, and they would have had little chance of success if Cambodia had remained isolated from the Indochinese war. Again, it was the tragedy of an externally imposed war that created the chaotic conditions necessary for the success of a tyrannical ideology.

One result of the communist uprising was that it swung power within the Sihanouk government toward the army and General Lon Nol, its conservative commander. The army and the conservatives, who were themselves bitterly anti-Vietnamese and strongly nationalist, gradually became the main power in Phnom Penh. By the time he formally overthrew Sihanouk in 1970, probably with the approval if not through the direct intervention of the Americans, Lon Nol was already the effective ruler of Cambodia. But on the communist side, though the Khmer Rouge needed Vietnamese help, they were also becoming increasingly hostile to the Vietnamese who were urging them, for their own tactical reasons, to stop their revolt, to rely more on the Russians than on the Chinese, and to follow Vietnamese policy more closely. The collapse of Sihanouk and the increase in direct American intervention may have made the ultimate victory of the Khmer Rouge possible, but it was their resentment of the Vietnamese, more than anything else, that shaped their long-run thinking.[129]

Though Sihanouk had lost much of his legitimacy in the cities, he remained a revered figure in the countryside, and the fact that after being overthrown he moved to China and formally allied himself with the Khmer Rouge to combat the Lon Nol government helped the communists greatly. Then, also, the Lon Nol forces proved to be a military failure almost from the start. The Cambodian army under Sihanouk had been small. Now it was hugely enlarged and fed with American equipment. But it lacked enough trained officers. It was corrupt and sold much of its equipment to the communists. And most of all, it came to rely far too much on American and South Vietnamese air support rather than adapting to the guerrilla tactics of the Vietnamese and Cambodian communists. It was a repetition of everything that was wrong with the American effort in Vietnam. As increased bombing, particularly the indiscriminate and frightening, though militarily large-ly ineffective B-52 strikes spread throughout the country, it created refugees and outraged peasant recruits who joined the Khmer Rouge. The bombing came to be the primary defense of the anti-communist government in Phnom Penh, but it could not improve its long-run situation.[130]

It was an extremely cruel war. Sylvana Foa, one of the outstanding American reporters in Phnom Penh at that time who, much to the resentment of the American government, uncovered the true nature of the war going on, has described to me how she saw Lon Nol soldiers tying up a Khmer Rouge prisoner and making an incision to take out some of his intestine. Then they slowly pulled it out, wrapping it on a stick, and left him there to die. Similar atrocities were committed on both sides. (Later, the American government had Foa expelled from Cambodia for discovering that the bombing of Cambodia was being directed by radio from the American Embassy in Phnom Penh, in con-travention of American Congressional orders.)[131]

For the Khmer Rouge, as for many peasants, the Lon Nol army and government came to be viewed as alien and cruel forces from the city who were the tools of Chinese businessmen, American officials, and corrupt aristocrats from the old regime.

The scene was set for what followed in 1975. Because of mounting opposition within the United States to the Nixon presidency and to his secretive war policies in Indochina, the level of aid to Lon Nol decreased and, after 1973, American bombing ceased. In 1974 the Khmer Rouge were not yet strong enough to seize Phnom Penh, and tensions between them and the North Vietnamese increased. But in 1975, as South Vietnam began to collapse in the face of North Viet-namese attacks, and the Americans were unable to help, the situation of the Lon Nol regime also deteriorated further. Phnom Penh, which by then had over two million people, was slowly starving to death, and when the final attack came in April, the city fell. By then the government scarcely controlled any territory except for the capital and a few other towns.[132]

Within a few days after they had marched into Phnom Penh, the communists ordered everyone out—the sick, the wounded, the old, the young, the refugees, the established urbanites—everyone. Over two million people set out on the roads to rural areas.[133] The Khmer Rouge had already been applying their rigorous policies of social reorganization, collectivization of all aspects of life, and very harsh discipline, with frequent use of the death penalty, in areas they had been occupying before 1975. Now, they applied them to the newly liberated cities as well.[134]

A Nightmarish Utopia

One of the main reasons for evacuating the cities was because there was not enough food, and since a return to any kind of market economy, which would have reestablished food distribution, or appeals for foreign aid were ruled out, this meant that people would have to go out and grow their own. Another reason was that dispersing the population would make Cambodia less vulnerable to a feared Vietnamese or possibly American attack. The Khmer Rouge leadership genuinely believed that by mobilizing the unsullied peasant purity and strength of the Khmer, they would be able to fight off any Vietnamese attacks, and then sweep into the parts of southern Vietnam they claimed (including Saigon), to establish a strong and independent country, and to recapture the glories of the past. The cities were the home of corruption and foreign influence, and they were a blight on Cambodia. The refugees from the countryside in the cities might be salvaged if they returned to their villages; the urban population had to be ruralized.[135]

A lot of people died on the way to their new rural homes. A few were killed outright. The ill and the weak died en route. In some areas there was enough food, in others not, and many more died. Once the survivors were resettled, there continued to be considerable differences between regions in how they were treated. But everywhere, strict class categories were established that determined how people were treated. Poor peasants and the few "workers" who were living in communist-controlled areas before April 17, 1975, were eligible to become what the Khmer Rouge labelled "full rights" and "old" or "base" people. They were subjected to rigorous discipline and harsh communal living like everyone else, but they also had more privileges, lighter work loads, and more rations. Somewhat less favored people, from better off peasant or "petit bourgeois" families, could become "candidates." This curious terminology was taken partly from the language normally applied in communist states to the elite: there were full, or voting members of the central committees and political bureaus, and "candidate" or nonvoting members. But nowhere else was this terminology used for the entire population. The term "base" people referred to the Maoist notion of a guerrilla organization with a secure base that could launch attacks against the enemy.

Others—the rich, those who had served the Lon Nol regime, ethnic minorities, and all those who had been refugees in the cities, no matter what their class origins—were called "depositees" and "new" people. They had no political rights, were subjected to harsher disciplinary actions, and to more brutal work conditions. To be from a family of one of the "depositees" put one in a low category, too, just as in China bad family blood could taint an individual for life. Intermarriage between "full rights" people and "depositees" was not allowed.[136]

There is no need to repeat what has been said about the similar practice of labelling people in China. Such a system of strict social categories that consigns vast portions of the population to inferiority as class enemies, often because they happened to be in the wrong place at the wrong time, produces a sense of massive despair and hopelessness. It also encourages constant denunciations and searches for "bad" backgrounds. These categories become the basis of social competition, and to be classified in an unfavorable way may mean death, or, at best, increased suffering for oneself and one's family. Michael Vickery says that such denunciations were a "bad habit" left over from the pre-revolutionary past. David Chandler says that the Cambodian revolution failed not because it was Marxist-Leninist but because of the "persistence of . . . so much counterrevolutionary behavior."[137] Though both these writers are knowledgeable experts on Cambodia, in a comparative context such statements are absurd. Only if one believes it is possible for people to be utterly selfless, devoid of ambition except for the collectivity, and entirely uninterested in helping their families can one seriously believe that application of such social categories can lead to anything other than a vicious struggle for survival at all levels of the society, to denunciations, and to cruelty and persecution.

Life was strictly regimented; families were often, though not always broken up; money and exchange disappeared; a puritanical morality was imposed; private property was eliminated.[138] In some areas cadres began to force individuals into marriages they thought suitable for the community. By 1977 in some jurisdictions children as young as seven or sometimes even six were being taken away from their parents to live in separate groups. Communal eating was imposed, partly in conjunction with the lowering of food rations, but also to attack "privateness." Mao had thought such a practice was a good idea during the Great Leap Forward until it proved so unpopular. In Cambodia it was applied to a greater extent than in China, but it was just as unpopular.[139]

Of course it could not work properly. Without markets or incentives of any kind people will work to survive, but without enthusiasm. Only fear made the social structure hold together, and in the long run that is a poor way to motivate workers. As almost all skilled people were in bad social categories, and their talents considered useless, at least until 1978, the Cambodian economy had no chance of recovering and gaining ground.

Almost from the very start of Khmer Rouge rule, the Chinese and Vietnamese minorities in Cambodia were targeted for elimination as foreign elements. Later, this was extended to those who were only part Vietnamese, and to the Chams. In a talk at the University of Washington in Seattle in 1992, Ben Kiernan said that he believed that no ethnic Vietnamese who did not manage to escape the country survived within Cambodia's borders. Tens of thousands were deliberately murdered. Half of the Chinese (some 200,000) perished, and about a third of all Chams were killed.[140] In view of the racial or "blood" notion of the nation that was held by the Khmer Rouge elite, this is not surprising. They felt that to survive they had to eliminate racial as well as class enemies. Indeed, in some respects this regime, so dominated by a small number of French-trained intellectuals, combined all of the ideological elements from European thought that had led to catastrophe in the first half of the twentieth century. This was a delayed and ironic effect of intellectual colonialism. The Khmer Rouge anthem itself stressed these elements, and might have pleased any good fascist ideologue:

Bright Red Blood which covers towns and plains
Of Kampuchea, our motherland

Sublime blood of workers and peasants,
Sublime blood of revolutionary men and women fighters!
The Blood changing into unrelenting hatred
And resolute struggle,
On April 17, under the Flag of Revolution,
Free from slavery![141]

In 1976 an anti-Pol Pot coup attempt was made by some other leading Khmer Rouge, perhaps to reverse harmful past policies. It failed,
and in December of 1976 Pol Pot promised to uncover the "microbes"
buried in the Party. This initiated a set of purges which picked up
steam in 1977 and resulted in the elimination of many of the most
experienced cadres. Pol Pot and his immediate circle moved to destroy
all possible opposition within the Party, and, as in other such cases,
when the economic and political situation began to deteriorate, they
had to find scapegoats as well. Now the standard purge trials, accompanied by torture and forced confessions, began. Chandler has written:

> Inevitably, more conspiracies were found. . . . Its documents fed the
> leadership's paranoia. Documents led to more arrests, arrests produced
> more documents, and so on. In 1977–78, those pulled in included many
> people quite close to the leaders themselves. . . . The talent pool for car-
> rying out a revolution was drying up. So were the possibilities of anyone
> trusting anyone. As Pol Pot and his colleagues tightened their grip, their
> perceptions became blurred. They were obsessed with purifying the
> party and imposing "socialism."[142]

Of the five top leaders of the Khmer Rouge in 1973, Pol Pot, Khieu
Samphan, Ieng Sary, Hu Nim, and Hou Yuon, the first three survived
in power, though Khieu Samphan is believed to have been a figure-
head. Pol Pot and Ieng Sary were related by marriage. Hou Yuon was
killed in late 1975 because he was a popular figure; Hu Nim was tortured and killed in 1977.[143] The other main leader, who became Pol
Pot's second-in-command, was Nuon Chea (born as Lau Ben Kon).
Chea was a Sino-Khmer (which may have made him less of a threat to
Pol Pot) from a prosperous urban family. He had been educated not in
France, but in Thailand, where he had gone to law school and joined
the Communist Party. He had returned to Cambodia in 1951 and
become a close friend of Pol Pot in the mid-1950s.[144]

At the main interrogation and torture center in Phnom Penh, Tuol

Sleng, pictures, tape recordings, and dossiers were kept of the pro-
ceedings. In all, 20,000 men, women, and children were put through
this facility. Much of this material is available for inspection.[145]

In the Eastern Zone of Cambodia which touched South Vietnam,
and which until 1977 seems to have been governed somewhat more
benignly, the purges were particularly ferocious. A later eyewitness
told Ben Kiernan, "They killed all the Eastern Zone cadres and ordinary people who committed the most minor offenses, such as talking
about family problems at night. Every day they would take away three
to five families for execution . . . we would hear them screaming for
help."[146] Kiernan believes that in this province of Cambodia alone,
100,000 were murdered in six months in 1978. Teenagers, who until
then had been favored to lead the way into the future, were not spared,
even many who had been active in the Party. They were dispatched in
batches because, living near Vietnam, they were thought to have had
their minds contaminated.[147]

From 1977 on, it seems that widows and families of those executed
were also executed in other parts of the country.[148]

To those who know about the history of the Stalinist purges in the
1930s, this is not an entirely unfamiliar story, but with one important
difference. At the same time as he was purging the Party, and ruthlessly eliminating whole categories of people on the mere suspicion that
they might have been associated with traitors and enemies, Stalin was
also abolishing egalitarianism and allowing ever greater pay differences
to reward the skilled. He was promoting higher education and
research, and decreasing family- or class-based criteria for admission
to higher education. Stalinism failed ultimately, but compared to Pol
Potism, it was far more rational and worked a lot better.

There were other differences between Pol Potism and Stalinism, as
well as many differences between the way in which the Khmer Rouge
conducted business and the way other communist regimes, including
Mao's, conducted theirs. For one thing, there was never a cult of the
leader. Pol Pot remained so anonymous that for the first few years of
Khmer Rouge rule very few people even knew what he looked like or
who he really was. Only in 1977, more than two years after taking
power, did his identity become known from pictures taken of him during an official visit to China.[149] Even now there are very few pictures of
Pol Pot. Only Nuon Chea, "Brother Number Two," remained more
hidden and less photographed than Pol Pot among the top Khmer

Rouge. This secretiveness has never been explained and stands in sharp contrast to Stalin, Mao, Ceausescu, Kim Il Sung, Fidel Castro, Enver Hoxha, Tito, and to almost all of the notable noncommunist dictators in the twentieth century. Probably it was Pol Pot's obsessive concern with security that prompted the anonymity, though there is evidence that in 1978 the makings of a real cult of personality were getting under way, only to be aborted by the loss of the war with Vietnam.[150] After all, the cult of Stalin only began in the 1930s, and even that of Mao only after 1959.

Whatever its causes, from 1975 to 1978, the passion for anonymity existed even at the local level, where people often did not know the name of the local cadres.[151] Decisions handed down were ascribed to "The Upper Organization" (*Angkar Loeu* in Khmer, often just called *Angkar*, "The Organization") which was "distant, mysterious, arbitrary, and impossible to question."[152] In a way, as commendable as such anonymity might seem when compared to the sickening cults of personality in many tyrannies, it removed yet one more possible source of hope for the people. However wrongly, people in Stalin's Soviet Union or Mao's China felt that if only the benign great leader knew, perhaps things would go better. Ordinary people were genuinely saddened by Stalin's death. In Cambodia, the element of anonymity added to all the suffering by making the situation seem even more hopeless.

What finally brought down the regime, however, was not an internal revolt but its attack against Vietnam which began on a large scale in 1977, even though there had been skirmishes from the very start of Khmer Rouge rule. The Vietnamese fought back, of course, but the tenacity of the Khmer kept the fighting confined to border regions throughout most of 1978. In May of 1978 Cambodian Radio proclaimed, "So far, we have succeeded in implementing this slogan of one against 30: that is to say, we lose one against 30 Vietnamese killed. We need only two million troops to crush 50 million Vietnamese—and we would still have 6 million people left."[153] This bizarre calculus turned out to be as deluded as all other Khmer Rouge notions. In late 1978 the Vietnamese launched a serious counterinvasion using their immense superiority in tanks, artillery, men, and aircraft, and they swiftly conquered most of Cambodia, reducing the fleeing Khmer Rouge to guerrilla strongholds near the Thai border. The Vietnamese had their own reasons to denounce the Khmer

Rouge, but they were quite right when in 1978 they said that Cambodia had turned into "hell on earth."[154]

Remarkably, however, the crushing defeat inflicted on the Khmer Rouge did not destroy them, and they survived as guerrillas and in refugee camps along the Thai-Cambodian border. One reason may be that from the start the Khmer Rouge had relied very heavily on very young soldiers, some barely in their teens, to carry out their policies. Youths with no other home or family than the Party, and used to being treated with greater respect than the adults they terrorized may have stuck with the "Organization" despite its policy failures because they knew no other life. When asked why the Khmer Rouge had been so cruel, Sihanouk told William Shawcross that one reason was that "many of the soldiers I saw were only twelve or thirteen years old."[155] Sylvana Foa, who has held interviews with Sihanouk and Khieu Samphan, told me that perhaps it would be better to study William Golding's *The Lord of the Flies* (a novel by the Nobel Prize winner about the cruelty of boys marooned without adults) than any Marxist texts in order to understand the utter viciousness of the Khmer Rouge. Though this insight does not explain the ideology that drove the Khmer Rouge leadership, it helps us understand that leadership's ability to survive.

The story of what followed the defeat of early 1979 is complicated, and remained unresolved into 1993. Supported by the Chinese, who feared a Soviet-Vietnamese alliance against them, Pol Pot's guerrilla army remained fed and armed along the borders. Even Sihanouk, much of whose family was killed by them, said he preferred the Khmer Rouge to Vietnamese puppets. After a decade of trying to pacify Cambodia, the Vietnamese pulled out, leaving many of the old contending forces vying for power: Sihanouk, still popular with the peasants; the Khmer Rouge, still led by the same murderers; former Khmer Rouges who had defected to the Vietnamese; and some Lon Nol conservatives (though Lon Nol was long dead). The Khmer Rouge, cynically used by the Chinese, and for a time even by the Americans and their close allies, the Thais, who saw in them a counterweight to Vietnamese hegemony in Indochina, remain a potent force. Sihanouk is still trying to play all sides off against each other. An election under United Nations supervision brought him back to power as king, but despite a temporary respite, the fighting and killing are not over. In the zones they control, the Khmer Rouge continue to impose the same communal, harsh discipline as before; and they have not given up their utopian dreams. It is a terrible story without a moral or an ending.[156]

Little Communist Tyrannies: A Comparative Comment

What happened in Cambodia was worse than, but not entirely unlike, what happened in a number of other communist tyrannies. In particular, several other small nations that fell into revolutionary communist hands turned into examples of particularly harsh regimes.

Albanian communism came to power because of another "big brother" that, like Vietnam, conducted its own, highly successful communist insurgency, Yugoslavia. During World War II, when Yugoslav and Albanian Partisans fought the Germans and Italians as well as their domestic enemies, the Yugoslavs also used the Albanians for their own purposes, patronized them, and threatened to absorb them in a "friendly" way, much as the Vietnamese did with the Khmer Rouge. The Albanian Communist Party's reaction under Enver Hoxha's leadership was not simply anti-Yugoslav but fiercely uncompromising and led Albania into being the most isolated, violent, and xenophobic communist country in Eastern Europe.[157]

North Korea, whose communist movement spent its formative years as a part of the Chinese Red Army, only survived the Korean War because of Chinese help. But the intense nationalism of its leadership also produced a level of isolation and self-reliance that have marked it as Asia's most extremist and intransigent communist regime after the Khmer Rouge.

It is not, of course, as if Maoist China and the Stalinist Soviet Union did not pass through such stages combining intense nationalism and a great sense of insecurity. But in the cases of the North Koreans, Albanians, and Cambodians, the smallness of these countries made their nationalist-communist leaders even less willing to compromise with the outside world, and even more determined to lock out all foreign influences.

In the next chapter we will explore the North Korean example, and also that of another small, paranoid communist tyranny that felt itself surrounded by racial enemies and not given its proper due as a great power by the world—Nicolae Ceausescu's Romania.

Chapter 7

Little Stalins?

Socialist Corporatism at the Service of the
Nation and the Leader

C ommunism has fooled a lot of people, not just the credulous or the ideologically blind. It was not only those who wished to find a better world in it who were mistaken; many of its most bitter enemies thought that communism would be much more durable than it turned out to be. Though it is untrue that no one at all foresaw the dramatic fall of communism in Eastern Europe in 1989, followed by its even more precipitous collapse in the Soviet Union, very few specialists, scholars, statesmen, journalists, or others really believed that such a thing could happen so quickly. The long-term problems of communism—such as the failure of collectivized agriculture, the tendency to rely on mammoth and inefficient industrial projects, the enormous proportion of all national expenditures that had to be devoted to security forces, the decline in public services ranging from transportation to health care, the pervasive cynicism and corruption—all these were known. But it was not until some time in the late 1980s that it became evident that they had accumulated to such a degree that the whole system might crack quickly.[1]

Until the late 1960s and early 1970s many intellectuals throughout the world hoped that communist societies, despite their many imperfections, were precursors of a new and better type of society.[2] And among those who disliked communism there was some fear that indeed it might be just that, the future, because it could create economically strong states able to expand their political power and influence everywhere. It used to be said that once the communists were in power, they never gave it up. Reverses were temporary, triumphs permanent. For those on the left, this was proof that Marxist historical science was essentially true. For those on the right, George Orwell's *Nineteen Eighty-Four* was widely read as prophecy. In his nightmarish totalitarian world, it was clearly impossible to defeat the state. A typical statement to that effect, published in 1988, now sounds embarrassing.

> Jeane Kirkpatrick was vilified for asserting that totalitarian systems were far more resistant to change than normal autocracies and therefore posed a unique danger to democracy. But events have demonstrated the essential accuracy of her thesis that . . . communist countries have been the most stubbornly opposed to change: Ethiopia with its war against the peasantry; Cuba, with its re-centralization of economic control; Romania, with its reversion to Stalinism; North Korea, with its terrorism and Stalin-like personality cults; Czechoslovakia, with its disgraceful persecution of independent culture; and Bulgaria with its "abolition" of minority groups.[3]

Three years later, of course, the Ethiopian regime had collapsed in civil war, the Czech and Bulgarian communists had given up power without fighting back; and the reign of the Ceausescus in Romania had ended with their being pushed against a wall and shot by a firing squad. Dictatorial regimes do not generally give up power willingly, and the better organized and the more ideologically coherent, the less likely that they will be overthrown. Yet, in the wake of the events from 1989 to 1991, the notion that communists are so repressive that they are almost impossible to overthrow has turned out to be as much of a fantasy as Hitler's Thousand Year Reich.

All these visions of paradise, or hell, depending on one's tastes, were based on the notion that Stalinism had worked to produce a modern, advanced, industrial power, even if at great cost. But this was not correct. Stalinism, and those who modelled their economic development on Stalinist lines, with an unrelenting emphasis on heavy industry and as much national self-sufficiency as possible, enforced isolation of the population from external influences, and an emphasis on nationalist solidarity in the face of a hostile world, did not create strong and viable modern industrial structures. Instead, what Stalinism created was a vast industrial structure that imitated what he and his fellow Bolsheviks had admired before the First World War, the German Ruhr, the great coal and steel Middle West of the United States, and similar areas in Western Europe. In the Soviet Union, large parts of Eastern Europe, parts of China, and North Korea, this program succeeded all too well and created super rust belts. Steel and coal, giant electrification projects and chemical factories, and massive concentrations of capital into very centralized firms were already becoming obsolete in the advanced capitalist world by the 1970s. The technological changes of the last part of the twentieth century required greater flexibility, faster technological change, and ever greater attention to the changing needs of consumers. By then the communists had succeeded in creating the world's leading early twentieth-century industrial states, but fifty to seventy-five years too late. This contributed to their collapse by finally making it clear that the ideology on which it was all based, Marxism-Leninism, was mistaken, and did not point to the future. Thus, among those who ruled Soviet-type systems, there was a corrosive loss of faith in what they were doing, and this destroyed their morale or ability to fight to save themselves.[4]

But long before the collapse, when Stalinism appeared to be working, it seemed to be a scientific way of making a country's backward economy catch up quickly, without in the least sacrificing national independence or pride. A look at how this particular vision contributed to the creation of two rather similar tyrannies in very different settings—the reign of Nicolae Ceausescu in Romania and Kim Il Sung in North Korea—confirms this. Looking at these cases will show some of the common threads that tie together most of the ideological "tyrannies of certitude" in the twentieth century.

SOCIALISM IN ONE FAMILY: THE CEAUSESCUS AND THE KIMS

Bruce Cumings has shown with extensive research that even though Kim Il Sung's North Korean communist regime was established under Soviet occupation in 1945, by 1946 it was making most of its own decisions. Its leaders found Stalinism appealing for its own sake, not because it was forced down their throats. Cumings has written that, despite the cultural and historical differences between Russia and Korea:

> Stalinist ideology did have one thing to teach the Koreans that fit like a glove with their own preconceptions. This was the Platonism of Stalin, the architectonic, engineering from on-high quality that marked his thought and praxis. Stalin was a hegemon in the era of "late" heavy industrialization, and his discourse, like his name, clanked with an abased, mechanical imagery that valued pig iron over people, machines over bread, bridges over ideas, the leader's will over the democratic instincts of Marx.[5]

Kim Il Sung was never the Soviet puppet the West imagined him to be, but rather had been an independent and experienced communist guerrilla leader. Korea was a Japanese colony from 1905 to 1945, and Kim, then in his early twenties, escaped to Manchuria in the 1930s to fight against the Japanese who had recently extended their empire to that part of China. Kim developed close relations with the Chinese communists, and Korean communists contributed tens of thousands of soldiers to the Chinese civil war in the late 1940s.[6]

The adoption of the closed, Stalinist model, with its emphasis on heavy industry, appealed to the Korean communists because it fit so well with their nationalism. After the Korean War South Korea, as it happens, also pushed heavy industrialization, and a high degree of concentration into the hands of a few giant firms. This it also did to promote national strength, especially during the military dictatorship of Park Hung Chee. But because it was allied to the United States and was part of the capitalist system, South Korea also emphasized exports, technology exchanges, foreign investment, and full participation in the competitive world market.[7] That forced South Korea to adapt much better than the closed Stalinist North, but this hardly means that the Northern strategy was forced on its leaders by the Soviets. Nor was it possible to tell until some time in the early to mid-1970s which model would work best in Korea. Only in about 1990 did it become obvious that North Korea had fallen catastrophically behind and was threatened with economic collapse.

Ken Jowitt, who invented the phrase "socialism in one family" to describe Romania's and North Korea's similar systems of rule by an all-powerful leader and his family (the phrase is a parody of Stalin's claim

to be constructing "socialism in one country," while putting world revolution aside in the 1920s), noticed in the early 1970s that these two
medium-sized communist societies, despite very different histories,
cultures, and geographic situations, seemed to have a peculiar affinity
for each other.[8] Yet, in the case of Romania, communism was not only
imposed by the Soviet army, but, unlike in North Korea, its leaders had
virtually no internal standing of their own in Romania. The Communist
Party of Romania had no legacy of guerrilla struggle, no popular
nationalist cause to which to tie itself, and in 1944, it had, at most, one
thousand members, of whom most were not actually ethnic Romanians, but members of various minorities—mostly Jews, Hungarians,
Bulgarians, Germans, and Ukrainians.[9]

Cumings argues that the North Korean regime can be likened to
revolutionary guerrilla communist governments that came to power on
their own, as in China, Yugoslavia, Albania, Vietnam, and Cuba, even
though it was installed during the Soviet occupation of North Korea.
His contention is backed by evidence that there was a substantial
insurrectionary communist peasant movement in the South after
World War II, though with American aid it was kept under control, and
was in the process of being eliminated by 1950. It was probably in
order to use the help of its supporters in the South, before it was too
late, that the North invaded the South and sought to unify the entire
country under communism in June of 1950. That Kim expected and
received Soviet aid, and then direct Chinese military help, does not, in
Cumings's view, remove the fact that the war began as a primarily
indigenous affair.[10]

Cumings's position is controversial, and does not correspond to the
official American and South Korean position that claims that the Korean War was part of Stalin's aggressive drive to spread communism. Nor
does it conform to the official history in North Korea, that sees it as
"imperialist" American aggression and nothing else. Nevertheless, the
notion that by 1945 Korea was in revolutionary ferment, especially in
the countryside, is supported by other social historical research.[11]

Unlike with the North Korean regime, the way in which the Romanian communists came to power and ruled in their early years is hardly
open to debate. They would not have had the slightest chance of success without the presence of Soviet occupying troops. On the contrary,
the Romanian Communist Party was almost certainly the weakest communist formation in all of Eastern Europe in 1945.

But despite these different origins, by the 1970s, Romania and North Korea had similar regimes, both bent on heavy industrialization and autarky at almost any cost, both extremely nationalistic and intolerant of any external influences, and both dominated by leaders who presented themselves and their families as gods incarnate—omniscient, omnipotent, models of perfection whose rule was the culmination of millennia of glorious national history. To be sure, they were still Marxist-Leninist socialists, but it was their own ideas, not those of the dead theoreticians of the past, that mattered most, and it was the works of Ceausescu and Kim that were cited by everyone as guides to proper action. Nicolae Ceausescu made his wife the second personage in the country, and began to prepare one of his sons for the succession. Kim Il Sung made his son crown prince, and began to give him increasing prominence. This neither Stalin nor any other communist leader had ever done, though, of course, it was common practice in monarchies and in some of the corrupt dictatorships of the twentieth century such as Haiti and the Dominican Republic. Also, Ceausescu and Kim became personally fond of each other, and particularly close ideological allies.[12]

HOW CEAUSESCU CAME TO DISCOVER KIM IL SUNGISM

Ceausescu was not the founding ruler of communist Romania, but the successor of Gheorghe Gheorghiu-Dej, a plodding old-time communist picked to head the country by the Soviets because he was one of the few genuine Romanians in the Party. Dej, who had been active in the labor movement in the 1930s, was supposed to be a front man for the "Moscow" communists who had been in exile in the Soviet Union until 1944 and were trusted by Stalin. Ceausescu, who came from a poor village family, and was born in 1918, was also an ethnic Romanian. He had gone to primary school and moved to Bucharest to work. There, at fifteen, he had joined the Communist Party. He was in prison during the war, and afterward, from the start of the communist period, as one of the few young Romanian veterans of the movement, he was trusted by Dej and given a top role.[13]

But Gheorghiu-Dej outmaneuvered the Moscow communists and the intellectuals in the Party, and, by the time Stalin died, he was in full command. His main rivals were purged. Some, like Anna Pauker (who was Jewish), went into obscure retirement. Others, like Lucretiu

Patrascanu, an ethnic Romanian, an intellectual, and a popular lawyer who was considered more dangerous to Gheorghiu-Dej, were shot.[14]

From 1947 to the early 1960s, thousands were killed, tortured, and sent to concentration camps. Some of these were members of Romania's large fascist movement, the Iron Guard. Others were part of the pre-communist political elite or from "bourgeois" or aristocratic families. Many were intellectuals. But many others were peasants who had gotten in the way of collectivization efforts, or rural people who happened to belong to outlawed Protestant sects, priests and ministers from the many religions that existed in Romania, or those associated in some way with losing communist factions. In the early 1950s about 180,000 people were in jails or concentration camps, out of a total population of 16 million. Of these, 40,000 were doing forced labor on the Danube-Black Sea Canal, which was originally begun by political prisoners under the right-wing military dictatorship that had ruled from 1941 to 1944.[15]

Lena Constante has written a moving account of the tortures, humiliations, and deprivations she underwent during this period. She was sentenced to eight years of solitary confinement in physically brutal conditions. Her crime? She was a friend of Lucretiu Patrascanu's wife and had worked with her in setting up a children's theater in Bucharest in the late 1940s. Petru Dumitriu, one of Gheorghiu-Dej's favorite authors who wrote convincing historical novels that conformed to the demands of socialist realism, later escaped, and once in the West, wrote a devastating account of the terror, bleakness, and utter hopelessness of life in Romania in the 1950s.[16]

This was the period Ken Jowitt has described as the "breakthrough" stage of revolutionary development: "Breaking through means the decisive alteration or destruction of values, structures, and behaviors which are perceived by a revolutionary elite as comprising or contributing to the actual or potential existence of alternative centers of political power."[17] Communists thought this was necessary in order to remold the society and make it capable of rapid Stalinist industrialization. Romania in 1945 was about three-quarters peasant and overwhelmingly rural. "Breaking through" would prepare the way for something more modern, as it had the Soviet Union in the 1930s.

The actual number of prisoners and dead in Romania, as in other Eastern European countries, was considerable but proportionately well under the numbers who died and were imprisoned in the Soviet

Union in the 1930s. The Soviets now had their procedures well worked out, and they wanted to create usable allies, not devastated and broken societies. But also, Stalin never felt particularly threatened by any East European figure except Tito of Yugoslavia, and this may have eased the terror. Or it may have been that Stalin was biding his time, consolidating Soviet rule, and the terror would have worsened had Stalin lived. In any case, it was bad enough.

Ceausescu became Gheorghiu-Dej's favorite, and by 1957 was in line for the succession. But then something quite unexpected happened. Khrushchev was in charge in the Soviet Union, and he was trying to rationalize both the Soviet economy and its system of foreign trade with the countries of Eastern Europe. According to the new Soviet plan Romania, which was less developed than the more northern communist countries of Czechoslovakia and East Germany, was supposed to specialize in agriculture, lumber, lighter industries, and petroleum extraction. Romania had substantial oil reserves, and was still Europe's biggest petroleum producer after the Soviet Union itself. This was a complete violation of the Stalinist conception of progress. Without a lot of smokestacks, without steel, there could be no economic success. Romania's leadership began trying to get out from under Soviet control in the late 1950s in order to avoid having Romania become economically dependent on the Czechs and East Germans. This was supported by the new communist elite, the semi-educated engineers promoted quickly to the top in the 1950s. It also meant a reassertion of previously suppressed nationalism. This pleased the country's intellectuals, even the many who were still anti-communist.[18]

In 1965 Gheorghiu-Dej died, and under Ceausescu, the drive toward nationalism and full industrialization (Ceausescu's phrase for this was "multilateral development") accelerated. But the danger was that because this was not supported by the Soviets, and because communism's legitimacy in Romania was low, the regime would be feeble. So, in order to strengthen his independence vis-à-vis the Soviets, Ceausescu courted the West, from which he hoped to get modern technology, and Romania's intellectuals were now given more independence and asked to join in the effort to develop the nation. He also allowed more consumption goods to be made, and the standard of living went up noticeably. Most remaining political prisoners were freed, and even some of the old fascist intellectuals were forgiven and put back in university positions. Romania became one of the "liberal" East European countries, relatively open, somewhat anti-Soviet, and on what seemed to be a path toward a brighter, more pragmatic future. Even *Time* magazine thought so and in 1966 featured Ceausescu on one of its covers.[19] Richard Nixon came to Bucharest where he was received as a conquering hero; in return, Ceausescu was invited to the White House in 1970.[20]

When I lived in Romania from January of 1970 until January of 1971, I found that Ceausescu was genuinely popular. The Soviets were blamed for everything bad that happened, and Ceausescu was given credit for his nationalism, for his courage in standing against the Soviet invasion of Czechoslovakia in 1968, for his pro-American attitude, and for the improvement of conditions. He was particularly well liked by many intellectuals, even those who had been communism's most bitter enemies. Traian Herseni, a sociologist who had been a major propagandist for the Iron Guard, one of Eastern Europe's most viciously anti-Semitic fascist movements in the late 1930s, and someone who had served a prison term under the communists, was put back in the university to teach social psychology. He told me, "I used to write things praising 'The Captain' [Codreanu, the putative Romanian Führer] and now I write pretty much the same thing, but praising Ceausescu. I'm not a Marxist, you understand, but I have to admit that I like what he's doing."[21]

Ceausescu was not a born-again liberal. Trained as a Stalinist, with almost no formal education except that of the Communist Party, but shrewd and ambitious, he had absorbed the overwhelming lesson of the 1930s. Romania was a backward society, and it had to be modernized at all costs. Stalin knew how to do that with Russia, and now it would have to be done with Romania. In a long, taped interview with Kenneth Auchinloss of *Newsweek* in 1988, Ceausescu would say that Stalin had been proved right by history.

Ceausescu's ostensible liberalism and friendliness with the West was tactical, a way of insuring Romanian interests against not only Soviet meddling, but mostly against that of the hard-line Czechs (put back in power after 1968) and East Germans who seemed to be favored by the Soviets. He did not want Romania to become anyone's colony, and this is what so appealed to the intellectuals. Ordinary peasants and workers, of course, were happy to be able to live better, whatever the ideology behind the new course.

But the new openness and contact with Westerners that resulted undoubtedly bothered Ceausescu because they brought a surge of consumerism, ideological laxness, and contentious pronouncements from some of the intellectuals, particularly some young ones, who thought they should be allowed to use their new freedoms. Ceausescu had different goals for Romania, calling for more investment in heavy industry and more sacrifice. This required privation and discipline. He no more wanted Romania to become a Western dependency than a Soviet one. Already in the late 1960s there were many signs that liberalism was not part of his agenda. But the full force of what his neo-Stalinism really involved would not become evident until the summer of 1971 when he visited North Korea, and came back enchanted by his inspiring "beloved friend," Kim Il Sung.

I have been told that on the plane coming back from Asia Ceausescu and his wife, having visited China and North Vietnam as well as North Korea, were enormously enthusiastic about what they had seen, especially in Korea. The discipline, the cleanliness of Pyongyang, the obedient marching masses, the enormous degree of self-reliance and independence, and most of all, the ability of the Party to mobilize such a tremendous effort on behalf of national development was something they wanted to emulate. As they were talking about this, one of Ceausescu's closest advisors, a representative of a younger, better educated class of technocrats, Ion Iliescu, pointed out that after all Romanians were not historically or culturally that similar to Koreans or Chinese. Romanians might not be so easily moulded. Supposedly, Elena Ceausescu became furious and accused him of not understanding. Iliescu, whom many had seen as a possible heir to Ceausescu, and a force for far-reaching change, was never officially purged. But from then on, he began a long slide toward obscurity. He would reemerge as Romania's first post-Ceausescu president, and its most important political figure in the early 1990s.

On Ceausescu's return, he began a "little cultural revolution," which was not, however, anything like the induced disorder and questioning of bureaucratic authority that was going on in China, but rather, a sharp move back toward classical Stalinism, with strong elements of Kim Il Sungism.[22]

COLLECTIVISM AND RESENTMENT AS THE BASIS OF NATIONAL AWARENESS AND THE CULT OF THE LEADER

Neither Ceausescu nor Kim Il Sung made up their doctrines out of thin air. Nor were either of them devoted Stalinist theoreticians who arrived at their positions by reading and studying. What both shared was a lot of practical experience from their youth in the cause of nationalist communism, and a desire to make their nations great. But in both Korea and Romania, there were intellectual and ideological histories to back this nationalism, and in both cases, the nationalism corresponded closely to the type identified in previous chapters as being conducive to tyranny.

Romania's Intellectual Tradition

Despite the mostly Latin language spoken by the Romanians (with the addition of a very substantial Slavic vocabulary), their agrarian and social history, as well as the majority's Orthodox Eastern religion, are much more like Russia's than the social histories and religions of Central or Western Europe. Conformity, communal solidarity, and a long history of serfdom preceded the emergence of modern intellectuals and a nationalist movement in the mid-nineteenth century.[23] The new intelligentsia was also much like Russia's. It prided itself on its modernity and ability to handle French, but it was also a deeply humiliated group aware of Romania's backwardness and history of subservience. In reaction to the first wave of enthusiasm about the West, and the continuing poverty of Romania, a distinctly "Romanophile" branch of thought developed, like the "Slavophiles" in Russia. Its most distinguished poet, who became a nationalist hero in the twentieth century under fascist as well as communist rule, was Mihai Eminescu, who wrote in 1881:

> [T]errible ignorance and corruption above, black ignorance and deep misery below. And this is the Romanian people? Our people of 50–60 years ago, with its healthy barbarity, rare and god-given quickness of mind, great vigor of spirit, cheerful, industrious, ironical? . . . And whence all this change? . . . Superimposed upon our people sits a foreign layer without tradition, without a fixed homeland, without fixed

nationality, which did away with what is a people's most precious possession, its historical sense of ongoing and organic development. . . . The
true civilization of a people consists not in the wholesale adoption of
laws, forms, institutions, etiquette, foreign clothes. It consists in *the natural, organic development* of its own powers and faculties. If there is
ever to exist a true civilization on this soil, it will be one that arises from
the elements of the ancient civilization. From its own roots, in its own
depths, arises the true civilization of a barbarian people; not from the
aping of foreign customs . . . [24]

Never mind that the notions of a past paradise, and the idea that in
some sense nineteenth-century Romania had anything in common
with the tribes that had lived there two thousand years earlier were
utter nonsense. This was the stuff of nationalist mythology, and is no
sillier than the Hitlerian belief in the mystical power of pure Germanic
blood to overcome all obstacles.

Romania's economic modernization in the nineteenth century
attracted a substantial Jewish immigration from Central Europe and
the Ukraine, so Eminescu and most of his fellow nationalists blamed
them for Romania's modern woes and became anti-Semites.

One of Romania's most influential poets and essayists, who would
become a veritable icon of the Ceausescu regime's intellectuals,
Lucian Blaga, wrote in the 1920s and 1930s about the soul of Romanian peasants. The mixture of different personality types that came from
"lucid and rational" Latin blood, mixed with the "seething" blood of
exuberant and vital Thracians and Slavs had produced a wonderfully
pure, authentic Romanian, untouched by the pollution of foreign influences. The peasant had to be the basis of national reconstruction.[25]
That Blaga knew very little about what really went on in Romanian villages, and cared less, made no difference to his intellectual followers in
the Ceausescu years. Nor did it matter that this is the kind of absurdity
that fed fascist fantasies about blood, race, and the need to privilege
the mythologized collectivity ahead of individuals. During the Ceausescu years, such notions were deemed perfectly acceptable.[26]

Reflections about the past, about blood and the wonderful qualities
of the rural Romanian had to face the problem of explaining why this
great Romanian people, so endowed with limitless virtue, was nevertheless weak, divided, and backward. From the late nineteenth century
until the late twentieth, the answer was clear: it was all the fault of out-

siders. Ilie Ceausescu, the leader's brother, who was the regime's official military historian and ideological watchdog in the army, said in the summer of 1979 that the Romanians had been striving for national unity for 2,049 years since the days of the Dacians (who lived in this part of Europe and are thought to have been related to the Thracians), but that their efforts had been impeded by many invaders, starting with the Romans, and going through various Germanic and Central Asian invaders, then the Turks, and finally the many Russian invasions. But none had succeeded in destroying the essential unity of the Romanians, who were now strong and happily united in their quest for multilateral development.[27] In 1980 Romania celebrated the 2,050th anniversary of the Dacian state.[28] Nicolae Ceausescu put it this way in a speech in 1983: "The migration of foreign tribes and populations . . . checked for hundreds of years the development of the Romanian people."[29]

Korea's Intellectual Tradition

Korea's intellectual tradition at first seems quite different from Romania's. Isolated for many centuries, Korea was only brought into close contact with the modern world in the twentieth century by Japanese colonization. It was amid brutal, if efficient Japanese rule, and particularly in reaction to Japanese contempt for Koreans, that modern nationalism evolved. But of course, the resentment built up was substantial, and led to a vision of Korea as victim. Kim Il Sung said in a speech in 1946 that Koreans were "a superior people" whose backwardness had been caused by the Japanese.[30]

Kim Kyong-Dong (Kim is the most common family name in Korea), a South Korean sociologist, has written:

> Perhaps the most interesting and unique factor [in explaining Korean behavior] happens to be what is called *hahn* in Korean. . . . *Hahn* refers to a mixture of feelings and emotional states, including a sense of rancor, regret, grief, remorse, and revenge; and grievances or grudges. These feelings may have to do with an accumulated sense of frustration, repeated deprivation of need gratification, or constant suppression of one's own desires. . . . For the nation as a whole the state of *hahn* has been historically due to frequent invasions and occupations by foreign forces. Especially strong is the emotion of *hahn* acquired from the bitter

experience of colonization by the Japanese. Also notable would be *hahn* caused by the realization through acculturation that Korea has remained too long as a poorer nation in the global society, in spite of her pride of having been a nation of high civilization for thousands of years.[31]

Kim Kyong-Dong ascribes much of South Korea's economic success and energy to the channelling of this resentment and consequent drive to excel by the Park regime.[32]

But the tyrannical instincts of Park's government, and its successor, were somewhat curbed by the need to maintain the friendship of the United States, to keep Japanese investments flowing in, and to maintain markets abroad. There were no such restraints in the North where, furthermore, there was an extra cause for resentment and bitterness, the destruction of much of the country by American bombing during the Korean War. Memory of the suffering this imposed has been carefully nurtured by the North Korean regime, and constantly brought up to exhort the people to persevere against foreign abomination.[33]

To overcome backwardness and weakness, Kim Il Sung developed the concept of *Juche*. This means "Putting Korea first in everything," and, as Cumings puts it, "its goal [is] a subjective, solipsistic state of mind, the correct thought that must precede and that will then determine correct action."[34]

In North Korean documents the term that is normally translated as "liberalism" implies "a kind of license in which the individual departs from the group, benefits his interests at the expense of others, and lacks a proper conception of morality." Emphasis on individualism against collective interests is deemed counterrevolutionary. But in premodern times, the Confucian ideal was identical.[35] Nor was it so different in South Korea, at least until very recently. At a conference of scholars in 1965 the South Koreans insisted that capitalism was something unnatural for Koreans, and had only been introduced to Korea by the Japanese; at the very moment when South Korean capitalism was beginning to transform the economy, the consensus among South Korean economists and philosophers was that capitalists were nothing more than speculators and dishonest profiteers.[36]

Recently Ezra Vogel has done comparative research a great favor by pointing out that the fantastic economic success of the East Asian "little dragons," including South Korea, was not so much due to their

Confucian heritage as to the fact that the hold of the old Confucian morality and ethical system was decisively broken in the post–World War II years.[37] Evidently, in North Korea, as in Romania, older philosophies seem to have survived quite well under communism.

In 1990, reacting with horror at what had happened in Eastern Europe, deeply disturbed by the fate of its best friends, and particularly the execution of Ceausescu, the North Koreans issued a statement saying that they would never open themselves to the evil influences of the capitalist world, but remain virtuous socialists. Their society would remain one where "there is nobody who is exceptionally better off, nobody who goes ill-clad and hungry . . . no jobless people, no people who go bankrupt and wander around begging, no drug addicts, alcoholics and fin-de-siècle faggots who seek abnormal desires."[38]

From Collectivism to the Deification of the Leader

It now becomes easier to see what Ceausescu and his wife, looking for a doctrine that would underpin their own instinctive nationalism, found so appealing about the doctrine of strong self-reliance they saw in North Korea. Both shared a sense of historical persecution and resentment as well as a distrust of individualistic liberalism.

But aside from these general values, Ceausescu also shared with Kim Il Sung the memory of the condescension with which the Soviets in the 1930s had treated Romanian and Korean communists. Stalin and the Comintern had considered these movements quite marginal and untrustworthy, and though it was not possible to mention this in the late 1940s and 1950s, it certainly fed continuing resentment by old Party leaders.[39] Yet Romania, which had so many of the same goals as North Korea, had not been as successful in becoming strong, independent, and disciplined.

It is easy to see, in retrospect, what the Ceausescus must have surmised, and why, on their return from their visit, they launched a determined attempt to reform Romanian intellectual life. It was one thing to rely on intellectuals for nationalist support, but quite another to trust them to lead Romanians into self-sufficient and disciplined grandeur. Indeed, Romania's intellectual tradition is based on a self-pitying denial of responsibility and an unwillingness to believe that much can be done to remedy the situation. Claude Karnoouh, a French anthropologist, has written:

Too cleverly able to "resist the terror of history" by inventing "methods of camouflage," Romania's intelligentsia has adopted the comfortable role of the eternal victim of powerful others. It has lost all sense of belonging and responsibility for any historical change. Romanian intellectuals look at the Romanian as if he has never been the subject of history, but merely a toy in the hands of the Evil One . . . betrayed in 1917 by the Russians, and again, this time by the West in 1944, but never at fault.[40]

This hardly fit the voluntarism and dynamism that Ceausescu needed, and he surely must have admired Kim and the Koreans for showing no such weakness. He therefore set out to reform thought as well as structure in his Romania. This was the final step toward making him a thorough tyrant.

In July of 1971, when he launched his post-Asian reforms with his "July theses," Ceausescu reversed the cultural opening that had occurred in the late 1960s and reestablished an Index of prohibited books and authors. Tightening continued for the rest of his rule. Sociology was removed from the university, and what remained was placed within the Communist Party's special academy of political studies; the number of those allowed to study nontechnical subjects at the university was sharply cut; fewer books were published; and the privileges formerly accorded to intellectuals were scaled back. In 1974, Elena Ceausescu was imposed on the Academy of Sciences as a member (she had training as a low-level chemical engineer), and then as head of this institution. She so politicized it that its prestige and much of its serious research were destroyed.[41]

A perusal of the Romanian press in the 1980s shows that along with daily mention of the leader's brilliance and devotion to the nation, there was also very frequent mention of Elena Ceausescu's scientific accomplishments, of the many "famous" scientists coming to Romania to ask her advice and pay her homage, and of the honors supposedly bestowed upon her abroad. By the late 1980s, Elena Ceausescu was officially "comrade, academician doctor engineer, beloved mother of the Romanian people."[42]

In North Korea, where there never seems to have been a period of cultural liberalization, such reassertion of control was unnecessary. The worship of the leader began almost from the start, but became overwhelming in the 1950s after the Korean War. That was when Kim was able to remove any trace of internal opposition. The surviving leadership of what had once been a major local communist movement in the South and had fled to the North was executed. Only those who had been with Kim from the beginning, and had been associated with him and the Chinese in Manchuria, remained in the top ranks of the leadership. One of Kim's followers had already written, in 1946, that Kim was "at our center the Great Sun . . . great leader, sagacious teacher, and intimate friend."[43]

Romania actually once had a fairly lively tradition of open intellectual discourse. The 1920s and 1930s saw a wealth of competing schools of thought and great progress in higher education; Romania produced a number of distinguished artists, writers, and scientists who gained world fame. There were liberals and socialists, communists and fascists, and most varieties of political thought in between. But Romanian intellectuals gradually became overwhelmingly fascist in the late 1930s. This corresponded to similar trends elsewhere in Europe that have already been discussed above.[44] That left them vulnerable to Ceausescu's nationalist appeals which seemed to promise a return to their favored status of the pre-communist period.

But after 1971, as their privileges were taken away, and they were humiliated by the constant pressure to conform and pay obeisance to the royal family's genius, they withdrew into sullen passivity, and Ceausescu's rule became ever more dependent on his family, on cronies, and on hypocritical opportunists because his legitimacy among other potential elites was falling. This was the common pattern all tyrannies, as Plato wrote in *The Republic*. It became a kind of vicious spiral until, finally, by the late 1980s, only those closest to his family were loyal. Despite the paucity of public protest, the regime came to be widely despised and perceived as corrupt.

Perhaps in Korea, where there was no time for modern intellectual life to flourish because of Japanese rule, control of all thought by a "Confucian sage," which, as Cumings emphasizes, is the way Kim presents himself, was more natural. In South Korea it was only in the 1980s that a genuinely open intellectual life began to flourish. One can wonder, however, if such behavior was genuinely legitimate, why it was necessary to have such an overwhelmingly heavy emphasis on leader worship in the North. Perhaps the drift to nepotism, reliance on old cronies, and artificial inflation of the leader's reputation in North Korea reflected the same growing absence of genuine support seen in other tyrannies, and particularly in Romania. It is much harder to tell what people really think in North Korea than in Romania because contacts between unsupervised North Koreans and outsiders have always been so strictly controlled and rigorously limited. What is known, however, is that the degree of official hero worship is staggering. Cumings writes about one of his visits to the North:

> Kim is everywhere. He greets you from large murals in the foyers of government buildings and schools. Buildings and rooms within them have plaques over the door showing the dates of his visits, and lately, his son's. Family bedrooms have portraits of Father and Son on the wall. . . . His photo is everywhere, and yet none can be ripped up. . . . Quotations are everywhere, ranging from rip-offs of Marxist-Leninist slogans to quaint homilies. . . . We visited the Museum of the Revolution, with a sixty-foot statue of Kim towering over the entry plaza. I witnessed kindergartners assembling before it and bowing, chanting "thank you father." The alpha and omega of the revolution is Kim's life, which modern Korean history merely adumbrates. He is shown in the van of a mass uprising against the Japanese in 1919, when he was exactly seven years old.[45]

Similar efforts were made in Romania on behalf of the Ceausescu family, but I never saw any mention of his "leadership role" among the revolutionary masses until he was at least in his mid-teens. The patent falsification of history, and the exclusion of other leaders from mention in the history produced for popular consumption, were nonetheless quite similar to what Cumings observed in North Korea.

If one is only a visitor in such a place, it is possible to see the grotesque humor of this kind of personification of the leader as the incarnation of all national and revolutionary virtues. The lies become so preposterous that it is hard to believe anyone takes them seriously. Yet their consequences are anything but funny for the inhabitants of countries ruled by such megalomaniacs.

THE THEORY OF REVOLUTIONARY CORPORATISM

Mature communism, after the instability of the early purges and restructuring of society is completed, would have seemed the fulfillment of the dreams of those who styled themselves corporatists in the first third of the twentieth century. To say that these corporatists were fascists, and that, supposedly, communism is the Marxist antithesis of fascism, is to miss the point of how narrow a range of possibilities exist for organizing nonmarket, centrally coordinated, modern industrial societies.

Corporatists such as Benito Mussolini argued that the most natural, and in their terminology "organic" way of organizing modern society was along occupational lines, so that everyone would be integrated into vertical corporations that would defend their interests. This would eliminate class struggles, and bring together the powerful and the weak in "functional" groups. Those at the top would benevolently look out for the interests of those in their corporations who were less powerful. And to coordinate and arbitrate potential disputes between corporate groups, there would be the wise ruling party and its leader acting as an impartial inspiration to all.

Communists found it impossible to treat their societies as one undifferentiated mass of people, simply because there were too many specialized sectors of the economy, too many types of occupations, and even within the most dictatorial, centralized system, too many competing interests to dispense with all intermediate bodies. But as the ideologies on which communist regimes were based claimed to be able to engineer perfect societies on the basis of the leadership's superior understanding, allowing spontaneous interest groups to form and compete was ruled out. And both fascism and communism set out to remedy the class conflict and disorder of capitalism. The result was the official establishment of functional organizations into which the entire population was eventually supposed to be incorporated, depending on the branch of the economy in which they were active. Limited competition between these sectors was allowed, and was to be resolved at the top by the leader and the Communist Party who were supposed to have the interests of the entire society at heart, not that of any restricted sector. Such a structure also made it easier for the Party to mobilize the population for great efforts.

Mussolini, had he seen it, would have envied North Korea's all-encompassing and rigid corporatism. Every individual was placed into a specific category according to occupation, political reliability, and family background. Everything was determined by one's category—place of residence, size of living unit, vacations, health benefits, and so on.[46]

The other major point of 1930s corporatist theory, also taken up by communist and many other nationalist dictatorships in such disparate places as Argentina and Burma, was the conviction that "dependency theory" explained the nation's economic backwardness. It was because the outside capitalist world, the "plutocratic nations" as Mussolini called them, unfairly dominated markets that "our" superior people (whoever these might be) had not reached their full potential.

The origins of dependency theory lie in Central European Marxist thought. Rosa Luxemburg, and later Lenin, based their theories of imperialism on the notion that the rich capitalist economies need to exploit poor primary exporters. But Italian nationalist writers, and Mussolini himself, took up the same idea, and in the 1930s a distinguished Romanian corporatist, Mihail Manoilescu, developed it further. Manoilescu's work was widely translated in the major European languages, including Portuguese and Spanish, and it was extensively read in Latin America as well. The conclusion was that in order to overcome backwardness it was necessary to close off an economy from the exploitative world market, and rely more on internally generated demand while industrialization occurred.[47]

Most modern economists do not accept the theory, preferring instead to adhere to classical notions of comparative advantage and the efficiency of free trade. But dependency theory made intuitive sense, and it has been widely practiced by many governments who accept the old notion, originally elaborated by Friedrich List, a mid-nineteenth-century German economist, that protecting infant industries through trade barriers is the only way to meet the competition from more advanced economies.

In its extreme version dependency theory became much more than a mere economic argument. Its political and social ramifications suited nationalists perfectly because they blamed most of the economic and social ills of the nation on foreign intervention. Was there poverty? That was because foreign interests were milking the nation dry. Were some local entrepreneurs becoming rich? That was proof that they had sold out to foreign interests. Was labor repressed? That was because foreign investors wanted labor costs kept down, and they were using local elites to enforce their will. Was foreign capital flowing in? That was to better rob and weaken the nation. Was it flowing out? That was proof that the imperialists were exporting their profits and not investing.

Mihail Manoilescu, who was a great admirer of Mussolini, ended his days in a Romanian communist prison after World War II. But in fact, Ceausescu's Romania was organized along many of Manoilescu's principles and with the same ideology of corporatist nationalism.[48] This way of structuring society was common to all communist societies, not because their leaders directly read Manoilescu, but because the corporatist theorists of the 1930s had understood how to combine resentful nationalism with a plausible theory of economic development that emphasized authoritarianism, mass mobilization of the population, and the retention of supposedly traditional, pure, non-Western values. So neither North Korea nor Romania were unusual in this respect; but only some communist regimes—Enver Hoxha's in Albania, Stalin's in the Soviet Union, Mao's in China, Kim's in North Korea, and Ceausescu's in Romania—so thoroughly combined an intense drive to modernize with such ruthless coordination and subjection of the entire society and the cult of the omniscient leader.

It is most unlikely that Kim Il Sung ever read Manoilescu. But he did have intimate knowledge of two good examples of intensely nationalist corporatism: the Soviet Union under Stalin, and Japan in the 1930s. For Koreans, the combination of extreme nationalism, suspicion of the outside world, rejection of capitalism, and a sense that there ought to be a harmonious coordination of society headed by a paternalistic leader made corporatism an entirely natural ideology.

No doubt that is why leftist South Korean students and young academics in the 1970s and 1980s remained so devoted no only to dependency theory, but also to anti-Americanism and anti-capitalism, and why they retained a touchingly uninformed faith in Kim Il Sung. They desperately wanted Korea to be reunited and freed of outside influence, but also, they deeply resented their own society in which Confucian virtue and learning were no longer the keys to high status, believing in their dreams that North Korea still functioned in that way under its wise emperor and father Kim. Some distinguished specialists of contemporary China, it should be noted, believe that the supposedly "liberal" Chinese students in 1989 had a similar ideological orientation.[49]

All this is very fine in theory, but what does it mean for people who are subjected to such all-encompassing coordination? Does it work? Is it tyranny? After all, some excellent political theorists, for example Peter Katzenstein, have argued that a mild form of corporatism has been compatible with democracy, economic progress, and social peace in Western Europe after World War II. And many have claimed that some form of closed autarky is a perfectly good strategy for the national development of poor societies. Clearly, not all governments that combine elements of corporatism and nationalism are tyrannical. What drives some toward bloody suppression of their people and gross abuses of power that ultimately do far more harm than good?

It may serve as a reminder of what all this really means to look at some instances of how general policy in Ceausescu's Romania and Kim's Korea affected ordinary people.

THE REAL CONSEQUENCES OF
REVOLUTIONARY CORPORATISM

The following story was told to me by a Japanese Korean woman in Osaka, Japan, in 1989, when she was about thirty years old. Hundreds of thousands of Koreans live in Japan. The younger ones were born there, speak Japanese, and are indistinguishable from their Japanese peers, except that the Japanese refuse to give most of them citizenship and treat them as resident aliens. The Japanese do not hesitate to express outrightly racist sentiments against the Koreans. In most cases, the parents and grandparents of the Japanese Koreans came during the colonial period, often but not always as forced laborers. Some wanted to be assimilated as Japanese. After World War II, they stayed because of the unsettled conditions and poverty at home. After the Korean War, and particularly in the 1960s and 1970s, the North Korean government made great efforts to establish contact with the Japanese Koreans and help them organize community activities. It eventually began to encourage them to return to North Korea, and many thousands did. This woman's father, who was dissatisfied with Japan, decided to go back. His wife, however, wanted to stay. With the help of North Koreans, he took his small boys on board a ship, essentially kidnapping them from the mother. But his daughter, who was older, managed to escape and stay in Japan with her mother.

For years she and her mother heard nothing about the fate of the father and the two boys. Then, through a friend who was prominent in Japanese Korean leftist activities, and could therefore travel back and forth to North Korea, they got news. The father, who had often complained about Japan, was not happy in North Korea because once they got there, the Japanese Koreans were sent off to poor, remote areas and kept together in groups, a special category of people not allowed to travel about, presumably so that they would not infect other North Koreans with stories about what it was really like in the outer world.

The father had complained, and though the details were not clear, probably expressed a desire to go back to Japan. This was totally unacceptable, and he was executed. Now the two brothers were young men, still living in the same part of North Korea, among resettled Japanese Koreans. Eventually, they were allowed to send letters, which were quite bland. I was shown pictures they had sent of themselves and their young wives, also from Japanese Korean families, smiling and sporting the required Kim Il Sung buttons that everyone wears.

Hearing such a story directly confirms reports that corporatism has been taken further than almost anywhere else. It is entirely believable that only the proper categories of people are allowed to live in the shiny new capital of Pyongyang, that social mobility, in fact, is tightly controlled, and that corporate familism extends much further than just among the elite, but throughout the society, so that those born of the wrong kind of family are stuck in those roles for their own lives, too. After all, we know from the Chinese and Cambodian examples how Marxist class categories and traditional notions of hereditary status passed on by the family line can be merged, and with what devastating effect.

It may be that on the whole there have been fewer mass killings, and perhaps less torture in North Korea than in some other communist dictatorships, certainly less than in China and the Soviet Union, though North Korea has had its share of brutal repression.[50] But the degree of regulation and control is extraordinarily high.

No doubt, when this regime collapses sometime in the next decade, we will learn the full details. For the time being, however, we can only guess at what the Koreans think of this. We know that in the end, the sacrifices will not have been worth it, because North Korea will not emerge from decades of Kim Il Sungism as a prosperous and modern society, but as an archaic industrial catastrophe, like the other Stalinist societies.

Because Romania was never as closed or as tightly controlled as North Korea, we have known about some of the consequences of Ceausescu's policies for a long time. The extent of the economic disaster and its social consequences, however, surprised even the experts when the protective blanket of communism was violently cast off in December of 1989. One of the most egregious and intrusive of Ceausescu's policies began even before the turn toward a "North Korean" style of rule in 1971, and it is worth mentioning because it became the basis for one of the most sickening set of exposés that followed the general collapse of communism in Europe.

In early 1990 terrible stories began to come to light of Romanian orphanages packed with starving, abandoned, children, including small babies. Many were receiving virtually no care. Further, it turned out that Romania had a high incidence of infantile AIDS. This was the result of the fierce pro-natalist policies of the Ceausescus. Contraceptive devices, never widely distributed, had been made almost completely unavailable since 1966. At that time, abortion, which had been the main method of contraception, was made illegal, except in a very small number of cases (if the mother's life was threatened, if there had been rape, in the likelihood of hereditary diseases, or if the mother had already had four or more children).[51]

When abortion was first declared illegal in 1966, and divorce made very difficult, it was to stop the decline in Romania's birthrate. Ceausescu believed that Romania needed people, as workers, as soldiers, and as a barrier to encroachment by the Slavs and Hungarians who surrounded it.[52] In 1967 the birthrates had shot up, but over time, most Romanians had adapted, and between smuggled contraceptives, illegal abortion rings, and changed sexual mores, birth rates had come back down. In 1985, the anti-abortion law was tightened, and by its last years the regime was ordering forced periodic gynecological inspection of women between 16 and 45. This way, in principle, pregnancies could be discovered early and women watched to prevent illegal abortion. In practice, as Gail Kligman points out, in this respect, as in most of the increasingly bizarre set of commands issuing from the top, the practice was far from being carried out fully, and many doctors falsified reports to pretend that they had fulfilled their "planned" number of inspections. (Everything, of course, was in the plan—taxi drivers had a planned number of customers per day, factories had planned outputs, and doctors had planned inspections for pregnancies. The state even tried to get peasant households to sign contracts for planned numbers of future children they would produce, but this did not work very well.)[53]

Many found ways of evading the state's intrusion into their personal lives, but many did not, especially the urban poor. There were many unwanted children, and as the economy deteriorated in the 1980s because of Ceausescu's obsession with forcing ever more investment out of national production, and thus reducing consumption, growing numbers of these were simply abandoned in hospitals, from which they were moved to orphanages. But the orphanages were poorly staffed and inadequately provisioned, and aside from boys picked to be raised as future special guards for Ceausescu, for many infants, this was just a slow death sentence. Many thousands of women also died of complications from illegal, poorly performed abortions.

AIDS was a further complication. Romanian doctors routinely gave newborns microtransfusions of blood. This practice, which was once thought to be beneficial, was abandoned decades ago in the West, but somehow, Romanian doctors, largely cut off from Western journals and contacts, never found out, and they continued the practice. Hospitals did not have enough needles, or proper sterilizing equipment, and blood for transfusions was not tested, even after the danger of AIDS became known throughout the world, so a lot of newborns contracted AIDS. We do not know how many caught hepatitis or other diseases, or how far such diseases have spread throughout the general population.[54]

In the 1970s people with the right Party connections could easily get safe abortions by bribing doctors working in the special Central Committee hospital. (There were also special Central Committee farms to grow food, special shops, vacation lodges, and so on.) By the late 1980s, it had become more difficult for everyone, and even some highly placed doctors were prosecuted for violating the law. Ceausescu was deadly serious about his goal of producing more Romanians for the national good.

All this was only part of a general plan to create a new and more vigorous Romania. Ceausescu wanted to homogenize the population, to make everyone live in apartment blocks with communal dining rooms. He wanted Romanians to abandon all ideas of personal property, and to this end he decreed that throughout Romania the villages were to be destroyed and replaced by small towns so that individual housing would be replaced by mass housing. This program was just barely beginning to get under way when he was overthrown. He also at one point projected moving retired people out of Bucharest, presumably to get the fresh and sparkling look that he had seen in Pyongyang.[55]

In Bucharest itself, a vast construction project got under way. Much of the inner city was torn down, and replaced by apartment buildings and huge public buildings. Those dispossessed of their old houses were often given twenty-four hours to move, and then they were shipped out to new apartment blocks on the outskirts of the city.[56] But as Kligman noticed upon later inspection, the new apartment buildings, which on the outside looked like ordinary, if somewhat shabby typical Eastern European socialist constructions, did not have running water. Their inhabitants had to carry their own water in buckets up stairs. Nor were they heated in winter.

By the late 1980s, the Romanian economy was in collapse. The plans for the 1990s at that time called for relying more on horse-drawn transportation than on trucks in the countryside, because there was not enough fuel.[57] The cities had no heat or light in winter. Food became scarcer and scarcer, and the lines longer than ever.

Yet, as qualified observers noted, there was little protest, and virtually no dissident movement as elsewhere in Eastern Europe. And when Ceausescu fell, it turned out that the number killed or imprisoned had been relatively small. Under Ceausescu the population had been largely compliant, and the threat of sanctions had been, on the whole, sufficient to keep the country in line. There were only two major outbreaks of strikes and protests, in 1977 and 1987. In both instances the regime had moved quickly and suppressed the uprisings with force. Leaders had been executed. But this was not one of the bloodier regimes in communist history. On the contrary, until the late 1980s, when everything began to go wrong, and the intellectuals, as well as substantial portions of the Party elite, began to suffer from the lack of heat and light, and had their privileges gradually removed, the overwhelming majority went along. This is why a number of commentators believe that the events of December 1989 were just a Party coup against the Ceausescus, not a real revolution as elsewhere in Eastern Europe. And indeed, whatever the truth of that assertion may be, the fact is that the former Party apparatus still largely controlled the country in the early 1990s.[58]

More telling, perhaps, is that during the 1970s and 1980s Romanian intellectuals came up with theories to justify the Ceausescu regime. They admired his nationalism, and fabricated evidence that Romania had always been a great center of civilization, inventing many aspects of modernity at the same time as Western Europe. Therefore, the increasing autarky and isolation were implicitly justified because Romania had within itself all it needed to accomplish Ceausescu's grand ambitions. Much of what these intellectuals wrote on behalf of the regime was based on pre-communist right-wing ideologies and mythologies, and many of those most active under Ceausescu came up with these analogies and theories on their own, without being told what to do. This is what Katherine Verdery found in her study of intellectual life under Ceausescu, and it is one of the most distressing aspect of his rule.[59]

What was the price paid in terms of human suffering, humiliation, and the destruction of both resources and the environment? All the Romanians got for their pains were more inefficient factories, more pollution, more moralizing lectures from the Ceausescu family, and more claims that they had reached the apogee of national glory.

The official economic growth rate from 1951 to 1975 was 13 percent per year, one of the highest rates in the world. Romanian economic statistics claimed that only Japan was growing faster than they were, and not by much. They were proud to point out that according to their (somewhat bizarre) calculations, Romania was second in the world, behind only the United States, in per capita steel production.[60]

Romania did not become a great and modern nation. Despite the impressive statistics, which were as much self-deception as conscious lies, it remained a pathetically isolated and impoverished state, filled with internal hatreds and pathologies. It remains exactly that in the 1990s, and it may well have been set on a course from which it will take a very long time to recover, if it ever does.

Yet, after Ceausescu was overthrown, the Western press largely misunderstood him and his wife. They noted that he had lived very well, that he had palaces, and foreign bank accounts. They assumed that he was just a typically corrupt tyrant. But he was not. His style of life was far above that of ordinary people, of course, but no more so than that of other heads of state. In his later years he had Bucharest's main street permanently closed off to traffic so that he could be taken along it when he wanted, and he came to be protected, like Stalin, or Hitler, by extravagant security measures. Toward the end, there is no doubt that he was ill, frequently out of touch with reality, and that for his people his rule had turned into a grotesque nightmare of deprivation and fear. His aim, however, was not to enrich himself, but to transform his society. Though not an intellectual, he had adopted the ideas that prevailed in nationalist intellectual circles, mixed them with his own practical brand of Marxism-Stalinism, and come up with a disaster. As everything soured, rather than giving up his early model of how to proceed, he clung to it ever more tenaciously, and practically no one dared tell him that his life had been devoted to a cause that could not work. It is not only tyrants who end their days like this, but because they have so much power their personal errors and refusal to adapt cause misery for millions. There is no way to get rid of them except by revolution or assassination, or simply by waiting until they die. At the end, before he was shot, Ceausescu was subjected to a hasty show trial. He claimed to have done wonders for Romania, and demanded to be heard before parliament, sure that his greatness would be recognized. He died believing in his cause.

And North Korea? Kim Il Sung lives well too, naturally, in elegant villas, but that is not his goal in life, either.[61] He is animated by a dream, a great national ideal to which he has devoted his life, as did his friend Ceausescu. What price have the North Koreans paid for this? We will see, no doubt, in the next decade, when the system he has built collapses. Everything we know about such regimes suggests that the price paid has been much higher than most of those who have studied it really know. But as yet, in this case, unlike with Romania, there is no proof.

COMPARING ROMANIA AND NORTH KOREA TO SIMILAR CASES THAT MIGHT HAVE EVOLVED INTO TYRANNIES

In view of their common past it is certain that if historical tradition and culture alone caused tyranny, there ought to be equal amounts of it in South and North Korea. Without going into any detail, it is easy to establish that South Korea's several post-independence governments have indeed had tyrannical elements. Suppression of the opposition, military rule, killings and torture for political reasons, the construction of a powerful secret police apparatus, and bloody repression of protests have occurred.[62] It is only in the late 1980s, except for a brief interlude in about 1960, that real democracy has emerged in South Korea. There is no guarantee that this tentative democracy would survive a political or economic crisis. Nevertheless, South Korean society has evolved toward greater democracy, and regimentation has been much less severe than in North Korea. As in Thailand and Taiwan, also run by military dictatorships for many years, the pressures of rapid economic development and the rise of a new, modern middle class have had a liberalizing effect.[63]

What distinguishes the North from the South is that South Korea fell into the American and capitalist orbit. This necessarily made it more open, and imposed a capitalist model of development. As Jung-en Woo has shown, the South Korean version of capitalism was heavily protected and state influenced, to be sure, yet it was also export oriented, and economic managers had to interact with their American and Japanese counterparts.[64] North Korea, on the other hand, drastically isolated itself, even from other communist societies. Furthermore, what ideology it did get from the outside, namely the Stalinist version of Marxism, tinged with ideological admiration for Mao's China, emphasized violent conflict as the mainspring of history. Combining isolation, a strong memory of wrongs imposed on it, xenophobia, and a vision of the world as one of inevitable revolutionary conflicts, it would seem probable indeed that North Korea would have even stronger leanings toward tyranny than South Korea, regardless of the personality of the individuals in command of these two states.

There is another element to this. However protected a version of capitalism may have developed in South Korea, it did produce a consumer-oriented modern society. This necessarily fragmented the old social order and decreased communal values. As Ezra Vogel has suggested, it is not the perpetuation of the old Confucian system which has allowed the South Koreans, and other East Asians, to develop so fast, but its partial replacement by a newer, more individualistic orientation. This may have outraged South Korea's politically active students, who like their counterparts in much of the West rejected the alienation and selfishness of modern society, but in many ways these students were quite out of touch with the changing realities of modern South Korean life. On three visits to South Korean universities in 1989 and 1990, I was repeatedly struck by the tenacity with which young South Korean leftist academics could deny the progress going on under their noses, even as they admired a North they believed to be the genuine representative of Korea. The South, in their mind, was only an American colony. In a sense, of course, they were right, but that is what made the South less tyrannical and economically so much more successful.

What I am suggesting, then, is that it is not the increasing individualism and destruction of old communal values that has produced modern tyranny, but the attempt to reverse these trends by reimposing mythologized and exaggerated old solidarities. Kim Il Sungism, for all that it wants to modernize the North Korean economy, rests on a rejection of the individualism that underpins modern economies. South Korea, for all its cultural biases against capitalism, individualism, and the destruction of older Confucian values, has been unable to hold on to its past because it is too entangled in the capitalist world system.

It is more difficult to contrast the Ceausescu regime to similar cases because there is no analogous "South Romania." There are, however, the surrounding countries of Eastern Europe that all had communism imposed on them by force. None of them went as far as Romania in creating personal tyrannies, except Albania. Some, like Hungary and Poland, became relatively benign dictatorships in their later years, certainly far more open, far more tolerant, and much less repressive than either the Stalinist Soviet Union or Ceausescu's Romania. It was precisely as it became more independent and nationalistic, and there-fore more anti-Soviet, that Romania lapsed into the Ceausescu tyran-ny. The assertion, sometimes made, that nationalism and communism are antithetical, is entirely wrong, even if it has some substance for those who compare the original theoretical doctrines from which these ideologies emerged in the nineteenth century.[65] But in the twen-tieth century, nationalism and communism combined made tyranny inevitable, whereas communist regimes that never gained nationalist credentials turned into flabby, illegitimate, and ineffective forms of government.

To Romania's north lies Hungary. Despite many differences, both countries shared some historical and cultural similarities, though Hun-gary's nationalists would be quick to deny this, as would Romania's. Mircea Eliade, a member of the fascist Iron Guard in Romania before the war, wrote in 1938 that the Hungarians were the second most imbecilic people on earth, surpassed only by the Bulgarians, who are the Romanians' southern neighbors. Later, Eliade became a renowned professor at the University of Chicago, and his books on religion and mysticism were favorites of American undergraduates for a whole gen-eration.[66]

Hungary had right-wing authoritarian regimes before and during World War II, as did Romania. It was one of Hitler's allies during the war, as was Romania. And both were subjected to communist rule for exactly as long. Has Hungary exhibited similar tyrannical tendencies?

Andrew Janos has described the fundamental reason for which throughout the late nineteenth and early twentieth century Hungarian intellectuals drifted ever more toward the far right, that is, toward cor-poratism and fascism.

[I]mages and expectations are disseminated faster than the means of material improvement, creating a deep sense of relative deprivation, indeed bitter frustration. . . . in the long run, pent-up frustrations are likely to resurface time and again, to act as the single most important destabilizing factor in peripheral societies.[67]

By "peripheral" societies Janos means those that are not the most developed, that is, those whose leaders and intelligentsia are the most likely to suffer the kind of *ressentiment* which is one of the causes of xenophobic and angry nationalism. Hungary, Janos emphasizes, was hardly unique. This has been the lot of nationalists in most of the world in the twentieth century, in Korea as in Russia, in Central and Eastern Europe as in Africa and Latin America.

Hungary was occupied by the Soviets in 1945. It revolted in 1956, but the Soviet army reimposed communism and installed János Kádár in power. His regime initiated economic reforms after 1958, and then gradually liberalized. Kádár never turned himself into a demi-god; he downplayed Hungarian nationalism in favor of a kind of cynical accommodation with a system no one really liked, but which could not be overcome without the threat of another Soviet invasion. Marxism, though it certainly remained the official ideology, was something that few continued to believe in. The Soviet Union, for its part, was slipping into the corruption and sloth of the Brezhnev years, and was happy enough to have peace and quiet in Hungary. That sort of messy accommodation, while it did not produce a liberal democracy, saved the Hungarians considerable pain. There were relatively few in prison by the 1970s, and Hungarians were generally free to travel and talk, if not to consider forming opposition parties. Before 1988 Hungary had gone further in introducing market reforms in its economy than any other country in the Soviet Bloc, and it therefore emerged from the 1989 collapse of communism with the least trauma.[68]

The contrast between Hungary and Romania could hardly be greater in view of the fact that they were both supposedly communist. Hungary was led by a communist elite that gave up all ambition to act as a big power, and that abandoned Hungary's previous territorial illusions. In part, this was because of the catastrophic outcome of its alliance with Hitler, followed by the brutality of early Soviet rule and the war of 1956. Romania, on the other hand, resurrected its pre-war nationalism, and Ceausescu's dream of making his nation a great power gained a considerable measure of legitimacy in the eyes of his citizens.[69]

I recognize that this explanation may strike many as offensive and unfair. It may be that the willingness of the Hungarians to fight in 1956, before their spirit of resistance was broken, contributed to the Soviets' willingness to let them experiment with gradual liberalization. The Czechoslovaks, who did not fight back in 1968 when their reforms were stopped by another Soviet invasion, had to suffer through humiliation and repression for two decades after that, though even there, they certainly did not have to bear the economic decline and pathetic personalization of power that Romania underwent. My point is less to moralize than to say that among the many forms of bad government that have existed, the combination of Stalinist industrialization, cultural isolation, and ultra-nationalist grandeur is among the most likely to produce tyranny. And tyranny imposes a steeper price on those so ruled than most other types of bad government.

There have been many communist leaders in Eastern Europe who could have been much worse. Constrained by their continued dependence on the Soviets, by conditions in their countries, and, to some unmeasurable degree, by their personalities, they did not take Ceausescu's path. In some cases, for example that of General Jaruzelski who imposed martial law on Poland in 1981 and ruled until 1989, and of Kádár in Hungary, they were so reviled by their anti-communist opponents that we may forget that, in difficult circumstances, they saved their people from much worse outcomes. Nationalist purity has little virtue in such circumstances.

The most appropriate analogy to Ceausescu in Eastern Europe was Enver Hoxha of Albania. Unlike Ceausescu (or for that matter, Kim Il Sung), Hoxha was a genuine intellectual, educated in France. During World War II he led a resistance movement against the Italians and Germans. This movement relied heavily on aid from the Yugoslav resistance movement led by Tito, and after 1945, Yugoslavia came close to absorbing Albania.[70] Albania narrowly escaped because it was protected by the Soviets after Tito's break with Stalin in 1948, but the attempt provoked a violently nationalistic reaction by Hoxha. Later, when the Soviets tried to regain Tito's friendship in the mid-1950s, Hoxha became a bitter enemy of the Soviet Union.[71] This led to the most closed regime in all of Europe, and one of the most isolated in the world. Hoxha promoted a fantastic cult of his own personality, autarkic development, hatred of all things foreign, and extreme collectivistic regimentation.[72] No one paid much attention because Albania is such a little country. The results were even worse than in Romania; after communism fell in Albania in 1991 it was revealed that its economic progress was without substance. By 1992 Albania was totally dependent on foreign food donations to keep its people alive. It had few motor vehicles, and its small industrial sector built up at great cost under Hoxha had collapsed.[73]

It would seem, then, that Ceausescu's regime was not as unique as some thought when its horrors were first exposed. In the Balkans, where nationalism was born angry and frustrated in the nineteenth century, where no ethnic or religious group was fully satisfied with the boundaries it got, where the ravages of World Wars I and II were severe, where economies were backward compared to Western Europe, and where communism then ruled for over four decades, there has been a general tendency toward tyranny. Nor did that tendency vanish with the end of communism, as the troubles of the 1990s demonstrate. Slobodan Milosevic's rule in Serbia, and the attendant horror, brutality, and persecutions in former Yugoslavia attest to this.

Throughout the modern world all societies have a variety of cultural strands. Extreme nationalists exist everywhere, but they are always opposed by some who are less extreme. Collectivistic tendencies are always present, more or less, as are those who would reject modernity. But such ideological strands are never uniformly accepted. Ideologies of blood and violence also exist everywhere, as do those who believe in the inevitability of racial, ethnic, religious, national, or class warfare, but sometimes they are widely accepted, and in other times and places, they are marginal. In the case of Romania we know, and for North Korea we can suppose, that not everyone agreed with direction taken by the leader. At least we are certain that in South Korea, with the same history and culture as the North, there have been a variety of ideologies. Yet, both Ceausescu and Kim, whatever their personal failings, relied on deep national traditions and appealed to some significant portion of their nationalist intellectuals. Neither was an anomaly in his society. And both were guided by a vision of economic and political development that almost inevitably pushed them toward personal tyranny. Though neither of them was an intellectual as such, they were not bereft of ideas, and both were visionaries who stuck to their ideals for their entire careers. Many other potential Romanian and Korean leaders would have followed the same course.

In the discussion of European totalitarianism, of Maoism, and of the Khmer Rouge, a few general propositions about the causes of ideological, modern tyranny have emerged. These are strengthened by adding the examples of North Korea and Romania.

One proposition is that the presence of nationalist ideologies that stress resentment of the outside and blame external forces for perceived domestic failures are likely to condone and even welcome dictatorial, brutal national saviors who promise to overcome the evil external world and venge the nation for past wrongs. Intellectuals who believe in such ideologies are particularly likely to accept tyranny as a solution. This was certainly the case in Romania and Korea.

Another general conclusion drawn from the study of Hitler, Stalin, Mao, and Pol Pot is that a worldview that believes in the inevitability of conflict between races or classes makes the emergence of tyranny more likely. Marxism, however modified and personalized by Ceausescu and Kim Il Sung, remained an ideology that promised inevitable conflict. The very ideology on which their rule was based promised that they would be assaulted by forces trying to reverse their utopian, revolutionary plans, and so they had to build garrison states, closed off from outside influence, in order to carry out their dreams.

The study of modern tyranny also shows a strong association between anti-individualistic, communal ideologies and acceptance of regimes that consider individual rights insignificant. As the ruler and his party come to be the interpreters of what the community and nation really want, this means, in effect, that the abuse of power becomes almost inevitable. Tyranny is justified as the true expression of the community's interests against recalcitrant and historically obsolete individualism. That most cultural traditions have emphasized group or communal rights over individual ones has increased the probability of tyranny throughout most of the world. But the specifically modern versions of communalism advocated by fascist and communist rulers have been far more coercive than older, traditional versions because they have been connected to ideologies that promise to transform society according to established scientific principles in order to bring about utopias. Elevating the community and nation at the expense of the individual, and trying to mobilize the entire population for great transforming efforts is a mixture particularly likely to create tyranny.

It is evident that nationalist elites who believe that discipline and social purity, defined as the exclusion of "foreign" values and habits, can solve the complex problems of adapting to the modern world are likely to become both increasingly frustrated and tyrannical once they achieve power. We know that this is exactly what happened to Ceausescu, as it did with the other cases we have studied. The frustration is inevitable because, in fact, adaptation to the modern world requires understanding, accepting, and using ideas and habits that are "foreign." Whatever one may think of Western individualism and capitalism, it is impossible to keep up with modern technology without being intimately exposed to what happens in the West, and more recently, in the most developed capitalist societies of East Asia.

Yet, it is important to remember that cultural traditions and the presence of certain ideologies do not make tyranny inevitable. Korea had to experience the chaos of decolonization, foreign occupation, and war to turn into a full-scale tyranny. Even then, the accident that the North fell under Soviet rather than American occupation played a key role in determining the outcome. Romania also had to be occupied by Soviet troops to emerge with the particular communist tyranny that it got under Ceausescu. In both cases, economic and political chaos, as well as foreign occupations played key roles.[74] We can never predict precise historical contingencies such as wars and their outcomes. But by understanding the ideological and cultural legacies that make tyranny more or less likely, we can know whether, given certain catastrophic events, the probability of tyranny is high or low.

We know, therefore, that in places like Romania, and elsewhere in the Balkans and large parts of the former Soviet Union, the emergence of new tyrannies in the near future is at least highly likely, if far from certain. Resentful nationalism, collectivistic ideologies, mistrust of liberalism, and the prospects of economic and political chaos all co-exist. The history of tyranny in these regions, which did not begin with the Bolshevik Revolution, will not end with the demise of communism, either. We will return to this theme in the book's concluding chapter.

Chapter 8

Little Hitlers?

Elite Fantasies in Argentina and Iraq, and Their Realization

The politics of angry, resentful, and vengeful nationalism have been so widespread in the twentieth century as to change the way in which nationalism is understood. What was once associated with liberation and greater freedom, with the opening of new possibilities for democratic development, and with greater dignity for all has come to be seen by many analysts, particularly but not only in the richer Western countries, as a monster of irrational passion waiting for its chance to break out of the civilized bonds that try to control it. Once loose, it wreaks havoc and death. The collapse of the Soviet Union and some former East European communist states, most obviously Yugoslavia, into competing states that are often at war with each other and even within their own boundaries, as well as the sad experience of postcolonial liberation in Africa, have been added to the older memories of the chaos left in the wake of dissolved empires in Central Europe in 1918 and the terrible civil and international wars spawned by the withdrawal of Great Britain from its Indian Empire in 1947.

Almost all, certainly most of the new nationalisms that have developed in the late nineteenth and early twentieth centuries have been based partly on jealous admiration for and resentment of the successful

West. It was the West, that is Western Europe and the United States, that first made the transition to modern industrial society. Whatever problems this raised, however serious the social disequilibrium which followed, industrialization made these societies rich and powerful beyond anything that had ever been seen in the world before. As a result, by 1900, almost all of the non-Western world was either directly controlled by Western powers, or indirectly controlled through foreign investment and frequent political interference. Only a few isolated places, and only one major non-European power (including in the word "European" overseas settler colonies) escaped this kind of domination—Japan. A few other places, including Thailand, Persia, what was left of the failing Ottoman Empire, and China (then being slowly dismembered) remained at least formally independent. But even when independence was preserved, the example of the West as a source of envy, fear, and admiration predominated.

It is not surprising, then, that of all the types of nationalism which developed in the late nineteenth and twentieth centuries, most should resemble Russian and German nationalism based on *ressentiment* more than the Anglo-American, more liberal type. This might suggest, then, that most of the world has had at least one of the important elements likely to produce tyranny for most of the twentieth century.

Add to this the strains placed on many non-Western societies as they tried to modernize their economies and create functioning, efficient administrations in a few short years, often with poorly educated, ill-prepared populations thrust into the modern world by its intrusion from the outside instead of by slow internal development, and the probability of tyranny increased. Economic insecurity, administrative disorganization, political instability—all of these common elements that contribute to ideological extremism and make conditions ripe for potential dictators were widely present.

And finally, there is the fact that it was only in the Western intellectual tradition that a sense of the worth of the individual over the community developed. Though this is not a sure barrier against tyranny, it helps, and its absence makes it that much easier for tyranny to establish itself.

The political histories of most of the non-Western states in the twentieth century make it abundantly clear that tyranny has been common. Not all have suffered tyrannies, but the majority have, at one time or another, been subjected to abusive and murderous governments. Given the fact that even some relatively favored European states—Germany and Italy among them—have been subject to such rule, and that in the case of Germany this was one of the worst governments to ever exist, is it any wonder that tyranny has repeatedly occurred elsewhere, in less fortunate societies?

It is not enough to throw up one's hands and say that for most of the world tyranny is a natural form of government, or that by liberal twentieth-century standards "bad kings" were very common in the past and therefore remain likely in the present. That may be true, but it is equally correct to note that people have fought against tyranny everywhere, and that tyrannical rule has not existed uniformly or constantly throughout most of the world. Just as, in the case of Germany, Italy, Russia, or China there have been considerable variations over time, so at any one time great variations exist in the types of regimes that rule countries at roughly comparable levels of economic modernization. The likelihood of tyranny is a function of several factors that may vary quite independently of each other: ideological tendencies, differing degrees of economic and political stability, external interference and war, and, at least in part, the personality of individual leaders who come to power.

Comparing such widely different countries as Argentina under Juan Perón from 1945 to 1955, and later during the rule of military juntas who conducted its "dirty" internal wars from 1976 to 1982, Syria under Hafez al-Asad, and Iraq under Saddam Hussein shows the great variability of conditions that can produce tyranny, and how the various contributory factors interact. These cases reinforce the notion that ideology has often been the principal, though never the sole cause of modern tyranny. We will illustrate this by looking at Argentina and Iraq in detail, and adding some comparative comments about Syria.

ARGENTINA: THE COUNTRY THAT IMAGINED ITS CRISIS

The modern history of Argentina is proof that a country need not be poor or short of human and physical resources to be an economic failure; a nation may be thoroughly divided within itself, to the point of civil war, without any major ethnic or religious divisions; foreign invasions and international threats are not necessary to produce a sense of persecution by imagined outside forces; and ultimately, unrealistic ideologies can triumph over even the best of objective conditions to produce catastrophe.

Although it was thinly populated and quite marginal in the Spanish colonial empire, and after independence in 1810 divided and misruled by various caudillos (local semi-feudal bosses), in the second half of the nineteenth century Argentina was transformed into a great success. Its almost empty great plains, the pampas, turned out to be excellent grazing land for beef, and exceptionally fertile, rich farmland. Argentina became one of the world's major cereal and meat exporters. The country was politically united, local caudillos were brought under control, and an educated, Europeanized, enlightened elite ruled it as foreign investment poured in to develop its railroads, food processing plants, and the infrastructure of its cities. Argentina was open to both European investment (mostly from England) and immigration (mostly from Spain and Italy).

The economy boomed, and it became one of the world's ten richest countries. By 1914 Argentina's per capita income was close to that of the advanced parts of Western Europe, much higher than Spain's or Italy's, and at least four times higher than Japan's.[1]

Oil was discovered, and in the first quarter of the twentieth century the size of the industrial labor force increased at an average rate of 6 percent a year, while installed horsepower in industry, a measure of its overall potential, increased at over 20 percent a year. The future was bright. Buenos Aires was by then one of the world's great cities, and Argentina enjoyed relatively stable politics, and increasing democracy, especially after 1912 when the franchise was extended. The prevailing political ethos was liberal and open to reform; the small army stayed out of politics.[2]

Though the elite showed little love for the abstract idea of democracy, and there was considerable electoral fraud and manipulation, by the standards of its day, Argentina before 1930 was one of the world's more democratic societies.[3]

Above all Argentina was a land of high social mobility, where those who worked hard could, with a little luck, get ahead, move into the middle class, and, for a few, even into the ranks of the elite. And because of social mobility and economic growth, immigrants, both those from Europe and those who moved in ever larger numbers from the rural areas to the cities, were more or less successfully integrated.[4]

In 1916 a party called the Radicals came to power because for the first time substantial portions of the middle class could vote. They were moderate reformers who opened politics to the middle class, but despite some anti-elite rhetoric, did not seriously threaten the interests of the rich. Peter Smith has summarized the situation in the late 1920s by suggesting that the generation of older Radicals still considered themselves in the opposition because of their hostility to the landed elite, while the new generation of Radical politicians were more concerned with their personal advancement than with finding useful compromises. But at the same time, the old elite was still disproportionately powerful, and angry about the way in which the Radicals had changed the traditional political system that had been so successful during the great era of rapid growth and progress.[5]

Most important of all, however, was a general ideological shift that had begun early in the century, increased after 1919 in reaction against mass strikes and popular mobilization by the Radicals, and continued to grow during the 1920s. This was an ultra-nationalist, nostalgic glorification of mythical "Hispanic" and "gaucho" (a Pampas cowboy) values, combined with a dislike for modern industrial, urban society, a distrust of foreign investment, and a rejection of liberal values. Combined with this, there also developed a more populist version of nationalism. Largely an offshoot of the Radical Party, this was equally anti-foreign, blaming social and economic problems of Argentine modernization on the control of so much of its economy by English and other outside investors. These two currents of thought reproduced much of the growing anti-liberal intellectual current in Europe at that time.[6]

In 1924 the nationalist poet and defender of "gaucho" values, Leopoldo Lugones, issued a call to the army: "Fortunately for the world the hour of the sword has rung again. . . . Pacifism, collectivism, democracy are synonyms of the emptiness which gives those destined to lead an opportunity. . . . Military men are better than politicians, and I want a government of those who are the best." In his massive study of the Argentine military, Alain Rouquié notes that in 1924 Argentina was not a militaristic nation, and it was very far from undergoing the kind of crisis which had already brought fascism to Italy.[7] But some officers were sympathetic. One of them was Juan Perón.

On his graduation from the military college in 1913, Perón had received three books from his father. Along with Plutarch's *Lives* (which, when he was 60, he tried to get his bored teenaged mistress to read), and Lord Chesterfield's *Letters* to his son, there was the 1870s epic poem about the beleaguered gaucho, *Martín Fierro*, a work much admired by Lugones. Perón's father had inscribed it: "So that you will never forget above all things that you are a Creole [a Spaniard born in America]."[8]

The Radicals themselves were also nationalists, and in 1922 they founded a state petroleum company meant to exclude the previously dominant American and British companies. It never succeeded, but oil was to become a major symbol of Argentina's new drive toward self-sufficiency, and its new state company, plagued by growing corruption and featherbedding, an equally appropriate symptom of the state's inability to carry out its nationalist economic policies efficiently.[9]

The corruption of the Radicals, the general dislike of democracy by a small elite, the growing nativist nationalism, and the ideological drift toward fascism came together in a movement called *Nueva República* which admired Mussolini and the authoritarian, corporatist regime of Primo de Rivera in Spain. The movement enlisted an important general, Uriburu, who was also one of the few top military men closely connected by family ties to the rich oligarchy. Uriburu and "New Republic" plotted to overthrow the government, and gathered around them some eager junior officers. With a tiny number of men, Uriburu seized power in September of 1930.[10]

Some historians have tried to connect this coup with the coming of the Great Depression. But Peter Smith has shown that when the plot was hatched in early 1930, the Depression had not made itself felt in Argentina, and even by September, its effects were mild. The price of beef was holding up, strike activity by workers was insignificant, and though wheat production was down, this was because of a drought.[11] Ultimately, Argentina would suffer far less from the Depression than the more industrialized countries. Unemployment never rose much above 5 percent; and though agricultural export prices did fall, Argentina continued to industrialize in the 1930s.[12]

In Smith's terminology, 1930 was the result of a "crisis of legitimacy." An ideologically motivated little group of military men put up a show of force, and a democratic system without much support or legitimacy at the top simply collapsed.

Uriburu's group was too small to keep control, and despite the loss of democratic legitimacy that had occurred, there was not yet much sentiment for anything close to a fascist solution. Instead, that wing of the army and oligarchy which wanted to return to the old days took over, manipulated the next set of elections, and by 1932 the old system seemed safely back in office. But Argentina was now too urbanized, the middle and working classes were too large, and the ideological mobilization that had begun had gone too far to allow a simple return to the days when a small group of members of the prestigious Buenos Aires Jockey Club ran politics while disenfranchised immigrants produced growing wealth. Furthermore, the army itself was becoming more professionalized, and during the 1930s was impressed by the German and Italian examples, so that its disdain for political manipulation and for civilians grew. The crisis of legitimacy remained unresolved.[13]

Along with increasing industrialization in the 1930s a new ideology of self-sufficiency also arose, this time not just from romantic nationalists but from reasoned economic analysts. Argentine economists (with contributions from Brazilians), inspired by earlier Central European economic theorists, developed a way of looking at economic growth and development which has come down to us in the form of Latin American "dependency theory." The intellectual roots and underlying assumptions of dependency theory as it developed in Europe have already been discussed in the previous chapter on Romania and Korea. It is only necessary to repeat the key points.

According to the theory, foreign investment produces an economy that funnels profits to foreigners. Primary resources and agricultural goods are exported, while more complex industrial goods are imported. Consequently, economies that export primary goods never get to develop their technology, and always remains backward. Further, over time, the price of primary exports tends to fall relative to advanced industrial goods, so that formerly rich primary exporters gradually get poorer. This occurs because rich, industrial countries, chiefly England in the nineteenth century, and the United States after World War I, have the political and military muscle to impose themselves. They force unfair trading agreements on weaker countries, oblige them to allow the repatriation of profits, and prevent developing economies from imposing the necessary tariffs and policies to develop their own industries.[14]

The most famous Argentine economist, Raúl Prebisch, who would become one of the world's most influential economists by mid-century, began his career in the 1920s in agreement with the basic assumptions of the nationalist economists. He was never as extreme as some of his associates and followers, and when called back to advise the government of Argentina in the late 1950s, he would propose a classically liberal solution to its problems. But by then it was too late. Nationalist closure and protectionism had created what Carlos Waisman calls "hothouse capitalism," that had bred strong resistance to an economic opening.[15]

In the 1930s and 1940s, many Argentines became convinced that most of their problems were due to their being subordinated to foreign capital and markets. Along with this assumption, as we have already seen in previous cases, was a sense that local institutions and ways of thinking were somehow superior those of the degenerate and evil great capitalist powers like England. So along with economic closure, there was growing ideological contempt for liberalism and democracy in general.

There is no question that foreign, mostly British capital played an immense role in Argentina's development, and that by the 1930s, the decline of Britain was endangering old trading and investment patterns. Nor did the British hesitate to use their power to retain privileges for their investors. But whatever the theory said, the fact was that foreign investment, combined with Argentina's excellent resources and its open immigration policy, had made it rich, and set it on the road to industrialization.

Then, capital formation, which had been very high before World War I, decreased during the war, and again in the 1930s. The reason was that foreign investment became negative during the war and again during the Great Depression. Argentina was becoming economically more independent, and forced to rely on its own capitalists for investment. And because of the effects of the Great Depression and World War II on international trade, Argentina experienced very substantial import substitution industrialization during this period. All this might have combined to make the Argentine economy a more balanced, independent one in the 1940s and 1950s.[16]

Despite the conservative governments of the 1930s, the growing urban working class did succeed in organizing itself into unions, though wages stagnated during most of the 1930s. Nevertheless, here also, Argentine workers by the early 1940s were not only the best paid in Latin America, but their diets were not appreciably lower than those of workers in the United States at that time.[17]

So what was the problem? For one thing, the legitimacy crisis of 1930 was never solved because government after the coup remained unrepresentative. Army officers continued to be dissatisfied with political corruption and inefficiency, businessmen wanted labor repressed, the old elite did not accept democracy, and labor wanted more benefits. All these were ordinary problems of rapidly industrializing countries, but without either truly democratic institutions or stable government, there was no way of reaching compromise.[18] Underneath, there was the growing conviction from most sides that it was necessary to pursue a more nationalistic policy to overcome these problems. In 1943, army officers carried out another coup, meeting opposition as feeble as in 1930. Again, it was not that there was much of a crisis, but rather, that the government had such little legitimacy at any level.[19]

Juan Perón: The Populist Who Ruined Argentina

A small group of officers called the United Officers' Group (GOU) quickly took charge of the new regime. The GOU consisted mostly of mid-ranking officers who wanted to combine Hispanic, Catholic nationalism and corporatism to solve Argentina's social and political ills. They admired the Axis powers during World War II. Their leader was Juan Perón, a rising colonel and military intellectual who had written several books on military history, and one on the etymological origins of Patagonian place-names. He had also been a military attaché in Italy in 1940 and had been impressed by Mussolini's regime as well as by Franco in Spain.[20]

The military wanted to resist pressure from the United States to enter the war against the Axis, but Brazil, Argentina's rival as the preponderant power in this part of the world, was an ally of the United States, and consequently received arms and aid. This worried the Argentine military and convinced it that it was all the more necessary to build up Argentina's heavy and military industries.[21]

Perón, who came from a middle-class family, had grown up outside Buenos Aires, partly in the frontier area of Patagonia. He felt a genuine affection for ordinary Argentines. While higher officers took the ostensible lead in the government, he took the second position in the Ministry of Defense, and asked to become head of the obscure National Labor Department. Then he used his influence to initiate a vast series of changes. Workers were given significant wage and benefit increases, while Perón began to cultivate union leaders and promote the unification and rapid growth of the organized labor movement.[22]

Under such slogans as "Honesty, Justice, Duty," the army grew from 30,000 in mid-1943 to 100,000 by 1945, military industries were started, and it became official policy to promote virtual self-sufficiency in the economy. But whereas the more traditional military officers also wanted to repress labor, Perón prevented this. Instead, as he gave labor more privileges, he began to attack the capitalists, and particularly the old elite for having been unpatriotic and greedy.[23]

In November of 1943 Perón said:

Personally, I am a syndicalist, and as such, an anti-communist, but I think that we have to organize those who work into unions such that the workers and not the bosses or the agitators get the main benefits.[24]

In August 1944, he said:

If we fail to carry out the Peaceful Revolution, the People will accomplish the Violent Revolution. . . . And the way to do this is to carry forward Social Justice for the Masses. . . . Naturally this is not a popular idea among rich men. . . . Undoubtedly this path will meet with their resistance. But they are their own worst enemies. Better to offer 30 percent now than in several years or perhaps even months to lose all they have, including their ears.[25]

And in August 1945:

In the Stock Exchange they are some five hundred people who live by trafficking in what others produce. In the Unión Industrial they are some twelve gentlemen who never were real industrialists. And among the ranchers there are other gentlemen, as we all know, who have conspired to impose a dictatorship on this country. . . . This is the notorious behavior, you see, of these gentlemen who have always sold out our country. These are the great capitalists who make it their business to sell us out: the lawyers who work for foreign companies . . . the handful of men working with certain ambassadors [here referring to the ambassador of the United States] to fight people like me because we defend our country. They include the hired press. . . . It is an honor to be opposed by such bandits and traitors.[26]

This was like Mussolini at his simultaneously anti-plutocratic and anti-communist best, but unlike the Italian fascist, Perón actually believed in helping the working class. Wages and salaries, which had been about 45 percent of total national income in the decade before 1946, shot up to 60 percent between 1949 and 1954.[27] For an economy that was already quite advanced, this was a very significant jump.

Worried conservative forces in business and among the officers pressured General Farrell, the president, to fire Perón on October 9, 1945. But Perón's supporters rallied the Buenos Aires working class and within a week there were huge strikes and demonstrations. These culminated in a demonstration with over a quarter of a million people on October 17, and the president brought him back. Soon after Perón married his mistress, Eva Duarte, a radio actress who had been with him for a few months, and then, he prepared to run for president. The election was held in February of 1946, and it was honest. Perón won 52.4 percent of the vote. He was by far the most popular political figure in Argentina.[28]

During World War II Argentina had benefitted from high prices and demand for its agricultural exports, and had accumulated substantial foreign currency reserves. Perón's government used these to buy the foreign, mostly British-owned utilities companies in Argentina, chiefly the now antiquated railway system. Though not a very good buy, this purchase delighted the nationalists because it freed Argentina of "foreign" control. Then, taking advantage of the substantial development of industry in the previous couple of decades, and not particularly aware of the fact that Argentina now suffered from inadequate capital formation to keep up growth, the Peronists pressed forward with redistributive policies to the working classes, both urban and rural.

It did not work, and could not have unless Perón had been willing to go much further and become totalitarian. The privileges given to labor produced massive labor insubordination and lowered productivity. Workers could no longer be disciplined, but the cost of labor went up. So, for more money they worked less. The growing number of government-owned enterprises, especially the railways, became thoroughly corrupted by the massive featherbedding. Not only external but also domestic investors were frightened away by the policies of the regime and its rhetoric. Government spending increased, and when the foreign reserves accumulated during the war vanished, the government simply inflated the money supply. As the economy began to visibly sour after 1949, Perón resorted to ever more heated, demagogic appeals to class hatred, thus further alienating potential investors.[29]

In Russia the Bolshevik reaction to capital flight and labor insubordination had been Stalinism. Hitler and Mussolini had not been obliged to face labor indiscipline because, whatever their rhetoric, they had maintained tight control over their workers, and had directed any potential class disputes away from internal concerns to external dreams of glory. Argentina had a sizable Jewish community (over 2 percent of the population in the late 1930s), and there was considerable anti-Semitism, especially within the army, but Perón had little interest in using Jews as scapegoats. Unlike Hitler, he did not believe in any biological theories of race and human behavior. And unlike Stalin, he had no global revolutionary Marxist goals.

Perón was, after all, what he claimed to be, a friend of the workers and the poor who believed in a self-sufficient Argentina free of foreign influence. He did not mean to provoke class war, capital flight, and a stagnant economy. In fact, after 1952, he began to try to be more reasonable, to strike deals with large companies in the United States who would invest in Argentina; and for all of his vitriol directed against the rich businessmen, he never expropriated, much less physically destroyed them.[30] He had the power to make himself a tyrant, but his own ideology and ambitions did not drive him as they had the European fascist dictators he admired.

His wife Eva, known as Evita, was a different matter. She did not come from a comfortable middle-class background, but was poor and born out of wedlock, facts she bitterly resented and tried to conceal her whole life. Her sympathies for the poor were equally genuine, but she went much further than her husband and set up a foundation which used government funds, and money squeezed out of both unions and the business classes to redistribute it. This made her hugely popular, and the subject of a fantastic, religious cult. Marysa Navarro has described it this way:

> Blond, pale, and beautiful, Evita was the incarnation of the Mediator, a virgin-like figure who despite her origins, shared the perfection of the Father because of her closeness to him. Her mission was to love infinitely, give herself to others and "burn her life" for others, a point made painfully literal when she fell sick with cancer and refused to interrupt her activities.[31]

She was also a religious fanatic who, by the late 1940s, was giving vent to her resentments and rages. She began calling for purification and elimination of those opposed to Perón, and indeed after 1948 the regime became more repressive even though it was at the height of its popularity.[32] Had she remained healthy, the regime might well have become much more brutal. But by 1951 she was seriously ill, and she died in the summer of 1952 at the age of 33. She was embalmed, and her corpse became the subject of a cult. In 1956 her coffin would disappear after Perón's overthrow, only to reappear fifteen years later in Perón's house in exile in Madrid. There, with Perón's new wife Isabel, and his closest advisors, a pair of monks, and Isabel's magician-astrologer present, the casket would be opened and the body recognized. This reassured Perón and became the prelude to his march back to power in 1973.[33]

Alone, Juan Perón was neither vengeful nor vicious enough to carry out massive purges and impose the totalitarianism he could have gotten away with. After Evita's death, he went through a period of conciliation and reversal of his economic policies. But he took a 14-year-old mistress, and there were false rumors that he was engaging in mass orgies. In fact he was a lonely old man. Some thought that he stole hundreds of millions of dollars. There was shameful corruption around him, but he does not seem to have gained much from it personally, as would be shown by his very modest life-style after he was forced from power. He alternated between calls to violence against the oligarchy, accompanied by increasing repression, and attempts to calm the situation. Finally, he attacked the Catholic Church because he feared it would establish a Christian Democratic opposition. This was one enemy too many, and it increased the plotting against him by discontented army officers.[34]

When the army overthrew him in 1955, Perón, who still had the fierce loyalty of the workers, and of some elements in the army, did not fight back, just as he had never instituted plans drawn up in 1952 to create a genuinely repressive dictatorship. Instead, he meekly went into exile.[35]

By then Argentina had been ruined. The economic problems of stagnation and lack of investment were severe enough, but they might have been remedied by the kind of liberalizing plan drawn up for the new government by Prebisch, the former theoretical champion of partial closure and dependency theory who was now called back.[36] It was not so easy, however, to ease the social conflict between the working class and the rest of society, nor to uproot entrenched nationalist belief in the virtues of autarky. Some military men believed that it was necessary to have an open, liberal economy, while others believed in corporatist fascism, though in a less populist form than Perón. Finally, the business and ranching elite loathed populism and confused it with democracy. This made for an endless, bitter political stalemate. Even within the military there were continuous divisions and frequent disputes between its branches. The next eighteen years, until 1973, would consist of "the politics of deadlock: like the economy the political system ha[d] fallen to the ruthless mathematics of a zero-sum equation."[37] Without adequate growth, there was an increasingly bitter fight over how to divide the economic pie. But with strong ideological biases against taking measures that would reopen the Argentine economy to competition in order to make it more efficient, without getting rid of the now vast and wasteful state sector, and without encouraging investment, growth could not pick up.[38]

There continued to be a core of labor and populist support for Perón because, after all, he had delivered what he had promised, and with time, the failures receded and the memory of wage increases and populism grew. Some 25 percent of the electorate, and in some cases far more, would vote for Perón or his candidates in free elections. The army sometimes tried to liberalize the economy, but many of the officers did not believe in that. The old Radical Party, which was the only viable non-Peronist political party, was afraid of losing popular support if it suppressed wages too much, or dismantled the bloated public sector. And most intellectuals generally accepted the well-worked-out tenets of dependency theory, which continued to blame multi-national firms and the United States for Argentina's economic stagnation and increasing inflation, even though these were generated by government subsidies to the grossly incapable state sector. It did not matter if the critique came from the left, from young Catholics who admired liberation theology, from the Peronists, or the ultra-nationalist and fascist far right, because none of them had any affection for an open economy or for capitalism. They all missed the main point that Argentina's problems were self-induced.[39]

By the late 1960s the endless stalemate, characterized by periodic swings between free and inconclusive elections and army coups, between timid economic liberalization and regression to autarkic policies, was producing severe strikes and disorder.[40]

Among the most disillusioned and alienated were young student intellectuals, who, in the late 1960s, began to form revolutionary groups. The two main ones were the Trotskyite Revolutionary People's

Army (ERP) and the Peronist Montoneros, established without the exiled Perón's guidance, but nevertheless loyal to his memory and to what they imagined was his working-class, autarkic nationalism. The Montoneros, who were almost entirely middle- and upper-middle-class urban students, wanted to return to the original, pure vision of Peronism, and overthrow the power of the now thoroughly corrupt unions. Many had been active in Catholic youth groups. Mario Firmenich, who would become their top leader, was the ex-president of the Catholic Action youth group and a former seminarian. Many young Catholic priests who thought it was their duty to promote revolution and return to the socialist teachings of the early Church sympathized with and helped the Montoneros.[41]

On the other side, a very different type of Catholic intellectual, allied to the army, linked to Francoist Spain and to elements in the Church who believed in a modernized form of authoritarianism, led the attack against liberalism and in favor of nationalism. One of their leaders was Nicanor Costa Méndez, foreign minister of Argentina in the late 1960s, and again in the early 1980s under the vicious military dictatorship which eventually took power.[42] In the spring of 1982 he would be a frequent guest on "Nightline," the television news show in the United States, promising that his "gaucho" boys were going to carve up the English in the Falkland (Malvinas) Islands war.

In this deadlocked society, the student revolutionaries began to organize kidnappings for ransom and armed robberies to raise funds for their operations. In the 1970s the Montoneros kidnapped a former general and president, Pedro Aramburu, and executed him. A new military government took power and tried to bring the guerrillas under control by the use of counter-terror. Torture and arbitrary arrests to try to uncover secret cells began in 1971. But they did not work, and in desperation, the military began to consider bringing back Perón, in exile all these years. Perhaps he could establish labor peace, lead a legitimate and popular government, and allow the economy to right itself. A long process of increasing concessions to Perón culminated in free elections in September of 1973. Perón won 62 percent of the vote, and assumed office a few days after his 78th birthday.[43]

Perón had a bad heart, but he thought he could bring social peace and make the Montoneros obey him. His vice president was his third wife (the first, before Evita, had also died of cancer very young). Isabel Perón's most trusted and omnipresent advisor was an astrologer who proclaimed himself a wizard, José López Rega. "It would be amusing," Paul Lewis has written, "to imagine what daily life was like [in Perón's household], with a crazy wizard spouting nonsense to an aging demagogue and his ignorant dance-hall wife—except that the consequences were to be so horrifying."[44]

From Perón to Death Squads, Torture, and War

Perón's call for conciliation did not work because it was predicated on the assumption that the Montoneros would be satisfied with symbolic gestures, whereas they were intensely committed to drastic change. Had they come to power, they would have been truly revolutionary. In May and June of 1974, Perón denounced them openly, and the campaign against them resumed. The unions, some of whose leaders were murdered by the Montoneros, loathed the young intellectual revolutionaries and backed Perón. But Perón died on July 1, 1974.[45]

The war picked up. López Rega, who controlled the Ministry of Social Welfare, set up death squads to murder leftists. In the outlying provinces the Montoneros and the ERP killed hundreds. With about 5,000 heavily armed fighters and 60,000 sympathizers in the ERP, plus 25,000 armed Montoneros backed by up to 250,000 sympathizers, the revolutionaries were a serious threat. The ERP actually took over parts of Tucuman province, and in 1975 the army launched full-scale military operations against them. Despite their ideological differences, the ERP and Montoneros became allies.[46]

Isabel Perón was no Evita, and she withdrew into passivity, leaving López Rega in charge. He was not only behind the death squads, but he was also corrupt, so that finally the army forced him out. Inflation soared out of control, at up to 700 percent a year. Then, in March 1976, with the economy in chaos and violence still increasing, the army took power under General Jorge Rafael Videla. They threw out the old government but incorporated López Rega's death squads into their own operations.[47]

Most Argentines were relieved. Jacobo Timerman, a liberal journalist and editor, who would soon become one of Argentina's most famous torture victims, and one of the lucky ones to get out alive, welcomed what he hoped would be a coordinated fight against the revolutionary terrorists.[48]

Instead the military, which consisted of competing factions, fell into the hands of those who decided that Argentine society had to be purged of all ideologically baneful influences. The left and the Peronist Montoneros were, of course, the first targets, but so were others: liberals, anyone identified with human rights, those who protested the increasing terror, relatives of revolutionaries, and Jews. Some were picked up simply because they were pretty girls whom bored officers tortured, raped, and killed for fun.[49] An account of what happened was later collected by an Argentine commission and published under the title *Nunca Más* (Never Again) in 1984. In all, the commission found that tens of thousands had been arrested, and many tortured. Nine thousand had disappeared, murdered by their jailers. Over 90 percent of these abductions occurred between the 1976 coup and 1979.[50] Undoubtedly, many more thousands died without leaving any trace for the commission to find.

The frenzy of brutality and torture was as bad as what happened in the Nazi death camps, though the scale was far smaller. The guerrillas, who did not expect this kind of onslaught, were eliminated, and their remnants fled abroad.[51] But why the killings spread so far, to include so many who clearly were not revolutionaries, and why there was so much utterly useless and repulsive torture are not things that are easy to explain. It is not possible to say that Argentina had a brutal political tradition, because, in fact, nothing like this had ever happened before. Before the 1970s, very little blood had actually been shed in the various coups and uprisings.

Some of the documented cases in *Nunca Más* are hard to believe, but nevertheless, they happened. Here are a few examples:

—Then I heard another voice. This one said he was "the Colonel." He told me they knew I was not involved with terrorism or the guerrillas, but that they were going to torture me because I opposed the regime, because: "I hadn't understood that in Argentina there was no room for any opposition. . . ." For days they applied electric shocks. . . . [T]hen they began to beat me systematically. . . . One day they put me face-down on the torture table, tied me up, and calmly began to strip the skin from the soles of my feet. . . . I passed out. From then on, strangely enough, I was able to faint very easily. As for example on the occasion when, showing me more bloodstained rags, they said these were my daughters' knickers, and asked me whether I wanted them [the daughters] to be tortured with me or separately.

—They were put into an empty swimming pool with high-powered searchlights trained on them. In the pool there were hundreds of dead bodies.

—He could hear men and women screaming. "The German" [the torturers used nicknames to identify themselves] tried to stick a length of pipe up his anus. . . . "The Spaniard" applied the [electric] prod to his armpits. . . . "The Spaniard" was laughing and said to the woman, "Since you like the privates you carry on." Then he felt the woman grab his penis and pour in some sort of caustic liquid.

—They threatened me for having uttered Jewish words in the street (my surname) and for being a bloody Yid, whom they would make soap out of. . . . They took me straight away to the torture room where I was subjected to the electric prod. They kept asking me for the names of people travelling with me to Israel. . . . I could hear the screams of my brother and his girlfriend . . . whose voices I could hear perfectly. . . . I never heard of him [his brother] again. Days later, they told me my arrest had been a mistake, but not to forget that I had been there.[52]

Many babies belonging to women under arrest were kidnapped and disappeared, probably distributed to favored individuals who wanted to adopt them. Some of them are still being searched for by their parents and grandparents. Older children were also seized, and often tortured and sexually abused.[53]

In *Nunca Más*, some attempt is made to link this nightmare to the spread of anti-communist national security doctrines which originated in the United States. Indeed, the Argentine generals seemed to believe that they were part of a great global crusade to save Western, Christian civilization against communism and other "exotic" ideologies.[54] But their notion of the "civilization" they wanted to uphold was not exactly North American.

Jacobo Timerman reports that in their efforts to define themselves, military ideologues said:

Argentina has three main enemies: Karl Marx, because he tried to destroy the Christian concept of society; Sigmund Freud, because he tried to destroy the Christian concept of the family; and Albert Einstein, because he tried to destroy the Christian concept of time and space.[55]

Both the Argentine military and their Uruguayan counterparts who were committing similar atrocities considered that their anti-terrorist doctrine was actually more French than North American. They particularly admired the way French paratroopers had broken apart underground guerrilla cells in Algiers during the Algerian War.[56]

But there is little evidence that either the United States, much less France, or any other foreign power had much influence over the Argentine military. In fact, during most of the worst of this period, Jimmy Carter was president of the United States, and of all American presidents he was the one most serious about conducting a human rights campaign. Alain Rouquié, probably the foremost expert on the Argentine military, and no great admirer of the United States, feels that ultimately it was the Argentines themselves who determined their counter-insurgency tactics. He has written that "the internalization of 'Western and Christian' values and of a counter-revolutionary ideology was not imposed from the outside. The myth of the Latin American officer *brain-washed* [he uses the English word] at Fort Gulick hardly stands up to comparative analysis."[57] Lawrence Weschler, writing about Uruguay and Brazil, where similar events occurred, agrees, and even points to the fact that if anything it was Latin American military extremists who influenced some North American officers and intelligence men, like Oliver North, and got them to accept the necessity of being brutally harsh to fight domestic subversion in Latin America.[58]

Counter-terrorist, national security doctrines were not the only important parts of what was actually a rather loose and unsystematic military ideology. Some of the military still preferred Nazism, and many of those tortured report having seen pictures of Hitler posted on the walls. Some of the military seemed to want an open, capitalist economy, and justified their murderous activities as the only way to bring back an open market. Others were devout Catholics who disliked open-market capitalism almost as much as they disliked communism, and who insisted on extending, not decreasing, state control over industry. What all of them had in common, it seems, was simply outraged nationalism and a desire to purify Argentina from all those polluting influences that they blamed for the failures of the past quarter of a century. They also had in common what Rouquié calls a "Manichean" attitude that seems to be part of all military training around the world: there is a right, and there is a wrong, a friend and an enemy, and all problems are amenable to clear technical solutions. Finally, of course, the military, which had built up so many privileges for itself, including control over large parts of the economy, wanted to keep these, and identified its interests with those of the nation.[59]

The fact that frustrated nationalism was the cementing ideology of the military, rather than the bits and pieces of doctrine taken from elsewhere, is shown by the fact that in 1978, Argentina and Chile came very close to war over a minor territorial issue in their far south. Only arbitration by the Pope resolved this conflict. Yet, it would be difficult to claim that Chile under General Pinochet was part of a communist world conspiracy or in any way ideologically at odds with his Argentine counterparts.[60] And in 1982, the Argentine military government did go to war, this time against Margaret Thatcher's United Kingdom, an equally unlikely target for anti-Marxist crusaders.

There are no studies of who actually participated in the tortures, and what their attitudes may have been, because in Argentina, as elsewhere in Latin America, the military, when it gave up power, managed to protect itself from retribution. No thorough examination of their files has yet been possible. But given what is known about such activities elsewhere, particularly in Nazi Germany, it is probable that some soldiers took part because that is what they were ordered to do. Others probably agreed with the general ideology. Still other military and nonmilitary torturers were no doubt sadists and opportunists who took advantage of the situation, but were tolerated, even encouraged by the leadership so that they could carry out the most distasteful tasks. We do know from studies of what happened elsewhere that there is no point in wondering how all this was possible. There are always enough torturers around, in any society, whatever their motives, to carry out the wishes of leaders. This is not said to remove the responsibility of those who carried out the actual work, but to stress that the orders and impetus for the whole thing came from the top, and had an ideological purpose.

Carina Perelli quotes the general who was governor of Buenos Aires province in 1977:

> First, we will kill all subversives, then all their collaborators, then those who sympathize with them, . . . immediately afterwards those who remain indifferent and finally, we will kill all those who are lukewarm in this matter.[61]

Terror was used deliberately to reshape the ideological profile of Argentina. This was clearly a totalitarian project, and large sectors of the population, including leaders of the Catholic church and Peronist unions, agreed with its general goals.[62]

But this was a form of totalitarianism that did not match the "scientific historicism" of either Nazism or Stalinism. It had no well-worked-out racial theories, even though it was obviously anti-Semitic. It had no theory of how classes interacted, except that it considered the poor dangerous, and anyone who wanted to help them subversive. The regime did not even have a coherent theory of economic development, and remained divided about what measures to take to salvage the economy. This explains its fragility. When compared to what modern totalitarian regimes can really accomplish when their leaders are ideologically sure of themselves and united, the Argentine army must be judged, on its own terms, as a pathetic failure.

The distance between ideological enthusiasm and corruption was very short, and almost immediately many of the abductions, tortures, and killings were directed more at forcing property out of the hands of the well-off than at any ideological goal.[63]

After 1979, the repression eased; the revolutionaries had been destroyed, and the more accommodating sector of the military gained the upper hand. It decided to court popular opinion by manipulating the currency to make imports cheap. For a while, there was a boom of consumer imports that took the minds of the population off the recent past, and then a crash caused by trade deficits and inflation. The government borrowed massively abroad, but by late 1981, that too was leading to disaster. So, a "firmer" group of generals led by Leopoldo Galtieri and backed by the hard nationalist right conducted another coup, and drove out the "moderates." Looking for a quick way to boost their popularity, and to head off protest over the collapsing economy, Galtieri's regime invaded the Falklands. This worked; it was immensely popular. But then the British counter-attacked, and the Argentine army turned out to be as incompetent and stupid in military matters as in its handling of economic, diplomatic, and ideological problems.[64]

The resultant debacle drove the military out of power, and brought back democracy. It would be hard to argue, however, even in the 1990s, that Argentina has overcome its troubled recent history. The army is still there and still powerful. The Peronists are still the strongest political force, though now, finally, after decades of error, it is following a market-oriented and open economic policy. The economy is in better condition, but progress is far from being secure. Argentina still has the potential to be a great success, but only if it avoids the mistakes of its recent past.

A country may be turned in the wrong direction by the bad decisions of its leaders. Frustrated nationalism is likely to produce simplistic solutions, and these are often wrong. When combined with bits and pieces of modern totalitarian ideology loosely stitched together, such nationalism, though unlikely to produce total social transformations, can, nevertheless, lead to vicious tyranny.

The most important lesson of Argentina is that army officers, because of their training and the nature of their profession, are very likely to believe in collectivistic, simplistic, and ultra-nationalistic solutions to social, political, and economic problems. Argentina did not have to experience a tyrannical regime in the late twentieth century. There were many elements in its history that pointed in exactly the opposite direction, toward liberal democracy and successful industrialization. By misunderstanding the situation in 1930 and 1943, when there were no major emergencies in Argentina, the army turned what could have been minor crises of legitimacy into a legacy of economic mistakes, political deadlock, and social intolerance.

SADDAM'S IRAQ: THE DESPERATION OF NATIONALISM WITHOUT A NATION

There is no obvious similarity between modern Argentina and Iraq, except that if both had been well managed, they would now both be among the world's wealthier places. But neither has been well governed, and both have been subjected to tyrannical rule. Iraq's tyranny, however, has been much worse. It has lasted much longer, and is much more solidly entrenched than Argentina's ever was. In Iraq, a far smaller country, hundreds of thousands have been killed, and certain populations have been subjected to genocidal attacks more similar to what the Nazis did than to the persecutions carried out by the Argentine army. Also, even though the American army defeated the Iraqis in a war in 1991 that bore some superficial resemblance to the Falkland Islands war, in fact the Iraqi military is a far more formidable instrument than its Argentine counterpart. It took a massive American effort to defeat it, not a small expeditionary force, and all of Iraq's neighbors fear its military potential.

If the histories, economies, geographies, religions, and politics of

Argentina and Iraq were compared, very few commonalities would emerge. Iraq began the twentieth century as a backwater of the collapsing Ottoman Empire. It then became a British protectorate before being granted independence. It was very poor and had a very small modern economic sector until huge petroleum deposits made it wealthy after mid-century. Its population is diverse and split along many linguistic and religious lines, and it has never been united by a common nationalism that all its people could share. That this country should have suffered misfortunes and bad government is far easier to understand than what happened to Argentina.

My purpose, then, is not to suggest that the two places have had much in common, but by contrasting them to show some of the different ways in which nationalist elites determined to impose their glorious visions of unity, discipline, and grandeur on recalcitrant subjects produce tyrannies. The two cases also illustrate how short a distance there is between ideological fervor and gross corruption once tyrannical rule is installed.

The simplified images of the "nation," conceived in modern times as a response to the intrusion of the Western world, has almost everywhere produced self-appointed elites capable of the greatest savagery in the pursuit of their historical myths and dreams. In a country like Iraq, which is not, as a matter of fact, characterized by anything close to a unified culture or historical tradition, that nationalist dream fell into the hands of an elite that came primarily, eventually almost entirely, from a minority segment of the population. This made it necessary for them to apply much more drastic means than those of the Argentine military. Therefore, even though this nationalist Iraqi elite has never fully adopted the pseudo-scientific Marxist or racist theories that made some European tyrannies so terrible, it has managed to produce a quite monstrous totalitarianism.

If Argentina is an object lesson in what harm a misguided elite may do in the name of saving national honor, Iraq is a demonstration of the nightmare that a similar ideology of national salvation can impose in a state that has never had a reasonable chance of becoming a real nation.

To explore this, it is as usual necessary to step back a little and find the origins of Arab Iraqi nationalism. And because of their close connection, the overlap of ethnicities, and their partially common modern histories, a few words have to be said about Iraq's ideological soul mate and bitter rival, Hafez al-Asad's Syria.

Arab Nationalism and the Ba'th in Greater Syria and Iraq

Arab nationalism in the Fertile Crescent developed in shocking and frustrating circumstances in the early twentieth century. It was barely in the process of being born when the Ottoman Empire was dismembered by the French and British. For Muslims it was difficult to be ruled by non-Muslims, who by definition adhered to an inferior religion, and this was worsened by the overwhelming evidence of Arab economic and political backwardness that the European presence suddenly revealed. Then, just as the first political victories were being won over the Europeans in the 1940s, there came Israel, ruled by what had historically been a tolerated but despised minority, the Jews. As Palestine, along with Lebanon and Jordan, was part of the land claimed by Syrian nationalists, and Iraq and Syria developed their Arab nationalism along very similar lines, with many of the same people playing leading roles in both places, this made Israel's success all the more galling, a permanent, hateful reminder of Arab failures.

Arab intellectuals travelled the familiar road of those exposed to the Europeans: first, resistance, then acceptance and a wish to imitate, followed by a growing awareness of the contradictions between their own culture and the Western Enlightenment, and frustration bred by the failure to catch up to the West. Finally, a synthesis has emerged combining a modern definition of nationhood with romantic, anti-Western myths about historical glories, racial and cultural purity, and religious community. Born of frustration and humiliation, Arab nationalism continues to be nourished by these same sentiments.

Iraq, like Syria, was an artificial colonial creation. There was no particular ethnic or even religious unity in either one. Why Kurds in both states were not united with their Iranian and Turkish fellow Kurds, why Iraq's Shi'ite Arabs were not united with Iran or granted their own independent state, or why Syrian Alawites and Druzes did not wind up in Lebanon has more to do with the military and political balance of power in the Near East in the 1920s and 1930s, and between France and England, than with any ethnic or linguistic logic. This is common throughout the world, but Syria and Iraq came into being particularly fragmented and under precarious circumstances.

Syrian nationalism originated among a class of absentee landowners who felt they were losing their elite positions. They were the urban notables in the late Ottoman period, and then rallied to King Faisal, the first ruler of post-Ottoman Syria. But Faisal was overthrown in Syria by the French. It is only a measure of the double-edged sword of nationalist pseudo-history that the French general who occupied Damascus in 1920, Gouraud, went to the tomb of Saladin, who had vanquished the Crusaders, and announced, *"Saladin, nous voici de retour"* (Saladin, we have returned).[65] Saladin, as it happens, was a Kurd, something which was of no particular consequence in a pre-nationalist age when religion, tribe, and clan defined a person, not nationality.

In 1921 Faisal, an ally of the British during World War I, and a friend of Lawrence of Arabia, was given the newly formed kingdom of Iraq, which consisted of three former Ottoman provinces stuck together, as a post-war British mandate under the League of Nations.[66]

Syria, Lebanon (which was included in the French mandate of Syria) and Iraq were anything but culturally homogeneous. On the contrary, this was one of the most religiously, linguistically, and socially split parts of the Ottoman Empire and the world, similar in its complexity to the Balkans or the Caucasus. There were many different kinds of Muslim and Christian communities, as well as Jews, living among each other, but each keeping its own habits and laws, and none quite trusting the others. A variety of linguistic groups were present, with Arabic predominating, but also including various Syriac languages, Kurdish, Turkish, and others spread around in small communities. Under Ottoman rule, which was tolerant of diversity, at least until infected by Western ideas of nationalism in the latter part of the nineteenth century, this worked, more or less. When confronted with the modern world, and with the demands of national homogenization, the old model of distinct groups interacting but also living separate communal existences broke down.[67]

In French Syria and Lebanon, in the late 1920s and 1930s, European-trained Arab intellectuals, especially ones who had higher education in France, at the American University of Beirut, or at other European institutions, banded together to create a more united, less communally or class-oriented liberation movement. From the start, this was aimed at the larger Arab world, particularly because the newly educated, Western-trained youths from these areas gathered together in universities where their common experiences outweighed old communal ties. Nationalism aimed at higher goals than narrow, traditional interests, it seemed more modern and progressive, and it offered hope for the future.[68]

At this stage nationalism was heavily influenced by European secular social philosophy, and Christian Arabs, with superior access to Western educations, were disproportionately represented among the ranks of the young nationalists. This created a contradiction that has yet to be resolved. Wishing to modernize Arab society along Western lines conflicted with the Islamic ideal of returning to the original Sunni historical community, the 'Umma based on divinely guided law. (The Sunni Muslims are the vast majority of the world's Muslims, but in Persia and southern Iraq, the Shi'ites are in the majority. The split occurred in the seventh century, and has at times been the cause of bitter conflict, much like the Orthodox-Catholic, or the Catholic-Protestant breaks in Christianity.)[69]

Whereas both secular modernists and Islamic traditionalists could agree that foreign domination was bad, their conceptions of the ideal Arab nation-state were radically different from each other. The Muslim Brotherhood, which began in Egypt between the two world wars, and then spread elsewhere in the Muslim world, became the chief representative of the latter side.[70]

The first of the successful secular modern nationalist parties in Syria was the Syrian Social National Party (SSNP), founded in 1932 by a Lebanese Greek Orthodox, Antun Sa'adah, while he was teaching at the American University in Beirut. Starting with only university students, the SSNP's membership grew until it became an influential movement in the 1940s, though its appeal remained largely limited to intellectual elites in Lebanon and Syria.

Sa'adah's theory of nationalism was secular and based on his understanding of biological evolution. Within Syria, by which he meant the entire Fertile Crescent (Iraq, Syria, Palestine, Jordan, and even Sinai and Cyprus), a unique culture had risen that characterized the Syrian "race." Reviving that Syrian "nation" was the primary goal of the party. He was hostile to wider pan-Arabism, but also to individualistic Western democracy. His concept of social nationalism was militaristic and unitary, a society where the national interest was above the individual's. It is not surprising, then, that observers have considered it to be similar to the fascist movements and parties in the Europe of the 1930s. It was a deliberate attempt to create a new collectivistic, ethnic nation.[71]

The pan-Arabic Ba'th (Renaissance) Party was founded in the early 1940s. Three schoolteachers who had gone through French universities in the 1930s, where they were influenced by Marxist as well as right-wing nationalist philosophies, created it. Michel 'Aflaq was a Greek Orthodox, Salah al-Din al-Bitar, a Sunni Muslim, and Zaki Arsuzi, an Alawi. (Alawites follow a schismatic, mystical religion that combines elements of Christianity and Islam and is practiced in what used to be one of the poorest and least developed parts of Syria, the mountains between the Mediterranean coast and the richer inland plain of the Orontes River and of Aleppo. It is now considered to be a Shi'ite sect, but that is largely an attempt to legitimize it in the eyes of Muslims who did not, in the past, consider it to be part of Islam at all.)[72]

Like the SSNP, the Ba'th was an elite movement that only spread to a mass base once it was in power, but whose program of independence and Arab renewal in general had a wider appeal. For the Ba'th, the ideal state would incorporate all Arabs. In the writing of 'Aflaq, its chief theoretician, Arab nationalism transcended all material and practical interests. It was a mystical love for the Arab nation. Western culture was rejected, and the organization of society was to be based on vaguely socialist lines. It was also an inherently dictatorial, brutal doctrine. 'Aflaq wrote:

> The nation is not a numerical sum, but an "Idea" embodied either in the total or in part of it. The Leader . . . is not to appeal to a majority or to a consensus, but to opposition and enmity; he is not one to substitute numbers for the "Idea," but to translate numbers into the "Idea"; . . . he is the master of the singular "Idea" from which he separates and casts aside all those who contradict it.[73]

'Aflaq understood the difference between a "scientific" and a romantic conception of the nation. He entirely rejected the notion that nationalist goals should be based on anything approaching an analysis of economic and political reality. He castigated other Arab intellectuals for their "verbal investigations" which caused them to lose "the force of nerve and the heat of emotion." 'Aflaq wrote, "Nationalism is not a science; it is . . . a living remembrance."[74]

That is why, despite their "socialist" ideals, which were really a means of promoting collective national solidarity against class divisions and of building up strong state power, 'Aflaq and the Ba'th were always bitter enemies of Marxism and communism, which were viewed as divisive and anti-national. "We represent the Arab Spirit against materialist communism," wrote 'Aflaq. Marxism was not only

Jewish, but also represented the European Enlightenment, which was antithetical to what 'Aflaq believed. Communism was likened by 'Aflaq to

> the *shu'ubi* [Arab-hating] movements which appeared in the Abbasid period [eighth to tenth centuries] advocating equality in women and wealth, anarchy, sabotage, dissolution of family ties and religious teachings, and the debasement of Arab history, its heroes, and the qualities of the nation that gave rise to them.[75]

In 1964 Michel 'Aflaq, who had become the chief theoretician of the Ba'thist movement, recommended that Saddam Hussein be elevated to the regional command of the Iraqi branch of the party.[76] Later, as an old man he lived in Iraq under Hussein's protection, and continued to be an honored sage until his death.

Though small, the SSNP and Ba'th had only two serious rivals in Syria for the attention of the intellectuals: communism and the Muslim Brotherhood. While the latter stood for a return to the historical Islamic community, the former were the ultimate "scientific" Westernizers. In a sense, the debate among Arab intellectual nationalists had some parallels with the earlier debates between Russian "Slavophiles" and "Westernizers," and in both parts of the world, the issue remains far from settled.

After World War II Syria gained independence from France. Ba'thism became popular with military and civilian officials looking for a doctrine to transcend deep, old communal divisions. These had, if anything, become worse because the French had tried to capitalize on them in order to keep Arab nationalism at bay. Ba'thism particularly appealed to a group of Alawite military officers, among them Hafez al-Asad, who was to become ruler of Syria in 1971.

The Alawites were a despised, marginal, poor minority who made up about 10 percent of the Syrian population. Many of its notables had tended to be pro-French, but among those who received some modern education, Ba'thism was attractive because it merged their identity into a larger Arab unity without consigning them to inferiority. Of course, the same was true of the SSNP which also gained adherents among Alawite and other minority officers and idealistic young nationalists. Through a series of bitter struggles, the Ba'thists became dominant and ultimately gained power. But in fact there was not much difference between them and the SSNP, either in terms of followers or ideology.

And the resentment of these Alawite, Druze (another large, semi-Muslim religion whose adherents are concentrated in the mountains of Syria and Lebanon), and Christian-educated officers and officials eventually succeeded in mobilizing substantial numbers of impoverished, landless Sunni peasants who resented their absentee landlords from the old urban, Sunni elite.[77]

It would be difficult to exaggerate the effect of Israeli success on the development of Syrian nationalism. Coming from an intellectual doctrine that was already inherently anti-Western, authoritarian, frustrated by Arab backwardness, and romantically attached to dreams of past historical glories, Ba`thist nationalism had all the elements necessary for being aggressive and warlike. Its followers rejected Syria's borders, either on the grounds that all Arabs were not included, or, in the case of those who had believed in the SSNP, because much of Greater Syria was left outside, including the district of Alexandretta, where many Alawites lived but which the French gave to Turkey in 1939. Even if there had been no Israel, it is unlikely that these larger aspirations could have been satisfied, and in any case, achieving desirable boundaries was not a solution to economic backwardness or to the continuing domination of the world economy by the West. But the success of Israel confirmed and strengthened what had been, from the start, a worldview shaped by *ressentiment*. The success of an anti-Arab, small, Western, Jewish state only increased Ba`thism's tendency toward paranoia.

In the case of Syria, of course, this has been compounded by the fact that Israeli military might does directly threaten the army on which Ba`thist rule came to be based. But even beyond this, resentment of Israel and the West was almost the only doctrine that Asad's Alawite military elite could use to try to win over the old Sunni urban elite which loathed him. It was the only doctrine which might be able, also, to overcome the extreme division of Syrian society. Indeed, in the late 1970s and early 1980s, the Muslim Brotherhood, which was strong in these Sunni circles, came close to overthrowing Asad. He brutally repressed them in a civil war that culminated in the massacre of some 10,000 inhabitants of the city of Hama in 1982. That made Asad's nationalistic Arab foreign policy all the more important as a way to try to win back some level of legitimacy among the urban Sunni.[78]

Asad's Syria has been a society in a state of constant war—within Lebanon, with Israel, with the Palestinians, with Jordan, with the Americans, with Iraq, and with itself—because its fragile and artificial identity is based on a larger conception of nationalism than what can be accommodated within its borders.

Ultimately, Asad essentially merged Ba'thism with the SSNP's ideal of a Greater Syria.[79] In the divisive context of Syrian politics, the combination of militarism, frustrated nationalism, ideological extremism, and the nearly complete lack of broadly based democracy or open discussion, it is not surprising that Ba'thist Syrian politics have been secretive, bloody, and repressive. Torture and mass executions, assassination of political enemies, both in Syria and abroad, long and cruel prison terms, and general intimidation have been used to keep the Asad regime in power. (In September of 1980 I tried to visit the citadel in Aleppo, Syria's second city and a major center of anti-Asad sentiment, much to the amusement of its special forces guards who were running a political prison and torture center within its spectacular medieval walls. I was told that probably the only reason I wasn't shot for getting so close to the gate was that I was with my wife and we looked like stupid tourists instead of natives.)

Iraqi Arab nationalism was born under King Faisal who never gave up the dream of uniting the Fertile Crescent under his rule, and who brought some of his officials with him from Syria. A major problem from the start, however, was that Faisal, as an orthodox Muslim from Mecca, received his main backing from Sunni Arabs. But unlike in Syria, the Sunni Arabs in Iraq were no more than 20 percent of the population. Shi'ite Arabs were about 50 percent, Sunni Kurds another 20 percent, Christians about 3 percent, Jews 2 percent, and the rest a mixture of other ethnicities, mostly Turks.[80]

Sunni Arabs occupied the leading military and political ranks of Iraq because the Ottomans had favored them, and because they happened to predominate in the Province of Baghdad, whereas Kurds were the majority in the Province of Mosul to the north and Shi'ite Arabs in Basra to the south. Faisal and his successors came to rely on three groups: a new class of military officers, the old urban elite of officials, and tribal leaders who controlled vast parts of the hinterland. The other prop for royal rule in the 1920s was the British army.[81]

The introduction of modern economic forces turned tribal communal lands into individual property monopolized by a small group of landowners, the multiplication of state offices created opportunities, but also competition between various ethnic and religious groups for jobs, and the new schools and universities turned out idealistic, angry young men who had an easy target for their frustrations—the British and the ruling elite. But even the elite, particularly the military officers nurtured by the royal regime, shared the anti-British nationalism of the young idealists. Unlike Syria under the French, Iraq had substantial internal autonomy from the start of the British mandate, and was granted independence in 1932. The British had never intended to keep Iraq as a colony, but only wanted to protect their strategic and petroleum interests. It was precisely because at that time most of Iraq's oil deposits were thought to be in the Province of Mosul that the British were so insistent on keeping it in Iraq, despite Kurdish rebellions. As it was, only force kept the country together, and by the late 1920s and early 1930s there had already been serious inter-communal violence, in which the government had used the Iraqi army to impose centralized, Sunni Arab domination.[82]

Of critical importance was the creation of a modern school system. In the 1920s and 1930s a Syrian pan-Arab intellectual, Satia' al-Husri, was the chief organizer of Iraq's schools. He imported many better educated Palestinian and Syrian teachers to staff these schools, and he insisted on weeding out the Turkish and Persian influences in Iraq. King Faisal backed Husri, whose work contributed significantly to shaping successive generations of schoolchildren.[83]

In the 1930s, the major political fault line of the growing nationalist movement became clear. On the one hand were the "Iraqi" nationalists whose aim was to create a stronger nation-state based on a blend of Sunni Arabs, Shi'ite Arabs, and Kurds. Opposed to them were the pan-Arabs, who looked primarily to the larger Sunni majority in the Arab world, especially to Syria and Palestine which produced surpluses of Arab nationalist intellectuals who could be imported as teachers and civil servants. The conflict was fought at first in the officer corps, then later among the radical intelligentsia who added programs for social reform to their nationalism. But repeatedly, at crucial junctures in modern Iraqi history, this split proved more important than the lesser one between radical and more moderate reformers.

In the 1940s and 1950s, another split opened within the "Westernizing" forces between the communists and the Ba'thists, as in Syria. The communists could count on substantial support from the poor in the rapidly growing cities, but the Ba'thist appeal to pan-Arabism was more reassuring to Sunni officers and officials. Ba'thism also corresponded better to the generalized pan-Arabic nationalism that was

taught by Iraqi schools. The communists sided with the "Iraqi" nationalists against the pan-Arabs.

The monarchy was overthrown in 1958 by military officers, largely
because of its failure to break with the British or to support an effective
anti-Israeli Arab coalition. The first period of military rule under 'Abd
al-Karim Qasim relied heavily on communist support and was "Iraqi"
rather than pan-Arabic. In 1963 Qasim was overthrown and murdered
by Sunni Ba'thist military officers, despite the substantial popularity of
the regime, especially among the Shi'ite majority and with the Kurds.
To prove to the population that Qasim was dead his body was shown
on television with a Ba'thist soldier spitting on the corpse's face. The
Ba'th then engaged in the large-scale slaughter of communists, arrests,
and torture of its political enemies. One of those torturers was a young
Ba'thist militant, Saddam Hussein, whose determination and ruthlessness caught 'Aflaq's attention.[84]

The political struggle had little to do with the population at large;
rather it was an internal debate within a small elite. The Ba'th did
not, at first, manage to keep control, and it was ousted. But it
returned to power because its pan-Arabic ideology reflected the frustrations of military officers faced by yet another defeat at the hands of
Israel in the 1967 war. When the Ba'th took power a second, and
decisive time in 1968, it had no more than about five thousand members.[85] But they were well placed in the army and this time they consolidated their power by building an effective party-police state
based on terror. This was where Saddam Hussein, who was not an
officer, excelled—in building up the machinery of repression and
controlling it. He became president in 1979, and since then Iraq has
been almost constantly at war in pursuit of the Ba'thist goal of Arab
unity and grandeur. But perhaps not surprisingly, because Ba'thist
rule in Iraq also marked the perpetuation of Arab Sunni domination
over Kurds and Shi'ites, and also because Syria is viewed as Iraq's
rival for Arab leadership, Asad's Alawite regime also became an
intensely hated enemy.

Neither Syria nor Iraq is by any means a secure nation. Though
both are ruled by extreme nationalists, their leaders are actually members of minorities who hold on to power by terror, all the while struggling to justify themselves by appealing to much broader
constituencies at home and in other Arab lands.

Saddam in Power: Nepotism, Brutality, and Terror in the Service of Ba'thist Nationalism

Saddam Hussein's regime soon became the rule of a tiny minority, not just of Sunni Arabs, but of a small number of related families from his home area of Tikrit. Whereas older regimes had had a sprinkling of Kurds and Shi'ites, and Qasim had been half Kurdish (on his mother's side), of fifteen members of the Ba'th Revolutionary Command Council from 1968 to 1977, the period during which Ba'thist rule was consolidated, fourteen were Sunni Arabs, and six were Tikritis. Tikritis held all the top positions. In large part, this can be explained by the many Tikritis who entered the army. Tikrit lies in the middle of the Sunni region, but it is poor and has offered few other opportunities for its aspiring educated young men.[86] In this respect, the Tikritis are similar to, though fewer in number than, the Syrian Alawites. Like the Syrian regime, they must hold on to a larger nationalism that transcends their minority status in order to legitimize their rule.

The popularity of the mirage of Arab unity is the key to understanding the Ba'th's success. Unlike the communists, who distinguish between classes, the Ba'thists could claim unmatched universalism that appealed to the small number of military officers, officials, and school teachers who saw themselves as the vanguard of Arabism. They could play on the broadly held resentment against Western imperialism (first French and British, more recently American) and Zionism, which have been used to explain the repeated failure of Muslim and Arab culture to catch up to and overtake the West. But since the Ba'thist regimes in Syria and Iraq have been economic and political failures, imposing heavy military costs on their populations but never quite catching up to their own image of themselves, they have had to continue to rely on the perceived threats from their enemies to mobilize their people and energize their party structures. Nor is their poorly thought-out socialism any help, because insofar as actual socialist policies and Soviet economic aid were used to further industrialization, they worked as poorly in Syria and Iraq as in the communist world itself.[87]

The contradictions of Ba'thism are astounding. The two Ba'thist regimes are controlled by small minorities trying to pretend that they are majorities; Ba'thists have laid claims to being secular modernizers whereas, in fact, with time they have had to fall back on the crudest sort of Islamic traditional resentment of non-Muslims. They have claimed to be acting on behalf of the masses, but they have killed large numbers of their own people, and repressed even the most rudimentary expressions of democracy.

But as Samir al-Khalil has pointedly shown, this should not surprise us. He has written, "Stalinism is the 'original' Third Worldism that Ba'thism as well as other post–World War II nationalisms sought to emulate."[88] Stalinism made many of the same claims, and in the end came to represent a highly intellectualized *ressentiment* cultivated by Russian nationalists against the West. It claimed to be the instrument that would help the nation catch up to the hated West, but instead it militarized society, terrorized it, and put it through unspeakable misery. Yet, the Ba'th never developed a "scientific" theory of economic behavior, much less a class-oriented set of policies. In that respect, perhaps, it resembles Hitlerism more than Stalinism, though here it lacks as thorough a racist explanation of history. Whether Ba'thism is "leftist" or "rightist," however, matters little. Its essence has been a belief in the Arab community's essential unity, past glory, and future revival as a great power, and its use of extremely brutal methods of repression in order to carry forward its nationalist agenda and keep its ruling minorities in power.

But if instead of looking only at the great sweep of ideology and Ba'thist foreign policy, we examine the inside of Saddam's regime, it is possible to come to a very different conclusion. In their quick book about Saddam produced at the time of the invasion of Kuwait and the American war against Iraq, Judith Miller and Laurie Mylroie wrote that Saddam's favorite movie was *The Godfather*, and Don Corleone a kind of model. And indeed, every work on contemporary Iraq stresses the extreme nepotism and corruption of the ruling clique. Saddam's family and retainers have the power to take anything they want, and they have not been shy about doing it. They murder, bully, and extort for private gain on a large scale.[89]

Corruption always goes hand in hand with tyranny, whether in Nazi Germany, in the Soviet Union, or under military rule in Argentina. But does this mean, as it has in cases such as Haiti's which we will explore later, that ideology is merely a cover for theft, and that no one really takes it seriously? In the case of Iraq that is not so, anymore than in Hitlerite Germany or in Argentina in the late 1970s. What these regimes have in common is that the ideal of national unity was seized by a small group which then used its power for its own benefits, but continued to believe that they were the essential saviors of the nation, and that, therefore, whatever excesses they committed, these were entirely justified because without them the nation would fail.

The Iraqi Ba'th may not hold firmly to its socialist ideals, but it is organized along the lines of a Leninist party. A Middle East Watch report on the absence of human rights in Iraq has noted that "hierarchy, discipline, and secrecy are its dominant characteristics." There is an omnipresent secret police, the Mukhabarat, and a Party Militia which is almost as large as the army itself. Its task is to make sure the army does not revolt. Civilian informers are everywhere. As in communist countries, there is a *nomenklatura*, a list of trusted party members eligible for promotion to significant positions.[90]

Saddam himself is an extremely brutal, vain, and utterly ruthless man, characteristics that have served him well in the violent world of Iraqi revolutionary politics, marked by purges and killings since the monarchy's overthrow in 1958. He is also capable of breaking into sentimental tears as he sentences former friends and relatives to death. The many books about him since he was catapulted to the world's attention by his invasion of Kuwait in the summer of 1990 emphasize his early poverty, the abuse and beatings he evidently suffered at the hands of an unfriendly stepfather, and the humiliation he felt.[91]

No doubt these explain much of his personal attitude toward life, though alone they do little to clarify his political success. As we have seen, Stalin also had a difficult youth, and an abusive father, but it is not as obvious that this was so for Hitler, and it was certainly not the case for Pol Pot. Nevertheless, for whatever reason, Hitler, Stalin, and Pol Pot also nurtured inner rages that emerged as a propensity for political violence.

Millions of people are prone to jealous rages and immoderate desires for revenge, whether because of their family past, or because of other reasons. Nevertheless, it is only when the prevailing ideology of an entire political and intellectual elite is focussed on resentment and frustrated, bitter jealousy that political figures who incarnate those sentiments come to the fore and succeed in carrying out their vengeful fantasies.

Saddam Hussein, like Hitler and Stalin, matured with an inner rage that fit his political surroundings well. A personality like that in a stable, nonrevolutionary environment, might have been equally fearsome, but not as a political leader. As it happens, accounts of Syria's Asad suggest that his is not a similar personality, but that out of political necessity he has been forced into similarly brutal policies.[92]

In part, Hussein's policies may be due to the fact that Iraq's national existence has always been so fragile, so that more extreme measures are accepted by the ruling political elite. But there is also a personal element, and to deny it would be to fall into the trap of some historical theories that believe individual action to be inconsequential.

While I am unable to explain how it is that an individual becomes extremely bitter and vengeful, it is obvious that combining a leader so inclined with an atmosphere of nationalist *ressentiment* is likely to produce horrible results. This is, of course, all the more so if this leader achieves supreme and unchallenged power.

The combination of dictatorship, an ideology of revenge, political insecurity caused by deep divisions within the society, and a leader who combines personal bitterness with a strong ideological commitment to national success spell almost sure disaster. Aside from the proliferation of secret police informers, brutal repression, and constant purges, this mixture is also very likely to lead to something which often amuses Western observers because of its absurdity, but which is a sign that something sinister is taking place underneath, namely, an exaggerated cult of the leader. This is because the extreme policies of such regimes, as well as the purges at the top, threaten their legitimacy. So, in part to make up for this lack, the leader is turned into a god. Stalin, Hitler, and Mussolini perfected this technique in the 1930s, and it has been repeated many times since. But the other aspect of this deification is that the most brutal and vengeful personalities also need the most personal reassurance that they are indeed the saviors they claim to be, and the best way of delivering that is to be surrounded by fawning praise and public acclaim.

Anyone who has visited both Asad's Syria and Hussein's Iraq is struck by the difference. Asad is praised, of course, and his picture is hung up in offices, but there is no overwhelming and nauseating cult of Asad, no proliferation of ridiculous monuments that overshadow everything else. And so it was in Perón's Argentina, where there was a small cult of personality, but nothing that went as far as in Nazi Germany, much less in Stalin's Soviet Union or Hussein's Iraq.[93]

Before Saddam Hussein pushed out his Tikriti relative and predecessor as Ba'thist president, Ahmad Hasan al-Bakr, in 1979, there was little personalization of power, but since 1979, the Iraqi regime has become one of the most highly personalized in the world. Hussein's picture appears on the front page of daily newspapers, and hundreds of songs have been written about him, such as the one that begins the nightly television news:

Oh Saddam, our victorious;
Oh Saddam, our beloved;
You carry the nation's dawn between your eyes. . . .
Allah, Allah, we are happy;
Saddam lights our days. . . . [94]

Huge posters of Saddam are everywhere, and in Baghdad there is a giant model of his hands holding crossed swords in a triumphal arch.[95]

In September of 1980, taking advantage of the disarray in Iran that followed the overthrow of the Shah and the massive purge of the previous regime's military and bureaucratic officials, Saddam invaded Iran to seize the rich provinces on the Persian Gulf which contain most of Iran's huge petroleum deposits. Partly because of the disorder in Iran, but also, perhaps, because these provinces contain many Arabic speakers (though mostly Shi'ite ones), Iraq was supposed to gain an easy victory. Instead, it turned out that the Iraqi army, though well equipped, was incapable of conducting major offensive operations, and it was held to fairly small advances. Then, the religious enthusiasm sweeping Iran and the tenacity of its leadership led by the Ayatollah Khomeini mobilized hundreds of thousands of courageous, mostly very young volunteers who were thrown into the frontline. There ensued a long, terrible war that in some ways reproduced World War I, with massed infantry charges against fixed artillery positions, gigantic slaughters, very little movement, and finally, use of poison gas by the Iraqis. In the end, the Iranians, who greatly outnumbered the Iraqis, would have won if it had not been for massive financial help to Iraq from other Arab states, the purchase of weapons from the Soviet Union and Western Europe, and help from the United States. The war ended after eight years in an exhausted stalemate. Rough estimates suggest that about 200,000 Iraqis, and somewhere between 400,000 and 600,000 Iranians were killed. Iraq emerged with no gains, and a debt of 60 to 80 billion dollars.[96]

Iran's religious regime, itself based on a nationalism of almost pure resentment and hatred of Western influence and modernization, was perhaps as brutal as Saddam's, but it was, at first, enormously popular. It was able, therefore, to demand almost unbelievable sacrifices from its fighting men who went to their deaths expecting to be holy martyrs. But Saddam's propaganda machine, his appeal to Arab nationalism against the Persian enemy, and the swift punishment imposed by his loyal party militias on deserters, shirkers, or those who did not obey his orders, were also successful in keeping his troops fighting, especially once they had been driven out of Iran and were defending their own territory. Furthermore, neither army mastered the logistics or techniques of modern warfare, despite the ready availability of modern weapons. The combination of enthusiasm and incompetence produced the frightful carnage, as bad as anything in World War I or II. "Fear and faith are among the most elemental and primordial of all human drives; under certain circumstances they have the force to make men die in droves for no other reason than that they cannot imagine otherwise," concludes Samir al-Khalil.[97]

But the war was not the only mass killing that resulted from Saddam's rule. Chemical warfare was used against the Kurds in the north in 1987 and 1988, killing thousands, mostly unarmed civilians. Middle East Watch reports that in March 1988, "Western television crews filmed ghastly scenes of bodies strewn along Halabja's streets, families locked in an embrace of death, lifeless children, doll-like with blackened mouths, eyes, and nails, and the upended carcasses of domestic animals."[98] At least a half million Kurds, perhaps many more, have been forcibly removed from their villages, many of them to places that were little more than concentration camps. Vast parts of Iraqi Kurdistan were burned, in all about 75 percent of its villages and towns. In 1989 Iraqis tested some of the chemical warfare compounds they were working on by poisoning the water supply in Kurdish camps.[99] This is the regime that was so tactfully helped and encouraged by the government of the United States until the invasion of Kuwait because it was a force for moderation in Middle East, and because to have been too harsh would unnecessarily have pushed it back toward radicalism![100]

Naturally, torture has been applied to thousands of other Iraqis. The usual methods—beatings, electric shocks, exposure to extreme heat and cold, deprivation of food, water, and sleep, rape and other forms of sexual abuse—have been documented. At times, and somewhat unusually for this type of regime, the mutilated bodies of victims have been returned to their families, so that the stories would get out and terrify the population. A mother who went to pick up her son's body in 1982 later reported seeing

> bodies on the floor . . . one of them had his chest cut lengthwise into three sections . . . from the neck to the bottom of the chest was slit with what must have been a knife and the flesh looked white and roasted as if cooked. Another had his legs axed . . . his arms were also axed. One of them had his eyes gouged out and his nose and ears cut off . . . [101]

Children have been tortured, particularly Kurdish ones, and the families of political enemies of the regime have been tortured and killed. Public executions have been a hallmark of the regime since it came to power. Tens of thousands have died in this way.[102]

Whatever one may think of Saddam Hussein, however, it is certain that he always had goals that went far beyond the pure enjoyment of power and wealth for their own sake. Saddam's career has not been that of a classical Aristotelian tyrant, in it "for the money," though perhaps some in his family were. Given Iraq's wealth, and the absolute control over the machinery of repression, Saddam might have shown less ambition. But he went to war to fulfill greater goals; he never considered giving up and retiring in luxury, as he could have done with ease. And after the near disaster of the war against Iran, he launched another adventure in 1990, not because he personally needed more loot, but because Iraq had to command greater resources if it was to move closer to the dream of Arab unity and power under the Ba`th.

There is little need to go into details of Saddam's invasion of Kuwait in 1990. After the stalemate with Iran, he was short of money and prestige needed to continue on his quest for leadership of the Arab world, despite the vast sums he could count on from the sale of Iraqi oil. He tried to pressure the Kuwaitis to fund him more generously, and when they did not, he guessed that the corrupt, fabulously rich ruling families of the Arab Gulf would be an easy prey. They were not popular in the Arab world, they were militarily weak and completely dependent on foreigners who worked for them, including large numbers of Palestinians, and he had a large, modern army.

All these calculations were correct, but the threat of having the world's largest petroleum resources along the Gulf controlled by this regime finally forced the United States into action, and there resulted another humiliating setback for Saddam. Yet, because the Americans and their allies (including Asad's Syria) did not actually occupy Iraq or destroy Saddam's army after defeating it, he remained in power. Unlike the Argentine military, he had built up such a thorough repressive machine that he could not be overthrown. To be rid of his regime required the physical destruction of its leadership.

His relatives who ran the country as their private preserve, the mostly Sunni Arab nationalists who believed, correctly, that without the Ba'th the country would disintegrate, and the thousands of officials who were involved in the killings and tortures supported him. They had no choice. In late 1993, Saddams's ultimate fate and that of his regime remain unknown. But whatever happens, it will not change the record of his long rule, which has left Iraq as far from any real national unity as ever.

THE TRAGEDY OF APPLIED FANTASY

Comparing Argentina, Syria, and Iraq highlights an important conclusion. Trying to create a nation where there is really no basis for one, for example in Iraq, is a dangerous business. By the time Argentine nationalism developed, it already existed as a Spanish-speaking, Catholic state with its own economy and society. It was not a perfectly integrated society; few ever are; nonetheless as immigrants began to enter in large numbers, there was a basis for gradually assimilating them, a task which was particularly easy in the case of the Italians and Spaniards.

Arab nationalism, on the other hand, was born frustrated and became more so as artificial boundaries were established by the outside European powers, as Israel was established, and as the promises of easy economic growth and social stability failed to materialize. However much one might wish to condemn the Ba'thists, theirs was a response that is easy to understand. Arab unity, communal solidarity against the outside world, unrelenting emphasis on the glorious past as well as on the shining future to come appealed to that select group of intellectuals and officials, particularly military men, who sought to bring order and pride to their world. And who could their models be? Hitler, Mussolini, later Stalin, Mao, and Tito, brutal dictators who had imposed totalitarian solutions on their nations to make them great.

But what could be done with recalcitrant human material? There was no way to be both ambitious for and proud of Arab nationalism while being accommodating to the various split interests and communities that existed in Iraq; even under the supposedly pro-Western monarchy there were severe repressions against those who were not Sunni Arabs. Later, in the climate of intense ideological competition between the communist world and the West, between Nasser's Egypt and the more traditional Arab states that remained loyal to the Britain and the United States, it seemed that national unity was all the more important, and that populations had to be mobilized for great efforts.

Even without a personality like Saddam's, the outcome for Iraq would have been severe dictatorship, and probably some variety of tyranny; lacking this there would have been internal collapse. We can see this from the Syrian example, which has been stabilized by Asad's brutality, or better yet, from Lebanon, which did split apart and destroy itself. In the short term, Saddam's brutality worked, though without resolving the long-term problem.

That is not to say that a culturally secure, ethnically united nation cannot produce tyranny. Germany is the proof of that. But the mixture of a form of nationalism based on extreme resentment of the outside world, a political elite that is an identifiable religious and ethnic minority within its state, and a heated atmosphere of constant political crisis is much more likely to produce tyranny than if any one of these factors exists alone.

This is the story of Iraq. It could equally well be the story of Serbia in the late 1980s and 1990s, of Ethiopia in the 1970s and 1980s, and it has been, as well, an important part of the story of Burma since independence.

In the case of Argentina in the 1970s, or in the neighboring South American countries of Chile, Uruguay, and Brazil at about the same time, there were already real nations with little realistic fear of fragmentation. The Argentine case, like many, perhaps most of the tyrannies of the twentieth century created by self-styled "national saviors," was based on its military's notion that it could solve Argentina's problems with a good dose of discipline and cultural purification to remove "foreign" influences. In most cases, and certainly in Argentina's, this was as much a fantasy as any nationalist dream ever imposed on a society.

These are disturbing conclusions. The world is not only full of multi-ethnic, multi-religious states that are poorly integrated, but if anything, the number of such states is growing in the 1990s because of the collapse of European communism. To most of Africa, large parts of the Middle East, South Asia, and Southeast Asia, as well as some Andean South American countries, one must add the Balkans and the new states formed from the failed Soviet Union. But in many places, the formation of determined nationalist elites risks producing many more Ba`thist parties. And everywhere, there are military men convinced that somehow, a good show of discipline and the judicious application of force would set things right.

Chapter 9

An Inadvertent Catastrophe:

Burma's Confrontation with Colonialism, Modern Nationalism, and Ne Win

On April 23, 1992, Radio Rangoon announced that the head of Burma's governing body, often called by its English acronym, SLORC, the State Law and Order Restoration Council, had replaced its "ailing" leader, General Saw Maung. It was believed that he had suffered a nervous breakdown in December of 1991 when he had been heard screaming at a golf tournament "I am the great king Kyanzittha! I am great King Kyanzittha!" Later, Saw Maung was observed by foreign diplomats to be incoherent. But behind the scenes the elderly General Ne Win, who had led a successful military coup in 1962 and ruled directly until 1988, was still pulling the strings. Some political prisoners were then released. An unnamed source was quoted as saying, "Ne Win will turn 81 in May. He hasn't got much time left to avoid going down in history as a tyrant." Or, perhaps, his main goal was to assure the succession for his daughter, Sanda.[1]

By 1992, SLORC was widely recognized as one of the more vicious regimes in the world, running a brutal military-police state that jailed, tortured, and killed thousands of its political opponents, kept the Burmese population impoverished, and, as the need arose, turned on ethnic and religious minorities with wanton brutality to rally ethnic Burmese loyalties. In 1991 and 1992 about 200,000 Muslims from the Burmese province of Arakan were driven into exile into neighboring Bangladesh (itself one of the world's most overcrowded and destitute lands) by fear of being impressed to carry out forced labor, by large-scale raping by the Burmese army, and by outright expulsions from their home villages.[2] Such tactics had been used before by Ne Win to rally Burmese support.

In May of 1990 the military regime had allowed a remarkably free election in Burma in response to extremely widespread revolutionary protest riots in 1988. These protests had led to Ne Win's formal renunciation of power and the formation of SLORC. But the election was a fiasco for the ruling military who had expected to win. A democratic alliance led by Aung San Suu Kyi, daughter of Burma's chief nationalist hero of the 1940s, Aung San, won 392 of 485 contested seats to what was supposed to be a new national assembly. SLORC reacted by jailing almost the entire leadership of the democratic movement, including most of those who had won elections, and by cracking down on the opposition. For a while it had seemed that Burma was going to rejoin the modern world, but the army, and Ne Win, refused.[3]

The opprobrium heaped on SLORC by international public opinion in 1990 culminated in the awarding of the Nobel Peace Prize to the imprisoned Aung San Suu Kyi in 1991. This did not deter some Asian powers, namely China, Thailand, Singapore, and Japan, from giving continuing aid to the regime. Japan even contributed a modern planetarium in Rangoon to help Ne Win's astrologers, on whom he relied for advice, to cast their horoscopes more precisely.[4]

But this is only the surface of a complicated and tragic story that hinges on Burma's repeated failure to adapt to its contact with a modern world. And Saw Maung was not the first Burmese leader to go mad trying to grapple with the contradictory and ultimately insupportable pressures imposed on his society by outsiders, just as Ne Win was not the first to try to isolate his people from the evil outside world, or to become a recluse as his failure became ever more obvious and his regime unravelled.

WITHDRAWAL AND SUBJECTION: A HARSH
INTRODUCTION TO MODERNITY

The geography of Burma has kept it relatively isolated. Jungle-covered, thinly inhabited mountains exist along its eastern, northern, and western borders. Only in the south is Burma easily accessible, by sea. Its river valleys, however, have been the home of advanced states based on peasant rice cultivators and modelled on Indian patterns for over a thousand years.[5]

King Kyanzittha, whose glory General Saw Maung wished to emulate, was the greatest of the rulers of Pagan, a major Burmese Empire centered on the upper valley of the Irrawady River from the eleventh to the late thirteenth century.

The boundaries of Kyazinttha's Empire were roughly the same as of modern Burma, but kingdoms of this sort did not create well-integrated national cultures. On the contrary, they tended to leave local customs and notables in place as long as they received the tribute they demanded.[6]

The Empire of Pagan was itself largely based on older Mon statecraft and Mon Buddhism. The Mon are linguistically related to the Khmer, whereas the Burmese, or more properly, the Burmans, more recent arrivals from the north, speak a language related to Tibetan. The Mon remain as a linguistically distinct population in southern Burma.

The existence of Pagan has played an important role in the mythology of modern nationalist Burma, just as modern Cambodian nationalism has idealized the ancient temple city of Angkor Wat, the capital of a long-faded Khmer Empire. Mussolini's glorification of Rome, Ceausescu's idealization of pre-Roman Dacia, and Hitler's promotion of Wagnerian operas based on mythologies about wandering German tribes played similar legitimizing nationalist roles in their regimes. Stalin's image of himself as a combination of Ivan the Terrible and Peter the Great was not dissimilar to the tendency of modern Burmese rulers to identify themselves with great kings from their own past. Whatever the reality of history, always more complex and less based on unified nationalistic passions than modern legend would have it, the real past matters less than its reinterpretation. Models offered to a nation and taught in its schools by its nationalist intellectuals become goals for leaders who come to evaluate their success on the basis of these historical tales.

The ethnic composition of Burma is exceedingly complex, as is much of Southeast Asia's. Various peoples have migrated into the area, and many have never been assimilated into the dominant Burman culture. There are peoples who speak languages related to Tibeto-Burman, chiefly the Chin and Kachin, who remain in the relatively inaccessible mountains around the more Burman and Mon lowlands. There are Karen, of the same linguistic family, some of whom live in the mountains, others in the plains among the Burmans, but who consider themselves a distinct people. There are T'ai speakers such as the Shan and some Lao. (The word T'ai refers to a linguistic group, whereas "Thai" refers to the modern nationality of those living in Thailand, Burma's eastern neighbor. Most but not all Thais speak T'ai languages, and not all T'ai speakers are the same as the dominant Siamese in Thailand.) Over time, various of these peoples, most often the Mon or Shan, periodically took over the Burman kingdom, and split it up. This, of course, was a common pattern in all agrarian empires and kingdoms, but because such a large part of Burma consists of difficult mountains, the proportion of unassimilated peoples with different ways of life remained relatively larger than in neighboring Thailand, Cambodia, Vietnam, or the Malay states.[7]

Burma was also more isolated from the outside world than the other Southeast Asian societies. The sea routes from India and China to the spice islands of Indonesia bypassed Burma, and China made only minor use of the hard mountain passes between Burma and the Chinese province of Yunnan. Later, when the Europeans, beginning with the Portuguese, followed by the Dutch, the English, and the French seized the lucrative trade routes to and from Southeast Asia, Burma was again left more alone than other major Southeast Asian civilizations. This was reinforced by the fact that the main Burman (as opposed to Mon) population base was in the northern valleys hundreds of miles from the coastline, and in difficult times, this is where the monarchy retreated.[8]

In the latter part of the eighteenth century there was a great revival of Burman strength. A new dynasty set out on a series of astounding conquests that for a time broke the power of the Siamese Kingdom of Ayutthya, the ancestor of modern Thailand, whose capital just north of modern Bangkok was seized, looted, and burned in 1767. Shan and Lao petty states in the northeastern hills were subjugated, and several attempts by the great Manchu Empire of China to invade Burma were repulsed and amicable diplomatic relations were established. The Mon in southern Burma were brought under greater control than ever before, and to the west Burma successfully invaded mountain valleys that are now part of India.[9] This success, coming so late in a world that was already being taken over by the Europeans, and based on the strength of the relatively isolated Burman heartland, contributed powerfully to the ensuing debacle. It persuaded the court, insulated from the rising power of the Europeans, that Burma was a great world power.[10]

The Kingdom of Burma was a fairly typical agrarian state, with much cruelty and violence; but in the villages of Burma, whether Burman, Mon, Karen, or Shan, people retained considerable freedom of action. Their headmen were locals, and villages had their Buddhist monks to educate the population and maintain communal solidarity. The non-Buddhist hill tribes maintained an even looser relationship with the valley kingdoms, paying some form of tribute but essentially ruling themselves. Though by the late eighteenth century the Burmese monarchy was trying, with some success, to change this pattern and centralize its power in order to meet foreign challenges, it had few mechanisms available to homogenize the population quickly. Nor was there much friction between ethnic groups except at the level of high elites competing for control of the larger state. Even there, considerable mixing, intermarriage, and adoption of each other's habits occurred, and the competition for power was more between elite families than between ethnicities as such. In fact, the very looseness of the political structure, the permeability of ethnic lines, and the mixture of Buddhism and old spirit worship confused the British when they conquered Burma in the nineteenth century. It seemed illogical and backward to them, and they tried to fix firmer boundaries between various peoples and to centralize administrative and legal practices.[11]

It is only through the efforts of anthropologists such as E. R. Leach in Burma that it gradually dawned on the Europeans, usually much too late, how new the concept of the modern "nation" actually was for most of the world. Nevertheless, it was this strange idea of a nation-state, based on a dominant culture and ruling ethnic group, which was adopted by local intellectuals who became the first nationalists after Burma was incorporated into the British Empire and set on its course toward political modernization. Not only did the colonizers impose such ideas, but it evidently made sense to assume that the political unity of the modern nation-state was a principal source of the Europeans' strength. So local nationalists made this their model, too.

The first invasion of Burma by the British in 1823–1826 was the result of tensions created by Burmese raids into border areas of Bengal, by the refusal of the Burmese court to accept the English East India Company in Calcutta as their diplomatic equal, and by the Burmese's confidence in their ability to handle what they thought was a minor power. The British invaded from the sea to the south and forced the King to sign a peace treaty ceding two coastal provinces, Arakan and Tenasserim. Still, the Burmese did not grasp the lesson, and told a British diplomat "The English are rich, but they are not so brave as we are." The Burmese waffled about their treaty obligations, refusing to give the East India Company trading privileges and delaying payment of promised indemnities. To the Burmese, the British were incomprehensible, their Indian subjects were considered contemptible weaklings, and the fiasco of the first war was thought to be an anomaly that was bound to be corrected.[12]

The King at that time, Bagyidaw, seems to have been more realistic than many of his nobles and officials, and he tried to follow the terms of the treaty and get along with the English. But he failed, and after 1831, he was afflicted by insanity and he withdrew from the daily task of governing as his unpopular Queen and brother-in-law took control. They were overthrown by the King's brother, Tharrawaddy, who caused a break in diplomatic relations with the English in 1840. Then, he too became insane, an unusually common affliction among modern Burmese rulers who have been unable to understand the pressures imposed on them by the outside world. He was replaced by his son who executed thousands in order to insure his hold on power. The combination of insults and provocations against the British, combined with the eagerness of European merchants to expand into what was now recognized as a potentially rich source of teak lumber, led to another war, in which the British seized the remainder of southern Burma in 1852. This new defeat caused the Burmese King to try to modernize and reform his kingdom, much as the neighboring Siamese Kingdom of Thailand was doing at this time. But Burma had lost many of its most productive rice lands, and it was now an entirely inland kingdom.[13]

The contrast with Thailand is instructive. Though similar in religion, historical origin, and economic base, the Thai state was more open to the West, had a few more decades to adapt than the Burmese because it did not happen to have the British as immediate neighbors, and perhaps it was lucky to have two outstanding kings in the middle and late nineteenth century, Mongkut (who was unfairly portrayed as a buffoon in the famous American musical *The King and I*) and Chulalongkorn, his successor. Thailand slowly reformed itself, and cleverly traded territorial and trade concessions in treaty after treaty in order to preserve the Siamese core of the kingdom. In the end, it survived as a successful modern nation-state, the only one in Southeast Asia to avoid being colonized by the Europeans.[14]

In some ways King Mindon, who ruled from the Second Burmese-English War until his death in 1878, tried to follow a policy similar to that of the Thais under Mongkut. But he had less room for maneuver. In 1878, under the newly installed King, Thibaw, there was the usual massacre of other members of the royal family. The British claimed to be outraged. Much more serious, however, was the fact that the Burmese court tried to negotiate with the French, who were establishing their Indochinese Empire. Then, there were border problems with the British, and continuing misunderstandings between them and Burmese about how to conduct relations with each other.[15]

By the 1880s it was unlikely that the Burmese could have done anything to save themselves. This was the high age of European imperialism, characterized by a desperate scramble for territory throughout the world. The competition was sharpest in Southeast Asia and Africa, with the French, British, Germans, and Dutch all trying to outmaneuver each other in Southeast Asia. In the 1890s the Japanese and Americans would join the competition, whose ultimate prize, coveted by Russia as well, was going to be China. It would have taken exceptional luck and skill to avoid colonization at this time, and the Burmese lacked both. On top of this, some British merchants and officials got the mistaken idea that Burma's Irrawady and Salween rivers would provide access to an inner route to China via a planned railway over the mountains.[16]

The Thai monarchy, much better prepared to handle the crisis of colonialism, survived it; the Burmese did not. Britain invaded Burma in late 1885 and quickly seized the capital of Mandalay. In 1886 Upper Burma was annexed to the British Indian Empire. But Burmese soldiers fought a protracted guerrilla war for another five years before peace was established. This greatly astonished the English who assumed that native Burmans would welcome them as liberators from the tyranny of misrule. In the event, the Burmans never really accepted either foreign rule or the joys of liberal capitalism which England proceeded to impose.[17]

English colonial rule was a disaster for much of Burmese society, partly because it marked such a sudden shift to a capitalist, market economy for which few Burmese were emotionally prepared, and also because the English rulers, firm believers in liberal theories about the benefits of the market and of administrative rationalization, never quite grasped what it was that was going wrong.

John S. Furnivall's work, one of the best accounts ever given of the disintegrative effects of modern European colonialism, was focussed primarily on Burma. In a study published in 1948 comparing Burma to the Netherlands East Indies (Indonesia) he wrote:

> On the liberal theory that economic progress guarantees the general diffusion of welfare, the rapid development of Burma after the opening of the Suez canal should have multiplied prosperity. One might expect to find the people far better off in 1900 than in 1870, and again during the present century achieving a still higher standard of comfort. . . . That, on the whole, was the official view, as expressed in successive annual reports.[18]

And indeed, the quantity of imported cotton goods went up six-fold from the 1870s to the 1910s, and the import of shoes, cigarettes, and other small consumer goods boomed during this period.[19] Petroleum was discovered and became an important export, while teak output also went up six-fold from the 1870s to the late 1890s. The number of acres under rice production went up nine-fold in Lower Burma from the 1850s to the 1910s, and in Upper Burma, after the English conquest, it doubled in three decades. Population also increased rapidly. In Lower Burma, which had been depopulated by wars before the conquest, land was reclaimed from swamp and opened to large-scale settlement by migrants from other parts of Burma and from India. From the early 1860s to 1911, the population of Lower Burma grew from about two to six million; in Upper Burma it grew from about four to six million from the early 1890s to 1911.[20]

This was not, however, the full story. Before the advent of colonialism land was occupied and handed down by families, but remained ultimately under the control of the village, which could take land that was not being worked, redistribute fallow land, which tended to be plentiful in most places, and otherwise control the sale and alienation of property.[21] In fact, this type of arrangement was common throughout much of the world in agrarian societies where population densities were relatively low and land was plentiful. In very substantial portions of Eastern Europe, particularly in the Balkans and Russia, in most of Africa, and in much of South and Southeast Asia, as well as in the pre-Columbian Central American and Andean civilizations, such patterns of semi-communal land tenure were disrupted in the modern era by a combination of marketization and population growth. In practice, this meant that the more powerful members of the community seized land and turned themselves into landlords while the safety afforded by communal redistribution vanished and left the poor peasants in a weak bargaining position.[22]

In the case of Burma, and in many others throughout the world in the nineteenth and twentieth centuries, growing population pressure further weakened the bargaining position of the peasant faced by landlords. So did his general lack of understanding of how markets and money lending operated, and how to tackle modern bureaucratic procedure in order to take advantage of new law courts and administrative systems. On the other hand, some foreigners from commercially more sophisticated societies often grasped the new requirements for getting ahead better. This is how East Indians came to dominate so much of the commerce of Uganda and other East African colonies, how Jews became moneylenders, tavern keepers, and estate managers in Eastern Europe, and how the Chinese and East Indians worked their way into similar situations in all Southeast Asia, including Burma.[23]

In Burma, however, the Chinese immigrants who came into the colony as merchants and coolies were greatly outnumbered by Indian immigrants. The Indians could take advantage of the colony's proximity, its formal incorporation into British India, their greater familiarity with British procedure, and not least, the overwhelming poverty of India which had accustomed poor Indians to work at levels much closer to subsistence than what the Burmese were used to.

In 1881 there were about a quarter of a million Indians in Lower Burma, but very few in independent Upper Burma. By 1901, in all of Burma there were more than a half million, and by 1931 slightly over one million out of a total population in the colony of 14.7 million. In 1931, there were also almost 200,000 Chinese in Burma, but only 30,000 Europeans. But in the largest cities, by 1931 50 percent of the

population of were Indians, 7 percent Chinese, 4 percent mixed Indo-
Burmese, and only 36 percent indigenous. Rangoon, the administrative
capital and chief port, where the little industrialization that occurred
was located, became a foreign city. In smaller towns the Indians were
only 19 percent, and in rural areas 4 percent of the population. The
Chinese made up, respectively, 4 percent of the small towns and 1 percent of rural villages.[24]

Again, this situation was not unique. Phnom Penh in Cambodia,
Saigon in Vietnam, Batavia (now Djakarta) in Indonesia, Manila in the
Spanish Philippines, and even Bangkok in independent Thailand were
heavily Chinese as immigrants became the main traders and urban
laborers throughout Southeast Asia. Malaya under British rule also had
an enormous influx of Indian and Chinese immigrants. In fact, in many
of the weakly industrialized parts of the world where indigenous populations were largely peasant, large proportions of the major urban centers were occupied by foreigners of one type or another. The Jews in
Vienna and Budapest played similar roles, as did Indians in East Africa
and Armenians throughout vast parts of the Near East. (Armenian merchants in the early modern period were important in Burma and Thailand, too.)[25] In that sense, what happened to Burma was only an
extreme example of the transformation generally wrought on pre-
industrial agrarian societies when they are abruptly introduced to the
modern capitalist market, particularly but not just under conditions of
colonialism.

The English, who could not understand what was happening, tended, as all colonial masters did, to blame the Burmese, saying that they
were apathetic and incompetent. "The exclusion of the Burman from
modern economic life was not deliberate, was indeed frequently
deplored; it just happened."[26]

The land-holding situation was even worse, particularly in Lower
Burma which grew most of the exported rice. There, moneylenders
from India, the Chettyars, became the chief, and often the only
providers of credit which was needed to clear land, build protective
dikes, and obtain tools and seed. Because so much of the land was
cleared by immigrants from Upper Burma, or colonists who were not
Burman, particularly Karen and Indian cultivators, and because British
rule was older than in the north, traditional social ties were weak. They
were further weakened as the moneylenders gradually took possession
of more and more land. The British claimed to favor a policy of pro-

moting small indigenous peasant owners, but they also believed in allowing a free market in land and credit. The problem was that the moneylenders, protected by the colonial legal system, were in a stronger position than the cultivators when market conditions or natural misfortune provided too little money for the peasants to pay their loans back. At the other end of the rice trade, since there were few buyers and many producers, the foreigners who controlled the mills, generally Europeans, could conspire to keep prices down. Under such difficult conditions, the rate of default on loans rose steadily. In the early 1900s, 18 percent of the land in Lower Burma was rented, and the rest cultivated directly by its owners. But after the closing of the frontier, that is, as newly available virgin land disappeared, the proportion of the land rented in Lower Burma rose and by the early 1930s it was just over 50 percent. And a growing number of the largely absentee landowners, who lived in the towns, were foreigners.[27]

In the early 1930s came the Great Depression, and the world price of rice collapsed. As the number of defaults rose, the moneylenders took over much of the land directly, so that by 1937 one quarter of the land in Lower Burma was directly controlled by Chettyars.[28] But the cultivators still had to pay taxes, rents, and debts. The result was a large-scale uprising which took almost two years to crush. This began with communal riots between Burmans, Indians, and Chinese in the cities in 1930, and spread into the countryside.[29] James Scott has described what happened in the Irrawady River Delta this way.

> The fact that much land had passed from the hands of the bankrupt Burman landlords into the hands of their Chettiar creditors and that the competition between Burmans and Indian laborers for a diminishing supply of jobs was so ferocious, lent a strong communal tone to the violence there. . . . Violence erupted in those provinces where the economic dislocation was most severe and the competition with Indians most intense—that is, in the East and Central Delta.[30]

Finally, the whole fabric of village life which had been weakened by the penetration of the new economy was also damaged, particularly in Lower Burma, by the decline of Buddhist religious institutions which had been central to community life in the past. The collapse of the old monarchy removed state support for the monasteries and temples, and the new colonial regime, while not hostile to the Buddhists, did little to help. By the late nineteenth century, three-quarters of all villages in

Lower Burma had no monastery, while in Upper Burma almost every village did. But in the twentieth century, the same dissolving forces of money and cash cropping, the penetration of Indian immigrants, and the implicit devaluation of Buddhism by the colonial education system were weakening the connection between organized religion and the people in the north, too.[31]

Also Christian missionaries were active, but they were successful primarily among non-Burmans, and this further weakened the prestige of the Buddhists as well as loosening ties between indigenous non-Burmans and the overwhelmingly Buddhist Burmans. As Furnivall pointed out, partial conversion of this sort increases divisions and reinforces all the weakness of what he called a "plural" colonial society, that is, one in which various ethnic groups have little to do with each other except as direct economic competitors or as political rivals competing for favors from their powerful but isolated foreign European masters.[32]

The Karen, along with the mountain Chin and Kachin, had been more trusted by the British than the Burmans, partly because as outsiders in the old Kingdom they had been less hostile to colonialism, and also because there had been many more conversions to Christianity among them. By the 1930s over 80 percent of the indigenous soldiers serving with the British were non-Burmans, and of these the Karen were the largest group, almost half, with most of the rest being Chin or Kachin, even though only 9 percent of the general population were Karen, 2 percent Chin, and 1 percent Kachin.[33]

That there would be a reaction might have been expected. Perceptive Englishmen such as George Orwell saw that this was a sick society filled with ethnic hatreds, economic inequity, and ruled at the top by Europeans who had little understanding of what was going on. The colonial authorities, however, were not prepared for what was coming. And unfortunately, neither were the Burmese.[34]

NATIONALISM AND INDEPENDENCE: BUDDHIST SOCIALISM ON THE ROAD TO RUIN

The reaction that set in among Burmans was similar to that which eventually developed in all colonial societies. It consisted of a search for cultural roots in their past that would validate their claim to independence and greatness as a people against the dismissive attitude of their European masters. And with this was the recognition that it would be necessary to modernize society in order to face the challenge of the advanced European world. It was thus, like most nationalisms of the nineteenth and twentieth centuries, a combination of deep resentment of and admiration for Europe and the West. The great importance of Buddhism, the fact that traditionally most young men had received some sort of formal religious training and many had served for a time as monks, made reformed Buddhism a central element in this search.

A simplified version of the history of Pagan provided, as Robert Taylor has put it, "a semi-mythical but also historically grounded claim that a state called Burma had long existed and was not therefore a colonial creation incapable of self-rule." Further, the development of a printing industry, and the relatively high level of literacy in traditional Burma (due to the training boys received from the monks) meant that a Buddhist nationalist literature could spread quickly once it was elaborated.[35]

The first identifiable modern nationalist organizations began to appear in the late 1890s, and in 1906 a Young Men's Buddhist Organization (modelled on the European YMCA) was formed with branches throughout Burma.[36] After 1916 Buddhist monks became deeply involved with the nationalist movement, and in the 1920s they organized protests and boycotts modelled on Gandhi's movement in India. But beyond mere nationalism, both secular and religious young nationalists found Marxism particularly appealing. A young man active in this movement, who later became important in independent Burma, U Ba Swe, has claimed that "Marxist theory is not antagonistic to Buddhist philosophy. The two are . . . not merely similar. In fact they are the same in concept."[37] Thakin Kodaw Hmaing, a former monk turned socialist, said in the 1930s that an independent socialist Burma would mean "nirvana-within-this-world."[38] The belief that Buddhism, nationalism, and socialism could be reconciled and provide a uniquely Burmese solution to the problems of the modern world remained deeply ingrained for the next half-century.

In an essay on intellectuals during colonialism, Aung San Suu Kyi has tried to explain the appeal of Marxism in the 1930s:

It was the view that socialism was opposed to imperialism which made [Marxism] attractive to young nationalists. The Burmese were caught up

in the tide of the times that saw leftist ideologies as progressive alterna-
tives to capitalism and colonialism. In addition . . . young Burmese were
very new intellectuals, and their minds longed to grapple with theories,
concepts, challenges.[39]

It was partly a matter of coincidence that at the moment of early
nationalist ideological awareness, Marxism happened to be available as
a convincing ideology, particularly during the Great Depression when
it seemed that capitalism was finished. This was the case throughout
most of the colonial world, though before it was defeated during World
War II the fascist version of nationalistic anti-capitalism was also popular. What was important was not so much the precise content of Marxism but that it seemed modern and scientific while also being
anti-capitalist.

Comparing Burma to India Aung Sang Suu Kyi notes that Indian
elite intellectuals, who were also widely enamored of Marxism, nevertheless underwent a much longer period of English rule and a more
thorough anglicization. This produced a substantial number of Indian
leaders who actually believed in the possibility of democratic tolerance. This tempered their Marxism and made it more pragmatic.
Burma lacked such a moderating influence.[40]

In the early 1930s the "Thakin" movement was organized by students at the University of Rangoon. "Thakin" originally meant "master"
and was applied to the British. The title was adopted by nationalist student leaders in defiance of colonialism. In 1936 they formed the Rangoon University Students' Union, with Thakin Nu, later known to the
world as U Nu (U is a more traditional honorific term) as the leader.
Thakin Nu had translated Dale Carnegie and Karl Marx into Burmese.
The secretary of the Students' Union, and soon the most effective leader of the Thakin movement, was Aung San. These students organized
in the cities and countryside, brought the Buddhist monks in on their
side, and demanded independence. They also organized some major
strikes, particularly in the oil fields.[41]

In 1938 students in Rangoon, demonstrating against an obscure
pamphlet written by a Burmese Muslim who had belittled Gautama
Buddha, turned against Indian shopkeepers (some of whom were Muslims) and initiated "an orgy of looting, arson, and murder."[42] However
grand the promises of universal brotherhood may have been, the
unfortunate fact was that much of the resentment against colonialism

was also directed against the non-indigenous Asians who were the most visible carriers of capitalism.

World War II offered new opportunities. Burmese nationalists, like others in colonial Asia, had long admired the Japanese for their ability to stand up to the Europeans. In 1940 and 1941 Aung San and twenty-nine others (the "Thirty Comrades," who were later called the "Thirty Heroes"), including Ne Win, were trained by the Japanese in occupied China, and in late 1941 they formed a small army in Thailand (which had become an ally of Japan), near the Burmese border, with the aid of the Japanese. In 1941 and 1942, this Burma Independence Army participated in the conquest of British Burma by the Japanese Imperial army.[43]

The collapse of British rule in 1942 as the Japanese invaded left a void. A colonial pluralistic society is a fragile construction because it lacks integrating mechanisms except through the top, that is by the exercise of the central state's power. The sudden removal of this presence, particularly in the tense and ethnically mixed rice-growing regions of Lower Burma, produced an explosion of ethnic conflict. Before effective Japanese control could be asserted, Burman nationalists took over. In the Irrawady Delta, there were many Karen settlers as well as Indians and Burmans. The newly formed Burma Independence Army, nominally under the control of nationalist Thakins, but actually only loosely under any command at all, were fearful and resentful of the Karen, and communal violence broke out which soon degenerated into massacres, looting, and burning of villages. Though the Japanese central command eventually reasserted control and stopped the slaughters, the Karen understood that the end of colonial rule would be a disaster for them. Though Aung San and some of the other Thakins called for tolerance and solidarity between ethic groups, the memories of the hostilities in 1942 remained.[44]

Burma was badly damaged during the war, but the nationalist movement was greatly strengthened. On August 1, 1943, formal independence was declared under Japanese tutelage, and by the end of the Japanese occupation, Aung San and his army, commanded by Ne Win, were a major force. In March 27, 1945, with a full-scale British invasion of Burma under way, and after the fall of Mandalay to the British army, Aung San and his troops officially changed sides, turned against the fallen Japanese, and presented themselves as the champions of an independent Burma.[45]

Though there seem to be no good studies of the ideological influence of the Japanese on the Burmese independence movement, it was obviously much more significant than the glossing over of the facts in accounts offered by sympathetic writers such as Frank Trager, Aung San Suu Kyi, or Maung Maung. The anti-Western, explicitly anti-capitalist, communal orientation of fascism in Europe appealed broadly to anti-colonial forces. The Japanese version, because of its anti-Europeanism and promotion of Asians was doubly attractive, and throughout Southeast Asia, including Thailand, Japan was greatly admired as a suitable model. There were various minority groups who had accepted colonial masters as their protectors who remained loyal to the Europeans, and there were communists and even a few liberal intellectuals who saw the flaws of fascist militarism. Yet, on the whole, the nationalists in Burma, Vietnam, and Indonesia joined with and were armed by the Japanese.[46] But the defeat of Germany in Europe and Japan in Asia meant that for those who took their anti-liberalism seriously the only alternative ideology left was some kind of socialism. Thus, the anti-capitalist, anti-British, Buddhist-Marxist orientation of the Thakins before the war could be reconciled quite easily with pro-Japanese sentiments during the war (except among those who became outrightly loyal to the international communist movement); and without any hypocrisy, these same idealists could claim to be genuinely leftist after the war, just as they had been genuine allies of the Japanese in 1941–1942.

The British did not intend to give Burma immediate independence after 1945, but Aung San's movement had become too well entrenched during the Japanese occupation to be overcome. It could initiate strikes and protests at will, and the exhausted British, facing far bigger problems in their empire, quickly gave in to its demands. On July 19, 1947, however, Aung San was murdered in a plot organized by a political rival.[47]

On January 4, 1948, at 4:20 am, a time chosen by astrologers because it was propitious, Burma became independent, with U Nu (formerly Thakin Nu), who had succeeded Aung San, as its first prime minister.[48]

Civil war broke out in March of 1948. The communists, soon joined by a portion of the military arm of the ruling party, attempted to take power in order to institute socialism immediately. Shortly after, there was a Karen uprising. Some say that Aung San would have kept the peace had he lived. But despite his personal charisma, and his ability to negotiate with many factions, as well as with the British and Japanese, he was committed to the same ideology that was pursued by his successors, U Nu and Ne Win, and he would have faced the same problems.[49]

Within a few months, rebels were close to taking the capital, Rangoon, itself, but they were ethnically and politically split among themselves, and Ne Win's army slowly pushed them back. By 1951, the rebellions had been reduced to the peripheries of the country. The fact that the British and Americans had been sympathetic to some of the rebel movements, which were seen as old allies and potential anti-communists, soured relations with the West and made the Burmese even more suspicious of Western intentions than before.[50]

But a commitment to neutrality and suspicion of outside capitalist investment discouraged foreign capital from returning to Burma to rebuild the war-damaged economy; and most of the many Indian moneylenders and merchants who had fled along with Indian civil servants during and after the war also stayed away. The government had few resources for investment, and the peasants who got their own land concentrated on feeding themselves rather than producing for the export market. Thus, the Burmese economy only recovered the level of production it had before the war in the mid-1950s, and despite slight improvements after this, especially in the cities, population growth meant that by the early 1960s per capita wealth was still no higher than in the 1930s.[51]

Furthermore, even though a considerable number of Indians had left during the war, the Indians and Chinese still played key and highly unpopular roles as merchants and moneylenders. So it seemed by the late 1950s that the ideals and goals of independence had not produced the results expected. This fragmented the ruling party and increased the size of the opposition, so that U Nu's electoral majority was reduced and paralyzed. There was little agreement about what to do to redress the economic problems facing the country, or how to end the chronic unrest in the hill and mountain regions. Unable to push through a program for reform, or perhaps threatened by the army's discontent, U Nu turned to Ne Win in 1958 and asked the army to take over the government.[52]

NE WIN: FROM NATIONAL SAVIOR TO MILITARY DICTATOR

Not much is known about Ne Win's youth. He is probably part Chinese. But Maung Maung, Ne Win's political ally and favorite intellectual, has ridiculed this notion, as has Ne Win himself, because with age he has increasingly identified himself with the traditional Burmese monarchy.[53] He was born in 1911. His father was a government revenue surveyor who seems to have been comfortably middle class. He owned some land to which he retired. Ne Win was born with the name Shu Maung, and he was sent to good schools by his parents. He entered the University College of Rangoon in 1929 with the intention of studying science and becoming a doctor. At about this time student activism was rising, and students were consciously espousing anti-British nationalism. In 1931 he failed his examinations in biology, and left the university, feeling some resentment toward his European biology professor. He had a number of jobs and became a postal clerk, but he also became active in the nationalist movement and one of the early Thakins. He collaborated in the publication of Karl Marx's *Communist Manifesto* in Burmese.[54]

He was recruited by a Japanese agent, Colonel Suzuki, in 1940. Later Suzuki would become the Japanese advisor to Aung San's new army. Ne Win went off to China to be trained by the Japanese in 1941. This was when he took the name Bo Ne Win (the Son of Glory General).[55] His career since that time indicates that he was a good organizer, a clever political tactician, a devoted nationalist, and an officer who was popular with his troops.[56]

Particularly telling is Ne Win's period of rule after he took command of Burma in 1958. He set out with the idea of bringing order to the political infighting and divisiveness of the 1950s. Army leaders all over the world often have the same idea about democratic party politics. It is messy, petty, and it seems corrupt. Programs do not get carried out as they should. Compared to the orderly chain of military command, it seems to them that they ought to be able to do things better than mere civilians. Despite this, Ne Win promised that military rule would be temporary, and that once everything was straightened out, power would be returned to democratically elected politicians. And that is exactly what happened, though it took sixteen months instead of the six months that Ne Win promised in the beginning. During those months administration was tightened, services were improved, the power of hereditary princes in the Shan states was ended and replaced by free elections for local leaders, and control over the frontier zones was improved. The army took over a number of commercial ventures to make them work better. On the whole, Ne Win's first period of rule was honest, straightforward, and effective. It was not, however, very popular because it was, as Josef Silverstein has put it, "lack[ing] compassion . . . direct and legalistic . . . firm and centralized."[57] In elections at the end of this period, U Nu regained power, and although it was against the military's wishes, Ne Win handed over power in 1960.[58] This was not the behavior of a tyrant, of a corrupt leader, or of a personality addicted to supreme power.

U Nu, however, was no better able to solve Burma's problems after 1960 than before 1958. The seeming efficiency of military rule from 1958 to 1960 had only improved matters on the surface. The basic conflicts between Burmans and non-Burmans were not solved. They were actually aggravated by the dispossession of some traditional Shan leaders who then rebelled. The economic problems were not solved by increasing state intervention because this brought neither new capital nor greater market flexibility. U Nu's ideology was the same as Ne Win's and Aung San's; all were anti-capitalist, suspicious of the outside world, and nationalistic. The new U Nu regime was therefore not ideologically offensive to Ne Win, it merely seemed to slip back into inefficiency and political bickering.[59]

Two parts of U Nu's political program finally provoked a military coup against his democratic regime. One was his increasing commitment to making Buddhism the state religion. That had been part of his electoral campaign, and he increasingly came to believe that it was his duty to acquire merit in order to help his subjects reach nirvana. This was an ancient duty of Burma's kings, and U Nu wished to accomplish the same thing.[60]

Many Burmans believed that U Nu was himself on the way to achieving Buddhahood. He did not thereby give up socialism as an ideal, because it was widely believed that socialism and Buddhism were entirely compatible; but Marxism-Leninism, with its emphasis on class struggle and warfare, was rejected in favor of a more benign, democratic, and religious doctrine. During Ne Win's military rule from 1958 to 1960, the army had stressed the incompatibility between communism and Buddhism as part of its campaign to eliminate the communist guerrillas. But when U Nu used his parliamentary majority in

1961 to declare Buddhism the official state religion, problems arose. The Christian, Muslim, and Hindu minorities protested. Among the hill tribes, animists, Christians, and even some Buddhists who interpreted the move as an assertion of Burman chauvinism, joined in the protests. Various compromises were sought to insure the protection of the non-Buddhist religions, but militant monks who had supported U Nu demonstrated against attempts to weaken Buddhist religious supremacy.[61]

This provoked a second initiative opposed by the army. To broaden support for his policies, to keep protesting non-Burman minorities in line, and to bring the remaining ethnic uprisings, chiefly among the Karen, under control, U Nu then initiated discussions in 1962 that were to lead to greater autonomy for the various non-Burman provinces.[62]

This was too much for the army. Despite his popularity and saintliness, U Nu had gradually abandoned socialist economic principles in favor of Buddhism; the country's economy was still stagnating; and now the very survival of the Burmese state seemed threatened by proposed decentralization. This was a betrayal of Aung San's original vision for a united, socialist Burma. Ne Win and his officers believed that their previous period of rule had demonstrated their greater capacity to administer the country, and they seized power again in a military coup on March 2, 1962.[63]

Ne Win's intentions were soon made clear, to realize the vague synthesis of socialism, Buddhism, egalitarianism, and Burmese nationalism that had been at the heart of the Thakin movement since the 1930s, but that U Nu had been unsuccessful in implementing. On April 30, 1962, *The Burmese Way to Socialism* was published by the government. It said:

> The Revolutionary Council of the Union of Burma does not believe that man will be set free from social evils as long as pernicious economic systems exist in which man exploits man and lives on the fat of such appropriation. The Council believes it to be possible only when exploitation of man by man is brought to an end and a socialist economy based on justice is established.[64]

The Burmese Socialist Programme Party (Lanzin) was soon created to lead the way to socialism. Its organizing principle was "democratic centralism," that is, control from the top down. In early 1963, the political philosophy of the regime was spelled out in *The System of Correlation of Man and His Environment*. But its convoluted language was an unsystematic, confused synthesis of the ideals of the 1930s and 1940s, combined with an attack against the "mistakes" of both communists and socialists in the period from 1948 to 1962. At one point, it attacked "pragmatism, dogmatism, opportunism, fellow travellerism, charlatanism, superficialism, bourgeois reformism, bureaucratic stylism, anarchic stylism, 'leftist' infantile disorder, bourgeois militaristic style, and such evils and 'isms.'"[65] It was almost as if, by reciting this stale list, it could conjure up something new. But there was nothing new, only a stricter application of neutralism, isolation, and socialism.

In practice, since its leadership was almost entirely military, and lacking practical experience in economic matters, this meant that the government tried to run Burma "like a military post exchange [rather than as] a complex national organization and commerce." In one of his speeches in 1969, Ne Win would say, "Internal trade is our real problem. I say trade only by convention. Internal distribution may be more appropriate for socialism."[66]

In practice, eliminating trade meant the seizure of big shops, wholesalers, banks, and brokerage businesses as well as what remained of foreign-owned large enterprises, chiefly the 49 percent of the Burma Oil Company owned by British interests. Also, large bills (50 and 100 Kyat notes) were declared to be void, and had to be traded in. But only a very small compensation was offered, so that "hoarders" were supposed to be ruined.[67]

These measures hit the remaining Indian urban community hard, and there resulted another mass exodus of about 200,000 Indians and Pakistanis in 1964. To replace the private shops and industries, "People's Shops" were established. The distribution system and much of the consumer goods manufacturing sector rapidly broke down.[68]

In the first few years of military rule the government retired two thousand of the top civil servants because they were considered "effete." To replace them, and staff a rapidly growing bureaucracy to handle all of the state's economic enterprises, the government and ruling party appointed politically reliable individuals, usually connected to army officers. This greatly reduced the efficiency of the civil service, and made a significant portion of the trained intelligentsia, who were not trusted, ineligible.[69]

Along with the elimination of trade, Ne Win's government was intent

on really making Burma independent of outside influence, and free of
corrupting Western consumerism. From 1961/62 to 1969/70 exports,
already much lower than in 1938, fell by 60 percent and imports by 25
percent. The government decided that it needed to concentrate on
building industry to make Burma self-reliant, and from 1961/62 to
1964/65 it increased the share of government-owned process and manufacturing industries from 29 percent of the total to 41 percent. After a
few years, however, dreams of building up heavy industry were abandoned because of meager results. Even so, fewer consumer goods were
available by the late 1970s than before the coup.[70]

Ne Win's regime never collectivized the land for fear of provoking
new uprisings. This probably saved Burma from the large-scale killings
and ensuing starvation that occurred in the Soviet Union, China, and
Cambodia. But marketing of the major crop, rice, was taken over by
the state, and government procurement quotas were imposed on the
peasants. At the same time, village "People's Councils" were established to redistribute land. This meant that local politics determined
who would control the land, and it made investment dangerous
because land tenure was not secure. Marketing of surplus rice beyond
what the government took, possible for peasants with enough land, was
discouraged by a prohibition on the transportation of rice without government approval. This made it difficult for the most efficient peasants
to increase their holdings, and uneconomical to increase production
beyond a certain point because to do so might run into political resistance.[71] Further, it became official Lanzin Party policy to move slowly
toward collective ownership by restricting the right of inheritance.
This further decreased the effort made by peasants to improve their
land.[72] In 1992, the same system, with only minor changes, was still in
effect. Per capita rice production fell significantly.[73]

Burma has an abundance of fertile land and, by Asian standards, a
low population density. In the past it never had trouble feeding itself,
but by 1988 I observed some children in towns, including Rangoon,
who seemed to show signs of malnutrition—crinkly hair and swollen
stomachs. Bertil Lintner reports that by the late 1980s peasants were
planting rice at gun point as the government was trying to procure
more for exports, and there were reports of rural riots.[74]

By the late 1970s the per capita Gross Domestic Product was the
same as it had been in the late 1930s, though probably this decreased

in the 1980s, and the economy was no closer to being modernized in any sector.[75]

The contrast with Thailand is striking. During this period, from the 1960s through the 1980s, Thailand experienced booming economic growth, somewhat over 6 percent a year for the entire period, and significant industrialization. Burma, on the contrary, applied for and obtained formal status at the United Nations in 1987 as one of the world's "least developed countries," that is, at a level of development that places it in the company of Africa's poorer countries and Asia's "basket cases" such as Bangladesh.

But until recently Burma's socialist idealism, its claim to Buddhist modesty, and the contrast between the decayed, slowly crumbling, but austere city of Rangoon and the crowded, polluted, traffic choked, vice-ridden city of Bangkok made some Western observers admire Burma's path of development. E. F. Schumacher, in his best-selling book *Small Is Beautiful*, specifically admired Burma's intention to practice "Buddhist economics" which was to be self-reliant, nonwasteful, and free of the ugly constraints of international trade. He was sorry that the Burmese had not gone far enough in that direction, and that they still paid some attention to conventional economics.[76]

The problem with this idyllic view is that the Burmese themselves lost their faith in it. It is not possible, in a world where governments are expected to increase the well-being of their populations rather than simply maintaining virtuous behavior, to fail so badly at economic development and to retain the loyalty of the population.

The failure Ne Win's policies became evident very soon after the military took power in 1962, and yet, rather than adapting and changing policies, he insisted ever more on isolating his country and behaving like a traditional Burmese king. Perhaps once "socialism" began to fail, he had no other model in mind and resorted to the historically familiar pattern of a closed, increasingly xenophobic monarchy, just as Stalin began to view himself as Ivan the Terrible, Mussolini believed he had become a conquering Caesar, and Hitler in his last days identified himself with Frederick the Great. It is not so much that any given society remains so unchanged over time as to repeat old patterns over and over, but that the past, or rather the imagined past, provides models that shape a leadership's image of itself and of its duties. And when failures occur, it is comforting to retreat into that heroic, imagined past.

The population then pays the price imposed by the continuation of catastrophic policies.

Shortly after taking power in 1962, Ne Win had all Western foreign agencies such as the Ford and Rockefeller Foundations expelled because they were centers of evil, "decadent" Western influence. Tourist visas were limited to twenty-four hours, thus effectively eliminating most visits by foreigners. In 1970 it became possible for foreigners to be tourists for seven days, so that Burma could gain some necessary foreign exchange. But Burma has remained one of the more difficult countries in the world to visit. English was removed from the school curriculum, and reinstated only in 1979 after Sanda, Ne Win's daughter, failed her English test for admission to a British medical school. To further contribute to the elimination of Western decadence, horse racing and beauty contests were outlawed.[77]

In the mid-1970s Ne Win married a descendant of the last Burmese royal family and began to appear at state functions in "full classical regalia." He became convinced that the last royal family were among his ancestors. Lintner writes that Ne Win "clearly viewed himself as an absolute monarch rather than a military usurper who had overthrown an elected government."[78]

One modern trend which was not abandoned, however, was centralization of state power. Begun but not very advanced by the old monarchy, the process had been greatly accelerated by the British, and adopted as a goal by the nationalists. Ne Win's administration set out to recover the loss of authority that had occurred under U Nu. But this only increased the level of ethnic rebellion as minorities resisted. The constant warfare was a persistent running sore taking substantial amounts of money and energy, and it contributed to the brutalization of political life in Burma.[79]

A story told to Bertil Lintner by a young Shan soldier fighting against the government typifies the situation, and explains why it was never resolved:

A Burma Army unit had come to Than Aung's home in . . . a rebel stronghold in northern Shan State. His father, for some reason, was apprehended and accused of helping the insurgents. No evidence was presented, but the government soldiers hung him by his feet and beat him to death in front of his family. "I will never forget that," Than Aung said simply. "I ran away from home to join the SSA [the Shan army]. I

wanted to kill as many Burmans as I could to take revenge." That had
been more than ten years before, when the boy had been nine.[80]

It is only fair to point out that Ne Win's fear and suspicion of outsiders, and his distrust of ethnic minorities, are understandable. The
Indians, who were such a hated minority in colonial times and have
been largely expelled, are still represented by two enormous, poor, and
overcrowded nations on Burma's western borders, India and
Bangladesh. The hereditary Thai enemies to the east have become
America's favorite and most successful ally in Southeast Asia, with a
booming economy that puts Burma to shame. To the north and north-
east there is China, whose government supported communist insurgents in Burma for a time, and which used to claim Burma in the
eighteenth century.

But neither the insurgencies nor the foreign problems faced by
Burma can explain its domestic economic failure or the growing opposition faced by Ne Win from the Burmans themselves. After all, Thailand was in even greater danger for a time because of the success of
the communists in Indochina. It also has its share of ethnic minorities,
including Karen, Shan, Lao, and Malay Muslims who might have
rebelled, and at one time it had two communist rebel groups within its
territory. The very survival for three decades of Ne Win's military rule
shows that its power base was solid, and that it had an opportunity to
do better. Comprehensible as Burma's errors may be, the fact remains
that wrong policies are most responsible for the catastrophic outcome
of the "Burmese Way to Socialism." And if Ne Win did not begin as a
ruthless seeker of absolute power, his continued hold on power and his
determination to retain his original ideological orientation are responsible for the continuing stagnation and growing discontent. That is the
problem with having a powerful king and no mechanism for getting rid
of him when his rule fails to solve his state's problems.

XENOPHOBIA AND BRUTALITY:
FROM BAD KING TO TYRANT

Ne Win has never resorted to genocide, as did the Khmer Rouge in
Cambodia, or Hitler. He has not engaged in mass purges against his
countrymen as did Stalin, Mao, and Saddam Hussein. He has not glorified war and provoked self-destructive international behavior. Though

it is a dictatorship guided by an ideology, his regime has not been characterized by all the excesses of what have been the genuinely totalitarian regimes of the twentieth century. It is understandable that Ne Win's main democratic opponent in the 1990s, Aung San Suu Kyi, should call his rule one of "totalitarian socialism."[81] But the charge seems excessive if Ne Win's Burma is compared to the more extreme Leninist cases. Nor is there is evidence that he enjoys sadistic killings. It cannot be said that his aims are simply those of a gangster looting his country. Though he may live quite comfortably, as do other top army officers, they are not an ostentatious group of wastrels, as were some of the corrupt tyrants and their followers we will be looking at in the next chapters, such as the Duvalier and Trujillo families. And yet, Ne Win and the army have had to resort to growing brutality to stay in power, and their policies continue to ruin the country.

The brutality began early. Shortly after the 1962 seizure of power there was a student protest that was suppressed by the army and hundreds of Rangoon University students were gunned down.[82]

In 1974, popular discontent exploded in Rangoon on the occasion of the burial of U Thant. Thant had been a Burmese diplomat at the United Nations in 1962. Had he been home at that time, he would have been arrested. Later he became Secretary General of the United Nations. After his retirement he was unable to go home, but after his death his body was brought back to Burma. Ne Win considered him a political opponent and provided only a small cart to pick up the body at the airport. Spontaneous student demonstrations erupted, and they were joined by irate monks. The protests grew quickly until tens of thousands were involved. Ne Win temporarily backed down, but crowds of over 100,000 in Rangoon turned out to hear speeches against the regime. Finally the army cracked down. There were waves of arrests in Rangoon and other major cities. Over a thousand were killed, many thousands were arrested, and hundreds more "disappeared," never to be seen again.[83]

The U Thant affair was not the only instance of violent protest. Earlier in 1974 there had been strikes in the oil fields (one of the original bases of the anti-British movement, along with the students and the monks) that had been put down with force, and over one hundred had been killed. In 1975, strikers and students gathered together at the Shwe Dagon Pagoda, Burma's most sacred Buddhist temple, and demonstrated. They were dispersed by the army, and hundreds were arrested, some for many years. Political prisoners were subjected to routine torture, beatings, and humiliation. A common form of torture was "the motorcycle," forcing prisoners to crouch as if on a motorcycle while being beaten and mocked. Electric shocks were commonly administered, and some prisoners were made to drink their own urine.[84]

The continuing unrest and the decay of the economy led to some very partial liberalization of economic policy, and eventually to an attempted coup within the army. But the coup failed, and Ne Win promoted a new generation of younger officers to top positions. The only basis for promotion was total loyalty to the military regime, and these new men were less well educated, less idealistic, and more brutal than their predecessors. One of those who rose to the top in the late 1970s was Saw Maung, who would later pronounce that he was King Kyanzittha. On the other hand, since there was ever less money with which to pay the soldiers, they were given free reign in frontier areas, where they were fighting insurgents, to enrich themselves. Amnesty International concluded in a 1988 report that systematic looting, rape, and burnings were the rule in these areas, while extortion and the illegal trade in opium and jade made money for the officers. What this did was to begin to change the nature of the regime. The original idealism of the officers, and presumably Ne Win's as well, were subverted by the brutality and corruption. But the army was becoming dependent on its power to sustain itself, and ever less willing to give up its privileges. The regime was turning into a typical tyranny of corruption.[85]

Ne Win retreated into greater seclusion, paying more attention to his astrologers and relying on his secret police to keep him in power. In 1980, he declared a political amnesty and released some prisoners. He called together a meeting of Buddhist monks for the "First Congregation for the Purification, Perpetuation and Propagation of Buddhism." Then in 1981 he formally resigned the presidency, but he kept the substance of power, and nothing really changed. In the early 1980s Military Intelligence was purged to keep it subservient, but then the regime hardened again.[86]

In 1987, it began to seem as if the system would crack. With a deteriorating economy, Ne Win publicly admitted that there were failures with the "Burmese Way to Socialism," and soon after trading of basic foods was allowed. To prepare for the remarketization of the economy, merchants withdrew money from their bank accounts. Then, it was announced that the three highest denominations of notes, 25, 35, and 75 Kyat bills, were officially demonetized, and therefore worthless. (Burma's 35 and 75 Kyat bills had been introduced in the mid-1980s because of Ne Win's numerological superstitions—these were supposed to be luckier numbers than 50 or 100, and the 75 Kyat bill was introduced on Ne Win's 75th birthday!) Something between 60 and 80 percent of Burma's money vanished. The supposed reason was to strike at insurgents and black marketeers along the Thai and Chinese borders, but because Kyats had long been unconvertible, neither smugglers nor insurgents held much Burmese money. Those hit hardest were ordinary people. The move really represented Ne Win's continuing suspicion of markets and his commitment to austere socialism. There might have been another element. After the demonetization, new bills were introduced. They were 45 Kyat and 90 Kyat notes. Ne Win's lucky number is 9; 4+5 and 9+0 equal 9! (Had I not been in Burma in 1988, seen these bills, and heard the same explanation for what happened from monks at Shwe Dagon Pagoda, I admit I would have found this story told by Bertil Lintner hard to believe.) There was a wave of outrage and sporadic demonstrations in response to the demonetization in late 1987, mostly led by students, so universities and higher schools were closed down until the spring of 1988.[87]

In March 1988, riots broke out. Thousands of students demonstrated against the one-party system, against what they called "fascism," and in favor of democracy. There were the usual beatings, killings, and arrests by security forces. These culminated in a deliberate massacre of demonstrators near Inya Lake, on the outskirts of Rangoon, where Ne Win has his villa. This time many of the dead were mere schoolchildren, not only university students.[88]

The demonstrations only lasted a week, but the stories that began to circulate after these events further weakened the regime's remaining legitimacy. Beatings, deaths, torture, suffocations in crowded cells and army trucks, and gang rapes of female students were reported.[89] In June the demonstrations began again, this time joined in Rangoon by large numbers of nonstudents. Some soldiers were killed. Rioting spread to other towns, and continued throughout the summer as monks joined in. As the situation got out of control Ne Win announced that he would retire as head of the Lanzin Party. Sein Lwin was named the new president. But Sein Lwin was one of Ne Win's most brutal and hated henchmen. He had led the troops who had repressed student uprisings before, and he was considered a poorly educated, uncouth killer. Hundreds of thousands of demonstrators in Rangoon protested, and a general strike broke out. The army responded by opening up on crowds with machine guns. There were cases of soldiers and policemen caught by the crowds who were beheaded. By mid-August thousands had been arrested and over one thousand demonstrators had been killed. Finally, Sein Lwin resigned.[90]

Over the next few weeks it seemed as if the regime would fall. Aung San Suu Kyi emerged as a popular leader of the opposition, prisoners were released, there were constant strikes, and demonstrations brought out hundreds of thousands of protestors. But Ne Win and his men were only reorganizing themselves. In September, SLORC, the State Law and Order Restoration Council, was formed, and its nominal leader, General Saw Maung, declared martial law. Throughout the country, the army cracked down, and many thousands were killed.[91]

Over the next year, the army gradually pacified the country, despite the renewal of serious warfare along the borders and the escape of thousands of students who tried to set up an opposition army in cooperation with ethnic insurgents. Aung San Suu Kyi was placed under house arrest in July of 1989.[92] But the outside world was shocked, and the military government felt it needed to make some concessions to regain some foreign aid. It decided that the situation was sufficiently under control to allow free elections. The actual date was set by Ne Win, May 27 (2+7) on the fourth Sunday of the fifth month of 1990. Unexpectedly, the opposition won overwhelmingly, obtaining 392 out of 485 seats in the putative assembly. The government then refused to admit the results, and arrested the leaders and many elected members of the opposition. Several died soon after in prison, allegedly after having been tortured. The international outcry led to Aung San Suu Kyi's being awarded the Nobel Peace Prize in October of 1991, even as she remained under house arrest.[93]

Through 1991, with Ne Win and the army still in control, the economy remained mired in deep crisis despite some loosening of state control, and endemic warfare continued along the borders with ethnic insurgents and young anti-SLORC Burmans. The slow decay of the infrastructure also continued, and the educational system virtually collapsed because it was starved of funds. A growing proportion of all revenues was going directly to the army.[94]

In May of 1992, in neighboring Thailand, demonstrations also broke out against a military regime. The Thai military are brutal and corrupt, and they have dominated politics in Thailand since the 1930s. But because they took a radically different path to development than the Burmese, Thailand has become substantially Westernized and modernized. A large middle class has developed. Foreign investment and tourism have been encouraged, and have contributed to growing prosperity. Increasingly, also, some measure of democracy was allowed, though the army clearly remained in control. Finally, in marked contrast to Burma, the old monarchy survived, though the King retained only ceremonial powers after an army coup in 1932. Yet, he remained a powerful symbol of nationalism and legitimacy.[95]

In some ways the Thai and Burmese armies have much in common. Both have been accused of trafficking in opium, of being involved in extortion, and of mistreating protestors. Corrupt Thai generals have helped SLORC by engaging in teak lumber smuggling across the border, contributing to the plundering of Burmese resources, and paying off the Burmese army in return.[96] Needless to say, the Thai army has had vastly greater opportunities for making money because of the economic boom. After 1989, the Thai military were particularly eager to reestablish good relations with the Burmese army in order to get the smuggling of precious stones, opium, and teak along the border going again. But in 1991, fearing that it was losing control over politics, the Thai army conducted a coup to stop the gradual democratization of the country. In May of 1992, a general was named prime minister. This had happened many times before, but this time, opposition politicians and students led a mass protest that brought out enormous crowds in Bangkok.

The Thai army reacted as did the Burmese, by killing demonstrators. But within a few days, the King had publicly intervened, the army had split, and the military government had failed. Thailand could hardly afford the kind of isolation that the Burmese army was quite willing to tolerate; the middle class, especially in the cities, was just too large to be ignored; the country was far too open to conceal brutality; and the economy was much too dependent on tourism and outside investment to let a Burmese type of development occur.[97]

The different outcomes in Thailand and Burma ought not be a surprise. The two countries, so similar in religion and tradition, have been on different paths since the late eighteenth century. Burma's tragedy is that its path has been such a failure. Though some of what happened is certainly the fault of British colonialism, and the humiliating and abrupt way in which it imposed modernization on the country, much of the failure of the past three decades is Ne Win's responsibility.

Well intentioned at the beginning, he chose an ideology that had developed among the fighters for independence in the 1930s and 1940s, but that was entirely unsuited to the modern world. What was at first a benign form of dependency theory eventually ruined the country. Then, when it began to fail, Ne Win reacted like a classically corrupt tyrant, like an evil monarch incapable of ruling properly and instead inflicting only harm. He retreated into the neo-traditional trappings of monarchy and refused to take into account the growing protests of his people. He resorted to what other disappointed rulers have done; he promoted yes-men and brutal, corrupt enforcers to keep himself in power, and they, in turn, were willing to do anything to keep that power on which they thrived. Ne Win went from being a national savior, with what at one time passed as a liberating nationalist ideology, to resembling the type of tyrant Plato described in *The Republic*.

The harm he has done to his people will remain long after his passing, and it will take many decades to undo.

Chapter 10

Race and Corruption on the Island of Hispaniola

Two Caribbean Nightmares

There are countries where illusory visions of utopia based on false notions of scientific certainty come to be accepted by many thinkers and political idealists, and conditions become so unsettled that masses of people turn to such ideologies for salvation. From such cases are born ideological tyrannies. There are others in which well-intentioned but catastrophic policies combined with dictatorship result in the tyranny of incompetence. And there are those many cases where entrenched dictatorships become increasingly corrupt and evil because that is the only way they have of holding onto power.

We have seen that corruption is endemic to all tyrannies, even ideological ones; however, there are many cases in which the original ideological component is feeble, even entirely absent, and corruption is the principal motivation of the regime from the start. But because the standards of political morality imposed on the world by the powerful liberal Western democracies in the twentieth century have made such governments less acceptable, what were once considered the prerogatives of ordinary kings are now thought to be examples of illegitimate corruption. Particularly egregious cases of corruption or incompetence

341

are considered tyrannical instead of merely being examples of old-fashioned bad kings.

Partly in response to more rigorous international standards of legitimacy that no longer just accept corrupt tyrants as normal, but also because no society, no matter how poor and remote, has been spared the influence of modern ideological trends, corrupt tyrants in the second half of the twentieth century have generally claimed some sort of ideological justification. At the very least, corrupt tyrants now call themselves national saviors, though they sometimes also claim to be "socialists" or "anti-communists" to gain international and domestic acceptance.

Cases of corrupt tyranny do not "just happen" any more than do ideological ones. There are always histories behind them, long-term causes that increase the probability of tyrannical outcomes. Some of these are actually similar to the causes of ideological tyranny: chaotic political and economic conditions, the accidents of war and foreign conquest, the presence of vengeful and resentful nationalism, and the absence of respect for individual rights against those of the community.

In this chapter and the next we will look at four such cases. All of them have happened in societies that entered the twentieth century with troubled pasts filled with conflict and tragedy. All of them have been colonies of European powers at one time or another, and their exposures to European rule have left disorienting legacies. In the past, all four of these tyrants might have been judged to be "bad kings," or even mad ones because of their excessive cruelty. One of these cases, that of Rafael Trujillo of the Dominican Republic, might have been called a fairly successful and normal, though highly autocratic and often cruel king. By our modern standard, however, all four of the rulers we will examine were tyrants whose control over modern state structures and weaponry, combined with elements of modern ideology, made their rule worse than it would otherwise have been had they existed in the past.

We will begin with two Caribbean cases, those of François Duvalier of Haiti and Rafael Trujillo of the Dominican Republic. These two neighbors on the island of Hispaniola have shared many experiences, but they also have quite distinct histories and are different from each other today. Therefore, comparing the two yields insights that might not be so obvious if only one were examined.

THE WORLD'S RICHEST COLONY AND
WHAT HAPPENED TO IT

The island of Hispaniola was called Ayiti by its natives, but was renamed by Christopher Columbus who established the New World's first European colony there in 1492. The Spaniards enslaved, killed, and infected the natives with new diseases so thoroughly that virtually all of them were dead within a half century. Slaves from Africa were imported to replace the dead Indian labor force, but the island, which lacked gold or silver, was not systematically exploited by the Spaniards. Only after the French seized the western third of the island in 1697 did this part, Saint-Domingue, became valuable. Eventually it would become the Republic of Haiti. The Spanish two-thirds, Santo Domingo, which would later become the Dominican Republic, continued to languish as an insignificant colonial backwater.[1]

In the three decades before the French Revolution of 1789 the French colony of Saint-Domingue became the richest, most lucrative colony in the world. It provided over 40 percent of France's foreign trade, it was Europe's main source of sugar, France's only source of coffee, the source for the cotton that was fueling French Normandy's textile revolution (which economic historians believe was not far behind England's at that time), and a major source of indigo and tobacco as well. The foreign commerce of tiny Saint-Domingue was worth as much as all the foreign commerce of the United States in 1790, and the great commercial cities of the French coast—Nantes, Bordeaux, Marseille—were dependent on that trade and the industries that it fed. One estimate claims that over a sixth of France's population, when France was the biggest and most populated country in Western Europe, relied on the trade with this single colony for its prosperity.[2]

There was only one problem with this gold mine. Ninety percent of the population of about 520,000 were black slaves who lived under terrible conditions—overworked, underfed, often beaten, even tortured to keep them submissive. Stories of owners stuffing recalcitrant slaves with gunpowder and blowing them up, roasting them on fires, pouring hot wax on them, and mutilating them were common. The black death rate was so high that their number had to be constantly replenished with new slaves brought from Africa, and as the accounts of the trans-Atlantic slave trade make clear, the voyage itself was a terrible one in which many died.[3] Of the nonslave population in Saint-Domingue, about half were whites, and the other half freed mulattoes (of mixed race) and freed blacks. The whites lived in fear of a revolt, and passed increasingly restrictive laws trying to make sure that the free blacks and mulattoes did not gain enough privileges to make them the equal of the whites. The colony, therefore, was a cauldron of suspicion, hostility, and fear, but it generated fabulous fortunes for the lucky few.[4]

Aimé Césaire has aptly called the elaborate racism that developed in the colony "picturesque and scientifically puerile." Well before racism as a biological "scientific" doctrine became popular in France or the rest of Europe in the mid- and late nineteenth century, the French colonists on Saint-Domingue were formulating such a doctrine, and trying to label people according to grotesquely refined racial criteria. All the authors who discuss this cite the key work of Louis Élie Moreau de Saint-Méry published in Philadelphia in 1798, *Description topographique, civile, politique et historique de la partie française de l'île Saint-Domingue*. He listed ten racial classes below pure whites, calculated according to what portion of their 128 ancestors seven generations earlier had been white or black. These were: *noir* (in English, black—0–7 parts white), *sacatra* (8–23 parts white), *griffe* (24–39 parts white), *marabou* (40–48 parts white), *mulâtre* (in English, mulatto—49–70 parts white), *quarteron* (in English, quadroon—71–100 parts white), *métis* (101–112 parts white), *mamelouc* (113–120 parts white), *quarteronné* (121–124 parts white), *sang-mêlé* (in English, mixed-blood—125–127 parts white).[5]

To be sure, these categories were hallucinatory, or as Césaire put it, the product of a "*délire classificateur*." It was impossible to know who someone's ancestors had been two hundred years earlier in a colony that was less than a century old, and the mere existence of such labels, meant to take into account such mixtures as those between a mulatto and a black (a *griffe*) or a white and a quadroon (a *marabou*), betrays the chronic insecurity of the dominant whites, who, of course, contradicted their own principles by mixing enthusiastically with their black and mulatto mistresses and concubines. Another sign of insecurity was the attempt to impose sumptuary laws, which prohibited the wearing of certain types of clothing by nonwhites, or of laws prohibiting mulattoes from sitting at the same tables as whites, but evidently not from sleeping with each other. (The German racial laws under Nazism were to be far more consistent.)[6]

But free mulattoes (using the term to mean mixed race in general) were a vital part of the society. The whites needed them to keep the black slaves under control. They could own property; France itself was not a legally racist society, however much the local whites may have been. And in the south of Haiti that had been developed after the north, there was a prosperous class of free blacks and mulattoes. As might be expected, within black and mulatto society there was also extreme color consciousness, with whiter skin being much valued because of the higher status it brought. Mulattoes were on the whole freer, richer, better educated, more Europeanized, and more politically conscious than black slaves, particularly because so many of the latter were recent arrivals from Africa.[7]

Many of the most bizarre racial pathologies of this society were reproduced in the southern United States, including the classification by fractions of ancestors, the loathing and fear of free blacks by whites, the sexual mixing of races, with whites taking black women, accompanied by a fear that white women might be polluted by blacks, the tortured attempts to justify the unjustifiable ethic of slavery, the wanton brutality, and the extreme consciousness of color among both whites and blacks.[8] But in Saint-Domingue, the situation was far worse because France was so far away and the proportion of slaves was so high, thus making the whites even more fearful than in the United States. Also, there was so much money to be made so quickly by colonists who hoped to be able to make their fortunes and return to Europe that there was little incentive on the part of whites to treat their slaves decently.

In 1791, because of the revolutionary turmoil in France and consequent internal splits among the French in Saint-Domingue, between officials and planters and between rich whites and poor ones, a successful slave revolt broke out. There was an informal, secretive network of black priests and leaders based on *vodun* (which comes from Ewe—a language in Benin on the west coast of Africa—in which it means a deity or demon, and from which is derived the English "Voodoo"), a syncretic mixture of religious and magical practices of largely African origin, and black leaders were able to mobilize followers as order broke down in the colony. Then free mulattoes rose in revolt, and confused fighting erupted, with blacks sometimes joining whites against mulattoes, or sometimes allied to them, with white royalists joining revolutionary black slaves against white Jacobins, and with the British and Spaniards invading to try to seize this richest of all colonies. There were terrible, cruel slaughters, cities and plantations burned down, and general anarchy. Finally, there emerged a black state in the north led by Toussaint Louverture, a former slave, who allied himself first with the Spaniards, then with the French to drive out the British. In the south there arose a state led by a former free mulatto who had fought in the American Revolution, André Rigaud.[9]

By 1799 Toussaint had united the entire island after a long war with the south, followed by a rapid conquest of the lightly populated Spanish Santo Domingo to the east. He attempted to reconcile the races, to bring back plantation cultivation through a system of forced (but remunerated) labor, and to get France to recognize him as the colony's legitimate governor-general. To a surprising extent, he succeeded, and some prosperity returned even though two-thirds of the whites had been killed or had fled, and one-third of the blacks had been killed or had died in the wars. Many other slaves had fled into the mountains and had become marginal subsistence farmers.[10]

Then in 1802 Napoleon decided to retake the island and reimpose slavery to make it as profitable as it had been. Toussaint was tricked into negotiating, captured, and then sent into exile in France where he died. But Napoleon's great fleet and invading army faced bitter black resistance, and killing, burning, looting, and horrible massacres became the rule once more. In the war of 1802–1803, what was left of the old plantation economy was practically wiped out. Toussaint's successor was Jean-Jacques Dessalines, a charismatic, though illiterate former slave who had been badly abused by his masters (unlike Toussaint, who had been one of the more favored slaves) and who hated whites. The stories of torture and mass murder on both sides (as reported, for example, by Marcus Rainsford in his 1805 work, *An Historical Account of the Black Empire of Hayti*) suggest that the society largely disintegrated. Mulattoes and blacks finally joined against the French, Napoleon's army was decimated by yellow fever, shortages of food, and collapsing morale, and the European peace between France and England ended with a resumption of the great war between the two. All this forced Napoleon to abandon Saint-Domingue in 1803, and also, not coincidentally, his attempt to create a continental American empire based on Louisiana—he sold that territory to the United States.[11]

Dessalines became the first leader of the renamed, now free Haiti, and declared himself emperor. But ruling Haiti was difficult. The British and Americans were suspicious of the new country because they feared it would cause slave revolts in their own Caribbean and southern territories. The United States would not grant diplomatic recognition until Lincoln's time in 1862. No longer valuable, newly isolated, and ruined, the world's first modern black state based on European forms of government languished. In 1806 mulatto officers from the south led by Alexandre Pétion assassinated Dessalines, and the country broke into two parts, a southern republic dominated by mulattoes, and a northern one dominated by blacks and led by another of Toussaint's former generals, Henri Christophe.[12]

Pétion ran a relaxed regime that allowed the former slaves to divide up the land and become small subsistence farmers, while mulattoes moved to the towns and became a commercial and administrative elite. Christophe, on the other hand, tried to maintain an export plantation system as well as the class distinctions necessary for this. In 1811 he had himself crowned king, and a titled nobility was created. But despite the relative economic success of his policies, he seems to have sunk into paranoia fostered by racial resentments and the poor prospects of his country. Aimé Césaire, one of the French Caribbean's best-known twentieth-century intellectuals, wrote a play portraying him as overcome by guilt, self-doubt, and racial insecurity. He used forced labor to have a spectacular castle built for himself high on a virtually inaccessible mountain. In 1820, he committed suicide. In Haiti's periods of calm, when it has a tourist trade, his castle is the most popular attraction on the island.[13]

Christophe was a figure that would become familiar in the twentieth century, a well-meaning, autocratic modernizer who cracked under the strain of trying to do the impossible, and whose fears and pretensions eventually overcame his beneficial policies, which were not, however, particularly popular with his subjects. After his death Haiti was reunited by the new ruler of the southern republic, the mulatto Jean-Pierre Boyer.

Boyer was an even more familiar type, a corrupt military dictator who tried to make up for his lack of a domestic policy by foreign successes. He reconquered the Spanish two-thirds of the island, got France to recognize Haiti by agreeing to pay a ruinous indemnity that put Haiti into debt, and he continued Pétion's policy of benign economic neglect, allowing the land to be divided into ever smaller plots, and the economy to stagnate. The educated mulattoes continued to widen their advantage over the blacks. Government service became just a way of stealing, and the very large army, which was the only avenue of upward mobility for poor blacks, plundered whatever surplus funds it could find. In 1843 Boyer was overthrown by other officers, and in the ensuing confusion, Spanish-speaking Santo Domingo escaped Haitian misrule and became the independent Dominican Republic. There followed a series of military coups and unusually incompetent presidents who were installed by the troops but were manipulated by the southern mulatto elite.[14]

In 1847 the Senate, dominated by the elite, picked an illiterate black soldier, Faustin Soulouque, to be president. He was a capable leader with much military experience, well connected to the Voodoo priesthood which he used to mobilize support, and he was vain. He purged the army, created a group of thugs called *zinglins* to enforce his will, and massacred mulattoes who tried to rebel against him in 1848. In 1849 he had himself pronounced Emperor Faustin I. He ruled by corruption and intimidation, and invaded Santo Domingo in 1855. In 1856 he was badly defeated in this war. A southern general, Fabre Nicholas Geffrard, overthrew him in 1859 and reestablished the more tolerant, but equally corrupt and inefficient regime of the republic. Emperor Faustin's rule foreshadowed Duvalier's a century later, but it was not as thorough. Faustin was one of Duvalier's models.[15]

The pattern of coups, uprisings, and continual corruption persisted into the twentieth century. Robert Rotberg has called this the period of "institutionalized chaos." An interesting comparison can be made with Jamaica, a British island with similar geographic conditions, and a similar history until 1791. Jamaica remained a colony, the slaves were eventually freed in 1834, and the plantation sugar economy also declined. On the whole, the Jamaican economy stagnated in the nineteenth century, but the British government took over direct control of the colony in 1866 and built up the basic infrastructure, particularly roads and railways. Thus, Jamaica emerged in the twentieth century as a far more prosperous and better educated Caribbean country. Its per capita Gross Domestic Product in recent times has been somewhat more than five times as high as Haiti's.[16]

Haiti continued to take out foreign loans, and to hover on the edge of bankruptcy. Nor did the situation inside Haiti improve. One Haitian president was blown up in 1912 with three hundred of his guards in the presidential palace, a successor was thought to have been poisoned to death, and there were frequent invasions of the cities by *cacos*, guerrilla bands based in the mountains and at the disposal of anyone who paid them off. In 1915, another president massacred 167 of his political prisoners, which resulted in his being seized by the population of the capital and torn to pieces by the mob which ran through the streets displaying various of his parts.[17]

This last event provoked an occupation of Haiti by American Marines. Partly this was the result of President Woodrow Wilson's sense of imperial righteousness. Wilson believed that civilized whites had a duty to bring order to the rest of the world. But there were strategic reasons for the intervention, too. Wilson feared that German or other Europeans might use the excuse of Haiti's debts to seize it and use it as a naval base. The Dominican Republic had had its financial affairs taken over by the United States on similar grounds in 1905, and it would be militarily occupied in 1916. This also happened to Nicaragua. Then, there were many secondary actors involved—the usual assortment of shady American speculators, French and German agents handing out bribes, and the interests of a big American bank that wanted to secure its loans.[18]

Fundamentally, the reasons for American intervention in Haiti and elsewhere in the region were less economic than strategic—to ring the Panama Canal with naval bases and exclude European naval forces— and moral, at least as far as the Americans understood international morality. Woodrow Wilson, like his immediate predecessors Roosevelt and Taft, genuinely believed in the superiority of white Anglo-American democracy. He thought it his duty to spread its institutions and benefits.[19]

On the occupied ground, however, the reality of the new American Caribbean Empire did not always match the purity of Wilsonian ideals. The American occupation certainly straightened out Haiti's finances, and began to build a modern infrastructure of schools, roads, bridges, railroads (which were never finished), and telephones. The army was reformed and better trained. On the other hand, the American Marine officers who ran Haiti were dictatorial, adhered to strict segregationist policies, and were openly racist. The president of Haiti was not allowed into the American Club, and American white women never went to formal ceremonies in the presidential palace. There was a *caco* rebellion in 1918 against the imposition of forced labor to build roads, and the Americans killed several thousand Haitians to bring it under control. And as the peasantry was antagonized by the authoritarianism and demands of the Americans, so was the small mulatto and black elite scandalized by the failure of the Americans to learn proper French as well as by their blatant racism which applied equally to all Haitians, no matter what their skin color or level of French education. To the Americans all Haitians were "niggers."[20]

Embarrassed by a rising level of protest in the late 1920s and serious riots in 1929, Herbert Hoover's administration made plans to leave Haiti, a move which was accomplished by his successor, Franklin Roosevelt. After almost twenty years of occupation, there were two main American legacies. One was a stronger army, the Garde. The other was a new and powerful ideological movement among Haitian intellectuals.

This movement was in some ways a product of the Darwinian and racist trends in early twentieth-century Europe and North America, but to these it added a deep sense of resentment against the whites who had bullied and demeaned Haiti. In some sense it resembled the Marcus Garvey movement in the United States, which flourished at about the same time, and a later anti-colonial ideology which Garvey and the Haitians inspired in Africa.[21]

NOIRISME, DUVALIER, AND THE REIGN OF THE TONTON MACOUTES

Haiti may have been poor and wretchedly ruled, but it had a well-developed culture of its own, both at the elite level, where it was Francophone and highly literate, and at the popular level, where Voodoo remained widespread despite the distaste felt for it by most of the elite, particularly the mulattoes and the Catholic church. The gross disrespect of the American occupiers for any aspect of Haitian culture, their crude materialism and utilitarianism, as well as their racism, produced a strong reaction. One of its leaders was the writer Price Mars, who was later called the "Father of *Négritude*" by Léopold Senghor, the Senegalese poet, nationalist leader, and president who would be the key figure in the creation of a Francophone theory of black culture and power in Africa.[22]

The theory of *négritude* claimed special cultural and esthetic virtues for Africans and had old roots in the Caribbean, but it became a major force in the 1920s and 1930s among black intellectuals in the United

States, the Caribbean (there were French, English, and Spanish, particularly Cuban versions), in colonial Africa, and of course in the European capitals of the colonial powers to which the brightest and most fortunate black intellectuals went to study.[23] It was meant to counter white racism and domination, but it was also inspired by the promise that fascism and communism seemed to offer as opposition to the dominant liberalism of the main colonial powers—England, France, and for the Caribbean, the United States.

The theory was better able to spread in Haiti because, for all its faults, the American occupation created a more diverse and practical school system, and some Haitians, particularly previously excluded blacks, were able to gain training they would not otherwise have had. An educated black middle class emerged, less Francophile than the old elite. It adopted a particularly black-centered version of the theory of *négritude* which was called *noirisme* (literally, "black-ism"). In the late 1920s, three men called "The Three Ds" because their last names began with "D" began to study the traditions and cultures of Africa and Haitian blacks. One of them was a medical student, François Duvalier, born in 1907, who earned his degree in 1934. In 1932 this group began to call itself the *Griots*, a West African word for a teller of tales, keeper of genealogies, and possessor of magical powers. *Griots* were common in many West African societies, particularly in Senegal, France's main base in Africa since the seventeenth century. In 1938, these intellectuals founded a journal, *Les Griots* which published articles about great African civilizations of the past, the subjection of blacks in the modern world, and the coming renaissance of black culture and power. "Duvalier," Nicholls has written, "agreed with Gobineau that the races are significantly different from one another, and that this difference has its roots in biological factors." Even though Haitians were of mixed blood, Duvalier and his friends believed they were essentially black, and this endowed them with a special, superior "sensibility." They also wanted to rehabilitate popular Haitian culture, especially those parts that came from Africa. "Voodoo was, for Denis and Duvalier, 'the transcendent expression of racial consciousness before the enigmas of the world.' "[24]

Duvalier went on to spend a year at the University of Michigan, where he was considered a mediocre, quiet student, and then worked in public health campaigns in Haiti. He also developed a theory of society and government which combined Voodoo, admiration for authoritarian modernizers like Kemal Ataturk, and a bitter denunciation of the mulatto elite for its lax ways and betrayal of black aspirations. He particularly hated the Catholic church because of its campaigns against Voodoo and because so many of its priests in Haiti were foreigners. His writings strike many familiar chords, particularly in the context of the 1930s. He was an increasingly xenophobic nationalist who believed in the importance of race and of racial struggle, he was anti-liberal, convinced that a strong leader who could embody the true desire of his people was superior to democracy, and he thought it important to cleanse his nation of its corrupt ways. In 1946 he published a work co-authored by him and Lorimer Denis, another of the original three "Ds," called *The Problem of Classes in Haitian History*, in which blacks, particularly Toussaint and Dessalines, as well as later, populist black leaders, were seen as heroes, while both the mulatto republic of Rigaud in the south, and later mulatto presidents were seen as traitors. Though some of this work was couched in socialist language, race and color were the main determinants of class, and solidarity on the basis of color was to save Haiti.[25]

In 1946 Dumarsais Estimé was elected president in an unusually fair and open election. He was black, the first nonmulatto in that office since the unfortunate Jean Vilbrun Guillaume Sam, the one torn to pieces in 1915, and he promised to bring important reforms to Haiti.[26]

Black intellectuals supported him, and he was widely popular. Duvalier became his director of pubic health and later secretary for labor and health. But the elite was unwilling to cooperate with Estimé, the peasants remained traditional subsistence cultivators, the bureaucracy was corrupt, and the army as well as the commercial classes were antagonized. The economy made no progress, and when Estimé tried to raise taxes on salaried workers, many fled back into rural areas. He invested in poorly thought-out, wasteful projects. He alarmed the neighboring Dominican Republic by reviving claims to its territory, and the Dominican dictator, Rafael Trujillo, backed mulatto exiles plotting against Estimé. He was forced out in 1950.[27]

The next president, Paul Magloire, was also black. He was a soldier trained under the Americans, and for a time the economy revived because of the rise in primary product prices during the Korean War. But in 1954, when he misappropriated the funds sent to Haiti to help it recover from a bad hurricane, strikes and protests erupted. He left in 1956, was replaced by an unstable regime, and there followed a long campaign for president in which François Duvalier presented himself as the popular champion of the black masses, of the nationalist intellectuals, and of the aspiring, technically trained black middle class against the old mulatto elite. With the support of the army, he won an overwhelming victory in 1957. He was, in fact, the best candidate. He had had administrative experience, he had performed adequately and honestly in public service, he had plans for reform, he had the interest of the previously disenfranchised blacks at heart and was supported by Voodoo priests, he was a distinguished intellectual, and even many Americans who had dealt with him trusted him.[28]

Duvalier's personal past gave no hint of what he would do in power. His father had been a schoolteacher and then a judge, and François had been favored with a good education. He had no history of personal suffering. His ideological hatred of mulattoes, the Catholic church, and foreigners in general was known to those who had read his work, of course, but the depth of his resentment was not evident to those who had worked with him. As with other twentieth-century tyrants, particularly the ideological ones such as Hitler and Stalin, it seems that many experienced politicians and observers failed to realize that strong words written in ideological tracts really mean something, and that a reasonable demeanor and willingness to compromise on the part of a leader who has not yet reached supreme power is no guarantee that he will be so reasonable later on.

Once in power, Duvalier moved quickly. He purged the army high command and promoted semi-literate young black officers entirely beholden to him. By 1958 he had organized nighttime raids by masked *cagoulards* (hooded ones—named after a French fascist organization of the 1930s). These later were formalized under the name "Volunteers for National Security," or more popularly as *tonton macoutes*, literally "uncle bagmen," bogeymen who got rid of their victims in the night. These sinister figures were entirely under the control of the president and his most loyal followers. They could rob, torture, and kill almost at will, and often did. They became the stuff of horrifying tales in Haiti and abroad, for example in Graham Greene's famous novel, *The Comedians*. Greene also wrote an article about Haiti entitled "Nightmare Republic."[29]

By repeated purges, and capricious raids against the old elite, against intellectuals, or anyone else they disliked, the *macoutes* instilled fear throughout the country. Very quickly, Duvalier saw that the means for thorough social change of the sort he had promised would not be available unless the power of the old elite and of the army was broken. But having engaged on this path, the idea of reform was abandoned in favor of a new type of corruption on an even larger scale than ever before, this time for the benefit of a new elite of gangsters.[30]

Yet it was not that simple. Some of the *macoutes* were Voodoo priests with genuine roots in the community; the hatred of many blacks for the old system was quite genuine, and the Duvalier regime offered them revenge as well as new possibilities for advancement. The army probably could not have been brought under presidential control without drastic purges.[31] Perhaps, if the means for reform had been at hand, if Duvalier had not had before him the example of so many failures, of such intransigence by old elites, he might have been less ruthless. Certainly, once he let loose a force like the *macoutes*, he was faced by the old dilemma of how to reward his men from what were rather meager resources. On the other hand, if his hero was Dessalines, as he claimed, he had a model of terror and race war in mind from the start. And since his ideology was more one of resentment than of any specific model for reform, it is possible that there was never any other alternative. But whatever the interpretation of what Rotberg calls Duvalier's "predatory state," however corrupt it became, this does not negate the fact that Duvalier probably intended something better when he became president. Here, too, there was once an idea, but it was so quickly corrupted that hardly anyone remembers it.

Duvalier found his Beria, his Himmler, in Clément Barbot, who was:

> utterly ruthless, terribly vindictive, very nationalistic, and unceasingly bitter about his own childhood treatment at the hands of the Roman Catholic Church. [H]e was whipped by priests for suggesting in school that Dessalines was a patriot.[32]

In 1959, Duvalier suffered a heart attack, and this may have affected his judgement. Barbot, however, was totally loyal, perhaps because he believed in the *noiriste* cause, and maintained Duvalier in power during his illness, for which he was rewarded by being arrested in 1960 as a potential rival. He was kept in prison for eighteen months. Later, Barbot tried to rebel, but his family was destroyed and he was gunned down in 1963.[33]

After 1960 all hope for social reform vanished, and was replaced, instead, by what Rotberg calls "the gods of destruction, brutality, and sadism." But Duvalier was different from past Haitian presidents. He was not interested in women or in having a good time. On the contrary, he remained a puritanical figure, appearing in dark suits (often resembling a Voodoo cult figure, Baron Samedi), and using corruption only to strengthen his rule and pay off his supporters.[34] He deliberately encouraged fantastic stories about his occult powers, which undoubtedly gave him a mysterious, frightening, but also legitimate image among believers in Voodoo. Laguerre refers to the "Voodooization" of Haitian politics.[35]

Duvalier also created a cult of his personality, though with fewer visible monuments than many other twentieth-century dictators. After the start of his concerted attack on the Catholic church from 1959 to 1966, in which many prominent churchmen were expelled, he began to encourage a kind of deification which resulted in a veritable "catechism" of Duvalierism spelled out in a book by Jean Fourcand, published in 1964 in the capital, Port-au-Prince, entitled *Catéchisme de la révolution*. A translation of the Lord's Prayer from this work is cited by Nicholls:

> *Our Doc, who art in the National Palace for life,*
> *hallowed be thy name*
> *by generations present and future,*
> *thy will be done*
> *in Port-au-Prince and in the provinces. . . .* [36]

In 1962 a night watchman who had refused to give the *macoutes* equipment from a warehouse was bound with barbed wire, hung up, and left to bleed to death. In 1963, university students who had distributed anti-Duvalier leaflets were tortured, along with their families. A war over turf between two gangs of *macoutes* ended with the losers' bodies dumped on the steps of a Catholic church with their genitals stuffed in their mouths. One government execution was shown on television. After an assassination attempt against his family, Duvalier decided that the culprit must be the army's best marksman (who had nothing to do with it). He escaped but his family was machine-gunned. People walking past the presidential palace had to hold their hands over their heads or risk being shot. So many Haitians began fleeing that the *macoutes* cleared a zone several miles deep on the Dominican

border and began shooting anyone in it. The president himself travelled only escorted by armored personnel vehicles. The total numbers
killed are not known, but at the height of the terror, in the one month
of May 1963, 196 were murdered by the *macoutes*, 103 sought asylum
in foreign embassies, and several hundred fled across the border. At
this rate, in a country with somewhat over four million people, it is
obvious that a significant portion of the society was being affected. All
this was punctuated by bouts of presidential puritanism in which he
sent out a "morals squad" to arrest prostitutes, homosexuals, or anyone
caught making love in Port-au-Prince. This regime continued until
1966, when it began to ease, though more limited use of terror never
ceased, and the *macoutes* remained powerful.[37]

There was also corruption on a grand scale. Money was extorted
from businesses by the *macoutes*; funds were skimmed off government
salary checks through a compulsory "national lottery"; tolls were collected on bridges and roads, and eventually inside urban areas as well;
foreign aid was stolen; and Duvalier pocketed a portion of the salaries
paid by the Dominican Republic for Haitian sugar cane cutters imported every season. If Duvalier himself was not interested in enjoying
great luxury, his children and their friends and spouses were, and he
lavished millions on them. The major *macoutes* built themselves huge
villas.[38]

In 1964, Duvalier became "President for Life." He said:

> It is not easy to find a man who has complete confidence in himself, and
> in his country, and who decides to maintain its dignity and prestige;
> such a revolutionary is found only every 50 or 75 years. . . . I knew that I
> had to fulfill a holy mission, a mission which will be fulfilled entirely.[39]

Perhaps he believed it. Even some foreign students of Haiti, who
know all the terrible details, find redeeming features in his reign. He
tried to limit American influence in Haiti. He ended foreign domination of the Catholic church. He gave the peasants a sense "that they
were really citizens and that what they did was important." He certainly knew how to play on the resentment of blacks against the mulattoes,
and he kept up his connections with the villages through his network
of clients and Voodoo priests. It is true that there was little resistance
to him in the 1960s, and almost none by his death in 1971, so that the
many attempts to foment rebellion from the outside failed miserably.[40]

But he had alienated the United States, despite his repeated claim to being a champion of anti-communism, and aid was drying up. The economy was suffering. The flight of the elite had reached such proportions that there were more well-trained Haitians working abroad than at home, and by 1966, Duvalier was so securely in power that he felt he could relax the terror and begin to try to refurbish his image. He made his peace with the Americans, and some investments followed in manufacturing for export items that required cheap, low-skilled labor. Tourism picked up after falling through the early Duvalier years, and the general economy improved.[41]

Nevertheless, these slight improvements in the late 1960s did not change the fact that Haiti had America's highest death rate, an official infant mortality rate of 150 per 1,000 per year (though it was probably much higher than that as infants who die soon after birth often remain unreported), the lowest rate of urbanization in the Americas, and a per capita Gross Domestic Product half of Bolivia's and 40 percent of Honduras's, the next two poorest countries in the western hemisphere. Most telling, its per capita product was less than one-third of the Dominican Republic's, a neighbor that had once been much less developed. The infant mortality rate in the Dominican Republic was one-fifth that of Haiti's.[42]

Haiti's population by 1970 was about eight times that in 1824, and was continuing to grow at about 2 percent a year. But given the primitive methods of cultivation, the mountainous terrain, and the lack of irrigation or agricultural investment, this was a disaster. Cultivation moved ever higher into the mountains that were stripped of their forest cover, and massive erosion destroyed the soil. There was simply not enough land to go around. Underfed, ridden by diseases, the population nevertheless continued to grow because inoculations and foreign aid kept epidemics in check. Illiteracy was over 75 percent. In the Dominican Republic, by contrast, it was about 34 percent. Even assuming that these figures are not very accurate, there is little question that Haiti continued to lose ground compared to other similar, poor Caribbean and Latin American societies, as it had been doing since some time in the nineteenth century.[43]

In 1959, there were 500 kilometers of paved roads in Haiti. By 1969 there were 370. It would be difficult to find a statistic that speaks more eloquently about infrastructural investments in Haiti under the Duvalier regime. Robert Rotberg's book on Haiti, published the year François Duvalier died, said that the regime was still kept in power by some 7,500 *macoutes*, of whom about 1,500 were "the hard core—the trusted killers." They remained the "eyes, ears, and arms of the regime," its Gestapo, KGB, and Mafia rolled into one.[44]

But to the surprise of many foreign observers, when Papa Doc died in April of 1971, the succession passed smoothly to his son, widely mocked as "Baby Doc," the young, pudgy Jean-Claude Duvalier. He became the new President for Life, and was to rule for fifteen more years. Unlike his predecessors, Papa Doc had combined a touch of populist ideology with a muscular police state. This gave him some popularity, but also a core of thoroughly corrupted killers determined to hold on to the fruits of power. This is why his regime long survived his death.

Postscript: Baby Doc Betrays His Legacy

Baby Doc was not at all like his father. He enjoyed the pleasures of wealth, married a spectacularly beautiful, very light mulatto woman, and began to rely increasingly on an educated, business-oriented elite, that is, largely the heirs of the old mulatto elite.[45]

This brought some rewards. In the 1970s, unlike in the 1960s, Haiti had a reasonably healthy economic growth rate, and by 1980, it seemed to be headed for sustained growth. But because there had been so little investment in education or infrastructure, the prosperity was entirely dependent on just a few agricultural exports, and on manufacturing which could only use unskilled labor. Furthermore, the few families who controlled the economy, estimated at between eight hundred and four thousand, sent their profits abroad to escape the depredations of the still active *macoutes*. Thus, there was virtually no domestic investment. What this meant was that when the economy of the United States went into recession in the early 1980s, Haiti's was badly damaged.[46]

Discontent resurfaced, and though there was severe repression, Baby Doc tried to be somewhat more moderate and more understanding of international (that is, American) sensibilities about the evils of torture and murder. But the old supporters of Papa Doc were increasingly at odds with the new crowd of mulatto sophisticates around Baby Doc and his extravagantly spendthrift wife. By 1985, the combination of renewed economic crisis, ever more blatant corruption and waste on the part of the Duvaliers, disputes among the regime's supporters, and renewed courage and hope within an opposition supported by international human rights groups and by the Catholic church combined to destabilize Baby Doc's hold on power. Even the United States government belatedly insisted that the *macoutes* be disciplined.[47]

Baby Doc was not the tough, bitter, nasty man that his father had been. He had tried to adapt to the modern world in order to continue to enjoy his inherited throne. A much less complicated, more purely corrupt, and quite traditional little dictator, when things became too difficult, in early 1986, he fled to France with his wife, his entourage, and unknown millions of dollars. He continues to live there happily.

In Haiti, the addition of a more modern ideological base to traditional corruption and misrule backfired and produced an outcome even more terrible than what existed before. Since the expulsion of the Duvaliers, it has proved difficult to be rid of Papa Doc's legacy. The *macoutes*, a revived army, the old elites, the Church, black populist sentiment, Voodoo priests—all are involved in complicated power struggles that have brought more killing, more horrors, and continuing misery for most Haitians. Because of its poverty and diseases, Haiti has been hard hit by a new plague, AIDS. With thousands upon thousands of Haitians trying to flee political turmoil and growing economic distress by taking their chances on dangerously small boats heading for Florida, and being rounded up to be sent back, the world in the 1990s can see the final result of Haiti's long, sad two centuries of history and of its tragic culmination, the Duvalier dynasty.

GOOD KING, BAD KING? WAS RAFAEL TRUJILLO A TYRANT?

On June 16, 1955, the Embassy of the Dominican Republic in Washington issued a pamphlet written by a certain Rev. Zenón Castillo de Aza in Rome to commemorate the signing of a Concordat between the Vatican and the Republic exactly one year earlier. Then, Rafael Trujillo had been received with great pomp and honor by Pope Pius XII. Later Trujillo would be singled out by Cardinal Spellman of New York, in 1956, as an exemplary leader because of his religious and anti-communist policies.[48] The pamphlet began like this:

> In the centuries upon centuries of its history, few men have entered triumphantly through Rome's gates. . . . Trujillo, the Dominican Republic's great leader, though, is one who entered that city proudly, wearing

the laurels of his merits and achievements, and left it triumphantly. . . . With his martial bearing, firm stride and alert look which impressed high Vatican dignitaries, Trujillo went up the broad marble stairway and crossed the spacious halls decorated with paintings by the world's greatest masters, and the Swiss Guard and other palace warders presented arms with medieval military pomp, rendering honors reserved for great heroes.[49]

In the several pages that follow there are references to the unfortunate plight of the Church in some other, less blessed Latin American countries, compared to the happy state of affairs in the Dominican Republic. And:

There is a parallel between what Trujillo has achieved and what was accomplished many centuries ago by two heroes of history— Constantine the Great, and Pepin, VIII century (*sic*) king of the Franks surnamed The Short. Like the former, Trujillo has recognized the Church as a juridical person. . . . Trujillo's enlightened policies in this wise are inspired by both tradition and sheer statesmanship. By tradition, he is a staunch Catholic; this he inherits from his illustrious forbears who were eminently loyal to the Church which Christ founded upon Peter and who were intimately linked to outstanding Dominican churchmen.[50]

There are many ironies in this pamphlet, and they provide important clues about Trujillo's regime.

Far from being a good Christian, Rafael Trujillo was known throughout his domain as an exceptional lecher who had to be provided with a steady supply of young, mostly virgin women for his use, generally for only one or two nights. Once or twice a week a group of about thirty eligibles would be gathered in the National Palace, to be reviewed by Trujillo, and he would pick those to be used that week. Evidently, he liked plump mulatto women, and enjoyed reciting poetry to them. He rewarded them generously, and by all accounts, his tastes were straightforward. Only when he became old "did his taste turn strongly to very young women."[51]

Rafael Trujillo had torturers and hired murderers to maintain him in power and get rid of his enemies from the very start of his rule.

Hans Magnus Enzensberger, quoting a report by a former foreign minister of Costa Rica sent to investigate the Dominican Republic in the time of Rafael Trujillo's dictatorship, wrote:

There were electric chairs which forced out confessions with the help of high voltage shocks; cigarettes pressed into the skin; women raped in front of their husbands; tanks filled with stinking water in which prisoners were immersed up to their necks for hours or even days; shark pools into which prisoners were thrown in the presence of Rafael Trujillo Junior and friends; vaults especially equipped for the purpose of torturing; dungeons with hunting dogs trained to bite off the genitals of their victims; and concentration camps on remote islands where there was practically nothing to eat.[52]

Long before this report was issued, in three days during October of 1937, Trujillo had ordered one of the most horrifying massacres in the bloody history of the Caribbean. Some 20,000, or perhaps as many as 25,000 Haitians in border areas had been murdered—some shot, many beheaded by machetes. Later Trujillo smiled when describing his negotiations with the Haitian government at that time, and said, "While I was negotiating, out there they were going sha-sha-sha"— imitating the chopping sound of the machete cutting through necks.[53]

This incident was the result of the long hostility and suspicion between the two countries produced by their earlier conflicts, and a continuing, residual fear of Haiti by the Dominicans, even though the balance of power between them had shifted by this time; the Dominican Republic had almost as many people as Haiti and was richer. The massacre was also to keep poor Haitian immigrants out of his territory, except at such times when they were needed to cut cane. Trujillo had negotiated a new boundary agreement to settle old claims, and wanted the border areas cleared of Haitians. But mostly, the slaughter was prompted by his bad temper. He had been bribing and suborning high Haitian officials and businessmen to get his way with their government, and just before the massacre, he learned that some of his key agents in Haiti had been exposed and killed. The Haitian government was in no position to press claims against the Dominican Republic, however, and the awful slaughter was not publicized. Later, one of Trujillo's paid Haitians, Élie Lescot, became president of his country in 1941, but then turned against Trujillo, who tried to have him murdered. Trujillo eventually contributed to his overthrow in 1946. Needless to say, this may have had something to do with Duvalier's suspicion about important people around him once he achieved power in Haiti in 1957.[54]

Aside from having a moral record that threw some doubts on his staunch Catholicism, there were other aspects about Trujillo's past that must have amused historically inclined readers.

Despite claims to the contrary, Rafael Trujillo's forbears were not particularly illustrious. One grandfather had been a Cuban police captain who, because of his illegal activities, had had to take refuge in the Dominican Republic, and had lived with Trujillo's grandmother for a year. Later, this captain had returned to Cuba, participated in the repression against the independence movement, and finally fled to Spain. The grandmother in question had then been involved in local politics as one of the supporters of the brutal dictator Ulises Heureaux, whose plumed hat Trujillo would wear on his first inauguration as president in 1930. His other grandmother was the illegitimate daughter of a Haitian officer and a Haitian woman who had lived in the Dominican Republic during the Haitian occupation. There was nothing unusual or disgraceful about this heritage, but it bothered Trujillo, particularly the fact that he was part black and Haitian. In his official biography, Trujillo was said to be descended from a Spanish military family on his father's side and French nobility on his mother's.[55]

Then, too, there was the historical allusion to Pepin the Short. Pepin had overthrown the decrepit Merovingian Frankish royal dynasty in the mid-eighth century, and started a new line, the Carolingians, whose most illustrious ruler would be Charlemagne. To legitimize his action, he had allied himself to the Church. Evidently, that is how Trujillo viewed himself, as the founder of a glorious new dynasty that would obtain legitimation from a Pope looking for allies.[56]

The preposterous historical allusion to an early medieval European dynasty brings up an important question: was Trujillo just a traditional, brutal king who treated his state as a personal domain, or was he really a tyrant? He was a lecher, a hypocrite, and a torturer, but then, so were many, perhaps most rulers of agrarian monarchies. On the other hand, he did not leave his country in ruin, as did the Duvalier dynasty. There was no particular ideology behind his regime, and he certainly was not a revolutionary who tried to create a new type of society by reshaping his people into something they did not want to be, or by waging war against certain classes or races. Most of his murderous activities, aside from the massacre of Haitians in 1937, were not, like those of the *tonton macoutes*, or of Stalin's police, randomly applied to spread terror.

They were directed largely against those who hated him, often members of the old Dominican elite, whiter, richer, and more Hispanic than the mass of the population. His economic record, in fact, was not bad. In slightly over thirty years in power he built many roads and bridges, stabilized the fiscal situation, encouraged investment, and improved the general well-being. The Dominican Republic became one of the major sugar producers in the world, and on that basis, began to industrialize.[57]

Building on his substantial achievement, the Dominican Republic was able to double its per capita Gross Domestic Product in the twenty years after Trujillo, a record better than that of any of the Central American countries except Panama, and better than that of most of the major independent Caribbean countries, including Jamaica, Haiti, Cuba, and Guyana.[58] Indeed, his most eloquent critic, who was subsequently murdered by Trujillo, Jesús de Galíndez, pointed out in his book that in terms of public order, material well-being, and education, the Dominican Republic made significant progress under Trujillo.[59]

This ought not suggest that the Trujillo's Republic was a fair place. Trujillo and his family involved themselves with such a wide array of enterprises in the Republic that by 1938 they controlled some 40 percent of its wealth, not counting the (largely foreign-owned) sugar plantations. Whether this amount is correct or not, there is no question that Trujillo's income was enormous, and that through preferential treatment, he and his family became overwhelmingly rich. As Galíndez put it, *"Trujillo es el primer hombre de negocios del país"* (Trujillo is the country's first businessman).[60]

Germán Ornes, a one-time member of the Dominican parliament who left his country and wrote about Trujillo, estimated that the family fortune was worth about $500 million in the mid-1950s. They engaged in sordid cruelty and wastefulness, and repulsive hangers-on gathered about them like flies.[61]

Trujillo's brothers and sisters behaved like a family of utter gangsters, taking advantage of their brother's power to plunder the country, as did his wife's family. Pétan, the worst, set himself up in the district of Bonao as a kind of feudal lord forcing every woman who wanted to get married to be inspected, and sexually taken by him if he wanted, before permission would be granted. Finally, carried away by his ambitions, he plotted to take power from his brother, and was subsequently exiled for a time. Others in the family were only marginally better, and one sister, Nieves Luisa, amused herself by running a prostitution business in Cuba.[62]

But Trujillo was not an unusual character in Latin American history. The Somoza family in Nicaragua comes to mind immediately, as do dictators like Batista in Cuba, and a long list of nineteenth- and twentieth-century rulers elsewhere in this continent.[63] Trujillo was more able than many of them, and actually ruled better than most, because, unlike his family, he was disciplined and had a good sense of how to protect the long-range future of his property.

It is only by modern democratic standards that Trujillo appears to us to be a vicious dictator who committed countless atrocities, who stole public funds, took unfair advantage of his power, and corrupted his society. But had he lived in Europe in the eighth century, or for that matter, in the eighteenth, his behavior would not have seemed unreasonable. He was careful about his patrimony. He invested in the economic infrastructure. He built grand buildings. To be sure, he confused public and private property, but then, in the past there were no solid distinctions between what the king owned and what was the state's. He did not involve his country in ruinous wars. And most of all, in a country that had had a history of internal divisions, that had been weakly integrated, he solidified the state and united the nation. This is why, when he exiled his brother, he made a special trip to Pétan's fiefdom in Bonao to say that he would no longer tolerate local bosses. From now on, he said, "I desire that all the authorities, all the members of the Dominican Party, and all my friends should know that there is a sole authority that embodies the ideals of the people and the aspirations of the Party. . . . "[64]

Any king or emperor trying to hold together his realm against ambitious kin, refractory local notables, officials trying to take advantage of the ruler behind his back or exploiting the inertia of regional customs and separatism in a weakly unified state would have understood Trujillo. Trujillo was a perfect monarch for the age of state building, a worthy if minor political soul mate of Louis XI of France, or Ivan the Terrible of Russia, of Henry VIII of England, and of many of their successors. They were also preoccupied with trying to keep their brothers, cousins, queens, and mistresses under control without being forced into civil war, balancing the demands of their Church with their own ambitions, and trying to pay their soldiers and officials enough to keep them loyal without overtaxing the peasants and destroying the economy. Some of them were as cruel as Trujillo, some perhaps less. None of them would have passed muster as twentieth-century defenders of human rights or democracy. Of course, Trujillo did not live in the fifteenth or sixteenth century, or even in the nineteenth. His most significant and powerful ally was the United States of America in the time of Franklin Roosevelt, Harry Truman, Dwight Eisenhower, and John Kennedy. And Trujillo's subjects, at least the ones who were literate, knew something about what life and politics were like in the country to the north.

Trujillo, like some other modern state builders, for example the Shah of Iran, ran into this problem, that what was acceptable in the past was considered shameless corruption and criminal cruelty by the standards of the Americans, and that could, from time to time, worry the government of the United States and cause serious internal debates in that country. If Ivan the Terrible or Peter the Great had depended on the United States as allies, sooner or later a congressman would have gotten up to complain that it wasn't right to be allied to a foreign potentate who was wont to lose his temper and murder his own children, and who, furthermore, relied on serfs for his revenues.

There is little doubt that Trujillo would have been more at home with medieval potentates than with American diplomats and presidents. By 1960, afraid that this longtime ally of the United States would provoke a second leftist revolution in the Caribbean (Fidel Castro had come to power in 1959), the Eisenhower State Department was describing Trujillo to the American Congress as "a tyrant, a torturer, and a murderer." Only some powerful southern congressmen and senators, who understood monarchy and autocracy better than most of their fellow Americans, came to his defense.[65]

THE RISE AND FALL OF TRUJILLO

The history of the Dominican Republic predisposed it to dictatorship in the same ways as in most other Latin American and Caribbean societies. The Spaniards had ruled it autocratically, particularly during the Bourbon period in the eighteenth century, when Spain had tried to reassert centralized control over its loosely governed American

Empire.[66] It became a sugar-exporting economy like the French part of Hispaniola, but it had only about one-fifth as many people as Haiti, and only one-third of them were black slaves.[67]

In 1795 the French took Santo Domingo, and most of the next fifty years were spent under various forms of French or Haitian occupation, interspersed with a period of inefficient Spanish rule. The Haitian occupations left bitter memories of pillage, rape, and torture. The Hispanic population considered Haitians to be uncivilized foreign blacks.[68]

After Haitian rule was overthrown in 1844, things did not go much better. The Dominican Republic was underpopulated and felt vulnerable to continuing Haitian threats. It tried repeatedly to get itself annexed, or at least protected by another foreign power—the French, the British, the Spaniards, and the Americans. American observers sent to investigate the situation in 1844 said there were not enough "white" Dominicans to recognize the Republic.[69]

Spain took over Santo Domingo in 1861, but there was a revolt, a destructive war of independence, and in 1865 the Republic became independent again.[70]

Subsequently, the country was neither united nor prosperous enough to support a modern government and administration, and it experienced endemic warfare between local strongmen and the central government, as well as chronic instability at the center. There were foreign loans which could not be paid on time. In 1868 and 1869 the United States almost annexed the Republic, but was stopped by the refusal of abolitionist Republican senators to go along and confirm the relevant treaty.[71]

In 1882 the government was seized by a military dictator, Ulises Heureaux, who happened to be black. In his major book on the history of the Dominican Republic, Sumner Welles (an American diplomat who was one of the State Department's top Latin American specialists, and during Franklin Roosevelt's presidency an under secretary of state) described the Heureaux period as "the most pitiless tyranny known to the Republics of the American continent."[72] This is certainly an exaggeration prompted by Welles's negrophobia. In fact, Heureaux was the typical capable soldier who used his troops to bring some order to his country, and in the process to enrich himself, his family, and his friends. To be sure, he used torture, intimidation, and bribery to keep himself in power, but he seems to have been more able than most of his predecessors. In 1899, however, he was assassinated, leaving behind chaos and a bankrupt government.[73]

The American seizure of the Republic's finances in 1905 to prevent European powers from interfering straightened out the fiscal conditions of the country. A military occupation, ordered by Woodrow Wilson to prevent renewed revolution and chaos and the country being seized as a naval base by Germany, began in 1916. It set the base for a new type of Dominican government.[74]

Rafael Trujillo was born in 1891. From his late teens to his mid-twenties, from about 1910 to 1916, he was involved in what sounds like gangsterism—petty theft, graft, and blackmail, and local politics. There was nothing unusual or particularly damning about this pattern, which has been a common one in weakly integrated, economically poor states throughout much of the world. This might have been Sicily and Trujillo would have been an aspiring member of the Mafia, or China, where he would have joined a local warlord. He was a good rider, was fond of nice clothes, and had a few years of education. He was also tremendously self-disciplined and capable of hard work.[75]

Almost from the start, the American occupation proved unpopular. There were some killings and abuses, particularly in the eastern part of the country where a Marine captain responsible for atrocities had to be court-martialed in 1922. He wound up committing suicide. As in Haiti, the racism of the American troops did not win them friends in a society that was largely of mixed blood. American attempts to bring order were not popular with local bosses; and the white, Spanish elite took no more liking for the Americans than did Haiti's Francophone elite. To overcome some of these problems, the United States established a National Guard which was supposed to become the local guarantor of law and order.[76]

In late 1918 Trujillo applied to join the National Guard, which later became the National Police, and which was under American command. He was immediately accepted and became a lieutenant in early 1919. The National Guard was desperate for capable Dominicans, and he fit very well. His exemplary neatness appealed to American officers, he learned passable English, and his discipline and hard work won him quick promotions. By the time the Americans left in 1924 he was a high officer, and he became commander of the National Police in 1925. In 1928 this force became the National Army, with General Trujillo in command.[77]

His good ties to the American military helped him in the next two years as he maneuvered to take complete power, against the wishes of the American State Department which preferred a nonmilitary democracy. But there was really no countervailing power in the country, and in 1930, after a campaign that included a number of murders and disappearances, as well as considerable intimidation, Trujillo became President. He quickly set about destroying all vestiges of possible opposition, including the remnants of the local bosses, and subordinated the old, white, social elite.[78]

Trujillo was not accepted by this old social elite, largely because he was from a partly black, lower-middle-class rural family. Once in power, he expressed his contempt for them, and deliberately humiliated many of them.[79]

It is certain that race was a sore point with him. He wanted to be considered white, even though, depending on the definition used, some two-thirds of the Republic population is mulatto, and the rest about evenly divided between whites and blacks.[80] This means very little in a mixed population anyway, because within a single family, for example Trujillo's, brothers and sisters may be of different colors. It is part of the Dominicans' mythology that they are white and civilized, whereas Haitians are black and not. This was Trujillo's rationale when he posed as a defender of Catholic European values against the "barbarous" black republic next door.[81]

Perhaps Trujillo's inner insecurity about his social origins contributed, as it did in the case of many dictators, to his almost childish desire to surround himself with useless luxuries. When Imelda Marcos, wife of the Philippino dictator Ferdinand Marcos, was driven from power, it was discovered that she owned 3,000 pairs of shoes. Rafael Trujillo had 10,000 ties.[82]

Trujillo proved himself to be a good administrator who worked hard and got results, whether in organizing hurricane relief, building roads, or getting rid of his enemies. Soon after he secured power, there began a systematic campaign of public adulation. Eventually, his long reign came to be called the "Era of Trujillo." Monuments were built to his glory, titles assigned to him, medals pinned on his uniforms, the name of the Dominican Republic's highest mountain was changed to Trujillo—all these have been so much a part of so many dictatorships that it is hardly worth going through the list. Trujillo also created a single mass party which anyone who wanted to get anywhere had to join, and which produced its own version of the communist *nomenklatura*, or list of those acceptable for appointment and promotion to significant jobs. But this was not a mobilizing party designed to change the society, only another mechanism for Trujillo to collect funds (from compulsory dues) and redistribute them as he saw fit.[83]

But Trujillo's nasty temper, rancor toward those who had hurt his interests or pride, and unwillingness to tolerate criticism often got the better of him. This tendency worsened in his later years, and it finally destroyed him because it pushed him into behavior that was unacceptable to the United States.[84]

The last years of Trujillo turned a regime that had been a vicious but reasonably efficient dictatorship into something more grotesque. Now his name had to be put everywhere, on streets, buildings, parks; his birthday and the anniversaries of his coming to power had to be celebrated with great pomp; and everyone had to pay him court. He had to be addressed with all his titles:

> Meritorious Son of San Cristobal; Benefactor of the Fatherland; the First and Greatest of the Dominican Chiefs of State; Restorer of Financial Independence; Commander in Chief of the Armed Forces; Father of the New Fatherland; Loyal and Noble Champion of World Peace; Chief Protector of Dominican Culture; Maximum Protector of the Dominican Working Class.[85]

In 1956, a former Dominican resident, then living in New York and lecturing at Columbia University, Jesús de Galíndez, who had just finished an excellent doctoral dissertation exposing the nature of Trujillo's reign, was kidnapped off the streets of New York, brought to the Dominican Republic, and murdered. One version of the story is that he was lowered into boiling water inch by inch after being beaten by Trujillo himself. His body was then fed to the sharks.[86]

Galíndez's book, which remains the best institutional analysis of the Trujillo regime, was published posthumously. Later, in an effort to cover up the incident, Trujillo had the American pilot who had flown the mission to pick up Galíndez murdered, too. These outrages were publicized in the United States and badly damaged his image.[87]

Trujillo began to involve himself in irresponsible plots against other Latin American heads of state in order to avenge various slights to his person; he was becoming an international nuisance and menace. He began treating the United States with disdain. When his old ally cooled toward him, he made overtures to Castro in 1960, using as an intermediary one of his most notorious killers, Johnny Abbes. The Dominican Communist Party was legalized. Dominican Radio began to broadcast Soviet propaganda. Though the Soviet Union proved to be uninterested in obtaining this kind of ally in the Caribbean, Trujillo did manage to worry the Americans.[88]

Meanwhile his sons and daughters cavorted and spent millions on their pleasures. Ramfis, the heir apparent, pursued Zsa Zsa Gabor and Kim Novak; he spent nights in debauched drinking; he also participated, with Johnny Abbes, in a gruesome massacre of political opponents.[89]

The American government decided it was time to be rid of Trujillo, who had become a menace, if only because it was thought that there would be a revolution in the Dominican Republic. The old tyrant was losing his grip on reality, it was thought, and there was no obvious successor. There was a CIA plot to get rid of him, by smuggling weapons into the country to be used by his political enemies. Supposedly President John Kennedy called it off, but the weapons were there. Trujillo was warned that the United States wanted change, but he refused. He could have retired gracefully to Europe with a fortune worth hundreds of millions of dollars, but he had no intention of doing so.[90]

Trujillo was courageous to the end. He liked to be driven alone by his chauffeur. On the night of May 30, 1961, as he was being driven to one of his homes, he was ambushed by a group of plotters who consisted of military men, officials, and businessmen who, over the years, had been insulted, injured, or had family members hurt by the Trujillo family. Hit, Trujillo jumped out of his car with a pistol in his hand, and he was gunned down. The Trujillo family, however, was able to hang on to power long enough to have some of the main plotters captured, horribly tortured, and killed. Then, on the insistence of the United States government, the Trujillo family left for exile.[91]

Rafael Trujillo was hardly one of the worst tyrants in the modern world, or even in Latin America, though for his political enemies, and especially those he tortured and killed, he was nightmarishly evil. But Papa Doc Duvalier was worse and did his country far more harm. Duvalier would have been considered a tyrant in any age. Trujillo, however, illustrates an important, though often forgotten point when corrupt dictators in small, poor, and weak modern countries are discussed.

Western liberal democracies, in this case the United States, have often stepped into situations where their overwhelming strength has given them the power to pick local rulers. Very commonly, these have turned out to be corrupt dictators. This certainly happened in the Dominican Republic. But in fact, local conditions have been such that almost any choice would have resulted in similar tyrannies. The historical and institutional legacies of these societies have not been conducive to democracy, and those in charge of the military have almost inevitably wielded enough power to do as they wished, unless a politician like Duvalier could manage to build up a countervailing terror organization. But ultimately, and this is particularly obvious with the case of Trujillo, the rising standards of political morality that came from public opinion in the democracies, and spread into the ranks of the educated locals, redefined these corrupt regimes as unacceptable tyrannies. For Trujillo and his family, that proved to be their undoing.

The phenomenon of liberal democracies helping old-fashioned, corrupt tyrants into power, sustaining them, and then turning against them in horror because they violate modern norms of political decency partly explains the seeming proliferation of corrupt tyranny in so many less industrialized societies in the second half of the twentieth century. It is not that suddenly there are more traditional tyrants, but that what was considered normal for so long has become less so, and also that many places that were colonies, or virtual colonies in the first half of the century turned into independent states in the second half. In so doing, they reverted to rather traditional autocracies, but in the new political moral climate that emanates from the richest democracies, this is no longer considered acceptable.

This might offer hope for the future, though it may be that the unacceptability of corrupt tyranny will only increase the tendency toward ideological tyranny in desperately chaotic, resentful, and poor societies. Before turning to that theme, I intend to take up two more cases of corrupt tyranny, and to show the complicity of European colonial powers in creating them. These examples will demonstrate how likely it was that tyranny would emerge in many new African states after decolonization, and also how the addition of a modern type of state-centered organization along with Western influence made what would have otherwise been quite traditional bad kings something considerably more sinister.

Chapter 11

Colonialism, Resentment, and Chaos

Two African Studies

The rapid conquest of Africa by Europe in the late nineteenth and early twentieth centuries generated a set of contradictory feelings on the part of both the colonizers and colonized. Africans confronted by the open racism and condescension of the Europeans were deeply resentful, but this was combined with admiration for these foreigners who ruled brutally, yet who had managed to make themselves so powerful. On the European side there was an overwhelming sense of superiority mixed with fear and insecurity, because there were so few whites in the colonies to maintain order in hostile circumstances. And increasingly in the twentieth century, especially in the French and British colonies, but to some extent in the others, too, there was a growing sense of guilt. After all, the rising standards of political morality which increased the scope of democracy in the Western world made the discrepancy between colonies and the home country ever larger. The Spaniards and Portuguese whose home countries did not become democratic until the 1970s felt less guilt than the Belgians, French, and British, but even they were not left untouched by the growing sentiment that colonization was somehow wrong.[1]

Africa's colonial experience was not unique. Similar complex feel-

373

ings of resentment and admiration on the part of subject people, and of superiority and insecurity accompanied by brutality and a growing sense of guilt by the masters played a role in the history of slavery in the Americas in the nineteenth century, and modern colonialism practically everywhere.

Generally, after a first wave of revolts against the Europeans, colonized people learned that the whites' technological superiority could not be matched. Ambitious locals then tried to learn the ways of the Europeans in schools, and invariably, it was from the ranks of such Westernized, educated youths that the successful anti-colonial movements emerged. We have seen how this happened in Burma and Cambodia. Very often these new potential elites combined a European education with continuing, intense resentment of the whites for their racism (except, of course, in Japanese colonies like Korea where the Japanese were the hated and admired masters), for their brutality, and for their exploitation. This did not lessen their admiration for Western technologies and scientific prowess. That is why Marxism seemed so appealing, and why it fit so easily with understandably bitter forms of nationalism. At the extremes, this nationalism could be violently racist and preach exclusion of anything foreign, as in Burma, Haiti, Cambodia, or North Korea, even as it hoped to be able to catch up to the power of the past or present colonial masters.[2]

In many parts of Africa the problem was compounded by the absence of pre-colonial states within the rough boundaries of the colonial ones. Mixing together various ethnic groups with very different political institutions may have been convenient for the Europeans; for Africa it was a prescription for disaster. Contradictory and dangerous as the colonial legacy may have been in Burma and Cambodia, or in much of Asia, in most Asian cases the Europeans had conquered established states that more or less survived within colonial boundaries. They had their own established histories, bureaucratic traditions, and common unifying cultures, at least at their cores, to hold together the states after they achieved post-colonial independence. But this was not so in most of Africa. Furthermore, Africa was effectively ruled by Europeans for a very short period of time. Even where the whites had controlled coastal forts or islands well before the twentieth century, the interior was brought under colonial rule only from about 1890 to 1910. With independence coming a mere two generations later, few of the new states in Africa had been sufficiently Westernized to have an adequate number of educated civil servants, businessmen, or other leaders to cope with the immense problems of economic backwardness, ethnic divisions, and political insecurity.

Since the early 1960s, when most African colonies achieved independence from their European rulers, many of their leaders have fit the definition of "corrupt tyrant." In a continent and at a time when almost every government was in some way despotic and undemocratic, where ethnicity, religion, and kinship played a leading role in the distribution of power and privilege, where national identities were weak, and where bureaucratic probity was scarce, almost all the grandiose schemes for economic and social improvements have failed and produced, instead, a long list of wars, famines, and economic catastrophes. But even in a region of the world where abuse of trust by those in power has been routine, and where government exercised primarily for the benefit of favored kin, clansmen, or one's own tribal group is almost normal, a few leaders stand out because of the harm they caused and because their corruption was so debased. The viciousness of their regimes seemed particularly disgusting because they had so little justification except for naked greed and obsessive cruelty. As we will see, in some of the most egregious examples it was almost inevitable that awful forms of government would emerge. The actions of the colonial powers increased the probability of such an outcome. But in the worst cases, also, there was a personal element—those who happened to seize power were exceptionally unprepared to rule and particularly likely to abuse their positions.

Two of the most notorious African tyrannies in the 1970s were those of Idi Amin of Uganda and of President, later Emperor Jean-Bédel Bokassa of the Central African Republic (C.A.R.) and Empire. The West European and North American press covered the rise and fall of these men with relish and in gruesome, titillating detail.

There was more than a touch of racism in the Western press's reaction to Idi Amin and Bokassa. Their vanity, which was no more grotesque than that of scores of other leaders around the world in the twentieth century, was only amusing because in some ways it seemed to be trying to put insignificant African states at the same level as established European ones. Of course, no one mocked the grandiose fantasies of Nicolae Ceausescu and his wife during the 1970s because

Romania was useful in the game of international diplomacy. The Shah of Iran, who intended to make Iran one of the world's five great powers by the end of the century, and who gloried in extravagant pomp and ceremony, had oil to sell and offered a huge market for Western military and other goods, so the Western press treated him as if his claims to grandeur were somehow legitimate. Nor did many laugh at the grotesque cults of personality fostered by Stalin, Mao, and Hitler, all of whom had legions of domestic and foreign admirers. Only after these tyrants' deaths did it suddenly become obvious that there was something bizarre about the image they presented to the world, as supermen who could do no wrong.

In comparison, not only were Uganda, and especially the Central African Empire, of little significance in world affairs, but their leaders so conformed to the European image of half beastly, half comical, imitative, but fundamentally stupid blacks that it was difficult for the press to resist mockery. At a time when overt racism was no longer acceptable in respectable Western publications, it was possible to make the kinds of snide remarks about Idi Amin and Emperor Bokassa that expressed what many Westerners still felt about Africans in general. In a typical article with the subtitle "Fireworks and Bare-Breasted Maidens," *Newsweek* magazine lampooned the Napoleonic coronation of the Central African Empire's "bandy-legged new emperor" and his "1,000 man army."[3] The coverage of Amin was often equally mocking.

But what seemed to many Westerners to be buffoonery manifested itself in Uganda and the Central African Empire as vicious cruelty, uncontrolled corruption, and erratic policies that caused severe suffering for the populations ruled by these two men, and in Uganda, mass murder on a very large scale.

Both were the products of twentieth-century European colonialism. Both, but particularly Idi Amin, ruled states that were not culturally united or economically integrated nations. That explains much about the ways in which they ruled, as well as something about their personal attitudes toward power.

The Central African Republic's colonial past prepared it poorly for independence. Uganda's colonial history seems, on the surface, to have been more positive, but it also sowed the seeds for a nasty harvest. It is therefore necessary to begin with a brief description of what the French and British found when they came to Africa, and what they did with their colonies.

SLAVERY, FORCED LABOR, AND THE PAINFUL BIRTH OF AN INDEPENDENT CENTRAL AFRICAN REPUBLIC

The C.A.R.'s tragedy began before the European conquest. Located in the heart of the immense Savannah that extends from the Atlantic almost to the Nile below the Sahara desert, but also containing some of the tropical forest which predominates further south, the territory was part of the great slave-raiding zone of Africa devastated during the late nineteenth century. Whereas in an earlier period it was the coastal Atlantic part of Africa that was most beset by European slavers, during the nineteenth century slave raiding came to be dominated by the Muslim kingdoms of Central and East Africa. They penetrated deeply into the interior in their search for the human merchandise which they used themselves or exported to the Arab lands along the Nile, where the slaves were used chiefly in cotton fields producing for export to Europe, and in the Middle East. The northeastern quarter of what would become the Central African Republic, touching on the Sudan, was virtually depopulated during this time because of slave raiding and warfare, and even today, it is almost empty.[4]

The territory was assigned to France in the late nineteenth-century treaties that divided Africa, and it became a part of a larger unit, French Equatorial Africa.[5] But the French were no more benign than the Muslim slave merchants they gradually replaced. Not only in the ravaged north and east of the territory, but also in the south and west, which had escaped the worst of the slave wars, the French imposed new and harsh demands on the population. The colony of Ubangui-Shari, as the territory was then called, was one of the least profitable in France's Empire, but it contained a useful African variety of rubber. The rubber was extracted from wild plants, and the colony was divided into concessions given to French companies that simply used forced labor to get it. New plantings did not replace what got used up, and large areas were devastated. Company policemen would round up Africans, tie them together, and force them to harvest the rubber and carry it to the rivers for transportation to the coast. Not only did this cause substantial numbers of deaths through maltreatment of the workers, but the gangs of famished quasi-slaves being moved about contributed to the spread of serious diseases, including sleeping sickness, which devastated the country from 1910 to 1930 and virtually depopulated southeastern Ubangui-Shari.[6]

In the 1920s the French also used forced labor, much of it rounded up as virtual slaves in Ubangui-Shari, to build a railroad in their neighboring colony of Congo. This particular scandal was one of the main subjects of the great André Gide's famous book denouncing colonialism in Equatorial Africa, *Voyage au Congo—Carnets de route*. But Gide was labelled a communist in France, and despite periodic attempts at reform, legal forced labor continued until 1946, and effectively into the 1950s. Nevertheless, gradually the rudiments of a health control system slowed the ravages of epidemics and reversed the demographic decline which had characterized the late nineteenth and early twentieth centuries. Missionary schools were established, and the improvement of the road network, combined with the introduction of motor vehicles, somewhat eased the burdens of forced labor for transportation of goods. Still, as this happened, new products to be exploited were found—lumber, gold, and diamonds—and these also required labor.[7]

From 1928 to 1931 there was an African revolt that spread through French Equatorial Africa, including the French Congo, Ubangui-Shari, and southern Chad. Fighting was widespread, and full peace was not reestablished until 1935.[8]

In the late 1920s the mother of Barthélemy Boganda, who would become the C.A.R.'s preeminent political leader in the 1950s, was beaten to death by a French company's policeman while collecting rubber. One of Boganda's uncles was seized by the colonial police in 1927 because of his supposed resistance to work, taken to a police station, and also beaten to death. This uncle had a son who later joined the French colonial army, and fifty years after his father's death, had himself crowned as Bokassa the First, Emperor of the Central African Empire.[9]

Generations of forced migrations, confiscation of lands, new taxes, the subordination of village institutions, and war had all created a kind of a social vacuum in which it was easier for the French to rule. The countryside's power of organized resistance was largely destroyed. In effect, the process begun by the wars and raids of the Muslim slave raiders was completed by the French who were to leave behind a fragmented population hostile to any exercise of state power, but too weak to do much about it.

World War II brought important changes to French Africa. The governor of French Equatorial Africa, a black man from the French

Caribbean, Félix Éboué, who tried to liberalize colonial policy, kept it loyal to de Gaulle against Vichy France.[10] The post-war government of liberated France intended to maintain its empire after the war, but it recognized that the old method of ruling was no longer possible, or morally acceptable. Efforts were made to co-opt potential indigenous leaders by allowing African representation in the French parliament.

The first African delegate to the French parliament from Ubangui-Shari was Father Barthélemy Boganda, who had been trained as a priest by French Catholic missionaries, and was therefore thought to be docile. But once in France, he broke with the Church and became a forceful champion of African rights. In the late 1950s, in order to head off potential revolutions against their rule, such as the one they were fighting in Algeria, the French increased the autonomy of their African colonies and promised eventual independence. Boganda would have become the first president of the independent C.A.R.[11]

Unfortunately, in 1959, the year before independence, Boganda was killed in an air crash that was probably caused by a bomb set by local French interests in Ubangui-Shari, though it remains unclear who was actually responsible. Boganda was campaigning for a continuing union with the other French colonies of Equatorial Africa, and his presence in power might have given Africans throughout the region a stronger bargaining position against the French.[12]

Boganda's successor was his cousin, David Dacko, a young former schoolteacher who lacked Boganda's popularity, experience, or strength. Dacko was installed by the French to block a more nationalistic and popular politician, Abel Goumba, who would have succeeded Boganda had the French not intervened. With French help, in 1959 and 1960, Dacko overthrew the constitutional provisions established in the late 1950s. In order to repress opposition to his rule, by 1961 he had established a presidential dictatorship almost entirely dependent on French technicians, soldiers, and aid.[13]

The C.A.R. was of no immediate value to France. Its cotton and coffee were not highly significant, and though there were minerals and lumber, their exploitation was not well organized. But quite aside from its potential wealth, the C.A.R. bordered on Cameroon, a much richer, more developed former territory. Gabon, one of the most resource-rich countries in Africa (chiefly oil and uranium), was nearby. The French, with fine strategic insight, knew that weak former colonies could become useful bases for France in Africa, and that the costs of maintaining their influence in a country like this—with under two million people in 1960, a fragmented, impoverished society, and no other sources of aid—were low.[14]

Dacko's problems were not solved by the French. The economic situation was poor. The C.A.R.'s cotton, coffee, and diamond production were stagnant. No other commercial crop seemed available for development. A few French enterprises continued to dominate trade, but it was difficult to imagine that displacing them could have made the situation anything but worse. Within this context, the pressure to Africanize the civil service and to provide government jobs for those with some education proved expensive. Not only were the resources for paying these new functionaries scarce, but once in place, they were also inexperienced and often incompetent. This was a common enough situation in Africa, but in the C.A.R., with its scattered, small population, it was particularly acute. The already poor road network began to deteriorate, cash crop production fell, and the diamond business began to attract a growing number of shady characters from abroad whose dealings escaped taxation. Dacko's regime became desperate for resources, and the French were not willing to contribute the very large sums that would have been necessary to transform the situation.[15] Much of the French aid was wasted on sustaining imported French personnel at a standard of living far above what they could have obtained in France itself, in sums paid for French consultants, for lavish conferences, imported cars, and expensive diplomatic activities.[16]

In 1962, Dacko began to try to seek more aid. After a desperate round of visits to Europe and pleas to China in 1964 and 1965, and rising discontent at home, the regime collapsed in bankruptcy.[17] If Dacko had been a more forceful person, he might have resorted to the more naked use of force to stay in power. Subsequent events were to show that the French would have backed such a strategy. But that was to be left to his successor.

Dacko and the French seem to have decided on the head of the national gendarmerie as the new leader who might be able to handle the situation, but the army's commander, Colonel Jean-Bédel Bokassa, discovered the plot and took power himself on January 4, 1966. Though this was not part of the original script, Bokassa, a relative of Dacko, was acceptable to the French; soon, he too became the recipient of continued French aid. For some years, it seemed that not much had changed. The French remained the ultimate power, they provided just enough aid to keep the government in power, but not nearly enough for serious reform, and in fact the same sorts of people ran the government as before.[18]

For the French, Bokassa seemed an ideal African head of state. He had been a highly decorated noncommissioned officer in the French army, and had fought loyally for them in Indochina. He even publicly identified himself as a Frenchman, and this had played an important role in getting him appointed as head of the Central African army. He was less well educated, less ideological than the intellectuals who might have radicalized the political situation. In short, he was deemed to be safe by the French, just as Idi Amin had been judged to be a loyal if none-too-bright soldier who would further British interests.

ENLIGHTENED BRITISH POLICY AND THE ATTEMPT TO CREATE A NONEXISTENT NATION: THE CASE OF UGANDA

Compared to the sad modern history of the C.A.R., Uganda's colonial experience was happier. But the colony's relative economic success and political stability were based on severe and hardening ethnic divisions. These could be contained as long as there was a strong colonial power, Great Britain. Yet, the British did more than arbitrate between conflicting ethnic claims; they also used them, and in many ways exacerbated them in order to strengthen their hold on power. After their departure, the problem became insoluble.

Uganda's geography was quite favorable and could support a relatively high population density in some areas. This and the availability of labor made the development of lucrative export crops—coffee, cotton, tea, tobacco, and sugar—feasible during the colonial period.[19]

Also, the southern part of the country already had well-developed states at the time of the British conquest. The presence of kings, officials, and established systems of administration made the transition to colonial rule easier because the Europeans had existing structures available for their use through indirect rule.[20] This made for a more effective and bearable colonial administration.

Finally, there is the fact that the British in the early twentieth century were able to invest more capital into developing their African possessions than the other European powers in Africa. England not only took the best parts of Africa, but it built railways and other infrastructures faster than the other Europeans.

Because of these favorable conditions, Uganda's colonial society achieved a relatively high level of education and prosperity for an African colony. It became the home of one of Africa's finest universities, and in the late 1950s the proportion of children in primary school was one of the highest in sub-Saharan Africa.[21]

Having learned from their successful imperial venture in India, and because of their immense power in the late nineteenth century, the British were particularly good at assimilating well-populated but culturally different regions together into colonies, and then using indirect rule and differentiated policies toward various ethnicities to create administrative units that would later prove to be ethnic powder kegs. To the example of Uganda one might add India-Pakistan-Bangladesh, Sri Lanka, Burma, Cyprus, Nigeria, South Africa, Sudan, and Malaysia. This is not to say that the British were the only Europeans to leave such countries in their wake. The French wish to give Christian Lebanon bigger borders and more resources, and the Russians' ability to hold together their nineteenth-century conquests in the Caucasus and Central Asia into the late twentieth century have left equally flammable mixtures, as did Belgian rule in its Congo (now Zaire).

Even without deliberate discrimination in favor of one or another ethnicity by the colonial authorities, the greater mixing that takes place in cities and in commercially developed areas as economies and societies are modernized increases competition between religiously or linguistically defined peoples whose traditional relations tended to be much more limited and compartmentalized. If, in combination with this, the colonial authorities actually encourage differences by giving various groups differential privileges, the stage is set for violent ethnic warfare when colonial rule disintegrates.[22] This is what happened in Uganda.

The term "tribe" has been much abused in the writing of African history. Ethnic identification may be fluid, particularly in places where there is much migration and disruption. New groups and alliances form, intermarriage occurs, and languages change. The myth of long-lasting cultural and biological purity is as absurd in Africa as it is in Europe, or in most of the world. Yet, if the myth is believed, it may become a powerful organizing force, and once open conflict occurs along well-defined cultural lines, it may persist for a long time, especially as power and privilege are distributed along such lines. This means that "tribal" hostilities in many African countries were not determined by fate centuries ago, and that they are constantly being reshaped by the exercise of political power. It is also true that often tribal lines were fixed, and tribal hostilities created during the period of colonial rule. This does not, however, make such hostilities any less real.

The British came to an agreement with the most powerful of the Bantu kingdoms on the shores of Lake Victoria, Buganda. The King, or Kabaka, retained many of his privileges, and some power, as did his aristocracy. Buganda was also the locus of economic and administrative development, and became the richest, most educated, best endowed part of the country. European settlers were not granted lands as they were in nearby Kenya. In return for this, Buganda, which had been the great military power in the region, disarmed, and left its security in the hands of the colonial army.

At the time the Europeans were first arriving in Buganda in the late nineteenth century at the apex of the kingdom's power, the Kabaka was in the habit of dispatching hundreds, even thousands of victims as a way of asserting his power. Many of those killed were first tortured, then burned to death. Whether this had any direct influence on events a century later is doubtful, but certainly, the idea of political terror was well rooted in pre-colonial statecraft.[23] In this, there was nothing unusual. Shaka, the great Zulu conqueror who created the mightiest of the nineteenth-century Bantu states, was renowned for his extraordinary cruelty and vengefulness.[24] This seems to be the rule in the early stages of state construction, when people who have been used to greater freedom are likely to resist the new impositions of a state. Rulers try to awe them into submission with great and seemingly capricious terror.

Partly as a matter of British policy, to insure that the colonial army would not become a danger in its own right, and partly because the people of Buganda had better opportunities by receiving modern educations and going into other sectors, few of the African colonial soldiers were recruited from there. Instead, soldiers tended to come from northern Uganda, where populations were culturally very different.[25]

Northern Uganda consists largely of people who had no state structures at the time of the Europeans' arrival, much like many of the people of northern Burma studied by Leach. These recently segmentary (nonstate) peoples speak Nilo-Saharan languages from an entirely different linguistic family than the Bantu kingdoms of the south. Within this family there is another important split, between the Eastern or

Nilotic branch (the Luo and Masai are part of this branch, as are the Acholi and the Langi) and the Central Sudanic branch related to languages spoken in southwestern Sudan and southern Chad. During British rule the north, and especially the Central Sudanic peoples, remained poorer, less developed, and less Christianized than the Bantu, particularly those of Buganda.[26]

The people of Buganda had higher status than others because of their special relationship with the British, their greater degree of Christianization (though there developed a split between Catholics and Protestants), and their more advanced economy. They took this as their natural right. But the colonial army recruited far more Northerners, partly because they had fewer other opportunities for a job, partly because they tended to be physically bigger, but mostly because they were thought by the British to be less dangerous than the more advanced Southerners.[27]

To further complicate the situation, the British imported immigrants from India, originally to help build the Kenya-Uganda railway, and this population, which generally spoke better English than the Africans and adapted more easily to the demands of the European market, came to dominate in the small commercial and service sector.[28] Again, this is an extremely familiar pattern, and we have seen how a similar development with emigrants from India and China affected Burmese nationalism, while similar immigrations of Chinese and Vietnamese embittered the Cambodian nationalists. V. S. Naipaul's A Bend in the River is a superb description of how these successful, hard-working "pariah capitalists" came to embody everything that was hated about economic modernization, even as they became an essential part of the more developed African economies. The story might have been written about Jews in Central and Eastern Europe, Chinese in Indonesia, or Lebanese and Syrian Christians in West Africa.

In conclusion, then, Uganda had a particularly complicated set of linguistic, cultural, and regional divisions that were also class, that is, economic and occupational divisions and rivalries. It might have been wiser of the British to recognize this, but of course, when they determined the boundaries of the colony of Uganda, they were hardly thinking of what might happen if it ever became independent.

As might be expected, it was in the Kingdom of Buganda that modern anti-colonial nationalism first developed in Uganda. Those with Western educations led the way, so at first there was considerable tension between them and the Kabaka and his traditionalist supporters. But as the British colonial administration tried to use the Kabaka against the nationalists, he joined with the growing demands for greater independence that would secure Buganda's interests. However, the British were loathe to see their empire break into little pieces, and especially in East Africa they thought more in terms of maintaining regional ties between colonies, rather than in terms of further subdividing their territories. Thus, while willing to grant Buganda an exceptionally important role in Uganda, they were unwilling to allow outright separation.[29] In retrospect, redrawing colonial boundaries, and breaking up countries like Uganda might not have been such a bad idea.

With the accelerating trend toward independence in Africa in the 1950s and the formal decolonization of the early 1960s, political maneuvering in Uganda came to be based on three different sets of cleavages: ideology, ethnicity, and class. As these did not automatically overlap, at first, when Uganda's politics were open and based on free elections, the various alliances seemed confusing and opportunistic. What finally emerged was an uneasy compromise between those who believed in a more modern, unitary, less traditional Ugandan political system and the monarchists in Buganda. The Kabaka was able to rally to his side most of his people, whatever their class or ideological interests, while the political "modernizers" came to be led by Milton Obote, a Northerner with socialist leanings. Both Obote and the Kabaka, therefore, could count on support from ethnic interests that might not have agreed with their ideologies. Obote became the country's first prime minister, and the Kabaka its first president after independence in 1962.

The most important class-based interest group in the new Uganda was the army which mutinied for higher pay soon after independence. Whereas similar mutinies in the other former British East African colonies, Kenya and Tanganyika (soon to become Tanzania), resulted in stricter government control over the military, Obote understood that he would need the army in what was going to be an inevitable conflict with Buganda, so he gave it increased benefits. He then used a combination of ethnic politics, capitalizing on old resentments between Buganda and other Bantu kingdoms in the south, plus the resentment of Northerners toward the arrogant and wealthier Southerners, to isolate the Kabaka. Using the army, he took over Buganda, overthrew the

King, and established a more unitary state in 1966. By so doing, he permanently alienated an important part of his country, and also the most advanced.[30]

The army chief of staff at that time was General Idi Amin, a popular, loyal professional soldier who had had a long, distinguished career in the British colonial army. An exceptionally big man, Amin had been a champion boxer, which appealed to his men as well as to his sports-minded British officers. He appeared to be a cheerful if not too smart fellow, and certainly he was no intellectual. This, no doubt, pleased the British officers, too. Amin had been an active participant in the suppression of the Kenya Mau Mau rebellion. As independence approached, he was picked to become an officer, and quickly promoted to the top by his British patrons. Obote, like the British, evidently felt he was an ideal commander because he was poorly educated, and therefore appeared politically unsophisticated.

Ali Mazrui has described the post-1966 political system in Uganda as an alliance between the intellectuals and the army. The problem with this alliance, however, was that no matter how clever the intellectuals, led by Obote, may have been, they did not have the power to resist army demands. Obote therefore began to move on two fronts. In 1969 he proclaimed a more socialist, egalitarian doctrine that would try to win the good will of the peasantry, and he began to try to maneuver Amin out of power. A large part of the army consisted of soldiers and officers from Obote's ethnic base, the Acholi-Langi alliance (Nilotic speakers), whereas Amin was from the Central Sudanic area. Time should have been on Obote's side as he tried to build an ethnic and class alliance that would have given him control over the army and a broader popular base. But Amin turned out to be much more clever than anyone thought, and he outmaneuvered Obote.

Amin had been a poor boy from a small, marginal ethnic Sudanic group in the north, the Kakwa, with no social prestige, education, or social grace. Many were misled by this, and even recent analysis, such as that by Samuel Decalo, has dismissed him because he was almost functionally illiterate and unable to handle standard bureaucratic paperwork. Yet, he not only understood how to win the trust of his subordinates, but he knew how to please his superiors as long as that was necessary. He had impressed the British, and later Obote, as being tractable. He had known how to be ruthless as well, engaging in torture during the Mau Mau repression and having military enemies murdered. Now, faced by Obote's attempt to purge him, he secretly recruited men from his part of Uganda and from neighboring Sudan to form units loyal to him.[31]

There was also a foreign element to Amin's rise. Israel had played an important role as a provider of aid to Uganda and many other black African countries after independence to gain international legitimacy. But gradually, as the Arab countries built alliances in Africa, and particularly after 1967, Israel was squeezed out of Africa. In Uganda, Israelis had been military advisors, too, and they were unhappy about Obote's increasingly militant Third World rhetoric. Some Israeli officers became direct Amin advisors. The British had also become disenchanted with Obote's left-wing talk which threatened their interests. Though there is no direct evidence of British participation in the Amin coup which eventually took place, the British knew what was coming and approved. The Israelis, on the other hand, gave direct assistance in the form of intelligence information to Amin, and an Israeli team participated in the operation that captured the central army barracks. A former Israeli military advisor to Amin, Colonel Bar-Lev, later boasted that he had made Amin president.[32]

When Amin overthrew Obote in January of 1971, just as he was about to be purged himself, the British, the Israelis, the still monarchist people of Buganda, and the East Indian community (which had also felt threatened by Obote's incipient socialism) all rejoiced. Many other Ugandans did too, because Obote's plans had frightened away investments and the economy, still overly dependent on a few cash crops, was no longer growing as in the early 1960s. The plans to accelerate industrialization by government action, and to give a substantial portion of agricultural investments to state-run centralized farms were both failing, despite their extensive use of scarce investment resources.[33]

In short, when Amin came to power, he seemed to offer considerable hope to many groups. He was both more friendly to Buganda than Obote and still a Northerner. He was popular with his own men, and seemingly more accessible to the masses than the distant, intellectual Obote. The British liked and trusted him, and the Asian community had no reason to fear him.[34] The only problem was that his only real power base was from a part of the army, not even the whole of it; many officers and soldiers were still Nilotic Acholis and Langis who were Obote's primary supporters. Obote was a Langi. To remedy this, Amin had to take rapid and drastic steps.[35]

Almost immediately after taking power, Amin began a massive purge of Acholi and Langi soldiers. As the army was poorly disciplined to begin with, the purge turned into brutal internal fighting. Amin recruited thousands of new Sudanic soldiers, both from within Uganda, and from two neighboring countries, the Sudan and Zaire, where endemic rebellions had produced large numbers of available, armed fighters. In 1971, as many as 10,000 soldiers died in an army that had only about that many at the start of the year, and not many more at the end. During that time, almost 16,000 new men were recruited, though obviously, many of them died, too.[36]

To stay in power, Amin had let loose a poorly disciplined, ethnically largely foreign, mercenary force on his country. That probably prevented his being overthrown by the old army, but it also created new economic and political problems to compound the old ones that had not been solved by Obote's overthrow. The increasingly brutal behavior of the army also began to damage Amin's original popularity.

To redress the situation and regain his popularity Amin then took the drastic step of expelling the East Indian community in 1972. This proved to be a fatal blow from which the Ugandan economy has never recovered.[37]

The expulsion of the Asians was accompanied by the seizure of their property by the army. But the economic basis of the East Indians' wealth could not be sustained for long without their work and skills. So, new loot had to be obtained in order to sustain the expected gains from the previous confiscations and to keep Amin's restive mercenaries happy.[38]

In the fall of 1972 Obote's supporters (Obote was living in exile in Tanzania) launched an invasion. Their assumption that Amin's rule would alienate the population was correct, but premature. The full horror of what was happening had not yet begun to affect the majority which still thought well of Amin for having expropriated the Asians, and had few regrets about Obote. In any case, the new army was, at that time, satisfied with its recent acquisitions, and it triumphed easily. But the invasion made Amin feel even more insecure, and he began a new wave of killing and repression in order to solidify his rule. Then, to offer new rewards to his army, he started to expropriate British hold-ings.[39] By then, the nightmare was well under way.

Despite the great differences between the Central African Republic and Uganda, there were obvious similarities. In both, independence had come to poorly integrated societies. In both, men trusted by the colonial powers because of their servility and intellectual mediocrity had been helped up the ladder to political power, and then turned out to be deeply resentful, with good reason, of their European mentors toward whom they had humbled themselves. Both Bokassa and Idi Amin were also hostile to the nationalist intellectuals in their countries, to whom they felt inferior. These were definitely not cases of utopian intellectuals seizing power and then imposing catastrophic policies on their people, but rather of anti-intellectuals who found themselves unable to rule except through corruption and increasing brutality. Finally, in both cases, it turned out that once in power, ruthless leaders with control of military forces to loot and reward their immediate fol-lowers were able to stay in power for a long time. There were no orga-nized groups able to resist. As the cases of Haiti and the Dominican Republic showed, and to some extent also Burma, there is no need to have a coherent ideology in order to maintain tyranny.

In the African examples we are looking at, tyrannical rule was accompanied by such deep resentments and hatreds on the part of the supposedly "docile" men put in power that they turned into particular-ly evil regimes.

TYRANNY AND RESENTMENT UNCHAINED

Once in power Idi Amin and Bokassa behaved in ways that suggested serious psychological imbalances—grandiose claims, vicious personal cruelty, an absolute disregard for the welfare of their people, and even-tually, a lack of realism that eventually led to their overthrow. But their behavior was no more megalomaniac, destructive, or unrealistic than Hitler's. For that matter, Stalin and Mao, despite their much more coherent ideological plans, were personally no better, only much more successful in their lifetimes. In this respect, much of the behavior of these African rulers corresponds to the typical behavior recognized by the classical analysts of tyranny, from the early Greeks to the present. We can always expect leaders corrupted by unrestrained power to be driven to wretched excesses in order to keep it. And in situations of disorganization and conflict such as those that prevailed in the post-colonial states we are examining, the squeamish or timid, like poor David Dacko of the Central African Republic, simply lost power to more ruthless men.

This is not to deny that these African leaders were in some sense unbalanced, just as were the great ideological tyrants of our century. But as in the cases of Hitler, Stalin, Pol Pot, and Duvalier, their particular form of "madness" actually reflected the strains of their societies. With time, like all tyrants, they began to lose touch with reality because of their isolation and growing, justified fear of retribution, so that these negative traits were accentuated.

Because both of these Africans lacked ideological pretensions, and because they were ruling insignificant little countries, they never had any defenders who could point to doctrinal excuses for their excesses. It is therefore uncontroversial to denounce their rule. But for the tortured and humiliated subjects of tyrants, whether the cause is ideologically or simply selfish, evil corruption, the consequences are remarkably similar.

The Destruction of Uganda

Idi Amin's strategy of expropriating the businesses and investments that had been the basis of Uganda's wealth in order to pay his mercenaries was a losing game that could not be sustained for long. As the economic effects of the expulsions, confiscations, and looting took hold, the economy retreated to subsistence and black marketing, there was less and less with which to pay the army, so that the vicious circle had to be intensified.[40]

As Amin saw in 1971 that his original Western allies, the British, Israelis, and West Germans, would be unwilling to subsidize his troubled economy, in 1972 he turned to Arab, particularly Libyan sources. This eventually led him into an extreme anti-Israeli position, partly to gain Arab support, but also, undoubtedly, because of his anger over being turned down by his original supporters. The twisting byways of his foreign policy after this were often interpreted in the West as proof of his inconsistency and even madness. His support for Palestinians led to his accepting a hijacked French airplane coming from Israel, and the subsequent embarrassing Israeli raid at Entebbe to rescue the passengers in 1976 humiliated his inept army, and in the eyes of the world paired him with the bombastic Qadhafi of Libya.

But far from being the actions of a madman, these policies could be interpreted as an increasingly desperate search for funds, and progressive frustration as promises of aid failed to materialize. Meanwhile, his domestic policies were driving refugees out of Uganda and causing problems for his African neighbors, Kenya and Tanzania.[41]

During Amin's last years in power, the army became a vast instrument for torture and extortion, an uncontrolled set of loosely organized groups of mercenaries destroying Uganda. He was using the same tactics as always—rotating officials, shifting allies to keep them off balance, randomly killing to keep the population quiet. All this was not just a matter of either mental imbalance or Amin's lack of education, as Samuel Decalo has suggested, or an amoral lack of understanding of the common rules of civility, as Jackson and Rosberg have suggested. Certainly Amin was uneducated, and if not unbalanced, he lacked a sense of civility. But beyond this, given the situation in Uganda, and the circumstances under which he took power, Amin had few other choices. Had he been more educated he might have been more successful in cloaking his behavior under an ideological mask, as were the equally brutal and destructive Sékou Touré of (former French) Guinea or Colonel Mengistu of Ethiopia.[42]

In the last days of British and French rule, it was possible for some moral and idealistic African intellectuals to appeal to the colonizers' sense of decency and take power peacefully. Some of them, like Julius Nyerere of Tanzania and Léopold Senghor of Senegal, turned out to be rather better at holding power than others, like Milton Obote. But by the time Amin came to power, ethnic tensions were too acute in Uganda, and economic rot had advanced too far. It was no longer possible to hold the situation together without resorting to a high level of violence, and the army was the only institution left that could rule. It is quite true that his lack of education and his personal ruthlessness were such that he was unable to imagine any solution other than increasing corruption and intensifying brutality. But in this he was not so very different from the supposedly more sophisticated Argentine military, or the socialist, Buddhist, Burmese General Ne Win, though both of these other regimes had begun with far better prospects for stability than Uganda. And after all, ideological tyrants in Germany, Russia, and Cambodia, among others, committed atrocities as bad as Amin's. So it is not necessary to assume that Amin was some kind of strange psychopath.

By late 1978, at least 300,000 had been killed. Hundreds of thousands more had fled. In frustration and desperation, to try to provide fertile new fields for plunder for his mercenaries, Amin invaded Tanzania. His army was poorly led and trained, however, and the Tanzanians counter-attacked and conquered Uganda, driving Amin from power in 1979.[43]

When the Tanzanian army entered Uganda, the enormity of Amin's crimes were revealed. Tony Avirgan, inspecting the headquarters of Amin's secret police, the "State Research Bureau," next to Amin's favorite presidential lodge, wrote:

> [There were] 20 to 30 bodies scattered around the room in varying states of decay and mutilation. Almost all showed signs of torture and the floor was covered with bloodstains. . . . On some days, up to 200 corpses were taken from headquarters to the mortuary.[44]

Files on thousands of individuals killed by the Bureau's agents were found, as well as bodies. It turned out that Amin had set up a vast spy network throughout the country.[45]

Martha Honey, also of the *Guardian*, filed a report from one of Amin's homes entitled "Spy files and porn magazines beside a president's bed," which described the luxurious residence. It had many bedrooms for Amin's various wives and children, with wind up plastic boats, board games, costly foods, and crates of light weapons and ammunition all intermingled. In his hastily abandoned chief mistress's bed there was a teddy bear.[46]

A later *Guardian* story described prison cells where prisoners had been forced to eat the bodies of those who died to stay alive. They got nothing else. Broken, starved, incoherent prisoners were released. Mass graves of thousands were found, victims of the State Research Bureau. Most exhumed bodies had beaten heads. Many had been killed by strangulation. Children's bodies were found impaled on stakes.[47]

In the end, Amin was defended by many Arab states because he was a Muslim. Libyan troops tried to save his regime, and were the last troops to withdraw as it collapsed. He wound up in exile in Saudi Arabia where, in the early 1990s, he was still living a luxurious life in retirement.[48]

Amin's removal did not solve Uganda's economic problems or endemic internal warfare. Uganda had been ruined, and for most of the decade that followed Amin's overthrow, killings, political instability, and economic regression accelerated. Probably another 300,000 were killed in the civil wars that ensued, or died from war-induced famine in the early 1980s.[49] By the mid-1980s, too, roving armies were spreading AIDS into the countryside, compounding the misery. In 1986, Yoweri Museveni, a Southerner (though not from Buganda) led his army into Kampala, the capital, and seized power. Since then, however, some fighting has continued, and parts of the north are not under full government control.[50] Over two decades, this country of ten million that was once fairly promising has been destroyed and shows few signs of recovery.

The Napoleonic Farce of Emperor Bokassa

Bokassa did not kill and torture on the scale of Idi Amin, though he tormented, jailed, and murdered his opponents from the start of his reign, and at the end, as he began to let his frustrations get out of hand, he committed some notable crimes. Despite his brutality, there is a sense of pathos about his vain and silly attempts to create a national historical tradition for his country. His tyranny illustrates the common danger of giving any man too much power, and feeding his delusions in order to sustain what was essentially a purely corrupt regime from the start. But what marks Bokassa as something a little more than just an old-fashioned bad and corrupt autocrat is that in his desperate search for legitimacy in the modern world, he picked a totally inappropriate model, thus subjecting himself and his people to the derision of the world.

In 1925 the great Italian historian and philosopher Benedetto Croce wrote:

> Neither individuals nor peoples can live without a myth of their past, present, and future potentialities, and when there is no tradition near at hand they search for one in remote times and places or in records of the whole human race, which speaks to us in universal history.[51]

We have seen how nationalist mythologies of blood and race have shaped some of the worst tyrannies of the twentieth century, and how the wish to imitate and surpass great historical figures from the past have driven whole nations into disaster. Every single one of the tyrants examined in this book's previous chapters, even corrupt and old-fashioned ones like Duvalier and Trujillo, tied himself to a certain mythological conception of the nation he ruled and his role in reshaping it. The particular African leaders we are examining in this chapter had a harder time of it, partly because they were specifically picked by their colonial masters for their seeming lack of attachment to any sort of national or independent consciousness. Amin eventually turned to Islam in hopes of finding a substitute national tradition, which is, no doubt, why the Saudi Arabians allowed him to retire in peace to Arabia.

Other African leaders faced by the lack of any national or cultural identity in the states they inherited from their colonial rulers often tried to force through a kind of artificial, purely symbolic Africanization. A master of this approach has been Mobutu Sese Soko, who, in 1993, still rules Zaire, the Central African Republic's big southern neighbor. He has led one of the most nakedly corrupt and predatory regimes in the world. But he survived in power for three decades, partly by leaning heavily on African symbols to legitimize his rule and impress his subjects. He ordered all Christian names to be changed to African ones (he himself was born as Joseph Désiré Mobutu); he surrounded himself with the trappings of traditional African chieftainship and began appearing everywhere with a leopard skin cap; and he repeatedly emphasized what he called "authenticity." This did not save him from rebellions which had to be put down with French, Belgian, and Moroccan troops, but it contributed to his being considered with some respect by many of his people, and also by other African leaders. By manipulating symbols, leaning on European and American aid, appointing only the most slavishly loyal and corrupt officials, and brutally repressing discontent, Mobutu held on to power and amassed a personal fortune (invested mostly in Europe) estimated in the many billions of U.S. dollars.[52]

Mobutu, supposedly characterized by Bernard Kouchner, a high French official, as a "walking bank account wearing a leopard skin cap," has been shrewd, but also lucky. His immense domain in the heart of Africa is one of the great mineral treasure houses in the world, and such a vital economic and strategic asset that the United States and France felt it necessary to prop him up as long as the Cold War lasted, no matter how corrupt he was.[53]

Bokassa had no historical tradition to lean on, or enough intellectuals close to him to make one up, and because of his own psychological, financial, and military dependence on France, he took a turn exactly opposite to that of most African leaders. He tried to become even more French and renounce his origins. And when this did not work, he became bitter and vicious. Had he not been a murderer, too, he might have inspired more pity than hatred.

After Bokassa took power in 1965, for a long time he behaved exactly as he was supposed to, a loyal servant of the French, ruling a territory that was of strategic and perhaps of potential economic value because of its minerals. Continuing French aid paid salaries, and Bokassa did nothing to upset the existing balance.

Bokassa had joined the French colonial army in 1939 at the age of 18, and had had a distinguished career as an enlisted man and much-decorated noncommissioned officer. He had served in Indochina, but only been promoted to lieutenant as the French prepared to give their colonies independence, in 1960. Nevertheless, he was one of the most senior and most trusted of the military men in the C.A.R., and it was pressure from the French military that got him appointed as Dacko's military chief of staff. He never renounced the French citizenship he had been granted in the French army.[54]

It is only possible to speculate about the psychology of a man whose career from the age of 18 until he was almost 40 was that of an exceptionally loyal professional soldier in a colonial army operated by the power responsible for his father's death. He received a rudimentary education, but not much more as Africans were not deemed capable of holding high positions in the French army, at least until the very last years of colonialism. He was indoctrinated in French military mythology, however, and his success suggests he properly assimilated the views that were imposed on him.

Bokassa seems to have loved France. The French army was his family, and he substituted its heroes for his own father beaten to death by the French when he was little. When Charles de Gaulle, whom he revered, died in 1970, he is said to have sobbed, "Papa est mort! Papa est mort!" (Daddy is dead!)[55]

Once in power, he at first tried to remedy the fiscal problems of his state by contributing a part of his own salary to the public, and by trying to open better communications with the general population. But the problems faced by his predecessor (and eventual successor), David

Dacko, did not disappear. In fact, there was no real way to solve them. On the contrary, now a new group of functionaries, the military, had to be paid off. Alexandre Banza, Bokassa's chief assistant, tried to clean out the endemic corruption that prevailed, but Bokassa had to fire him, and in 1969 he had him tortured and executed.[56]

To reform a state like the C.A.R. would have required new revenues, but these were simply not available. Gradually, Bokassa, who probably meant to do better when he first took power, slipped into deeply corrupt ways, becoming a direct participant in many businesses, and collaborating with the foreign, chiefly French interests in his country's economy. This easy solution guaranteed continuing cooperation with the Europeans extracting resources from the country, it provided funds with which to reward supporters, starting with the army, and it made the imposition of heavier taxes on the largely peasant population less necessary. Neglect of basic administrative needs was less dangerous in such circumstances than a concerted attempt to extract more resources directly from the population. For some time, the strategy worked and Bokassa was accepted by the French. He even seems to have developed a special relationship with the new president of France, Valéry Giscard d'Estaing, who often visited the C.A.R. for hunting trips and who received diamonds as presents from Bokassa. Bokassa thought that Giscard considered him to be a virtual family member. The French government paid about 90 percent of the civil service salaries in the C.A.R.[57]

Later, in 1985, while Bokassa was in exile he wrote a book claiming that Giscard d'Estaing had been quite corrupt. Giscard, by then no longer president, but still a prominent political figure, sued on grounds of defamation and got a court to order all copies of the book burned. Giscard also claimed that the diamonds he had received as presents had been sold, and the proceeds given to charity.[58] It is clear that in some way Giscard had at one time singled out Bokassa, whose personal devotion to all things French may have amused him, for special flattery.

But, try as it might, Bokassa's government did not succeed in gaining a greater measure of legitimacy for itself. Domestically, the C.A.R. continued to be poorly integrated, with most of its people viewing the state as a foreign, brutal, and exploitative superimposition. Internationally, the C.A.R. continued to be seen as an insignificant French neocolony, despite Bokassa's attempts to open bridges to various other African and Arab countries.

Bokassa's rule was oppressive and harsh, but no more so than in most classical agrarian societies of the past. There were some political prisoners who were tortured for months. From the start his men had beaten and strangled to death some opponents. A former chief of police was castrated and had his eyes poked out in front of his family. Looting and raping by the army was common. But if neither the brutality nor corruption was unusual, he and the small coterie around him took a growing portion of what funds were available, so that the government became less and less able to cover its operating expenses. Bokassa also came to demand increasing adulation. He accumulated titles, "savior of the Republic," "man of steel," "unparalleled engineer," "artist and guide of Central Africa," "man made to create nations," and so on.[59]

Combining his increasingly desperate search for authority and prestige with a vague, and not terribly well-informed conception about what might finally show his French masters that he, Bokassa, was a great man, he decided to make himself emperor. As Thomas O'Toole has written in a very suggestive essay, this step probably seemed to Bokassa to combine several advantages. He would be able to present himself to his people as a great traditional war leader; but he would do this in a "civilized," that is, French way that would legitimize him in the eyes of the Europeans, too. Unable to find his own legitimizing historical myth, he picked one he had heard about from the French. He would become Africa's Napoleon.[60]

There were precedents, but not contemporary ones. If Bokassa had pronounced himself a great Marxist theoretician, or an anti-imperialist savior, his rule might have been no different, but it would have attracted less mockery. If he had limited himself to wearing a leopard skin cap and making his civil servants adopt African names, he might have drawn less attention to himself, and so his subsequent brutality would have been less embarrassing to his French patrons. The desperation of a head of state lacking legitimacy and resources is fairly easy to understand. It was Bokassa's personal tragedy that he was so out of touch with history that he was a century behind in his imitation of the French. For this, his French advisors, who acceded to his wishes and helped finance the whole affair, while mocking him behind his back, bear much responsibility. Bokassa's thinking was anticipated in Aimé Césaire's play about early nineteenth-century Haiti, *La Tragédie du Roi Christophe*.

Ostensibly about King Christophe of Haiti in the early nineteenth century, this play is actually part of a trilogy about decolonization. In it, a Haitian is haranguing a crowd and says:

> The whole world is looking at us, citizens, and other nations think that blacks lack dignity. A king, a court, a kingdom—that's what we need to show them if we want respect. A leader as head of our nation. A crown on his head. This, believe me, will calm those whose unsavory ideas could at any moment, right here, bring a storm down on our heads.[61]

Bokassa's coronation cost his country a third of its annual budget in 1977. Everything was imported from France—the food, the horses (who died soon after because of sleeping sickness), the uniforms, and the bands. After all this, the country was even poorer, though certainly more famous than before.[62]

Partly to raise his personal revenues, but also to impose the kind of order and discipline he thought appropriate for a great new nation, Bokassa mandated the wearing of school uniforms to be purchased from a factory he owned. As most schoolchildren were too poor to afford them, and protested, he had hundreds of them arrested in January 1979, and again in April. By that time, we can assume that His Imperial Majesty Bokassa the First was out of control. Over one hundred children died. Some suffocated to death, others were bayonetted, still others beaten to death with whips and sticks studded with nails. His imperial guard, previously trained by the Israeli army, did the grisly deed, and he personally participated. He used his imperial cane of ebony and ivory to poke the eyes out of some of the children. Word leaked out and was published by Amnesty International, and the French government, which had gone along willingly enough until then, was publicly shamed. An African commission of inquiry was set up, and found, that summer, that the story was true.[63]

By then, Giscard, who had been quite willing to have Bokassa call him his "dear relative," was facing a presidential election in France, and wanted to be rid of Bokassa who was proving to be a major liability. The coup was carried out in September of 1979 by French troops who were flown in while Bokassa was on a state visit to Libya where he was pleading for more aid. Only one Libyan foreign aid technician in Bangui was killed, but no Central Africans. David Dacko, Bokassa's predecessor in office, was brought in on a plane that landed shortly after that of the French soldiers, and he once again became president.[64]

In a similar situation ten years later, the United States also felt obliged to remove a dictator it had long supported but who had become a public embarrassment. But when George Bush had Manuel Noriega removed, he used a large number of troops, and several thousand Panamanians were killed. One has to say of the French that they are better at this type of cynical operation than the Americans, perhaps because they have had more practice.

Bokassa's overthrow produced an orgy of self-questioning in the French press. After all, they had subsidized Bokassa until the end, flattered him, and encouraged him to behave foolishly so that he would remain under their control. Albert de Schoe, a former French ambassador to the C.A.R., wrote in *Le Monde*:

> We must be aware that our western civilization stuck on top of African civilization creates an explosive alchemy and a deep disequilibrium. Rare are those Africans able to synthesize the two civilizations. Is it, after all, possible? Well, often the problem in talking to a Bokassa is to know whether one is dealing with the African or the Westerner. . . . I have heard Bokassa saying publicly "Before the arrival of the French colonizers, we were monkeys." And not long after, in front of the same audience, he was to say, with indignation, "Well, before the French came we were somebody, something significant."[65]

This elegant statement does not answer the question of why the French tolerated and encouraged such a phenomenon, though, as the example of Amin shows, had the French dropped Bokassa without overthrowing him, it is entirely possible that the massacres initiated by him in early 1979 could have turned into something much worse, and he might have been able to hold on to power a lot longer.

After Bokassa's overthrow, *Le Monde*, generally considered the most authoritative and intellectual major newspaper in France, printed a story entitled "Corpses in the Emperor's Refrigerator."

> Is Bokassa the First a cannibal? That is the question being asked in Bangui after the discovery of four mutilated cadavers in one of the refrigerators of one of the former emperor's residences. . . . Central Africans asked about this are unanimous. These bodies, with their arms and legs cut off, their guts ripped open, were going to be eaten by the ex-dictator.

> Several witnesses testify that several vanished persons were indeed eaten by the former emperor. . . . Everyone knew it, these witnesses said. Only fear . . . kept the people silent.[66]

On the same page there was an article saying that Libya was accusing France of having overthrown Bokassa as part of a "fight against Islam."

The next day, *Le Monde* hedged. There were only two corpses, and they were in a freezer. And maybe it was only a rumor.[67] No matter that this particularly gruesome story has never been verified. More people remember it than the story of the children who were really killed by Bokassa, though a few days later one of Bokassa's closest French aides gave *Le Monde* an interview and claimed that Bokassa had told him, "I killed fewer children than they said, and they were older than they said." This Frenchman, Jacques Duchemin, doubted the cannibalism story, though he said that there had long been a rumor that as a joke Bokassa had had human flesh served to an unknowing high French dignitary at his imperial coronation.[68]

A few weeks later, the leading French-language African news magazine, *Jeune Afrique*, published in Paris, rightly attacked the world press for paying so much attention to rumors of cannibalism, while it had long ignored the genuine atrocities and plundering of his regime. Rather that falling into such stereotyped racism, the editorial concluded, it would be better to express sorrow for "the families of those unfortunate schoolchildren he killed and had killed. Even without eating them."[69]

Bokassa was refused asylum in France, despite his French passport, which he had always kept because of his admiration for the French. He was, however, allowed to go the Ivory Coast, where France's closest ally in Africa, the elderly President Félix Houphouët-Boigny, protected him. But after he tried to return to the C.A.R. in 1983, Houphouët expelled Bokassa and he moved to France.[70]

Bokassa probably believed that he was viewed by his own population as a father figure, just as he had viewed de Gaulle that way. He had said in a public address in 1976, "What counts most in life is God, money, and me, your daddy."[71] In 1986, bored and frustrated, and thinking that his country needed its father back, he flew to Bangui even though he had been sentenced to death *in absentia* in 1980. The new government, which by that time was again being run by the army, put him on trial. In front of the court he admitted that he had not been a "saint," and said that "being chief of state is an extremely thankless job," but that he had not committed all the crimes he was accused of. Witnesses recounted tales of torture, beatings, and starving prisoners in his jails, but despite the rumors, there was no evidence of any cannibalism. One of the *New York Times* articles about the trial, however, was entitled "Trial Revives Memory: What Was in the Freezer?"[72]

He was sentenced to death once more in June 1987, on charges of murder. With tears in his eyes, he said he had returned to clear his name, to explain to the outside world that Africans were not cannibals, and because he wanted to be home. In March 1988, the C.A.R.'s leader, General Kolingba, commuted the death sentence to life in solitary confinement.[73] In late 1993, he was released.

In many other African states, and elsewhere in the world, there have been and continue to be regimes responsible for many more deaths than Bokassa's ill-fated empire. This does not excuse him, or the French who cynically tolerated and sustained him for so long. But it raises many question about the nature of power, and why such grotesqueries can occur. Why did his own people not overthrow Bokassa? But why, also, did Idi Amin have to be removed by a foreign invasion? And why did the international community, including some democratic countries, tolerate these monsters and many others? Why did they, and many others like them, continue to be received as visiting dignitaries on state visits; why did they continue to get aid? Were they, after all, such bizarre anomalies in the world, or did they, in their excesses, simply highlight the basic nature of political power in that majority of the world where democracy does not exist? These tyrants did not fall because they tortured and stole, or because they ruined their countries. They fell because with time they went too far, partly out of desperation, but also because they were losing touch with reality after many years in power. In this respect, they were no different from Hitler or Pol Pot, even though they had no particular social theory to justify their behavior.

Chapter 12

Some Propositions, Lessons, and Predictions about Tyranny

H ow could such heinous governments as the ones we have studied
have come to power and endured so long in the twentieth century? Tyrannies have come to power in states both big and small; in rich
industrial and very poor agrarian societies; in countries with many centuries of statecraft in their tradition, and in brand new ones; in culturally united nations with a firm sense of identity, and in ethnically split
states with almost no basis for common solidarity. What generalizations
can be drawn from these thirteen sad and diverse histories? Are there
common causes of tyranny that can be shown to be valid in all, or at
least most cases? Are there lessons to be drawn about how to avoid
tyranny in the future? And is it possible, from this review, to improve
our ability to see tyrannies in the making?

THE CAUSES OF TYRANNY

A venerable theory contends that democracy only survives when there
are strong countervailing powers to those of the central state. European history strongly supports this notion. The delicate balance
between king, church, the nobility, and the towns in parts of Western

Europe during the Middle Ages explains the unique development of capitalism, of parliamentary regimes, and ultimately, of democracy. This holds most of all for England and the Netherlands, less for those European states that acquired absolutist monarchs able to override the powers of other parts of their societies, and not at all for militaristic, absolutist states in Eastern and Central Europe such as Prussia and Russia, where no such balance evolved.[1]

The notion that liberty required a balance between the parts of the society, and that these ought to have some representation in government was so commonplace in eighteenth-century America that the absence of a nobility was often cited as the principal reason for the uncontrollable power of the crown. In England, the aristocracy restrained the tyranny of the king, it was thought, while it also balanced the dangerous popular instincts of the democratic, "licentious" commons. The absence of aristocracy in the colonies had thrown the fine machinery of English government out of balance and allowed the crown, through its agents, to become "tyrannical."[2] If, by our modern standards or those that prevailed in most of the kingdoms and empires of the world at that time, the charge of "tyranny" levelled at King George III by the American Declaration of Independence seems overwrought, to its authors, raised on English political tradition and Enlightenment philosophy, it was serious.

Long before the eighteenth-century Enlightenment, Aristotle knew that stable, moderate government was the best insurance against tyranny. He believed that positions of power should not be held too long by any individuals or families. He wrote that divisions within the society opened the way for demagogues, oligarchs, or soldiers to seize excessive power. A substantial and independent class, neither too rich nor too poor, and thus acting as a mediating influence between the sharply divergent interests of rich and poor, could stabilize society and inhibit the emergence of tyranny.[3] A society in which power was balanced between various interests, and in which consensus between these interests existed on the issue of how to operate government, was unlikely to be subjected to tyranny.

The idea that balancing forces are necessary to maintain human liberty and prevent the emergence of an excessively strong state remained influential in the nineteenth and twentieth centuries, from Alexis de Tocqueville to Friedrich Hayek, who, by the time he died in

1992, had become the prophet of anti-statist worshippers of free markets throughout much of the capitalist and formerly communist world.[4]

Such a historically well-grounded theory must be taken seriously. It
obviously explains how democracy evolved over time in a few Western
societies. Nevertheless, our examples suggest that for most twentieth-
century cases of tyranny it is at best an irrelevant theory, and on the
whole more wrong than right.

Weakness and Disorder

Countervailing powers within the state may lead to disintegration
rather than to democratic stability. If they do, in an era dominated by
idealized models of the nation-state as the best form of government,
many of the most patriotic nationalists will turn to dictatorial modes of
government and drastically undemocratic ideologies in order to save
the nation. In moments of crisis and weakness, government based on
Anglo-American notions of the division of powers seems slow and inefficient. It is not surprising, therefore, that most elites of new and struggling states trying to build strong nations should reject such forms.

The Bolsheviks did not take power in a strong bureaucratic state,
but in a collapsing one, with pieces of the old Russian Empire falling
away, internal civil war, and a disintegrating economy. By reimposing
order, at a terrible cost, they won the allegiance of a sufficient proportion of the educated elite to carry on, and begin to build a new society
according to their own utopian vision. Then, and only then, did Stalin
succeed in building the monstrous bureaucratic machine that carried
out his crimes. He had the model of the Tsarist autocracy, and the
expertise of much of the old administrative and intellectual elite to
help him at first, but the institutions he built were new, and he had
new personnel placed in positions of power as quickly as possible.
Tyranny preceded its administrative apparatus, not the other way
around. Exactly the same conclusion can be drawn from the regimes of
Mao, Pol Pot, and Kim Il Sung. They consolidated their power in war-
ravaged societies whose administrative structures had been massively
disrupted, and they built new state machines.

Even the Argentine generals, who seized power in what should have
been a reasonably efficient and unified nation-state, actually took over
after a series of exceptionally bungling, ideologically confused govern-

ments had brought Argentina to the edge of economic ruin and civil war. The ineffectiveness of its government, not its overwhelming bureaucratic power, led to tyranny.

Saddam Hussein's Ba'th did not begin the centralization of the Iraqi state machine, but it greatly accelerated a process that was not far advanced at the time the Iraqi monarchy was overthrown in 1958. Before Ba'thist rule, Iraq suffered more from instability and division than from an excessively centralized bureaucracy. Much the same, though to a lesser extent, could be said of Romania before it was turned into a communist state by Soviet power. It was neither highly bureaucratized nor particularly well administered before 1945, and the communist state built a whole new structure that allowed it to be far more dictatorial and tyrannical than anything which had existed in Romania's past.

Nor did Duvalier and Trujillo seize strong, bureaucratized states, but almost incoherent administrative machines incapable of doing much of anything. Their tyranny centralized power in a way that had never before been done in their nations' histories.

That was also the intent of the two African tyrants we examined—to centralize state powers. In the case of Uganda, the process was started by Obote when he demolished the political power of Buganda. But ultimately, both of these tyrants failed to create effective state machineries, and in Uganda, where strong regional and ethnic loyalties survived and were exacerbated by the rule of Obote and Amin, the attempt led neither to a balance of power and democracy, nor to a centralized, bureaucratic state, but to anarchy and a terrible civil war.

The Burmese case suggests the same conclusion. It was not that the state was too centralized, but that it was falling apart that led to Ne Win's assumption of power. His success in controlling, though never in eliminating regional challenges to central rule, made his tyranny possible. Yet, the alternative was never a carefully balanced set of regional interests coexisting democratically and peacefully, but a disintegration of the state.

Whether or not, as Hayek maintains, it is a fairly small step from the social democratic welfare state that the Western democracies pioneered in the twentieth century to the enslavement of the population by the tyranny of centralized planning is not a question I can answer. I am skeptical, simply because in the late twentieth century we have seen that the strongest welfare states of Western Europe are capable of pulling away from central control when their populations have become tired of such policies. As long as democracy and free elections survive, and as long as communalism does not overwhelm individual rights, bureaucratization can be partly reversed, excesses controlled, and tyranny prevented long before it occurs. Whatever the merit of Hayek's case, it is hard to see what application it has to the examples of tyranny we have studied, because none of the cases of twentieth-century tyranny have come out of democratic welfare states like those of Western Europe.

On the contrary, twelve of our thirteen cases do not suggest that tyrannies emerge from democracies that gradually allow their centers to become too powerful, and so upset the careful balance of forces that created democracies in the first place. Rather, they have come from societies either without democratic institutions at all, or with very weak and insecure ones. In all cases these societies were struggling to overcome serious problems, sometimes verging on the edge of what looked like or what had actually become chaos.

However, there is Germany, where it may seem that the theory of over-bureaucratization really does work. Germany had regional political institutions stronger than in most European states, it had a substantial middle class, and a functioning, albeit insecure democracy. But it also had a very powerful, centralized civil and military bureaucracy, and when these went along with Hitler, it was an easy matter for him to eliminate both democracy and the remnants of regional political power. The strength and willingness of the bureaucracy to follow the Nazis made it easier for Hitler to rule, and made it unnecessary for him to create revolutionary new institutions, as Stalin had to do. If it is impossible to base a whole theory of modern tyranny on one case, Hitler's, nevertheless this exception must be accounted for. (Perhaps the case of the tyranny imposed on Japan by its military in the 1930s might be similar.)

On closer inspection, however, the exceptional German case is not quite as different from the others as it seems. The reason Hitler came to power was that he offered a coherent ideology of national salvation to a people who felt that their world had almost totally disintegrated between 1918 and 1932. The catastrophes of the lost war, followed by the inflation of 1923, capped by the depression of the early 1930s convinced a substantial portion of the Germans, and by all accounts a probable majority of the social, political, intellectual, and economic elite, that a chaotic collapse was next. If Volkish ideology had not been so strong, if notions of history as conflict had not been so prevalent, if German nationalism had not been so self-pitying and resentful, if the military and higher civil service had not been so hostile to democracy, and if the cumulative shocks that preceded Hitler's rise to power had not occured, the mere existence of a strong centralized bureaucracy would not have produced tyranny. And even then, without Hitler's racial theories, any German dictatorship would have been quite different. Tyranny in Germany cannot be explained simply by saying that there was a critical breakdown, and this gave an opportunistic politician his chance to take power. But it cannot be explained, either, by claiming that any strong central bureaucracy is a potential instrument of tyranny.

Where does this leave the theory that the best protection against tyranny is a careful balance of political and social forces, and resistance to any form of centralized state power? It cannot be doubted that a state which functions smoothly and has many sources of power other than the center is unlikely to become tyrannical. But such wonderful balances, where they exist, as they do in the United States of America, are the result of long, idiosyncratic histories. They cannot be created artificially, they are rare, and there is no guarantee that once they exist they can survive major ideological changes and severe crisis. Keeping central governments and bureaucracies weak is certainly no guarantee at all that tyranny can be avoided.

This was a conclusion reached by Jacob Burckhardt in 1860 when he described how Florence, the most enlightened of Italy's Renaissance republics, failed to preserve its republican form of government no matter how hard it worked to find the right constitutional balance. He wrote:

> When Dante compares the city which was always mending its constitution with the sick man who is continually changing his posture to escape from pain, he touches with the comparison a permanent feature of the political life of Florence. The great modern fallacy that a constitution can be made, can be manufactured by a combination of existing forces and tendencies, was constantly cropping up in stormy times. . . . [5]

Those experts who believe that by finding the perfect constitutional balance in new states, whether recently decolonized ones, or in Russia and Eastern Europe after communism, they can insure the future of democracy and avoid the renewal of tyranny, are fooling themselves.

If the majority of the people of the United States were ever to feel that their political system was collapsing in chaos, if America's elites came to believe that communal needs had to override individual rights, and that democratic procedure was too cumbersome to meet the emergency at hand, all the division of powers would not help save democracy. If, along with this, there existed a widely accepted utopian faith that it was possible to bring back a lost paradise, and a desperate sense that the nation was engaged in a life-and-death struggle against terribly dangerous internal and external enemies, the dictatorship would soon turn into tyranny. Not increasing bureaucratic interference, which can always be corrected in a democracy, but an ideological transformation combined with economic and political catastrophe would be required to bring about such an outcome.

Institutional defects do not explain the rise of tyrannies, though they may contribute to economic and political failures. The corollary to this is that the survival of democracy is not a function of perfectly invented constitutional mechanisms, but of an ideological faith in the worth of democracy and the rights of the individual combined with reasonable success in conducting the affairs of state.

It is possible to summarize this argument in the form of two propositions about the likelihood of tyranny:

Proposition One: The more chaotic the economy and political system, the more they seem to be failing, the more likely it is that a tyrant will emerge as a self-proclaimed savior.

And, leaving aside Germany, which fell to tyranny despites its strong administrative apparatus, not because of it, the other cases suggest the related proposition:

Proposition Two: The weaker the administrative apparatus of the state, the more likely it is that there will be the kind of chaos that leads to the emergence of a powerful potential national savior, and the easier it will be for him to turn into a tyrant once he has seized power.

These two propositions apply to all modern tyranny in general, whether ideological or more purely corrupt.

National Rage

Russian and German nationalism in the nineteenth century were largely based on resentment. On one hand, they admired and wished to be considered the equals of France and England, but on the other they felt they were not recognized as equals. Particularly in the case of the Russian nationalists, they felt themselves both inferior, but at the same time morally superior to the "degenerate" West. In a sense Russia never caught up to the West, but Germany certainly did, and became the most powerful economy and state in Western Europe. But this did not assuage the feelings of hostility and resentment which continued as a belief that German superiority was not fully recognized or given its due place in European affairs.

Liah Greenfeld uses the word *ressentiment* to characterize this type of nationalism. Coined by Nietzsche and later defined and developed by Max Scheler, it refers to a psychological state resulting from suppressed feelings of envy and hatred. The first condition necessary for it to exist is that the subject and the object of envy should be seen by the subject as essentially equal. The second condition is that the actual inequality between them rules out the practical achievement of the theoretically existing equality. When a group perceives itself unequal and in some sense inferior to another, when it is envious, but when it believes that the inequality is neither fundamental nor justified, it is prone to *ressentiment*, no matter what the psychological predispositions of the individuals in the group.[6]

As Greenfeld explains it, nationalisms characterized by *ressentiment* interpret unsatisfactory internal situations as well as perceived international slights as the result of foreign influence. The pure and ideal nation could not be at fault, so that an external community, or its perceived internal agents, become the chief object of *ressentiment*. Pride in the mythologized nation, combined with growing frustration and jealousy directed against these foreign forces, result in intense xenophobia.

The catastrophe of the First World War and Germany's problems in the 1920s and early 1930s greatly reinforced this aspect of German nationalism. The same happened in Russia. Both Hitler and Stalin were genuinely representative of the rage and lust for revenge that these events produced among German and Russian nationalists. Therefore it was not just bad luck that they came to power, particularly not Hitler. Nor is it simple coincidence that when anger, jealousy, and blaming external agents for all of the nation's ruin are the basis of nationalism, the more successful politicians will be those that embody those very attitudes.

But Russia and Germany were not alone. The incipient, not fully formed nationalism in the European colonies of Africa has also been based on *ressentiment*. And in the case of Africa, this has considerably more objective justification than in the case of Germany. When we look at the biographies of the two African tyrants we have studied, we can see ample reason for them to have been prey to this emotion. They concealed or repressed it, but at least in the case of Amin, it broke out virulently once he was in power, and he exploded with rage.

The same inner rage and resentment obviously acted as a basis for Haitian nationalism from the late eighteenth century through the emergence of *noirisme* in the twentieth, and with good reason. Similarly Burman and Cambodian forms of nationalism, which emerged out of colonial situations that humiliated Burmans and Khmer and stripped them of economic and political power, also have many of the same elements. In fact, it ought to come as no surprise that the domination by a few Western societies over the entire world produced a very widespread sense of nationalist rage and suppressed desire for revenge. When this desire could emerge, if the great Western powers who were to blame could not be reached, real or imagined internal "agents" of Western imperialism and corruption were identified and attacked. These might be Indians in Burma or Uganda, Jews in Germany, Russia, or Argentina, Vietnamese and Chinese in Cambodia, Hungarians in Romania, Kurds in Iraq, or simply, in the absence of any easily identifiable ethnic enemy, hereditary "bad elements" in China.

Colonial subjection, lost wars, and economic failures have all contributed to the proliferation of tyranny in the twentieth century because *ressentiment* has become such an important part of many political communities' identities. Some of the most bitter "tribal" wars in our century have been the result of attempts to create strong nations on the basis of *ressentiment*. Misha Glenny, for example, has shown how the carefully nurtured sense of persecution by Croatian and Serbian nationalists lies at the heart of the ghastly war that broke out over the corpse of Yugoslavia in the early 1990s, and how expertly it has been manipulated by leaders who have turned themselves into local tyrants.[7]

The more strongly manifested the degree of *ressentiment* as a basis for national self-consciousness, the more likely it is that political or economic crisis will lead to tyranny. Vengeance may take on a strongly ideological, utopian appearance, as under Stalin and Hitler, or it may simply be an expression of almost incoherent hatred and bitterness by a corrupt dictator, as in the case of Idi Amin. But in neither case is it simply a function of that one individual's personality. It corresponds, rather, to a widely shared emotion, and this is what makes the rage of an individual leader so potent, and allows him to rule as a national savior claiming to represent the people.

From this we can derive a general proposition:

Proposition Three: For any nation, new or old, we can judge the extent to which its political and intellectual elite's identity is based on jealous and vengeful resentment, on memories of past wrongs, real or imagined, and estimate that the more this is so, the higher the probability of future tyrannies.

Communal Ideologies of Conflict, Virtue, and Heredity

The presence and widespread acceptance of utopian theories of society that demand perfection, and believe that it is possible to obtain it, are also a good predictor of tyranny. Most of the twentieth-century's tyrannical ideologies, beginning with Europe's, have been based on popularized science and a misplaced faith that it was possible to engineer the ideal society. But it was not just a matter of idealism carried to excess. The specific content of these theories, their neo-Darwinian belief that history consists of struggles to the death between competing classes or races, was necessary in order to transform them into such deadly instruments of tyranny.

Utopian idealism about Lockian liberalism may produce a bullying majority, as Alexis de Tocqueville warned, and as Louis Hartz heatedly proclaimed in his classic attack on American liberalism, but there is nothing in such an ideology to encourage its followers to label whole parts of their society as deadly menaces that have to be exterminated.[8] We have seen that liberal Western states are capable of behaving in atrocious, tyrannical ways in their dealings with small, weak foreign societies, as the French did in their African colonies and in Indochina, or as the United States also did in Indochina, particularly Cambodia. But to get away with this, they had to conceal their activities from their populations, and to violate the principles of their own democratic political systems in ways that would have been unacceptable at home.

In the past there were religious ideologies capable of inspiring massacres and persecutions on a large scale in order to bring about perfection, though the religious traditions that came out of the Near East, especially medieval Christianity, seem to have been more prone to this than others. Yet, for all the bloodshed in the past, most of it due to the famine and disease that resulted from wars, there are no cases of deliberate mass slaughter for ideological reasons on the scale of what the twentieth century has witnessed.

A neo-Darwinian sense of history as a struggle to the death has spread well beyond those intellectuals who think of themselves as being in the Western scientific tradition. The idea that various categories of people—races, classes, ethnicities, religions—are the equivalent of species of organisms fighting for survival, and therefore justified in taking the most extreme measures, has become widespread. Thus, even though it adopts the position that it is only reviving an old tradition, the fundamentalist version of Islam, when it achieves power, is a type of modern utopian totalitarianism.

The fundamentalist Arab Muslim revival in recent decades has been led by, and enrolled as its militants, those with university educations, primarily in the sciences and engineering.[9] The ideological underpinning of the Islamic Iranian regime that took power in 1979 combined enraged nationalism with a Marxist view of what determines the distribution of power in the world.[10]

Why is it that the worst of the Western ideological tradition, its aggressive nationalism and pseudo-scientific totalitarian fantasies, has been adopted so much more easily outside the West than the best of that tradition, faith in genuine democracy? In large part this is because outside the West there never developed strong philosophical traditions that allowed the rights of the individual to stand against those of the community. The community has been seen not only as the supreme, but the only legitimate social actor. The individual, except at the top of each social hierarchy where one individual acts for the community as a whole, has been viewed as inconsequential. Thus, the king or political ruler acts an authoritarian but protective father, making society a larger reflection of the authoritarian family. This has been the pattern in all agrarian states, including those in Europe until the beginning of the modern era.[11]

We can see the power of this attitude in a regime such as Kim Il Sung's. The more closely it is examined, the more its leader seems to take on many of the traditional, authoritarian virtues of a traditional Confucian ruler. This appeals to national tradition, of course, and fits well with a sense that the interests of the community so far outweigh those of any individual that repression of the population for the good of the nation is justified. This was part of Mao's appeal in China, and Stalin's as well in the Soviet Union. It has, in fact, been an integral part of every ideological tyranny in the twentieth century.

The story of how a contrary philosophy that promotes individual over group dignity managed to develop and flourish in a few European societies, even against continual, widespread opposition, is very long. I shall not try to explain it because that would take us too far away from the subject at hand, and also because there are so many good accounts of it by intellectual historians and political philosophers. That this tradition survived, and continued to inform the legal and political practices of a few European democracies, particularly in their Anglo-American versions, is closely related to the survival of democracy. It also contributed to the skepticism among genuinely liberal intellectuals about the value of utopian totalitarian ideologies.[12]

Radical individualism, of course, has never been the rule in any political system. In practice, some sense that community needs must often prevail, and that individuals are not capable of acting alone without being grouped into communities, has tempered the defense of individual freedom. As Isaiah Berlin has pointed out, discussions about the proper limits between individual liberty and community needs have made up the substance of many of the most interesting philosophical and political debates in the West in the past several centuries. This continues, for example, in the work of such theorists of justice and liberty as John Rawls and Brian Barry. Nevertheless, in a few societies, there emerged from that debate a sense that it is not proper to deal with individuals as mere members of their communities. This inoculates liberal thought against ever taking too seriously the theory that to be a member of a certain community is to be possessed of indelible characteristics. It also makes it impossible to believe in the scientific or moral inevitability of wars to the death between communities based on race, class, or religion.

There is little question that part of the revolt against liberal, democratic capitalism in Europe in the late nineteenth century was also an expression of despair against the apparent disintegration of community. When the market and impersonal money become the determinants of an individual's fate, the comforting social bonds that protected and nurtured individuals were dissolved.[13] Yet, the search for a return to community, understandable as it may be, became an attachment to the values of community over freedom. Marxist collectivism was not, in the end, so different from the German demand for a return to the *Volksgemeinschaft*, an imagined perfect people's community.

That the intellectual traditions in most of the world never went through the debates about individualism and communalism which have been a staple in Western literature for so long has meant that the argument was generally decided in favor of communalism by non-Western intelligentsias. The Russian case may be considered as typical for the non-Western world, even though Russian intellectual tradition was in other ways so influenced by Western Europe's. This explains why it has been common for those parts of the European tradition most likely to lead to tyranny to be widely adopted throughout the world, while an understanding of democracy and individualism has been rare.

Knowing this suggests a fourth proposition:

Proposition Four: The more strongly communal values are held to be superior to individual rights, and the more it is believed that every individual is determined by traits he or she automatically inherits from his or her community, the more likely it is that tyranny will be found morally acceptable for the greater good of the community.

It follows that in such a moral climate, theories about the inevitability of group conflict are more likely to be accepted than otherwise. After all, it is not a large step to go from a belief that one's hereditary community is the source of all virtue to believing other communities are the source of all evil. This suggests a fifth proposition closely related to the fourth.

Proposition Five: The stronger the ideologies of inevitable conflict between communities—be they races, nations, economic classes, or religions—the more likely it is that tyranny will occur.

Though it may not seem necessary because it follows so logically, in order to be quite clear I think it useful to combine propositions three, four, and five into a sixth.

Proposition Six: Reactive nationalism that is based on fear and resentment of the outside world, that demands communal solidarity of the entire nation, regardless of the cultural and individual differences which exist, and that faces serious internal ethnic and religious diversity is likely to impose itself by force. This will produce resistance, and in turn, acceptance of increasingly tyrannical methods of rule by those in power in order to sustain the nationalist ideal.

The unending ethnic and religious conflict in Iraq and Burma shows that creating strong state machines to impose nationalist unity on culturally diverse states, when the ideals of nationalism are born fearful, communal, and resentful of the outside world, leads to disaster. The ensuing conflicts are bound to produce crises that will result either in tyranny or in anarchic collapse, as in Uganda. Once such a process has begun, there is nothing that can be done to stop it except the virtual extinction or expulsion of some communities, because each ethnic, linguistic, or religious group begins to define itself in opposition to those that are persecuting it, and what were once imagined, ideologically imposed conflicts to the death become, quite literally, exactly that. In the ensuing wars, civil wars, massacres, and persecutions, every group can find reason enough to turn to a tyrannical savior in order to preserve its identity and very life.

Order and Cleanliness at Any Cost

One of the important causes of both anti-democratic and anti-capitalist ideologies in the nineteenth and twentieth centuries has been the perceived messiness of parliamentary democracy and the wastefulness of individualistic, consumer capitalism. This was part of the anti-liberal critique in late nineteenth-century Europe, and it has remained a staple ideological tool throughout the twentieth century. The rather strange quote from a recent North Korean commentary (cited above in Chapter 8) proclaiming that state to be a true socialist vanguard is worth repeating. North Korea, it asserts, is a place where "there is nobody who is exceptionally better off, nobody who goes ill-clad and hungry . . . no jobless people, no people who go bankrupt and wander around begging, no drug addicts, alcoholics and fin-de-siècle faggots who seek abnormal desires."[14] Much of the original appeal of the Argentine generals was that they promised to overcome the corruption, disorder, and degeneracy of "foreign" Western culture.

Hitler's appeal to a disoriented German population, beset not only by financial and political chaos, but also by the open manifestation of new cultural tastes and sexual mores, was that he would bring back traditional order, a simple and comprehensible culture, and a clear public morality. This promise was warmly welcomed not only by the broader population, but also by the majority of intellectuals whose depreciation of democratic capitalism and the confusions of modern life made them happily renounce their individual liberties.[15]

We know that the promises of modern totalitarian ideologies to clean out corruption and disorder are false. In the long run corruption and administrative chaos flourish far more in tyrannies than in open political systems. The constant lying and deception subvert morality more than the public exhibitionism in liberal societies that so shocks those from unliberal traditions. We have seen how Nazism was corrupt from the start, and how Stalinism degenerated because it was impossible to confront corrupt officials or subject the political process to honest examination. We know that the Argentine generals, despite their promises to clean out corruption, made it worse, and that Ne Win's regime in Burma became increasingly criminal and dishonest in its attempt to hold on to power.

And yet, the search for order, cleanliness, and simplicity are seductive, and when this search becomes a national obsession, the likelihood of a tyrannical outcome is greatly increased.

Military men are particularly prone to this delusion because of the nature of their profession which presents them with clear lines of authority and an artificially imposed sense of discipline. The Argentine and Burmese armies' notion that they could solve their nation's problems by imposing military order and discipline, and by removing complex, corrupting "foreign" influences, was as much of a fantasy as any other twentieth-century utopian dream. Once army men with such an agenda are in power, their frustrations will grow as they discover that problems which seemed so simple to begin with are actually intractable. They will be tempted to use increasing force to carry out their will. This illustrates the particular danger of allowing military solutions to complicated political and economic problems, and suggests a seventh proposition:

Proposition Seven: Nationalist elites who believe that discipline and social purity, defined as the exclusion of "foreign" values and habits, can solve the complex problems of adapting to the modern world are likely to become both increasingly frustrated and tyrannical once they achieve power.

Probabilities and Personalities

This is a good place in which to emphasize that these propositions are only probabilistic statements. There have been dictators who have presented themselves as national saviors, who have promised to bring order to messy situations, who have been strong nationalists, and who have succeeded in carrying out many of their promises without becoming abusive tyrants. Many have been military men, but have had the suppleness of intellect, the flexibility to tolerate dissent and temporary reverses, and the innate decency to avoid imposing humiliation, corruption, and mass killings on their populations.

General Charles de Gaulle of France had the potential, and for a time the power to become a dictator, perhaps even a tyrant, but he had no such inclination. Marshal Pilsudski who took power in Poland in a military coup in 1926, and Kemal Atatürk, who used his army to establish himself as Turkey's dictator after World War I, both used dictatorial methods and knew how to be ruthless. But by our definition, they were not tyrants. They did not have inflexible theories of human behavior that might have led them into excessive brutality, and they were not particularly corrupt. They were successful in strengthening their states without destroying the well-being of their populations; and they furthered the cause of their nations without resorting to excessive intolerance.[16]

There are borderline cases, for example Francisco Franco of Spain and Augusto Pinochet of Chile, who killed on a substantial scale to promote their ideological visions. Yet, they created the conditions for a return to prosperity and democracy in their countries. For a foreign and distant observer, they may or may not have fit our definition of tyrants. They were leaders whose abuse of power went well beyond what was strictly necessary to promote the general well-being of their countries, and yet, they did not produce disasters. Naturally, for those who were tortured or killed in their prisons because they were on the losing side of deeply ideological struggles, the question does not arise: Franco and Pinochet were tyrants.

The point is that no single proposition, alone, has much explanatory power, and even together, they only point to conditions that increase the likelihood of tyranny, but do not make it inevitable. There always remains an entirely unpredictable element, the personality of the individual who eventually takes power in a moment of crisis. Will it be a de Gaulle, who preferred to resign when public opinion swung against him, or a Ne Win, who decided to hold on to the bitter end, a Bukharin who saw the error of Bolshevism carried to extremes, or a Stalin, a Julius Nyerere who tempered his nationalism and socialism in Tanzania with a certain humane vision, or an Idi Amin? Of course, the prevailing ideologies and national traditions play a role. A Stalin was more likely to win in Russia than a Bukharin, and it is doubtful that a regime such as Ne Win's could have survived long in France in the late twentieth century. But de Gaulle could have been much worse than he was, and Ne Win could have been better.

To show how personalities can affect the final outcome, and prevent what might have been tyranny from asserting itself, we need only look at the last years of the Soviet Union, when Gorbachev, a believing communist, had the levers of power necessary for reimposing a much more brutal, totalitarian regime. There is little question he could have swung much of the military and the KGB to his side. That would not have solved the long-run problems of the USSR, but it would have kept him and the Communist Party of the Soviet Union in power a lot longer.[17] Why did he not do it? Ultimately, no broad generalizing propositions can explain this. Even as we recognize that there is much in Russia's political and cultural tradition that makes the probability of some sort of return to tyranny very high, we also have to admit that there was something about Gorbachev which made him renounce such a path.

Corruption and Anti-Intellectualism

Though the role of ideas and of intellectuals has been stressed from the start, not all the tyrants we have examined have been intellectuals or have been inspired by them. Idi Amin, Trujillo, and Bokassa may have been nationalists in their own way, but they lacked both the training and inclination to be proponents of well-worked-out ideological programs.

The smaller the role of intellectuals in establishing tyranny, the more quickly will a tyrannical regime become corrupt. This is rather obvious, but it leads to an important generalization. Tyrants in general persecute and fear intellectuals, even if that is what they are themselves, because intellectuals are a likely source of opposition. But in poor societies where there are few educated people, corrupt tyrants are particularly harmful. They will, from the start, suppress intellectuals capable of organizing opposition and making ideological claims against the ruler. In doing this, corrupt tyrants are likely to destroy the very basis of education and therefore all hope for improving the society. That is certainly what Idi Amin did to Uganda where he destroyed one of Africa's most promising universities and school systems, and that is also what Duvalier did in Haiti.

This can be phrased as a final, eighth proposition:

Proposition Eight: A tyrant who is not an intellectual, or ceases to identify himself as one, and who rejects the influence of the ideological intelligentsia, will be corrupt because that will become the only basis of his power. He will feel threatened by intellectuals and persecute them because they have more coherent ideological programs that threaten his rule.

But presumably, in more economically developed societies, the higher average level of education, and the larger the size of the educated elite make it essential for a potential tyrant to have a convincing ideology in order to gain power. That was certainly the case in Germany as well as Russia, and even, somewhat, in Argentina. On the other hand, even in poorly developed economies with low levels of education, intellectuals play a disproportionate political role. Intellectual elites are the carriers of nationalism, of utopian programs, and of revolutionary dreams. These have spread all over the world, and are continuing to increase their hold on politically aware people.

What this suggests is that, with time, the incidence of purely corrupt tyranny that begins with almost no ideological agenda will become rarer. It would not have been possible for such a tyranny to establish itself in Europe in the twentieth century, and it is becoming much more difficult in Latin America, most of Asia, and the Near East. In Africa, too, levels of education and urbanization have been rising, and with them, awareness of higher standards of political morality. This makes pure corruption less acceptable; it also makes intellectuals and ideology more important.

The issue for the future, then, is not whether or not there will continue to be corrupt tyrants. Yes, there will be, but eventually, the breed will become rare, and corrupt tyranny will tend to occur only as ideologically tyrannical regimes degenerate. But the reverse of that will be that the conditions that created ideological tyranny in the twentieth century will not disappear. On the contrary, they are likely to get stronger.

AVOIDING TYRANNY

To be able to listen, to tolerate dissent, to adapt to changing circumstances—these are the marks of good leadership. Most of the tyrants we have studied possessed this quality early in their careers. That is how they reached high positions. Hitler, Stalin, and Mao were all thought to be exceptionally skillful at adapting to new circumstances, listening to other opinions within their parties, and learning from their experiences. Pol Pot and Idi Amin appeared to be unusually reasonable and able to take direction from their seniors. With time, all of these tyrants lost this quality. In some cases, this was out of ideological conviction. Having achieved power, ideological tyrants pressed forward with their programs, convinced that they possessed the ultimate truth. Less ideological tyrants, like Duvalier and eventually Ne Win, discovered that to stay in power they had to become brutally corrupt, so they closed off dissent and retreated into lies and personal isolation.

All dictatorships have the potential to turn into tyranny because they discourage open discourse and complaint, and because they do not provide a way of limiting either the terms or powers of those at the top of the political hierarchy.

Machiavelli was well aware of this and advised princes to be wise enough to listen to criticism. He wrote:

> [T]here is no other way of guarding one's self against flattery than by letting men understand that they will not offend you by speaking the truth; but when every one can tell you the truth, you lose their respect. A prudent prince must therefore take a third course, by choosing for his council wise men, and giving these alone full liberty to speak the truth to him, but only of those things that he asks and of nothing else; but he must ask them about everything and hear their opinion and afterwards deliberate by himself in his own way. . . . Beyond these he should listen to no one.[18]

But this proposal demands that the Prince have superhuman virtue. The leader who can pick only the wise from whom to ask advice, who knows what questions to ask, and who can then make the appropriate decision may need no restraints. How many such leaders are there? How many know that, as they age and lose their judgement, they ought to retire? They may exist, but they are so rare that it is the height of folly to build a theory of government on them. Machiavelli himself understood this perfectly well, and in his *Discourses* advised that it was better to have elected than hereditary princes, because it was more likely that in this way "an infinite number of most competent and virtuous rulers one after the other" would be selected.[19]

If picking the ideal ruler is almost impossible, choosing the right science of society by which to guide it is even more difficult. The French Encyclopedists, from whose ranks came some of the best of the Enlightenment political philosophers, believed that "morals and politics were not sufficiently rigorous branches of knowledge to allow for the drafting of ambitious models of perfect societies."[20] They were right, and it is a pity that their advice was not more widely heeded in the twentieth century.

The only sure way to avoid tyranny is to follow democratic procedures, to insist on regular elections and the periodic rotation of office, and to make sure that no minority is stripped of its rights to vote and protest against injustice. As John Rawls has observed, no reasonable theory of justice claims that majorities are always right.[21] That way, not even a "tyranny of the majority" is possible, much less the tyranny of a single despot or party.

None of the tyrannies we have examined would have survived regular elections and an open press, a fact they knew very well. The only exception was the deluded Burmese regime of Ne Win, which allowed free elections it thought it would win, and then redoubled its tyranny in angry frustration at the unfavorable results it obtained.

But we know that establishing and maintaining democracy is not just a matter of making the right rules, of writing the perfect constitution, or of pointing to the successful Western democracies and telling everyone else that they should simply follow this special model of government. To sustain democracy requires a widespread acceptance of ideologies that are tolerant, that admit the frailty of all human institutions, and that recognize the impossibility of finding perfect solutions. There must be a faith, and ultimately it is just that, a kind of religious belief rather than a logically worked out position, that the individual has a value beyond merely being a functioning member of the community.

More than this, social theories that claim with absolute certitude that human history is based on competition and inevitable conflict between clearly identifiable groups—be they classes, races, ethnicities, or religions—will, in the long run, be unfavorable to tolerant democracy. They will promote ruthless conflict and demands for revenge against historical wrongs, real or imagined, imposed by one group against another. They also place individuals in group categories from which they cannot escape, thus making them subjects of persecution, and instigating further intractable conflicts.

All this is much easier said than done. It cannot be accomplished by pontificating, but only by showing over and over again what have been the sad results of ideologies of blood and revenge, of pseudo-scientific social theories that see group conflict as the law of history, and of contempt for the messy disorder of modern liberal democracy.

AND IN THE FUTURE?

In late October 1992, I went to Zagreb, the capital of Croatia, to give a lecture on the economic history of capitalism. While there I walked into one of the city's main bookstores and picked up a little book called *Historical Maps of Croatia* put out by an organization acting on behalf of the newly independent government of Croatia. In it I found a chronology of Croatian history. It contained several astonishing claims. One of the strangest was the first item in the chronology, "500 B.C. Croatian name first mentioned on the inscription of Persian ruler, Darius the Great."[22] As the first historical suggestion of a south Slavic people called by that name occurred more than a thousand years later, this item might have seemed to be a silly, but harmless piece of self-promotion by nationalist intellectuals. A distinguished local historian in Zagreb immediately pointed out to me that it was anything but harmless.

Before World War II Croatian nationalists trying to define themselves as better than their linguistically almost identical Serbian neighbors came up with the notion that Croatians were somehow descended from the ancient Persians, and that they were therefore "Aryan." (The Persians were considered Aryans—in fact the word "Iranian" is the same as the word "Aryan.") This myth was used to justify the alliance of extremist Croatian fascists during World War II with "Aryan" Nazi Germany, and to provide a pseudo-scientific basis for the brutal mass murders the Croatian fascists carried out against Serbs. This reference, which would be an obscure and silly piece of legend if it had not been for the terrible experiences of the Second World War, is hardly reassuring to those who know the history of the fable. In case anyone should miss the point, the historical chronology cites only massacres by Serbs during World War II, and leaves out any mention of the killings conducted by the Croatian fascists led by Ante Pavelić. Pictures of Pavelić in his fascist uniform, modelled on the Nazi military uniform, were being sold in the bookstore, as well as in tourist shops in the quaint old part of Zagreb.

No Serbian intellectual could miss the point of this symbolism. Ultra-nationalist Serbs, needless to say, have been quick to exploit the persistent insensitivity of the Croatian government toward the grim fascist past to warn all Serbs in Croatia that they are slated for another round of extinction unless they fight back.[23]

I mention this story not to place exclusive blame for what has happened in Yugoslavia on Croatia, because the Serbs, and in fact all the parties, have been guilty of historical mystification about the recent as well as the ancient past, boundary claims based on distorted demographic and linguistic claims, and calls for blood revenge.[24] Misha Glenny has described how these frightening calls to arms persuaded mountain peasants throughout former Yugoslavia that the time of slaughter, as during World War II, had returned, and that they had to defend themselves by destroying their religiously different neighbors or be killed themselves. Once that idea was firmly established, and "ethnic cleansing" begun, the nightmarish mythologizing of the intellectuals became real, and the war fed on itself, thus making the local extremist politicians all the stronger.[25]

The reason the story about Croatia has such significance is that under communist rule Croatia was neither poor nor isolated from the economic and intellectual currents of Western Europe. On the contrary, because of its spectacular natural beauty it was one of the world's main tourist attractions, and there was almost completely unrestricted freedom of movement in and out Croatia, as well as the rest of Yugoslavia, for at least two decades before the collapse of communism. Croatia was actually one of the most Westernized and modernized places in all of Eastern Europe. Yet, it reverted to the kind of ideology that promotes militaristic authoritarianism at best, and tyranny at worst, very quickly, as did its neighbors the Serbs. In Serbia, as in Croatia, this regression was not begun by illiterate peasants, but had its roots among intellectuals at the University of Belgrade, particularly history professors, and highly educated, well-trained professional politicians like Slobodan Milosevic.

But if this is the case in relatively prosperous, heavily Westernized parts of the former communist world, what is it like elsewhere? We have seen the cultural and intellectual basis of Russian tyranny while examining the background of Stalin's rise to power. Now, Russia has emerged from seventy years of isolation more backward than ever, more chaotic than at any time since 1918–1919, its dreams of being a great power equal to the West shattered. Is there any reason to assume that its nationalist intellectuals have been magically transformed into liberals at peace with themselves and the world?

Liah Greenfeld, who is conducting research on this issue, has found that there is every reason for the greatest pessimism because in fact the Russian intelligentsia is no more democratic or liberal than it was in the past.[26] And what about in Islamic Central Asia, where the sense of historical persecution by outside forces is far more justified than in Russia, and where an Islamic revival is competing with secular forces to capitalize on these grievances?

Far from being on the decline, the grievances of the poorer parts of the world against the rich are greater than ever. The Shining Path in Peru, one of the most brutal, centralized, and tyrannical political movements in the world, has a program that might seem to be a perfect replication of all the ideological nightmares of the twentieth century. It claims that Peru's problems are caused by outside imperialism, that total communism is the scientific solution for poverty and inequality, and that violence will cleanse the old society of its foreign sins and corruption. The Shining Path are deeply nationalist and have created a myth of a communal Inca past which they see as being a sound base for creating a future Maoist utopia. Finally, even though they have been able to capitalize on the poverty and isolation of Peru's largely Indian peasantry, on the squalid conditions in its urban slums, and on the real corruption and ineffectiveness of Peru's government and army, the Shining Path were created by and have remained largely led by intellectuals. Their founder, Abimael Guzmán, was a philosophy professor at a provincial university.[27]

And now, along with the persistence of ideologies similar to those of the Khmer Rouge, along with the continuing power in much of the world of resentful nationalism and theories of history that claim that ethnic groups must rid themselves of impurities and dangerous others in order to survive, there has been the adaptation of religious ideologies to these same principles. We have already seen that ultra-nationalism and modern totalitarian methods of government have more to do with Iranian Islamic fundamentalism than any genuinely traditional aspect of Islam, and this applies equally well to the growth of extremism in other parts of the Muslim world. The leaders of this bitterly anti-Western, anti-liberal fundamentalism are not the isolated and illiterate, but sophisticated intellectuals who often have great familiarity with the West. In their calls against parliamentary democracy, against toleration of minorities, and in favor of a return to purity, they are also, in effect, demanding that new tyrannies of certitude be imposed on their people. What is going on in the Sudan is a perfect example.[28] But it is not only Islam that is subjected to such trends.

In India there is a powerful Hinduist revival that demands the extermination, or at least expulsion of India's huge Muslim minority. The contrast between this growing movement and the old Indian political elite that was more secular, more tolerant, and therefore also democratic, is stark. If the Hindu revivalists ever take power, India will be subject to mass killings, internal and external wars, and certainly, to political tyranny.[29]

As this is not a book about contemporary politics, it would not serve much purpose to continue to go through similar examples in many parts of the world, or to point to the revival of crude racism in Western Europe itself as a reason for alarm. The fact is that the causes of tyranny in the twentieth century have not vanished, and in many parts of the world, they are as active as ever. If Marxism is a greatly diminished force, religious tyrannies of certitude are more common than in the past, ethnic intolerance is on the increase, nationalistic *ressentiment* has in no way diminished, and the specter of countless local wars bringing economic and political chaos is greater than at any time since the end of World War II.[30] All this means that the twenty-first century will have its share of tyrannies.

We cannot even say with any assurance that pseudo-science will play a lesser role in the future than in the recent past. Carl Degler has shown that Darwinian thinking has made a very strong comeback in American social thought.[31] This does not mean that Darwinism is either wrong or that in its scientific content it is conducive to tyranny. After all, it would be foolish to blame Charles Darwin for Nazism. But the immense appeal of pseudo-scientific biological thinking on those poorly trained in rigorous scientific thought has been demonstrated before. Now that the worst consequences of extreme biological historicism to date have receded into the past, the revival of a respectable form of social Darwinism, along with the tremendous technological and scientific progress being made in the field of biology, make it likely that this will be the historicism of choice in the early twenty-first century.

Intellectuals in West European and American universities, especially those involved with the humanities and some of the social sciences, have become enamored of new forms of anti-liberal rejection of their Enlightenment tradition. To those outside the world of universities this may appear to be largely irrelevant and amusing. But then, who paid attention to Nietzsche while he was alive?

Twentieth-century tyrannies were defeated because Enlightenment liberalism survived in a very few places, most importantly, in the United States and Great Britain, when much of the rest of the world was overrun by fascism and communism. Liberal societies in Western

Europe and North America are not now likely to fall prey to tyrannical ideological movements, even though these exist. But if their faith in their liberal traditions is weakened, if they lose confidence in the rightness of their solutions to human problems, they will also lose the ability to fight back against tyrannical abuses of power, abuses that may arise again at home and certainly will elsewhere in the world.

NOTES

Chapter 1: On Modern Tyranny

1. Fried, *The Evolution of Political Society*, 71–75, 99–107, 178–184, 213–226; Service, *Origins of the State*, 47–102.
2. Carneiro, "A Theory of the Origin of the State,"; Smith and Young, "The Evolution of Early Agriculture and Culture in Greater Mesopotamia," Service, *Origins*, 166–264.
3. Sagan, *At the Dawn of Tyranny*, xxii, 118, 163–164; Nigel Davies, "Human Sacrifice."
4. Boserup, *Population and Technological Change*, 31–33, 61–62; Harris, *Cannibals and Kings*, 20, 113–143; Adams, "The Origin of Cities."
5. Michael Mann, *The Sources of Social Power*, I, 58, 63–70.
6. Sagan, *Dawn*, 367–376.
7. Ibid., 243, 297.
8. Cited in Chaliand, *Anthologie mondiale de la stratégie*, 680.
9. Cited in Kung-sun Yang, *Lord Shang*, 185, 186, 188.
10. Hobsbawm, *The Age of Revolution*.
11. Spencer, *Principles of Sociology*, Part V, #565, 608.
12. Gilbert, *First World War Atlas*, 158; Kuper, *Genocide*, 105.
13. Gilbert, *Jewish History Atlas*, 88; Rosefielde, "Excess Mortality in the Soviet Union"; "War's End Stirs Memories for China," *New York Times*, August 20, 1985, A3; Woytinski and Woytinski, *World Population*, 44, 47.
14. Rosefielde, "Excess Mortality in the Soviet Union." For those interested in claiming that things were not that bad in Stalin's Soviet Union, see Robert Thurston, "Fear and Belief in the USSR's 'Great Terror' "; and Conquest's scathing answer, "What Is Terror?"
15. Lardy's conservative estimate is from 16 to 28 million: *Agriculture in China's Modern Economic Development*, 41–43, 150–152.
16. Chandler, *The Tragedy of Cambodian History*, 1.
17. Kuper, *Genocide*, 78–79.
18. Jansson, Harris, and Penrose, *The Ethiopian Famine*, try to present an even-handed account that stresses the blame of the pre-revolutionary regime as well as of

foreign aid donors as well as the crude policies of the Ethiopian revolutionary regime. See especially pp. 108–110, 115–123, 126–129, 156, 171–176.

19. Crouch, *The Army and Politics in Indonesia*, 97–157; Anderson and Kahin, eds., *Interpreting Indonesian Politics*; Hefner, *The Political Economy of Mountain Java*, 209–217; Chalk and Jonassohn, *Genocide*, 408–411.

20. Lardy, *Agriculture in Economic Development*, 164-166, 176, 186–187.

21. Many of these examples are discussed by Kuper, *Genocide*, and in Chalk and Jonassohn, *Genocide*.

22. For brief descriptions of most of these examples and accompanying bibliographies, see Wheatcroft, *The World Atlas of Revolutions*. The story about the unspeakable tortures in Bosnia was told to me by a high official of the United Nations in Geneva who had just returned from Bosnia in January 1993.

23. Cited in Chaliand, *Anthologie*, 550.

24. Morgan, *The Mongols*, 93.

25. Barrett, *Caligula*, 213–241.

26. Sagan, *Dawn*, 320.

27. Ibn Batuta, *The Rehla of Ibn Batuta*, translated by Mahdi Husain, 94.

28. Ibid., 97–98.

29. Rizvi, *The Wonder That Was India*, 45–50.

30. Ivo Andrić has a description of impaling in his great novel *The Bridge on the Drina*, 48–55. On Vlad the Impaler and the stories about him, see Chirot, *Social Change in a Peripheral Society*, 38.

31. Wedgwood, *Thirty Years' War*.

32. McNeill, *The Human Condition*.

33. Goldstone, *Revolution and Rebellion in the Early Modern World*, chapter 1, reviews the theories of revolution in agrarian societies.

34. Aristotle, *Politics*, McKeon edition, 1252–1253.

35. Liss, *Isabel the Queen: Life and Times*, shows the deeply ideological and transforming ideology of th Spanish Inquisition in the fifteenth century, as well as the pre-occupation with "blood" and race.

36. Cohn's classic work, *The Pursuit of the Millennium*, remains the best study of this aspect of medieval and early modern Christianity.

37. Cecil Roth, *A History of the Marranos*, 145.

38. Riley-Smith, *The Crusades: A Short History*.

39. This and what follows about the history of nationalism in Europe is a summary of Greenfeld's *Nationalism*.

40. Fritz Stern, *The Politics of Cultural Despair*; Greenfeld, *Nationalism*, part IV.

41. Greenfeld, *Nationalism*, Part III.

42. Greenfeld and Chirot, "Nationalism and War," paper prepared for the National Academy of Sciences, Washington, DC, 1991.

43. Popper, *The Poverty of Historicism*.

44. Fukuyama, for example, in *The End of History*.

Chapter 2: Moderation Abandoned

1. Cited in Hamerow, *German Unification*, 204–205.

2. Hobsbawm and Ranger, eds., *The Invention of Tradition*; Hobsbawm, *The Age of Empire*, 165–191.

3. Schumpeter, *Capitalism, Socialism and Democracy*, 23.

4. Chirot, *Social Change in the Modern Era*, 59–65.

5. Mitchell, *European Historical Statistics*, 389.

6. Hobsbawm, *The Age of Empire*, 35–46.

7. Ibid., 36

8. Chirot, *Social Change*, 86–92.

9. Burke, *Reflections on the Revolution in France*, 160.

10. Marx, *Manuscripts of 1844*, in *Early Writings*, 323–324.

11. Mosse, *Crisis of German Ideology*, 16.

12. Cited in La Capra, *History, Politics, and the Novel*, 37–38.

13. Rogger and Weber, eds., *The European Right*, 71–74, 89–90.

14. In Mendes-Flohr and Reinharz, eds., *The Jew in the Modern World*, 276–277.

15. Marx, "On the Jewish Question," in *Early Writings*, 239.

16. On the numbers of Jews in Europe, see Mendes-Flohr and Reinharz, eds., *The Jew*, 525–535; Gilbert, *Jewish History Atlas*; Mitchell, *European Historical Statistics*; Gilbert, *Illustrated Atlas of Jewish Civilization*.

17. Sorel, *Violence*, 246–247.

18. Nietzsche, in *The Philosophy of Nietzsche*, 565–567, 802.

19. Again, I am using the theory developed by Greenfeld in *Nationalism*.

20. Greenfeld, *Nationalism*, Part I.

21. Weber, *The Protestant Ethic*; Merton, "Puritanism, Pietism and Science" and "Science and Economy of 17th Century England."

22. Greenfeld, *Nationalism*, Part II.

23. Ibid., Part IV.

24. Cited in Mendes-Flohr and Reinharz, *The Jew*, 257.

25. Lilley, "Progress and the Industrial Revolution" and Landes, *Unbound Prometheus*, 269–276.

26. Hamerow, *Restoration, Revolution, Reaction*.

27. Fritz Stern, *The Politics of Cultural Despair*, 291–292.

28. Gunst, "Agrarian Systems of Central and Eastern Europe."

29. Von Laue, "Imperial Russia."

30. Kochanowicz, "The Polish Economy and the Evolution of Dependency"; Norman Davies, *Heart of Europe*, 291–306.

31. Blum, *Lord and Peasant in Russia*, 135–151, 219–246; Billington, *The Icon and the Axe*, 47–77.

32. Greenfeld, *Nationalism*, Part III.

33. Greenfeld, "The Formation of the Russian National Identity: The Role of Status Insecurity and *Ressentiment*."

34. Leikina-Svirskaya, *Intelligentsia v Rossii*, 70, cited in Katz and Wagner, "Introduction" to Chernyshevsky, *What Is to Be Done?* 2.

35. Frank, *Dostoevsky*, 310–347; Schapiro, *Russian Studies*, 192–196, 214–219.

36. Schapiro, *Russian Studies*, 329–330.

37. Ulam, *In the Name of the People*, 35–36.

38. Schapiro, *Turgenev*; Schapiro, *Russian Studies*, 321–343.

39. Gay, *Enlightenment* I, 127–159; II, 126–187.

40. Kelly, *Descent of Darwin*, 10–18.

41. For an interesting comparison of their systems, and their antecedents, see Manuel and Manuel, *Utopian Thought*, parts VI and VII.

42. Berlin, *Four Essays*, 51–57.
43. Ibid., 77–78.
44. Kelly, *Descent*, 30.
45. Hobsbawm, *The Age of Capital*, 285.
46. Fritz Stern, *Despair*, 63–65.
47. Popper, *The Poverty of Historicism*, 3.
48. Cited in Kelly, *Descent*, 124.
49. Kelly, *Descent*, 125.
50. Ibid., 37.
51. Kaye, *Social Meaning of Biology*, 37–39.
52. Higham, *Strangers in the Land*; Hofstadter, *Social Darwinism*; Zmarzlik, "Social Darwinism in Germany," cited in Holborn, *Republic to Reich*, 441–448.
53. Chirot, *Social Change*, 74–84.
54. Cited in Fieldhouse, "Imperialism," 120.
55. Luxemburg, *The Accumulation of Capital*.
56. Lenin, *Imperialism*.
57. Hobsbawm, *The Age of Empire*, 102, 121.
58. Rosenberg, *Imperial Germany*, 69; Judt, *Marxism and the French Left*, 106.
59. Judt, *Marxism and the French Left*, 19–20.
60. Guenther Roth, *Social Democrats*, 163–192.
61. Szamuely, *The Russian Tradition*, 169–170.
62. Ibid., chapters 14–15.
63. Ulam, *In the Name of the People*, 392–393; Louis Fischer, *Lenin*, 17.
64. Levy, *The Downfall of the Anti-Semitic Political Parties in Imperial Germany*.
65. Cited in Wolfe, *Three Who Made a Revolution*, 558.
66. Fest, *Hitler*, 67–86.
67. Ibid., 115–124.
68. Ulam, *Stalin*, 129–157.
69. Ibid., 234–288.
70. Lenin, *Imperialism*.
71. Mitchell, *European Historical Statistics*, 179–181, 223–225, 271; Bureau of the Census, *Historical Statistics of the United States*, 667, 692–694.
72. Hobsbawm, *The Age of Empire*, 56–73.
73. Schumpeter, "The Sociology of Imperialisms."
74. Sked, *The Decline and Fall of the Habsburg Empire*, especially chapter 6; on the tangled diplomatic story, see A. J. P. Taylor, *The Struggle for Mastery in Europe 1848–1918*, especially 518–528.
75. Fritz Fischer, *Germany's Aims in the First World War*.
76. Kennedy, *The Rise of Anglo-German Antagonism 1860–1914*, in particular 464–470.
77. Vyvyan, "The Approach of the War of 1914," 149.
78. Kennan, *The Fateful Alliance*.
79. Chirot, *Social Change*, 76–80.
80. Asquith in Parsons, ed., *Men Who March Away*, 41.
81. Chirot, *Social Change*, 136; Gilbert, *First World War Atlas*, 52–61, 90–93, 100–103, 158–159.
82. Sassoon in Parsons, ed., *Men Who March Away*, 86.

83. Gilbert, *First World War Atlas*, 144–155.
84. Butler, "The Peace Settlement of Versailles."

Chapter 3: In the Beginning Was the Word

1. Nolte, *Three Faces of Fascism*, 289, 291.
2. Fest, *Hitler*, 24–35.
3. Ulam, *Stalin*, 16–27.
4. Ibid., 100, 158.
5. Fest, *Hitler*, 238.
6. William Carr, *Hitler*, 2–3.
7. Ibid., 4, 6.
8. Langer, *The Mind of Hitler*, 153–233, 240–241.
9. Waite, *Psychopathic God*, particularly 55–63.
10. Speer, *Inside the Third Reich*, 83–101.
11. Mannheim, "The Problem of Generations"; and more recently Hyman, *Political Socialization*; or Delli Carpini, "Age and History: Generations and Social Political Change."
12. Schorske, *Fin-de-Siècle Vienna*, chapter 2.
13. Deak, "Pacesetters of Integration: Jewish Officers in the Habsburg Monarchy."
14. Beller, *Vienna and the Jews*, chapter 2.
15. Schorske, *Vienna*, 119, and more generally, 116–146.
16. Fest, *Hitler*, 76–77.
17. Holborn, *A History of Modern Germany*, 578.
18. Ibid., 509–515.
19. Ibid., chapter 10.
20. Fest, *The Face of the Third Reich*, 145.
21. Neumann, *Behemoth*, 199–218; the Marxist thesis has been pushed furthest by Abraham in *The Collapse of the Weimar Republic: Political Economy and Crisis*.
22. Turner, *German Big Business and the Rise of Hitler*.
23. See Fest's *The Face of the Third Reich*, chapters on Schirach, Heydrich, and Speer, as well as Speer's own account of how he joined the Nazis in *Inside the Third Reich*, 3–31.
24. Merkl, *Political Violence under the Swastika*, 14.
25. Ibid., 13.
26. Holborn, *History*, 533–606.
27. Gay, *Weimar Culture*, 81–86; Spengler, "Prussianism and Socialism."
28. Kershaw, *Hitler*, 16–18.
29. Flood, *Hitler*, 131, 268.
30. See the extract in Mendes-Flohr and Reinharz, eds., *The Jew in the Modern World*, 296–299, that contains these themes.
31. Hitler, *Mein Kampf*, 269–270; Fest, *The Face of the Third Reich*, 165–168.
32. Hitler, *Mein Kampf*, 307.
33. Ibid., 325–236.
34. See the family tree in Bullock, *Hitler*, 6–7.
35. Waite, *Psychopathic God*, 151–152; William Carr, *Hitler*, 125.
36. Hitler, *Mein Kampf*, 642–643.

37. Ibid., 637–638.
38. Most notoriously, A. J. P. Taylor in *The Origins of the Second World War*.
39. Hitler, *Mein Kampf*, 431–433.
40. Ibid., 577.
41. Ibid., 543.
42. "Introduction" to ibid., xi.
43. Ringer, ed., *German Inflation of 1923*.
44. Mitchell, *European Historical Statistics*, 390; Aldcroft, *From Versailles to Wall Street*, 31–33.
45. Thomas Mann tries to convey the disorientation of the solid middle classes at that time in his story "Disorder and Early Sorrow."
46. Angress, *The Stillborn Revolution*.
47. Fest, *Hitler*, 160–220.
48. Bullock, *Hitler*, 104–105.
49. Fest, *Hitler*, 221–237.
50. Fest, *The Face of the Third Reich*, 86–93; Bullock, *Hitler*, 107–108.
51. Bullock, *Hitler*, 104–106.
52. Görlitz, *History of the German General Staff*; Craig, *The Germans*, 238–239; Hamerow, *Social Foundations of German Unification*, 60.
53. Moore, *Social Origins of Dictatorship and Democracy*, chapters 7 and 8; Meinecke, *The German Catastrophe*, 12–15.
54. Deak, *Beyond Nationalism*.
55. Meinecke, *Catastrophe*, 12.
56. Carsten, *The Reichswehr and Politics*, 103–250.
57. J. P. Stern, *Hitler*, 52, 104.
58. Fest, *The Face of the Third Reich*, 252.
59. Müller, *Hitler's Justice*, 10.
60. Maddison, "Economic Policy and Performance in Europe, 1913–1970," 460–463.
61. Mitchell, *European Historical Statistics*, 65–68.
62. Hamilton, *Who Voted for Hitler?* 476.
63. Ibid., 462–464.
64. Rosenberg, *Imperial Germany*, 10–14; Guenther Roth, *Social Democrats*, chapter 5.
65. All figures are from Hamilton, *Who Voted for Hitler?*, 476.
66. Ibid., 88–89, 122, 387.
67. Ibid., 90, 108–110, 121, 218–219.
68. Kater, *The Nazi Party*, 12, 241, 272 (figure 10).
69. Guenther Roth, *Social Democrats*.
70. Hamilton, *Who Voted for Hitler?* 350, 356, 377.
71. Arendt, *The Origins of Totalitarianism*, 315–318; Mann, "Disorder and Early Sorrow," 189.
72. Tucker, *Stalin*, I, 76.
73. Ibid., I, 71–75, 78.
74. Ibid., I, 79–82.
75. Shanin, *Russia, 1905–1907*, II, 103–107.
76. Tucker, *Stalin*, I, 123–126.
77. Shanin, *Russia*, II, 218.
78. Ibid., II, 21–23, 219.

79. Ibid., II, 219–222; Schapiro, *Russian Studies*, 253–260.
80. Schapiro, *Russian Studies*, 261.
81. Ibid., 262.
82. Bonnell, *Roots of Rebellion*, 393–434.
83. Haupt and Marie, *Makers of the Russian Revolution*, 65–75.
84. Medvedev, *Let History Judge*, 31–32.
85. Schapiro, *The Communist Party of the Soviet Union*, 126.
86. Medvedev, *Let History Judge*, 28.
87. Tucker, *Stalin*, I, 137–141.
88. Bottomore, ed., *Dictionary of Marxist Thought*, 344, 346–349.
89. Stalin, "Marxism and the National Question," in *Works*, II, 300–381; Tucker, *Stalin*, I, 154–156.
90. Stalin, *Works*, II, 364.
91. Wolfe, *Three Who Made a Revolution*, 582.
92. Tucker, *Stalin*, I, 107–108, 158–159; Ulam, *Stalin*, 548–549.
93. Avrich, *Russian Rebels*; Szamuely, *The Russian Tradition*.
94. Shanin, *Russia*, II, 200.
95. Mitchell, *European Historical Statistics*, 40–43.
96. Rogger, "Russia," 473.
97. Bonnell, *Roots of Rebellion*, 106–110.
98. Shanin, *Russia*, II, 122–123.
99. Ibid., II, 248–249.
100. Hobsbawm, *Primitive Rebels*.
101. Shanin, *Russia*, II, 243–245.
102. McDaniel, *Autocracy, Capitalism, and Revolution in Russia*, 142.
103. Shanin, *Russia*, II, 207.
104. Ibid., II, 234.
105. Schapiro, *Russian Studies*, 95.
106. Rogger, "Russia," 483–499.
107. Trotsky, *The Russian Revolution*, 52–53.
108. Solzhenitsyn's novel, *August 1914*, describes the mess.
109. Gilbert, *First World War Atlas*, 104, 158.
110. Fitzpatrick, *Russian Revolution*, 38–40.
111. McDaniel, *Autocracy*, 313–319.
112. Ibid., 222, 322–326.
113. Ibid., 378–379.
114. Haupt and Marie, *Makers of the Russian Revolution*, contains brief biographies of each of the important Bolshevik leaders.
115. Ibid., 100–105.
116. Fitzpatrick, *Russian Revolution*, 69.
117. Schapiro, *History of the Communist Party*, 187.
118. Shanin, *Russia*, II, 200–201.
119. Ibid., II, 202.
120. Schapiro, *The Communist Party*, 186; also Tucker, *Stalin*, I, 197–210.
121. Avrich, *Kronstadt 1921*.
122. Tucker, *Stalin*, I, 240.
123. Cited in ibid., 261–262.
124. Tucker, *Stalin*, I, 270–277.

125. Lewin, *Lenin's Last Struggle*.

126. Cited in Tucker, *Stalin*, I, 190–192.

127. Deutscher, *Stalin*.

128. Tucker, *Stalin*, I, 289–290.

129. Ibid., 300–301; Cohen, *Bukharin*, 160–212; Erlich, *The Soviet Industrialization Debate*.

130. Tucker, *Stalin*, I, 393.

131. Cohen, *Bukharin*, 147–148.

132. Tucker, *Stalin*, I, 322–323, 386.

133. Von Laue, *Why Lenin? Why Stalin?* 186–187; Tucker, *Stalin*, I, 389.

134. That, at least, is what Trotsky argued. See Mitrany, *Marx against the Peasants*, 69–70.

135. Trotsky, *The Revolution Betrayed*, 273.

136. Hayward, *Writers in Russia 1917–1978*, 86–87; Zamiatin, *We*.

137. E. H. Carr, *Studies in Revolution*, 219–220.

Chapter 4: Death, Lies, and Decay

1. Cited in Fest, *Hitler*, 746–747.

2. Ulam, *Stalin*, 684, 730–731.

3. Ibid., 700–714.

4. Djilas, *Conversations with Stalin*, 151–153, saw signs of senility in Stalin as early as 1948.

5. Ulam, *Stalin*, 735–739; Volkogonov, *Stalin*, 517–529.

6. Webb, *The Truth about Russia*, 16–19.

7. Webb, *The Truth*, 44, 68.

8. Davis, *Behind Soviet Power*, 59.

9. Conquest, *Harvest of Sorrow*, 3, 301.

10. Shanin, *The Awkward Class*.

11. Conquest, *The Great Terror*, 708–709.

12. Tolstoy, *The Secret Betrayal*, 408–409.

13. Conquest, *Terror*, 710–713.

14. Antonov-Ovseyenko, *The Time of Stalin*, 205–213.

15. Moscow, February 4, 1989, cited in Hosking, *The Awakening of the Soviet Union*, 164.

16. Quoted in Conquest, *Harvest*, 248–249.

17. Cited in Maier, *The Unmasterable Past*, 30.

18. Maier, *Past*, 75–75

19. Cited in J. P. Stern, *Hitler*, 223–224, 250.

20. Trotsky, *The Revolution Betrayed*, 273.

21. Fest, *Hitler*, 449–480.

22. Ibid., 561–563.

23. Padfield, *Himmler*, 227.

24. Kennan, *Russia and the West under Lenin and Stalin*, 322.

25. Hitler, *Hitler's Table Talk 1941–43*, 72, 299–300.

26. A. J. P. Taylor, *English History 1914–1945*, 435.

27. Fest, *Hitler*, 596.

28. Ibid., 601–603; A. J. P. Taylor, *English History*, 454, 458.

29. Kennan, *Russia and the West*, 324–336; Fest, *Hitler*, 601–603.
30. Fest, *Hitler*, 641–644.
31. Ibid., *Hitler*, 607.
32. Shirer, *Berlin Diary*, 189–193.
33. Maier, *Past*.
34. Mayer, *Why Did the Heavens Not Darken?*
35. Deak, "Jews, Catholics, Nazis, and the Holocaust"; Browning, "The Holocaust Distorted."
36. Dawidowicz, *The War against the Jews*, 118–119.
37. Burleigh and Wippermann, *The Racial State*, 136–153; Browning, "The Decisions Concerning the Final Solution," 101.
38. Hitler, *Hitler's Table Talk*, 624; Speer, *Inside the Third Reich*, 306.
39. Cited in Mayer, *Why Did the Heavens*, 208.
40. Jäckel, *Hitler*, 51–54.
41. Turner, ed., *Hitler: Memoirs of a Confidant*, 71.
42. Padfield, *Himmler*, 228, 306.
43. Kershaw, *The 'Hitler Myth'*, 243–248.
44. Padfield, *Himmler*, 333.
45. Browning, *Ordinary Men*, 9.
46. Dawidowicz, *The War*, 200.
47. Marrus and Paxton, "The Nazis and the Jews in Occupied Western Europe," 183.
48. Cited in Padfield, *Himmler*, 238–239.
49. Mendes-Flohr and Reinharz, eds., *The Jew*, 520.
50. Burleigh and Wippermann, *Racial State*.
51. Ibid., 125, 196–197, 304–308.
52. Adam, "Nazi Actions Concerning the Jews," 88–89.
53. Browning, *Ordinary Men*, 50.
54. Marrus and Paxton, "The Nazis and the Jews," 183; Burleigh and Wippermann, *Racial State*, 103–104.
55. Fest, *The Face of the Third Reich*, 100–102.
56. Padfield, *Himmler*, 20–24.
57. Cited in Mendes-Flohr and Reinharz, eds., *The Jew*, 506.
58. Arendt, *Eichmann in Jerusalem*, 26–27, 100–101.
59. Cited in Fest, *The Face of the Third Reich*, 115.
60. Browning, *Ordinary Men*, 52.
61. That is the whole theme of Browning's *Ordinary Men*.
62. Dawidowicz, *The War*; Wiesel, *Night*; Fink, *A Scrap of Time*.
63. Hilberg, "The Statistics," 170–171, and his definitive study, *The Destruction of the European Jews*, III, 1201–1220.
64. Dawidowicz, *The War*, 149; Maier, *Past*, 75.
65. Gross, *Polish Society under German Occupation*.
66. For example, see Paxton, *Vichy France*.
67. Hitler, *Hitler's Table Talk*, 332.
68. *The Dialogues of Plato*, "The Republic," Book 8, I, 826.
69. Laqueur, *Stalin*, 34–37.
70. Ibid., 35; Ken Jowitt calls the Stalinist period a "castle regime" for this reason in "Moscow 'Centre,'" 306.
71. Cited in Tucker, *Stalin*, II, 85.

72. Laqueur, *Stalin*, 34, quotes Nikolaevsky, *The Letter of an Old Bolshevik*, to emphasize the point. Though there is controversy about this document, the consensus is that it reflects much of what was going on at that time within the mind of high Party people, and in particular, Bukharin, the "Old Bolshevik" whose views are supposedly expressed. See Liebich, " 'I Am the Last,'" and Tucker, "On the 'Letter of an Old Bolshevik'."

73. Tucker, *Stalin* II, chapter, 3, 266, 317–318.

74. Conquest, *Terror*, 730–733; Vaksberg, *Vyshinski*, 85.

75. Alliluyeva, *Twenty Letters to a Friend*.

76. Tucker, *Stalin*, II, 215–217.

77. Ibid., II, 218.

78. Ibid., II, 238–254; Conquest, *Kirov*, 22–36.

79. Medvedev, *Let History Judge*, 866.

80. Conquest, *Kirov*.

81. For details, see Conquest, *Terror*; Tucker, *Stalin*, II; Ulam, *Stalin*; Volkogonov, *Stalin*; Medvedev, *Let History Judge*.

82. Cited in Vaksberg, *Vyshinski*, 71–72.

83. Tucker, *Stalin*, II, 333–335, Volkogonov, *Stalin*, 331–335.

84. Tucker and Cohen, eds., *The Great Purge Trial*.

85. Ulam, *Stalin*, 389; also Tucker, *Stalin*, II, 547.

86. Tucker, *Stalin*, II, 102–103, 482.

87. Cited in *Time*, January 1, 1940, 16.

88. Getty, *Origins of the Great Purges*.

89. Tucker, *Stalin*, II, 447.

90. Djilas, *Conversations with Stalin*, 105.

91. Volkogonov, *Stalin*, 155.

92. Laqueur, *Stalin*, 165.

93. See Walter Schellenberg's memoirs, *The Labyrinth*; Laqueur, *Stalin*, 85–100.

94. Tucker, *Stalin*, II, 514–515.

95. Laqueur, *Stalin*, 91.

96. Arendt, *Totalitarianism*, 126.

97. On the inefficiency of the camps, see Swianiewicz. *Forced Labour and Economic Development*.

98. For some details, see Ginzburg, *Journey into the Whirlwind*, and of course, Solzhenitsyn, *The Gulag Archipelago*.

99. Conquest, *Terror*.

100. See, for example, Constante, *L'Evasion silencieuse*, on the Romanian version or London, *The Confession*, on the Czech version.

101. Medvedev, *Let History Judge*, 490, 491.

102. Browning, *Ordinary Men*, chapter 18.

103. Cited in Toranska, *"Them": Stalin's Polish Puppets*, 206.

104. Dahrendorf, *Society and Democracy*, 381–396.

105. Schoenbaum, *Hitler's Social Revolution*, 77–158; Grunberger, *Social History of the Third Reich*, 167–202.

106. Grunberger, *Social History*, 267–284.

107. Speer, *Inside the Third Reich*, cites numerous examples.

108. From a speech he gave in 1937, in Mosse, ed., *Nazi Culture*, 11–16.

109. Medvedev, *Let History Judge*, 445–449; Shostakovich, *Testimony*; Mandelstam, *Hope Abandoned*.
110. For some interesting parallels in totalitarian Arab architecture and art, see al-Khalil, *Art, Vulgarity, and Responsibility in Iraq*.
111. Sagan, *At the Dawn of Tyranny*, 319–343.
112. Zinoviev, *Radiant Future*.
113. Medvedev, *Let History Judge*, 617–623.
114. Peukert, *Inside Nazi Germany*, 76.
115. Jäckel, *Hitler*, 94.
116. Fest, *Hitler*, 710.
117. Medvedev, *Let History Judge*, 868.
118. Peukert, *Inside Nazi Germany*, 46.
119. Hosking, *Awakening*, 16.
120. Solzhenitsyn, *Gulag*, especially 565–587.
121. Herling-Grudzinski, *The World Apart*.
122. Medvedev, *Let History Judge*, 836–846.
123. See Vaksberg, *The Soviet Mafia*; and the wonderful review essay on the topic written by David Remnick, "Dons of the Don."
124. Grunberger, *Social History*, 90–107; On Göring, see Speer, *Inside The Third Reich*, 322.
125. Speer, *Inside The Third Reich*, 199.
126. Ibid., Part 3.
127. Djilas, *Conversations*, 147–161, 174–185.
128. Medvedev, *Let History Judge*, 861–63.
129. Chirot, *Crisis of Leninism*; Hosking, *Awakening*.

Chapter 6: Imagined Egalitarian Hells

1. Judt, *Marxism and the French Left*, 195–196.
2. Wakeman, *History and Will*, 68–69.
3. Jowitt, "Moscow 'Centre,'" 324–327; MacFarquhar, *The Origins of the Cultural Revolution*, II, 255–292.
4. Kiernan, *How Pol Pot Came to Power*, 258–260, 297–302.
5. Chandler, *The Tragedy of Cambodian History*, 149–150.
6. Lardy, "Is China Different?"
7. Perry, *Rebels and Revolutionaries in North China*, 10–15; Wakeman, *Fall of Imperial China*, 105–106; and more generally, Elvin, *The Pattern of the Chinese Past*.
8. Goldstone, *Revolution and Rebellion*.
9. Wakeman, *Fall of Imperial China*, 55–69.
10. Spence, *The Search for Modern China*, 147–164; Graham, *The China Station*.
11. Cited in Shih, *Taiping Ideology*, 6.
12. Wakeman, *Fall of Imperial China*, 153–154; I heard Stevan Harrell in a discussion with Ben Kiernan suggest the utility of comparing the similar ideologies of the Taiping and the Khmer Rouge.
13. Perry, *Rebels and Revolutionaries*, 96–151.
14. Spence, *The Search for Modern China*, 250–256, 271, 285.
15. Nathan, *Peking Politics*; Eastman, *The Abortive Revolution*.

16. Schwarz, *Chinese Enlightenment*; 39–46; Wakeman, *Fall of Imperial China*, 199–202.
17. Wakeman, *History and Will*, 99.
18. Ibid., 130–134.
19. Schwarz, *Chinese Enlightenment*, 12–23.
20. Ibid., 102–115.
21. Ibid., 145–176.
22. Ibid., 170–194.
23. Dirlik, *The Origins of Chinese Communism*, 156–190; and more generally, Dirlik, *Revolution and History*.
24. Schram, *The Political Thought of Mao Tse-tung*, 28–29.
25. Meisner, *Li Ta-chao and the Origins of Chinese Marxism*.
26. Wakeman, *History and Will*, 63.
27. Snow, *Red Star over China*.
28. Salisbury, *The New Emperors*, 22.
29. Johnson, *Peasant Nationalism*, 1–70; Perry, *Rebels and Revolutionaries*, 208–247.
30. Salisbury, *New Emperors*, 84–95.
31. For the general story, see Eastman, *Seeds of Destruction* and Levine, *Anvil of Victory*; also Johnson, *Peasant Nationalism*, 176–187.
32. Most explicitly in Skocpol, "Old Regime Legacies and Communist Revolutions in Russia and China."
33. North and Pool, "Kuomintang and Communist Elites," 381–382.
34. Salisbury, *New Emperors*, 130–131; Spence, in *Search for Modern China*, 517, estimates a million deaths during this period.
35. Schram, *Political Thought*, 78–83; MacFarquhar, *Origins*, II, 3–4.
36. Moore, *Soviet Politics—The Dilemma of Power*, 182–188, 236–246.
37. MacFarquhar, *Origins*, I, 57–74.
38. Schram, *Political Thought*, 171–172.
39. Ibid., 339, 343–346, 350–351.
40. Ibid., 162–63.
41. Ibid., *Political Thought*, 374.
42. MacFarquhar, *Origins*, I, 118–121.
43. Dittmer, *China's Continuous Revolution*, 48–49.
44. Ibid., 54.
45. Cited in Schram, *Political Thought*, 308–309.
46. Dittmer, *Continuous Revolution*, 30.
47. Ibid., 65.
48. Heng and Shapiro, *Son of the Revolution*, 8–9.
49. Salisbury, *New Emperors*, 137.
50. MacFarquhar, *Origins*, II, 21–24.
51. Cited in ibid., II, 53.
52. Hanson, "Gorbachev," 37–41.
53. MacFarquhar, *Origins*, II, 88–90, 128.
54. Cited in Dittmer, *Continuous Revolution*, 32.
55. Chan, Madsen, and Unger, *Chen Village*, 94–96.
56. MacFarquhar, *Origins*, II, 124–125.
57. Ibid., 79–82.
58. Cited in ibid., 103.

59. Salisbury, *New Emperors*, 218–219; Terrill, *White-Boned Demon*, 152–153.
60. Heng and Shapiro, *Son of the Revolution*, 162; MacFarquhar, *Origins*, II, 116.
61. Dittmer, *Continuous Revolution*, 35, especially note 59.
62. Lardy, *Agriculture in Economic Development*, 41–43, 150–152; Salisbury, *New Emperors*, 166–167; MacFarquhar, *Origins*, II, 330.
63. Chan, Madsen, and Unger, *Chen Village*, 25–26.
64. MacFarquhar, *Origins*, II, 126–127, 154–155.
65. Ibid., 128, 144–159.
66. Ibid., 173–174, 216; Dittmer, *Continuous Revolution*, 34–36.
67. MacFarquhar, *Origins*, II, 322–325.
68. Cited in Dittmer, *Continuous Revolution*, 37.
69. MacFarquhar, *Origins*, II, 336.
70. White, *Policies of Chaos*, 7; Anne Thurston, *Enemies of the People*, xv–xix.
71. Dittmer, *Continuous Revolution*, 79.
72. Anne Thurston, *Enemies of the People*, 22.
73. Lee, *The Politics of the Chinese Cultural Revolution*, 11–21.
74. Salisbury, *New Emperors*, 276–277; and Terrill, *White-Boned Demon*, especially 237–301.
75. White, *Policies of Chaos*, 225; the quote is by Salisbury, *New Emperors*, 222–223.
76. Lee, *The Politics of the Chinese Cultural Revolution*, 4–5, 26.
77. Ibid., 17, 27–29.
78. Cited in White, *Policies of Chaos*, 226.
79. White, *Policies of Chaos*, 227.
80. Cited in ibid., 228.
81. Ibid., 222.
82. Cited in Lee, *The Politics of the Chinese Cultural Revolution*, 70.
83. Lee, *The Politics of the Chinese Cultural Revolution*, 68–75.
84. Heng and Shapiro, *Son of the Revolution*, 46.
85. Hinton, *Hundred Day War*.
86. White, *Policies of Chaos*, 241–243.
87. Salisbury, *New Emperors*, 268–275.
88. Anne Thurston, *Enemies of the People*, has many representative accounts.
89. Salisbury, *New Emperors*, 320–321.
90. Cited in Heng and Shapiro, *Son of the Revolution*, 73.
91. Kristof, "A Tale of Red Guards and Cannibals," A-6.
92. Dittmer, *Continuous Revolution*, 96, 174–181; Salisbury, *New Emperors*, 292–306.
93. Chan, Madsen, and Unger, *Chen Village*, 141–166.
94. Salisbury, *New Emperors*, 287–288.
95. Ibid., 340–374; Terrill, *White-Boned Demon*, 374–406.
96. Wakeman, *History and Will*, 7.
97. Based on his article, "Genocide in Cambodia, 1975–1979."
98. Chandler, *Brother Number One*, 4.
99. Vickery, *Cambodia 1975–1982*, 184–188.
100. Chandler, *Brother*, 4.
101. Chandler, *Brother*, 1.
102. Shawcross, *Sideshow*.
103. Chandler, *Brother*, 6.

104. Coedès, *The Indianized States of Southeast Asia*; Steinberg, ed., *In Search of Southeast Asia*.

105. Kiernan, *How Pol Pot*, 1–3.

106. On Vietnam at this time, see Scott, *The Moral Economy of the Peasant*, 120–130.

107. Kiernan, *How Pol Pot*, 2–7, 18–21.

108. Ibid., 23–33.

109. Benedict Anderson, *Imagined Communities*, 106–111.

110. See various issues of *La Pensée*, particularly Sédov, "La société angkorienne et le problème du mode de production asiatique."

111. Kiernan, "Myth, Nationalism, and Genocide in Cambodia"; Groslier, *Angkor, hommes, et pierres*.

112. Vickery, *Cambodia*, 1–2.

113. Chandler, *The Tragedy*, 6.

114. Kiernan, "Myth"; Chandler, "Seeing Red," 50–51.

115. Cited in Kiernan, "Wild Chickens," 164.

116. Kiernan, "Wild Chickens," 165–166.

117. Kiernan, *How Pol Pot*, 169–235.

118. On Indonesia, see Crouch, *The Army and Politics in Indonesia*.

119. Kiernan, *How Pol Pot*, 118–124.

120. Chandler, "Seeing Red," 35–36, 44.

121. Chandler, *Brother*, 231 (note 5); Kiernan, "Wild Chickens," 166.

122. Chandler, "Seeing Red," 44.

123. Chandler, *Brother*, 7–25; Chandler, *The Tragedy*, 51.

124. See Banac, *With Stalin against Tito*.

125. Kiernan, *How Pol Pot*, 120–121; Chandler, *Brother*, 30–31; Vickery, *Cambodia*, 275–276.

126. Vickery, *Cambodia*, 266–268.

127. Chandler, *Brother*, 57.

128. Ibid., 74–77.

129. Kiernan, *How Pol Pot*, 258–260, 297–302.

130. Ibid., 302–368; Chandler, *The Tragedy*, 197–235; Shawcross, *Sideshow*, especially 209–235.

131. Shawcross, *Sideshow*, 270, 276.

132. Ibid., 344–364.

133. Ibid., 365–367.

134. Kiernan, *How Pol Pot*, 368–393, 412–421.

135. Chandler, *The Tragedy*, 246–261.

136. Vickery, *Cambodia*, 81–82, 175.

137. Ibid., 164; Chandler, *The Tragedy*, 237.

138. Chandler, *The Tragedy*, 238–246, 261–265.

139. Kiernan, "Wild Chickens," 142–143, 146, 148, 153.

140. Kiernan, "Myth."

141. Cited in Shawcross, *Sideshow*, 383.

142. Chandler, *Brother*, 138.

143. Kiernan, *How Pol Pot*, picture 18, between 286 and 287; Chandler, *The Tragedy*, 293.

144. Chandler, *Brother*, 56–57.

145. Ibid., 130.

146. Cited in Kiernan, "Wild Chickens," 147.

147. Kiernan, "Wild Chickens," 138, 197.

148. Vickery, *Cambodia*, 124.

149. Chandler, *Brother*, 2.

150. Ibid., 158–159.

151. Vickery, "Democratic Kampuchea," 104.

152. Chandler, *The Tragedy*, 246.

153. Cited in Kiernan, "Myth."

154. Cited in Shawcross, *Sideshow*, 389.

155. Ibid., 391.

156. Chandler, *The Tragedy*, 312–316.

157. Griffith, *Albania and the Sino-Soviet Rift*, 9–34.

Chapter 7: Little Stalins?

1. Chirot, "What Happened in Eastern Europe in 1989?"

2. On the decline of the left, see Lipset, "No Third Way."

3. Cited in Puddington, *Failed Utopias*, 264.

4. Chirot, "What Happened"; there is a vast literature on this by now. Some of the major works are summarized in Brand, "Why the Soviet Economy Failed."

5. Cumings, *The Origins of the Korean War*, II, 296–297.

6. Cumings, *Origins*, I, 32–38, 397–403; II, 350–376; Dae-sook Suh, The Korean Communist Movement.

7. Jung-en Woo, *Race to the Swift*.

8. Jowitt, "Moscow 'Centre,'" 320.

9. Shafir, *Romania*, 25–27.

10. Cumings, *Origins*, I, 267–381; II, 268–290, 569–621.

11. Gi-wook Shin, *Social Change and Peasant Protest in Colonial Korea*.

12. Jowitt, "Political Innovation in Rumania," 133–135.

13. Castellan, *Histoire de la Roumanie*, 123.

14. Tismaneanu, "The Tragicomedy of Romanian Communism," 360–364.

15. Chirot, "Social Change in Communist Romania," 465; and more generally on this period, Ionescu, *Communism in Rumania*.

16. Constante, *L'Evasion Silencieuse*; Dumitriu, *Incognito*.

17. Jowitt, *Revolutionary Breakthroughs*, 7.

18. Chirot, "Social Change in Communist Romania," 490–491.

19. *Time*, March 18, 1966. The upbeat story is on 34–48.

20. Shafir, *Romania*, 192. I was given many glowing accounts of what a wonderful man Nixon was by high Romanian Communist Party people in 1970.

21. Personal conversation with Herseni in April 1970.

22. Shafir, *Romania*, 107, 121.

23. Stahl, *Traditional Romanian Village Communities*; Radulescu-Motru, *Românismul*; Verdery, *National Ideology under Socialism*, 30–40.

24. Cited in Verdery, *National Ideology*, 38.

25. Ibid., 49, 57.

26. Verdery, *National Ideology*, 49, 57, 209, 210. For those who read Romanian, Stahl's *Eseuri Critice* are the best exposé of the obscurantism favored by Blaga, Eliade, and others like them.

27. I heard him say this to a small gathering of American specialists on Romanian history and Romanian historians in Cluj in August 1979.
28. Castellan, *Histoire de la Roumanie*, 4.
29. Cited in Verdery, *National Ideology*, 129.
30. Cumings, *Origins*, II, 314.
31. Kim Kyong-Dong, "The Distinctive Features of South Korea's Development," 206–207.
32. Ibid., 208–209.
33. Cumings, *War and Television*, 214–217.
34. Cumings, *Origins*, II, 313.
35. Ibid., II, 332.
36. Asiatic Research Center, *International Conference on the Problems of Modernization in Asia*.
37. Vogel, *The Four Little Dragons*.
38. Cited in Cumings, *War and Television*, 230.
39. Verdery, *National Ideology*, 118; Tismaneanu, "The Tragicomedy," 342–353; Jowitt, "Moscow 'Centre,'" 320–321; Cumings, *Origins*, II, 333.
40. Karnoouh, *L'Invention du peuple*, 188–189.
41. Verdery, *National Ideology*, 113–115.
42. Kligman, "When Abortion Is Banned."
43. Cited in Cumings, *Origins*, II, 291, 319–320.
44. Chirot, "Ideology, Reality, and Competing Models of Development in Eastern Europe," 406–411.
45. Cumings, *War and Television*, 194–195.
46. Cumings, "Corporatism in North Korea."
47. Love, "Raúl Prebisch and the Origins of the Doctrine of Unequal Exchange"; Schmitter, "Reflections on Mihail Manoilescu."
48. Chirot, "The Corporatist Model and Socialism"; Chirot, "Social Change in Communist Romania."
49. Esherick and Wasserstrom, "Acting Out Democracy"; Perry, "Casting a Chinese 'Democracy' Movement."
50. See Asia Watch, *Human Rights in Korea.* The portion on North Korea is authored by Cumings, and the one on South Korea by Palais.
51. Kligman, "The Politics of Reproduction in Ceausescu's Romania," 364, 372–379.
52. George Schöpflin, "Rumanian Nationalism."
53. Kligman, "The Politics of Reproduction," 379–389.
54. Ibid., 390–406.
55. This was part of the general process of socialist "homogenization." See Kligman, "The Politics of Reproduction," 366–371. The plan to remove the old from Bucharest was reported in a Radio Free Europe broadcast in 1985, but was never carried out.
56. Chirot, "Romania: Ceausescu's Last Folly"; Kligman, "The Politics of Reproduction," 369.
57. Hunya, "New Developments in Romanian Agriculture," 265–271.
58. Shafir, "Political Culture and the Romanian Revolution of December 1989."
59. Verdery, *National Ideology*, chapters 5, 6, and 7.
60. Castellan, *Histoire de la Roumanie*, 124–125.
61. Cumings, *War and Television*, 195.

62. See Asia Watch, Human Rights in Korea, section authored by Palais.
63. Vogel, *The Four Little Dragons*.
64. Woo, *Race to the Swift*, particularly 85–106.
65. On the original differences between Marxism and nationalism, see Szporluk, *Communism and Nationalism*, particularly 152–168.
66. Manea, "Happy Guilt: Mircea Eliade, Fascism, and the Unhappy Fate of Romania," 33.
67. Janos, *The Politics of Backwardness in Hungary*, 315.
68. Rothschild, *Return to Diversity*, 204–207; Bauer, "Hungarian Economic Reform."
69. Gilberg, *Nationalism and Communism in Romania*, 209–225.
70. Djilas, *Conversations with Stalin*, 133–136.
71. Griffith, *Albania and the Sino–Soviet Rift*, 9–34.
72. Halliday has collected and written introductions to some of Hoxha's writings in *The Artful Albanian: The Memoirs of Enver Hoxha*.
73. Merit, "Albania," *International Herald Tribune*, October 10, 1992, 4.
74. Gross has explained how World War II and Nazi control actually contributed substantially to what happened later under communist rule in "Social Consequences of War."

Chapter 8: Little Hitlers?

1. Chirot, *Social Change*, 102–103.
2. Lewis, *The Crisis of Argentine Capitalism*, 33–78; Peter Smith, *Argentina and the Failure of Democracy*, 4–22.
3. Waisman, "Argentina: Autarkic Industrialization and Illegitimacy," 64–69.
4. Shumway, *The Invention of Argentina*.
5. Peter Smith, *Failure of Democracy*, 96–97.
6. Rock, *Argentina*, 202–203, 207, 215–216; Crassweller, *Perón*, 78; Potash, *The Army and Politics in Argentina, 1928–1945*; Ibarguren, *La Historia que he vivido*.
7. Rouquié, *Pouvoir militaire*, 158.
8. Cited in Crassweller, *Perón*, 51, 68.
9. Solberg, *Oil and Nationalism*.
10. Rouquié, *Pouvoir militaire*, 168–182.
11. Peter Smith, *Failure of Democracy*, 97.
12. Rock, *Argentina*, 231–233.
13. Peter Smith, *Failure of Democracy*, 98–99.
14. Chirot and Hall, "World System Theory"; Bunge, *Una Nueva Argentina*; Scalabrini Ortiz, *Historia de los ferrocarriles argentinos*.
15. Lewis, *The Crisis*, 87–89, 275–277; Waisman, "Argentina," 74.
16. Lewis, *The Crisis*, 48–49; Diaz Alejandro, *Essays in the Economic History of the Argentine Republic*, 443.
17. Lewis, *The Crisis*, 117–123; Smith, *Failure of Democracy*, 101; Fillol, *Social Factors*, 77.
18. Peter Smith, *Failure of Democracy*, 102.
19. Rock, *Argentina*, 247.
20. Crassweller, *Perón*, 81–90; Rouquié, *Pouvoir militaire*, 331–336.
21. Rock, *Argentina*, 245–248.
22. Crassweller, *Perón*, 114–120.

23. Rock, *Argentina*, 249–258.
24. Cited in Rouquié, *Pouvoir militaire*, 350.
25. Cited in Rock, *Argentina*, 258.
26. Cited in Lewis, *The Crisis*, 144.
27. Peter Smith, *Failure of Democracy*, 104.
28. Crassweller, *Perón*, 136–182.
29. Lewis, *The Crisis*, 144–203.
30. Crassweller, *Perón*, 261–263.
31. Navarro, "Evita's Charismatic Leadership," 62.
32. Crassweller, *Perón*, 198, 209–217.
33. Ibid., 347.
34. Ibid., 248–260, 269–276.
35. Ibid., 288–289; Lewis, *The Crisis*, 223.
36. Lewis, *The Crisis*, 274–276.
37. Peter Smith, *Failure of Democracy*, 108.
38. Rouquié, *Pouvoir militaire*, 434–539.
39. Waisman, "Argentina," 72–80.
40. Lewis, *The Crisis*, 276–286.
41. Ibid., 376–378, 385, 403, 407–408. For details, see Gillespie, *Soldiers of Perón: Argentina's Montoneros.*
42. Rouquié, *Pouvoir militaire*, 576.
43. Ibid., 602–614.
44. Lewis, *The Crisis*, 432.
45. Ibid., 433–435.
46. Ibid., 436–437.
47. Crassweller, *Perón*, 370–371; Timerman, *Prisoner without a Name*, 44–45.
48. Timerman, *Prisoner without a Name*, 26.
49. Dworkin, "Introduction," to *Nunca Más*, xvi–xvii.
50. *Nunca Más*, 10.
51. Lewis, *The Crisis*, 449.
52. *Nunca Más*, 21–23, 44, 45, 69–71.
53. Ibid., 286–320.
54. Ibid., 442–445.
55. Timerman, *Prisoner without a Name*, 130.
56. Weschler, *A Miracle, a Universe*, 120–121; Perelli, "Settling Accounts with Blood Memory: The Case of Argentina," 421.
57. Rouquié, *Pouvoir militaire*, 668.
58. Weschler, *A Miracle*, 119–120.
59. Rock, *Argentina*, 370–371; Lewis, *The Crisis*, 448–457; Rouquié, *Pouvoir militaire*, 666–677.
60. Perelli, "Settling Accounts," 426–427.
61. Cited in ibid., 422.
62. Perelli, "Settling Accounts," 423.
63. *Nunca Más*, 272–283.
64. Rock, *Argentina*, 373–380.
65. Pipes, *Greater Syria*, 25.
66. Kedourie, *England and the Middle East*; Silverfarb, *Britain's Informal Empire*, 3–10.

67. Khoury, *Syria and the French Mandate*; Batatu, *The Old Social Classes*.
68. Khoury, *Syria*, 397–433.
69. Zuwiyya Yamak, *The Syrian Social Nationalist Party*, 11; Gibb, "Some Considerations on the Sunni Theory of the Caliphate," in Gibb, *Studies*, 141.
70. Ahmed, *The Intellectual Origins of Egyptian Nationalism*.
71. Zuwiyya Yamak, *The Syrian Social Nationalist Party*, 53–110.
72. The classic work on the Alawites remains Weulersse's two volumes, *Le Pays des Alaouites*.
73. Cited in al-Khalil, *Republic of Fear*, 195–196.
74. Ibid., 189–190.
75. Ibid., 191, 226.
76. al-Khalil, *Republic of Fear*, xiv.
77. Seale, *Asad*, 49–50; Ma`oz, *Asad: The Sphinx of Damascus*, 24–27.
78. Seale, *Asad*, 316–338, 492–495; Middle East Watch, *Syria Unmasked*, 17–21.
79. Pipes, *Greater Syria*, 193.
80. Batatu, *The Old Social Classes and the Revolutionary Movements of Iraq*, 40.
81. Silverfarb, *Britain's Informal Empire*, 11–22.
82. Marr, *The Modern History of Iraq*, 29–94; Ibid., 13–15, 35–47.
83. al-Khalil, *Republic of Fear*, 151–160.
84. Ibid., 58–59; Batatu, *Old Social Classes*, 981–982; Miller and Mylroie, *Saddam and Crisis*, 31.
85. Marr, *History of Iraq*, 213.
86. Batatu, *Old Social Classes*, 1085–1088.
87. al-Khalil, *Republic of Fear*, 242–257.
88. Ibid., 97.
89. Miller and Mylroie, *Saddam and Crisis*, 24–25, 38–40.
90. Middle East Watch, *Human Rights in Iraq*, 10–13.
91. Miller and Mylroie, *Saddam and Crisis*, 26–28, 44–45.
92. That is the whole theme of Patrick Seale's political biography, *Asad*.
93. On Iraq, see al-Khalil's *The Monument*; the observations about Syria are mine, and correspond to the descriptions in Seale, *Asad*.
94. Cited in Middle East Watch, *Human Rights in Iraq*, 15.
95. Partner, "In Saddam's Arms."
96. Middle East Watch, *Human Rights in Iraq*, 4–7.
97. al-Khalil, *Republic of Fear*, 276–289.
98. Middle East Watch, *Human Rights in Iraq*, 83.
99. Ibid., 69–96.
100. Miller and Mylroie, *Saddam and Crisis*, 147–153; Middle East Watch, *Human Rights in Iraq*, 102–114.
101. Middle East Watch, *Human Rights in Iraq*, 47.
102. Ibid., 39–68.

Chapter 9: An Inadvertent Catastrophe

1. Lintner, "The Secret Mover"; Shenon, "Burmese, After Years of Terror, Hope Things May Soon Change for the Better."
2. Lintner, "Diversionary Tactics"; Lintner, "The Secret Mover."

3. Lintner, *Outrage*; Lintner, "Mock Turtle"; David I. Steinberg, *The Future of Burma*.

4. Lintner, "The Odd Couple."

5. Coedès, *Indianized States*; Hall, *Burma*, chapter I.

6. Robert Taylor, *The State in Burma*, chapter 1.

7. David J. Steinberg ed., *In Search of Southeast Asia*, chapter 1.

8. Chaudhuri, *Trade and Civilisation in the Indian Ocean*; Hall, *Burma*, 34-37, 66; Trager, *Burma*, 11.

9. David J. Steinberg ed., *In Search*, 97–99.

10. Harvey, *History of Burma*, 303.

11. Furnivall, *Colonial Policy and Practice*, 17; Leach, *Political Systems of Highland Burma*, 238–246.

12. David J. Steinberg, ed., *In Search*, 100–102.

13. Ibid., 103–105; Hall, *Burma*, 108–117.

14. Keyes, *Thailand*, 39–61.

15. Hall, *Burma*, 124–130.

16. Furnivall, *Colonial Policy and Practice*, 62–70.

17. Ibid., 71.

18. Ibid., 99.

19. Ibid., 100–101.

20. Fenichel and Huff, *The Impact of Colonialism on Burmese Economic Development*, 45–46, 52–53.

21. Furnivall, *Colonial Policy and Practice*, 109–110.

22. For examples, see Migdal, *Peasants, Politics, and Revolution*; and more generally, Marx, *Capital*, I, chapters 26–29.

23. For example, see Hillel Levine, *Economic Origins of Antisemitism*, on the rise of anti–Semitism in Poland.

24. Furnivall, *Colonial Policy and Practice*, 116–123; Suu Kyi, *Freedom From Fear and Other Writings*, 102; Fenichel and Huff, *The Impact of Colonialism*, 44, 51–52.

25. Hall, *A History of South-East Asia*, 405–406, 409, 432–433; Beller, *Vienna and the Jews*; Horowitz, *Ethnic Groups in Conflict*.

26. Furnivall, *Colonial Policy and Practice*, 119.

27. Adas, *The Burma Delta*, particularly 127–153; Furnivall, *Colonial Policy and Practice*, 109–116; Fenichel and Huff, *The Impact of Colonialism*, 54.

28. Furnivall, *Colonial Policy and Practice*, 111.

29. Ibid., 196–197.

30. Scott, *The Moral Economy of the Peasant*, 89.

31. Furnivall, *Colonial Policy and Practice*, 56–58. 103, 105–106, 109.

32. Ibid., 303–312, 546–547.

33. Ibid., 184.

34. Orwell, *Burmese Days*.

35. Robert Taylor, *The State in Burma*, 150–151.

36. Trager, *Burma*, 44–45.

37. Cited in Keyes, "Buddhist Economics and Buddhist Fundamentalism in Burma and Thailand."

38. Cited in Lintner, *Outrage*, 30.

39. Ibid., 131.

40. Lintner, *Outrage*, 133–135.
41. Trager, *Burma*, 54–57.
42. Adas, *The Burma Delta*, 206–207.
43. Trager, *Burma*, 58–63.
44. Guyot, "Communal Conflict."
45. Maung Maung, *Burma and General Ne Win*, 134–136; Trager, *Burma*, 62–63; Suu Kyi, *Freedom from Fear*, 20–22.
46. David J. Steinberg et al., *In Search*, 337–338; Keyes, *Thailand*, 68.
47. Trager, *Burma*, 59.
48. Lintner, *Outrage*, 41.
49. Silverstein, *Burma*, 20–21.
50. Trager, *Burma*, 97–131.
51. Silverstein, *Burma*, 78, 81.
52. Ibid., 26–28.
53. Lintner, *Outrage*, 87; Maung Maung, *Burma and General Ne Win*, 306–307.
54. Maung Maung, *Burma and General Ne Win*, 26–49.
55. Ibid., 73–85.
56. Silverstein, *Burma*, 44–46.
57. Ibid., 79.
58. Trager, *Burma*, 187–189.
59. Silverstein, *Burma*, 76–79; Ibid., 190–191.
60. Donald Smith, *Religion and Politics in Burma*, 25.
61. Ibid., 117–136, 235–280.
62. Ibid., 320–322; Silverstein, "Minority Problems in Burma since 1962," 52–53.
63. Silverstein, *Burma*, 80; Lehman, Preface, *Military Rule in Burma since 1962*, 1–5.
64. Cited in David I. Steinberg, *The Future of Burma*, 27–28.
65. Cited in Robert Taylor, *The State in Burma*, 297.
66. Ibid., 297–299.
67. Trager, *Burma*, 204–208.
68. Lintner, *Outrage*, 59–60.
69. David I. Steinberg, *The Future of Burma*, 164–165.
70. Ibid., 37–38, 137–145, 151, 154.
71. Robert Taylor, *The State in Burma*, 351–353.
72. David I. Steinberg, *The Future of Burma*, 116.
73. Ibid., 105, 113.
74. Lintner, *Outrage*, 94–95.
75. David I. Steinberg, *The Future of Burma*, 78.
76. Keyes, "Buddhist Economics"; Martin Smith, *Burma: Insurgency and the Politics of Ethnicity*, 24–27; E. F. Schumacher, *Small Is Beautiful*, 48–56.
77. Maung Maung Gyi, "Foreign Policy of Burma since 162," 12, 24; Lintner, *Outrage*, 89; Liang, *Burma's Foreign Relations*, 83–84, 163, 223–226.
78. Lintner, *Outrage*, 87–88.
79. Robert Taylor, *The State in Burma*, 300–304; Lintner, *Land of Jade*, xv.
80. Lintner, *Land of Jade*, 172.
81. Suu Kyi, *Freedom from Fear*, 169.
82. David I. Steinberg, *The Future of Burma*, 25.
83. Selth, *Death of a Hero*.
84. Lintner, *Outrage*, 74–76.

85. Ibid., 78–82.
86. Ibid., 94.
87. Ibid., 95–97.
88. Ibid., 9–23.
89. Ibid., 98–100.
90. Ibid., 122–146.
91. Ibid., 147–195.
92. Ibid., 196–215; Suu Kyi, *Freedom from Fear*, 235.
93. Martin Smith, *Burma*, 26, 412–419; Suu Kyi, *Freedom from Fear*, 236–237.
94. Martin Smith, *Burma*, 419–425.
95. Keyes, *Thailand*, 61–66, 141–144.
96. McDonald, "Partners in Plunder," 16–18.
97. Handley, "An Uneasy Calm," "March of Democracy," and "The Markets Speak," 10–13; Shenon, "Thai Legislators Curb Role of Military," A3.

Chapter 10: Race and Corruption on the Island of Hispaniola

1. Logan, *Haiti and the Dominican Republic*, 10–12.
2. Rotberg, *Haiti*, 32; Logan, *Haiti and Dominican Republic*, 85–86; See, *L'Evolution commerciale et industrielle de la France*, 227–229.
3. Curtin, *The Atlantic Slave Trade: A Census*.
4. James, *Black Jacobins*, chapters 1–2; Rotberg, *Haiti*, 33–36.
5. Nicholls, *From Dessalines to Duvalier*, 25; Césaire, *Toussaint Louverture*, 31.
6. James, *Black Jacobins*, 36–42.
7. Ibid., 43–46.
8. See, among others, the interesting psychoanalytic explanation of the origin and nature of Southern racism in the United States in Dollard, *Caste and Class in a Southern Town*; and the classic Myrdal, *An American Dilemma*, II, 558–569.
9. James, *Black Jacobins*, tells the story well, as does Césaire, *Toussaint*.
10. Rotberg, *Haiti*, 43–51.
11. Ibid., 52–56.
12. Ibid., 57–58.
13. Césaire, *La Tragédie du Roi Christophe*; Rotberg, *Haiti*, 60, 181.
14. Rotberg, *Haiti*, 65–82.
15. Ibid., 83–88.
16. Ibid., 89, 98–99; Hopkins, *Latin America and Caribbean Contemporary Records*, IV, *1984–1985*, 987.
17. Rotberg, *Haiti*, 103–108; Nicholls, *From Dessalines to Duvalier*, 146.
18. Buell, "The American Occupation of Haiti"; Logan, *Haiti and the Dominican Republic*, 54–60, 118–132.
19. See Wilson's speeches on Latin America and China in Commager, ed., *Documents*, II, (8th edition), 85, 87–93, 97–98, and the Treaty with Haiti of 1916, 112–114; DeConde, *A History of American Foreign Policy*, 426–429; Rostow, *The United States in the World Arena*, 23–24.
20. Rotberg, *Haiti*, 109–140; Schmidt, *The American Occupation of Haiti, 1915–1934*, especially 137.
21. Rotberg, *Haiti*, 140–146; Kilson and Hill, *Apropos of Africa*, 68–75.
22. Nicholls, *From Dessalines to Duvalier*, 152–158.

23. Ibid., 164.
24. Ibid., 167–170.
25. Rotberg, *Haiti*, 162–166; Ibid., 194–196.
26. Logan, *Haiti and the Dominican Republic*, 201–202.
27. Rotberg, *Haiti*, 173–176.
28. Ibid., 177–196.
29. Ibid., 215; Greene, "Nightmare Republic."
30. Ferguson, *Papa Doc, Baby Doc*, 38–41.
31. See Laguerre, *Voodoo and Politics in Haiti*.
32. Rotberg, *Haiti*, 217.
33. Ibid., 217–218, 226–228.
34. Ibid. *Haiti*, 208, 224.
35. Laguerre, *Voodoo and Politics*.
36. Nicholls, *From Dessalines to Duvalier*, 221–232, the quote is on p. 233.
37. Rotberg, *Haiti*, 227–230.
38. Ibid., *Haiti*, 240–242.
39. Cited in Rotberg, *Haiti*, 234.
40. Nicholls, *From Dessalines to Duvalier*, 236–237.
41. Rotberg, *Haiti*, 300–306.
42. Hopkins, *Latin America*, I, *1981–1982*, 554, 586, 806–807.
43. Ibid., 554, 586; Rotberg, *Haiti*, 258–270, 395.
44. Rotberg, *Haiti*, 332, 353.
45. Ferguson, *Papa Doc, Baby Doc*, 60–89.
46. Hopkins, *Latin America*, I, *1981–1982*, 807; II, *1982–1983*, 698–710; III, *1983–1984*, 808–831; IV, *1984–1985*, 727–741. Articles titled "Haiti," on those pages are written by Jean-Claude Garcia-Zamor for II, and by Michael S. Hooper for III and IV.
47. Hopkins, *Latin America*, III, 809–810; IV, 727–29, articles by Hooper, "Haiti."
48. Crassweller, *Trujillo*, 325.
49. Castillo de Aza, *Trujillo, Benefactor of the Church*, 5.
50. Ibid., 7–8.
51. Crassweller, *Trujillo*, 79–80.
52. Enzensberger, *Raids and Reconstructions*, 112.
53. Galíndez, *La Era de Trujillo*, 373–381; Crassweller, *Trujillo*, 154–156.
54. Ferguson, *Papa Doc, Baby Doc*, 66; cited in Crassweller, *Trujillo*, 149–163.
55. Rodman, *Quisqueya*, 130; Crassweller, *Trujillo*, 26–29.
56. On Pepin, see Burr, "The Carlovingian Revolution," 586–587.
57. Logan, *Haiti and the Dominican Republic*, 189–193.
58. Hopkins, *Latin America*, I, 807; II, 965; also World Bank, *World Development Report 1991*, 204–205.
59. Galíndez, *La Era*, 421–427.
60. Ibid., 348–366; Crassweller, *Trujillo*, 127–128.
61. Ornes, *Trujillo, Little Caesar of the Caribbean*, 211–226, 234–268; Diederich, *Trujillo: The Death of the Goat*.
62. Crassweller, *Trujillo*, 137–142.
63. Galíndez, *La Era*, 11–15.
64. Cited in Crassweller, *Trujillo*, 141.
65. Crassweller, *Trujillo*, 428–430.

66. Herr, *The Eighteenth-Century Revolution in Spain*.
67. Rodman, *Quisqueya*, 19–29; Logan, *Haiti and the Dominican Republic*, 30–31.
68. Rodman, *Quisqueya*, 30–58; Logan, *Haiti and the Dominican Republic*, 32–33.
69. Logan, *Haiti and the Dominican Republic*, 34.
70. Rodman, *Quisqueya*, 71–81; Ibid., 40–42.
71. DeConde, *Foreign Policy*, 284–286.
72. Welles, *Naboth's Vineyard*, I, 444.
73. Rodman, *Quisqueya*, 91–105; Logan, *Haiti and the Dominican Republic*, 48–52.
74. DeConde, *Foreign Policy*, 386–388, 427–428.
75. Crassweller, *Trujillo*, 32–37.
76. Rodman, *Quisqueya*, 122–125.
77. Galíndez, *La Era*, 27–28; Crassweller, *Trujillo*, 39–51.
78. Crassweller, *Trujillo*, 68–72.
79. Ibid., 57–58, 104; Logan, *Haiti and the Dominican Republic*, 69.
80. Logan, *Haiti and the Dominican Republic*, 13–14.
81. Nicholls, *From Dessalines to Duvalier*, 167.
82. Bosch, *Trujillo: Causas de una tiranía sin ejemplo*; Crassweller, *Trujillo*, 78, 82–83.
83. Galíndez, *La Era*, 287–292, 342–347; Crassweller, *Trujillo*, 90–107.
84. Crassweller, *Trujillo*, 111–119, 311–312.
85. Ibid., 290–291.
86. Diederich, *The Death of the Goat*, 3–9.
87. Ornes, *Trujillo*, 309–338.
88. Crassweller, *Trujillo*, 334–339, 409–425.
89. Ibid., 361–366.
90. Ibid., 430–431; Diederich, *The Death of the Goat*, 40–72.
91. Crassweller, *Trujillo*, 436–446; Diederich, *The Death of the Goat*, 189–264; Rodman, *Quisqueya*, 155–162.

Chapter 11: Colonialism, Resentment, and Chaos

1. See Mannoni, *Prospero and Caliban*.
2. Fanon gave voice to the rage this ambivalence could produce. See his *Wretched of the Earth* and, particularly, *Black Skin, White Masks*, 83–108.
3. *Newsweek*, December 19, 1977, 42–44.
4. Kalck, *Histoire de la République Centrafricaine*, 16, 73, 103–125, 177–211.
5. See Coquery-Vidrovitch, *Le Congo au temps des grandes compagnies concessionaires*; and Kalck, *Histoire*, 179–220.
6. Kalck, *Histoire*, 16, 221–231.
7. Ibid., 231–254.
8. Ibid., *Histoire*, 235–238.
9. Ibid., 244.
10. Weinstein, *Éboué*.
11. Kalck, *Histoire*, 273–274; O'Toole, *The Central African Republic*, 32. On the general process of decolonization in Africa, see Wallerstein, *Africa: The Politics of Independence*.
12. *L'Express*, May 7, 1959; Kalck, *Histoire*, 290–302; Chafford, *Les Carnets secrets de la décolonisation*, 171.

13. O'Toole, *C.A.R.*, 40–44.
14. See Kelley's book on neighboring Chad, *A State in Disarray: Conditions of Chad's Survival*, 88–98, for a description of how the French have held together their colonial empire long after independence.
15. Kalck, *Histoire*, 306, 312–314.
16. O'Toole, *C.A.R.*, 45. I witnessed this phenomenon myself working in another former French colony, Niger, from 1964 to 1966.
17. Kalck, *Histoire*, 320–330; O'Toole, *C.A.R.*, 44–48.
18. O'Toole, *C.A.R.*, 48–49.
19. 29. Murray, ed., *Cultural Atlas of Africa*, 187.
20. On indirect rule in the colonies, see Mair, *Native Policies in Africa*.
21. Mitchell, *International Historical Statistics: Africa and Asia*, 38–42, 692–698.
22. This is the same issue that came up already in the chapter on Burma and the inevitability of growing ethnic conflict in colonial "plural societies." See Chapter 9.
23. Cited in Sathyamurthy, *The Political Development of Uganda*, especially, 96, from Kagwa, *The Kings of Buganda*. More generally, see Sagan's argument in *At the Dawn of Tyranny*, discussed above in Chapter 1, on the brutality of rule in early states. Buganda is one of Sagan's key examples.
24. Mazrui, *Soldiers and Kinsmen in Uganda*, 201.
25. Sathyamurthy, *Political Development*, 138–181, 207; Ibid., 36–41, 58–64.
26. Murray, ed., *Cultural Atlas of Africa*, 25, 187; See Sathyamurty, *Political Development*, 71–88, on political differences in pre-colonial Uganda.
27. Sathyamurthy, *Political Development*, 243–245.
28. Mazrui, *Soldiers and Kinsmen*, 234–236; Sathyamurthy, *Political Development*, 245.
29. Sathyamurthy, *Political Development*, 295–346. See Apter, *The Political Kingdom in Uganda*, for a more sympathetic interpretation of the liberal policies of the reforming British governor in the 1950s, Andrew Cohen.
30. Decalo, *Coups and Army Rule in Africa*, 150–164.
31. Ibid., 169–171.
32. Omara-Otunnu, *Politics and the Military in Uganda*, 98–100. See also, *Private Eye*, April 27, 1979, *Washington Post*, February 24, 1978.
33. Sathyamurthy, *Political Development*, 495–511.
34. Ibid., 611–612.
35. Omara-Otunnu, *Politics and the Military*, 87.
36. Ibid., 102–108.
37. Jackson and Rosberg, *Personal Rule in Black Africa*, 254–255.
38. Omara–Otunnu, *Politics and the Military*, 119.
39. Ibid., 121–122.
40. Sathyamurthy, *Political Development*, 689, shows the growth of the extra–legal, barter economy.
41. Omara-Otunnu, *Politics and the Military*, 113–117, 131–134.
42. Decalo, *Psychoses of Power: African Personal Dictatorships*, 24; Jackson and Rosberg, *Personal Rule*, 260.
43. Jackson and Rosberg, *Personal Rule*, 258–264.
44. *The Guardian*, April 14, 1979, "Carnage exposed at Amin's torture base," 1.
45. Ibid., 1, 22.

46. Ibid., 15.

47. *The Guardian*, April 21, 1979, 6.

48. *Jeune Afrique*, April 11, 1979, 12–13; an account of the war between Tanzania and Uganda is to be found in a book by *The Guardian*'s reporters there, Avirgan and Honey, *War in Uganda: The Legacy of Idi Amin*. On Amin's current life, see Anderson and Van Atta, "Idi Amin Living High in Saudi Arabia," *Washington Post*, March 31, 1991, B7.

49. Decalo, *Coups and Army Rule in Africa*, 190.

50. Decalo, *Psychoses*, 116–119.

51. Croce, *History of the Kingdom of Naples*, 41.

52. Young and Turner, *The Rise and Decline of the Zairian State*, particularly 168–182; and more recently, see the exposé written by Braeckman, *Le Dinosaure*.

53. On the American role in bringing him to power, see Weissman, *American Foreign Policy in the Congo, 1960–1964*.

54. O'Toole, *C.A.R.*, 48.

55. Cited in *Jeune Afrique*, October 10, 1979, 43.

56. O'Toole, *C.A.R.*, 51.

57. *Le Canard Enchaîné*, a French satirical weekly, claimed that Giscard was more interested in local women and diamonds for himself than in hunting wild game. See also, *Le Matin*, Sept 25, 1980, *Asie Afrique*, March 2, 1980; *Jeune Afrique*, 31 January, 1979, 18–19.

58. *New York Times*, October 24, 1986, A3.

59. Comte, "L'Heure de l'examen de conscience," 1–2.

60. O'Toole, "Jean-Bédel Bokassa; Neo-Napoleonic Cult or Traditional African Ruler?" 95–106.

61. Césaire, *La Tragédie du Roi Christophe*, 28.

62. *Newsweek*, December 19, 1977, 42–43; *Jeune Afrique*, October 3, 1979, 28–29.

63. *Jeune Afrique*, 23 May, 1979, 18–19; 6 June, 1979, 16–17; 20 June, 1979, 14–15; 11 July, 1979, 17; 18 July, 27.

64. Ibid., October 3, 1979, 24–40.

65. *Le Monde*, September 21, 1979, 1, 4.

66. Ibid., September 26, 1979, 3.

67. Ibid., September 27, 1979, 3.

68. Ibid., September 29, 1979, 6.

69. Dahmani, *Jeune Afrique*, "Editorial," October 10, 1979, 7.

70. *New York Times*, October 24, 1986, A3.

71. *Jeune Afrique*, 14 March, 1979, 71.

72. Brooke, *New York Times*, " 'Not a Saint' Bokassa Says at His Trial," December 16, 1986, A3, and December 17, 1986, A4.

73. *New York Times*, June 13, 1987, A5, and March 1, 1988, A3.

Chapter 12: Some Propositions, Lessons, and Predictions about Tyranny

1. Chirot, "The Rise of the West"; Anderson, *Lineages of the Absolutist State*.

2. Bailyn, *The Ideological Origins of the American Revolution*, 274–277.

3. Aristotle, *Politics*, McKeon edition, 1221, 1247–1252.

4. Hayek, *The Road to Serfdom*.

5. Burckhardt, *The Civilization of the Renaissance in Italy*, 68.

6. Greenfeld, *Nationalism*, 15–17; and more generally, Scheler, *Ressentiment*.

7. Glenny, *The Fall of Yugoslavia*, 31–97.

8. For that attack see Hartz, *The Liberal Tradition in America*, particularly 56–57, but in general throughout the book. This is as good an expression of the danger of a "tyranny of the majority" as any. It should be obvious that I believe that, if compared to the real tyrannies of our century, this is one form that I consider relatively benign.

9. Sivan, *Radical Islam*, 118–119.

10. Abrahamian, " 'Ali Shari'ati: Ideologue of the Iranian Revolution," and Keddie, "Iranian Revolution in Comparative Perspective."

11. Sagan, *At the Dawn of Tyranny*.

12. Berlin, *Four Essays on Liberty*.

13. I thank Paul Heyne for showing me that both the political right and left hate the idea that money is so powerful because it is so impersonal.

14. Cited in Cumings, *War and Television*, 230.

15. J. P. Stern, *Hitler: The Führer and the People*, 52–55.

16. Rothschild, *Pilsudski's Coup d'État*; on Ataturk, see the favorable interpretation of his rule in the essays published by Rustow, ed., in *Political Modernization in Japan and Turkey*.

17. Hanson, "Gorbachev."

18. Machiavelli, *The Prince and the Discourses*, 87–89.

19. Ibid., 175.

20. Manuel and Manuel, *Utopian Thought in the Western World*, 414–415.

21. Rawls, *A Theory of Justice*, 356.

22. Beljo, ed., *Historical Maps of Croatia*, 32.

23. Kaplan, "Croatianism."

24. For example, see Stokes, ed., *From Stalinism to Pluralism*, 226–228.

25. Glenny, *The Fall of Yugoslavia*, 1–30.

26. Greenfeld, "Kitchen Debate."

27. Articles by Michael Smith, "Shining Path's Urban Strategy"; de Wit and Gianotten, "The Center's Multiple Failures"; Isbell, "Shining Path and Peasant Responses in Rural Ayacucho."

28. For anyone doubting the grim outlook in the Sudan, it is useful to read the recent story by Bonner, "Letter from Sudan," 70–83.

29. McDonald, "Saffron Nationalism," 22.

30. Jowitt, *New World Disorder*.

31. Degler, *In Search of Human Nature*.

BIBLIOGRAPHY

Abraham, David. *The Collapse of the Weimar Republic: Political Economy and Crisis*. Princeton: Princeton University Press, 1981.

Abrahamian, Ervand. "|'Ali Shari'ati: Ideologue of the Iranian Revolution." In Edmund Burke, III and Ira M. Lapidus, eds., *Islam, Politics, and Social Movements*. Berkeley and Los Angeles: University of California Press, 1988.

Adam, Uwe Dietrich. "Nazi Actions Concerning the Jews between the Beginning of World War II and the German Attack on the USSR." In François Furet, ed., *Unanswered Questions: Nazi Germany and the Genocide of the Jews*. New York: Shocken, 1989.

Adams, Robert M. "The Origin of Cities." In C. C. Lamberg-Karlovsky, ed., *Old World Archeology: Foundations of Civilization*. San Francisco: W. H. Freeman/Scientific American, 1972.

Adas, Michael. *The Burma Delta: Economic Development and Social Change on an Asian Rice Frontier*. Madison: University of Wisconsin Press, 1974.

Ahmed, Jamal Mohammed. *The Intellectual Origins of Egyptian Nationalism*. Oxford: Oxford University Press, 1960.

Aldcroft, Derek H. *From Versailles to Wall Street 1919–1979*. Berkeley and Los Angeles: University of California Press, 1981.

Alliluyeva, Svetlana. *Twenty Letters to a Friend*. New York: Harper and Row, 1967.

Anderson, Benedict R. *Imagined Communities: Reflections on the Origin and Spread of Nationalism*. London: Verso, 1983.

Anderson, Benedict R., and Audrey Kahin, eds. *Interpreting Indonesian Politics*. Ithaca: Cornell University Press, 1982.

Anderson, Jack, and Dale Van Atta, "Idi Amin Living High in Saudi Arabia." *Washington Post*, March 31, 1991, p. B-7.

Anderson, Perry. *Lineages of the Absolutist State*. London: New Left Books, 1974.

Andric, Ivo. *The Bridge on the Drina*. Chicago: University of Chicago Press, 1977.

Angress, Werner. *The Stillborn Revolution*. Princeton: Princeton University Press, 1963.

Antonov-Ovseyenko, Anton. *The Time of Stalin: Portrait of a Tyranny*. New York: Harper Colophon, 1981.

Apter, David E. *The Political Kingdom in Uganda: A Study in Bureaucratic Nationalism*. Princeton: Princeton University Press, 1961.

Arendt, Hannah. *Eichmann in Jerusalem*. New York: Viking, 1963.
——. *The Origins of Totalitarianism*. New York: Meridian, 1958.
Aristotle. *The Basic Works of Aristotle*. Edited by Richard McKeon. New York: Random House, 1941.
Asia Watch. *Human Rights in Korea*. (South Korean section by James Palais; North Korean section by Bruce Cumings.) New York: Human Rights Watch, 1986.
Asiatic Research Center, ed. *International Conference on the Problems of Modernization in Asia*. Seoul: Asiatic Research Center, 1965.
Avirgan, Tony, and Martha Honey. *War in Uganda: The Legacy of Idi Amin*. London: Zed Press, 1982.
Avrich, Paul. *Kronstadt 1921*. Princeton: Princeton University Press, 1970.
——. *Russian Rebels 1600–1800*. New York: Shocken, 1972.
Bailyn, Bernard. *The Ideological Origins of the American Revolution*. Cambridge: The Belknap Press of Harvard University Press, 1967.
Banac, Ivo. *With Stalin against Tito: Cominformist Splits in Yugoslav Communism*. Ithaca: Cornell University Press, 1988.
Barrett, Anthony A. *Caligula: The Corruption of Power*. New Haven: Yale University Press, 1990.
Batatu, Hanna. *The Old Social Classes and the Revolutionary Movements of Iraq*. Princeton: Princeton University Press, 1978.
Bauer, Tamàs. "Hungarian Economic Reform in East European Perspective." *Eastern European Politics and Societies* 2, 3 (1988).
Beljo, Ante, ed. *Historical Maps of Croatia*. Zagreb: Croatian Information Center, 1992.
Beller, Steven. *Vienna and the Jews, 1867–1938*. Cambridge: Cambridge University Press, 1989.
Berlin, Isaiah. *Four Essays on Liberty*. London: Oxford University Press, 1969.
Billington, James H. *The Icon and the Axe*. New York: Knopf, 1966.
Blum, Jerome. *Lord and Peasant in Russia from the Ninth to the Nineteenth Century*. New York: Atheneum, 1964.
Bonnell, Victoria. *Roots of Rebellion*. Berkeley and Los Angeles: University of California Press, 1984.
Bonner, Raymond. "Letter from Sudan." *New Yorker*, July 13, 1992.
Bosch, Juan. *Trujillo: Causas de una tirania sin ejemplo*. Caracas: Libraria Las Novedades, 1959.
Boserup, Ester. *Population and Technological Change*. Chicago: University of Chicago Press, 1981.
Bottomore, Tom, ed. *A Dictionary of Marxist Thought* Oxford: Blackwell, 1983.
Braeckman, Colette. *Le Dinosaure*. Paris: Fayard, 1991.
Brand, H. "Why the Soviet Economy Failed." *Dissent* (Spring 1992).
Brooke, James. "'Not a Saint' Bokassa Says at His Trial" (two articles). *New York Times*, December 16, 1986, p. A-3 and December 17, 1986, p. A-4.
Browning, Christopher R. "The Decisions Concerning the Final Solution." In François Furet, ed., *Unanswered Questions: Nazi Germany and the Genocide of the Jews*. New York: Shocken, 1989.
——. "The Holocaust Distorted." *Dissent* (Summer 1989).
——. *Ordinary Men: Reserve Police Battalion 101 and the Final Solution in Poland*. New York: Harper Collins, 1992.

Buell, R. L. "The American Occupation of Haiti." In Foreign Policy Association, *Information Service*, Volume V. Washington: Foreign Policy Association, 1927.

Bullock, Alan. *Hitler: A Study in Tyranny*. New York: Bantam, 1961.

———. *Hitler and Stalin: Parallel Lives*. New York: Knopf, 1992.

Bunge, Alejandro E. *Una Nueva Argentina*. Buenos Aires: Guillermo Kraft, 1940.

Burckhardt, Jacob. *The Civilization of the Renaissance in Italy*. New York: Modern Library, 1954.

Bureau of the Census (U.S.A.). *Historical Statistics of the United States, Colonial Times to 1970*. Washington: U.S. Government Printing Office, 1975.

Burke, Edmund. *Reflections on the Revolution in France*. Indianapolis: Bobbs-Merrill, 1955.

Burleigh, Michael, and Wolfgang Wippermann. *The Racial State: Germany 1933-1945*. Cambridge: Cambridge University Press, 1991.

Burr, G. L. "The Carlovingian Revolution" In *Cambridge Medieval History*, Volume II. Cambridge: Cambridge University Press, 1957.

Butler, Rohan. "The Peace Settlement of Versailles." In *The Cambridge Modern History*, Volume XII. Cambridge: Cambridge University Press, 1968.

Carneiro, Robert L. "A Theory of the Origin of the State." *Science* 169 (1970): 733–738.

Carr, E. H. *The October Revolution Before and After*. New York: Vintage, 1969.

———. *Studies in Revolution*. New York: Grosset and Dunlop, 1964.

Carr, William. *Hitler: A Study in Personality and Politics*. London: Edward Arnold, 1978.

Carsten, F. L. *The Reichswehr and Politics 1918-1933*. Berkeley and Los Angeles: University of California Press, 1973.

Castellan, Georges. *Histoire de la Roumanie*. Paris: Presses Universitaires de France, 1984.

Castillo de Aza, Zenon. *Trujillo, Benefactor of the Church*. Ciudad Trujillo, 1955.

Césaire, Aimé. *Toussaint l'Ouverture: La Révolution Francaise et le problème colonial*. Paris: Présence Africaine, 1961.

———. *La Tragédie du Roi Christophe*. Paris: Présence Africaine, 1963.

Chafford, Georges. *Les Carnets secrets de la décolonisation*. Paris: Berger-Levrault, 1967.

Chaliand, Gérard. *Anthologie mondiale de la stratégie: Des Origines au nucléaire*. Paris: Robert Laffont, 1990.

Chalk, Frank, and Kurth Jonassohn. *The History and Sociology of Genocide*. New Haven: Yale University Press, 1990.

Chan, Anita, Richard Madsen, and Jonathan Unger. *Chen Village: The Recent History of a Peasant Community in Mao's China*. Berkeley and Los Angeles: University of California Press, 1984.

Chandler, David. *Brother Number One: A Political Biography of Pol Pot*. Boulder: Westview, 1992.

Chandler, David P. "Seeing Red: Perceptions of Cambodian History in Democratic Kampuchea." In David P. Chandler and Ben Kiernan, eds., *Revolution and Its Aftermath in Kampuchea*. New Haven: Yale University Southeast Asia Studies Series #25, 1983.

———. *The Tragedy of Cambodian History: Politics, War and Revolution since 1945*. New Haven: Yale University Press, 1991.

Chaudhuri, K. N. *Trade and Civilization in the Indian Ocean: The Economic History from the Rise of Islam to 1750*. Cambridge: Cambridge University Press, 1985.

Chernyshevsky, Nikolai G. *What Is to Be Done?* Ithaca: Cornell University Press, 1989.

Chirot, Daniel. "The Corporatist Model and Socialism." *Theory and Society* 9 (1980).

———. "Ideology, Reality, and Competing Models of Development in Eastern Europe between the Two World Wars." *Eastern European Politics and Societies* 3, 3 (1989).

———. "The Rise of the West." *American Sociological Review* 50, 2 (1985).

———. "Romania: Ceausescu's Last Folly." *Dissent* (Summer 1988).

———. "Social Change in Communist Romania." *Social Forces* 57 (1978).

———. *Social Change in the Modern Era*. San Diego: Harcourt Brace Jovanovich, 1986.

———. *Social Change in a Peripheral Society: The Creation of a Balkan Colony*. New York: Academic Press, 1976.

———. "What Happened in Eastern Europe in 1989?" In Chirot, ed., *The Crisis of Leninism and the Decline of the Left: The Revolutions of 1989*. Seattle: University of Washington Press, 1991.

Chirot, Daniel, and Thomas D. Hall. "World System Theory." *Annual Review of Sociology* 8 (1982).

Coedès, Georges. *The Indianized States of Southeast Asia*. Honolulu: University Press of Hawaii, 1968.

Cohen, Stephen F. *Bukharin and the Russian Revolution: A Political Biography, 1888–1938*. Oxford: Oxford University Press, 1980.

Cohn, Norman. *The Pursuit of the Millennium*. New York: Harper Torchbooks, 1961.

Commager, Henry S., ed. *Documents of American History*. New York: Appleton-Century-Crofts, 1968.

Comte, Gilbert. "L'Heure de l'examen de conscience." *Le Monde*, September 23–24, 1979, pp. 1–2.

Conquest, Robert. *The Great Terror: Stalin's Purges of the Thirties*. New York: Collier Books, 1973.

———. *Harvest of Sorrow: Soviet Collectivization and the Terror-Famine*. New York: Oxford University Press, 1986.

———. *Stalin and the Kirov Murder*. Oxford: Oxford University Press, 1989.

———. "What Is Terror?" *Slavic Review* 45 (1990): 235–237.

Constante, Léna. *L'Evasion silencieuse*. Paris: La Découverte, 1990.

Coquery-Vidrovitch, Catherine. *Le Congo au temps des grandes compagnies concessionaires, 1898–1930*. Paris: Mouton, 1972.

Craig, Gordon A. *The Germans*. New York: G. P. Putnam's Sons, 1982.

Crassweller, Robert D. *Perón and the Enigmas of Argentina*. New York: W. W. Norton, 1987.

———. *Trujillo: The Life and Times of a Caribbean Dictator*. New York: Macmillan, 1966.

Croce, Benedetto. *History of the Kingdom of Naples*. Chicago: University of Chicago Press, 1965.

Crouch, Harold. *The Army and Politics in Indonesia*. Ithaca: Cornell University Press, 1978.

Cumings, Bruce. "Corporatism in North Korea." *Journal of Korean Studies* 4 (1982–1983).

———. *The Origins of the Korean War*. Volume I, *Liberation and the Emergence of Separate Regimes 1945–1947*. Princeton: Princton University Press, 1981.

———. *The Origins of the Korean War*. Volume II, *Liberation and the Emergence of Separate Regimes 1947–1950*. Princeton: Princeton University Press, 1990.

———. *War and Television*. London: Verso, 1992.

Curtin, Philip D. *The Atlantic Slave Trade: A Census*. Madison: University of Wisconsin Press, 1969.

Dahmani, Abdelziz. "Éditorial." *Jeune Afrique*, October 10, 1979, p. 7.

Dahrendorf, Ralf. *Society and Democracy in Germany*. Garden City: Doubleday/Anchor, 1969.

Davies, Nigel. "Human Sacrifice in the Old World and the New." In Elizabeth P. Benson and Elizabeth H. Boone, eds., *Ritual Human Sacrifice in Mesoamerica*. Washington, D.C.: Dumbarton Oaks Research Library Collection, 1984.

Davies, Norman. *Heart of Europe: A Short History of Poland*. Oxford: Oxford University Press, 1986.

Davis, Jerome E. *Behind Soviet Power: Stalin and the Russians*. New York: Reader's Press, 1946.

Dawidowicz, Lucy S. *The War against the Jews 1933–1945*. New York: Bantam, 1976.

Decalo, Samuel. *Coups and Army Rule in Africa: Motivations and Constraints*. New Haven: Yale University Press, 1990.

———. *Psychoses of Power: African Personal Dictatorships*. Boulder: Westview, 1989.

Deák, István. *Beyond Nationalism: A Social and Political History of the Habsburg Officer Corps*. New York: Oxford University Press, 1970.

———. "Jews, Catholics, Nazis, and the Holocaust." *New York Review of Books* 36, 14 (September 28, 1989).

———. "Pacesetters of Integration: Jewish Officers in the Habsburg Monarchy." *Eastern European Politics and Societies* 3, 1 (1989).

DeConde, Alexander. *A History of American Foreign Policy*. New York: Scribner's, 1971 (2nd edition).

Degler, Carl N. *In Search of Human Nature: The Decline and Revival of Darwinism in American Social Thought*. New York: Oxford University Press, 1991.

Delli Carpini, Michael X. "Age and History: Generations and Social Political Change." In Roberta S. Sigel, ed., *Political Learning in Adulthood*. Chicago: Chicago University Press, 1989.

Deutscher, Isaac. *Stalin: A Political Biography*. London: Oxford University Press, 1967.

Diaz Alejandro, Carlos F. *Essays in the Economic History of the Argentine Republic*. New Haven: Yale University Press, 1970.

Diederich, Bernard. *Trujillo: The Death of the Goat*. Boston: Little, Brown, 1978.

Dirlik, Arif. *The Origins of Chinese Communism*. New York: Oxford University Press, 1989.

———. *Revolution and History: Origins of Marxist Historiography in China, 1919–1937*. Berkeley and Los Angeles: University of California Press, 1978.

Dittmer, Lowell. *China's Continuous Revolution: The Post-Liberation Epoch 1949–1981*. Berkeley and Los Angeles: University of California Press, 1987.

Djilas, Milovan. *Conversations with Stalin*. New York: Harcourt, Brace and World, 1962.

Dollard, John. *Caste and Class in a Southern Town*. New York: Doubleday, 1957.

Dumitriu, Petru. *Incognito*. New York: Macmillan, 1964.

Dworkin, Ronald. "Introduction," to *Nunca Más*. New York: Farrar Straus Giroux, 1986.

Eastman, Lloyd E. *The Abortive Revolution: China under Nationalist Rule, 1927–1937*. Cambridge: Harvard University Press, 1974.

———. *Seeds of Destruction: Nationalist China in War and Revolution, 1937–1949*. Stanford: Stanford University Press, 1984.

Elvin, Mark. *The Pattern of the Chinese Past*. Stanford: Stanford: Stanford University Press, 1973.

Enzensberger, Hans Magnus. *Raids and Reconstructions*. London: Pluto Press, 1976.

Erlich, Alexander. *The Soviet Industrialization Debate*. Cambridge: Harvard University Press, 1960.

Esherick, Joseph W., and Jeffrey N. Wasserstrom. "Acting Out Democracy: Political Theater in Modern China." In Jeffrey N. Wasserstrom and Elizabeth J. Perry, eds., *Popular Protest and Political Culture in Modern China: Learning from 1989*. Boulder: Westview, 1992.

Fanon, Frantz. *Black Skin, White Masks*. New York: Grove Press, 1967.

———. *The Wretched of the Earth*. New York: Grove Press, 1963.

Fenichel, A. H., and W. G. Huff. *The Impact of Colonialism on Burmese Economic Development*. Montreal: McGill University Press, 1971.

Ferguson, James. *Papa Doc, Baby Doc: Haiti and the Duvaliers*. Oxford: Basil Blackwell, 1988.

Fest, Joachim C. *The Face of the Third Reich*. New York: Pantheon, 1970.

———. *Hitler*. New York: Vintage, 1975.

Fieldhouse, D. K. "Imperialism: An Historiographic Revision." In Kenneth E. Boulding and Tapan Mukerjee, eds., *Economic Imperialism*. Ann Arbor: University of Michigan Press, 1972.

Fillol, Tomás R. *Social Factors in Economic Development: The Argentine Case*. Cambridge: MIT Press, 1961.

Fink, Ida. *A Scrap of Time*. New York: Random House, 1987.

Fischer, Fritz. *Germany's Aims in the First World War*. New York: W. W. Norton, 1967.

Fischer, Louis. *The Life of Lenin*. New York: Harper & Row, 1964.

Fitzpatrick, Sheila. *The Russian Revolution*. Oxford: Oxford University Press, 1982.

Flood, Charles B. *Hitler: The Path to Power*. Boston: Houghton Mifflin, 1989.

Frank, Joseph. *Dostoyevsky: The Making of a Novelist: The Stir of Liberation, 1860–1865*. Princeton: Princeton University Press, 1986.

Fried, Morton H. *The Evolution of Political Society: An Essay in Political Anthropology*. New York: Random House, 1967.

Fukuyama, Francis. *The End of History and the Last Man*. New York: Free Press, 1992.

Furet, François, ed. *Unanswered Questions: Nazi Germany and the Genocide of the Jews*. New York: Shocken, 1989.

Furnivall, John S. *Colonial Policy and Practice: A Comparative Study of Burma and Netherlands India*. Cambridge: Cambridge University Press, 1948.

Galíndez, Jesús de. *La Era de Trujillo*. Santiago de Chile: Editorial del Pacifico, 1956.

Gay, Peter. *The Englightenment: An Interpretation*, 2 volumes. New York: W. W. Norton, 1977.

Gay, Peter. *Weimar Culture: The Outsider as Insider*. New York and Evanston: Harper Torchbooks, 1970.

Getty, J. Arch. *Origins of the Great Purges: The Soviet Communist Party Reconsidered*. New York: Cambridge University Press, 1987.

Gibb, Hamilton A. R. *Studies on the Civilization of Islam*. Princeton: Princeton University Press, 1962.

Gilberg, Trond. *Nationalism and Communism in Romania: The Rise and Fall of Ceausescu's Personal Dictatorship*. Boulder: Westview, 1990.

Gilbert, Martin. *First World War Atlas*. New York: Macmillan, 1970.

———. *Illustrated Atlas of Jewish Civilization*. New York: Macmillan, 1990.

———. *Jewish History Atlas*. New York: Macmillan, 1969.

Gillespie, Richard. *Soldiers of Perón: Argentina's Montoneros*. Oxford: Oxford University Press, 1982.

Ginzburg, Eugenia S. *Journey into the Whirlwind*. New York: Harcourt, Brace and World, 1967.

Glenny, Misha. *The Fall of Yugoslavia: The Third Balkan War*. New York: Penguin, 1992.

Goldstone, Jack A. *Revolution and Rebellion in the Early Modern World*. Berkeley and Los Angeles: University of California Press, 1991.

Görlitz, Walter. *History of the German General Staff, 1675–1945*. New York: Praeger, 1953.

Graham, Gerald S. *The China Station: War and Diplomacy, 1830–1860*. New York: Oxford University Press, 1978.

Greene, Graham. "Nightmare Republic." *New Republic*, November 16, 1963.

Greenfeld, Liah. "The Formation of the Russian National Identity: The Role of Status Insecurity and *Ressentiment*." *Comparative Studies in Society and History* 32 (July 1990): 549–591.

———. "Kitchen Debate: Russia's Nationalist Intelligentsia." *New Republic*, September 21, 1992.

———. *Nationalism: Five Roads to Modernity*. Cambridge: Harvard University Press, 1992.

Greenfeld, Liah, and Daniel Chirot. "Nationalism and War." Paper prepared for the National Academy of Sciences, Washington, D.C., 1991.

Griffith, William E. *Albania and the Sino-Soviet Rift*. Cambridge: MIT Press, 1963.

Groslier, Bernard-Philippe. *Angkor, hommes, et pierres*. Paris: Arthaud, 1956.

Gross, Jan T. *Polish Society under German Occupation: Generalgouvernement 1939–1944*. Princeton: Princeton University Press, 1979.

———. "Social Consequences of War." *Eastern European Politics and Societies* 3, 2 (1989).

Grunberger, Richard. *A Social History of the Third Reich*. London: Weidenfeld and Nicolson, 1971.

Guardian, The. "Carnage Exposed at Amin's Torture Base." *The Guardian*, April 14, 1949, p. 1.

Gunst, Péter. "Agrarian Systems of Central and Eastern Europe." In Daniel Chirot, ed., *The Origins of Backwardness in Eastern Europe*. Berkeley and Los Angeles: University of California Press, 1989.

Guyot, Dorothy H. "Communal Conflict in the Burma Delta." In Ruth T. McVey, ed., *Southeast Asian Transitions: Approaches through Social History*. New Haven: Yale University Press, 1978.

Hall, Daniel G. E. *Burma*. London: Hutchison University Library, 1960.

———. *A History of South-East Asia*. New York: St. Martin's Press, 1981.

Halliday, Jon. *The Artful Albanian: The Memoirs of Enver Hoxha*. London: Chatto & Windus, 1986.

Hamerow, Theodore S. *Restoration, Revolution, Reaction: Economics and Politics in Germany, 1815-1871*. Princeton: Princeton University Press, 1958.

———. *The Social Foundations of German Unification, 1858–1871*. Princeton: Princeton University Press, 1969.

Hamilton, Richard F. *Who Voted for Hitler?* Princeton: Princeton University Press, 1982.

Handley, Paul. "An Uneasy Calm," "March of Democracy," and "The Markets Speak." *Far Eastern Economic Review*, 21 (May 1992): 10–13.

Hanson, Stephen E. "Gorbachev: The Last True Leninist Believer?" In Daniel Chirot, ed., *The Crisis of Leninism and the Decline of the Left: The Revolutions of 1989*. Seattle: University of Washington Press, 1989.

Harris, Marvin. *Cannibals and Kings*. New York: Vintage, 1977.

Hartz, Louis. *The Liberal Tradition in America*. New York: Harcourt, Brace and World, 1955.

Harvey, Godfrey E. *A History of Burma from the Earliest Time to 10 March 1824*. New York: Octagon Books, 1983.

Haupt, Georges, and Jean-Jacques Marie. *The Makers of the Russian Revolution: Biographies of Bolshevik Leaders*. Ithaca: Cornell University Press, 1974.

Hayek, Friedrich A. *The Road to Serfdom*. Chicago: University of Chicago Press, 1976.

Hayward, Max. *Writers in Russia 1917–1978*. San Diego: Harcourt Brace Jovanovich, 1983.

Hefner, Robert. *The Political Economy of Mountain Java*. Berkeley and Los Angeles: University of California Press, 1990.

Heng, Liang, and Judith Shapiro. *Son of the Revolution*. New York: Vintage, 1984.

Herling-Grudzinski, Gustaw. *The World Apart*. New York: Arbor, 1986.

Herr, Richard. *The Eighteenth-Century Revolution in Spain*. Princeton: Princeton University Press, 1958.

Higham, John. *Strangers in the Land: Patterns of American Nativism 1860–1925*. New York: Antheneum, 1963.

Hilberg, Raul. *The Destruction of the European Jews*, Volume III. New York: Holmes and Meier, 1985.

———. "The Statistics." In François Furet, ed., *Unanswered Questions: Nazi Germany and the Genocide of the Jews*. New York: Shocken, 1989.

Hinton, William. *Hundred Day War: The Cultural Revolution at Tsinghua University*. New York: Monthly Review Press, 1972.

Hitler, Adolph. *Hitler's Table Talk 1941–1943*. Introduced by Hugh R. Trevor-Roper. London: Weidenfeld and Nicolson, 1973.

———. *Mein Kampf*. Translated by Ralph Mannheim. Boston: Houghton Mifflin, 1971.

Hobsbawm, Eric J. *The Age of Capital 1848–1875*. New York: Charles Scribner's, 1975.

———. *The Age of Empire 1875–1914*. New York: Pantheon, 1987.

———. *The Age of Revolution: Europe 1789–1848*. New York: Mentor, 1962.

———. *Primitive Rebels*. New York: W. W. Norton, 1959.

Hobsbawm, Eric J., and Terence Ranger, eds. *The Invention of Tradition*. Cambridge: Cambridge University Press, 1984.

Hofstadter, Richard. *Social Darwinism in American Thought*. New York: George Braziller, 1959.

Holborn, Hajo. *A History of Modern Germany 1840–1945*. Princeton: Princeton University Press, 1982.

Hopkins, Jack W., ed. *Latin America and Caribbean Contemporary Records*. Volume I, *1981–1982*. Volume II, *1982–1983*. Volume III, *1983–1984*. Volume IV, *1984–1985*. New York: Holmes and Meier, 1983–1986.

Horowitz, Donald L. *Ethnic Groups in Conflict*. Berkeley and Los Angeles: University of California Press, 1986.

Hosking, Geoffrey. *The Awakening of the Soviet Union*. Cambridge: Harvard University Press, 1989.

Hunya, Gábor. "New Developments in Romanian Agriculture." *Eastern European Politics and Societies* 1, 2 (1987).

Hyman, Herbert H. *Political Socialization*. Glencoe: Free Press, 1959.

Ibarguren, Carlos. *La Historia que he vivido*. Buenos Aires: Ediciones Péuser, 1955.

Ibn Batuta. *The Rehla of Ibn Batuta*. Translated by Mahdi Husain. Baroda: Oriental Institute, 1953.

Ionescu, Gita. *Communism in Romania 1944–1962*. London: Oxford University Press, 1964.

Isbell, Billie Jean. "Shining Path and Peasant Responses in Rural Ayacucho." In David S. Palmer, ed., *Shining Path*. New York: St. Martin's Press, 1992.

Jäckel, Eberhard. *Hitler in History*. Hanover: University Press of New England, 1984.

Jackson, Robert H., and Carl G. Rosberg. *Personal Rule in Black Africa: Prince, Autocrat, Prophet, Tyrant*. Berkeley and Los Angeles: University of California Press, 1982.

James, C. L. R. *The Black Jacobins: Toussaint L'Ouverture and the San Domingo Revolution*. New York: Vintage, 1963.

Janos, Andrew. *The Politics of Backwardness in Hungary, 1825–1945*. Princeton: Princeton University Press, 1982.

Jansson, Kurt, Michael Harris, and Angela Penrose. *The Ethiopian Famine*. London: Zed Books, 1990.

Johnson, Chalmers A. *Peasant Nationalism and Communist Power: The Emergence of Revolutionary China 1937–1945*. Stanford: Stanford University Press, 1962.

Jowitt, Kenneth. "Moscow 'Centre.'|" *Eastern European Politics and Societies* 1, 3 (1987).

———. *New World Disorder*. Berkeley and Los Angeles: University of California Press, 1992.

———. "Political Innovation in Romania." *Survey* 4 (1974).

———. *Revolutionary Breakthroughs and National Development: The Case of Romania 1944–1965*. Berkeley and Los Angeles: University of California Press, 1971.

Judt, Tony. *Marxism and the French Left: Studies in Labour and Politics in France, 1830–1981*. Oxford: Clarendon Press, 1986.

Kagwa, Apolo. *The Kings of Buganda*. Nairobi: East African Publishing House, 1971.

Kalck, Pierre. *Histoire de la République Centrafricaine*. Paris: Berger-Levrault, 1974.

Kaplan, Robert D. "Croatianism." *New Republic*, November 25, 1991.

Karnoouh, Claude. *L'Invention du peuple: Chroniques de Roumanie et d'Europe Orientale*. Paris: Editions Arcantère, 1990.

Kater, Michael H. *The Nazi Party: A Social Profile of Members and Leaders 1919-1945*. Cambridge: Harvard University Press, 1983.

Katz, Michael R., and William G. Wagner. "Introduction: Chernyshevsky, What Is to Be Done?" and the Russian Intelligentsia." In Chernyshevsky, Nikolai G., *What Is to Be Done?* edited by Katz and Wagner. Ithaca: Cornell University Press, 1989.

Kaye, Howard L. *The Social Meaning of Modern Biology: From Social Darwinism to Sociobiology*. New Haven: Yale University Press, 1986.

Keddie, Nikki. "The Iranian Revolution Comparative Perspective." In Edmund Burke III and Ira M. Lapidus, eds., *Islam, Politics, and Social Movements*. Berkeley and Los Angeles: University of California Press, 1988.

Kedourie, Elie. *England and the Middle East: The Destruction of the Ottoman Empire 1914–1922*. London: Bowes & Bowes, 1956.

Kelley, Michael P. *A State in Disarray: Conditions of Chad's Survival*. Boulder: Westview, 1986.

Kelly, Alfred. *The Descent of Darwin: The Popularization of Darwinism in Germany*. Chapel Hill: University of North Carolina Press, 1981.

Kennan, George F. *The Fateful Alliance: France, Russia and the Coming of the First World War*. New York: Pantheon, 1984.

———. *Russia and the West under Lenin and Stalin*. Boston: Little, Brown, 1961.

Kennedy, Paul M. *The Rise of Anglo-German Antagonism 1860–1914*. London: Allen & Unwin, 1980.

Kershaw, Ian. *Hitler*. London: Longman, 1991.

———. *The 'Hitler Myth': Image and Reality in the Third Reich*. Oxford: Oxford University Press, 1987.

Keyes, Charles F. "Buddhist Economics and Buddhist Fundamentalism in Burma and Thailand." In Martin Marty and Scott Appleby, eds. *Fundamentalism and the State: Remaking Politics, Economics, and Militance*. Chicago: University of Chicago Press, 1993.

———. *Thailand: Buddhist Kingdom as Modern Nation-State*. Boulder: Westview, 1987.

al-Khalil, Samir. *The Monument: Art, Vulgarity, and Responsibility in Iraq*. Berkeley and Los Angeles: University of California Press, 1991.

———. *Republic of Fear: The Politics of Modern Iraq*. Berkeley and Los Angeles: University of California Press, 1989.

Khoury, Philip S. *Syria and the French Mandate: The Politics of Arab Nationalism 1920-1945*. Princeton: Princeton University Press, 1987.

Kiernan, Ben. "Genocide in Cambodia, 1975-1979." *Bulletin of the Concerned Asian Scholar* 22, 2 (1990).

———. *How Pol Pot Came to Power*. London: Verso, 1985.

———. "Myth, Nationalism, and Genocide in Cambodia." Unpublished Paper presented at the University of Washington, Seattle, in the spring of 1992.

————. "Wild Chickens, Farm Chickens, and Cormorants: Kampuchea's Eastern Zone under Pol Pot." In David P. Chandler and Ben Kiernan, eds., *Revolution and Its Aftermath in Kampuchea*. New Haven: Yale University Southeast Asia Studies Monograph # 25, 1983.

Kilson, Martin, and Adelaide Hill, eds. *Apropos of Africa: Afro-American Leaders and the Romance of Africa*. (Garden City: Doubleday/Anchor, 1971)

Kim, Kyong-Dong. "The Distinctive Features of South Korea's Development." In Peter L. Berger and Hsin-Huang Michael Hsiao, eds., *In Search of an East Asian Development Model*. New Brunswick: Transaction Books, 1988.

Kligman, Gail. "The Politics of Reproduction in Ceausescu's Romania: A Case Study in Political Culture." *Eastern European Politics and Societies* 6, 3 (1992).

————. "When Abortion Is Banned: The Politics of Reproduction in Ceausescu's Romania." Washington, D.C., National Council for Soviet and East European Studies Report, 1992.

Kochanowicz, Jacek. "The Polish Economy and the Evolution of Dependency." In Daniel Chirot, ed., *The Origin of Backwardness in Eastern Europe*. Berkeley and Los Angeles: University of California Press, 1989.

Kristof, Nicholas D. "A Tale of Red Guards and Cannibals." *New York Times*, January 6, 1993, p. A-6.

Kuper, Leo. *Genocide: Its Political Use in the Twentieth Century*. New Haven: Yale University Press, 1981.

LaCapra, Dominick. *History, Politics and the Novel*. Ithaca: Cornell University Press, 1987.

Laguerre, Michael. *Voodoo and Politics in Haiti*. New York: Macmillan, 1989.

Landes, David S. *The Unbound Prometheus: Technological Change and Industrial Development in Industrial Europe from 1750 to the Present*. Cambridge: Cambridge University Press, 1969.

Langer, Walter C. *The Mind of Adolph Hitler*. New York: Basic Books, 1972.

Laqueur, Walter. *Stalin: The Glasnost Revelations*. New York: Scribner's, 1990.

Lardy, Nicholas R. *Agriculture in China's Modern Economic Development*. New York: Cambridge University Press, 1983.

————. "Is China Different? The Fate of Its Economic Reform." In Daniel Chirot, ed., *The Crisis of Leninism and the Decline of the Left: The Revolutions of 1989*. Seattle: University of Washington Press, 1991.

Leach, Edmund R. *Political Systems of Highland Burma*. Boston: Beacon Press, 1965.

Lee, Hong Yung. *The Politics of the Chinese Cultural Revolution: A Case Study*. Berkeley and Los Angeles: University of California Press, 1978.

Lehman, F. K., ed. *Military Rule in Burma Since 1962*. Singapore: Maruzen Asia, 1981.

Lenin, Vladimir I. *Imperialism: The Highest Stage of Capitalism*. New York: International Publishers, 1939.

Levine, Hillel. *Economic Origins of Antisemitism: Poland and Its Jews in the Early Modern Period*. New Haven: Yale University Press, 1991.

Levine, Steven. *Anvil of Victory: The Communist Revolution in Manchuria, 1945–1948*. New York: Columbia University Press, 1987.

Levy, Richard S. *The Downfall of the Anti-Semitic Political Parties in Imperial Germany*. New Haven: Yale University Press, 1979.

Lewin, Moshe. *Lenin's Last Struggle*. New York: Pantheon, 1968.

Lewis, Paul H. *The Crisis of Argentine Capitalism*. Chapel Hill: University of North Carolina Press, 1990.

Liang, Chi-shad. *Burma's Foreign Relations: Neutralism in Theory and Practice*. New York: Praeger, 1990.

Liebich, André. "'I Am the Last'—Memories of Bukharin in Paris." *Slavic Review* 51, 4 (1992).

Lilley, Samuel. "Technological Progress and the Industrial Revolution." In Carlo C. Cipolla, ed., *The Fontana Economic History of Europe*. Volume III, *The Industrial Revolution*. Glasgow: Fontana/Collins, 1973.

Lintner, Bertil. "Diversionary Tactics." *Far Eastern Economic Review*, 29 August 1991, pp. 26–28.

———. *Land of Jade: A Journey through Insurgent Burma*. Edinburgh: Kiscadale Publications, 1990.

———. "Mock Turtle." *Far Eastern Economic Review*, 15 November 1991, pp. 22–24.

———. "The Odd Couple." *Far Eastern Economic Review*, 11 July 1991, pp. 39–41.

———. *Outrage: Burma's Struggle for Democracy*. Hong Kong: Review Publishing, 1989.

———. "The Secret Mover." *Far Eastern Economic Review*, 7 May 1992, pp. 20–21.

Lipset, Seymour Martin. "No Third Way: A Comparative Perspective on the Left." In Daniel Chirot, ed., *The Crisis of Leninism and the Decline of the Left: The Revolutions of 1989*. Seattle: University of Washington Press, 1991.

Liss, Peggy K. *Isabel the Queen: Life and Times*. New York: Oxford University Press, 1991.

Logan, Rayford W. *Haiti and the Dominican Republic*. New York: Oxford University Press, 1968.

London, Arthur G. *The Confession*. New York: Morrow, 1970.

Love, Joseph L. "Raúl Prebisch and the Origins of the Doctrine of Unequal Exchange." *Latin American Research Review* 15 (1980).

Luxemburg, Rosa. *The Accumulation of Capital*. New Haven: Yale University Press, 1951.

MacFarquhar, Roderick. *The Origins of the Cultural Revolution*. Volume I, *Contradictions among the People 1956–1957*. New York: Columbia University Press, 1974.

MacFarquhar, Roderick. *The Origins of the Cultural Revolution*. Volume II, *The Great Leap Forward 1958-1960*. New York: Columbia University Press, 1983.

Machiavelli, Niccoló. *The Prince and the Discourse*. New York: The Modern Library, 1940.

Maddison, Angus. "Economic Policy and Performance in Europe, 1913-1970." In Carlo M. Cipolla, ed., *The Fontana Economic History of Europe*, Volume 5-2. Glasgow: Fontana/Collins, 1976.

Maier, Charles S. *The Unmasterable Past: History, Holocaust, and German National Identity*. Cambridge: Harvard University Press, 1988.

Mair, Lucy. *Native Policies in Africa*. London: Routledge, 1936.

Mandelstam, Nadezhda. *Hope Abandoned*. New York: Atheneum, 1974.

Manea, Norman. "Happy Guilt: Mircea Eliade, Fascism, and the Unhappy Fate of Romania." *New Republic*, August 5, 1991.

Mann, Michael. *The Sources of Social Power*, Volume I. Cambridge: Cambridge University Press, 1986.

Mann, Thomas. "Disorder and Early Sorrow." In Mann, *Death in Venice and Seven Other Stories*. New York: Vintage, 1954.

Mannheim, Karl. "The Problem of Generations." In Philip G. Altbach and Robert Lafner, eds., *The New Pilgrims*. New York: Doubleday, 1972.

Mannoni, Octave. *Prospero and Caliban: The Psychology of Colonization*. New York: Praeger, 1964.

Manuel, Frank E., and Fritizie P. Manuel. *Utopian Thought in the Western World*. Cambridge: Belknap Press of Harvard University, 1979.

Ma'oz, Moshe. *Asad: The Sphinx of Damascus*. London: Weidenfeld and Nicolson, 1988.

Marr, Phebe C. *The Modern History of Iraq*. Boulder: Westview, 1985.

Marrus, Michael R., and Robert O. Paxton. "The Nazis and the Jews in Occupied Western Europe, 1940–1944." In François Furet, ed., *Unanswered Questions: Nazi Germany and the Genocide of the Jews*. New York: Shocken Books, 1989.

Marx, Karl. *Capital*. Volume I, *A Critical Analysis of Capitalist Production*. Edited by Frederick Engels. New York: International Publishers, 1967.

———. *Early Writings*. Introduced by Lucio Colletti. Harmondsworth: Penguin, 1975.

Maung Maung. *Burma and General Ne Win*. New York: Asia Publishing House, 1969.

Maung Maung Gyi. "Foreign Policy of Burma since 1962." In F. K. Lehman, ed., *Military Rule in Burma since 1962*. Singapore: Maruzen Asia, 1981.

Mayer, Arno J. *Why Did the Heavens Not Darken? The "Final Solution" in History*. New York: Pantheon, 1990.

Mazrui, Ali A. *Soldiers and Kinsmen in Uganda: The Making of a Military Ethnocracy*. Beverly Hills: Sage Publications, 1975.

McDaniel, Tim. *Autocracy, Capitalism, and Revolution in Russia*. Berkeley and Los Angeles: University of California Press, 1988.

McDonald, Hamish. "Partners in Plunder." *Far Eastern Economic Review*, 22 February 1990, pp. 16-18.

———. "Saffron Nationalism." *Far Eastern Economic Review*, 11 March 1993, p. 22.

McNeill, William H. *The Human Condition: An Ecological and Historical View*. Princeton: Princeton University Press, 1980.

Medvedev, Roy A. *Let History Judge: The Origins and Consequences of Stalinism*. New York: Columbia University Press, 1989 (2nd edition).

Meinecke, Friedrich. *The German Catastrophe*. Boston: Beacon Press, 1963.

Meisner, Maurice. *Li Ta-chao and the Origins of Chinese Marxism*. Cambridge: Harvard University Press, 1967.

Mendes-Flohr, Paul R., and Jehuda Reinharz, eds. *The Jew in the Modern World: A Documentary History*. New York: Oxford University Press, 1980.

Merit, Giles. "Albania." *International Herald Tribune*, October 10, 1992, p. 4.

Merkl, Peter H. *Political Violence under the Swastika*. Princeton: Princeton University Press, 1975.

Merton, Robert K. "Puritanism, Pietism, and Science" and "Science and Economy of 17th Century England." In Merton, *Social Theory and Social Structure*. Glencoe: Free Press, 1949.

Middle East Watch. *Human Rights in Iraq* (written by David A. Korn). New Haven: Yale University Press, 1990.

————. *Syria Unmasked: The Suppression of Human Rights by the Asad Regime* (written by James A. Paul). New Haven: Yale University Press, 1991.

Migdal, Joel S. *Peasants, Politics, and Revolution: Pressures toward Political and Social Change in the Third World*. Princeton: Princeton University Press, 1974.

Miller, Judith, and Laurie Mylroie. *Saddam Hussein and the Crisis in the Gulf*. New York: Random House, 1990.

Mitchell, B. R. *European Historical Statistics 1750–1970*. New York: Columbia University Press, 1978 (abridged edition).

————. *International Historical Statistics: Africa and Asia*. New York: New York University Press, 1982.

Mitrany, David. *Marx against the Peasants: A Study in Social Dogmatism*. Chapel Hill: University of North Carolina Press, 1951.

Moore, Barrington, Jr. *The Social Origins of Democracy and Dictatorship: Lord and Peasant in the Making of the Modern World*. Boston: Beacon Press, 1967.

————. *Soviet Politics—The Dilemma of Power*. New York: Harper and Row, 1950.

Morgan, David. *The Mongols*. New York: Basil Blackwell, 1986.

Mosse, George L. *The Crisis of German Ideology: Intellectual Origins of the Third Reich*. New York: Grosset & Dunlap, 1964.

Mosse, George L., ed. *Nazi Culture*. New York: Shocken, 1966.

Müller, Ingo. *Hitler's Justice: The Courts of the Third Reich*. Cambridge: Harvard University Press, 1991.

Murray, Jocelyn, ed. *Cultural Atlas of Africa*. New York: Facts on File, 1988.

Myrdal, Gunnar. *An American Dilemma. The Negro Problem and Modern Democracy*. Volume II. New York: Harper Torchbooks, 1962.

Naipaul, V. S. *A Bend in the River*. New York: Vintage, 1980.

Nathan, Andrew. *Peking Politics, 1918–1923: Factionalism and the Failure of Constitutionalism*. New York: Columbia University Press, 1976.

Navarro, Marysa. "Evita's Charismatic Leadership." In Michael L. Connif, ed., *Latin American Populism in Comparative Perspective*. Albuquerque: University of New Mexico Press, 1982.

Neumann, Franz. *Behemoth: The Structure and Practice of National Socialism 1933–1944*. New York: Harper Torchbooks, 1966.

New York Times. "War's End Stirs Memories for China." *New York Times*, August 20, 1985, p. A-3.

Nicholls, David. *From Dessalines to Duvalier: Race, Colour, and National Independence in Haiti*. Cambridge: Cambridge University Press, 1979.

Nietzsche, Friedrich. *The Philosophy of Nietzsche*. New York: Random House/The Modern Library, 1954.

Nolte, Ernst. *Three Faces of Fascism: Action Française, Italian Fascism, National Socialism*. London: Weidenfeld and Nicolson, 1965.

North, Robert C., and Ithiel de Sola Pool. "Kuomintang and Communist Elites." In Harold D. Lasswell and Daniel Lerner, eds., *World Revolutionary Elites: Studies in Coercive Ideological Movements*. Cambridge: MIT Press, 1966.

Nunca Más. The Report of the Argentine National Commission on the Disappeared. New York: Farrar Straus Giroux, 1986.

Omara-Otunnu, Amii. *Politics and the Military in Uganda, 1890–1985*. Basingstoke: Macmillan, 1987.

Ornes, Germán E. *Trujillo, Little Caesar of the Caribbean*. New York: Thomas Nelson, 1958.

Orwell, George. *Burmese Days*. London: Secker and Warburg, 1949.

O'Toole, Thomas E. "Jean-Bédel Bokassa: Neo-Napoleonic Cult or Traditional African Ruler?" In Joseph Held, ed., *The Cult of Power: Dictators in the Twentieth Century*. New York: Columbia University Press, 1983.

————. *The Central African Republic: The Continent's Hidden Heart*. Boulder: Westview, 1986.

Padfield, Peter. *Himmler*. New York: Henry Holt, 1990.

Parsons, I. M., ed. *Men Who March Away: Poems of the First World War, An Anthology*. New York: Viking, 1965.

Partner, Peter. "In Saddam's Arms." *New York Review of Books* 38, 8 (April 25, 1991).

Paxton, Robert O. *Vichy France: Old Guard and New Order 1940–1944*. New York: Knopf, 1972.

Perelli, Carina. "Settling Accounts with Blood Memory: The Case of Argentina." *Social Research* 59, 2 (1992).

Perry, Elizabeth J. "Casting a Chinese 'Democracy' Movement: The Roles of Students, Workers, and Entrepreneurs." In Jeffrey N. Wasserstrom and Elizabeth J. Perry, eds., *Popular Protest and Political Culture in Modern China: Learning from 1989*. Boulder: Westview, 1989.

————. *Rebels and Revolutionaries in North China, 1845–1945*. Stanford: Stanford University Press, 1980.

Peukert, Detlev J. K. *Inside Nazi Germany*. New Haven: Yale University Press, 1987.

Pipes, Daniel. *Greater Syria: The History of an Ambition*. New York: Oxford University Press, 1990.

Plato. *The Dialogues of Plato* (two volumes). Translated by B. Jowett. New York: Random House, 1937.

Popper, Karl. *The Poverty of Historicism*. London: Routledge, 1961.

Potash, Robert A. *The Army and Politics in Argentina, 1928–1945: Yrigoyen to Perón*. Stanford: Stanford University Press, 1969.

Puddington, Arch. *Failed Utopias: Methods of Coercion in Communist Regimes*. San Francisco: Institute for Contemporary Studies, 1988.

Radulescu-Motru, Constantin. *Românismul*. Bucharest: Fundatia Regele Carol II, 1936.

Rawls, John. *A Theory of Justice*. Cambridge: The Belknap Press of Harvard University Press, 1971.

Remick, David. "Dons of the Don." *New York Review of Books* 39, 13 (July 16, 1992).

Riley-Smith, Jonathan. *The Crusades: A Short History*. New Haven: Yales University Press, 1977.

Ringer, Fritz, K., ed. *The German Inflation of 1923*. New York: Oxford University Press, 1969.

Rizvi, Athar Abbas. *The Wonder That Was India*, Volume II. London: Sidgwick and Jackson, 1987.

Rock, David. *Argentina 1516–1987: From Spanish Colony to Alfonsín*. Berkeley and Los Angeles: University of California Press, 1987.

Rodman, Selden. *Quisqueya*. Seattle: University of Washington Press, 1964.

Rogger, Hans. "Russia." In Hans Rogger and Eugen Weber, eds., *The European*

Right: A Historical Profile. Berkeley and Los Angeles: University of California Press, 1966.

Rosefielde, Steven. "Excess Mortality in the Soviet Union." *Soviet Studies* 35 (1983): 385–409.

Rosenberg, Arthur. *Imperial Germany: The Birth of the German Republic, 1871–1918*. Boston: Beacon, 1964.

Rostow, Walt W. *The United States in the World Arena*. New York: Harper, 1960.

Rotberg, Robert I. *Haiti: The Politics of Squalor*. Boston: Houghton Mifflin, 1971.

Roth, Cecil. *A History of the Marranos*. New York: Shocken Books, 1974 (fourth edition).

Roth, Guenther. *The Social Democrats in Imperial Germany: A Study in Working Class Isolation and National Integration*. Totowa, NJ: Bedminster Press, 1963.

Rothschild, Joseph. *Pilsudski's Coup d'État*. New York: Columbia University Press, 1966.

———. *Return to Diversity: A Political History of East Central Europe since World War II*. New York: Oxford University Press, 1989.

Rouquié, Alain. *Pouvoir militaire et société politique en République Argentine*. Paris: Presses de la Fondation Nationale des Sciences Politiques, 1978.

Rustow, Dankwart A., ed. *Political Modernization in Japan and Turkey*. Princeton: Princeton University Press, 1964.

Sagan, Eli. *At the Dawn of Tyranny*. New York: Knopf, 1985.

Salisbury, Harrison E. *The New Emperors: China in the Era of Mao and Deng*. Boston: Little, Brown, 1992.

Sathyamurthy, T. V. *The Political Development of Uganda 1900–1986*. Aldershot, Hants: Gower, 1986.

Scalabrini Ortiz, Raúl. *Historia de los ferrocarilles argentinos*. Buenos Aires: Reconquista, 1940.

Schapiro, Leonard. *The Communist Party of the Soviet Union*. New York: Random House, 1960.

———. *Russian Studies*. New York: Viking, 1987.

———. *Turgenev: His Life and Times*. New York: Oxford University Press, 1978.

Scheler, Max. *Ressentiment*. Glencoe: Free Press, 1960.

Schellenberg, Walter. *The Labyrinth*. New York: Harper, 1956.

Schmidt, Hans. *The American Occupation of Haiti, 1915–1934*. New Brunswick: Rutgers University Press, 1971.

Schmitter, Philippe C. "Reflections on Mihail Manoilescu and the Political Consequences of Delayed-Dependent Development on the Periphery of Western Europe." In Kenneth Jowitt, ed., *Social Change in Romania, 1860–1940*. Berkeley: Institute of International Relations, 1978.

Schoenbaum, David. *Hitler's Social Revolution: Class and Status in Nazi Germany 1933–1939*. Garden City: Doubleday, 1966.

Schöpflin, George. "Rumanian Nationalism." *Survey* 4 (1974).

Schorske, Carl E. *Fin-de-Siècle Vienna: Politics and Culture*. New York: Vintage, 1981.

Schram, Stuart R. *The Political Thought of Mao Tse-tung*. New York: Praeger, 1969 (second edition).

Schumacher, E. F. Small Is Beautiful. London: Blond and Briggs, 1973.

Schumpeter, Joseph A. *Capitalism, Socialism, and Democracy*. New York: Harper Torchbooks, 1962 (third edition).

———. "The Sociology of Imperialism." In Schumpeter, *The Economics and Sociology of Capitalism*. Princeton: Princeton University Press, 1991.

Schwarz, Vera. *The Chinese Enlightenment: Intellectuals and the Legacy of the May Fourth Movement of 1919*. Berkeley and Los Angeles: University of California Press, 1986.

Scott, James C. *The Moral Economy of the Peasant: Rebellion and Subsistence in Southeast Asia*. New Haven: Yale University Press, 1976.

Seale, Patrick. *Asad: The Struggle for the Middle East*. Berkeley and Los Angeles: University of California Press, 1988.

Sédov, L. "La société angkorienne et le problème du mode de production asiatique." *La Pensée* 138 (1968).

Sée, Henri. *L'Évolution commerciale et industrielle de la France sous l'Ancien Régime*. Paris: Marcel Giard, 1925.

Selth, Andrew. *Death of a Hero: The U Thant Disturbances in Burma, December 1974*. Nathan, Australia: Griffith University Research Paper 49, 1989.

Service, Elman R. *Origins of the State and Civilization: The Process of Cultural Evolution*. New York: W. W. Norton, 1975.

Shafir, Michael. "Political Culture and the Romanian Revolution of December 1989: Who Failed Whom?" Munich: Radio Free Europe paper, 1991.

———. *Romania: Politics, Economics, Society*. Boulder: Lynne Riener, 1985.

Shanin, Teodor. *The Awkward Class: Political Sociology of Peasantry in a Developing Society: Russia 1910–1925*. Oxford: Clarendon Press, 1972.

———. *The Roots of Otherness: Russia's Turn of the Century*. Volume I, *Russia as a Developing Society*. New Haven: Yale University Press, 1986.

———. *The Roots of Otherness: Russia's Turn of the Century*. Volume II, *Russia, 1905–1907: Revolution as a Moment of Truth*. New Haven: Yale University Press, 1986.

Shawcross, William. *Sideshow: Kissinger, Nixon and Destruction of Cambodia*. New York: Simon and Schuster / Pocket Books, 1979.

Shenon, Philip. "Burmese, After Years of Terror, Hope Things May Soon Change for the Better." *New York Times*, April 29, 1992, p. A-3.

———. "Thai Legislators Curb Role of Military." *New York Times*, May 26, 1992, p. A-3.

Shih, Vincent Y. C. *Taiping Ideology*. Seattle: University of Washington Press, 1967.

Shin, Gi-wook. *The Politics of Popular Protest: Roots and Legacy of Peasant Activism in Twentieth-Century Korea*. Seattle: University of Washington Press, forthcoming in 1995.

Shirer, William L. *Berlin Diary 1934–1941*. New York: Knopf, 1941.

Shostakovich, Dmitri. *Testimony: The Memoirs of Dmitri Shostakovich*. New York: Harper and Row, 1979.

Shumway, Nicolas. *The Invention of Argentina*. Berkeley and Los Angeles: University of California Press, 1991.

Silverfarb, Daniel. *Britain's Informal Empire in the Middle East: A Case Study of Iraq 1929–1941*. New York: Oxford University Press, 1986.

Silverstein, Josef. *Burma: Military Rule and the Politics of Stagnation*. Ithaca: Cornell University Press, 1977.

———. "Minority Problems in Burma since 1962." In F. K. Lehman, ed., *Military Rule in Burma since 1962*. Singapore: Maruzen Asia, 1981.

Sivan, Emmanuel. *Radical Islam: Medieval Theology and Modern Politics*. New Haven: Yale University Press, 1985.

Sked, Alan. *The Decline and Fall of the Habsburg Empire 1815–1918*. London: Longman, 1989.

Skocpol, Theda. "Old Regime Legacies and Communist Revolutions in Russia and China." *Social Forces* 55, 2 (1976).

Smith, Donald E. *Religion and Politics in Burma*. Princeton: Princeton University Press, 1965.

Smith, Martin. *Burma: Insurgency and the Politics of Ethnicity*. London: Zed Books, 1991.

Smith, Michael. "Shining Path's Urban Strategy: Ate Vitarte." In David S. Palmer, *Shining Path of Peru*. New York: St. Martin's Press, 1992.

Smith, Peter H. *Argentina and the Failure of Democracy: Conflict among Political Elites, 1904–1955*. Madison: University of Wisconsin Press, 1974.

Smith, Philip E. L. and T. Cuyler Young. "The Evolution of Early Agriculture and Culture in Greater Mesopotamia: A Trial Model." In Brian Spooner, ed., *Population Growth: Anthropological Implications*. Cambridge: MIT Press, 1972.

Snow, Edgar. *Red Star over China*. New York: Modern Library, 1938.

Solberg, Carl. *Oil and Nationalism in Argentina*. Stanford: Stanford University Press, 1979.

Solzhenitsyn, Alexandr I. *August 1914*. New York: Farrar, Straus & Giroux, 1972.

———. *The Gulag Archipelago, Volume I*. New York: Harper and Row, 1974.

Sorel, Georges. *Reflections on Violence*. New York: Peter Smith, 1941.

Speer, Albert. *Inside the Third Reich*. New York: Macmillan, 1970.

Spence, Jonathan D. *The Search for Modern China*. New York: W. W. Norton, 1990.

Spencer, Herbert. *The Principles of Sociology*. New York: D. Appleton, 1897.

Spengler, Oswald. "Prussianism and Socialism." In Spengler, *Selected Essays*. Chicago: Henry Regnery, 1967.

Stahl, Henri H. *Eseuri Critice Despre Cultura Populara Romaneasca*. Bucharest: Minerva, 1983.

———. *Traditional Romanian Village Communities*. Cambridge: Cambridge University Press, 1980.

Stalin, Joseph V. "Marxism and the National Question." In Stalin, *Works*, Volume II. Moscow: Foreign Publishing House, 1952.

Steinberg, David I. *The Future of Burma: Crisis and Choice in Myanmar*. New York: Asia Society/University Press of America, 1989.

Steinberg, David Joel, ed. *In Search of Southeast Asia*. Honolulu: University of Hawaii Press, 1985.

Stern, Fritz. *The Politics of Cultural Despair*. Berkeley and Los Angeles: University of California Press, 1974.

Stern, J. P. *Hitler: The Führer and the People*. Berkeley and Los Angeles: University of California Press, 1988.

Stokes, Gale, ed. *From Stalinism to Pluralism: A Documentary History of Eastern Europe since 1945*. New York: Oxford University Press, 1991.

Suh, Dae-suk. *The Korean Communist Movement, 1918–1948*. Princeton: Princeton University Press, 1967.

Suu Kyi, Aung San. *Freedom from Fear and Other Writings*. New York: Penguin, 1991.

Swianiewicz, Stanislaw. *Forced Labor and Economic Development: An Enquiry into the Experiences of Soviet Industrialization*. London: Oxford University Press, 1965.

Szamuely, Tibor. *The Russian Tradition*. New York: McGraw-Hill, 1974.

Szporluk, Roman. *Communism and Nationalism: Karl Marx versus Friedrich List*. New York: Oxford University Press, 1988.

Taylor, A. J. P. *English History 1914–1945*. Oxford: Clarendon Press, 1965.

———. *The Origins of the Second World War*. New York: Atheneum, 1962.

———. *The Struggle for Mastery in Europe 1848–1918*. Oxford: Clarendon Press of Oxford University, 1954.

Taylor, Robert. *The State in Burma*. Honolulu: University of Hawaii Press, 1987.

Terrill, Ross. *Madame Mao: The White-Boned Demon*. New York: Simon and Schuster/Touchstone, 1992.

Thurston, Anne F. *Enemies of the People: The Ordeal of the Intellectuals in China's Great Cultural Revolution*. Cambridge: Harvard University Press, 1988.

Thurston, Robert W. "Fear and Belief in the USSR's 'Great Terror': Response to Arrest, 1935–1939." *Slavic Review* 45 (1990): 213–234.

Time Magazine. "Eastern Europe: The Third Communism." *Time* Magazine, March 18, 1966, pp. 34–48.

Time Magazine. "Man of the Year: Russia." *Time* Magazine, January 1, 1940, pp. 14–17.

Timerman, Jacobo. *Prisoner without a Name, Cell without a Number*. New York: Vintage Books, 1982.

Tismaneanu, Vladimir. "The Tragicomedy of Romanian Communism." *Eastern European Politics and Societies* 3, 2 (1989).

Tolstoy, Nikolai. *The Secret Betrayal 1944–1947*. New York: Charles Scribner's Sons, 1977.

Torańska, Teresa. *"Them": Stalin's Polish Puppets*. New York: Harper and Row, 1987.

Trager, Frank N. *Burma: From Kingdom to Republic: A Historical and Political Analysis*. New York: Praeger, 1966.

Trotsky, Leon. *The Revolution Betrayed: What Is the Soviet Union and Where Is It Going?* New York: Doubleday, 1937.

———. *The Russian Revolution*. New York: Doubleday/Anchor, 1959.

Tucker, Robert C. "On the 'Letter of an Old Bolshevik' as an Historical Document." *Slavic Review* 51, 4 (1992).

———. *Stalin as Revolutionary 1879–1929*, Volume I. New York: W. W. Norton, 1974.

———. *Stalin in Power 1928–1941*, Volume II. New York: W. W. Norton, 1990.

Tucker, Robert C., and Stephen F. Cohen, eds. *The Great Purge Trial*. New York: Grosset and Dunlap, 1965.

Turner, Henry A., Jr. *German Big Business and the Rise of Hitler*. New York: Oxford University Press, 1985.

Turner, Henry A. Jr., ed. *Hitler: Memoirs of a Confidant* (by Otto Wagener). New Haven: Yale University Press, 1988.

Ulam, Adam B. *In the Name of the People: Prophets and Conspirators in Prerevolutionary Russia*. New York: Viking, 1977.

———. *Stalin: The Man and His Era*. Boston: Beacon, 1989 (second edition).

Vaksberg, Arkady. *The Soviet Mafia*. New York: St. Martin's Press, 1992.

———. *Stalin's Prosecutor: The Life of Andrei Vyshinski*. New York: Grove Weidenfeld, 1991.

Verdery, Katherine. *National Ideology under Socialism: Identity and Cultural Politics in Ceausescu's Romania*. Berkeley and Los Angeles: University of California Press, 1991.

Vickery, Michael. *Cambodia 1975–1982*. Boston: South End Press, 1984.

———. "Democratic Kampuchea: Themes and Variations." In David P. Chandler and Ben Kiernan, eds., *Revolution and Its Aftermath in Kampuchea*. New Haven: Yale University Southeast Asia Studies Monograph #25, 1983.

Vogel, Ezra F. *The Four Little Dragons: The Spread of Industrialization in East Asia*. Cambridge: Harvard University Press, 1991.

Volkogonov, Dmitri. *Stalin: Triumph and Tragedy*. New York: Grove Weidenfeld, 1991.

Von Laue, Theodore H. "Imperial Russia at the Turn of the Century: The Cultural Slope and the Revolution from Within." In Reinhard Bendix, ed., *State and Society*. Boston: Little, Brown, 1968.

———. *Why Lenin? Why Stalin?* New York:J. B. Lippincott, 1971 (2nd edition).

Vyvyan, J. M. K. "The Approach of the War of 1914." In *The Cambridge Modern History*, Volume XII Cambridge: Cambridge University Press, 1984.

Waisman, Carlos H. "Argentina: Autarkic Industrialization and Illegitimacy." In Larry J. Diamond, Juan Linz, and Seymour Martin Lipset, eds., *Democracy in Developing Countries*. Volume IV, *Latin America*. Boulder: Lynne Reiner, 1989.

Waite, Robert G. L. *The Psychopathic God: Adolph Hitler*. New York: Mentor, 1977.

Wakeman, Frederick, Jr. *The Fall of Imperial China*. New York: Free Press, 1975.

———. *History and Will: Philosophical Perspectives of Mao Tse-tung's Thought*. Berkeley and Los Angeles: University of California Press, 1973.

Wallerstein, Immanuel. *Africa: The Politics of Independence*. New York: Vintage Books, 1961.

Webb, Sidney, and Beatrice Webb. *The Truth about Soviet Russia*. New York: Longmans, Green, 1942.

Weber, Eugen, and Hans Rogger. *The European Right: A Historical Profile*. Berkeley and Los Angeles: University of California Press, 1966.

Weber, Max. *The Protestant Ethic and the Spirit of Capitalism*. New York: Charles Scribner's, 1958.

Wedgwood, Cicely V. *The Thirty Years' War*. Garden City: Doubleday / Anchor, 1961.

Weinstein, Brian. *Éboué*. New York: Oxford University Press, 1972.

Weissman, Stephen R. *American Foreign Policy in the Congo, 1960–1964*. Ithaca: Cornell University Press, 1974.

Welles, Sumner. *Naboth's Vineyard: The Dominican Republic, 1844–1924*. New York: Payson and Clarke, 1928.

Weschler, Lawrence. *A Miracle, A Universe: Settling Accounts with Torturers*. New York: Penguin, 1990.

Weulersse, Jacques. *Le Pays des Alaouites*, two volumes. Tours: Arrault, 1940.

Wheatcroft, Andrew. *The World Atlas of Revolutions*. New York: Simon and Schuster, 1983.

White, Lynn T. III. *Policies of Chaos: The Organizational Causes of Violence in China's Cultural Revolution*. Princeton: Princeton University Press, 1989.

Wiesel, Elie. *Night*. New York: Bantam, 1982.

Wit, Ton de, and Ver Gianotten. "The Center's Multiple Failures." In David S. Palmer, ed., *Shining Path of Peru*. New York: St. Martin's Press, 1992.

Wolfe, Bertram D. *Three Who Made a Revolution*. New York: Stein and Day, 1984.

Woo, Jung-en. *Race to the Swift: State and Finance in Korean Industrialization*. New York: Columbia University Press, 1991.

World Bank. *World Development Report 1991*. Oxford: Oxford University Press, 1991.

Woytinski, W. S., and E. S. Woytinski. *World Population and Production: Trends and Outlooks*. New York: The Twentieth Century Fund, 1953.

Yang, Kung-sun. *The Book of Lord Shang*. Translated by J. J. L. Duyvendak. London: A Probsthain, 1928.

Young, Crawford, and Thomas Turner. *The Rise and Decline of the Zairian State*. Madison: University of Wisconsin Press, 1985.

Zamiatin, Eugene. *We*. New York: E. P. Dutton, 1952.

Zinoviev, Aleksandr. *The Radiant Future*. New York: Random House, 1980.

Zmarzlik, Hans-Günter. "Social Darwinism in Germany Seen as a Historical Problem." In Hajo Holborn, ed., *Republic to Reich: The Making of the Nazi Revolution*. New York: Pantheon, 1972.

Zuwiyya Zamak, Labib. *The Syrian Socialist Nationalist Party*. Cambridge: Harvard University Press, 1966.

INDEX

Pavelić, Ante, 424
Peng Dehuai, 196–97, 207
Peng Zhen, 200, 201
Pepin the Short, 362
Perelli, Carina, 286
Perón, Eva Duarte, 200, 277, 278–79
Perón, Isabel, 279, 281–82
Perón, Juan: death of, 82; as dictator in
    Argentina, 275–82, 302; exile of,
    279–80; influences on, 271–72; as
    leader of United Officers' Group
    (GOU), 275; overthrow by army in
    1955, 279; return to Argentina from
    exile, 281–82; working class support
    for, 275–78, 280
Persia, 268, 292
Peru, 100, 426
Peter the Great, 5, 45, 47, 48, 147, 365
Pétion, Alexandre, 347
Peukert, Detlev, 163
Philippines, 368
Pilsudski, Marshal, 418
Pinochet, Augusto, 16, 286, 419
Pius XII, Pope, 359
Plato, 1, 6, 17, 145, 247, 339
Plutarch, 271
Pol Pot: anonymity of, 227–28; birth of,
    218; on Chams, 215; in communist
    underground in Cambodia, 220;
    deaths caused by, 8, 167, 226–27; edu-
    cation of, 218, 219; and extreme form
    of communism, 21; family of, 218–19;
    and image of past, 215; leadership
    qualities of, 421; and myth of Angkor,
    218; personality of, 220; visit to China,
    220; visit to Yugoslavia, 219; and
    weakness and disorder of Cambodia,
    405; youth of, 219, 301. *See also*
    Khmer Rouge
Poland: benign dictatorship in, 260;
    Berman in, 156; in 18th century, 44;
    German occupation of, 142; Hitler's
    takeover of, 130, 131, 135, 137;
    Jaruzelski in, 262; Jews in, 135, 137,
    141; Pilsudski in, 418; strikes during
    1950s, 191; after World War I, 77
Popper, Karl, 22
Portuguese colonies, 373

Poskrebyshev, Alexander, 153
Pravda, 111
Prebisch, Raúl, 273–74
Primo de Rivera, General, 272
Protocols of the Elders of Zion, The, 82
Proudhon, Pierre-Joseph, 34
Prussia, 27–28, 41–44, 81, 88, 89

Qadhafi, Muammar al-, 391
Qasim, 'Abd al-Karim, 298, 299
Qin state, 5
Qing dynasty, 179–81

Races: Duvalier on, 351; Hitler on racial
    purity, 81–85, 88, 121, 128, 133,
    137–38; in Saint-Domingue, 344–45;
    struggle of, 52, 53–55, 60–61, 84–85;
    theory about superiority of white
    races, 55; in United States, 345. *See
    also* Jews
Rainsford, Marcus, 346
Rasputin, Grigori, 108
Rawls, John, 414, 422
Renais, Alain, 128
Ressentiment, 410–12, 427
Revolutionary corporatism: consequences
    of, 252–58; theory of, 248–52
Revolutionary idealism, and tyranny,
    16–27
Revolutionary People's Army (ERP),
    280–81, 282
Ricardo, David, 29
Richelieu, Cardinal, 14
Rigaud, André, 346
Rockefeller Foundation, 332
Rogger, Hans, 106–07
Röhm, Ernst, 79, 130
Roma, 138, 142, 144, 209
Roman Empire, 10–12, 45, 56, 243
Romania: abortion as illegal in, 254–55;
    AIDS in, 254–55; Ceausescu's ostensi-
    ble liberalism and friendliness with
    West, 238–40; Ceausescu's regime in,
    1, 159, 168, 230, 236–40, 245–48,
    250–51, 253–58, 265; collapse of com-
    munism in, 253; Communist Party in,
    235; compared with Albania, 262–63;
    compared with Hungary, 260–62;